EDUCATION
IN A COMPARATIVE
CONTEXT
Studies of Israeli Society
Volume IV

EDUCATION IN A COMPARATIVE CONTEXT
Studies of Israeli Society
Volume IV

Editor

Ernest Krausz

Associate Editor

David Glanz

Publication Series of the Israel Sociological Society

Transaction Publishers
New Brunswick (U.S.A.) and Oxford (U.K.)

Sponsored by the Schnitzer Foundation for Research on the Israeli Economy and Society—Bar-Ilan University.

Library of Congress Catalog Number: 79-93045
ISBN: 0-88738-184-7 (cloth), 0-88738-709-8 (paper)

Printed in the United States of America

Library of Congress Cataloging in Publication Data

(Revised for vol. IV)
Main entry under title:

Studies of Israeli society.
    Vol. IV: Editor, Ernest Krausz; associate editor, David Glanz.
    Includes bibliographies.
    v. 1. Migration, ethnicity, and community—v. 2. The sociology of the kibbutz—v. 3. Politics and society in Israel—v. 4. Education in a comparative context. 1. Israel—Social and conditions—Collected works.
2. Israel—Emigration and immigration—Collected works.
3. Israel—Ethnic relations—Collected works.
4. Kibbutzim—Collected works. 5. Israel—Politics and government—Collected works. 6. Education—Israel I. Krausz, Ernest. II. Glanz, David. III. Series.
HN660.A8S83   306'095694   79-93045
ISBN 0-87855-369-X

Dedication

This fourth volume of *Studies of Israeli Society* is respectfully dedicated to the memory of Professor Joseph Ben-David, a founding member of the editorial board of this series. His death is a great loss to the sociological community in Israel and to his many students and friends in the field. He was a dedicated and distinguished scholar whose work was an inspiration to all who knew him.

Contents

Preface

The object of this series as defined in the previous three volumes is to identify the major areas of sociological research being conducted on Israeli society. As in previous volumes, the articles considered for inclusion in Volume IV were selected exclusively from among those appearing in international scholarly journals and books printed in English. As in the case of the preceding volumes, the selection of the overall topic for the collection has been guided by two principal criteria: (1) that the subject be specifically directed to a better understanding of Israeli society and generally contribute to the larger world of the social sciences; and (2) that a critical mass of literature be available to provide a comprehensive view of "the state of the art" in the field under review.

This fourth volume on Israeli education examines one of the most extensively-studied social institutions in Israel. Unfortunately, because much of the sociological literature in Israeli education has thus far appeared only in Hebrew, the valuable work of many distinguished scholars had to be omitted from this volume. Nevertheless, we believe this volume represents a milestone in the development of the sociological analysis of the socialization and educational processes at work in Israeli society.

The selected bibliography, specially prepared by David Glanz for this volume, represents the first comprehensive survey of English-language material on education and socialization in Israel and includes over 750 listings. We hope that this bibliography will serve as a significant resource for readers interested in studying the topic in greater depth.

The preparation and publication of this volume would not have been possible without the help of a number of organizations and individuals. First and foremost, we are most grateful to the Schnitzer Foundation for Research on the Israeli Economy and Society, Bar-Ilan University, for its generous support in sponsoring this volume. We also wish to express our gratitude to Professors James Coleman and E.O. Schild for their contributions of original introductory essays. The guidance of Professor Michael Chen and Dr. Abraham Yogev in the review and selection process was invaluable. We would also like to express our appreciation to Grace Hollander for her technical help, to the members of the Editorial Board, and to

Daniel Mann, Secretary of the Israel Sociological Society for his assistance. Finally, we gratefully acknowledge the generous cooperation we have received from all the authors and publishers who permitted us to reprint their works.

Joseph Ben-David: In Memoriam

Elihu Katz

Chairman of the Editorial Board

*Presented at the Memorial Meeting
at the Eleventh World Congress of Sociology,
New Delhi, August 18, 1986*

It is an honor to be asked to speak in memory of Joseph Ben-David, colleague and friend at the Department of Sociology at the Hebrew University. Joseph was also a professor of sociology and education at the University of Chicago. He was a member of the Israel Academy of Sciences and a foreign honorary member of the American Academy of Arts and Sciences. In the International Sociological Association, he served as President of the Research Committee on the Sociology of Science and as a member of the ISA Executive and Research Coordinating Committees. Joseph was the winner of many prizes for his achievements in the sociology of higher education and of science, the field in which he invested most of his energy and prodigious talents.

One of the foremost areas of Professor Ben-David's academic activities, which is generally not known in the sociological community, was his involvement in the establishment and direction of the Sidney M. Edelstein Center for the History and Philosophy of Science, Technology, and Medicine at Hebrew University over the last ten years. Due in large measure to his efforts, this center houses the Einstein archives among other significant collections. The Center is internationally known as an institute for advanced studies in the development of the philosophy and history of scientific thought.

Upon reading his last, still unpublished papers, one cannot but be impressed by Ben-David's dedication to the rehabilitation of the image of the ethos of science as a model not only for natural science, not only for social science, but for a libertarian theory of society. For Ben-David, the openness of science to all contributors, its striving for universal applicability, its public character, its rules for conducting debate and evaluating research, its dispassionateness and disinterestedness—in a word, its objectivity—are a model for the rational conduct not only of academic inquiry but also of social life. Empirically-oriented science, obliged by its own code to make way for change when change better fits the facts, is the very opposite of the dogma and ideology Ben-David feared, having experienced too much of it himself prior to his arrival in Israel in 1939.

His recent work constitutes an eloquent defense of the scientific ethos in an era that has seen science both over- and underrated. Ben-David shows how science was overvalued at certain periods, especially after World War II, when occasional "scientist-kings" walked in the land and certain ideologues claimed too much for the applicability of science to social planning, arrogating its name to bolster political power.

Even more than Ben-David was troubled by this overrating of science, he worried about its downgrading in the 1960s. In a brilliant paper on rationality in scientific research, he shows how radical and romantic critics tried to discredit the scientific enterprise by misreading and misunderstanding the works of Marx, Mannheim, and Durkheim. He counters the argument that knowledge is a function of the social location of the observer, and thus that science must reconcile itself to a doctrine of relativism, by reminding us that we fail to appreciate that the fallacies of relativism—in intelligence testing, for example—have themselves been exposed through the application of scientific method. He shows how Marx and Durkheim—far from any wish to create relativistic epistemologies—were interested in "how sociological interpretation could help to understand the emergence of knowledge, the conditions under which it develops in an increasingly universalistic and scientific direction, and the conditions under which it remains limited local knowledge, or deteriorates, according to Marx, into actually deceptive knowledge. These questions make sense only on the assumption that there is some kind of (relatively) valid and improving knowledge, such as science."

In the spirit of this reading of Durkheim, Ben-David then goes on to propose that society itself is an impetus rather than an obstacle to scientific creativity. The "rootedness" of scientific work in self-correcting communities illustrates the point. But it is not only communities bearing the standards of science that tend toward rationality; it is the ordinary human group itself that constrains individuals to behave reasonably, responsibly, and creatively.

It follows from this—and Ben-David's thought leads the way—that human societies, like science itself, strive for a rational understanding of the universe, if only in order to survive and progress. If so, says Ben-David, the ethnosciences of human communities deserve to be taken seriously—even if critically—not as exotic systems of mystification incapable of translation, but as variant models of universal patterns of coping and conceptualization. Society, unlike nature, provides its observers with a head start on concepts and classifications worthy of investigation; there are useful hypotheses to be found in magic and myth that may properly be viewed as precursors of science. Durkheim's group mind is not an arational imposition for Ben-David, but, on the whole, is a set of rules and proposals based on human experience and open to correction by members of the community. It follows that social scientists must work from within the situations they are observing, much as neo-Marxists faithful to Marx might expect, because of—not only in spite of—the bias implicit in each of the loci of observation that leads to dialogue, debate, and consensual validation.

Ben-David combined his sociology with a profound knowledge of history, with great familiarity with the sociological classics, with striking analytical ability, and with the talent to express himself. In the heady 1960s, he argued against the salon "chic" of many social scientists and with those who were all too ready to surrender to fashion some of the basic tenets of the great model of human endeavor in which they shared. There is no room for arrogance in the ethos of science, warned Ben-David; but the striving for cumulative knowledge, and its constant correction, must not surrender to self-doubt or to romantic yearnings either.

That social factors influence science is something we have learned lately from Ben-David among others. That science needs material but also moral support from other institutions; that scientists as individuals and groups may be misled by particularistic interests; that the dynamics of fashion and the constraints of job markets enter the scientific laboratory—all these are relevant and researchable concerns, but none of them should be allowed to overpower an institution whose norms guide us in the careful, systematic, unhysterical pursuit of knowledge and change.

There is a Jewish adage to the effect that giving proper credit to the sayings of another upholds the world. Ben-David upheld the world in his reanalysis of the sociologists of knowledge—Marx, Mannheim, Durkheim, and others. We can do likewise in paying the proper and due tribute we owe to Joseph Ben-David.

Acknowledgements

We wish to gratefully acknowledge the permission to use copyrighted material granted by the following journals and publishers:

"Israeli Education Addressing Dilemmas Caused by Pluralism: A Sociological Perspective," in *Education and Ethnic Minorities*, Eds. D. Rothermund and J. Simon, 1986, pp. 64-87. © F. Pinter Publishers.

"Conflict and Consensus in Educational Policy-Making in Israel," *International Journal of Political Education*, Vol. 4, 1981, pp. 219-32. © Elsiever Science Publishing.

"The Impact of Rapid Social Change on Technological Education: An Israeli Example," *Comparative Education Review*, Vol. 20, 1976, pp. 165-78. © The University of Chicago Press.

"Varieties of Orthodox Religious Behaviour: A Case Study of Yeshiva High School Graduates in Israel," *The Jewish Journal of Sociology*, Vol. 20, 1978, pp. 59-74. © The Jewish Journal of Sociology.

"Changing Socioeconomic and Political Conditions," in *Arab Education in Israel*, by Sami Khalil Mar'i, 1978, pp. 145-72 (footnotes pp. 202-203). © Syracuse University Press.

"The Israeli Armed Forces," in *The Political Education of Soldiers*, eds. H. Janowitz and F. Westbrook, 1983, pp. 99-127. © Sage Publications.

"Universities in Israel: Dilemmas of Growth, Diversification, and Administration," in *Studies in Higher Education*, Vol. 11, 1985, pp. 105-30. © Van Leer Institute and Carfax Publishing (published here with the permission of the Van Leer Jerusalem Institute). It is a chapter from a multi-author volume on *Education in Israel*, edited by W. Ackerman, A. Caromon, and D. Zucker, which had been published in Germany by Klett-Cotta Publishing Co. and in Hebrew by Hakibbutz Hameuhad Publishing Co. and is forthcoming in English.

"Determinants of Early Educational Career in Israel: Further Evidence for the Sponsorship Thesis," *Sociology of Education*, Vol. 54, 1981, pp. 181-94. © American Sociological Association.

"Classroom Intellectual Composition and Academic Achievement," *American Educational Research Journal*, Vol. 23, pp. 357-74. © American Educational Research Association.

"Tracking and Ethnicity in Israeli Secondary Education," *American So-*

1
Introduction

James Coleman

That research on education in Israel should constitute the basis for a volume in the English-language series *Studies of Israeli Society* is not remarkable in itself. What is remarkable is the quantity and quality of published work in this area, as represented by the papers included in this volume. These papers constitute a portion of the returns to society on its investment in social research—in the training of social researchers and the funding of social research.

That these returns have come to take the form of increasingly detailed and deeper inquiries into the structure and functioning of Israeli education is a measure of the growth and maturity of this work. The importance of education to the future of Israeli society is widely recognized. What is less widely recognized, however, is the potential importance of systematic research in education for improving and strengthening the educational process. Social research in education is a prominent part of the developing self-consciousness of Israeli society about the way its institutions function—a self-consciousness that can lead to embarrassing questions but can also lead, when these questions are addressed in social research, to better-functioning institutions.

Neither in Israel nor in any other society has this self-consciousness reached a stage of comprehensiveness and the social research attendant upon it a stage of maturity such that the most important questions about educational institutions are always asked and when asked are always answered well. But the papers in this volume constitute strong evidence that the process is rapidly becoming an important element in the improvement of Israeli education.

The social research reported here focuses on important questions in the functioning of Israeli education, and sheds light on these questions in the dispassionate way that is the hallmark of social research, distinguishing it from the variety of other forces for change in social institutions.

One of the important classes of questions that can be asked about education in Israel concerns integration: What is the state of social integration in Israeli schools? How does this integration in the schools contribute to the integration of Israeli society as a whole? These questions have been addressed by social research as reflected in several of the papers of this volume. Because some of my own research has addressed comparable questions in American society, and because I have some familiarity with the research on these questions in Israel, I will reflect on this class of questions in the remainder of this introduction.

School Integration and Social Integration in Israel

Observation on integration in Israel education by an outsider has a number of defects, but there is one virtue: the greater distance of an outsider can provide a perspective that is hard to attain otherwise. My aim will not be to examine the effects of particular policies—others are in a better position to do that than I, and have done so[1]—but to raise questions that arise from research on school integration inside Israel.

From the point of view of social integration, Israel is a society with unique problems and opportunities. The majority of its population, the Jews, consists primarily of those whose parents have come to one place from an enormously wide range of cultures, linguistic domains, and economic levels; these persons are held together only by religion, the sense of a common ethnic identity, and a common enemy. A significant minority, the Arabs (now 17 percent of the population; 20 percent of Israeli school children), consists of persons who are homogeneous in ethnicity and relatively so as to economic level. They are kept apart, however, from the majority by religious differences, language, and by ethnic identity with enemies of the state. The cultural and economic heterogeneity among the Jews in Israel, and the barriers between the Jewish majority and the Arab minority, create extraordinary problems of social and educational integration, and of providing equal educational opportunity.

It is useful to discuss problems of Arab education separately, because these problems are quite different from those of integration and equal opportunity within the Jewish sector. I will turn to Arab education later.

Jews from Asian and African backgrounds differ sharply in economic level and educational background from Jews of European or American origin. Most Asian and African Jews came to Israel much later than did most Europeans and were sometimes settled by government policy, in towns, communities, moshavim, or neighborhoods that were homogeneous by country of origin. Their children were more likely to be sent to state religious schools than were children of European or American Jews.

One might ask how integration in society or in the schools is possible under such unpropitious circumstances. Even among the European and American immigrants to Israel, there was a diversity of languages and cultural backgrounds, as there was among the Jews of African or Asian origin. Yet there is social integration in Israel among Jews from all parts of the world. This is the most important fact of all. The children attend schools with a common curriculum, are taught in a different language from the one their parents or grandparents learned, and have created a common culture. It is not perfectly integrated, but it does not consist, as it might well have, of physically and culturally isolated immigrant groups from different countries of origin.

Any discussion of educational integration among Jews in Israel must start with this striking fact. An integrated society has been created from an enormously diverse array of cultural and linguistic groups in a remarkably short period of time.

Integration in the Schools

The first question that arises is the importance of school integration in bringing about the social integration that exists. (I use the term "school integration" as it is commonly used in Israel: integration between Eastern and Western Jews.) In asking this question, it is necessary to separate the importance of the schools for social integration from the importance of integration policy in the schools for social integration. It appears that the schools have been extraordinarily important for social integration in Israel. They are, for many children if not most, the principal means of learning written Hebrew, Jewish history, national celebrations, and other socially unifying knowledge. Especially important in Israel is the inculcation of Hebrew, a different language for many children than their parents' native language. At least as much as in other nations, the schools are the central loci of interaction between the nation-state and the children within it. National holidays and their meanings are first introduced to children of immigrants in the schools. Museums and historic sites are visited as part of school activities. The sense of being an Israeli is first and most intensively transmitted by the schools.

It seems unlikely, however, that integration policy in the schools has been the principal avenue through which the schools have achieved their integrative effect. There have been few explicit policies for integration of Eastern and Western Jews at the elementary school level, and, for some time, elementary school through the eighth grade was the only compulsory and free public school. It is probably the fact that there was no single dominant national group either among the earlier Ashkenazi immigrants or among

the later Sephardi immigrants that made many schools culturally heterogeneous without an explicit integration policy. If anything, explicit policy
worked in a segregative direction. The diverse array of types of schools
(including kibbutz schools, independent religious schools, state religious
schools, and state secular schools) as well as residential settlement policies
of immigrants have increased the separation between children from different cultural backgrounds. Despite these policies, the elementary schools
show some integration. Although a significant minority of Asian-African
origin students attend schools without children from European or American origins, few of the latter attend schools without children from Asian
and African origins.

At the secondary level, the structure of the school system has not fostered school integration. The extensive use of vocational schools (compris-
ing about half of the total secondary school student body) has been a
strongly segregative force between Eastern and Western Jews. The importance and growth of these schools illustrates the policy dilemma in education for disadvantaged ethnic minorities. Vocational schools have been a
means of extending the education of these children in Israel, and preparing
them for productive occupations. As the number of Asian and African
immigrants to Israel grew, the number of vocational high schools also
increased. The vocational schools, however, reinforced the segregation of
these children from their European-American counterparts in the academic high school who prepared for a university matriculation examination in the traditional European pattern.

Altogether, social integration of Jewish Israeli children into society has
been greatly facilitated by the schools, but has been accomplished without
extensive integration policies in the schools. This fact emphasizes the difference between social integration of different groups into a common society on one hand and integration of different groups in the same school on
the other. The former has been extensive among Jews from different origins
in Israel, while the latter has been modest at best.

The principal policy of explicit integration in education has been the
junior high school reform conceived in 1963 and begun in 1968. The policy
had two goals: to extend compulsory education from eighth grade through
ninth grade, thereby redefining grades seven through nine as lower secondary school and making this compulsory; and to bring about integration.
The junior high schools, with several elementary schools as feeders, were
seen as the principal loci of integration between children of diverse economic and cultural backgrounds. The impact of this policy on higher
education was seen as important as well: with junior high schools as feeders
to particular academic high schools, the integration of junior high schools
would lead to increased integration of the academic high schools. Although

the integration policy has not been the extreme one of attempting to achieve racial balance throughout all schools in a town or city, as in some cities of the U.S., it has attempted to create feeder patterns that will increase integration, subject to reasonable distances of student travel.

Overall, the policy has had both difficulties and successes. The difficulties are reflected by the fact that the reform has been implemented slowly. The goals of the reform were particularly difficult to accomplish in the state religious schools for three reasons. First, as it comprises a smaller sector of education than the secular schools, the religious community finds it difficult except in the densest population centers to bring together children from a number of its elementary schools to a central junior high school. Second, children of Asian-African backgrounds are greatly overrepresented in state religious schools. As in many American cities, religious schools in many Israeli localities do not have sufficient number of "advantaged" students to achieve integration. Third, the philosophy of education in the state religious schools is not congenial to integration between advantaged and disadvantaged students. This philosophy has emphasized selection of an educational elite—often from lower economic backgrounds—with special attention and preparation given to this elite. Such a philosophy may or may not be less beneficial to a lower socioeconomic group than a philosophy of heterogeneous classes and non-selectivity. But it conflicts with a policy of non-selective integration of Asian-African and European-American children, a goal of the Israeli reform as well as of school integration in America.

Other problems with the reform have included reactions of some parents and teachers to integration, and, in their view, the educational dilution imposed by the reform. This belief has led in some cases to shifting among schools, a phenomenon like the "white flight" from integration in American cities. This flight, however, and negative parental reactions in general have not been great; in fact, it has occurred far less than in the U.S., and certainly not sufficiently to defeat the goals of the reform.

There have been policies of explicit integration in the elementary schools in a few localities, notably Jerusalem[2] though such policies are not general ones. As with the junior high school reform, these policies have not been universally accepted by the American-European origin families subject to them, nor have they provoked strong negative reaction.

Other policies to increase educational opportunities for the disadvantaged have been neutral with respect to integration. The principal such policy is one of compensatory funding for schools with large numbers of disadvantaged students. Israel has a centrally financed school system, so that there are no wide variations in school expenditures found in countries with decentralized systems like the U.S. Superimposed upon this general level of approximate equality in school expenditures is the policy of the Ministry of Education to provide extra resources for schools with high numbers of disadvantaged students. The aim is that of compensatory programs everywhere: to compensate for the lesser educational resources of disadvantaged children outside the school, principally in the family. Yet the same forces that brought about the differences in the first place (that is, parental and community support and supplementation of school activities, which is especially great in Israeli schools) still remain.

Despite some such differences that undoubtedly continue to exist, the reverse discrimination that has taken place in Israeli schools, giving more school resources to those students with fewer out-of-school resources, is impressive. It could exist only in a centralized system, but there are many centralized systems in which such compensatory policies do not exist.

Religion

Since the reform of 1968, there has come another "reform" in Israeli education. This is the increased importance of the religious-secular distinction in Israel. While the cultural separation of Jews from Eastern and Western origins is decreasing, the cultural separation of religious and non-religious Jews is increasing. To what degree is this cultural separation a consequence of the schools? And to what degree is it a consequence of segregation of religious and secular children in different schools?

The answers are not clear, but it is a question about which social research can provide valuable information. An outsider's conjecture is this: schools are extremely important in producing this cultural divergence, but not because of the physical separation of students in different schools—any more than physical separation of boys and girls in separate schools produces cultural divergence. Rather, it is the different goals and ideals of Israeli society transmitted through the different sets of schools that have this effect. This difference is pronounced between the secular and religious schools, and if my conjecture is correct, will produce an increasing religious-secular split in Israel.

Arab Education

Another disadvantaged group in Israel is the Arab minority. Arab education is conducted in a separate school system, in Arabic, under Arab teachers. Among Jewish students of Asian or African origin, the schools have, as described earlier, greatly faciliated identification with the state of Israel and integration into Israeli society as a whole. Among Arabs, the same cannot be said. Policies were established early in the history of the state to maintain a largely autonomous Arab educational system, containing overlaps in curriculum with the Jewish schools, but operated by Arabs and transmitting Arabic cultural traditions rather than those associated with the new state.

Some would argue that Israel made a serious error in its diffident stance with regard to the cultural content of Israeli Arab education. Yet the matter is a difficult one. The traditions and cultural content of the state of Israel are so intimately linked with those of Judaism that the infusion of Israeli traditions, culture, and national goals into the education of Israeli Arabs, who are 85 percent Muslim, 15 percent Christian, and a few Druze, would appear difficult indeed. It may not, however, have been impossible. What other options Israel had in the education of its Arab population is not clear. But the policy of a wholly separate and largely autonomous educational system for Israeli Arabs has left them apart from other Israelis, as a potentially fertile ground for the kind of anti-Israel attitudes and actions that would confirm the worst fears of some Israelis. If such fears were the source of the apparent diffidence in educational policy, they may have been self-confirming.

The possibility of linguistically and culturally separate school systems within a state depends very much on the nature of the society and economy. It may be possible if the society and economy are centered around the household and the neighborhood, as was much of Palestinian Arab society in the past, or if it is split into two geographically distinct sectors like Belgium or Switzerland. If the society and economy are modern, however, as Israel's is becoming, drawing Israeli Arabs into it and increasing Israeli Arab education, this separateness may not be viable in the future.

The problem is compounded by the increase in education experienced by Arabs under the Israeli educational system. Israeli Arabs may be among the best educated anywhere, for resources put into their education have paralleled those put into the education of Jews in Israel,[3] a much higher level of resources put into public education than in most Arab countries. This increase in education encourages the ambitious to move out of the villages and into modern society. This situation leads directly to frustration if barriers to that ambition exist, as they do to Arabs in Israeli society. And if the best-educated Israeli Arabs want to attend institutions of higher education in Arab countries outside Israel, they confront discrimination as Israelis. (They may choose to be educated at Israeli universities, as some do, especially at Haifa University, but this education is not easily used outside Israel in the Arab world.)

Altogether, the education of Arabs in Israel constitutes a perplexing problem, not only of providing individual opportunities to those students in a disadvantaged minority, but of educating good citizens for the state of

Israel. It is not a problem Israel has solved nor, despite its importance, is it one that Israeli policymakers have given the kind of sustained attention they have devoted to the problem of Israel's largest disadvantaged group, Jews of Asian or African origin. As the population of Arabs in Israel grows and modernizes, the problem is not merely a problem for Israel's Arabs; it is a problem for the state of Israel itself.

Conclusion: Integration in School and Society

Two conclusions can be drawn from the preceding discussion. First, social integration of Israeli society depends greatly upon the schools; and second, social integration in Israel depends much less on integration policy in the schools than is commonly believed. It appears to depend much more on the common language, common culture, common national goals, and common beliefs that are inculcated during the educational process, whether the degree of physical integration is high or low.

Both the evidence from comparisons within the Jewish sector and that obtained from Jewish-Arab comparisons lead to the first conclusion. The common language, culture, national goals, and beliefs inculcated in all Jewish secular and state religious schools that results in a high degree of cultural integration provides positive evidence. The lack of commonalities between Jewish and Arab schools and the resulting absence of social integration add weight to the conclusion that social integration depends greatly on the schools.

The evidence from the high level of integration between Jews of Eastern and Western origins in schools leads to the second conclusion, for the cultural integration has occurred *despite* the relatively low level of policy toward integration by country of origin in the school system.

It may in fact be that school integration is more a symptom than a cause: those divisions in a society that are so major that separate schools seem the only "reasonable" solution are precisely those divisions across which there are not shared goals and common beliefs. Where there are shared goals and common beliefs, as between Jews from East and West, integration in the schools appears a reasonable policy; but the very existence of the shared goals and beliefs that make it more feasible also make it less necessary for social integration.

Conclusion

It is clear that social research in education has reached a high level of maturity in Israel. It constitutes an important feedback mechanism for educational policy; the papers in this volume provide evidence of that fact.

Yet the articulation between educational research and educational policy has not reached a comparable level of maturity, which would enable the schools to profit as fully as they might from this instrument that Israeli society's investments have made possible. Perhaps the publication of this volume will hasten this maturity.

Notes

1. Besides papers in Section 3 and 4 of this volume, see Klein and Eshel, 1980; Amir et al., 1978a; 1978b; Amir and Sharon, 1984; Arzi and Amir, 1977; Chen and Fresco, 1977; Minkovich, Davis, and Bashi, 1977.
2. See Klein and Eshel, 1980.
3. I do not attempt here to directly compare the support of education for Arabs in Israel with that of education for Jews. It can be said, however, that there is no compensatory program of extra resources comparable to that provided in Jewish schools that have a high proportion of disadvantaged students.

References

Amir, Yehuda, Miriam Rivner, Aharon Bizman, and Rachel Ben-Ari.
  1978a.   Contact between Israelis and Arabs and its effects. Photocopy, Bar-Ilan University, Ramat-Gan.
Amir, Yehuda, Shlomo Sharan, Miriam Rivner, and Rachel Ben-Ari.
  1978b.   Attitude change in desegregated Israeli high schools. *Journal of Educational Psychology* 70: 129-36.
Amir, Yehuda and Shlomo Sharan, eds.
  1984.   *School Segregation & Cross-Cultural Perspectives.* Hillsdale, NJ: Lawrence Erlbaum.
Arzi, Yehudit and Yehuda Amir.
  1977.   Intellectual and academic achievements and adjustment of underprivileged children in homogeneous and heterogeneous classrooms. *Child Development* 48: 726-29.
Chen, Michael and Barbara Fresko.
  1977.   The interaction of school environment and student traits. *Educational Research* 20: 114-21.
Klein, Zen and Yohanan Eshel.
  1980.   *Integrating Jerusalem schools.* New York: Academic Press.
Minkovich, Avram, Dan Davis, and Joseph Bashi.
  1977.   *An Evaluation Study of Israeli Elementary Schools.* Jerusalem: Hebrew University.

2

Overview: A Policy Perspective

E.O. Schild

James S. Coleman, who prefaces this volume, asserted some twenty years ago in another context that "educational sociology . . . has long languished in the cellar of the discipline."[1] This may no longer be true for the discipline internationally; it surely does not hold for Israeli sociology today. The papers in this volume reflect, in one way or another, much of what characterizes Israeli sociology in general. Even their very heterogeneity, in content, approach, and method, is not untypical of sociology in Israel (and of Israeli society itself). Nevertheless, I believe that there is also something distinctive about educational sociology in Israel relative to other subfields of the discipline. Beyond the heterogeneity of the papers, one may discern the outlines of a social and intellectual context that is relevant beyond the content of the specific findings and analyses.

This belief is the background for the comments to follow. An "Overview" may simply offer convenient abstracts of the papers, and/or provide classification by things such as topic or method. In the present case, the organization of the volume already offers a broad classification by topic—and, to a certain extent, by method as well (note, e.g., the dominance of multivariate analysis in Part 3). Moreover, the original publications span a decade. It is thus not relevant to attempt to propose specific implications for issues at the frontiers of research; it is likely that in many cases the frontiers have moved since first publication. Rather, I expect that what the reader is interested in learning from this volume is something about the general nature of sociology of education in Israel.

Consequently, I shall offer a few suggestions to provide a perspective for the papers and possibly aid the reader in appreciating their place in the Israeli experience, both social and academic. More specifically, I shall propose a relationship between educational sociology and educational policy in Israel—at least in respect to the choice of topics for research. In this sense, the volume offers an insight into the state of education in Israel, and not only on the state of the sociological enterprise.

The starting point for such an analysis is the fact that education is a major focus of Israeli society. The national expenditure for education, as a proportion of the GNP, is higher (and in many cases considerably higher) than in most of the Western world.[2] The relationship of occupational prestige and the average schooling characteristic of the occupation, compared to the relationship of prestige and income, is considerably closer in Israel than say, in the U.S.[3] and is of particular relevance to several papers in the volume. Ethnic inequalities in *occupational* attainment are almost entirely linked to inequalities in *educational* attainment.[4] This correlation holds true for comparison between Jews and Arabs, as well as within the Jewish population: between those of "Western" (European-American) origin and those of "Oriental" (Asian-African) origin. Thus, when Israeli folk wisdom emphasizes the importance of education in Israeli society—it seems, for a change, to be correct.

But this fact can only be a starting point. It is not unknown for sociologists to focus their intellectual endeavors on topics far removed from the concerns and issues of society. But Israeli sociologists have been offered a temptation. Policymakers in education have been willing to pay attention to sociological research and to the opinions of sociologists. In many other countries, and in other areas in Israel, the potential contribution of sociologists to policymaking is an extremely indirect one, obtained by influence on the general intellectual climate. In Israeli educational policy, however, specific views and findings of sociologists have frequently been at least noted, and in not a few cases, even solicited. Some of my best friends would and do argue that, to a considerable extent, policymakers give lip service only to research, or that they utilize findings primarily in support of positions and attitudes taken on quite different grounds (cf., Coleman's conclusion in the Preface to this volume). Having been for a while between academe and government (as Chief Science Officer for the Ministry of Education), I tend toward a less skeptical evaluation. While acknowledging that this argument holds some truth, in a democracy scholars are not and should not be the ultimate judges of policy. Even so, the net opportunity for Israeli sociologists to have some kind of impact on educational policy has for long periods been greater than in many other countries. (One contributing factor is probably the small physical size of Israel, which facilitates interaction and direct communication between senior administrators and politicians on one hand, and researchers on the other.)

Thus, education in Israel is a promising field for the sociologist who feels a need and desire for involvement in the problems of his society. But, at the same time, the normative orientation of Israeli academe is "cosmopolitan" rather than "local," as described by Ben-David in this volume. These norms push the researcher toward topics and areas of high international visibility rather than toward those of immediate Israeli relevance. A possible solution to this dilemma is for the sociologist to focus on an issue of general import for current concerns of international sociology, but which at the same time has features relatively unique to Israel. The relative weight of uniqueness and generality will of course vary from study to study (including some studies that have an explicitly comparative focus, such as those in this volume by Lewis and by Harrison and Glaubman). Indeed, the papers to follow run most of the gamut. Gordon and Ackerman as well as Azarya focus on topics special to Israel; in fact, part of their concern is to highlight particularity and difference. This, of course, has general implications as well, in the sense of extending the scope of phenomena to be included in sociological explanation. But it is different from the concern of papers such as that by Dar and Resh or that by Shuval and Adler: the direct concern of these studies is a general issue, and the Israeli scene with its peculiarities is primarily important as the source of data. The majority of studies in the volume, nevertheless, do represent a mixture of Israeli and international concerns.

Moreover, most of the articles have, to a greater or lesser degree, policy implications, even if these are not explicitly spelled out, and even if the central interest of the author(s) is theoretical (such as in the paper by Yuchtman-Yaar and Semyonov). Frequently the presentation of the paper is addressed almost exclusively to the international community and its disciplinary concerns, as is required by the academic orientation of Israeli sociology. But at the same time, it is not difficult for the Israeli reader to "translate" the message into a policy-relevant statement. This is, of course, what could be expected considering the opportunity that exists—as suggested above—for Israeli sociologists to have an impact on policy. It also holds true for a paper such as that by Herzog and Shapira, which at first glance is addressed to the student of historical trends; in fact, the specific development described bears on issues on the present agenda of the educational system and on some public debate.

The implicit policy-orientation is particularly noteworthy in light of the criteria for the selection of papers as candidates for this volume. Only papers originally published in English are included. Many studies with a primary focus on policy evaluation, however, tend to choose Hebrew outlets. If, nevertheless, the majority of papers included are relevant to salient policy issues, this may be a not negligible indication of the conscious or unconscious orientation of educational sociology in Israel.

This policy feature of the papers to follow has implications for the reader: in several cases, the import of a study can only be fully appreciated on the basis of some familiarity with education and educational policy in Israel. In this respect, Part 1 of the volume, with the papers by Adler and by Elboim-Dror, provides an essential background for the subsequent sections: not only as a discussion of policy per se, but also as a way of setting the stage for what follows.

Prominent on this stage is the issue of educational equality. The major application in policy, as discussed by Adler, is (or at least has been) to the inequality in educational attainment between, on one hand, immigrants from Europe-America and their descendants, and, on the other hand, immigrants from Asia-Africa and their descendants. This issue is central to papers in Sections 3 and 4, and such aspects are found in other papers as well. It should be pointed out that in the Israeli context, the question is not only one of social ideology, but that there are national implications as well. An axiom of Zionism is the unity of the Jewish people, so that differences between Jews of different geographical origins are superficial or transitory, relative to their common bond and common destiny. This ought, of course, to be evident in the state of Israel, which is the crystallization of the Jewish national renaissance of the past century. If and when, nevertheless, inequality by origin is maintained in Israel, something central to the *raison d'etre* of the state is affected.

Moreover, the success of the Israeli educational system in overcoming this inequality has been limited. In spite of achievements described in some of the papers—such as school attendance—inequality has in important aspects not only persisted, but has even increased. Thus, while educational attainment at the post-secondary level has risen for all, it has risen most for the "Western" subgroup. Within the present-day population, the Western-Oriental inequality is greater in the generation of native-born Israelis than for their immigrant parents.[5] Or consider the difference between the probability of an Israeli-born youth of Western origin reaching university, and the probability for an Israeli-born youth of Oriental origin. This difference has increased over the last twenty years—not by much—but it has increased.[6]

These indications of growing inequality are found, despite the fact that over the years major policy steps have been taken to promote equality. The governmental budget is allocated differentially, with preference given to schools catering to socially deprived students, and funding provided for projects intended to raise the achievements of such students. The period of compulsory education has been extended, and high school made tuition-free. The structure of elementary school and of the transition to secondary school was changed—and changed in such a way as to accelerate ethnic desegregation, or "integration," in schools. The latter policy in particular has attracted the attention of the public at large, and of researchers. The papers by Schwartzwald and Amir and by Halper *et al.* are evidence of this interest. The initiation of the policy of integration in Israel was not unrelated to contemporaneous developments in the U.S. These studies thus illustrate a denominator that is common to most papers: the possibility of simultaneous contribution to the advancement of general knowledge and to issues on the Israeli scene. Indeed, studies such as these are frequently cited both in general public discussion and within the educational establishment.

The persistence of important aspects of inequality despite an apparently egalitarian policy has led to increased concern on the part of sociologists with the mechanisms of selection and tracking in the Israeli school system. The issue of tracking is in one way or another central to the papers by Yogev, Shavit, and Yogev and Ayalon. It is instructive to compare the perspective of these papers—all recent publications—with that of the older paper by Kahane and Starr, which also deals with vocational or technological education, but in a different vein. This difference in perspective parallels a difference in approach among policymakers—and, of course, a difference in method, to which I shall return below.

The inequality in educational attainment between Jews and Arabs has not been nearly as central—either to educational policy or to educational research. I would argue that this correlation is another instance of the responsiveness of educational sociology in Israel to the priorities in policy. The illustrations above demonstrate a tendency of research to pursue issues that have priority in policy. The case of Arab education provides the other side of the coin: less emphasis on policy is accompanied by less attention in research.

The argument is strengthened by very recent developments: issues of Arab-Jewish relations have gained prominence in the educational system—and at the same time several Israeli sociologists (including some represented in this volume) have initiated major studies of stratification in the Arab sector of Israeli society, with emphasis on the role and mechanisms of educational attainment. In the meantime, this volume can only offer one major contribution, the 1978 review by Mar'i.

This paucity is the more regrettable, as the Arab-language educational system, by its achievements over the last couple of decades, presents an intriguing question for educational sociology: in spite of its relative lack of resources, Arab education has been some kind of success story. Not that inequality has, by any means, disappeared. The general level of educational attainment of non-Jews in Israel, however, has risen sharply, as has this level when compared to that of Jews;[7] and school attendance among adolescent Christian Arabs has come close to that of their Jewish peers.[8]

Educational sociologists are probably less surprised than are policymakers when there is no clear correlation between allocation of resources and achievements; the positive factors accelerating Arab educational achievements are, however, unclear (or, at least, in dispute).

The Jewish religious school system is another case in which this anthology underrepresents the importance of an aspect of Israeli education. Although the distinction between the religious and the secular ("general") trends appears as a variable in other papers, only the study by Bar-Lev and Krausz is entirely dedicated to a feature unique to this system. "Unique" in two senses: first, in practice religious schools accord priority, more than do secular schools, to shaping the future values and behavior of their students—and this future is the topic of the paper; second, the yeshiva high schools studied are an innovation in Israel, striving to merge, in content as well as in pedagogy, tradition and modernity.

Actually, I am not aware of any major study by Israeli non-religious (i.e., non-observer) researchers (and they are in the majority in the sociological community) that is devoted to issues particular to the religious system; and this in spite of some features of the system that would seem to be of general interest—e.g., the application to advanced Judaic studies of principles (traditional to Jewish learning) of peer-teaching and cooperative learning in Judaic subjects, together with routine teaching in "secular" subjects. (Major studies of cooperative learning have indeed been carried out in Israel; e.g., Hertz-Lazarowitz, 1984. But they have not included the yeshiva high schools.) I am tempted to explain this by the closure of the religious system; it has enjoyed educational autonomy for more than 60 years, and the likelihood that the policy of its establishment would be greatly influenced by non-observer outsiders, be they sociologists or not, is probably not very high. Thus, again, the choice of topic for research may be influenced by the potential for policy impact (although a more prosaic explanation would focus on possible difficulties for outsiders to gain access to research in the religious system).

I have suggested that the choice of topics by Israeli educational sociologists—insofar as expressed in this volume—is related to factors on the local scene, and in particular to issues prominent in educational policy. Not so for approach and method. In this respect there are hardly surprises for the non-Israeli reader, except perhaps in the absence of certain approaches (or ideologies). Israeli sociology has not undergone major wars around Radical Sociology or Interpretative Sociology. This fact should not be taken to mean that its mission has been to strengthen the educational establishment and its policies. Nor does my assertion that issues of research tend to follow issues in policy imply that research has been geared to providing support for policymakers. The reader will easily see that most papers have a critical bent—but it is *differentiated* critique, which probably is good strategy by a criterion of desired influence on policy.

In Israeli sociology of education, macro and micro; "soft" and "hard"; structural equations and anthropological observation—exist together, and not only within the covers of the volume. Perhaps it should also be mentioned that the contributors to the volume have different institutional affiliations. I am not certain that the reader will be able to guess the departmental labels of the authors as "sociology," "education," or "psychology" on the basis of their writing only.

For those interested in predicting trends, I may, however, add that (judging by these papers) there is a negative correlation—albeit not perfect—between the age of the author and the use of "hard" data and multivariate techniques. This is hardly surprising, considering the affinity of Israeli sociology to the sociological community in the U.S., which constitutes the major normative as well as comparative reference group. Several of the contributors are Americans by origin, the majority have been trained in the U.S., and practically all commute—in mind, if not in body—between the two countries. I shall, of course, not venture to evaluate the qualitative level of Israeli educational sociology in general or as it is represented in this volume—either as an intellectual enterprise, or as a contribution to educational policy. This is the prerogative of the reader and of Israeli policymakers, respectively.

I do hope that the reader will conclude that sociology of education in Israel is not only an active field, but also is of some significance. At least, many colleagues—from the ranks of those represented in this volume, and others as well—would agree that it offers researchers a combination of applied importance and intellectual fun.

Notes

1. Coleman, p. 7.
2. Central Bureau of Statistics, 1986, Table XXII/4.
3. Kraus, 1976.
4. Kraus and Hodge.
5. Central Bureau of Statistics, 1986, Table XXII/2.
6. *Ibid.*, Table XXII/13.
7. *Ibid.*, Table XXII/1.
8. *Ibid.*, Tables XXII/11 and XXII/12.

References

Central Bureau of Statistics.
    1986.   *Statistical abstract of Israel, No. 37*, Jerusalem.

Coleman, James S. Preface, in Boocock, Sarane S. and E.O. Schild (eds.)
   1968.   *Simulation Games in Learning.* Beverly Hills, Calif: Sage.
Hertz-Lazarowitz, R. and S. Sharan.
   1984.   Enhancing pro-social behavior through cooperative learning in the classroom. In Karylowski, J., *The Development and Maintenance of Pro-Social Behavior*, New York: Plenum Books.
Kraus, Vered.
   1976.   Grading of Occupations in Israel. Ph.D. diss. Jerusalem: Hebrew University.
Kraus, Vered and Robert W. Hodge. Ethnicity and stratification in Israel, forthcoming.

Part I

THE SOCIAL STATE
OF EDUCATIONAL POLICIES

3.

Israeli Education Addressing Dilemmas Caused by Pluralism: A Sociological Perspective

Chaim Adler

I. Introduction*

Israeli society exhibits three main divisions which may be looked at as an expression of pluralism.[1] As in most similar situations these divisions are the result of demographic, religious and national differences or cleavages. More specifically:

(a) The Jewish majority of Israel includes in its composition the main subdivisions of the Jewish people as they existed in the Jewish communities all over the world from which the Jewish citizens of Israel (their parents or grandparents) emigrated. One such subdivision may be defined as 'ethnic' and traced to differences in religious practices, mores and traditions, or paths of the Jewish dispersion. Essentially it reflects the social and cultural context from which people (or communities) originated: those who immigrated to Israel *after* having assimilated the main elements of the Western industrial civilization (mostly of European and American background and those who immigrated to Israel after *partial* assimilation of such patterns or even *prior* to such processes of assimilation (mostly of Asian and African background). The dilemma which these differences pose for

* I wish to express my thanks to my colleagues, Mrs Lorraine Gastwirt, Assistant Director of the National Council of Jewish Women U.S.A. Research Institute for Innovation in Education and Dr Reuven Kahane of the Department of Sociology and the School of Education for suggesting alterations in the manuscript; to my colleague Mrs Ilana Felsenthal of the NCJW Research Institute and the School of Education for her careful reading of the manuscript and suggesting valuable changes and additions; to Dr Geulah Solomon of the Institute of Contemporary Jewry, and to Mrs Chaya Buckwold for her kind help and patience in typing and retyping the manuscript.

Israeli schools is how to contribute to equalization of opportunities and elimination of the educational and social gaps resulting from this ethnic division while at the same time preserving (and, perhaps, raising) standards of education.

(b) Another important subdivision of the Jewish majority of Israel is along religious parameters, essentially setting apart those who abide strictly by the faith and traditions from those who do not. These differences in religious adherence and practice, for reasons beyond the scope of this paper, have given rise to a quite divided social system. Differences in attitude toward religion are reflected in the structure of communities (housing and settlements), politics (parties) and even legal arrangements. Public schools, too, are subdivided into 'state religious' and 'general' schools.

The dilemma for the educational system results from its having been conceived as one of the main tools for integrating a new society born of immigration from eighty different countries. Education was expected to strengthen the purpose and ideals that constituted Israel's *raison d'être* as an independent contemporary state while simultaneously drawing on the age-old Jewish heritage to create a stronger sense of shared cultural roots.

Will the identity of the Israeli-born younger generation be shaped by the age-old Jewish religious tradition, or will there emerge a modern adapted secular blend? And is there not the looming danger that instead of treating such a modern Jewish culture, Israel's educational system will unintentionally contribute to the blurring of the Jewish identity of its students (at least of the majority who study in state secular schools)?

(c) A different kind of subdivision of Israeli society exists along the lines of 'nationhood', that is, the Jewish majority and the Arab minority. About 17 per cent of the 4,000,000 Israeli citizens are Arabs. This division creates a particularly difficult dilemma for the whole of Israeli society. On the one hand the social and cultural revolution which gave rise to Israel was essentially a Jewish one, resulting in the formation of an independent, democratic, creative, modern society based on a vision of social justice. On the other hand, however, the democratic and egalitarian elements of this vision surely call for the incorporation (at least in the realms of the polity and the economy) of any minority living within its borders. The dilemma is sharpened by the fact that while the Arabs of Israel are a minority among the

Jews, the Jews are a tiny minority in the Arab Middle and Near East. Unfortunately, moreover, the Jewish entity has so far been unwelcome in the Arab world, so much so that in thirty-five years of Israel's statehood five wars have erupted and a continuous state of war with at least part of the Arab world has persisted. The Arabs of Israel, consequently, while being Israeli citizens (by volition, in view of the option to emigrate), are also part of the Arab world (culturally, linguistically, religiously, and to an extent, politically). This feature makes for mutual ambivalences as to social incorporation on the part of both the Jewish majority (due to political and military sensitivities) and the Arab minority (due to their desire to keep their distinct and separate identity). Consequently, while schools are expected to play an integrative and equalizing role for the Jewish majority, the separateness of schools for Arabs and Jews may curtail their ability to provide equalization of social opportunities for Arab students.

II.   Background

Although Israel's statehood is only about thirty-five years old, its educational system dates back about eighty years. When Israel gained independence in 1948, there already existed a fully-fledged educational system from kindergarten through university that included teacher training institutions, a curriculum, a school inspectorate, and a quite elaborate examination system. Perhaps most important, from the early 1920s there existed a language — Hebrew — which was universally used as the vehicle of instruction and served as a symbol of the emergence of a revived culture.

Three prominent features characterized the pre-independence educational system:

Uniformity. The educational system of the pre-statehood Jewish community in Palestine was essentially uniform in structure and content. This uniformity coincided with the social, cultural and demographic homogeneity of the Jewish population in Palestine during the 1930s and 1940s. A basically non-differentiated educational system could meet the educational needs of most children. However, with the foundation of the state in 1948, and the tremendous growth of the population due to mass immigration from four continents, the almost perfect fit between students' needs and the opportunities offered by this uniform educational system began to come apart.

At the same time, the educational system from the 1920s until the 1940s was not expected to be responsible for the preparation and promotion of sophisticated manpower as needed by industry, scientific endeavours or complex bureaucracy. Most of the positions which required highly trained manpower were occupied by people educated in Europe who immigrated as adults. Since independence, however, Israel's educational system has been increasingly vested with responsibility for the development of such sophisticated manpower. It remains to be seen whether the system inherited from the Jewish community in Palestine was sufficiently equipped to fulfil this function.

Partisan affiliation. Secondly, the educational system which was handed down from the Jewish community in Palestine to the state of Israel was politically subdivided along partisan lines. The absence of centralized state institutions meant there was no centralized public schooling. Instead the school system was owned, conducted and supervised by the main political parties. This resulted in three major trends of schooling — socialist, religious (essentially orthodox) and general.[2]

This political subdivision, which was essentially of an ideological nature, did not countervail the far-reaching curricular and structural uniformity. Although schools were run by three different political movements, they did not differ dramatically in their curricular emphases and certainly not in their general structure, educational approaches or academic standards. In 1953 the political 'trends' in education were abolished, and a bipartite state school system was established, introducing 'general' and 'religious' (orthodox) state schools. One problem that emerged has been the segregatedness of those two distinct educational subsystems (both, as mentioned, part of state-run education)[3] Perhaps an even more critical issue concerns the nature, contents and flavour of the Jewish identity to be nurtured in the general, non-religious sector of public school education, the segment that caters for about 75 per cent of the school population.

Separateness of Arab education. As indicated, the educational system of the Jewish community in Palestine was essentially directed towards the creation of an independent Jewish political entity.

Schools were seen as a major tool for the stimulation and acceleration of the social revolution that was put into motion by Zionism. It is, therefore, not surprising that the Jews of Palestine preferred their own school system from kindergarten (almost universally attended) to a Hebrew university (which, of course, only very few attended).

The state schools run by the British mandatory administration were unsatisfactory to the Jews in terms of duration of schooling (only six compulsory years), in terms of language (a mixture of English, Arabic and Hebrew), and most importantly in that they did not serve the national-revolutionary fervour of the society. The Arabs of Palestine, on the other hand, many of whom were still illiterate, perceived these government schools as serving their needs perfectly. For some of these Arabs, many of whom were peasants, it was conceived as even too much schooling, especially as far as their daughters were concerned.

The growing momentum of Zionism, peaking with the holocaust and the end of the Second World War, came into increasing conflict with the Palestinian Arab national movement. Separate school systems, one private (Hebrew) and one public (the government's, almost exclusively serving Arabs) contributed to the growing segregatedness of the Jewish and Arab social systems in Palestine.

Against this background three basic challenges have existed for Israel's educational system to this day:

(1) The recognition that an egalitarian ideology calls for a democratic education system providing equal educational opportunities despite serious social and economic inequalities, stimulated extensive policy and curriculum adaptations.[4] At the same time Israel has had to mobilize all its potential for human and intellectual excellence so as to secure its very survival and sustain its economic, technological, cultural and structural growth. Equalizing opportunities and nurturing excellence, however, are directions that usually lead to conflicting or even opposing policies.

(2) Israel's educational system has had to address itself to the fact that between two-thirds and three-quarters of the nation's children grow up in secular homes and study in the general sector of the public school system. They thus need to acquire motivation and sources of legitimation for their Jewishness other

than the traditional religious-based ones that had predominated. The general school is being torn between a non-orthodox though traditional orientations, and a modern-scientific though Judaic orientation.[5]

(3) The Israeli educational system's democratic structure and commitments call for the provision of equal opportunities. At the same time, however, the separateness of the Jewish and Arab school systems (in view of the desire to preserve independent cultural, social and political entities) casts a shadow over the chances of providing equal educational opportunities.

In line with the basic theme of this book, the paper will concentrate on the first and third challenges only.

III.   Coping with the first challenge: bridging social gaps and coping with the manpower needs of an industrialized civilization

From the late nineteenth century until the establishment of the state of Israel in 1948, the Jewish settlers of modern Palestine were predominantly of European origin. In 1948 more than 90 per cent of Israeli Jewish inhabitants were of European background. Then mass immigration began, doubling the population in the first three years of statehood and trebling it over the first twelve years. It is the combination of the origin of the immigrants and their numbers which is of interest here. Since independence, only some 50 per cent of the new immigrants have been of European or American origin, the remainder coming from Near and Middle Eastern Jewish communities — mainly Iran, Iraq, Yemen, and North Africa. The chief ethnic division among Jews in Israel, therefore, is between citizens of European or Anglo-Saxon background and those of Asian or African origin.[6]

Because European cultural styles and institutional patterns prevail in modern Israel, immigration for many Asian and African Jews has meant an encounter with an unknown and basically different social system. Some characteristics of the Asian and African immigrant groups have constituted a priori obstacles to immediate social integration. For example, many Asian and African adults have enjoyed little or no formal schooling prior to immigration, and very few have undergone technological training congruent with the needs of a modern economy. In addition, many have arrived with very large families and often have been ignorant of, or opposed to, family planning. These characteristics have placed these immigrants in the lower socioeconomic strata of Israeli society. In consequence, a high correlation between socioeconomic status and ethnic origin has emerged, a correlation manifested in school performance as well as by other institutional indicators.[7]

At the same time the school system has been seen as one of the main agents of social integration.[8] Indeed, it was harnessed to that purpose from the early 1950s. The main strategies applied by the educational system to reducing the gap between ethnic groups may be subsumed under the following five categories:

(a) *Administrative measures*. In the first years, when mass failure showed up even in the low grades, the educational system was so overwhelmed by the growth in student numbers on the one hand and the wide gaps in achievement on the other that it could only respond administratively. For instance, the practice of holding over failing students was abolished. This measure indeed removed the obstacles faced by students of disadvantaged backgrounds from promotion to the following grade. It did not, however (like most other administrative measures), have any impact on the source of the problem.

(b) *Pedagogical measures*. Towards the end of the 1950s pedagogical intervention was initiated. Some of the measures introduced included:

   (i) early intervention, mainly through kindergartens and nurseries; home intervention programmes were introduced later;

   (ii) experimentation with didactic measures, remedial teaching methods, and curricular innovations;

   (iii) enrichment programmes aimed specifically at the upper achievement quartile of the disadvantaged.

(c) *Structural differentiating measures*. Schools faced with mounting numbers of 'underachievers' at the end of the 1960s, despite the pedagogic measures, applied instituted patterns of ability groupings. Even though such measures helped schools to overcome problems incurred by great gaps in achievement between students, they evidently contributed to the segregation of students by ethnic background without, at the same time, having any impact on their achievement levels.[9]

(d) *Structural integrative measures.* The continued existence of a social and economic division based on the ethnic origin of Jewish parents conflicted with the goal of a modern unified Jewish nation and the egalitarian principles on which it was founded. As structural differentiation seemed to perpetuate this division (although it did not grow larger), integrative measures were tried. Integrative efforts focused on enrichment, aiming at raising scholastic achievements and school retention rates of students of disadvantaged origin. At the same time these measures carried a symbolic message by offering all students in the integrated system, irrespective of their (or their parents') country of origin, shared school environments (the school building, the teachers, the curriculum). It thus symbolized structurally the commitment to national unity, social solidarity and equality.[10] In fact, as research shows, the quality of educational inputs into integrated schools is considerably better than that of the segregated ones.[11] A school reform, the core of which was the formation of integrated junior high schools, was introduced in 1968 as a result of a resolution of the Knesset.[12]

(e) *Intensive focusing on hard-core disadvantaged communities.* In the early 1970s, the Educational Welfare Programme singled out the most depressed and disadvantaged communities to receive intensive and concerted compensatory efforts (specifically decided upon by local steering committees). Secluded and mostly homogeneous cities or neighbourhoods, where integration is virtually impossible to achieve without massive bussing, became the target for this programme.[13]

Impact of these reforms

Although it is not possible to evaluate the total impact of these measures, perhaps the most impressive indicator is the expansion of the educational system.[14] Not only has school-leaving age been raised twice since 1948 — schooling is compulsory today between the ages of 5 and 16 — but all four-year-olds and almost all three-year-olds are in kindergartens or nurseries.[15] Ability grouping (from seventh grade) and tracking (from tenth or eleventh grade) result in school paths for students of Asian or African (AA) and European or Anglo-Saxon (EA) origin that are not necessarily identical, but 13 years of almost universal school attendance cannot but leave its imprint on students, even if differential school achievements persist.

With the abolition in 1978 of school fees up to age 18 and the essential success of many of the compensatory measures applied over more than a generation, almost two-thirds of seventeen-year-old Jews were completing twelfth grade! (It should be added, however, that about two-thirds of the AA students complete vocational, non-university directed, programmes while two-thirds of the EA students complete academic, university directed, programmes).[16] An additional 5–6 per cent combine study and work during their adolescent years.[17]

This expansion of the educational system can be viewed as a *policy* directed at creating opportunities for all young Israelis as well as equalizing opportunities for the disadvantaged. The dramatic diminution of drop-out rates in secondary schools during the 1970s, on the other hand, should be viewed as a *result* (at least in part) of educational policies (see Tables 6.1 and 6.2). Indeed, research clearly shows that length of participation in school is highly correlated with social mobility.[18]

Table 6.1 The development of transition rates from first to twelfth grade (two cohorts, commencing first grade in 1957–58 and 1967–68 respectively)

Year commenced			Percentage reaching				
1st grade	8th grade	12th grade	8th grade	9th grade	10th grade	11th grade	12th grade
1957–58	1964–65	1968–69	82.7	64.8	55.7	44.7	32.2
1967–68	1974–75	1978–79	95.5	91.2	77.9	64.6	55.9

Source: M. Egorzi and P. Bilezki, *The Educational System in the Mirror of Numbers,* Ministry of Education and Culture, Jerusalem, 1980, Table 11 (Hebrew, mimeo)

Another indicator of the impact of these democratizing educational measures is success of AA and EA candidates in the government-administered matriculation examinations. These examinations, taken mostly by the about-to-graduate students of academic high schools, are necessary for university admission. While in the late 1960s about 6 per cent of all the seventeen-year-olds of AA origin in Israeli society successfully passed these examinations (as compared with about 33 per cent of the EA seventeen-year-olds), this rate rose to about 15 per cent in the early 1980s while the percentage of EA seventeen-year-olds remained constant.[19]

Table 6.2 Transition rates from tenth to twelfth grade (per cent)

	Grade	Total	Israeli and European or American origin	Asian or African origin
		First cohort 1970–72		
		Secondary education – total		
1970	10th	100	100	100
1971	11th	78.5	84.8	72.8
1972	12th	59.6	68.4	48.2
		Second cohort 1975–77		
		Secondary education – total		
1975	10th	100	100	100
1976	11th	78.9	84.1	74.4
1977	12th	67.8	75.0	61.5
		Vocational and agriculture		
1975	10th	100	100	100
1976	11th	71.4	75.9	69.2
1977	12th	56.0	62.8	52.7
		Academic education		
1975	10th	100	100	100
1976	11th	88.7	89.4	87.4
1977	12th	83.1	83.0	83.3

Source: Egozi and Bilezki, *The Educational System in the Mirror of Numbers,* 1979, Table 16.

Table 6.3 The proportion of 14–17 year-old Asian and African adolescents in the population at large and in secondary education (per cent)

	Amongst 14–17 year olds	In secondary schools	9th grade	12th grade	Academic schools	Vocational schools	Agricultural schools
1966–67	49.9	35.6	45.3	18.9	25.4	47.0	52.4
1976–77	58.7	50.6	54.6	46.6	37.5	63.7	65.9
1977–78	58.4	51.3	55.0	47.5	38.4	64.1	65.3
1978–79	57.7	51.5	53.5	48.3	38.7	64.3	64.7
1979–80	57.3	51.9	54.9	49.6	39.9	64.4	64.6

Source: Egozi and Bilezki, *The Educational System in the Mirror of Numbers,* 1980, Table 25; and Bilezki and Ch. Turki, *The Educational System in the Mirror of Numbers,* 1982, Table 26.

Table 6.4 The participation of 14–17-year-old adolescents of Asian and African origin in academic secondary schools

	1966–67	*1973–74*	*1976–77*
The proportion of Asians and African adolescents among 14–17-year-olds	49.9	57.7	58.7
The proportion of Asian and African adolescents:			
Secondary schools – Total	35.6	46.6	50.6
Academic schools			
9th grade	33.9	37.2	39.7
12th grade	16.4	27.7	33.7

Source: Egozi and Bilezki, *The Educational System in the Mirror of Numbers*, 1978, adapted from Table 13.

As Table 6.3 clearly indicates, the rate of under-representation of AA adolescents (aged 14–17) in secondary schools changed from 14.3 per cent in 1966–7 to only 5.4 per cent in 1978–9. Table 6.4 shows that the underrepresentation of AA 14–17-year-olds in academic schools decreased from 24.5 per cent in 1966–7 to only 17.4 per cent twelve years later. Table 6.4 shows that in twelfth grade academic schools the rate of underrepresentation shrank from 33.5 per cent to 25 per cent over the same period. And Table 6.5 shows that the relative

Table 6.5 University attendance of 20–29-year-olds,* by continent of birth (rates per 10,000 in respective population groups)

	1964–65	*1974–75*
Israeli born – Total	893	951
Father Israeli born	524	997
Father Asian or African born	158	299
Father European or American born	1,074	1,405
Asian or African born	79	211
European or American born	535	842
Total	413	716

*   In view of the universal military services of Israeli youth, freshmen at Israeli universities are 20–21 years old.

Source: Egozi and Bilezki, *The Educational System in the Mirror of Numbers*, 1979, Table 33.

participation of 20–29-year-olds of AA origin in higher education expanded between the years 1965–6 and 1974–5 much more than did the participation among their counterparts of EA origin. Indeed, the rate of increase was about 100 per cent for Israeli-born young adults of AA origin and about 200 per cent for AA-born as compared to about 30 per cent growth among Israeli-born of EA origin and about 50 per cent for EA-born young adults.

This progress may be cautiously related to the emergence of an AA Jewish middle class in Israel and to the beginning of a penetration of people of AA origin into élite positions in politics, the military, business, and to a lesser degree the professions.

Nevertheless, essentially all of Israel's lower class is composed of people of AA origin. The policies enacted during the past decade to diminish inequalities and prevent the perpetuation thereof into future generations (such as that of Project Renewal) are therefore to be welcomed because they are directed at ecological pockets of lower-income or lower-class groups in Israel's population which exhibit signs of a self-perpetuating 'culture of poverty' rather than at entire ethnic groups. This statement does not contradict the fact that in recent years 'ethnic-consciousness' of people of AA origin has risen and been partially translated into political power. The analysis thereof, however, is beyond the scope of this paper.

To sum up, even though gaps in school achievements and inequality in the opportunity to attend academic secondary schools and universities have not disappeared, they certainly have not deepened and have in some respects considerably decreased. Although whether this shrinkage is socially significant (considering the very short time in which these developments took place and the circumstances under which they occurred) or not is a matter of value judgement, I strongly lean towards the opinion that it is.

Equal opportunity or selective excellence

Educational systems virtually everywhere are subject to opposing demands: one calls for efforts to democratize the system, offer mass education and equalize opportunities (which might lead to compromising standards); the other emphasizes maintaining high academic standards (and tends to be selective and even elitist). In the second case as few students will complete a fully-fledged academic course of study, fewer of them will have access to opportunities that require academic certification.

Israel was forced in its short history to try and satisfy both demands simultaneously. It undertook to reduce the serious social and economic gaps between groups of different ethnic origins and, at the same time, it also launched a rapid process of industrialization. Industrialization was complicated by the need to replace a generation of skilled manpower trained in Europe and America prior to their immigration by locally educated and trained workers. It is very hard to judge so far whether the results were merely a compromise between those essentially conflicting goals or constitute a development in which they successfully complement each other. As the following analysis will indicate, I tend to lean towards the latter conclusion.

Expansion of educational opportunity led to both the inclusion of the very young (three- to four-year-olds) in the system and the opening up of secondary education to all adolescents — clear strategies of democratization. Table 6.6 shows an annual growth rate of participation in education between 1970 and 1981 exceeding the population growth rates for respective age groups between 1970 and 1981, particularly in post-secondary and academic higher education institutions. At the same time, however, the educational system did not abandon the quite selective track of senior academic high schools. Only about 25 per cent of each year's age cohort successfully complete the course in those schools and thereby constitute the main pool of candidates for university admission. With the abolition of school fees in 1978, acceptance into this track has become almost

Table 6.6　Number of students by school rank (Jewish education) (thousands)

	1970–71	1975–76	1980–81	1981–82	Average annual growth rate 1970–81 (per cent)
Kindergartens	107.6	180.6	211.9	208.8	6.2
Elementary schools	409.8	441.7	509.6	523.0	2.2
Secondary schools	155.7	177.8	195.9	199.9	2.3
Post-secondary schools	18.3	31.6	34.9	36.7	6.5
Academic higher education	39.5	51.3	57.0	57.9	3.5
Total	730.9	883.0	1,009.3	1,026.2	3.1

Source: Bilezki and Turki, *The Educational System in the Mirror of Numbers*, 1982, Table 2.

Table 6.7 Numbers of 17-year-olds in the population and in the graduating class (12th grade) of academic high schools (1975, 1981)

	1975–76	*1981–82*
Numbers in population	about 52.000	about 55.000*
Numbers in graduating class of academic high schools	about 14.900	about 19.800**
Numbers of matriculated graduates	about 12.690 (24%)	about 16.800*** (30%)

*   Table 23 reports that the number of 14–17-year-olds in those years was 209.000 and 215.000 respectively. We assumed that each age cohort comprised about 25%.

**   Table 12 reports that the number of students in 12th grade in 1975 was about 27.500 and that about 55% of those studied in academic high schools; similarly in 1981 about 36.000 studied in 12th grades and 53% of them in academic high schools.

*** Based on the assumption that about 85% of the graduating class successfully pass the matriculation examination.

Source: Bilezki and Turki. *The Educational Systems in the Mirror of Numbers.* 1982.

solely dependent upon academic performance. Assuming that about 85 per cent of the graduating academic class successfully took the matriculation examination in 1975–6, this group would have included — according to Table 6.7 — about 2.700 students or about 24 per cent of that year's age cohort of seventeen-year-olds. In 1980–81 this number rose to about 16,800 or 30.5 per cent. Vocational education also contributes graduates who successfully pass the matriculation examination and thus increase the pool of university candidates (see Table 6.7).

Israel's system of higher education has dramatically expanded over the past thirty years from one university (the Hebrew University of Jerusalem) and one technological institute (the Technion) — both founded about twenty years prior to the establishment of the state — to include four additional universities. (Tel-Aviv, Bar-Ilan, Ben Gurion in Beer-Sheeva, and Haifa).

Many of the academic positions in these institutions are held by scholars and researchers who are products of Israeli secondary schools and undergraduate education. A growing number of the young faculty have even acquired their PhDs in Israel. At the same time, the rate of Israeli scholars' publications and their participation in international research teams, symposia or conferences is steadily rising. Thus, for instance, there were about 450 publications by Israeli

Table 6.8 Numbers of students in institutions of higher learning, by degree

	1948–49	1959–60	1969–70	1978–79	1980–81	1982–83
First degree	1,549	8,348	28,053	39,010	40,910	43,380
Second degree	*	*	5,156	2,370	13,550	11,155
Third degree	86	927	1,346	2,970	3,070	3,000
Diploma	—	—	819	1,390	4,390	4,830
Special programme	—	—	865	3,050	—	—
Total	1,635	9,275	36,239	55,790	58,970	63,365

* Included among those studying for degrees
Source: Statistical Abstract of Israel, 1980. Table XXII/26; *Statistical Abstract of Israel, 1983.* Table XXII/36; and Bilezki and Turki. *The Educational System in the Mirror of Numbers.* 1982. Table 21.

scholars until 1959, while in 1967 alone there were about 2,000 publications in the natural sciences.[20] The number of students in the Israeli institutions of higher education rose from about 200 in 1929 and 1,700 in 1949 to more than 63,000 in 1982–3 (see Table 6.8). This growth rate (almost thirty-five times) far transcends that of the population growth over the respective years (about six times). The growth rate of degree recipients is even more dramatic (see Table 6.9). In addition, the number of Israeli applications entered for registration of patents rose from 638 in 1949 to 2,917 in 1982.[21]

Parallel with this development an 'explosion' of technological and vocational training took place. These tracks became — certainly in the earlier years — the main avenue for educational promotion and mobility for adolescents of AA origin. Indeed, today about two-thirds of this student body comes from AA backgrounds. One could

Table 6.9 Recipients of university degrees, by degrees

	1948–49	1959–60	1969–70	1978–79	1981–82
First degree	135	779	4,064	6,602	7,396
Second degree	48	337	807	1,767	1,754
Third degree	10	81	238	401	353
Diploma	—	—	457	786	585
Total	193	1,237	5,566	9,556	10,088

Source: Statistical Abstract of Israel, 1980. Table XXII/32; and *Statistical Abstract of Israel, 1983.* Table XXII/42.

certainly argue that these statistics suggest a discriminatory selection procedure. However, we have already noted the growing penetration of young women and men of AA origin into post-secondary training and studies (alas, even if not rapidly enough), which suggests a general trend of upward mobility.[22]

The development of skilled, locally trained manpower has great social, economic and even military importance for Israeli society. Within that context the growing percentage of skilled blue-collar workers, foremen in industry, and technicians of AA origin is highly significant. Even if top management and most senior staff of Israel's industry are still of EA origin, Israel's emergence into modern industrial civilization cannot be explained without recognizing the impact of the massive expansion of vocational training and technological education and the critical role played by many young women and men whose families originated in North Africa and the Middle East. The importance of vocational education can be seen in the rise between 1970–71 and 1981–2 of the percentage of vocational school students from 29 per cent to almost 47 per cent of the total twelfth grade student population.[23] Moreover, in 1981–2 about 25 per cent of twelfth grade vocational students studied in the vocational academic stream, and of those, about 65 per cent (about 6,000 students) took a full matriculation examination.[24] Since the total number of students who took the matriculation exam in 1981–2 was about 16,000, the vocational track contributed about 38 per cent.[25] In many respects, Israel's internationally recognized success in science-based endeavours such as medicine, high technology or agriculture, not to mention the military, can be attributed to a secondary school system which has emphasized quality of education and standards of achievement in spite of understandable and surely legitimate efforts in the opposite direction.

In conclusion, Israel's massive investment in the expansion of public education and in making it available and accessible to all, as well as the deep commitment to education and willingness to share in the burden (through taxes or fees) of its maintenance and extension to growing parts of the population, may be a partial explanation for the relative openness and democratization of the educational system being able to coexist with its relatively high educational standards.

IV.   Coping with the third challenge: providing equal educational opportunities for Israel's Arab population

To understand the development of Arab education in Israel, some background information seems to be called for.

During the year-long Israeli War of Independence (in 1948–9) there was an exodus of about 750,000 Palestinian Arabs who feared being crushed by the combating forces (some, perhaps, hoping to return upon the victory of the four invading armies). The tendency of the educated Arab middle class (and other urban inhabitants) to leave the country was significantly higher than that of the rural and lower-class population. In consequence, the 250,000 Arabs who remained in the newly established state of Israel were bereft of their intelligentsia in general and teachers in particular. Consequently most of the teachers in Arab schools were unqualified during the first fifteen or twenty years of Israel's statehood. Indeed, many Arabic-speaking Jews were recruited so as to fill some of the vacancies. This situation has changed dramatically in recent years so that, by 1981–2, 72.5 per cent of Arab elementary school teachers, 91.7 per cent of Arab intermediate school teachers and 88.7 per cent of Arab secondary school teachers were graduates of either teachers' colleges or universities.[26]

Among the Arabs who chose to remain in Israel many were peasants. To this day Arabs tend to occupy lower socioeconomic positions in Israel to a greater degree than Jews. Although in 1982, for example, 24.5 per cent of the Jewish labour force (aged 14 and over) had only eight years' education or less, the corresponding figure for Israeli Arabs was 59.2 per cent.[27] This situation contributes to a vicious circle of low education of adults, leading to low socioeconomic employment opportunities, and again to relatively low achievements by the next generation in schools.

The language issue also needs to be discussed. As one of the two official languages of Israel, Arabic is the language of instruction for Arab students from kindergarten to twelfth grade. This policy is consistent with the existing situation in which neither the majority nor the minority wishes to lose its identity or to integrate socially or culturally with the other. Hebrew is taught as the main foreign language starting in the fourth grade and English in the sixth.

The Arab student is thus at a distinct disadvantage with respect to higher education. The language of instruction in all institutions of higher education in Israel is Hebrew. There are still far too few qualified Arab candidates to justify the opening of an Arabic teaching university. Both in competing for admission and, once admitted, in the university classroom, most Jewish students (except for recent immigrants) hold an edge not only in their command of Hebrew, which the Arabs learn as a foreign language, but in their ability to use English, which is essential to higher learning due to the almost complete lack of translated texts and scientific literature in either Hebrew or Arabic.

Additionally, the political situation and its social and cultural ramifications have influenced Arab education. On the one hand, the Arabs of Israel were almost entirely cut off from social, cultural, linguistic and ideological developments in the rest of the Arab world for nineteen years until the Six Day War of 1967 by the ongoing state of belligerence to which Israel was subjected by all its surrounding Arab neighbours. During that time the Arab minority in Israel also suffered from severe suspicion from the Jewish majority and even surveillance by the security forces. The relatively limited success of Arab children and youth in secondary and higher education in Israel's early years needs to be viewed against this background.

As of 1967, the state of the Arab minority in Israel changed dramatically. Israel's conquest of the West Bank of the Jordan and the Gaza strip opened up opportunities for contact between the 400,000 Arabs of Israel and the 1 million or so Arabs of the West Bank and Gaza. Moreover, the 'open bridges' policy of Israel *vis-à-vis* Jordan allowed for the emergence of a dialogue between the Arabs of Israel and the rest of the Arab world. These events did not, however, create a state of integration or mutual acceptance. The Arabs of Israel, with very few exceptions, decided to remain Israeli citizens. The Israeli Arabs' growing rate of modernization, rising standards of living and partial (perhaps, selective) absorption of Israeli lifestyle (as expressed in housing, dress, interpersonal behaviour and the like) were responsible for a growing ambivalence on the part of much of the rest of the Arab world and a reluctance to embrace them fully into their fold. In an almost tragic way the Arabs of Israel are regarded by many Jews of Israel as being hostile to Israel's independent statehood but are also regarded as alienated from Arab culture and the 'Arab nation' by major sectors of the Arab world.

The nationalistic extremism of certain Israeli Arabs does not, of course, increase chances for mutual Jewish–Arab acceptance. This growing militancy accounts for the continuous cautiousness of Israeli authorities toward the incorporation of Arabs into senior government positions. Furthermore, the exclusion of Arabs from the otherwise universal obligation to do military service — welcomed by them for obvious reasons — deepens the estrangement between the Arab and Jewish communities within Israel. It follows, therefore, that the growing participation of Israeli Arabs in education and their relative growing success in it is being frustrated by the limited available options for mobility into jobs congruent with that education.

The complete legal equality which the Arabs of Israel enjoy — exclusion from military service is the only exception — covers education as well. Thus, 94 per cent of Arab children aged 5–13 attended schools in 1980, as compared with 98 per cent among the Jews; even in the 14–17 age group there was an increase in attendance from 294 per 1,000 in 1970 to 573 per 1,000 in 1980.[28] Since the foundation of the state of Israel, elementary school attendance among Israeli Arabs has increased thirteen-fold or more than three times their rate of population growth.[29]

As in the Jewish sector, teachers' salaries are covered by the Ministry of Education; maintenance of schools and construction of new schools are paid for by local authorities. Among the Christian Arabs (who constitute about 10 per cent of all Arab children), there is a tendency to attend private schools (sponsored by the Church). Those, too, enjoy government support. In fact, 7 per cent of all Arab students attend private schools. The language of instruction is Arabic, and cultural studies are a basic component of the curriculum (literature, history and above all, the Koran).[30] Otherwise, the curriculum in Arab schools is identical to that in the Jewish sector. Indeed, in the early 1970s many critics complained about the heavy emphasis on Jewish studies in the curriculum of Arab schools.[31] As a result far-reaching revisions were implemented.

Arab education, nevertheless, suffers from certain structural disadvantages. First, Arab schools in Israel enjoy fewer educational support services than do Jewish schools, such as psychological counselling, special education and the like. Secondly, Arab secondary education is still much less diversified than Jewish education; specifically, vocational education — which caters among Jews for more than 60 per cent of all secondary school students — is still in the early development stage among the Arabs. The relatively lower rate of Arab participation in post-elementary education is certainly a consequence of this state of affairs. And thirdly, since most Arab local authorities are rural (or small towns), the financial means at their disposal are limited. Consequently, until about ten years ago, Arab communities had distinctly worse school buildings available for their students.[32] This situation has improved significantly over the past ten years.

Are these differences between the Arab and the Jewish sector in the quality of the educational inputs a function of deliberate discrimination? It is the author's conviction, shared by numerous observers, that they are not. The Arabs of Israel have been the victims of seriously disadvantageous conditions. Educational literature has documented that this explains much of the relative school failure of Arab children. Furthermore, some of the educational innovations aimed at the promotion and development of the underachieving segments of the Jewish sector have not been (or have only partially been) introduced in the Arab sector.[33] Teaching patterns in the Arab sector are, consequently, conservative to a large extent, featuring authoritative teachers, emphasis on discipline, frontal teaching, and repetitive daily routines.

Bashi, Cahan and Davis have performed the most comprehensive study of schooling in the Arab sector to date. One of the most interesting findings of their study was that the schools in Arab communities were homogeneous in terms of parents' education (which was medium to poor), and family size (six or more children per family on average, as compared to only 2.7 children on average in the Jewish sector). In consequence, very low correlations were found between students' socioeconomic background and their scholastic achievements. This finding differed dramatically from parallel findings in the Jewish sector. In Arab communities significant differences in scholastic achievement are to be found *within* and not *between* schools. A very important policy implication seems to be that compensatory or enrichment tactics ought to be directed at subgroups within each school class rather than at total classes or entire schools (as is the case in the Jewish sector).[34]

A contemporary study of Arab students' attitudes towards their schools[35] emphasizes the importance of expectations, which were found to be essentially instrumental. Unlike the prevailing sentiment among their Jewish peers, Arab students' sentiments were predominantly negative. They did not identify with their schools since their chances of successfully passing the matriculation examination were meagre.[36] It is interesting to note that, despite these low rates of success, Arab students tend to develop very high expectations. In view of their very limited chances of social mobility in Israeli society, these high expectations reflect the great prestige value that education carries within the Arab village or small town. University students displayed high expectations identical to those of school children, but comparisons between freshmen and seniors in college showed that confidence in fulfilling those expectations had shrunk as the students neared graduation.[37]

It is, therefore, not surprising that many of the approximately 50 per cent of the 14–17-year-old Israeli Arabs who are not in school are very critically oriented towards their environment. On the one hand, they have enjoyed nine to ten years of schooling (unlike most of the elders in their home communities) and are ambivalent towards their traditional setting; on the other hand, they cannot complete a full cycle of secondary education (or do not feel motivated to do so) and consequently do not foresee real chances for social participation congruent with education. It is likely that this conflict contributes to the relatively high (and rising) rates of juvenile delinquency in the Arab settlements.

Interestingly, Arab university graduates tend to face a similar though even more severe conflict. They have undergone an experience of modernization and consequently withdrawn from their traditional environment and find themselves to a degree in conflict with it. Yet they have only meagre opportunities for mobility within the broader Israeli society.[38]

In conclusion, Israel can legitimately claim that very significant improvements have taken place in the rates of Arab participation in the educational system. Table 6.10 clearly shows that in the twenty

Table 6.10 The educational achievements of adults (over 14 years), by national identity and number of years of schooling

			Number of years of schooling			
		Total	0–4	5–8	9–12	13–13	16+
Jews	1961	100	20.1	35.4	34.6	9.9	
	1972	100	13.6	29.3	42.6	9.1	5.4
	1980	100	10.3	21.3	47.6	12.3	8.5
Arabs	1961	100	63.3	27.5	7.6	1.5	
	1972	100	48.0	35.7	13.9	1.9	0.4
	1980	100	28.9	33.9	29.5	5.5	2.2

Source: Bilezki and Turki, *Education in the Mirror of Numbers.* The Ministry of Education and Culture, Jerusalem, 1982, Table 34 (Hebrew, mimeo).

years between 1961 and 1980, the percentage of uneducated Arab adults has more than halved; similarly, between 1970 and 1980 the percentage of adults who completed thirteen or more years of education has more than tripled. The respective rate of growth among the Jews in those ten years was about 30 per cent. It is, of course, true that the absolute rates of Arab participation in the educational system are, in spite of the mentioned dramatic trend, still significantly lower than those of the Jews.

Parallel with this expansion of educational services (and the concomitant processes of modernization), we witness — in both Jews and Arabs — heightened nationalism attended by ethnocentrism.[39] This polarization may well be explained against the social and political background briefly described in this paper. The Ministry of Education's recently proposed educational interventions, in and of themselves most welcome developments, may contribute, even if only moderately, to the emergence of a more or less satisfying mode of coexistence, despite the continuing difficulties.[40]

Notes

1. This discussion follows the model described and analysed by S. Smooha, *Israel — Pluralism and Conflict*, Routledge & Kegan Paul, 1978. To what extent and in which respect Isreal indeed is a pluralistic society is beyond the scope of this paper.
2. E. Rieger, *Hebrew Education in Palestine*, Dvir Publishing Co., Tel Aviv, 1940 (Hebrew), pp. 1–95; J. Bentwich, *Education in Israel*, Routledge & Kegan Paul, London, 1965; R. Elboim-Dror, 'Israel's Educational Policies' in W. Ackerman *et al.* (eds), *Education in Israel*, Klett-Cotta, Stuttgart, Germany, 1982 (German), pp. 54–74.
3. R. Elboim-Dror, 'Israel's Educational Policies', pp. 74–81.
4. Ibid.
5. R. Kahane, 'Patterns of National Identity in Israel' in S.N. Eisenstadt *et al.* (eds), *Education and Society in Israel*, Academon, Jerusalem, 1968 (Hebrew).
6. Central Bureau of Statistics, *Statistical Abstract of Israel, 1980*, Jerusalem, 1981 (Hebrew and English), Table V/2, p. 134.
7. See for instance: C. Adler, 'The Place of Education in the Integration of Ethnic Communities in Israel', in S.N. Eisenstadt and A. Zloczower (eds), *Ingathering of Exiles*, The Magnes Press, Jerusalem, 1969 (Hebrew).
8. See for instance: C. Frankenstein (ed.), *Teaching as a Social Challenge*, School of Education, The Hebrew University of Jerusalem, and the Ministry of Education and Culture, Jerusalem, 1976 (in memory of Z. Aranne, late Minister of Education and Culture).

9. Y. Dar in collaboration with N. Resh. *Homogeneity and Heterogeneity in Education*. The NCJW Research Institute for Innovation in Education. School of Education. The Hebrew University of Jerusalem. 1981 (mimeo).

10. Z. Klein and Y. Eshel. *Integrating Jerusalem Schools*. Academic Press Inc.. 1980. See also *Megamot: Behavioral Science Quarterly*, special edition, **XXIII**, nos. 3–4 (1977) (Hebrew, English Abstracts).

11. D. Davis. D. Sprinzak, and R. Osizon. *Who Benefits from Educational Resources: Allocation of Resources in Years 1973, 1978, 1981*. The Ministry of Education and Culture. Jerusalem. 1982 (Hebrew).

12. C. Adler. 'The Evaluation of the Israeli School Reform' in S. Goldstein (ed.). *Law and Equality in Education*. The Van Leer Jerusalem Foundation. 1980. pp. 53–9; E. Peled. 'The Educational Reform in Israel — The Political Aspect' in E. Ben-Baruch and Y. Newmann (eds). *Educational Policy and Policy Making*. Vinpress. Herzlia. Israel. 1982. pp. 85–109.

13. C. Adler and P. Melzer-Druker. *A Survey of Evaluations of Educational Intervention Programs Sponsored by Project Renewal*. The NCJW Research Institute for Innovation in Education. School of Education. The Hebrew University of Jerusalem. 1983 (mimeo).

14. Central Bureau of Statistics. op. cit.. Table XXII/9. p. 586.

15. P. Bilezki and Ch. Turki, *The Educational System in the Mirror of Numbers, 1982*. Jerusalem. 1982. Table 7. p. 7 (mimeo. Hebrew).

16. Central Bureau of Statistics. op. cit.. Table XXII/12.

17. Bilezki and Turki. op. cit.. Table 17. p. 17.

18. See. for example. F. Musgrove. *School and the Social Order*. John Wiley & Sons. New York. 1979.

19. The relevant statistics have never been officially published. This statement is thus my own approximated calculation, based on unpublished reports, as well as on growth rates in university attendance (see. for example. Central Bureau of Statistics. *Statistical Abstracts of Israel, 1982*. Jerusalem. 1983. Table XXII/39).

20. R. Kahane, 'Preliminary Reflections on the University in Israel: A Sociological Perspective' (mimeo. presented at the Symposium on the International Issues in University Administration. Ankara University. March 1979).

21. See Central Bureau of Statistics. *Statistical Abstracts of Israel, 1983*. Jerusalem. 1983. Table XXIII/9.

22. R. Kahane and L. Starr. *Education and Work: Vocational Socialization Processes in Israel*. The Magnes Press. Jerusalem. 1984 (Hebrew).

23. See Bilezki and Turki. op. cit.. Table 12.

24. Central Bureau of Statistics. *Statistical Abstracts of Israel, 1982*. Table XXII/28.

25. Ibid.. Table XXII/27.

26. Bilezki and Turki. op. cit.. Table 33.

27. Central Bureau of Statistics. *Statistical Abstracts of Israel, 1982*. Tables XII/5 and XII/8.

28. In 1970 the minimum school-leaving age was still 15. It was raised to 16 in 1978. See Bilezki and Turki. op. cit.. Table 19.

29. J. Bashi. S. Cahan. D. Davis. *Educational Achievements of the Arab*

Elementary School in Israel, The Hebrew University of Jerusalem, 1981 (Hebrew).

30. As Arab students study two foreign languages (Hebrew and English), about 50 per cent of teaching time is devoted to language instruction (compared with only about 35 per cent in the Jewish sector).
31. Y. Perez, 'National Education for Arab Youth in Israel: A Comparative Analysis of Curricula', *The Jewish Journal of Sociology*, **12**, no. 2 (1970); and Sami Mar'i Khalil, *Arab Education in Israel*, Syracuse University Press, New York, 1978.
32. A.F. Kleinberger, op. cit., Pergamon Press, Oxford, 1969, Ch. VII.
33. Ibid.
34. Bashi *et al.*, op. cit.
35. Azis Haider, 'Determinants of Identification with and Alienation from School of Arab High-School Pupils in Israel', thesis submitted for the MA degree, The Hebrew University of Jerusalem, 1981 (Hebrew).
36. In 1980, 21 per cent of all Jewish adults (over fourteen years of age) had enjoyed more than twelve years' of education, while only about 8 per cent of all adults in the Arab sector had.
37. R. Peleg and A. Benjamin, *Higher Education and the Israeli Arabs*, Am-Oved, 1977 (Hebrew).
38. Peleg and Benjamin, op. cit.
39. Lazarovitz-Herz, 'Identity and Educational Environment', *BaShaar*, vol. **2** (June–September 1981) (Hebrew).
40. *Guidelines for Educational Intervention on the Subject of Education for Jewish Arab Coexistence*, Pedagogical Secretariat, Ministry of Education and Culture, September 1983 (Hebrew).

4.

Conflict and Consensus in Educational Policy Making in Israel

Rachel Elboim-Dror

ABSTRACT

The Israeli educational policy-making system is distinguished by both a propensity to produce conflict and an ability contain it. The system's seven main conflict-managing strategies are: ignoring or veiling differences; responding to conflicting demands on the expressive level alone; deferring decisions; lingering and tortuous decision-making processes; compartmentalization and granting of autonomy; crisis as deliverance from conflict; and exchanging financial resources for political consensus.

The influence of the Israeli political system and its major interest groups — such as the religious parties, the Kibbutzim and oriental Jews — is examined in the light of efforts to obviate conflicting pressures.

The costs of consensus in a society engaged in an internal and external struggle are discussed. These include: fixation on consensual ideals and their consequent rigidification and non-reexamination; development of consensus on a symbolic level, concealing conflicts and disagreements on the behavioral and operational levels of educational policy-making; transformation of conflicts of ideas into conflicts of interests; and an enhanced role for lower bureaucratic and professional personnel resulting from the long drawn out decision processes employed to avoid conflict and manage it. This article explores the deficiencies as well as the advantages of such strategies in reducing friction and allowing the system to function without creating alienation despite its conflicting and unresolved dilemmas.

In a dialogue between educators from the United States and Israel, James Coleman stated that educational policy-making in the United States is the outcome of conflict between interest groups. In Israel, it would seem, educational policy-making is the outcome of efforts to avoid conflicts.

Utilizing Aaron Wildavsky's (1975, pp. 243–246) diversity-intensity and consensus-deference indices, it could be said that the Israeli educational policy-making system is high on both the propensity to produce conflict and the ability to contain it. Israeli educational policy-makers work hard to avoid conflict and achieve consensus, and are successful in doing so. This could, however, be called a quasi-consensus, as there is a difference between consensus attained after explicating policy differences, discussing and fighting over them, and one reached by avoiding, veiling and suppressing differences.

Observing educational policy-makers in Israel one might get the impression that their main objective is not to make policy but to obviate conflicting pressures. Perhaps this is what policy-making is all about.

Israel is considered to be a cohesive society with a high degree of consensus stemming from its background of common Jewish bonds and traditions and the shared ideals and values of Zionist ideology. In addition to these inner consensus-building mechanisms, such factors as the external pressures for cooperation and solidarity, the long history of Jewish persecution and a continuing war with the Arab states should be borne in mind. At the base of each of these consensus-facilitating forces, however, lie conflict-generating differences of ideology, attitudes and interests.

The novelist, A.B. Yehoshua, has gone so far as to suggest that conflicts drove the Jews to diaspora life and that, even today, living in the diaspora is regarded as a solution to conflicts between the national and the religious systems, between kings and prophets. The same holds true for the realization of the national "mission" as the chosen people, for while Jewish existence in the diaspora minimizes conflict, the comprehensive framework of national life in Israel demands decisions which we try to avoid. Life in Israel, in a Jewish state, forces one to give operational meaning to basic questions, some of which pose contradictory demands. The need to confront and tackle conflicts, resolving or tolerating them and learning to live with them, is a specially pressing and tangible task for the educational policy-making system, as its basic function is to translate values, norms and demands into objectives and make educational policy decisions accordingly.

The educational policy formation process in Israel is of special interest as it reflects the dilemmas, deficiencies, potentials, pitfalls, and challenges faced by a society engaged in a continuous struggle with itself and its surroundings. Consensus and conflict are the two major poles around which educational policy-making processes in Israel revolve and are held in a delicate and vulnerable balance. In order to maintain this balance and to function despite the pull of opposing factors, the educational policy-formation system is obliged to find a strategy which will cater to all tastes and be good for all seasons.

As it cannot answer all the demands all of the time, it tries to answer some of them some of the time. In doing so, the Israeli educational policy-formation system appears reminiscent of fairy tales in which the competing contenders for the princess's hand are given various impossible tasks to perform, such as, "to do and not to do," "to speak and not to speak," "to walk and not to walk." In order to be able to fulfill these contradicting tasks, the Israeli educational policy-formation system has developed a series of strategies designed to relieve tension and enhance solidarity. Although not actually resolving conflict, they keep the system functioning, albeit at a high cost.

The Zionist movement and its ideology brought about tremendous changes in traditional Jewish education. Despite these and other shifts in many aspects of Jewish life in Israel, certain features of educational policy-formation, and especially its modes of treating conflicts, reveal a striking resemblance to traditional Jewish patterns of dealing with consensus and conflict

especially those developed by East European Jewry. First and foremost is
the view that consensus must be maintained at all costs. This emphasis on consensus, which became a matter of life and death in the survival of Jewish culture after the destruction of the Temple and the dispersion of the Jews, did
not mean weeding out individualism and eliminating conflicts. On the contrary, there were always bitter internal disputes and fights, but since there
was neither political autonomy nor national sovereignty, the need for consensus regarding the authority of the Halacha (the religious laws) and the community, became vitally important. The rule: "Both are the words of the
living God but the Halacha [rule] is according to the House of Hillel,"
epitomizes the sensitive balance that had to be kept between freedom of
thought and ideas and the need for consensus and authority in a society de-
void of political sovereignty (Eisenstadt, 1977).

The centrality of consensus and the need to contain conflict and maintain
a united front also dominated the Zionist movement and the life of the
Yishuv in Palestine prior to the establishment of the State of Israel. The need
to attain consensus in the Yishuv and in the State of Israel has often been
explained as an outcome of the multi-party system in which no one party
has the majority needed to form a government. But, as Hurwitz and Lissak
(1978) claim in their study that the formation of coalitions in Israel did not
follow the rule of a "minimum winning coalition;" instead efforts were made
to achieve an absolute majority, and even "a wall-to-wall" coalition in times
of crisis, to express a national unity and consensus.

The pressure to avoid conflict in educational policy-making in Israel seems
to evolve from the basic norm of adhering to consensus, despite conflict and
disputes, which is deeply rooted in Jewish tradition and is reflected in Israeli
political culture.

Looking at the educational policy-making process from a conflict-avoid-
ance perspective, one can identify seven strategies employed by the system
to reach this end. These are:

1) ignoring, veiling and mitigating differences;
2) expressive response to conflicting demands and pressures;
3) avoiding decisions as critical committing events;
4) lingering, tortuous decision-making processes;
5) crisis as deliverance from conflict;
6) compartmentalization and autonomy;
7) exchange of financial resources for political consensus.

1. Ignoring, Veiling and Mitigating Differences

From the outset, Zionist education was troubled by different, sometimes
conflicting, ideologies and from the outset it adopted what Ahad Haam de-

scribed at the beginning of this century as a policy of obscuring and veiling differences. "Instead of really solving the issue at hand they seek refuge in diffuse, generalized decisions which do not touch the 'wound' or make it worse, but neither do they heal it" (*Hashiloah* (1903) Vol. 10).

Disputes centering on ideological differences which rocked the education system in the pre-State days, have all but vanished. Today all parties and interest groups, whether right- or left-wing, atheist or orthodox, doves or hawks, are all "for education." The active role played by political parties, the kibbutzim, the Histadruth (General Federation of Labour) and other groups and organizations has been taken over by "statism" *(mamlachtiut).* Education, the politicians claim, is "above politics," it is a sacred area kept apart from the "ugly facts of political life." Thus, efforts are made to remove questions of education policy from politics. To use Charles Lindblom's statement about another issue: "They do not press for agreement on the grand issues but for political silence on them" (Lindblom, 1977, p.204). The outcome of this process is "politicization without politics," as described by Aaron Wildavsky (1979, pp. 320–323).

This tranquility is regarded by some as an expression of consensus and solidarity, by others as a false or empty facade obscuring differences and symptomatic of the desire to let sleeping dogs lie and avoid touching the "wound" which might erupt in a "culture war."

2. Expressive Response to Conflicting Demands and Pressures

The educational policy-making system usually reacts to conflicting demands and pressures by expressing its willingness to oblige, discussing the issues and sometimes even considering what legislative action should be taken. This is, however, in many cases as far as it will go. The pattern of reaction can be described as primarily expressive, avoiding specific instrumental decisions which would commit the education system to act. (Salisbury (1969) describes as expressive actions those actions in which expression is given to the interests or values of a person or group rather than instrumentally or concretely pursuing interests or values.) This expressive response fulfills an important role in building consensus and strengthening the solidarity of different groups within the education system. It would, therefore, be correct to say that the threshold of the education policy-formation system to demands from its environment is very low as far as expressive reaction goes. Its threshold for decisions, however, is high. Although it reacts to and deals with many of the demands, it does not produce policy decisions which commit the system. The result is that the Israeli educational policy-making system "deals" with many problems but decides about very few. As this mode of dealing with issues does not meet the demands raised by the different groups, the same issues crop up time and again and are discussed repeatedly by committees which produce comments, suggestions, and thousands of pages of minutes.

Looked at from a conflict-resolution perspective, this strategy is most effective, releasing some of the pressures and relieving tension. It gives the various groups the feeling that somebody up there is listening and taking notice, while it does not commit the system to take action which might bring it into conflict with other groups' values or demands. On the other hand, although it restrains conflict, this strategy augments frustrations and burdens the system almost to the point of suffocation with endless discussions, meetings and committees constantly churning up the same issues.

3. Avoiding Decisions as Critical Committing Events

The Israeli educational policy-making system tries to avoid making decisions as far as possible. As a result, people in all segments of the system seem to be endlessly seeking decisions, especially with regard to aims and priorities in education. Both the coalition and the opposition repeatedly complain that the Government does not state its education policy, objectives and priorities. The opposition accuses the Minister of Education of not having a clear education policy. The coalition challenges the opposition to present its priorities for education, claiming that it has not made any decisions or commitments. The Minister of Education, on the other hand, puts the blame on society at large. Expressing his opinion on the subject, former Minister of Education, Aharon Yadlin has said: "The situation is such that society does not guide us, there is no system of values that binds all the different segments of society together, nor is there any spiritual, religious, or political leadership which has widespread national support . . . I think that it is preferable to avoid making decisions on basic spiritual issues, leaving them for the coming generations" (Yadlin, 1978).

Officials of the Ministeries of Education and Finance, as well as teachers and parents, all take part in this endless, general search for education policy decisions, each blaming the others for not taking a firm stand.

When the system is forced to make decisions and cannot satisfy demands by expressive modes only, it resorts to its alternative strategy of trying to gain time by delaying the decision-making process as far as possible. This approach is well known and used in Israel in many other fields and is justified by those employing it by the phrase, "time is on our side." The time gained by postponing decisions is supposedly used in order to build bridges between differences in attitudes and interests; however, on many occasions delaying decisions has increased costs rather than reducing them.

Delaying decisions in order to deal with conflict by reaching a compromise becomes a very expensive proposition in terms of manpower, time and energy. The inputs in time and energy thus incurred have been sometimes double or triple the resources at the heart of the dispute. (A striking example is the "thirty years question" about subsidies for the Israeli opera. The time and energy spent on this issue by committees, various Ministers of Education, Knesset members, artists and public figures is unbelievable.)

4. Lingering, Tortuous Decision-making Processes

The educational policy-making system's basic orientation of preventing conflict has led to the development of a strategy of long drawn out, twisting decision-making processes, one which both Wildavsky and Lindblom might describe as alternating incrementalism. This strategy is especially suited to responding to conflicting objectives and demands without antagonizing or alienating any group too much. It is the Israeli answer to satisfying most of the people some of the time. It is a kind of ongoing, slow-motion, never-ending decision process, evolving bit by bit, allowing each group to obtain part of its demands. The main advantage of this strategy is that it allows conflicting decisions to be made without being conspicuously inconsistent. During the lingering decision-making process, marginal changes are made in policy decisions in response to demands by interest groups, first to one group in partial fulfillment of its demands, then to another group, and so on. Sometimes this aggregate process of marginal incremental decisions leads to the erosion of major education policies or to the emergence of a new one which has never been considered but is introduced post factum. Thus, partial decisions in a given area are made, so that the education system finds itself committed to a policy it has not even considered. Numerous cases of this patchwork of decision-making processes can be listed.

An interesting case of a process of erosion and the rebirth of a new policy decision exists in the form of the 1978 Free Secondary Education Act. Till 1977, education in Israel was free and compulsory up to the age of fifteen. For the education of children between fifteen and eighteen years old, a graded scale of tuition fees was introduced and parents paid according to their income and family size. By a long drawn-out, incremental decision-making process, the Ministry of Education introduced special reductions in response to pressures from different interest groups, regardless of the family's economic situation and therefore in contradiction to its own policy. The population exempt from paying full tuition fees for secondary education gradually increased until only a negligible percentage of parents were still paying the full amount. When presenting its proposal for free secondary education for all, the Ministry of Education stressed the fact that it was unable to stop this process and by legitimizing it would eliminate the injustices caused.

The lingering, tortuous process of decision-making which enables the system to respond to conflicting demands, helps the system to navigate between opposing educational aims and interests without making a clear and unambiguous stand on colliding values and interests. Even if it does declare what its policy is, by its patchwork decision-making processes, it can contradict its own offical policy. This strategy of lingering decisions is also partly responsible for the prevailing feeling that so many issues are perpetually unresolved, waiting for decisions to be made.

5. Crisis as Deliverance from Conflict

Crises are extremely convenient for rescuing educational policy-makers from the pressures of conflicting objectives and demands. While crises narrow the options, they facilitate acceptance and save the decision-makers from the lengthy process of reaching a compromise. When a crisis is imminent, all conflicting views are subordinated to the more pressing problem at hand, consensus is reached swiftly and differences are set aside until a more appropriate moment.

It could be argued that education policy, unlike foreign policy, is not frequently exposed to crisis nor is subject to world-shattering decisions. While this may be true, the Israeli educational policy-making system often functions best in an atmosphere of panic, as if it were contending with a serious crisis. (Every time it transpires that three or four high-school pupils have been smoking hashish, the whole system — the Knesset, the Ministry, the press — are thrown into a crisis-like situation.) In this respect, Holsti's definition of a crisis as characterized by surprise, a threat to important values, and little time for making decisions, seems to accord with the way decisions are made in the Ministry of Education (Holsti, 1978). According to Holsti's analysis, crisis increases the tendency to stereotype situations and define problems in over-simplified, one-dimensional terms, allowing no time for detailed analysis, and serving as a good excuse both to forego former procedures and to circumvent the rigid structure and long processes of reaching consensus. Although cognitive abilities may be eroded, crisis liberates educational policy-makers from the necessity of accommodating conflicting interests and demands, legitimizing their unsystematic decision-making methods.

By adopting the strategies mentioned above, by ignoring issues, postponing decisions and drawing out the attendant processes, educational policy-makers cause more crisis situations to erupt.

The Ministry of Education is very fond of special operations and projects in which all energies are mobilized to meet a certain goal and conflicts are set aside until "normal times." This "operations" or "projects" approach contains many features of crisis management, a situation in which Israelis seem to excel.

Thus, decision-making processes alternate between delaying tactics and swift action, relieved of dealing with conflicts by the slogan: "There's no choice". Crisis situations are an important aid to creating cooperation and agreement.

6. Compartmentalization and Autonomy

The education system in Israel is divided into state education and religious state education. The ultra-orthodox party, Agudat Yisrael, has an independent education system outside the state education system. While it enjoys complete freedom from state intervention and supervision, it is largely financed by the state. The kibbutzim and moshavim (cooperative settlements) are granted wide autonomy in all matters of education policy in their schools, even if their policies sometimes contradict government education policies, as is the case with the integration of disadvantaged children and school consolidation policy.

By separating religious education from secular education, allowing each system to develop autonomously, and by allowing kibbutz schools considerable freedom, many potential conflicts and battles are avoided.

Peace through structural separation and autonomy for different ideological orientations has proved to be very effective in reducing conflicts, removing education policy issues from the top of the national agenda to a peripheral position. As everyone is "for education" and the various ideologies each get their "pound of flesh," opposition and public debates are minimal.

7. Exchange of Financial Resources for Political Consensus

The allocation of resources has played an important role in maintaining consensus through an exchange process among different groups from the very beginning of Jewish settlement in Palestine, as has been demonstrated in the research by Hurwitz and Lissak (1978) among others. This exchange process is conspicuous in education, especially in the relationship between the government and the religious parties.

The part played by the religious parties as a major interest group in educational policy-formation is well known, as are the ambivalent feelings and attitudes of most Israelis towards the Jewish religion. Two points which might add another dimension to explaining the attitudes of most of the secular population in Israel towards the Jewish religion as a binding force in maintaining consensus should be stressed.

First, the waves of young immigrants who came to Palestine at the beginning of the century, especially the Second and Third Aliyot (1905–1912, 1919–1923) which had a profound influence on moulding the new Israeli culture, were young rebels, the first hippies of the twentieth century, who had left their traditional, religious, bourgeois families in order to establish a new, just and secular Jewish society. They were strongly commited to secular values and the rejection of the Jewish religion was a dominant element in their negation of Jewish life in the diaspora. After the new society had been institutionalized and the young rebels had become the "establishment" of the new society, the fury of rejection died away to be replaced by nostalgic memories of childhood, parents, traditions, holidays and the synagogue, coupled with feelings of guilt like prodigal sons. This transformation was reflected in the sixties when the then Minister of Education, Zalman Aranne, a representative of the Labour Party, laid before the Knesset an ambitious study programme of "Jewish Consciousness" for the stream of secular education. The discussion in the Knesset for and against this programme should be studied and analyzed not only by students of policy-making but also by psychoanalysts interested in feelings of guilt and ambivalence.

A second point which intensified the feelings of guilt of the secular population was the Holocaust. Jewish life in a large part of the diaspora, especially in Eastern Europe, which was ridiculed and rejected by Israeli culture, (as is well documented in modern Hebrew literature and folklore), disappeared altogether in a cruel act of Nazi barbarism. In the words of Saul Bellow, recounting a conversation with Jacob Talmon:

> It all went into the graves and into the ovens. And when it was gone there were only the synagogues to give cohesion to Jewish life in these increasingly secular times. This is one reason for the success of Jewish clericalism in Israel. Our politicians are obliged to make use of everything that can draw us together (*To Jerusalem and Back*, p. 134).

Because of the diffusion of power among the many parties in Israel, it is difficult to form a coalition government, without the support of the religious parties. This situation gives them a leverage which they exploit to the full. In effect, the desire to include the religious parties in the government stems not only from their strategic electoral position, but also from the desire to enlarge the consensual basis of the government, as has been discussed above. The price paid for the consent of the religious parties is reflected in the field of education, extending the autonomy of the Division of Religious

Education in the Ministry of Education and allocating more resources to the religious school system, amongst other things. A replica of the bargaining and exchange process on the national level takes place at the local authority level.

Although the government rarely discusses education policy issues, one of the prime factors in the establishment and dissolution of governments are disputes regarding education policy or, more specifically, unwillingness to accept the religious parties' demands concerning education policy. Education policy questions, particularly the expansion of religious education and services, constitute a major part of all government and local authority coalition agreements.

Considerable financial resources are allocated each year both to state religious education and the "recognized" school system of the orthodox party, Agudat Yisrael, which enjoys complete independence while being almost totally financed by the state. In addition to these formal, institutionalized budget allocations, there are many other avenues for the allocation of resources to religious education and religious cultural activities. The kibbutz schools and the cultural activities sponsored by the Histadruth (General Federation of Labour) also have special arrangements for allocating resources, in some cases through regular budget procedures, in others through bypassing them.

As the religious parties, as well as the kibbutzim, are extremely efficient and powerful pressure groups, the price of their autonomy in terms of resource allocation is quite high, as expressed in school buildings, the spatial allocation of education services, staffing, programme developments, etc.

It is difficult to determine whether the National Religious Party uses political power primarily as a means of guarding and developing religious education because of its moral and ideological significance, or whether it uses the state religious education system as a means of mobilizing and expanding its political power. In previous years, when the "old guard" of Mizrachi leadership ruled the party, the first premise seemed true. However, in the present Knesset, with the shift of leadership to the new, younger generation which is more politically inclined and militant, the second assumption seems to hold.

8. The Cost of Consensus

Analysis and examination of education objectives stand in opposition to coalition governments, which give a feeling of security and belonging. Avoiding the examination and discussion of conflicts creates a fixation on consensual ideals and ideas which, because they are not aired through public debate and re-examination, tend to become rigid and fossilized. Only by the demystification of some social symbols is it possible to engage in a real debate.

An even more serious consequence is the development of consensus on a symbolic level, concealing conflicts and disagreements at the behavioural and operational levels of educational policy-making. The developments in regard to school integration policy, closing the gap between Oriental and Western Jews, may serve as an illustration.

The last decade has given rise to a great many interest groups in the West and could be called the decade of minorities, the poor and the weak. In Israel only one of these groups has developed into a fully-fledged effective pressure group, and consists of representatives of the "development towns" and poor neighbourhoods in urban centres, both of which are inhabited primarily by Jewish immigrants from North Africa and Asia.

The problems of the low socio-economic strata in Israeli society are especially complicated and emotionally charged because of the high correlation between ethnic origin, poor educational attainment, and low occupational status and income. Thus, being an Oriental Jew correlates with being disadvantaged. This fact threatens two of Israel's most cherished values: social justice and the integration of immigrants.

It is possible to distinguish three periods or phases in the development of attitudes towards the disadvantaged in Israel. The first period, prior to the establishment of the state is usually described as the time when the problem did not exist or was ignored. This, however, is not quite true. The social and educational aspects of the problem were already known and were even the focus of research, such as that undertaken by Carl Frankenstein and others in the thirties. The reason why such a grave social and educational problem was disregarded in a society that was so sensitive to social and educational ideals, was not because it was simply ignored, but rather because of what can be termed the Zionist version of the Protestant Ethic.

The belief that the Jews had to become productive and that everyone should make an effort and work hard created the naive assumption that willpower alone would erase social differences and improve the achievements of Oriental Jewish children within the educational system. (The centrality of the belief in willpower in Zionist ideology is well expressed in Herzl's epigram: "If you will it, it is no dream.")

The second period, when the failure of Oriental children in the schools became a serious problem because of its magnitude, began after the establishment of the state and the resultant waves of immigration of Jews expelled from the Arab countries. The pre-eminent ideology during this period was that Oriental Jews from traditional societies should change, adapting to the modern State of Israel and its Zionist ideology and becoming Israelis as quickly as possible. This absorption process resulted, among other things, in destroying the immigrants' family structure and religious traditions, increasing their passivity vis-à-vis the dominant Western culture and its values, and causing them to imitate primarily its external features.

The last period can be considered to have begun with the so-called 'Black Panthers' riots of 1971. Despite the tremendous efforts made by Israeli society to help Oriental Jews to better their economic, social and educational levels, and despite impressive progress in these respects, Oriental Jews still constitute the majority of the low income groups and their children form the bulk of under-achieving pupils. Although the level of achievement among Oriental Jewish children has risen, the level of Western Jewish children has done so too, thus leaving the gap as wide as ever. Four out of every five primary school pupils of North African origin are still defined as disadvantaged, while only one out of every nine pupils of European or American origin is so defined. The immigrants' high expectations, which were not fulfilled, caused feelings of failure, frustration and aggression towards the society that had robbed them of pride in their ethnic origin and culture and failed them in their new surroundings.

In additon, demographic changes partly account for the crystallization of the new pressure group and the changing attitude towards it in Israel. Today, Jews of Oriental origin constitute about half of Israeli society, numbering 47.4% in the last census taken in 1972, and 55% of children attending primary school in 1977.

The political impact of the values and orientations of the Oriental Jews was demonstrated dramatically in the last elections. Other changes that took place in Israel also had an effect, such as the erosion of the dominace of the Labour Party, and the development of universal criteria for the allocation of resources, weakening the power of traditional interest groups and allowing new groups to develop.

It is difficult to define who belongs to the new pressure group. Not only do people of Oriental origin and the inhabitants of "development towns" speak on their own behalf, but nearly every politician and public figure feels obliged to champion the underprivileged. This new interest group has had an important impact on education policy-making, reducing economic rationality in the allocation of resources while maintaining consensus.

Consensus regarding school integration policy in Israel seems to be very high: no opposition had developed nor have alternatives been suggested. However, disagreements exist and are expressed through pressures exerted by interest groups altering and circumventing accepted policy in a variety of ways. Thus, the cry for the integration of children from different ethnic and social backgrounds has served mainly as a political slogan, and despite decisions to allocate resources for programmes for the disadvantaged, better learning conditions are still to be found among the well-to-do, as was demonstrated by the Van Leer Study (Minkovich et al., 1977). Despite statements about positive discrimination, education policy is geared towards developing universal services for all, as exemplified by the 1978 Free Secondary Education Act.

The various interest groups active in education policy formation are geared to the styles of decision-making described above, investing their efforts in side-stepping the decision-makers, rather than in persuading them to change their policies. While approaching Knesset members for help, the leaders of interest groups try to enlist their help informally to put pressure on the bureaucracy, circumventing education policies to serve their own interests, rather than convincing them that education policy should be changed. Thus, conflicts of ideas degenerate into conflicts of interests. Similar patterns were observed in other areas too, such as physical planning. The interested parties in the domain of building, says Yael Azmon (1979, pp. 4–5) direct all their efforts not to changing outlines, but in getting permits to go ahead outside the rules. From the viewpoint of the administrative bodies responsible for physical planning, their authority is undermined as a result of the erosion of the existing laws and the creation of *faits accomplis* in defiance of the laws.

Among other consequences, the failure to examine the opportunity costs of education policies should be mentioned. As education is "above politics" and everyone is "for education," education policy implications are not fully discussed, analyzed and differentiated. To put it bluntly, the two guiding rules of Israeli politicians in regard to education services are: "the more the better" and "more of the same." The only exception to these rules is the critical attitude towards higher education. As a consequence, the education system is expanding quantitatively without the needed corresponding changes to fit the changing objectives, needs and characteristics of school populations. This is the case in expanding vocational education, kindergartens and the "long school day".

Conclusion

Avoiding conflicts by long drawn-out decision processes obliges lower bureaucratic and professional personnel, working on the implementation level, to make policy decisions. As a result, the ability to make decisions and influence policy of medium- and low-ranking bureaucrats and professionals in the education system is much higher, for example, than those of the chairman of the Pedagogical Secretariat, a central policy-making unit in the

Ministry of Education. Thus, although the education system is fairly free to initiate, intervene, innovate and decide, this fundamentally useful development is undefined, unsystematic and unrewarded. It is subject to a great many informal, subjective and random variables and circumstances. This also means that these decisions taken at a lower bureaucratic and professional level may facilitate narrow, short-range interests, such as the administrative convenience of the bureaucracy, and they may be damaging to major policies. Thus, some policies are created haphazardly, without assessment of their meaning and implications. They may help the system to progress towards its goals or they may hinder the process, making it further away than ever. They may aggregate in a positive, linear direction or they may contradict each other, disrupting and disturbing each other and creating a stalemate.

The deficiences of these strategies are obvious, as are advantages in strengthening consensus. They reduce friction in the system, allowing it to function without creating alienation and to progress despite its conflicting and unresolved dilemmas.

It could be said that many problems faced by the education policy-making system in Israel have no solution. It might be best to leave conflicts and disagreements open, and learn to live with open dilemmas and conflicts.

It could equally be said that it is time to stop making excuses based on the difficult political situation and to begin dealing with painful social and cultural conflicts, if Israel is not to become a static society, obsessed by past objectives and ideas.

I would venture to say that the function of Israel's education policy-formation system as a container of conflicts and a strengthener of consensus has outgrown its usefulness. It inhibits the search for different modes of change by being overprotective.

References

Azmon, Y. (1979). *Bargaining in Physical Planning in Israel.* Jerusalem: The Hebrew University.

Bellow, Saul (1976). *To Jerusalem and Back.* New York: The Viking Press.

Eisenstadt, S.N. (1977). *Comments on the Continuity of Some Jewish Historical Forms in Israeli Society* (in Hebrew). Jerusalem: The Institute of Contemporary Jewry, The Hebrew University.

Holsti, O.R. (1978). "Limitations of cognitive abilities in the face of crisis," *Journal of Business Administration* 9(2): 35–55.

Hurwitz, D. and Lissak, M. (1978). *Origins of the Israeli Polity.* Chicago: Chicago University Press.

Lindblom, C.E. (1977). *Politics and Markets.* New York: Basic Books.

Minkovich. A., Davis, D. and Bashi, J. (1977). *An Evaluation Study of Israeli Elementary Schools* (The Van Leer Study). Jerusalem: School of Education, The Hebrew University.

Salisbury, R.H. (1969). "An exchange theory of interest groups," *Midwest Journal of Political Science* 13 (Feb.): 16.

Wildavsky, A. (1975). *Budgetting.* Boston: Little, Brown & Co.

Wildavsky, A. (1979). *Speaking Truth to Power.* Boston: Little, Brown & Co.

Yadlin, A. (1978). *The Jewish Component in Israeli Education* (in Hebrew). Jerusalem: The Institute of Contemporary Jewry, The Hebrew University.

Part II

STRUCTURAL VARIETIES AND SOCIAL CHANGE IN EDUCATION

5.

The Impact of Rapid Social Change on Technological Education: An Israeli Example

Reuven Kahane and Laura Starr

PERHAPS THE TWO MOST CRUCIAL problems facing societies undergoing modernization are the preparation of manpower to master constantly advancing techno-economic development and the promotion of the integration of the lower classes. Educational systems expected to meet the needs of adaptation and integration[1] are often challenged by a situation in which the successful performance of one may reduce the effectiveness of the other.[2]

The simultaneous demands of rapid techno-economic change and of egalitarian participation conflict. Techno-economic development requires constant adjustment of the educational system to the increasingly sophisticated industry and agriculture which demands the provision of manpower that can supply a blend of technical and "organizational intelligence."[3] This creates the necessity for a highly academic, theoretical curriculum. However, such an emphasis frequently interferes with the educational system's integrative function, the provision of equal opportunities for all levels of the population.[4] Thus, educational systems often face a serious dilemma: If standards are raised and a theoretical approach is emphasized to meet techno-economic needs, education's capacity to integrate the lower echelons of the pupil population will be diminished; on the other hand, if academic standards are lowered to achieve integration of this population, education's capacity to meet techno-economic demands will be reduced.

In general, scholars have recommended that educational planning be geared to the simultaneous maximal fulfillment of these two functions. However scholars have not recommended specific programs for achievement of this goal, nor have they conducted much research into how these conflicting

---

[1] T. Parsons and N.J. Smelser, *Economy and Society* (New York: The Free Press, 1956).

[2] Due to the lack of aggregate wealth, no welfare or redistribution system is usually developed in the first stages of modernization and differences in wealth tend to widen. In the long run, however, when a developing society succeeds in promoting its economic structure, the initial contradiction between the two objectives of development and integration is mitigated. See W.W. Rostow, *Politics and the Stages of Growth* (Cambridge: At the University Press, 1971).

[3] See E.F. Denison, "Measuring the Contribution of Education to Economic Growth," in A.E.G. Robinson and J.E. Vaizey, *The Economics of Education* (London: MacMillan, 1966); F. Harbison and C.A. Myers, *Education, Manpower and Economic Growth* (New York: McGraw Hill, 1964); S.B. Saul, "Editor's Introduction," in *Technological Change: The United States and Britain in the 19th Century* (London: Methuen & Co. Ltd., 1970); T.W. Schultz, *Investment in Human Capital* (New York: The Free Press, 1971); and H.L. Wilensky, *Organizational Intelligence* (New York: Basic Books Inc. Publishers, 1967).

[4] See C. Jencks, *Inequality: A Reassessment of the Effect of Family and Schooling in America* (New York: Basic Books Inc., 1972); and H. Silver, ed., *Equal Opportunities in Education* (London: Methuen & Co. Ltd., 1973).

demands have been dealt with within various educational systems.[5] It is obvious that the most feasible solution to this dilemma is a system of streams adapted to the abilities of each segment of the population. Frequently, however, horizontal educational differentiation also carries hierarchical implications: social stratification can result from the different values attributed to various streams. Such a system is incompatible with the dominant values of egalitarian societies whose members believe in equality of educational opportunity. Furthermore, in such societies, aspirations appear to be increasingly similar across all strata,[6] and thus differential opportunities are often considered unfair by the lower echelons of society.[7]

In many countries this problem is particularly acute in the area of technological vocational training[8] which usually absorbs a high proportion of the "under-resourced" population while at the same time it is expected to prepare sophisticated technical manpower. The term "under-resourced" here refers to those students who lack certain assets necessary for educational, social, and economic mobility in a given society.[9] These resources include value commitment, power, wealth, prestige, along with various intellectual, emotional, and manual skills. Each may be utilized directly or may be converted into other resources. "Under-resourced" also refers to those people who possess these assets but do not possess the capacity to utilize them in given contexts. This term is preferable to that of "disadvantaged" or "underprivileged," because it is less biased and relates to the cause rather than the effect of maladjustment.[10]

It must be noted that because of their limitations, both educational and occupational choice for under-resourced students is not really "free" even in an egalitarian society. The problem is further accentuated because of the strong correlation between social class and the amount and nature of re-

---

[5] See, for example, D.J. Abernethy, *The Political Dilemma of Popular Education* (Stanford: The University Press, 1968); J.S. Coleman ed., *Education and Political Development* (Princeton, N.J.: Princeton University Press, 1965); P.J. Foster, *Education and Social Change in Ghana* (Chicago: The University of Chicago Press, 1965); A.M. Kazamias and B.G. Massialas, *Tradition and Change in Education* (Englewood Cliffs, N.J.: Prentice-Hall, 1965); A.M. Kazamias and E.H. Epstein eds., *Schools in Transition: Essays in Comparative Education* (Boston: Allyn and Bacon, 1968); and M.D. Shipman, *Education and Modernization* (London: Faber and Faber, 1971).

[6] W.G. Runciman, *Relative Deprivation and Social Justice* (Harmondsworth, Middlesex, England: Penguin Books Ltd., 1972).

[7] P. Selznick, *Law, Society and Industrial Justice* (New York: Russell Sage Foundation, 1969).

[8] Problems of technological education in developing countries have been investigated by few scholars. Some are C.A. Anderson and M.J. Bowman eds., *Education and Economic Development* (Chicago: Aldine, 1965); C.A. Anderson, "Technical and Vocational Education in the New Nations," in A.M. Kazamias and E.H. Epstein eds., *Schools in Transition: Essays in Comparative Education* (Boston: Allyn and Bacon Inc., 1968); E. Ginsberg, *Manpower for Development* (New York: Praeger Publishers, 1971).

[9] The writings on which this definition is based are T. Parsons, "On the Concept of Value-Commitment," *Sociological Inquiry* 38 (Spring 1968), pp. 135-160; J.S. Coleman, *Resources of Social Change* (New York: Wiley, 1971); S.N. Eisenstadt, *Social Differentiation and Stratification* (Glenview, Illinois: Little-Brown, 1971).

[10] See J.S. Coleman, *Resources of Social Change.*

sources possessed. The lower the socioeconomic status, the lower the resource cluster.[11] Moreover, even if the economic system requires manpower
who will operate at different levels and will possess varied occupational skills,
it is problematic in a dominantly egalitarian value system to define education
in such a way that it will be used as a mechanism which predetermines or limits educational and occupational free choice.

Because these problems are most salient in the technological education
system, we have chosen to analyze this system in Israel as a case study illus-
trating a type of response to the central-system dilemma.[12] Only the internal
processes of the educational system will be dealt with. A discussion of the
efficiency of the framework with regard to occupational placement of its
graduates, as well as a consideration of alternative channels of education for
under-resourced pupils, are beyond the scope of this paper.

A SYSTEM UNDER CROSS-PRESSURES

The technological education system in Israel provides us with a case in
which education's dilemma is quite salient and has become a focal point of
two basic problems confronting Israel today—integration and economic development. The problem of integration is quite intense because Israel is an
immigrant society with a very heterogeneous population characterized by
social, economic, cultural and educational differences. With regard to productivity, the Israeli economy has been in a constant process of development
since the establishment of the State, with the gross national product rising
approximately 10 percent yearly. Paralleling this growth is immense technological development and increasing structural complexity resulting in an
ever-growing demand for qualified manpower.

This demand is intensified even more by two additional factors. First,
the security situation in Israel demands manpower production on a high
technological level, beyond that which would be expected of the country
under normal conditions. Second, because of its small size and lack of natural resources, Israel is more successful in competing in world markets with
products requiring technological and scientific knowledge and skilled manpower rather than with those entailing mass production.[13] To deal simultaneously with the problems of integration and adaption under these condi-

[11] See J.S. Coleman, *Equality of Educational Opportunity* (Washington, D.C.: U.S. Department of
Health, Education and Welfare, 1966) and C. Jencks, *Inequality*.

[12] The Israeli technological education system is quite separate from the general academic oriented
system. The former system is almost completely vocationally oriented, adding a few hours in general
education, where the latter is built on the concept of the traditional European Gymnasium framework
directed mainly at academic-oriented knowledge and considered as passage to higher education.
Furthermore, the vocational system is perceived as having low status while that of the latter is defined
as an elitist one. Recently there has been an attempt to develop comprehensive schools with both
systems in one building, but this effort is still in its infancy.

[13] See E. Tal and Y. Ezrachi eds., *Science Policy and Development: The Case of Israel* (Jerusalem:
National Council for Research and Development, 1972).

tions, the goals of the technological educational system have been formulated in a dual way: to supply sophisticated manpower for the constantly developing economy and provide under-resourced youth with an educational framework which will promote their chances for integration and mobility within the society.

In an attempt to respond to the above goals, the educational system has been developed differentially on the secondary level. While most of the "achievers" enter the academic high schools, most of the "under-achievers" are directed by educational policy into the technological education system.[14] Since the number of pupils in the latter group has been far greater than that in the former, the technological education system has grown at a much greater rate than academic high schools. In 1948-49 technological high school students comprised 18.6 percent of the total post-primary student population in Israel; in 1971-72 they comprised 45.3 percent. Thus, with the expansion of this system, increasing numbers of under-resourced students were included.

TABLE 1. PUPILS IN HEBREW POST-PRIMARY EDUCATION
ACADEMIC AND TECHNOLOGICAL HIGH SCHOOLS IN ISRAEL*
1948/49–1971/72

Type of School	Post-Primary Education		Academic High Schools		Technological High Schools		Other Post-Primary Schools	
Year	Pupils Total	Percentage	Pupils	Percentage	Pupils	Percentage	Pupils	Percentage
1948/49	10,218	100.0	6,411	62.7	2,002	19.6	1,805	17.7
1951/52	24,958	100.0	12,936	51.8	4,315	17.3	7,707	30.9
1959/60	55,142	100.0	24,565	44.6	10,167	18.4	20,410	37.0
1964/65	99,837	100.0	46,661	46.8	25,601	25.6	27,575	27.6
1969/70	129,436	100.0	58,479	45.2	49,556	38.3	21,401	16.5
1971/72	132,488	100.0	54,333	41.0	60,039	45.3	18,116	13.7

Source: *Computed from C.B.S., The Statistical Abstract of Israel, no. 23, 1972, Table XXII/5, Page 578, and Table XXII/7, page 580.

Today, many students in the technological education system come from new immigrant families and/or those in the so-called lower echelon of society. Complicating matters further is the fact that these students are usually members of oriental Jewish communities (i.e., from North Africa, the Middle East, and Yemen), and are *a priori* socially, politically, and economically, disadvantaged in the basically technologically-oriented and largely modern Israeli society since they come from quite different cultural contexts.

[14] It should be noted that official educational policy from the 1960's directed under-resourced pupils into the technological education system by means of two mechanisms: (1) these pupils were not accepted into academic high schools, and (2) a system of tuition grants encouraging participation in vocational schools was instituted.

More importantly, many pupils originating from such sectors are impeded in their chances for scholastic success in Israeli society. Four characteristic indicators have been determined as significant for the Israeli population: low level of father's education, large families, poor housing conditions, and low level of consumption. About one-third of the children of oriental origin have three or four of these characteristics, while only two out of every 100 children of European origin are in the same situation.[15] Whereas in the academic schools, only 32 percent of the pupils are of oriental origin, 60 percent of the pupils in the technological education system are from oriental countries.[16] Students with three or four impeding characteristics are more likely to be found in this system. This propensity is further strengthened by the fact that pupils with higher achievement are less likely to choose, or be directed into, the technological education system. Under these conditions, it is clear that the system faces a difficult problem: how to develop highly sophisticated manpower from an under-resourced population.

THE RESPONSE OF THE TECHNOLOGICAL EDUCATION SYSTEM
TO CONFLICTING PRESSURES

Let us now examine the pattern of response employed by the technological education system in answer to these cross pressures. Since this system is officially committed to fulfill both the instrumental and the integrative tasks, the most efficient strategy of adjustment would be the development of differentiated systems of training. What we investigate here is which specific patterns of differentiation have been employed and whether high or low level "tracks" have been emphasized in this process. The term "track" refers to a study program within a given area of specialization divided according to the level of study. For example, pupils studying electricity can be found in (a) the matriculation program (which gives both a trade certificate and the possibility of university entrance), or (b) the non-matriculation program. With group (b) there are several levels of trade certificates available.

Two Patterns of Educational Differentiation

Over the years, at least two different patterns of differentiation have been adopted by the technological education system in Israel—differentiation according to length of the period of study and differentiation according to levels of study (although the employment of one pattern does not always preclude the existence of the other). Length of period of study refers to the period of time, usually the number of years, a pupil spends in a particular track. Level of studies refers to the academic standards of that track.

[15] Y. Haviv, *Children in Israel* (Jerusalem: The Szold Institute, Research Report 168, Publication 518, 1972) (in Hebrew) and C. Adler, "Social Stratification and Education in Israel," *Comparative Education Review* 18, no. 1 (February, 1974), pp. 10-23.

[16] C.B.S., *Statistical Abstract of Israel*, No. 23, 1972, Jerusalem, Table XXII/16, p. 589. In 1970, 53.2 percent of the Jewish population in Israel were of oriental origin. (C.B.S...Table II/21, pp. 48-9.)

Until the late 1960's the technological education system was differentiated principally according to tracks designated by length of study. Patterns of partial schooling (apprenticeship and evening schools, one to four year tracks, etc.) existed. This variety allowed pupils to participate in a program of study which could be individually suited to their intellectual ability and motivations. On the one hand, shorter tracks of study may have restricted a student's chances of further educational advancement. But, on the other hand, this structure had the advantage of creating a quick exit out of the educational system into the labor market. To some extent, early entry into the labor market may have compensated youth for what is considered a low educational level. In other words, by giving youth the opportunity for legitimate exit out of the educational system upon *completion* of some type of educational program, this system prevented the feelings of frustration which often accompany school failure or non-participation. It allowed youth to enter adult occupational roles, thereby instituting a new reference group and reducing emphasis on a youth's limited success in the student role.

Around 1969-70, as a result of a more rapid economic development, the Ministry of Education decided to change the system of technological education. The official policy declared:

(1) Most of the pupils would study for four or more years but would be placed into different tracks.

(2) The "highest" track would last four and one-half years, the successful completion of which would grant pupils a technician's certificate as well as a matriculation or governmental certificate.

(3) Aside from the highest track, there would be two other major tracks—the middle or "regular" track and the low, "practical" track. In addition, for those who could not be absorbed into one of the three tracks, special "directional classes" would be arranged. The length of study of all the tracks would be about four years, except in special cases.[17]

As a result, the old system, including two and three year schools and the apprenticeship program, was almost phased out. For example, whereas in 1968-69 only 43 percent of all pupils in the technological education framework were in four-year (or higher) tracks, by 1970-71 about 90 percent of all the pupils in this system were strongly encouraged to take four-year programs. This type of differentiation increased the pressures on the pupils, particularly the weaker ones, and postponed their entrance into the labor market. There is no evidence, however, of an improvement in achievement level for greater opportunities for occupational mobility.[18] Furthermore, with the

---

[17] *Vocational Schools in the Academic Year 1969-70* (Jerusalem: Ministry of Education and Culture).

[18] *Schools and Kindergartens—1968-69* (Jerusalem: C.B.S., Special Series Number 320), pp. 62-63; and *Schools and Kindergartens—1970-71* (Jerusalem: Data in Educational Statistics Number 32),

new pattern of differentiation, a tendency to discriminate against low level tracks developed. For example, in 1972 there were some sixty-three areas of specialization available in technological schools. Only twenty-one of these (33 percent) were offered on the lowest level.[19] Therefore, the number of educational options (from the point of view of lowest level tracks offered in the different areas of specialization) open to under-resourced pupils is quite limited under the new system and the limited availability of educational opportunities for these pupils may serve to reinforce their disadvantages.

Raising the Level of Studies

The new pattern of differentiation was accompanied by an attempt to raise the overall level of studies in technological schools. This tendency may be indicated by changes made in three aspects of the internal structure of the technological school: the pupils' study load, curricular emphasis, and the distribution of pupils according to areas of study.

STUDY LOAD. As noted above, technological education absorbs many pupils whose educational motivation and/or abilities are limited. Furthermore skilled and semi-professional occupations for which this framework trains workers do not carry a great deal of status in Israel or other societies. Therefore, everything else being equal, its power of attraction is relatively low.[20] Under these conditions, it is clear that the required study load, in terms of class hours, should not be heavy. A heavy load may cause an increase in the manifest or latent drop-out rate from school and alienate some segments of the student population. Furthermore, a heavier load is likely to discourage under-resourced pupils as well as applicants possessing the qualifications to enter the academic high school where the number of study hours is less.

Since all the limitations cited above are prevalent in the technological education system in Israel, it would be reasonable to assume that the study load in these schools should be relatively light. In reality, the opposite is the

---

p. 35. From partial investigations which have been made in Israel and in the United States, one may conclude that chances for occupational mobility among under-resourced students are increased if they enter the labor market after having completed a short training period at a school or in a specific training program, with most of their training being carried out in the factory itself after a period of experience-gaining. These problems have been discussed with regard to Israel by R. Klinov-Malul, *The Profit of Investment in Education* (Jerusalem: Falk Institute, 1966), and by the Ministry of Labor, the Manpower Planning Authority, *The Value of Investment in Vocational Education in Israel* (Jerusalem, 1969). With regard to the United States, see Berg, *Education and Jobs* (Boston: Beacon Press, 1971). The effectiveness of the technological education system in Israel has been analyzed by Guttman and Arad in terms of workers' continued employment in appropriate jobs. The problem of occupational elasticity in an economy undergoing rapid change has been neglected. See Y. Guttman and S. Arad, *A Follow-Up of Graduates of Three- and Four-Year Vocational Schools* (Jerusalem: The Szold Institute Research Report 141, 1970).

[19] Computed from *The Technological Trends in Post-Primary Schools in the Academic Year 1971-72* (Jerusalem: The Technological Education System, Ministry of Education and Culture) pp. 13-19.

[20] M. Lissak, *Social Mobility in Israeli Society* (Jerusalem: University Press, 1969). Recently, the earnings of people employed in the above occupations have increased to a large degree, and as a result, the attractiveness may have increased. Still, in most cases, the image of technological education is less favorable than that of other post-primary education frameworks.

case. An examination of the study load of pupils in all types of these schools shows that, on the average, pupils attend classes for about forty-five hours a week as opposed to thirty-six hours in academic high schools.[21] Study pressures on pupils in the technological education system in terms of hours of study are more intense for several reasons. First, practical work (shop or laboratory) takes up a great deal of time. Second, there is an underlying assumption that under-resourced pupils require a relatively greater number of hours in order to reach an achievement similar to that of other pupils. Third, among the dominant educational premises of the Ministry of Education is the assumption that there is a need to provide every Israeli pupil with humanistic-citizenship education (that is, history, civics, English, etc.), in addition to technological education. This adds yet another pressure. Paradoxically, then, study pressures on pupils are inversely related to abilities and rewards.

CURRICULUM. The above pressures pose a curricular dilemma. Since curriculum can be divided into two types, it is necessary to investigate the system effects of emphasis on one or the other. The first, or theoretical curriculum, is grounded in a basic body of general ideas or codes underlying scientific paradigms. These studies enable the student to understand the processes involved in specific tasks and to apply acquired knowledge to that task. The second, or practical curriculum, teaches the application of knowledge to concrete, specific tasks. In most cases, the first type of curriculum cultivates the intellect, while the second transfers skills. In many cases, the latter course of study leads to the use of knowledge without understanding and within limited areas. If the curriculum emphasizes "practical" skills, a majority of the under-resourced population will be certified. On the other hand, if the emphasis is on "theoretical" studies, the failure rate in the educational framework will increase. In either case, occupational and economic mobility are curbed.[22]

Until recently, the technological education curriculum was one in which theoretical studies were on a low or medium level in comparison with those of academic high schools, while practical studies were greatly emphasized. In the last few years, emphasis on theoretical studies has increased while stress

---

[21] *Report of the Committee for the Examination of Manpower Needs in Industry*, June 1969 (Horev Committee), Table III/I, p. 43.

[22] While most scholars discuss general versus technical education, they neglect the problem of the theoretical level of studies offered in each and its appropriateness for the absorbed population. A. Page, "Desirable Balance Between General Education and Technical and Vocational Training," in A.E.G. Robinson and J.E. Vaizey, *The Economics of Education* (London: MacMillan, 1966), p. 2. "Theoretical" knowledge includes two related groups of subjects—the theory of the pupil's major subject and pure academic subjects needed to understand this theory such as mathematics, physics, and chemistry. These two groups must be studied together. "Practical" knowledge includes some kind of application of theory such as technology of metal work, electricity, sewing, commercial art, carpentry, etc.. This is often taught in a shop or lab situation. It must be noted that the assumption that occupational mobility increases as the level of specialization decreases and as the theoretical level increases (to a certain threshold), has not been examined specifically in any research we know of. Also, this assumption has not been checked regarding different types of youth and industries.

on practical studies has decreased. In 1959, practical studies comprised 70 percent of the curriculum in most patterns of technological education. By 1970 it represented only 40 percent of the curriculum. In 1972, practical classes took up about 40 percent of the study hours in the highest track, 50 percent in the middle track, and 60 percent in the lowest track.[23]

This change in emphasis risks creation of a situation in which a high percentage of pupils could fail to grasp theoretical knowledge and thus be limited in their opportunities to acquire a wide range of practical skills. As one teacher commented, "Now not only do the pupils not know theory, they do not know the practical material either." It seems that the emphasis on theoretical over practical studies has increased the curricular pressures on under-resourced pupils. It probably has also decreased the functional relevancy which this type of pupil attributes to the technological education system.[24]

DISTRIBUTION OF PUPILS ACCORDING TO AREAS OF STUDY. As in the past, the largest number of vocational students today are concentrated in metal work and machinery programs. However, a re-distribution of students according to subjects of study has occurred which suits the present needs of industrial modernization in Israel.[25] Although changes have taken place in the delineation of various occupational roles, and consequently in the educational categories of classification, it appears that there is a tendency towards strengthening fields which require greater theoretical knowledge such as electronics, electricity, and textiles.

Likewise, it appears that the supposedly less complicated subjects, such as carpentry, printing, and even metal work, which demand more technical skill than theoretical knowledge, are becoming less available. However, the strengthening of the non-technical areas (clerical work, secretarial work, commercial art,) probably compensates for this trend by absorbing under-resourced pupils.

To conclude, increasing the emphasis on theory within the technological education system, even though enrollments are increased, can intensify contradictory pressures. To cope with these pressures, a particular strategy of differentiation was introduced. This strategy emphasized lengthy tracks characterized by a heavy study load and a theory-based curriculum. Such a tendency has decreased the structural opportunities for under-resourced youth to use education as an efficient channel for mobility.

[23] See *Vocational Schools in the Academic Year 1969-70* p. 8; and M. Avigad, *Vocational Technical Education—Its Planning in Accordance with the Needs of the Economy and Society* (Jerusalem: Ministry of Education and Culture, 1971) (in Hebrew), p.8.

[24] J. Maizels, *Adolescent Needs and the Transition from School to Work* (London: The Athlone Press, 1970).

[25] See *The Committee for the Evaluation of the Manpower Needs of Industry* (Jerusalem, 1969), and *The Committee for Expansion of Practical Engineering Education* (Jerusalem, 1970).

TABLE 2. THE DISTRIBUTION OF PUPILS IN TECHNOLOGICAL
EDUCATION ACCORDING TO AREAS OF STUDY
1957/58; 1965/66; 1970/71 (Rounded Percentages)*

	Year		
Areas of Study	*1957/58*	*1965/66*	*1970/71*
Electricity, Electronics, etc.	14	15	20
Metalwork and Machinery	36	37	33
Carpentry	17	5	3
Printing	2	1	1
Sewing, Fashion, Textile, Weaving	5	15	12
Office trades—Clerk, Secretary, Bookkeeper, etc.	1	18	20
Home Economics, Child Care	15	4	4
Other	10	5	7
Total	100	100	100

Sources: (1) 1957/58: C.B.S., Schools and Kindergartens 1947/48–1967/68, Special Series Number 186, Jerusalem, Table 37, p. 10.

(2) 1965/66 and 1970/71: Ministry of Education and Culture, Technological Education System, Vocational Schools in 1970/71, Jerusalem, March 1971, p. 3.

SOME CONSEQUENCES OF THE PATTERN OF DIFFERENTIATION

Having outlined the basic dilemma facing the technological education system in Isael and the subsequent pattern of differentiation adopted, we shall next investigate the consequences. These can be measured by several indicators such as changing rates of completion and certification.

First, an examination of completion rates in post-primary education shows that 68 percent of all pupils who entered the ninth grade of academic high schools in 1967 completed the twelfth grade in 1971, as compared with 50 percent from technological high schools.[26] If the technological framework was adjusted more toward the under-resourced (under the assumption that a basic aim now is the retention of the maximum number of pupils in school through the twelfth grade), one could expect retention rates in technological schools to be at least equal to those of other frameworks in the system. In any case, under the present conditions, at some stage, about 50 percent of the students who participate in technological education are labelled failures. This fact must be emphasized since, under the new system, one-to-three year tracks are not considered as alternatives, but usually as indications of incompletion.

Further, an examination of the official yearly drop-out rates in each grade of the major technological education network (ORT, acknowledged to be the most elite technological education sub-system and containing about 25 percent of the pupils in Israel) in the years 1968-69 and 1970-71 shows an insignificant decrease (except for the thirteenth grade). About 12 percent

[26] *The Technological Trends in Post-Primary Schools in the Academic Year 1971-72* (Jerusalem: Ministry of Education and Culture).

of the total number of pupils registered during the 1970-71 school year were officially defined as drop-outs.

TABLE 3. DROP-OUT RATES IN THE ORT TECHNOLOGICAL EDUCATION
NETWORK ACCORDING TO SCHOOL YEAR 1968/69, 1970/71*

	1968/69		1970/71	
Grade	Pupils Registered	Drop-Out Rate (Percentages)	Pupils Registered	Drop-Out Rate (Percentages)
9th	4,115	17.8	4,582	15.9
10th	3,038	19.6	3,716	16.3
11th	2,174	8.8	2,734	7.0
12th	1,161	2.8	1,317	2.0
13th	222	2.2	317	4.1
14th	173	—	225	0.9
Total	10,883	14.3	12,891	12.2

*Sources: (1) 1968/69: ORT Israel—Statistical Data 1970, Table 26.
(2) 1970/71: ORT Israel—Statistical Data 1972, Table 26.

This stratistic implies that the sub-system's absorptive power has increased, since the drop-out rate has remained relatively stable despite a probable increase in under-resourced pupils in this network. However, the ORT school system tends to absorb a relatively large percentage of the more resourced pupils in the technological education system. It is unclear what the consequences of the pattern of differentiation are in terms of drop-outs in the other networks containing larger percentages of under-resourced students. However, due to the expansion of the technological education system, it is obvious that the absolute number of drop-outs from this system has risen. Thus, an increased number of youth have experienced the frustration of failure.

Second, an examination of the results of final exams in technological high schools implies that a large number of pupils failed to obtain any certificate of completion from these schools. This phenomenon resulted from previously described changes initiated in the early sixties but not declared formal policy until the end of the sixties. For example, out of 4,427 pupils who submitted final examinations in 1969, approximately 57 percent received certificates.[27] The proportion of graduates who passed exams and received certificates varies according to areas of study. For example, in both

[27] A. Gor, *A Summary of the Results of Final Examinations in the School Year 1968-69* (Jerusalem: The Szold Institute, Research Report 155, Publication 507, 1970) (in Hebrew), p. 3. Data on the results of final examinations in technological schools in more recent years is not available at this time. However, there is no impression of change in recent years in the overall results. It should be noted that unlike American students who are generally examined at the completion of each subject year only, Israeli pupils must take a series of comprehensive examinations at the end of their last year of secondary school (whether academic or technological), in addition to yearly exams.

electronics and communication the percentage of pupils receiving certificates was 78 percent. Since it can be assumed that there is a concentration of relatively highly qualified pupils in these subject areas, the results are not surprising. More interesting is the fact that 83 percent of the pupils who submitted exams in carpentry as opposed to 47 percent in auto mechanics—subjects studied by pupils of supposedly limited abilities—received certificates. This fact suggests that carpentry is suited, and/or has adapted itself more than some areas to the characteristics of the under-resourced pupil population.

Compared to the types of study programs described above, the apprenticeship pattern[28] meets the needs of more under-resourced pupils; that is, it admits them into the labor market with an appropriate certificate. For example, in 1969-70, 90 percent of those who took final examinations in the apprenticeship framework passed.[29] This fact illustrates the major dilemma of the technological education system quite well: the apprenticeship pattern lowers the level of studies and therefore is able to award certificates of completion to a higher proportion of its graduates. In contrast, most of the programs in the technological education system seem to prefer to establish relatively high requirements, even if this reduces the percentage of graduates earning certificates of completion. Only a comparative study can determine which of the two systems is preferable, in terms of opportunities in occupational mobility for under-resourced youth.

Within the present vocational system, despite the given qualification of its students, educators have raised the standards of study by emphasizing "theory"; thus technological schools compete with the standards of the academic high schools. With the lack of alternative channels, the diminished absorptive power of technological education for under-resourced pupils, at least for the lower echelons, might be one of the causes, for the growing number of "non-affiliated" youth in Israel.[30] It may be hypothesized that the pattern of adjustment, including the specific pattern of differentiation that this sytem has adopted, has contributed to the increased alienation among under-resourced youth of lower socioeconomic classes—alienation which expresses itself partially in juvenile delinquency and partially in protest.[31]

[28] The apprenticeship system in Israel consists of the pupil attending classes one full day per week and working in his trade five days a week, at a shop, factory, etc..

[29] P. Krenot, *Results of Final Examinations in Apprenticeship for the School Year 1969-70* (Jerusalem: Ministry of Labor, The Section for Vocational Training, 1971), p. 10.

[30] In 1969, there were about 57,700 youth between the ages of fourteen and seventeen (27.4 percent of the age group) who did not participate in any program of study. Of these youth, 19,600 (9.3 percent of the age group) did not work either. See *Educational Level, Studies and Participation in the Labor Force Among the Age Group Between 14-17 in the Jewish Population* (Jerusalem: C.B.S., 1970).

[31] Recent research in Israel found an increase in the educational gap between the lower and middle classes, a gap which overlapped with ethnic divisions. A clear correlation was also received between the above phenomenon and a sense of frustration and tendency to protest among the lower classes. See

CONCLUSION

An analysis of the technological education system in Israel reveals increasing conflict between rapid social and economic change and integrative needs. These pressures pose a dilemma for the educational system: how to produce well qualified manpower while providing appropriate educational and employment opportunities for the under-resourced population. Most developing societies face a similar problem of solving conflicting economic and integrative needs by means of their educational policy; the problem is not unique to Israel.

In any educational system there are three possible patterns of problem-solving to the two pressures on the educational system:

(1) Increasing the differentiation between or within educational networks;

(2) Responding mainly to one side of the dilemma; and

(3) Developing mechanisms to bridge the gap between the goals of producing high-level manpower and adjusting to the needs of the under-resourced students.

The unique Israeli situation has fostered an educational system which combines option (1) and (2). Through its specific pattern of differentiation, it has responded more to economic pressures to maintain high standards than to those exerted by the under-resourced pupils. This response, as has been shown, seems to have had an aggravated impact on class and ethnic conflicts.

In many other developing societies one can detect an implicit or explicit tendency to choose a variation of the second alternative, usually to maintain lower standards and to absorb as many aspirants as possible.[32] By means of this policy, frustration resulting from limited access to education is prevented, but the risk of producing unsuitable manpower with exaggerated aspirations is increased. Thus, in either case, the solution may have socially injurious effects.

Y. Peres, "Politics and Ethnicity in Three Poor Areas," in R. Kahane and S. Kopstein, eds., *The Israeli Society—1967-1973* (Jerusalem: The Hebrew University, Acadomon Press, 1974).

The most salient expression of growing alienation among these youth in Israel is the so-called Black Panther Movement, which has already been politicized and was represented as a political party in last year's national elections. For a discussion of this movement, see E. Cohen, "Black Panthers and Israeli Society," *Jewish Journal of Sociology* 14 (1972), pp. 93-109.

Note, as opposed to most Western societies, alienation and protest in Israel are not diffused among the students and the upper echelons although recent protests after the Yom Kippur War were sporadic and institutionalized among the middle and upper classes. See C. Adler and R. Kahane, "A Portrait of the Israeli Youth" in C. Ormian ed., *Education in Israel* (Jerusalem: Ministry of Education, 1973).

Another expression of alientation is the rise in juvenile delinquency. The number of officially listed offenders in Israel grew from 5,062 in 1969 to 5,282 in 1970. The delinquency rate per 1,000 of the juvenile population dropped from 11.1 in 1969 to 9.6 in 1970. However, the rate for those whose fathers were born in Asia or Africa, many of whom are new immigrants and/or belong to the lower classes, was 18.5 per 1,000 as against 4.8 per 1,000 of those born in, or whose background stems from Europe and America (Statistical Abstract of Israel, 1972, p. 565).

[32] S.H. Rudolph and L.I. Rudolph eds., *Education and Politics in India* (Cambridge Mass.: Harvard University Press, 1972).

The third alternative remains the most difficult. The development of some mediatory mechanism which would allow the educational system to successfully fulfill both crucial functions simultaneously has received some attention to date. Modest progress in this direction can be seen in attempts at a redefinition of teacher role, development of informal education, and structured learning situations for the nurturing of the under-resourced.[33]

[33] See K. Frankestein, *Impaired Intelligence* (Jerusalem: The Hebrew University, and the Ministry of Education and Culture, 1970); R. Kahane, "Informal Youth Organizations: A General Model," *Sociological Inquiry* 45, no. 4 (1975); and R. Kahane and L. Starr, "Framework, Resources and Role Commitment: The Case of the Technical Teacher" (Jerusalem: The Hebrew University, 1975) (mimeo).

6.

Varieties of Orthodox Religious Behavior: A Case Study of Yeshiva High School Graduates in Israel

Mordechai Bar-Lev and Ernest Krausz

Introduction

IN traditional Jewish society, as in most other traditional societies, religious thought, action, and institutions were of supreme importance, both structurally and substantively. Generally, in any case of tension between sacred and secular elements, religious values and institutions were the dominant and decisive factors, since they were seen in traditional Jewish life as the sole source of social legitimation.[1] The central position of religion gradually led to the crystallization of a more or less homogeneous set of behavioural norms in the area of religious observance and the establishment of a stable pattern of religious standards and strictures, at least within specific geographic regions.

The development of modern society, and the strength of the processes of social change within it, brought about a radical decline in the status of religious values, and concomitantly shattered the consensus in the area of religious behaviour. In this new age, according to Bryan Wilson, religion and religious institutions have gradually lost their dominant status, and their social influence has declined dramatically, as 'religious thinking practice, and institutions lose social significance'.[2]

These processes of secularization,[3] as would be expected, affected Jewish life as well. Since the end of the eighteenth century, they have steadily eroded both the structural and functional integrity of traditional Jewish society as a 'total world'. In Palestine the secularization processes appeared only during a somewhat later period, with the intensification of the intra-communal strife for supremacy in the political, social, and ideological fields throughout the *Yishuv* (Jewish Settlement in Palestine) and in Jerusalem in particular.

This conflict began to develop at the end of the period of Ottoman rule and in the early years of the British Mandate in Palestine. On one side of the battle were the representatives of secular Jewish nationalism, Zionists and their supporters; among them were a significant percentage of the ideologues of the New *Yishuv*. Their opponents, primarily associated with the Old *Yishuv*, held to a traditional religious conception of Jewish life, which found its political expression in the positions taken by the Orthodox Agudat Israel party. The conclusion of this struggle produced a grave crisis in the legitimation of Orthodox Judaism in Palestine.[4] As a consequence, not only was there a decline in the social status of religious institutions and increased tensions between the religious and secular sectors; but in addition, changes took place in the religious behaviour of even those individuals who identified themselves with those very religious institutions and values.

We draw on the work of Peter Berger[5] to understand the problem of the tensions generated between the sacred and the secular, and to examine the effect of such tensions on religious behaviour.

Berger, in his analysis of the social situation of Protestant sects in America, focuses on the essential changes emerging as a result of the transition from a traditional religious society rooted in a specific locality, to a modern society which is pluralistic in terms of religious behaviour, both structurally and functionally. The existence of a variety of forms of religious expression in the same territorial area, none of which occupies a monopolistic position, places religion, according to Berger, in a 'market situation' of free competition. Each religion is therefore compelled to compete for 'consumers' ('customers'), whose loyalty to their 'product' is not guaranteed *a priori*. In such a situation of free competition, two alternative reactions are possible:

(a) The first is that of adaptation, at different levels, to the new pluralistic system and acceptance of the rational 'rules of the game' in a 'free market'. Such an adaptation necessitates fitting the 'price' to market conditions—that is, the concession of moderating any extreme religious demands, the tolerance of deviance from traditional religious norms, and the like. All this is done to 'sell' these religious values to both 'regular customers' and potential 'new consumers'.

(b) The alternative option involves the rejection of the basic principles of a pluralistic system, coupled with a voluntary and principled renunciation of any participation in the 'free market' game. The strategy usually takes the form of physical and/or social-structural isolation, as in various religious sects, and the continuance of activities in accordance with their traditional structures of meaning. A rejection demanding such a very high 'price', including the acceptance of extreme religious demands and a constant wariness against any deviations from traditional religious norms, means that only a small minority of individuals will be prepared to 'pay' the 'membership fee' for such social groups.

This study will explore the actual types of religious behaviour among a specific population of observant Jews who represent a very particular stratum within the religious Orthodox community in Israel.[6] The specific population investigated consists of the 'graduates' of Yeshiva High Schools, the latter being a novel type of educational institution established by religious Zionist circles in the early 1940's. In these schools, religious studies in the style of the traditional Yeshiva (Talmudic College) are combined with secular studies leading to University entrance examinations.[7] Pupils in the Yeshiva High Schools represent some 15 per cent of the total number of male pupils attending academic type high schools in Israel (that is to say, excluding those in technical and agricultural high schools). In addition there are female pupils in six parallel religious high schools for girls, called *Ulpana*.

The Yeshiva High Schools are fee-paying boarding schools, the fees being higher than those of secular boarding high schools; that is justified on the grounds of longer teaching hours owing to religious subjects being included in the curriculum. Although the Yeshiva High Schools differ from other high schools (including other non-Yeshiva religious high schools) in so far as the organizing of their curricula and time-tables is concerned, they are subject to the supervision and inspection of the Ministry of Education, which also sets the examinations. Their success may be seen in the steady increase in the number of pupils entering these schools in the 1960's (mainly at the expense of the non-Yeshiva religious high schools). The numbers have become stabilized during the 1970's. Here we will consider:

(a) Whether or not the religious behaviour of the respondents in a sample survey (described below) is basically uniform, and how it corresponds to the standards of religious behaviour of Jews in traditional societies.

(b) If their behaviour is of a mixed nature, what kinds of religious practice are displayed by the respondents? Specifically, in which particular aspects do the respondents maintain the religious rituals and norms, as they were kept in traditional Jewish life, and in what areas do they engage in various sorts of personal choice and selection among the traditional religious rituals and norms which they do observe?

The question of this 'mix' of traditionalism and personal decision will be examined in the social life of the sample respondents, who continue to subscribe to religious values and institutions while they live in the midst of a pluralistic cultural reality, confronted constantly by the basically secular values and social norms of Israeli society.[8]

Population and sampling procedure

The population investigated consists of 'graduates' of Yeshiva High Schools in Israel. This is an exclusively male population of high-school age (15–18 years) preparing for University entrance examinations (academic stream) of the Ministry of Education. A 'graduate' was defined as one included in the lists of students presented for examination purposes by these institutions; lists were obtained directly from the schools.

The sample was selected from 'graduates' of all the 22 Yeshiva High Schools in existence in 1975. The newer schools whose pupils had not reached matriculation examinations, and older schools (which for various reasons have closed down), were excluded. The first cohort chosen for the sample was the one which concluded its studies in 1955, since this was the first year when an organized group of students presented themselves for matriculation examinations from all the institutions in existence at the time. As for graduates after that date, proportional systematic random sampling was employed in order to select the sample from all the Yeshiva High Schools.

After ascertaining the number of graduates in each year, the following sampling procedure was adopted: (a) for the period 1955–64 all graduates in alternate years were selected—that is to say, five graduating years were included; (b) for the period 1965–74 half the graduates in every third graduating year were selected, alternate names being chosen from alphabetical lists. While this sampling method controlled for time-cohorts,[9] it left variables—such as religion, ethnicity, and educational specialization—uncontrolled. Thus the sample figure reached 1,832 graduates, drawn from nine graduating years and covering all Yeshiva High Schools. The final operative sample numbered 1,610 graduates.[10]

Research techniques

As a result of background information concerning the nature of the variables involved, the relatively homogeneous character of the population to be investigated, and especially considering the very wide geographical spread of the graduates, it was decided to adopt the technique of a postal survey. The questionnaire included only closed questions. (Graduates were told that the anonymity of the replies would be ensured.) A pilot survey, involving 84 pupils (from graduating years not included in the sample design) was first carried out. Its results helped to finalize the questionnaire design.

The survey itself was carried out during the months of January and February 1975. As an immediate response, 962 completed questionnaires were received. In order to ensure the representativeness of the sample, a sub-sample of the first-stage non-respondents, numbering 210, were contacted personally in their homes. Of these, 144 graduates produced completed questionnaires, thus bringing the total of respondents to 1,106, or 69 per cent of the operative sample of 1,610. First-stage non-respondents were compared with those who responded without personal contact. No significant differences were found between the two groups in either social background or level of religious observance.

The material gathered, involving 165 variables, was analysed by computer, and was subjected to statistical tests of significance. In addition, an index of religiosity was built on the principles of the Guttman Scale[11] based on ten questions involving religious ritual.

Findings

The ten closed questions mentioned above related to the index of religiosity[12] of the graduates and focused primarily on those *mitsvot* (commandments) possessing social characteristics. These included *mitsvot* of both positive and negative natures, among them commandments referred to colloquially as 'simple' or 'easy', as well as others termed 'difficult' or 'demanding'.[13]

The questions dealt with the following areas: the wearing of *tefillin* (phylacteries); the observance of the Sabbath; participation in public prayers; fixed times for the study of Torah (taken in the broadest sense to encompass Bible, Talmud, and rabbinic writings); the avoidance of social bathing in sexually mixed settings; the avoidance of mixed social dancing; the renunciation of television viewing because of halakhic (Jewish legal) considerations; the purchase and consumption of only kasher food; the strict separation of all dairy and meat utensils; and in the case of married men, the wife's covering of her hair (a traditional norm of modesty on the part of a married woman).

(1) *The wearing of tefillin.* According to the Orthodox interpretation of Jewish law, every male from the age of *bar-mitsvah* (13 years) and above must place phylacteries on his arm and his head *every* day, with the exception of the Sabbath and the Holy Days. The tradition holds that a Jewish male who does not put on his *tefillin* even for a single day—and even in the case where he is not rejecting the commandment but rather because he will lose some work, time, or money, or is simply lazy—is placed in the category of 'complete transgessors'.[14] (This does not apply in cases of illness.) Nevertheless, our findings demonstrate that a not insignificant percentage of the population studied is negligent in various ways in the total fulfilment of this important ritual: 6·3 per cent of the respondents report they do not conscientiously 'lay' (put on) *tefillin* every day, while another 10·2 per cent do so only irregularly or not at all.

(2) *Sabbath observance.* A somewhat higher level of uniformity was found among the subjects in terms of general Sabbath observance: 86·3 per cent of the sample claim to observe the Sabbath in strict accord with the *Halakha* (the totality of codified Jewish law). The commandment to observe the Sabbath has come to be defined exclusively in halakhic terms and to occupy such a central place in Jewish

law that only those who responded, 'Yes, absolutely', should be seen as falling in the category of Sabbath observers. Those who are partially observant ('In general, yes', 'I am not conscientious', 'I do not observe the Sabbath according to the *Halakha*', etc.) engage in some selected practices such as candle-lighting, *kiddush* (the blessing over the wine), and buying *hallot* (the special Sabbath bread which is generally blessed): these have become semi-secular, symbolic rituals and nothing more.[15] Even in the case of this fundamental *mitsvah* of Sabbath observance—which is strongly reinforced by extensive social control owing to the public nature of its observance or non-observance— there are some expressions of deviance in religious behaviour.

(3) *Participation in public prayer.* From a strictly formal legal point of view, the Jewish male must fulfil his obligation of prayer three times daily—*shaharit* (morning), *minha* (afternoon), and *maariv* (evening)— through individual private prayer. However, according to Katz,[16]

Private prayer was regarded as the exception. The proper form of worship in communities large enough to maintain a *minyan* (the quorum of ten males of the age of thirteen or over) was public prayer in the synagogue, in the *bet hamidrash* or house of study, or even in a private home ...

This traditional form of participation in public prayer for all three daily services is subject in modern society to very powerful economic pressures.[17] Consequently, Orthodoxy in recent times has shown some degree of tolerance and flexibility: there is a sort of implicit compromise to overlook non-attendance at public prayer on weekdays. Concomitantly, however, participation in public worship on the Sabbath and Holy Days is viewed as a minimal condition, and those who are not conscientious about meeting this limited obligation are viewed as transgressors. Table I below indicates the wide range of behaviour associated with this religious norm. (There were 46 'No reply'; 1,060+46=1,106.)

TABLE I.   *Participation in public prayer*

	Absolute Number	%
(1) I try to pray with a *minyan* every day or almost every day.	604	57·0
(2) I try to pray with a *minyan* every Monday and Thursday [when the Torah is read in public], in addition to the Sabbath and Holy Days.	58	5·5
(3) I try to pray with a *minyan* every *Rosh Hodesh* [the first of each month] in addition to the Sabbath and Holy Days.	83	7·8
(4) I try to pray with a *minyan* every Sabbath and Holy Day.	219	20·7
(5) I try to pray with a *minyan* in general on the Sabbath.	34	3·2
(6) I pray occasionally with a *minyan* on the Sabbath and Holy Days.	33	3·1
(7) I am accustomed to pray with a *minyan* only on *Rosh HaShanah* [New Year] and *Yom Kippur* [the Day Of Atonement].	17	1·6
(8) I do not go to the synagogue at all.	12	1·1
Total	1,060	100·0

(4) *Fixed periods for Torah study.* The fundamental halakhic requirement to be engaged in Torah study and learning, which is mandatory during every moment of an adult male's free time, with the exception of the time required to fulfil the so-called 'practical' *mitsvot*—those involving some physical action, to earn a livelihood, to satisfy basic needs, etc.—has never been expected of all individuals. As Katz points out,[18] this totalistic expectation was an ideal norm; it was realized in practice only by a small minority of rabbinic scholars who devoted all their time and energy to the *mitsvot*. The commandment to engage in Torah learning, as practised by the majority of the community in traditional Jewish life, was satisfied by the establishment of fixed times for study in the home, or in other frameworks outside the home, such as the synagogue, which was often termed 'the House of Study'. The behaviour of our respondents with respect to this *mitsvah* was also found to vary: while approximately one-third of them studied consistently every day, almost the same percentage did not have any regular schedule for religious learning. The remaining third tended to engage in Torah study one to three times a week.

(5) *Social bathing in mixed settings.* The type of religious behaviour we are concerned with in this section is best described as a prohibition growing out of a 'negative' *mitsvah* ('You shall not ...'), as are the sixth and seventh sections which follow this discussion.

In traditional Jewish society, almost any social meeting between men and women was perceived as a form of deviance and potential source of immoral sexual entanglements.[19] Therefore, participation in a mixed social event like bathing in the sea or a swimming pool (especially given the nature of swimming costumes) with members of the opposite sex was among the most strictly forbidden acts in the traditional Jewish community. The change of values in modern society in the general field of leisure activities, as well as in the status of women and in social relations between the sexes in particular, is clearly reflected in our findings: 65·5 per cent of those who were asked whether they bathed in sexually mixed settings said they did so or would not object to doing so.

(6) *Mixed social dancing.* The halakhic norms against mixed social dancing are also tied to the prohibition against social intercourse between the sexes.[20] Yet the research findings on the religious behaviour of the sample population are radically different in this area from the replies concerning mixed bathing. While about two-thirds of the subjects were untroubled about engaging in mixed bathing, only one-third participated in mixed social dancing:[21] 25·1 per cent in mixed ballroom dancing and 8·2 per cent in mixed folk dancing. Mixed ballroom dancing is perceived in Orthodox circles in Israel as representative of the worst in secular culture. Slightly more than half of the respondents—56·1 per cent—did not engage in any form of mixed dancing

whatsoever; and even restricted themselves still further to only traditional yeshiva-style dancing. A further 3·3 per cent engaged in folk dancing exclusively among males. Finally, there is a group whose behaviour in this respect is slightly atypical, although in keeping with elements of the traditional position: namely, the remaining 7·3 per cent of the respondents, who stated that they participated in folk dancing where men and women dance in separate circles. That is associated, especially in the last several years, with alumni of the religious youth movement.

(7) *Television viewing*. Television is a recent technological innovation which has been available in Israel only since the end of 1967. However, in a few years it has become a very influential medium in shaping the cultural norms of Israeli society.[22]

Despite the fact that traditional Jewish society in the past could obviously not have taken any position with respect to television viewing, contemporary extreme Orthodox circles have expressly forbidden the purchase of television sets, as well as the viewing of any television programmes—regardless of their nature.[23] Our findings indicate that 92·7 per cent of the Yeshiva High School graduates questioned watch television during their leisure time, without any apparent halakhic qualms, and are thus exposed to its cultural influence.[24] The remaining 7·3 per cent of the sample said that they did not watch television mainly because of religious reasons.[25]

(8) *The purchase of kasher food*. The details of the laws governing the *kashrut* (ritual purity) of the Jewish table acted at different periods as barriers to social contacts between Jews and Gentiles. At times, this was done with an eye towards maintaining maximal segregation from the Gentile population, while during other periods it was intended to reinforce the self-consciousness of the Jew who of necessity came into contact with Gentiles on a day-to-day basis.[26]

Even in Jewish society in Israel today, meticulousness in *kashrut* observance can present obstacles to social intercourse between 'religious' and 'non-religious' Jews. The position of our respondents, however, is clear on this question: nearly 98 per cent of them comply with the requirement by buying only certified kasher food for the home, or when eating out.[27]

(9) *The separation of all dairy and meat utensils*. In this area of ritual also, as in the buying of kasher food, we are dealing with a form of religious behaviour which reinforces the social exclusiveness of the observant Jew. The maintenance of separate sets of utensils for dairy and meat products not only serves to reassert the social distance between the Jew and the Gentile in the Dispora, and the 'religious' and 'non-religious' Jew in Israel; it also functions, in our view, as a mechanism for social integration of those who do structure their eating patterns in such a fashion.

It is, therefore, not surprising to discover that this is the most widely observed ritual among our research population. The fact that 98·3 per cent of the respondents maintain separate sets of dairy and meat utensils demonstrates the centrality of this practice, since many who are neither conscientious about, nor committed to, the other behavioural norms are observant only in the matter of *kashrut*.[28]

(10) *The wife's covering of her hair.* On the assumption that a correlation exists between the total religious behaviour of the Yeshiva High School graduates and the religious behaviour of their wives, each of the 580 married respondents[29] was asked whether his wife covered her hair. Jewish law views the married woman (including the widow and the divorcée) who does not cover her hair as 'transgressing the Jewish religious law'[30] and a legitimate object of scorn and social sanctions. However, our research demonstrates that only half of the wives of married respondents observed this practice.[31]

Classification according to the Guttman scale technique

The varieties of religious practice among respondents, presented earlier by means of an examination of the behaviour in respect of each particular ritual or observance, take on a much more concrete and meaningful form when we try to rank the individual rituals in a descending order, from what is in the respondent's eyes most 'difficult' to what is 'easiest' for him to accept.

The attempt to create such a ranking based on the Guttman scaling technique demonstrates that the particular items investigated all relate to the same substantive area of religious observance. All the earlier questions appear to be relevant to the relationships among the values

TABLE 2.   *Index of Yeshiva Graduates' Religiosity*[32]

Rank Order	Variable	Frequency	%	Cumulative %
10	For halakhic reasons does not view television.	47	4·3	4·3
9	No mixed social bathing.	210	19·0	23·3
8	Wife covers her head.	153	13·8	37·1
7	No mixed social dancing.	156	14·1	51·2
6	Studies Torah regularly.	184	16·6	67·8
5	Wears *tefillin* daily.	125	11·3	79.1
4	Observes the Sabbath according to *Halakha*.	63	5·7	84·8
3	Prays in a *minyan*.	56	5·0	89·8
2	Buys only kasher food.	52	4·7	94·5
1	Maintains separate sets of dairy and meat utensils.	42	3·8	98·3
0	Does not observe even one of the above rituals.	18	1·6	99·9
Total		1,106	99·9	—

of our 'global' religiosity variable and these relationships are systematic in their nature.

In addition, it was found that all the modes of behaviour in question ranged themselves according to their 'intrinsic' difficulty. Thus, for example, a respondent who replied that he observed a more 'difficult' ritual, also behaved in a 'religious' way with respect to those rituals which were 'easier'.

An examination of the coefficient of reproducibility showed that the number of deviant responses was very small in relation to the total size of the sample respondents who replied to the survey. The coefficient of reproducibility was 0·9586, and we therefore feel confident that our data base is sound when we propose Table 2.

Social profiles related to divergent patterns of religious observance

The ranking system developed on the basis of the Guttman scaling technique enables us not only to observe, as we mentioned earlier, ten different types of religious behaviour. It also permits us to collapse specific behavioural variables into more general categories, and thus to create a typology of divergent patterns of religious behaviour within our research population. In this way we discovered four separate groups, each representing a different pattern of religiosity of graduates of Yeshiva High Schools. The first group includes respondents who received a scaled 'religiosity grade' average of 7·000 and above—those who at the very least did not engage in mixed social dancing and may even have been still more 'traditional' in terms of our scale of religiosity. The next group represents those whose 'grade' was between 6·000 and 6·999 (having fixed times for Torah study). The third stratum received 'grades' ranging between 4·000 and 5·999 (those who observe the Sabbath according to the *Halakha* and wear *tefillin* regularly). Finally, the last group included those with scores of 3·999 and less (pray in a *minyan*, or do not do so, but observe *kashrut*)—or at the other extreme do not follow a single one of all the listed observances.

The attempt to group these different levels of religious behaviour can now be set against various aspects of the social backgrounds of these different sorts of Yeshiva High School graduates. Here we are referring to such variables as post-high school education, military service, occupation, nuclear family, residence pattern, leisure activities, etc., which typify the four groups, in the sense of a dominant pattern emerging within each of the different groups. We suggest that the basic findings presented here, tying the religious behaviour pattern to the social profile of each of the groups, may lead to a deeper understanding of the complex mechanisms and diversity we have found within a particular segment of Orthodox Jewry in Israel today.

(1) *The highly religious pattern.* Members of this group had studied in

post-high school, higher-level *yeshivot*, and did not plan to attend university. They did not do regular military service, nor did they serve in the framework of *yeshivot hesder* (which offer an opportunity of a combined programme of military service and Torah study). Their wives generally had received only a completely traditional Jewish education. They tended to reside in primarily religious sections of major urban areas and to send their children to the educational institutions of the more traditionally Orthodox, non-Zionist groups. In the Knesset and in local municipal elections, they voted for the Orthodox Agudat Israel party. It is also fair to characterize them as proponents of a specific sort of Orthodox 'Torah-true' culture in terms of their leisure-time activities. The only newspapers they read were those published by religious parties and their radio listening was confined primarily to programmes with a religious content. They did not maintain a library of 'secular' books at home, nor did they attend the cinema, theatre, concerts, light entertainment, etc. They accounted for slightly more than half the total number of respondents: 51·2 per cent.

(2) *The above-average pattern of religiosity* was found among 16·6 per cent; they had continued their full-time yeshiva studies beyond high school for longer than a year or two. Typically, they did their military service as privates (that is, not as officers) or in some sort of quasi-religious military framework, such as the military rabbinates, as members of a religious outpost settlement (*Nahal*), or in a *yeshiva hesder*. They tended to have sought higher education at Bar Ilan University (which was founded as a 'religious' institution) or at some other religious institution for post-high school learning, where they followed courses in Jewish Studies, education, humanities, or the natural sciences. Their wives did not have an exclusively religious education and the respondents in this group tended to dwell in urban areas with religious population clusters, in religious rural settlements, or in newer urban areas with a high percentage of religious Israelis and immigrants. Their children attended state religious schools within the general school system. The graduates themselves were mostly salaried employees, in upper-middle-class occupations. Many of them were members of religious political organizations and in elections they voted for *Mafdal*, the Orthodox-Zionist religious party. In almost every case, their parents were native-born Israelis of Ashkenazi origin, or had immigrated to Israel before 1954. This group may be said to have a traditionalist Orthodox cultural world-view concerning their free-time activities, although they allow themselves a limited degree of freedom and openness in those types of leisure activity which they perceive as being 'neutral' with respect to religious values.

(3) *The moderate pattern of religiosity.* Respondents in this category account for 17 per cent of the total; their pattern of moderate religiosity falls in the middle of our typology. In their army service

they were officers or senior non-commissioned officers. They did not attend any higher-level *yeshivot*, religious university, or other religious institutions for higher education. They tended to have studied in secular universities in the areas of the social sciences, medicine, law, architecture, and engineering. They lived in urban areas with a mixed population of the observant and the non-observant and were mainly professionals, generally self-employed. This category is particularly striking for the number of its members whose parents immigrated to Israel from North Africa or Asia between 1955 and 1966. Their fathers in the past often worked in low-prestige occupations and in contrast to the sons, had received only a very limited religious education at the *heder* (elementary school) level. They exhibit remarkable upward social mobility. The nature of their leisure-time activities may be described as completely secular without any restrictions whatsoever on general social patterns of leisure-time activity, which are perceived by them as being totally 'neutral' with respect to their religious values.

(4) *The pattern of minimal religious observance.* In this category (the remaining 15·1 per cent of the total), there are the sort of individuals whose wives served in the army. (Under Israeli law, women who choose to define themselves as 'religious' may obtain exemption from compulsory military service, since the army is viewed in traditional Orthodox circles as an environment unfit for a young girl.) These graduates also send their children to non-religious kindergartens and elementary schools. They were often active in non-religious political groups and voted in elections for secular political parties such as the Labour Party or Herut—and later, Likud. In their free time, they participated completely and unself-consciously in all aspects of society's secular cultural life, including such things as visits to nightclubs. They attended concerts of popular singers and performances of light entertainment at least once a month, and went to the cinema very frequently. The books in their homes were almost exclusively on secular subjects.

Conclusion

The results of our survey suggest clearly that religious pluralism has developed within the ranks of the Yeshiva High School graduates. An extremist attitude to religion—expressed in terms of strict adherence to traditional Orthodox precepts on the one hand, and the wholesale abandonment of religious practices on the other—is characteristic only of small groups out of the sample investigated. Nearly half the sample of Yeshiva High School graduates appear to have opted for a somewhat more diluted expression of Orthodoxy—an approach which does not regard television viewing or mixed bathing, for example, as anathema to Orthodox religious practice. In the Guttman scale, too, a fair measure of religious pluralism is reflected: the variable response in all the ten questions, dealing only with ritualistic behaviour, leads us firmly to the conclusion that a heterogeneous tendency is clearly evident in this religious population, and that this holds even for the more basic religious practices.

In the light of these conclusions we put forward the proposition that a Neo-Orthodoxy has become established and that this may be seen as an adaptive response to the demands of what Peter Berger calls the 'market situation', given Israel's secularized society. This Neo-Orthodoxy has evolved from the complexity of the behavioural style which is typical of the vast majority of the graduates. That complex identity, with leanings towards Western cultural norms, is gaining ground over the exclusively Jewish religious identity which character-izes members of traditional Jewish society. We should not overlook, however, the ambivalence which may ensue from this complex approach involving both religious and secular tendencies. Moreover, the ambi-valence may naturally reflect the structural tension inherent in this new type of religious educational institution,[33] so that both the institutional development and its products may be regarded as reflecting the 'cost' which has been incurred, or the 'price' which has been paid, by a section of religious Jews who are prepared to adjust to the 'market situation' in the secularized environment. Nevertheless, this Neo-Orthodoxy has produced an element possessing an intense Jewish identity carried by a 'Torah-schooled intelligentsia' moving between tradition and innovation.[34]

We wish to acknowledge gratefully the assistance we received from David Glanz; the support given by the Institute for the Study of Ethnic and Religious Groups at Bar Ilan University; and the Memorial Foundation for Jewish Culture, New York.

NOTES

[1] On the role of religion in traditional, non-Jewish societies (including Christian and Muslim), see Roland Robertson, ed., *Sociology of Religion*, Baltimore, 1972, pp. 115–38; and L. Huizinga, *Herbst des Mittlealters*, Munich, 1928.

[2] See B. R. Wilson, *Religion in Secular Society*, London, 1966, p. 14.

[3] Concerning the sociological meaning of 'secularization', see L. Shiner, 'The Concept of Secularization in Empirical Research', *Journal for the Scientific Study of Religion*, vol. 6, no. 2, 1967, pp. 207–20.

[4] On the social turmoil during this period in the Ashkenazi Old *Yishuv*,

whose members were centrally involved in the struggle and crisis over legitimation, etc., see M. Friedman, *Society and Religion: The Non-Zionist Orthodox in Eretz Yisrael (1918–1936)* (Hebrew), Jerusalem, 1977.

[5] See P. L. Berger, 'A Market Model for the Analysis of Ecumenicity', *Social Research*, vol. 30, no. 1, 1963, pp. 77–93. See also by P. L. Berger, *The Sacred Canopy: Elements of a Sociological Theory of Religion*, New York, 1967, p. 153, and his *The Social Reality of Religion*, London, 1969, pp. 137–49.

[6] In our research, we are not concerned with the various types of religiosity found among the 'secular' population (i.e. the non-Orthodox). On the problem of secular religiosity or 'non-religious religion', in the non-Orthodox sectors of Israeli society, see I. Shelach, *Indications Towards Secular Religion in Israel* (Hebrew), Jerusalem, 1975, pp. 39–40.

[7] For details, see Mordechai Bar-Lev, *The Graduates of the Yeshiva High School in Eretz-Israel—Between Tradition and Innovation* (Hebrew), Ph.D. thesis, Bar Ilan University, Ramat-Gan, 1977.

[8] Although some scattered religious norms operate within Israeli society in general as approved by the state legislature, the basic sources of legitimation in that society are secular in character. On the isolated instances of religious norms which play a role in the life of the society, see M. Elon, *Religious Law* (Hebrew), Tel Aviv, 1968, pp. 55–56.

[9] The first period (1955–64) was one during which the older institutions became well established; while the second period (1965–74) saw the fast growth in the number of institutions and graduates.

[10] 222 graduates were lost from the original sample owing to the following: 71 were overseas at the time of the research; 14 had died; and for 137 graduates it was not possible to obtain their addresses. Thus, 7·5 per cent of the graduates in the original sample were not located. This is a fairly small proportion when compared with other studies. See, for example, Elihu Katz and Michael Gurevitch, *The Culture of Leisure in Israel* (Hebrew), Tel Aviv, 1973, Appendix A, p. 2, in whose study 25 per cent of the original sample were not located.

[11] See C. A. Moser, *Survey Methods in Social Investigation*, London, 1968, p. 239.

[12] The choice of, and stress on, the ritual dimension and the conscious disregard of the other dimensions of religiosity, such as experiential, ideological, intellectual, and consequential—as formulated by C. V. Glock, ed., in his own essay on 'Dimensions in Religious Commitment' in *Religion in Sociological Perspective*, Belmont, Calif., 1973, pp. 9–11—are based on the hypothesis that Orthodox Jewish society in Israel judges and evaluates the success of the religious socialization of its members in terms of their actual behaviour. What we wish to stress is that from the perspective of the internal criteria of the Orthodox community, the fulfilment of halakhic norms is viewed as *the* most important and fundamental yardstick in measuring an individual's religiosity. The selection of these specific ten types of ritual was based on the authors' personal familiarity with both the subject area itself and the spiritual worldview of Orthodox circles.

[13] A number of the questions do not relate to *mitsvot* performed exclusively in public, such as wearing phylacteries or the study of Jewish texts at fixed times.

[14] See Rabbi Joseph Karo, *The Shulchan Aruch—Code of Law* (Hebrew), *Orach Haim*, section 37, paragraph 11.

[15] On secular rituals, see Note 6.

[16] See Jacob Katz, *Tradition and Crisis*, New York, 1974, p. 176.

[17] It should also be pointed out that even in traditional Jewish society some difficulties arose with respect to communal prayer on weekdays, especially in connection with the afternoon *minha* service. See Katz, op. cit., Note 16, pp. 178–79.

[18] ibid., p. 74.

[19] ibid., p. 162.

[20] On the prohibition against mixed social dancing see, for example, H. D. Halevi, *Find Yourself a Rabbi* (Hebrew), Tel Aviv, 1976, pp. 192–97; O. Joseph, *Yabia Omer I* (Hebrew), Jerusalem, 1954, p. 106; M. Feinstein, *Letters from Moshe, Even Haezer II* (Hebrew), New York, 1964, p. 326.

[21] Perhaps it is possible to explain these apparently contradictory findings by noting that Israeli society sees sea bathing as a clear case of an activity associated with health and popular relaxation; while on the other hand, in the case of mixed social dancing, the religious individual finds a much greater degree of social control operating on him from those who do not engage in such dancing—the family, peer group, rabbis, adults in general, etc. This is especially so in the case of mixed ballroom dancing, where a man usually holds his female partner very close to him. The *Halakha* forbids even the slightest contact.

[22] On the development and impact of television in Israel and the public's attitude towards it, see E. Katz and M. Gurevitch, op. cit., pp. 166–213.

[23] For an analysis of the formulation of this prohibition as being based on the *Halakha*, see Y. Didavoski, *Machneha Kadosh* (Hebrew), Jerusalem, 1976.

[24] 73·3 per cent of the subjects watched television regularly at least once a week.

[25] Only 3·7 per cent of the sample responded in this manner exclusively. A further 3·6 per cent who were non-viewers gave in addition other reasons such as, 'It is a waste of time', or 'Most of the programmes are at a low level'.

[26] On the social and religious distinctions between Jews and Gentiles, see Jacob Katz, *Between Jews and Gentiles* (Hebrew), Jerusalem, 1960, pp. 46–56.

[27] The uniformity of behaviour in this area of ritual life was defined simply in terms of the demand by the subjects that the food be certified kasher. With respect to the source of the rabbinic supervision, it is possible that different respondents will buy only food certified by certain groups or rabbis whose *kashrut* they personally trust (e.g. the Chief Rabbinate, the Beth Din Zedek of Jerusalem, etc.). In any case, no further data are available on this question.

[28] It is unquestionable that the desire to preserve social relations and commensality with parents and other close relatives (brothers, sisters, in-laws, etc.) plays a central role in the considerations of this group of respondents.

[29] The total sample of 1,106 consisted of 580 married respondents, 520 single men, 4 divorcés, and 2 'no answers'.

[30] For a review of the halakhic sources on the necessity for a married

woman to cover her hair, see G. Ellinsohn, *Women and the Mitsvot* (Hebrew), Jerusalem, 1974, pp. 117–20.

[31] There are variations in the fashion and style in which a woman conceals her hair from view. These range from a simple kerchief (partly or entirely covering the hair) to a wig (sometimes worn over a shaven head). In practice, most of the wives in this study did not concern themselves with more than the basic demand for a minimal covering of some sort.

[32] The most 'religious' respondent would score ten points on this scale, while the least 'religious' only a single point. Someone without a single 'religious' response would receive a rating of zero.

[33] See M. Bar-Lev, op. cit., pp. 142–46, 411–17.

[34] The founders of the Midrashia, one of the best known Yeshiva High Schools in Israel, used this expression in the 1940's. See Y. R. Etzion, 'Intelligentsia Toranit', in *15 Lamidrashia* (Hebrew), Tel Aviv, 1961, pp. 22–25 and M. Bar-Lev, 'The Social Profile of Midrashia Graduates as Compared with Graduates of Other Yeshiva High Schools' (Hebrew), in *Niv Hamidrashia*, no. 13, 1978.

7.

Arab Education in Israel

Sami Khalil Mar'i

ONE OF THE MOST CONSPICUOUS INEQUALITIES between Arab and Jewish education in Israel exists in the area of vocational-technological education, an inequality leading to, among other things, inequality in economic opportunities. In the cases of both education and jobs, a thorough analysis reveals that the status of Arab society and education in Israel is no longer determined by political issues and forces stemming from the Middle Eastern conflict as much as it is by internal Israeli social and economic forces. In addition, even the issue of security is manipulated to serve the majority's social and economic needs. Indeed, many researchers and scholars who belong to the majority in Israel have observed that the security rationale is often utilized to manipulate the Arab minority and deprive them of equal opportunity. This maintains superior opportunity for the majority which, in turn, has its own problems of inequality between the two major Jewish subcultural groups. Arieh Luva Eliav, an eminent Zionist and political leader in Israel, claims that Jewish society manipulates and controls the Arab minority to maintain superficial socioeconomic stability and avoid confrontation with problems of social unrest.[1]

The Arab minority in Israel is vulnerable to such manipulation because it lacks the political and economic power necessary to express any opposition to the majority's control. Moreover, the little opposition that Arabs in Israel are capable of expressing is automatically perceived by the authorities as subversive activity directed against the state and its existence. This rationale makes it easier for them to suppress any opposition by Arabs or any effort on the Arabs' part to organize politically to defend their rights to be equal citizens of the state of

Israel, and thus make better educational and job opportunities available to themselves, too.

THE ISSUE OF TECHNICAL EDUCATION

This study originated mainly as a consequence of a disagreement between educational authorities and Arab community representatives, all of whom were members of a committee formed in 1973 by the director general of the Ministry of Education in Israel. The task of this *ad hoc* committee was to define the goals and needs of Arab education in Israel during the 1980s. One of the major issues the committee found itself dealing with rather intensively was career (i.e., technological) education for Arab youth in Israel.

Through its surveys and data collection activities, the committee discovered a huge gap between Jewish and Arab educational systems in Israel; for example, in the Jewish educational system about 50 percent of the middle and high school pupils are enrolled in vocational-technological educational programs either in vocational schools or in vocational streams in comprehensive schools. In the Arab educational system, on the other hand, less than 10 percent of the middle and high school students are enrolled in such programs.

A few observations could be offered as possible explanations for this astonishing gap, each of which seems to have some validity. One of the explanations used most often by the central educational authorities is that Arab society in Israel is a developing rural one, and as such has a long history of placing a negative value on manual labor and a very high value on white collar jobs, even those jobs which are not highly prestigious (i.e., elementary school teachers, clerks, secretaries, and civil servants). This position may have basis because, as mentioned before, the basic role of secondary education during more than three decades of the British Mandate over Palestine was to prepare qualified personnel as elementary school teachers, civil servants, and clerical employees, not only to serve their own communities, but also to mediate between the British government and the Arab communities in Palestine.

This tradition of linking high school education and the attainment of a white collar job, goes the argument, is deeply rooted and still exists. Thus, the educational authorities are not ready to risk a fairly large investment in vocational-technological education in Arab schools because, based on the assumption that Arab parents would prefer academic over vocational training, such an investment would be in vain.

Those parents who express such a preference have already placed their children in a few available vocational programs in Arab schools in Israel. Indeed, the small percentage (10 percent) of pupils enrolled in such programs is a reflection of such parental attitudes. Moreover, no demand for such educational programs has been reported by the field representatives of the official educational authorities. Nor has there been a demand from communities or local organizations (municipal councils or parent associations). This lack of demand, again, supposedly proves that Arab society in Israel does not hold the kind of attitudes which favor manual labor, even though it is skill based.

A twofold assumption underlies this position. First, the Arab society has been for a long time associating postelementary education with the achievement of a job which does not require manual labor. Second, the first part of this assumption continues to be considered valid unless a community's demand is reported to the educational authorities by its field representatives for a different option of educational quality, a course of action which in itself assumes community awareness and involvement that is basically a Western type of community characteristic.

Another explanation is usually presented by Arab community representatives, however, for the gap between Arabs and Jews in the vocational-technological educational network. They maintain that the gap is due basically not to negative parental attitudes towards this kind of education, but rather to discriminatory policies which are being practiced against Arabs by Israeli authorities, particularly educational authorities. Vocational-technological education is costly, at least more so than the academic type of schooling, because it demands more personnel, updated equipment geared to the different technological vocations, and an adequate physical set-up to contain such equipment. And this is only one reason why educational authorities are not willing to invest in Arab technical education.

But, the argument goes, in the eyes of the Arab communities the educational authorities' assumptions as to the negative attitudes of Arabs toward labor, though erroneous, are of minor importance. The community representatives claim that the attitudes of central educational authorities in Israel towards Arab education are an extension of a larger policy towards the socioeconomic status of Arabs in Israel. With the academic trend increasing in importance, the relevance of postelementary education is gradually being lessened since it leads nowhere except to the university. With regard to university education, still other problems exist. The ultimate outcome is that more and more Arab pupils either drop out earlier or graduate, and in both cases they join their fellow

Arab cheap, unskilled laborers to serve the majority's economy. Thus, the Arab educational system in Israel helps keep the young Arab at the lower level of the country's socioeconomic spectrum which, in turn, insures that the opportunities for skill-based jobs remain exclusively to majority members.

This feeling, whether justified or not, on the part of Arab community leaders as to the attitudes of educational authorities, implies a few assumptions. One is that a discriminatory policy exists against the Arab minority with the educational system as the perpetrator of such a policy. Another assumption is that although the Arab community may have held attitudes which were not favorable to educational programs involving preparation for a future manual job, those attitudes were operative in the past. A third assumption is that Arab society, due to changes in the economic and social aspects of its life, has changed tremendously in that it has realized that one of the best ways to insure an economically secure future is through learning skills useful in the different technological jobs available in the Israeli job market. "The experiences which an Arab laborer gains in the Jewish society while working or hunting for a job, is that unless he owns the skills necessary, he is forced to accept lower paying and lower valued jobs out of necessity. When he interacts with his Jewish boss or fellow workers, he soon discovers that they had learned a job, or at least useful skills at high school. The first question which comes to his mind is why his high school did not have those helpful programs. . . . Is it because the authorities want him to serve in the lower unskilled jobs?" This is an excerpt from an interview with a young Arab journalist who is associated with a majority party's newspaper. During the interview he often referred to his many talks and experiences with Arab workers in the city of Tel Aviv. He was quite positive that a favorable attitude towards vocational-technological education exists among Arabs in Israel. "It is a necessity out of the continuous daily reality," he said.

A third explanation for the rather large gap in vocational programs and enrollment between Arab and Jewish educational systems, which is usually expressed by moderate professional Arabs and Jews in Israel, is that the Arab Education Department within the Ministry of Education is built in such a way that it is difficult for it to see the emerging needs of Arab society in Israel. Not only does this department not have a history of trying to make itself relevant to the needs of the society within which it functions, but also it is basically run by Jews and Arabs who are either remainders from the British mandatory educational system in Palestine or the products of it. Thus, the Department of Arab Education fails to recognize the changes which have taken place rather rapidly in Arab society in Israel, and as a consequence, fails to adapt curricula to the needs which have emerged from changes in the economic life of the Arab in Israel.

These shortcomings become more detrimental to Arab education in Israel in light of two conditions. First, the Israeli educational system is very centralized, and the quality of education, innovations in curricula, and goals are the responsibility of the centralized educational authorities, not the communities. Second, from an administrative point of view, the Arab educational system is an integral part of the overall Israeli system of education. It is anticipated that the subsystem for Arab education should approach planning and implementation with a rather high level of sophistication, at least as high a level as exists in the Jewish educational system in Israel. As far as vocational-technological education is concerned, it is maintained by Arab community leaders that the gap between Arab and Jewish educational systems is due to false or outdated assumptions concerning values of Arabs in Israel towards manual labor and vocational-technological education.

Apparently, in the argument between Arab communities and educational authorities, there are two central and opposing positions, each of which may have a certain validity. One is a position of hesitation and restraint on the part of the educational authorities from investment in vocational-technological education in Arab schools because of the fear that the very small number of pupils who will decide to choose this program does not legitimize the relatively large investment. The second more decisive position is pressing for just such an investment in vocational-technological education for Arabs. Under circumstances so wrought with contradictions, it is not easy to arrive at a decision in one direction or the other, when such a decision may necessitate large amounts of money for investment or when a lack of investment can be interpreted as supporting a position of neglect, deprivation, or even discrimination.

In an attempt to solve this dilemma and supply the educational authorities responsible for making decisions in this matter with dependable data, a survey was undertaken as to the attitudes of Arab society in Israel towards postelementary education in general and towards manual, skill-based labor and vocational-technological education in particular. This was done under the assumption that such an educational program corresponds to the changing values and needs of Arabs in Israel.

This study was requested by the Research Authority of the Ministry of Education in Israel and carried out within the framework of the Institute for Research and Development of Arab Education at the University of Haifa. The research report was published in Hebrew in 1975, and the data provided in this chapter are based on the report. Because of the sensitivity of the issue involved and its background, two researchers, one Arab and one Jewish, carried out this study, and the report was originally published under their names.[2] Since the study is expected to be used as a basis for decision making by the educational authorities, the combination of the researchers' backgrounds is also useful as a safeguard against any complaints of slantedness and subjectivity.

In addition, the secretary of the Research Authority of the Ministry of Education, the director of the Arab Education Department, and the chairman of the Ad Hoc Committee on Arab Education during the 1980s, all of whom are majority members, asked to preview the questionnaires which were to be used in the study. The latter two did complete the preview and made appropriate comments. The questionnaires were then revised accordingly, and when the revised edition was previewed again the reviewers had no objections. These individuals also approved of the subjects and methods of the study.

There were two reasons for this preview procedure. First, it is a general rule in the Israeli Ministry of Education that any research project which has to do with entering schools, whether sponsored by the ministry or not, be approved by the ministry's Research Authority. This study, of course, was not, and should not have been, an exception to the rule. Second, because of the controversial nature of the subject and because of the opposing claims and accusations, it was the wish of the authorities to make sure that the study tools and plan were not inappropriate as far as the level of desired objectivity was concerned.

A SURVEY OF ATTITUDES TOWARD TECHNICAL EDUCATION

Three hundred ninety-six eleventh grade pupils, 210 of their parents (fathers), and 67 teachers were administered the questionnaires which were constructed for this study in order to determine their attitudes towards technical education. The pupils were chosen from the eleventh grade Arab pupil population in Israel because at this level pupils have to make decisions concerning their future after the twelfth grade. Fathers were chosen because in a traditional patriarchal society, such as the Arab society, they influence decisions more than mothers as far as the future of children is concerned. More than 50 percent of the fathers were given the questionnaires on an interview basis on the assumption that some of them might have difficulties in reading and writing? Finally, all of the pupils' teachers were given the questionnaires based upon the assumption that they influence the decision-making process as far as their pupils' future is concerned by being consulted by the parents and the pupils as well.

The following were the points of emphasis in this study: attitude toward continuation in postelementary education; the identity of the person(s) who takes the major part in the decision making as to the continuation of education; attitudes toward work in general and manual skill-based labor in particular; differences as to attitudes toward the sexes; effects of occupation upon status; and finally, attitudes toward vocational-technological education in light of changing economic realities.

1. *Attitudes Toward Secondary Education in General*

The researchers tried to learn something about parents', pupils' and teachers' attitudes toward secondary education because such information would indicate how the society relates to secondary education, which includes both academic and vocational streams. The assumption is that to the extent that there is greater approval of secondary education one can expect the differences in attitudes towards academic and vocational education to be more discernible. In other words, the greater the approval, the greater the effort will be to exhaust all the possibilities and potentialities in secondary education.

Table 12 shows in percentages the attitudes of parents, teachers, and pupils to the statement: "It is preferable that a pupil with no chance of achieving his matriculation certificate should start working earlier." The three groups examined expressed themselves as very much in favor of secondary education. The issue was purposely put strongly: a pupil with no chance of achieving his matriculation certificate had better leave school and go to work early. Only 13.3 percent of the parents agreed that the youngster should drop out and go to work if he had no chance of getting his matriculation certificate. The same feeling was expressed by the teachers. However, almost 20 percent of the pupils examined agreed that in this given case the pupil better drop out and start working.

TABLE 12

Attitudes Toward Continuation in Secondary School

	Agree	Disagree	Undecided	N
Parents	13.3%	86.2%	0.5%	210
Teachers	13.4%	86.6%	—	67
Pupils	19.9%	78.0%	2.1%	396

SOURCE: Sami Khalil Mar'i and A. Benjamin, "The Attitudes of Arab Society Towards Vocational Education" (Haifa: The University of Haifa, Institute for Research and Development of Arab Education, 1976).

Apparently, the small gap between the position of pupils and that of the parents and teachers can be explained by the notion that the school experiences of the unsuccessful pupil are not particularly pleasant. Therefore, he finds it better to drop out and thereby escape frustrating experiences and make better use of his time. Despite acknowledging this possibility of dropping out, most of the pupils were still in favor of continuation of high school regardless of the absence of any significant chance of achieving the matriculation certification at the end of the twelfth grade. In conclusion, Table 12 illustrates that all the groups together and each one separately favored secondary education because of its intrinsic educational and its pragmatic values in a changing society, such as the Arab society in Israel.

2. The Decisive Factor in Decision Making

One of the important variables in the issue of attitudes toward vocational-technological education is the relative significance of the factor most affecting the decision in all matters touching on the continuation of studies and the type of studies to be undertaken.

Table 13 shows the distribution of the responses to the following item: "In your opinion, which of the following most determines the decisions in matters of study?" As shown in the table, in most cases both parents and pupils feel that the decision was arrived at by the pupil himself. Here also a small gap between parents and pupils in terms of the identity of the decision maker was found: 80.9 percent of the parents left the decision to their children, the pupils, while 72 percent of the pupils reported making the decisions independently. This gap can be explained by the fact that 14.4 percent of the pupils felt that decisions

TABLE 13

Determining Elements in the Decision to Study

	Parents	Pupils	Both	N
Parents	15.7%	80.9%	3.4%	210
Pupils	13.6%	72.0%	14.4%	396

SOURCE: Sami Khalil Mar'i and A. Benjamin, "Attitudes of Arab Society Towards Vocational Education," (Haifa: University of Haifa, Institute for Research and Development of Arab Education, 1976).

concerning their future education were reached by both parents and children.

In conclusion, a situation clearly exists in which the pupils themselves were primarily responsible for making the decisions in all matters having to do with their studies. The intervention of parents and other elements was minimal. This finding is interesting and even strange in the light of the fact that the society under discussion is a traditional and patriarchal one in which the father has ultimate and almost sole authority in everything connected with his family and its members. Because of rapid sociocultural change, however, it is difficult for those same parents—who, for the most part, studied in only the first few grades of elementary school—to keep abreast of the various developments in the fields of study and education and the opportunities these fields offer the pupil. In other words, the difficult conditions of a period of transition have resulted in many parents losing their ability to decide in matters about which they have insufficient knowledge and in which they have relatively little previous experience. In addition, in the transition from a traditional to a modern society there is also a change of values toward granting greater autonomy to children to make decisions and bear responsibility.

3. Attitudes Toward Work

There are in general two popular categories of occupation: the first, clerical work and other white collar jobs, and the second, an occupation which involves manual labor. It seems very important to clarify the positions taken in regard to these categories because of their direct influence on the positions taken with respect to vocational-technological education.

The position of parents interviewed toward the future occupation of their children was, in general, that they favored work in some trade and preferred it over clerical work or other office jobs. Thus, when parents were asked to state their reaction to the statement: "A good trade is better than a desk job," 65.2 percent (N = 210) answered in the affirmative and 30.5 percent didn't agree—that is, they preferred a desk job and clerical work to a trade. Of the parents questioned, 4.3 percent answered that it was difficult for them to decide. It is clear, therefore, that most of the parents preferred a good trade for their children to a desk job.

Another question attempted an examination of the degree of differentiation existing in the attitudes of parents towards their children of each sex. It is necessary to keep in mind, of course, that we are dealing here with a traditional society which had formerly preferred white collar work to manual labor even for their sons. How much difference was there in parental feelings towards the occupational future for their sons on the one hand, and for their daughters on the other? It was expected that their attitudes towards their daughters would remain more conservative.

Table 14 shows the distribution of parents' responses to the item concerning the kind of occupation considered desirable for their sons

TABLE 14

Parents' Attitudes Toward the Future Occupations of Sons and Daughters

	Trade	Clerical/nonmanual	Undecided	N
Parents toward their sons	64%	32.0%	4.0%	100
Parents toward their daughters	15.2%	77.3%	7.5%	110

Source: Sami Khalil Mar'i and A. Benjamin. "The Attitudes of Arab Society Towards Vocational Education," (Haifa: University of Haifa, Institute for Research and Development of Arab Education, 1976).

and their daughters. The interesting point is that the parents held contrary opinions concerning the future of each of the sexes. Whereas most of the parents (64 percent) were interested in a future in some trade for their sons, most of them rejected this kind of occupation for their daughters. They were interested (77.3 percent) in clerical work for them, and only 15.2 percent were interested in a future job for their daughters which would involve manual labor.

In this item the parents were divided into two groups: those who had sons in the eleventh grade and those who had daughters. This method of division was in itself significant: the sample included 210 parents who had a son or a daughter, each in the eleventh grade at the high school level. One would expect, based on many statistics concerning developing societies, that males would outnumber females in high school. However, among Arabs in Israel the ratio is also balanced at 50 percent each.

Two conclusions can be drawn from the analysis of the responses to this item. First, the parents questioned agreed to the notion that a skill-based job was far better than a lower ranking white collar job (clerical and desk jobs). This finding supports the notion that the society under discussion has indeed changed in the direction of accepting manual, skill-based labor over other usually nonmanual occupations. The second conclusion is that parents had opposing attitudes with respect to the sexes. For their sons they (64.0 percent) preferred a trade over clerical jobs. However, more than 77 percent of the parents interviewed objected to the idea that their daughters might have a manual job. They preferred clerical jobs for them. The expectation of conservative attitudes of parents towards the quality of jobs for their daughters was confirmed by the data.

It is worth examining this finding on parental attitudes toward female employment still further. A closer examination of interviews with parents reveals that this position on the future of their daughters was in no way a rejection of vocational-technological education for them. On the contrary, the parents viewed this type of education favorably on the condition that it would lead to clerical work rather than to manual labor. An effort to pursue this point in depth was made. In the city of Acre there are 37,000 inhabitants; 30 percent are Arabs, and the rest are Jewish. Acre has an Arab comprehensive school, one of the very few Arab schools in the country that has vocational training streams. For female pupils, it has two streams: one is home economics and the other is office management. However, the latter was introduced only in 1975, and is also very weak. The training does not exceed basic typing skills in Arabic and Hebrew.

In the city there are four Arab schools; most of their secretaries are Jews with a background in Arabic. This is not so much due to policy as it is to necessity. In the city there are more than twenty-five Arab lawyers' offices serving basically the Arab citizens of the city and the Arab population in the many villages surrounding Acre. Only 3 of the 25 lawyers have Arab secretaries in their offices. Office managers and chief secretaries are mostly of Jewish background, again out of necessity. Moreover, among the hundreds of clerical employees of the city municipal council, there is only one Arab female secretary.

In such a situation one wonders why a school which already has the minimum basis for establishing a quality training program for a needed vocation such as office management does not provide it. By doing so, the school would make itself relevant to its pupils' and community's needs. In a discussion with members of the parent organization it was learned that what is needed is money and good teachers. "Without having the first, we can't have the second; and money should come from the Department for Vocational-Technological Education in the ministry through the city government."

The discussion with fifteen eleventh grade girls was most enlightening. All of them attended the Arab Comprehensive School in Acre and at the same time enrolled in the vocational streams of both home economics and typing. Although they enjoyed the nice dishes and tasty cookies and cakes they learned to prepare in their home economics classes, they nonetheless felt resistance to such learning. "We don't need a class that reinforces our already inferior status in our society; we are sick of our role as housekeepers. We want some good quality vocational program, like office management, which would help improve our status by becoming independent. . . . This also will help us compete for the many secretarial jobs available in our city." Apparently, school was perceived by them as perpetuating their traditionally inferior status as females instead of improving it in their very male-dominated society.

4. *Vocation Contributing to Socioeconomic Status*

An attempt was made to find out to what extent, in comparison with other factors, vocation was viewed by parents and pupils as likely to contribute to raising a person's socioeconomic status. Six factors were listed and the subjects were asked to arrange them in order of importance in terms of their possible contribution to upward mobility in a person's socioeconomic status. Findings here show that both among parents and pupils technical occupation was listed in second place after higher education.

Ranking by Parents	*Ranking by Pupils*
Higher education	Higher education
Technical occupation	Technical occupation
Government connections	Government connections
Money	Money
Property (land)	"Hamoula" (clan) distinction
"Hamoula" (clan) distinction	Property (land)

A number of interesting points stand out in this ranking by parents and pupils. In fact, the marked congruence between the order of priority given by parents and that given by pupils is quite amazing. The parents and pupils related to these factors in a similar way in all but two cases. *Property* took fifth place and *"Hamoula" distinction* sixth place among the parents, while there was a reversal of this order among the pupils. However, these two factors were ranked at the bottom of the scale by both groups.

Another outstanding point is the value placed on *government connections* as a factor in mobility and social status; this factor was ranked in third place by both groups. It can therefore be said that not only were the two groups unified in their opinions, but also *government connections* were perceived as significant in an individual's attempts to rise on the social ladder. This attitude reflects the individual's feelings that it was not enough to succeed in studies and training, but that in many cases there was a need for association with government (the ruling group) for studies and success to become significant factors in social mobility. This supports Benjamin and Peleg's findings[3] that Arab high school pupils felt they couldn't actualize their aspirations because of political reasons.

It is interesting that in a society which only a few years ago feudalistic wherein the landowners almost automatically enjoyed the highest social status, *property* was now not considered a significant determinant of a person's social status. Similarly, *"Hamoula" distinction* was considered unimportant in determining social status in this society in which status is ascriptive rather than achieved. The transition from a traditional-feudalistic society to a more modern one has apparently required relinquishing feudalistic life patterns and abandoning class membership as important factors in consolidating social status; this transition has thereby allowed greater personal achievement and responsibility.

There was an attempt to examine further the variable of family position (the Hamoula distinction variable) as a factor considered important in contributing to a person's social status in which the following statement was presented to parents, teachers, and pupils for their reactions: "A good trade gives no honor to a man without position."

Table 15 shows that the decisive majority of parents, teachers, and pupils rejected the statement that a good trade grants no honor to a man without family position. This finding again strengthens and even confirms the contention that the processes of modernization are at work in Arab society in Israel, processes which gradually bring

TABLE 15

**Hamoula Membership Compared to a Trade as Potential
Contributors to the Individual's Social Status**

	Agree	Disagree	Undecided	N
Parents	15.6%	82.0%	1.5%	210
Teachers	13.4%	83.6%	3.0%	67
Pupils	21.2%	72.2%	6.6%	396

SOURCE: Sami Khalil Mar'i and A. Benjamin, "The Attitudes of Arab Society Towards Vocational Education," (Haifa: The University of Haifa, Institute for Research and Development of Arab Education, 1976).

about cultural and value changes as well as structural alterations within the society. The values have changed in that a man is not automatically seen in a positive way just because he is a son in an important Hamoula. Instead, his work is measured by his achievements and not by the position he inherited. There are, of course, various influences on the structure of Arab society in Israel. Its traditional class structure is being transformed in a way that is gradually replacing the traditional Hamoula which existed for so many years and continues even now to exist alongside of social systems more characteristic of modern rather than traditional society. To mention one example, a working class has emerged to replace the traditionally known fallaheen class which is Hamoula based.

5. *Attitudes Toward Vocational-technological Education*

The attitude toward the type of education given to children in school is determined, to a large extent, by the value system prevailing in the society, by the attitude of the society toward work of various kinds, by its conceptions of status and the connection between status and a given type of occupation and by the opportunities such an education offers.

Of course, the quality of vocational-technological education and the resources provided for it determine to no less a degree the attitude of the society towards this type of education. However, in this study there was an effort to differentiate between the actual situation which exists in regard to vocational education and the opinions of those questioned, regardless of the poor quality of the limited technological-vocational programs in Arab schools. In other words, subjects were asked to express their opinion regardless of the situation which exists in the school with which they are familiar.

From the attitudes expressed toward work and the contribution of trade to social status, it can be concluded that Arab society in Israel not only does not reject vocational training in the school, but in fact favors it. This conclusion can be reached indirectly on the basis of the findings mentioned above. It would seem, though, that this is not enough to ensure a conclusion of scientific credibility and pragmatic significance. Rather, the conclusion must be directly derived from data which make its formulation unavoidable. The survey, therefore, posed direct questions to parents, teachers, and pupils to determine their positions in relation to vocational-technological education. Table 16 expresses the difference in percentage frequencies in the reactions of

TABLE 16

The Position of Parents, Teachers, and Pupils in Regard to Vocational Education

	Agree	Disagree	Other	N
Parents	67.1%	30.5%	2.4%	210
Teachers	74.6%	22.4%	3.0%	67
Pupils	58.0%	39.9%	2.1%	396

SOURCE: Sami Khalil Mar'i and A. Benjamin, "The Attitudes of Arab Society Towards Vocational Education," (Haifa: University of Haifa, Institute for Research and Development of Arab Education, 1976).

those examined to the statement: "It's not so terrible if a good student in the academic stream continues in the vocational stream."

In a general way, most of the parents, teachers, and pupils agreed that there is nothing wrong in a good student in the academic curriculum transferring to a technological-vocational course emphasis.

It should be pointed out that the teachers were the most favorable to technological-vocational education (only 22.4 percent did not agree to a good student in academic studies transferring to vocational studies). On the other hand, the position of the pupils was less affirmative than that of parents and teachers (about 40 percent did not view with favor a change from an academic to a vocational curriculum on the part of good students). Apparently, the other two groups, particularly the teachers, were more aware of the potential and the implications inherent in vocational-technological education than were the pupils, who were inclined to identify the pupil in the vocational stream as relatively weak in academic studies.

In order to bring out a clearer and more unequivocal position, the question was made more rigorous, and the subjects were asked to react to the following statement: "A good student in academic studies would be making a serious mistake if he were to switch to vocational-technological studies." Table 17 reveals the distribution of the frequencies of the subjects' responses to this question in percentages. And, in fact, there is a shift to the affirmative. Only 2.5 percent of the parents and 25 percent of the pupils agreed that a successful pupil in academic studies would be making a serious mistake if he were to switch his studies to a vocational course. The teachers, on the other hand, remained unique in this case, too, in that they were even more in favor

TABLE 17

Attitudes Toward Vocational Education

	Agree	Disagree	Undecided	N
Parents	25.2%	72.4%	2.4%	210
Teachers	7.5%	89.5%	3.0%	67
Pupils	25.0%	70.5%	4.5	396

Source: Sami Khalil Mar'i and A. Benjamin, "The Attitudes of Arab Society Towards Vocational Education" (Haifa: University of Haifa, Institute for Research and Development of Arab Education, 1976).

of vocational education than the parents and pupils. Only 7.5 percent of the teachers agreed that a good student in the academic program would be making a serious mistake were he to switch to a vocational program. Here again the teachers demonstrated greater perception and awareness—because of their broader education—than the other groups questioned toward the problems which could stem from an overemphasis on academic studies on the one hand, and the advantages and possibilities of vocational education on the other.

It is noteworthy that although the two items concerning the attitudes toward vocational-technological training in the school differ in their wording, they have a common factor. It was the purpose of the researchers to draw the subjects' attention toward considering a successful student turning from academic to vocational-technological education, for, in general, vocational-technological education is identified with the low-achieving pupils. In this way, an attempt was made to reveal the attitudes of subjects towards vocational education in its broader sense, namely, as an educational quality which offers opportunities other than just providing a framework for the absorption of under-achieving pupils.

A third item in the parents' questionnaire probed their attitudes toward vocational-technological education in a direct personal manner: "What would you advise your child who is in the ninth grade before entering high school?" Four alternatives were provided: to continue in the academic stream; to continue in the vocational stream; to drop out and start working; or undecided yet. Of the parents questioned, 59 percent would advise their children to continue in the academic stream, 34 percent in the vocational-technological one, 5 percent to quit and start working, and 6.5 percent undecided yet. We see, then, that one-third of the parents would advise their children to continue in the vocational stream. This seems a very high and promising proportion considering that vocational-technological education in the Arab schools in Israel is in its beginnings and is still struggling with the most difficult problems of scope, equipment, quality, and diversification.

So far, the subjects' attitudes towards vocational-technological education have been revealed without any consideration, at least not an explicit one, of the current status of the economy and job opportunities. The following is an analysis which was specifically designed to evaluate parents' and pupils' attitudes when they were instructed by the questionnaire/interviewer to consider job opportunities and the economy as far as the Arab in Israel is concerned.

It is clear from Table 18 that when the job opportunities for Arabs in Israel are considered, 42 percent of the parents preferred

TABLE 18

Distribution of Responses of Parents and Pupils as to Attitudes Toward Vocational vs. Academic Programs

	Vocational-Technological Training	Academic Stream	Undecided	N
Parents	42.0%	18.5%	39.5%	210
Pupils	65.7%	28.5%	5.8%	396

SOURCE: Sami Khalil Mar'i and A. Benjamin, "The Attitudes of Arab Society Towards Vocational Education," (Haifa: University of Haifa, Institute for Research and Development of Arab Education, 1976).

vocational-technological training over an exclusive academic program; 18.5 percent preferred academic, and surprisingly, 39.5 percent of the parents could not decide. This is apparently due to the fact that many parents find themselves in a situation wrought with contradictions when it comes to decision making. On one hand, they favor academic programs because of the opportunity for the continuation of their children's education in higher levels and/or because of the possibility that an academic program may lead to an affiliation with office type of work. On the other hand, they are familiar with the difficulties involved in achieving a job such as this and with the many job opportunities available in the technological field. Thus, they found it difficult to decide. However, more than 40 percent of the parents in this study preferred vocational-technological education for their children.

The attitudes of the pupils are expressed in their responses to this item were much less equivocal and more fully appraised. The percentage of those who could not decide was very low (only 5.9 percent). Two-thirds of the pupils questioned preferred a vocational-technological stream over an exclusively academic one when asked to take into consideration the job opportunities available to them after graduation from high school. This fact is important in light of another finding in this survey, namely, that in the opinion of most parents (80.9 percent) and most pupils (72 percent), this decision was in the hands of the pupils themselves (Table 13).

It is worth noting that when parents asked what advice would they provide for their elementary school children, 59 percent responded in favor of the academic stream. These parents were then placed in a position where they had to take existing conditions into account. At that point, their support for academic studies decreased from 59 percent to only 18.5 percent. On the other hand, their support of vocational-technological streams increased. These observations clearly testify to the fact that society's attitudes are not static, but vary by degrees in accordance with living conditions and the possibilities that these conditions allow the individual.

In a summation of the findings of this study, it can be concluded that:

1. Secondary school education in general is highly advocated. The percentage favoring a "drop out and go to work" position is almost zero.

2. The pupils in secondary school (eleventh grade) are the ones who decide about their education, its continuation, and the stream to be chosen.

3. There is a clear preference for work in a trade which is skill based over work in clerical occupations.

4. Parents prefer trade to an office job for their sons, while they prefer an office job and clerical work to a trade involving physical work for their daughters.

5. The acquisition of a trade takes second place (after higher education) as a factor contributing to the improvement of the individual's socioeconomic status.

6. Property owning and Hamoula affiliation are least important among the factors contributing to upward socioeconomic mobility. Moreover, a person's lowly social origins are not thought to hurt his status if he has acquired a good trade.

7. About one-third of the parents are still torn between the heritage of the past and conditions of the present. They are struggling with a situation wrought with contradictions in that their attitudes of esteem and preference towards white collar work are in conflict with the existing conditions of the economy.

8. Both parents and pupils are sensitive to and aware of the present conditions of the economy and the job market, conditions which require a change from positions giving priority to academic studies to those giving priority to vocational-technological training.

9. Overall, not less than half the subjects of this survey preferred vocational-technological streams over exclusively academic ones. If the situation in the Jewish sector is taken as a model, it follows that half of the pupils in the Arab secondary school system should turn to vocational-technological programs provided that these programs are available for them at a comparable quality.

SOCIOECONOMIC CHANGES AND EDUCATIONAL NEEDS

The findings of this survey point to some of the indications of sociocultural change which Arab society in Israel is undergoing. One of the indisputable indications of transition from a traditional to a modern society is the existence of a state of conflict engendered by forces pulling towards the past and forces pushing toward the present and the future. In the case of the survey, the conflict was revealed in the uncertainties of many parents (almost 40 percent) when their traditional values conflicted with existing socioeconomic conditions.

Another indication of sociocultural change reflected by the findings of this study is that society emphasizes the achievement aspects of status more than the ascriptive aspects. Feudalism and Hamoula position were the outstanding indications of socioeconomic status in Arab society until a few years ago when, in general, the distinguished Hamoulas were also the feudalistic clans and the large land owners. However, these are no longer the exclusive or even the principal tokens of socioeconomic status in an ascriptive society. Higher education and the acquisition of a trade have taken the place of feudalistic affiliation and family position, and the two variables of education and occupation are the outstanding status tokens in a modern achievement-oriented society.

A third indication of modernization in Arab society in Israel is expressed in the right and freedom practiced by the youngsters to make decisions concerning their education and their occupational future. In the decisive majority of cases Arab youngsters are the main decision makers, an indication of modernization in the development of a more democratic family atmosphere and interpersonal relation. All this is taking place in a society in which family has traditionally been extremely patriarchal and strictly authoritarian. The father once almost exclusively determined everything concerned with his children, but today apparently he determines the decisions in a relatively minor percentage (15.5 percent) of the cases.

The agreement by most parents to let their daughters work outside the family and the home is also an indication of modernization, since women working outside the family domain is a relatively new development. The type of work preferred by these parents for their daughters testifies to the fact that the changes in attitudes are not uniform and equal in all cases. There is a certain degree of restraint affecting such changes. Thus, when living conditions necessitate changes in attitudes which are in sharp contradiction to a particular value, the attitudes change in a moderate and considered way. Arab parents, then, are opposed to their daughters working at various occupations which are incongruent with the value placed on white collar work. In other words, if a girl goes to work, it is preferable that she be employed in a job within the limits of traditional values, i.e., clerical work.

The high value placed on secondary education by the subjects questioned in this survey is in itself indicative of modernization. There has been a shift in the way education is viewed: in the past, if it was necessary at all, it was only for the sake of acquiring the "three Rs" and some religious training; now the whole process is extended and viewed positively not only as instrumental but intrinsic to the growth of the youngster. Moreover, it can be deduced from this position that the period of adolescence is prolonged. This is an obvious characteristic of a modern complex society, for it is well-known that the more traditional the society, the sharper and more abrupt is the transition from childhood to adulthood.

Finally, the positive shift in attitudes towards skilled labor and vocational-technological education is the most conspicuous indication that Arab society is going through accelerated processes of sociocultural change. And these attitudes, in conjunction with the opportunities available in the job market, will sooner or later bring about some far-reaching changes in the occupational structure of the Arab society in Israel, provided that the educational authorities are aware of and responsive to those attitudes expressed in this survey.

It is difficult to establish beyond any doubt why the gap in vocational-technological education between Arab and Jewish educational systems in Israel exists. It could be related to the fact that the educational authorities in charge of this educational sphere hold outdated assumptions about Arab society in Israel. If this is the case, one can't avoid the conclusion that should these false assumptions and misconceptions continue to be held, the outcome will be a gradual lowering of the level of relevance of education for Arab youngsters in Israel. And as the educational system becomes outdated, it will become isolated from the society it is supposed to serve. Whatever the case may be, one thing is obvious: the need is great and the attitudes are positive for Arab vocational-technological education. As a consequence, interest is assured. Therefore, an investment in a vocational-technological educational network in the Arab educational system in Israel is indeed a worthwhile one, at least from the minority's point of view.

The need for quality education in the vocational-technological sphere is becoming more and more intensified as a consequence of two separate yet related trends. The first trend is an external one: job opportunities, in terms of those jobs which necessitate specialized former training in school, are available in the larger Israeli job market. Arabs in Israel are aware of the many opportunities available in the Israeli industrial society, and they are motivated to enjoy them. Through relevant vocational-technological programs schools are an important means by which young Arab can make use of those opportunities. Because they are untrained, however, the masses of Arab youth and adults in Israel are occupying the less prestigious, lower paying, and less secure jobs in construction, restaurants and gas stations.[4] Moreover, these jobs occupied mainly by Arabs are the most sensitive to economic fluctuations in the country. For example, the first to be affected by an economic slowdown is the area of construction, both public and private, thus Arabs are the first to be jobless. By demanding a vocational-technological educational program, Arab parents are expressing a need for employment and economic security for their children.

The other trend is within the Arab society itself. The subordinated class in Arab society, traditionally known as *fellaheen* in the feudalistic days, awakened a long time ago. The society is no longer feudalistic, and farming is no longer the basic source of living. The fellaheen have become workers in the predominantly Jewish cities. They are not dependent on their former masters (landowners) anymore and have a strong ambition to develop and compete with the formerly distinguished class. Occupation is the arena for this competition. An occupational-technological educational program will not help them compete in the job market with majority members, but it is expected to help reinforce the improvement in their socioeconomic status as compared with their former masters within their own society. These internal tensions are being transformed into educational needs—needs which are magnified, of course, by the economic realities in a country where the Arab worker in the Jewish society observes and learns through the cross-cultural situation that a promising way to move upwards on the social ladder is to acquire a technical vocation.

By being at the crossroads of cultures, Arab society in Israel is undergoing many changes and transformations. The Arab educational system in Israel is at these same crossroads and, like the society within which it functions, is being challenged to become more relevant by being more responsive to the needs of the society, represented by a young generation which, for the first time in a few hundred years, is spending thirteen years or more in school. Whereas Arab society in Israel is affected by the cross-cultural situation as revealed by the many cultural and structural changes and transformations, the Arab educational system has been less responsive than Arab society to possibilities for changes. A major part of the reason for this rigidity is that the Arab educational system *is* on the crossroads of cultures, and, as such, the decisions are not made by the recipients of education from the system but by the representatives of the majority culture. And their decisions are based on the way they perceive Arab society and on their convictions and beliefs which are conditioned to a large extent by their background.

One could, of course, observe that majority domination over minority education is universally true. Examples are provided by the cases of black, Indian, and chicano minorities in the United States; the French minority in Canada; the Catholics and Asians in India; the North Africans in France; and the Basque people in Spain. Moreover, this is true to a large extent within Jewish Israeli society itself, which is dominated by the Western-oriented Ashkenazi culture though the non-Western Sephardic Jews are the majority. Like Arabs, Sephardic Jews are also thrown into a cross-cultural situation where another culture is dominant. Consequently, their younger generation constitutes the culturally disadvantaged group in the Israeli Jewish school.

It is clear from the findings of the study reviewed earlier in this chapter that Arab society in Israel is indeed interested in vocational-technological education, not as a substitute for, but as an alternative to academic education. Yet these attitudes in favor of vocational education may not seem consistent with the pattern of preferences among parents, i.e., their preference for academic over technical training. Nevertheless, because of the special situation of the Arab minority in Israel and because of the opportunities existing, yet not available in the Israeli job market, Arab parents and students would prefer to have the option of vocational training in order to avail themselves of such chances for advancement.

Furthermore, this preference for vocational programs expressed by at least 50 percent of Arab parents, is also due to the fact that many academics turn out to be simple workers without any helpful technical skills. The accumulation of frustrating experiences arising from this trend has helped endow education with a pragmatic value in the sense that it should prepare one for a future job rather than be irrelevant and lead nowhere for the many who cannot make it into higher learning institutions. As one Arab parent put it: "If the investment of 13 years in schooling does not lead a person to the university, it should lead him somewhere and not turn the high school graduate into a simple construction worker. . . . Even at this, he cannot compete with those who have not had as much education as he did because they are tough and he is soft for such a job."

TOWARDS AN EQUALITY IN JOB OPPORTUNITIES

The establishment and development of a vocational-technical educational network in the Arab educational system in Israel—both on the qualitative and the quantitative level—is of utmost importance. Such a network would not only contribute to solutions for educational and socioeconomic problems in the Arab sector in Israel, but would also strengthen the processes of integration of the Arab labor force into the wider Israeli economy on an egalitarian basis. Furthermore, development and enrichment of the vocational-technological educational network in the Arab sector would to a great extent prevent the intensification of those dangers which could accompany the appearance of a surplus of academics—a surplus which would be difficult for this society or any society to absorb satisfactorily because of their lack of specific vocational skills.

However, vocational education is often referred to as a "fallacy" in many developing societies.[5] Indeed, it has been discovered that this type of education, while thought of as the solution for the lack of relevance in many educational settings, is a creator of another, possibly more severe social problem. Through vocational education many expectations are created and raised as far as the achievement of jobs which require skills. But soon graduates of technical programs are faced with a frustrating reality: there are no jobs available due to the fact that the process of job creation through industrial development projects has not accomplished the establishment of vocational programs in the schools.[6] In other words, educational planning and industrial and economic development have not been compatible and mutually complementary.

Although in Israel industrial development is blooming and jobs are available for the trained, it is naive to assume that a quality vocational-technological education will solve the Arabs' socioeconomic problems and will meet their aspirations as far as socioeconomic upward mobility is concerned. Although such training is a necessary condition for the Arab in Israel to become integrated on an equal basis into the Israeli economy, it is not sufficient in itself. The equality of educational opportunities is just a necessary step towards equality of job opportunities.

It is this principle of equality in job opportunities between Jews and Arabs in Israel which is so difficult to achieve, for two reasons. One is the often used rationale of *security*. Because Israel and the Arab countries have been involved in a continuous state of war and because Israeli industry and other employment frameworks are involved with security, it follows that an Arab citizen cannot obtain a job because he belongs to the nation with which Israel is at war. This rationale, though it may be understandable, is nevertheless so broad and so fluid that it can be applied to almost any position. Moreover, as justifiable as it may or may not be, the security rationale gives rise to some definite absurdities as far as employment of Arabs in "security loaded" jobs is concerned. An Arab engineer or technician is often barred from obtaining a job in a factory because of security reasons, while the same factory is being guarded all night long by an Arab worker with a gun. It seems, then, that lower ranking jobs are available for minority members even though these jobs are "security loaded." Higher ranking jobs, on the other hand, are less attainable.

While discussing this problem as it negatively affects Arab-Jewish relations in Israel, Dan Shivtan of Tel Aviv University has suggested the following: "Take an Arab engineer for example. After he graduates, what can he do? Can he enter the ultra-modern industry of the State of Israel? Nowadays every modern industry in the State of Israel produces for the needs of defense. Maybe it is not written that in order to be accepted for a job you must not be an Arab. But, after all, if you are an Arab you will face many difficulties in being accepted for a job."[7] Aharon Kleinberger elaborates on the consequences of this apparent inequality of job opportunities and states that:

> The Arab sector itself has no industry and few social and administrative services of its own which can offer white-collar jobs to Arab graduates of secondary schools or universities. In the Jewish sector, social and cultural distance as well as alleged security reasons (which are not infrequently unfounded) and suspicion of Arab loyalty and reliability prevent their employment in any substantial number. In consequence not a few of the educated young Arabs remain unemployed or are forced to accept employment in manual labor. . . . This results in feelings of frustration, bitterness, and reinforced animosity against the State of Israel.[8]

A most inclusive as well as conclusive study of the Arab's economic situation, particularly job opportunities in Israel's economic structure was carried out by Yosef Waschitz of the Kibbutz Giv'at Haviva Institute of Arab Studies. He determined that the Arab labor force in Israel has started and remained as "guest workers" and "commuters." He concluded that:

> The higher we rise in the echelons of employment, the less we find Arabs: in civil service, in the Histadrut administration, on university

staffs. The Advisor for Arab Affairs has made a large effort to open middle and higher echelons of civil services to Arabs. But in general, the government and Histadrut have set the example for the private sector in their reluctance to employ Arabs in key positions in which Jews would be their subordinates. Openly, the reasons given are usually "security considerations". But the reluctance to employ white-collar Arabs in general and the fact that Arabs are employed in constructing security installations, seem to indicate a problem of status, not of security.

To sum up: Arabs are climbing, exasperatingly slowly, the institutional ladders of public institutions. They compare the snail's pace of·their advancement with the avenues open to Jews—quick advance, taking part in decision-making, self-fulfillment. All this is denied to most Arabs, especially the well educated ones.[9]

It is clear that the security rationale is applied indiscriminately to "security loaded" and to "security free" positions, thus depriving Arabs of the many existing job opportunities for which they qualify. The results of such deprivation are usually expressed in an estrangement from the state and its institutions, more polarization between the Arab and the Jewish sectors, and, most important of all, a feeling of despair as far as Arab-Jewish coexistence in Israel is concerned. As an indicator of this feeling, more than 50 percent of Arab youth, questioned in a late study by John Hofman, thought that they did not have any future in Israel.[10] They felt that because of existing inequalities and trends the possibilities of fulfilling their future professional aspirations were dim.

These economic, social, and political dynamics usually operating under the "security" considerations rationale are reinforced by another, yet no less powerful element in the process of depriving Arabs of equal opportunity. Indeed, Arieh Luva Eliav, a Knesset member of the majority ruling labor party, claims that due to a continuous and extensive reliance on Arab labor in Israel, Jewish society is becoming a society of bosses. The very basic values upon which the pioneers created the state of Israel are being neglected and reversed as younger Israeli Jewish generations relinquish the idea of labor to become masters of laborers. Eliav claims in *Land of the Deer*[11] that this is the most poisonous thing that could happen to the Jewish society in Israel. It is not only inhumane and unjust, but it is also harmful to Israeli society itself.

Moreover, Eliav in a later book[12] suggests that the Arab minority in Israel, through its labor force in the Israeli economy, is being manipulated in such a way as to solve some inconsistencies within the Israeli Jewish society. Thus, with Arab labor forces at the lower level, the Israeli Jewish Sephardic labor force occupies the middle, and the Ashkenazi maintains itself in the highest level of the occupational structure. The minority is being manipulated to serve as an outlet for the lowering of tensions existing within the two Israeli Jewish subcultural groups. Any noticeable changes in the direction of more equality of job opportunities between Arabs and Jews in Israel, although not expected to bring back the pioneers' values, would certainly shake the structure of the Israeli Jewish society and mean a reorganization of the occupational structure so that more Arabs could move up likely to be from the Sephardic group, a result which would intensify the job hierarchy. Fewer Jews would be privileged, then, and those are the already existing tensions within the Jewish society in Israel.

Nevertheless, although it may be difficult to implement the principle of equal job opportunities, it does not seem impossible. Lessening tension and conflict within Israeli Jewish society opened up and magnified the conflict between Arab and Jewish societies in Israel—a conflict by no means isolated from the larger one in the Middle East. Moreover, the maintenance of relative stability within Jewish society by reinforcing the status quo might quiet down potential social conflicts between the two Israeli Jewish subcultural groups. However, a situation of relative, yet superficial stability would not eliminate these tensions and conflicts caused by inequalities within Jewish society itself. And it is not illogical to expect that any sense of political stability, in the case of peace or even the absence of war, could help excite conflicts within Israeli Jewish society.

Finally, although some of the difficulties encountered by Arab society and education in Israel are attributed to the existing conflict between the Arab nation and Israel, it is also true that other conflict-independent socioeconomic forces within Israel are contributing to the amount and scope of the problems encountered by the Arab citizen in Israel. It seems that Arab minority status is becoming more and more dependent not only on political dynamics in the Middle East, but also on internal socioeconomic dynamics within Israel. And these problems are most likely to continue even when a Middle East peace settlement becomes real.

In conclusion, it is clear from the discussion presented in this chapter that Arab education in Israel is at the crossroads of cultures. It is influenced by the socioeconomic forces and cultural transformations which are taking place within Arab society itself; it is affected by political and socioeconomic dynamics operating within Jewish society; and it is sensitive to the cultural and political movements in existence within the Arab world in general and among Palestinians in particular. Arab education is caught in the middle of this triangle. The quality and direction of change in any of these dimensions will not only influence Arab education in Israel but will also, to a large extent, determine the political, cultural, and socioeconomic conditions in the lives of Arabs in Israel.

1. Arieh Luva Eliav, *Israel's Ladder* (Tel-Aviv: Zemura, Bitan, Modern Publishers, 1976) (Hebrew).

2. Sami Khalil Mar'i and A. Benjamin, "The Attitudes of Arab Society Towards Vocational Education," (Haifa: University of Haifa, Institute for Research and Development of Arab Education, 1976). The author assumes full responsibility for the data and interpretations presented herein.

3. Abraham Benjamin and Rachel Peleg, "Vocational Aspirations of Arab High School Seniors and Their Social Implications" (Haifa: University of Haifa, Institute for Research and Development of Arab Education, 1976) (Hebrew).

4. Yousef Waschitz, "Commuters and Entrepreneurs," *New Outlook* 18(7) (Oct.–Nov. 1975).

5. John Hanson, *Imagination & Hallucination in African Education* (East Lansing: Michigan State University, Institute for International Studies in Education, 1965).

6. P. J. Foster, "The Vocational School Fallacy in Development Planning" (Chicago: University of Chicago, Conference on Education and Economic Development, 1963).

7. Dan Shivtan, "Arab-Jewish Relations in Israel," in John Hofman, ed., *Proceedings of the Convention on the State of Research on Arab-Jewish Relations* (Haifa: University of Haifa, 1971), p. 38 (Hebrew).

8. Aharon Kleinberger, *Society, Schools & Progress in Israel* (Oxford: Pergamon Press, Ltd., 1969), p. 320.

9. Waschitz, "Commuters and Entrepreneurs," *New Outlook* 18(7)(Oct–Nov. 1975):47–48.

10. John Hofman, "Readiness for Social Relations Between Arabs and Jews in Israel," *Journal of Conflict Resolution* 16(2)(1972).

11. Arieh Luva Eliav, *Land of the Deer* (Tel Aviv: Am Oved Publishers, 1972).

12. Arieh Luva Eliav, *Israel's Ladder* (Tel Aviv: Zemorah, Bitan, Modern Publishers, 1976) (Hebrew).

8.

Civil Education in the Israeli Armed Forces

Victor Azarya

The Israel Defense Forces (IDF) are known to be a prominent educator in the Israeli society, both because of the educational effects inherent in the universal military service and reserve duties and because of the various programs of education carried out in the military framework (Lissak, 1971; Hanning, 1967; Glick, 1967). Nonvocational civic education has occupied an especially important place in the IDF because of its image as a nation-builder. Since their inception the Israeli armed forces have been regarded as the principal carriers of national goals and identity, the inculcators of nationalist consciousness, the integrators of various sectors of the population, and the most genuine representatives of the new culture and generation. Ben-Gurion called them "the workshop of the new Israeli society" (quoted in Peri, 1977: 38). He saw in the IDF a central force that would mold the shape of the nation, integrating Jews from different countries and educating the young generation, serving as a model of excellence, civic spirit, pioneering, and a source of pride to all (Peri, 1980: 93-94; Perlmutter, 1968: 623).

The task of being a model for the rest of society was combined with the "citizens in arms" concept based on universal conscription and large-scale active reserve duty which brought a large part of the population into close contact with the military. The armed forces were not to be sheltered from the rest of Israeli society as an island of higher quality. On the contrary,

AUTHOR'S NOTE: This research was carried out with the financial support of the Social Science Research Fund of the Hebrew University of Jerusalem. I wish to thank my research assistants, Tamar Kenet and Michael Feige, for their help in data collection.

they had to be sensitive to and participate in solving the central problems of the society. The IDF would not just open itself to all sectors of the population but would act as a channel for acculturation, education, and integration in the new society which it personified. It would also reach beyond those under arms and offer services to the entire Israeli population (Schiff, 1974: 54-57, 94-95; Bowden, 1976: 75; Perlmutter, 1969: 128).

The various welfare and development projects undertaken by the armed forces were most strongly felt in the early years after independence, since the objective hardships were most acute at that time and civilian agencies designed to deal with those problems had not yet been sufficiently institutionalized. Such activities sharply declined after the first decade of the state's existence, but the continuing military conflict with the country's neighbors and the concomitant centrality of the security issue kept the military at the forefront of national consciousness, a primary objective for identification and the vanguard of the nation's basic values and collective goals (Horowitz, 1977). The military was a model of operational effectiveness and of civic spirit, comparing favorably with the deficiencies of the civilian sector, but it was not a closed sphere of excellence, being open to extensive civilian participation. The military was attributed a certain superiority over the civilian sector without this leading to a separate corporate identity and antagonism with the parent society.

More than 30 years after independence, despite all the changes that have occurred in both the armed forces and the parent society, despite their bureaucratization, their institutional differentiation, and the formalization of the relations between armed forces and society, the IDF still acts as a "school for the nation." Hence, the goals of its civic education are different from both its Western and Soviet counterparts.[1] In Israel, civic education offered by the military is primarily conceived as a contribution to the entire society; it maintains the dual "national service" and "distinctive superiority" attributes of the military in society, rather than contributes to military performance per se. To the extent that military performance does improve as a result of civic education, this is a welcome side effect, but it is not the primary objective.

I do not mean to say, of course, that the military performance of the Israeli soldier is not related to civic consciousness. This would obviously be an untenable proposition. On the contrary, it is well known that civic consciousness and ideological factors play important roles in the Israeli armed forces' reputed high military qualities. However, this is a more diffuse civic consciousness acquired throughout one's socialization, in civilian life as well as in military service. It does not derive specifically from the civic education programs offered by the IDF. Those whose civic consciousness has to be aroused specifically by formal IDF programs are not very useful to the military and occupy a peripheral position in it. In this chapter, looking at the principal formal civic education programs conducted by the IDF, I will try to show (a) how prominent they indeed are, but (b) that a great number of them either do not differentiate between civilian and military audiences or are specifically offered to civilians, and (c) that even in those offered specifically to recruits, some disproportion exists between exposure to civic education and expected military contribution.

Civil-Military Cultural Permeability

The cultural permeability which characterizes Israeli civil-military relations is an important clue to understanding the IDF's role in civic education. In a recent study, relying on Luckham's (1971) typology of fragmented, permeable, and integral boundaries between the military and the larger society,[2] Lissak has tried to map the exact configurations of linkages between the Israel military and civilian sectors in different institutional spheres. In his analysis (1980) Lissak found much greater permeability in the cultural and educational spheres (and in informal social networks) than in the economic, professional, legal, and political spheres. He also found that in the educational and cultural spheres the Israeli military has a greater autonomy in determining the content of its activities while at the same time engaging in these activities mainly for civilian or general societal rather than military purposes. The linkages are solidary and cooperative; civilian and military sides perceive each other as completing one another's work rather than competing with it (with the major exception being the Military Broadcasting Service, to be discussed later). This cultural permeability strongly affects the socialization inherent in military service as well as the themes and targets of the IDF's formal civic education programs.

Military service is, apart from elementary school, the most universal experience of Israeli youth and it continues long into adulthood. One cannot stress enough the contrast to the volunteer army. In the United States and some Western European countries, the issue has been raised whether or not military service can be retained as a component of the civic ethic when it is meaningful to a dwindling fraction of the population (Little, 1969: 34). No such concern exists in Israel. On the contrary, military service has a diffuse but pervasive influence on the civilian sector. Of the Jewish men age 18, 92 percent, and 50 percent of the women, are conscripted to service—two years for women, three years for men, and another half a year to a year for male officers.[3] Compulsory service precedes college education and is looked on as an integral part of the growing-up process, a *rite de passage* into adulthood. Following their discharge, the great majority of the conscripts continue to be called up to active reserve duty for about a month per year. On the average they will spend a total of six to seven years in service between the ages of 18 and 55. Some of them also continue to serve on a voluntary basis in the Civil Guard patrolling their own neighborhood (Peri, 1980: 80; Horowitz, 1977: 71; Kimmerling, 1978).

There exists a strong similarity between army culture and civilian popular culture. Military slang and linguistic expressions are widely used in the civilian society. Army overcoats and other clothing items set the pace of young people's fashion. Military service experience and camp life are central themes of artistic and literary creation, especially in popular entertainment. It should also be noted that because of the small size of the country, the distances between camp and home are short and most military personnel return home on a daily or weekly basis (Luttwak and Horowitz, 1974: 86; Schild, 1973: 421-422).

The close encounter between the civilian and military sectors is not the only reason for the army culture's impinging on civilian life. In Switzerland, where a similar universal conscription and reserve system exist, we do not find the same extent of spillover between military and civilian culture, perhaps because the military and the security issue do not occupy the same prominent place in the national consciousness. Intensive contact is not enough; it has to be accompanied by a normative identification, the military being considered to perform a crucial instrumental function in society and upholding its highest values. The armed forces also personify the new Israeli generation and the break with Diaspora Jewish history. Few Jews outside Israel willingly seek military careers. For Diaspora Jews the military is the threatening expression of the non-Jewish majority's rule over them. In Israel, by contrast, it conveys a feeling of belonging and dominance (Azarya and Kimmerling, 1980: 470-473).

It should be stressed, however, that the cultural permeability between the Israeli military and the larger society works both ways. It "civilianizes" military service just as it extends to the whole society the informal education inherent in military service. Perlmutter (1968: 608, 622-623) has attributed to this fact the Israeli military's relative nonintervention in politics. Cultural permeability indicates the pervasiveness of the education inherent in military service, but, by the same token, it makes it difficult to detect the distinctive educational effect of military service.

Themes and Targets of Civic Education

Besides the latent socializational effects inherent in military service, the IDF maintains a widespread and institutionalized system of formal educational activities. It operates a range of schools, education centers, and field schools specializing in the knowledge of land and nature. Lecturers criss-cross military camps. Every unit of battalion size (in some corps even at company size) has its own specially trained education officer who is responsible for supplying educational and cultural activities to his or her unit (Bamahane, Aug. 3, 1977: 3 [Hebrew]). The Military Broadcasting Service successfully competes with civilian radio stations. Various books, pamphlets, magazines, and newspapers are published and widely distributed among service personnel. The IDF supplies preinduction military training to secondary school pupils and has its own paramilitary youth movement. As a sign of appreciation for its educational programs the IDF was twice granted (in 1966 and 1973) national education prizes (Bar On, 1967: 138; Bamahane, June 13, 1979: 4). Some of these activities are provided as part of military training. Others, such as the military broadcasting service, do not differentiate between civilian and military audiences. Some activities, such as teaching in the schools of border settlements and new towns, are exclusively oriented to civilian populations. In these activities civic education is often mixed with transmitting basic education (such as literacy, the Hebrew language, and elementary history). Closing gaps in one's general education is considered to contribute to one's civic consciousness. The underlying assumption is, of course, that these activities also contribute to the recipient's military performance, since they enable him or her to attribute *meaning* to his or her military service and thus enhance the motivation to serve (Lt. Gen. Raphael Eitan, interviewed in Bamahane, Sept. 2, 1978: 5-10 and Sept. 14, 1979: 8-11). But the principal focus of civic education remains contribution to the formation of an enlightened and loyal citizenship.

In Western democracies armed forces have played a more limited role in civic versus vocational or elementary education, partly because of the normative ambiguity about inviting the military into an area which might undermine the leadership of responsible civilian authorities. In Israel no such ambiguity exists. The centrality of the military in national consciousness and the lack of distinct military corporate identity legitimize the military's involvement in civic education. The IDF is active in professional education too, but this remains beyond the scope of this chapter and is less interesting from a comparative viewpoint. The civic aspects, more than the professional, are the ones which underline the special position occupied by the military in Israeli society.

Janowitz has proposed a distinction between patriotism, civic consciousness, and political ideology, and he suggests that much of the democratic societies' reluctance to military involvement in civic education stems from the inability to distinguish between them. Civic consciousness is differentiated from patriotism in being a more cognitive and critical attachment to a polity rather than a primordial and emotional tie to a territory, and it is differentiated from political ideology in stipulating loyalty and involvement in the entire polity rather than in the explicitly formulated beliefs and actions of different groups and sectors in it. Civic consciousness indicates sensitivity to and participation in the public domain as informed and responsible citizens while remaining nonpartisans of this or other political stands (Janowitz, this volume).

Important as these distinctions are as analytical constructs, they are not always easy to detect in practice. In Israel the element of patriotism is especially dominant in civic education, and it infiltrates civic consciousness because of the self-conscious nature of collective ties with the land. The Zionist ideal is surrounded by international controversy. The very survival of the national collectivity is at stake and has to be defended by military means. Moreover, the state was formed by mostly first-generation immigrants on a land with which they had ties that were more symbolic and ideological than organic. These lead to an overarticulation of the issue of national ties. The issue is raised to an ideological level compared with the more taken-for-granted attitude that generally characterizes patriotism. Ties with the land and the national collectivity are consciously thought of, planned, and legitimized in Israel. Hence they are inseparable from the civic consciousness and occupy a central place in civic education.

It is interesting to point out in this regard that an important difference exists between the civic education themes of the IDF and of its counterparts in Western democratic societies. In most Western societies ties with the land, traditions, and history are not much stressed, since they are taken for granted. In the case of the Federal Republic of Germany, they are perhaps underemphasized because they are "sensitive" subjects in view of the Nazi past. More emphasis is laid on the responsibilities of citizenship, on the democratic political values, on the legitimacy and operation of political institutions, and on the military's place in the political process (Wakenhut, 1979; Harries-Jenkins, this volume). This difference is also related to the fact that the IDF's civic education is not as limited to the military personnel as are those of its counterparts in Western societies (Bowden, 1976: 53). When the targeted audience is strictly military it is perhaps natural to expect greater emphasis on the organization of governmental institutions and the role of the military in the larger political system. When civic education appeals to both civilian and military audiences, one might expect greater attention to be given to general cultural values, group identifications, and the sense of collective membership in the society.

While patriotism is not clearly differentiated from civic consciousness, there exists great sensitivity to the distinction between civic consciousness and political ideology. Issues of political controversy are avoided as much as possible in order not to display a sectarian point of view. Until the 1970s this was not a difficult task because a broad national consensus existed on the basic collective goals and security-related policies (except, of course, the Arab citizens). But in the 1970s national consensus declined considerably, especially regarding the fate of territories occupied in the 1967 war and the requirements of a peace settlement with neighboring countries (Peri, 1980: 293, 304; Horowitz, 1974: 73). Interestingly, since a cognitive, reasoned discussion of these issues was bound to arouse controversy, the IDF shifted to more expressive education on these questions—for example, preferring ceremonial activities, nature trips, or visits to museums to lectures and debates. This appealed to basic primordial sentiments rather than reasoned critical views, in effect stressing patriotism even more over civic consciousness. In other words, in its attempt to keep the differentiation between civic consciousness and sectarian political ideology, the IDF's civic education further confounded primordial patriotism with civic consciousness. On the other hand, more attention was paid and more cognitive education was offered on social issues that had been relatively neglected until then, such as ethnic relations, social integration, and urban neighborhood problems. In these fields education offered by the IDF could lead to civic consciousness distinct from both patriotism and political ideology.

In the following pages the principal civic education activities of the IDF will be surveyed with regard to their purpose, their content, and their target audience.

Civic Education in Military Training

"EDUCATION SERIES"

Civic education is an integral part of military training in the IDF. Every military training program includes a number of days set aside for "education series" held in specially designed schools located in large urban centers away from camp. Different units are brought to these schools, according to a predetermined schedule, and are housed there for the duration of the series, usually about a week, during which they perform no other military functions. Trainees for noncommissioned positions receive about a week of education series in the course of their general training. Participants in the officer training course receive a total of three weeks of such education (Bowden, 1976: 57; Bamahane, Apr. 5, 1978: 8 and Mar. 14, 1979: 22-23). Education series are also offered to units which have completed their military training, but in this case the initiative rests more with the given unit's commander or its education officer.

Besides the concentrated education offered in special centers away from military bases, roving lecturers tour the units at their respective locations. In this way many university professors fulfill their reserve duty obligations. Another campside civic education activity is the commanders' weekly "conversation hour." Platoon commanders are expected to reserve one hour per week for conversation with their soldiers on current affairs of general interest. To help the commanders in their task, the IDF's Education Office periodically supplies them with pamphlets on subjects considered to be of general interest (Bowden, 1976: 57; Roumani, 1978: 44).[4] Complaints are often heard, however, that most commanders either do not hold the conversation hour or use it to discuss problems related to their unit and military life rather than the more general topics for which it is intended.

The topics covered in the education series are standardized according to the rank, unit, and sex of the recipients. Specific regulations predetermine the proportional coverage of various topics, though the specific content of what is taught depends on the individual educator. In education offered beyond the minimum training requirements, specific topics could be sought, but the repertoire of what can be obtained through military channels is limited. The topics of instruction could be divided into a number of basic categories: One, called "battle tradition" is clearly military-oriented. It deals with military history, the specific corps' or unit's history, reports on famous battles, and acts of heroism. A second category which we may call "human relations" includes group dynamics, leadership, and organization. While being a general topic, it is clearly related to developing certain capabilities needed in the military. A third category, civic education proper, includes Jewish and Israeli history, the Arab-Israeli conflict, current political problems (such as the energy crisis or the revival of Islam), and Israeli social problems (ethnic relations, social integration, delinquency, etc.). A related topic which has received a great boost lately is Jewish culture and traditions. These latter topics, which form the greatest part of the instruction, are also the least related to military performance. The education series are regarded as a necessary counterpart to, and a relaxing break from, the intensive military training, enabling trainees to view their military role and proficiency from a more distant and broader national perspective.

A topic to which special attention is paid is "knowledge of the land." In the course of their military service soldiers are frequently taken on trips to acquaint them with different parts of the country. They participate in nature trips and are taken on tours of museums, development areas, industrial centers, and so on. Special field schools of the IDF organize tours of the countryside and offer instruction on ecological and geographical topics, fauna and flora, and historical and archeological sites. Some soldiers are specially trained as field tour guides (Bamahane, Aug. 16, 1978: 5, Feb. 22, 1980: 5, Mar. 14, 1979: 22-23). Familiarity with the physical contours of the landscape and with its history gives a more tangible reality to an abstract patriotism; it establishes a more organic relationship between the individual and the land, and by association it strengthens one's right to that land (Roumani, 1978: 98-100; Rolbant, 1970: 218-219). This is especially important in the Israeli case, since the link between the nation and the land is not taken for granted, having been physically renewed only recently after a long interruption. This link is reaffirmed also by active interest in nature, both in terms of its preservation and its improvement through afforestation, drying of swamps, and refertilization of the soil (Kimmerling, 1974: 254-264). Service personnel are instilled with a strong ecological consciousness, and many high-ranking officers become actively involved in civilian ecological groups and in archeology after their retirement from the armed forces.

Civic education is in great demand among soldiers, not necessarily because of a genuine interest in the topics but for its recreational value. In the education series soldiers feel pampered in the special schools, whose accommodations are incomparably more comfortable than the camps. One can also enjoy the city lights, entertainment, and civilian atmosphere between lectures. The few attempts to set up such schools in smaller towns have invariably failed because these places offered no entertainment opportunities between classes. While these obvious advantages do not exist in activities brought to the military camp, they too are in great demand, since they break the routine and free the recipient from harder work. But for the same reason, civic education activities strain manpower allocation schedules and regularly lose out to other military tasks, especially among units which perform more important military roles. Thus combat troops rightly complain that they receive less cultural and educational activities than support personnel; the latter are more accessible and their education time is less costly to the military organization.

COMPLETING BASIC EDUCATION

Besides the civic education supplied to all conscripts as part of their military training, the IDF conducts programs designed to remedy basic educational deficiencies of certain groups of service personnel. These activities include Hebrew language courses, literacy programs, primary and secondary education completion courses, and special youth rehabilitation projects. In these examples elementary education is not differentiated from civic education. Instead, teaching elementary skills and knowledge is mixed in the curriculum with transmitting basic civic values and is regarded as a means by which recipients integrate more smoothly into society and develop individually. Those who are offered these special programs generally make a marginal contribution to the military. They serve a shorter compulsory service and some are never called up for reserve duty. The aim of the educational program is to salvage such personnel for society rather than directly profit from their improved military performance. Some are drafted as an educational service even though they fail to meet the minimum induction requirements.

Such activities on the part of the military are common in many societies. Military service is seen as a second chance for disadvantaged youth, at least as far as vocational training is concerned (see, e.g., Moskos, 1970: 171-172). But in Israel these activities are particularly developed and institutionalized. In assuming these functions the IDF maintains its "national service" image. It underlies its pivotal role in the nation-building process, serving as the agent of the common weal in problem areas while at the same time showing that it is best equipped to tackle problems the civilian sector failed to solve. Thus it maintains its superiority over the civilian sector in effectiveness and dedication to collectively cherished goals. This superiority of the military is readily acknowledged by the civilian leadership and is used as a further means of solidarity and national integration.[5] The special educational programs, as well as other extra-military tasks of the IDF, not only help the individuals in need but also act as an outlet to collective conscience; they give an assurance to the society that certain undesirable conditions are being taken care of by its most representative and most effective institution (Bowden, 1976: 78).

The principal special education institution of the IDF is located on Camp Marcus near Haifa. Camp Marcus was originally established in 1948 as a Hebrew language school for new immigrant recruits.[6] Since the 1950s it has also dispensed general elementary education to service personnel. The primary education completion program is offered to soldiers in the last three months of their term of service, thus showing that it is oriented toward helping recipients in their civilian life and is not aimed at improving their military performance or military job allocation. On the other hand, Hebrew courses given to new immigrants are held in the first months of service since knowledge of the language is indispensable to all subsequent communications and is more closely related to military performance.[7]

The armed forces also conduct special drafts for youngsters who have failed to meet the minimum induction requirements. Twice a year selected groups are sent to a special six-month-long basic training course which combines elementary education, group work, and military training. Following basic training, those found fit to continue their service are sent to various units to complete their compulsory service. In 1978 another program was established in Givat Olga for a similar special-draft population but this time without combining basic training with education (Kimmerling, 1979a: 30; Bamahane Nahal, Sept. 1979: 48, 63; Bamahane, Apr. 16, 1980: 5 and July 16, 1980: 4). Even though these educational services are given in the early stages of military service, they are nonetheless civilian-role oriented, aiming at the social rehabilitation of recipients especially recruited for this purpose.

The IDF has gradually become expert in the education of disadvantaged youth. It has gained increasing autonomy in determining the content and methods of education and it has had more input into civilian agencies than vice versa. The IDF trains its own staff for these educational programs. Over the years it has developed special syllabi and has published several textbooks and instruction manuals. Some of the instruction techniques first introduced into the armed forces were later adopted by civilian agencies (Lissak, 1970: 330-331; Hanning, 1967: 127).

This self-reliance and expertise of the IDF in education to specially deprived groups is contrasted with the much heavier reliance on civilian experts in the civic education offered to regular conscripts. Half of the teaching staff in the education series are civilians, either fulfilling their reserve duty obligations (though not wearing uniforms) or on contract with the IDF. The proportion of civilians rises even higher among lecturers visiting military camps. The military's attitude to the civilian educators is one of deference to their expertise. There are few attempts to intervene in the content of the instruction, and civilian experts are selected so as to represent a broad spectrum of political views. We are thus faced with the paradox of having a relatively larger civilian staff for civic education offered to regular conscripts while a larger military staff is used for the more civilian-oriented education offered to marginal populations. But we should not make broad generalizations on this point, since an opposite tendency is observed in the treatment of new immigrants. Civilian agents of the Ministry of Immigrant Absorption play an active role in the IDF's orientation meetings for new immigrants; they visit military camps and pass on to military authorities various impressions and requests from new immigrants. With regard to new immigrants, in contrast with other marginal groups, the IDF relies heavily on the outside help of the specialized civilian agency (Azarya and Kimmerling, 1980: 476-479).

The general picture of civic education offered as part of military training indicates a relatively high exposure of groups who are under-utilized in the military framework. This is true of general civic education series as well as special basic education completion programs. The disproportion has increased in recent years, as marginal groups have been the main beneficiaries of the recent expansion of the military's educational programs. Education is the only branch of the armed forces whose budget showed a net (inflation-adjusted) rise in the last three years. During the same period drastic cuts were made in the civilian Ministry of Education budget. The armed forces' education programs gained great publicity lately (unprecedented since the early 1950s). The present chief of staff is an enthusiastic supporter of these programs and states his views in frequent public appearances.[8] Television and radio stations carry public service advertisements praising the military's education efforts and urging the public to send financial contributions to a special Security Fund earmarked mostly for education. The military broadcasting service consecrated its entire 1981 Independence Day broadcast to a contribution campaign for this purpose. The lion's share of these resources and public attention goes to the more disadvantaged populations who, by the same token, are the least useful to the military. Soldiers with more suitable preinduction background receive a smaller share of the increased attention given to education.

A number of reasons can explain the greater emphasis laid on civic education to marginal groups. First, this education is the least costly in terms of demands made on the recipients' other military activities. Their time of service is less precious because it is not needed for more extensive military training or more central security functions. Second, such education can be conducted at a level that would not raise controversial issues because it transmits elementary knowledge and appeals to values and primordial attachments that are beyond debate. Third, the emphasis on marginal populations enjoys wider popular support in the larger society than does civic education offered to regular conscripts because the former are thought to be in greater need. It portrays the IDF as performing a national service, correcting the failures of the civilian sector without intervening in politics or being involved in differences of opinion.

It should be noted, however, that relative exposure to education rises again at the level of high-ranking career officers. The general picture of the relationship between civic education and assumed military contribution is that of a U-shaped curve. Officers of battalion commander or higher position participate in the School for Staff and Command which focuses on general staff work and problems of operational command. A university-level College for National Security was opened in the 1960s, closed after a few years, and then reopened in the 1970s. High-ranking officers are also sent to civilian institutions of higher learning in Israel and abroad (Luttwak and Horowitz, 1974: 88, 182; Bamahane, Aug. 16, 1972: 10-11). The education offered to high-ranking officers extends beyond conventional military topics. It includes such general topics as international relations, comparative government, economics, public administration, communications, and research methods, in addition to military strategy, weapons technology, and conflict management. The civic and professional aspects of education are harder to distinguish at this level, since they form part of the training for elite positions in the military. They are also necessary incentives to attracting high-quality elements to professional military careers. Moreover, high-ranking officers are groomed for civilian elite positions, since most of them will probably leave the service in a short time, in accordance with the IDF's characteristic high turnover at top military positions. Besides its military training and incentive aspects, the high education opportunities given to career officers thus help smooth their transfer to civilian occupations of comparable status in the middle of their adult life (Lissak, 1970: 331).

Civic Education and the Mass Media

Mass media of communications and artistic performances are widely used indirect agents of civic education in the Israeli armed forces (Shaler, interview in Bamahane, Mar. 15, 1978: 10-12, 26 and Mar. 14, 1979: 18-20). The IDF operates its own radio station, publishes various books, magazines and newspapers, and until a few years ago maintained a large number of musical and theatrical ensembles. The civic education objective is never lost in these activities, and a delicate balance is sought between education and recreation. However, paradoxically, the more successful these activities became, the more they turned to a civilian all-Israeli audience and adjusted to its demands rather than being specific military channels.

GALEI ZAHAL

The military broadcasting service, Galei Zahal, is by far the most important communications medium operated by the IDF. From a small radio station broadcasting a few hours a day it has developed into Israel's most popular radio channel (according to a poll published in October 1981 in Haaretz, Oct. 28, 1981).[9]

Galei Zahal does not differentiate between civilian and military audiences. Its programs vary in content, ranging from pop and rock music, Israeli songs and hit parades to political news reports, commentary, college-level educational broadcasts, theater reviews, and sports. It does not have its own hourly news service (it transmits the news from the state monopoly, Israeli Broadcasting Authority) but broadcasts its own newsreel (for two hours a day) and has its own correspondents stationed in Israel and abroad. With time, the hours consecrated to music grew at the expense of more educational programs. There was also a steady decline in the coverage of military matters. Galei Zahal makes great efforts not to display a special "military view" of things, and its proclaimed political neutrality is widely accepted in society. To be sure, there still exist some subtle differences between Galei Zahal and the civilian stations. The military station still carries more coverage of camp life, military maneuvers, military graduation ceremonies, and so on. It sounds more Israeli than the civilian stations and plays relatively more Hebrew songs. It also sounds more youthful, if for no other reason than because its broadcasters are younger, about half of the staff being 18-22-year-old conscripts (Shaley, interview in Bamahane, Mar. 14, 1979: 24; Yedioth Ahronoth, Oct. 1, 1980: 21; Zertel, 1980: 12-13).

Galei Zahal promotes a more Israeli and a more youthful image than other channels, but this is still a civilian image. While it is natural that its content be adjusted to its growing civilian audience, the important point here is that the growth of the civilian audience occurred in a situation of competition with civilian stations. Unlike other cultural and educational activities in which linkages with civilian institutions are cooperative and the military is expected to bring its distinctive contribution, here the military enters into competition with civilian institutions on the latter's own turf and has to adapt its content accordingly. We should also point out that private broadcasting is prohibited in Israel, and Galei Zahal is the only Israeli radio station that is not controlled by the state monopoly, Israel Broadcasting Authority (another radio station, the Voice of Peace, broadcasts from a ship on the Mediterranean). Galei Zahal is seen by some as a means by which the state monopoly on broadcasting is broken. Whatever the merits of this view, it is a telling indication of Galei Zahal's civilian image in the public eye.

In the fall of 1980 it was disclosed that preparations had been under way for Galei Zahal and the Educational Television (operated by the Ministry of Education) to co-produce a daily television news program called "Good Morning Israel" modeled on ABC's "Good Morning America" (Yedioth Ahronoth, Oct. 1, 1980: 21; Zertel, 1980: 12-13). The program has now been shelved, mostly for financial reasons, and it raised some political criticism when it was disclosed. Nonetheless, the very fact that Galei Zahal was considered as a possible co-producer of such a program is in itself of utmost interest, for several reasons. First, it heralded the military's entrance into the television medium, from which it has been excluded so far. Supporters of the program saw in it the precursor of the hoped-for private television channels. Second, the IDF was invited to supply a service that was almost exclusively oriented to a civilian audience, since the morning hours are not those in which military personnel are free to watch TV. Third, cooperation with the Educational Television acknowledged the educational purpose of the program. Finally, Galei Zahal was entrusted with running a politically sensitive program. This showed a reliance on Galei Zahal's ability to steer clear of partisan political bias while recognizing its general up-beat, morale-boosting, and more nationalistic influence, which were the admitted motives of the program's promoters.

Galei Zahal enjoys great autonomy in its operations and programming policies. While the military hierarchy has the formal authority to interfere, it has refrained from doing so. The great popularity of Galei Zahal in the general Israeli audience has created for it a "civilian constituency" which would discourage any attempt to give it a more military content. Galei Zahal is directed by a civilian on contract with the IDF. About half of its professional staff are likewise civilian employees. The rest are mostly young draftees selected for their journalistic skills demonstrated in high school or youth movement papers. Their work in Galei Zahal (or in the IDF's printed media) open journalistic career opportunities after their service (Bar On, 1967: 156; Yedioth Ahronoth, Oct. 1, 1980: 21).

The military framework influences civilian employees' conditions of employment much more than the content of their broadcasts. They cannot form labor unions and are forbidden to strike. These clauses make a difference in the Israeli context, where industrial conflict and related work stoppages are common. The military station is not affected by the frequent strikes of civilian radio employees. In a rare occurrence in fall 1979 when all the journalists in the radio, television, and newspaper fields went on strike together for about a week, Galei Zahal was the only medium which broke the total news blackout in the country. Similarly, the principal reason why Galei Zahal is the only radio channel broadcasting 24 hours a day is that unlike its civilian counterparts, it does not have to contend with the heavy financial demands of radio technicians for working through the night.

MILITARY PUBLICATIONS

Compared to Galei Zahal, the printed medium of the IDF is more limited in civilian audience and content. The weekly newspaper *Bamahane* (In the Camp) is also sold in general newsstands, but less than 10 percent of the total circulation goes to civilians. *Bamahane*'s inability to reach a larger civilian audience is related to the more general circulation difficulties faced by printed media compared with their electronic counterparts. After all, *Bamahane* has to be bought by civilians while Galei Zahal can be heard free of charge. More specifically, the demand for weekly newspapers is low in the Israeli public compared with a heavy demand for daily newspapers. Even though a small part of its circulation goes to civilians, *Bamahane* is still one of the leading Israeli weeklies. In a survey conducted in 1980 it occupied second place (being the first choice of 18 percent of the respondents) among the general audience (a women's weekly was the first choice of 34 percent of the respondents) (Feb. 15, 1980: 4).

Nevertheless, because of its overwhelmingly military audience, *Bamahane* has remained more military in content. Its chief editor and some of its staff are civilian professionals, but the paper bears a military mark. Unlike Galei Zahal, which is regarded as an all-purpose medium, *Bamahane* is read for its distinctive military camp flavor. *Bamahane* is somewhat bland and is not expected to deal with controversial issues, but unlike some of its counterparts in other armed forces (Moskos, 1970: 100-103, 157-158), it is not rejected by service personnel for representing the establishment. This is perhaps a tribute not so much to the newspaper's quality as to the relative lack of alienation of Israeli soldiers.

The IDF issues a range of other publications, most of which are accessible to civilians as well as military personnel but whose civilian circulation is even more limited than *Bamahane*. Different military corps issue their own magazines. More scholarly articles on military-related topics are published in the periodical *Maarakhot* (Campaigns), which is regarded as the professional communication medium of the career military. Another journal, *Skira Hodshit* (Monthly Survey) specializes in reporting the current regional and international political events. The IDF also publishes books on various subjects ranging from literature to battle histories and weaponry. It issues booklets on local geography, wildlife, archeology, and other subjects. It prepares films and slides, and its posters are exhibited in schools, youth clubs, and similar settings (Bamahane, June 13, 1979: 48-49; Lissak, 1970: 334).

Education Provided Exclusively to Civilians

The civic education activities discussed thus far either did not distinguish between civilian and military audiences or were offered as part of military service. The IDF also supplies educational services exclusively to civilians. These activities, which were very widespread in the first years after independence, have diminished considerably, but they still continue on a small scale. Every year a number of female soldiers who are trained in the IDF's own teacher course are sent to teach in the civilian schools of new towns and border settlements (Bowden, 1976: 75, 101; Bar On, 1967: 153). Female soldiers are also involved in adult literacy courses and work in community centers. Some are assigned to the field schools of the Society for the Preservation of Nature. Others are attached to youth movements and work in them as guides and group leaders (Bamahane, Feb. 29, 1980: 5). There is increasing doubt as to whether this military assistance to the civilian education system is really needed, but it is convenient for the IDF to continue to provide this small task force, which retains its national service image.

A different type of civic education is supplied to civilians in the framework of Gadna (Youth Battalions). Gadna operates under two schemes—one compulsory, the other voluntary. Secondary school students aged 14 to 17 (except for pupils of some religious schools) are required, as part of their regular education, to take part in preinduction military training. Instruction combines more narrowly military matters such as shooting practice, night reconnaissance, and drill in scouting, camping, first-aid, and civic action (Schiff, 1974: 104-107; Tadmor, 1976: 26-27, 65-70). It stresses discipline and such military symbols as wearing uniforms and posting guards at night when Gadna units are in the field. The training staff are service personnel, most of them conscripts commanded by a small cadre of career officers. Gadna professes to prepare trainees for the rigors of military life and to instill in them military values such as discipline and security consciousness. But it also provides general education designed to raise civic consciousness (Bowden, 1976: 122-124; Eaton, 1969: 472).

Beyond compulsory training, Gadna offers a wide range of voluntary activities, including summer camps, social meetings, and trips, similar to those undertaken by civilian youth movements. Gadna also undertakes various civic action campaigns, such as afforestation, participation in archeological excavations, and assistance to border settlements or to urban slums (Lissak, 1970: 333, Rolbant, 1970: 223).

The voluntary activities of Gadna reach beyond the secondary school population. One of the principal aims of Gadna is to reach youngsters who do not continue formal studies beyond the eight years of compulsory elementary education, on the justified assumption that these youngsters are less likely to enroll in the existing civilian youth movements. Gadna instruction is also given in institutions for juvenile delinquents, and some Gadna work is done with street gangs (Eaton, 1969: 478-481; Bowden, 1976: 131). In the latter cases Gadna activities are provided to populations which in great part will not be drafted into the armed forces. It thus shows the Gadna role expansion beyond preparation for military service. Gadna camps even include Jewish youth from abroad, thus extending its activities to people who are not Israeli citizens (Bamahane, Aug. 20, 1980: 7). We thus see that the civilian orientation of the IDF's civic education finds its expression in Gadna activities too. Gadna specializes in the youth movement aspects of these functions which in other aspects and for other groups are carved out by other military units.

Civic Education in Special Military Units

I will now discuss civic education offered specifically to people under arms in two special military units in which education is particularly stressed. In this case, civic education is directed to soldiers with great military promise. But the special education offered to them is not designed to improve their military capabilities. Rather, it is regarded as the continuation within the military framework of a more general ideological or religious socialization which started long before induction and will continue after military service.

This leads to another crucial difference between the IDF's general civic education and that provided in these two military units. In all the civic education activities discussed I stressed that the IDF acts as the supreme carrier of collective goals and values. In Nahal and Yeshivot Hahesder, by contrast, education is sectarian. It is intended to maintain the particularistic values and lifestyle of the specific sector with which service personnel are affiliated. The IDF does not act here as the agent of the commonweal, but rather accommodates itself to the special requests of certain sectors in the larger society. The examples of Nahal and Yeshivot Hahesder point up the paradox between the IDF's claim to be a general cultural model and socialization agent in the society and the fact that in certain cases military service is seen as potentially disruptive to the socialization of some of its soldiers. These units are specifically created to minimize this disruption. Members of certain collective settlement movements and religious schools are drafted together in special units, and their respective civilian bodies are allowed considerable control over their education. Also, as part of their socialization, a portion of their service time is spent in nonmilitary pursuits, either working in collective agricultural settlements, in the case of most Nahal units, or continuing high religious studies, in the case of Yeshivot Hahesder.

Nahal (Pioneer Fighting Youth) is the older and more institutionalized of the two military frameworks. It operates as a special military command but has no reserve duty system and its soldiers are incorporated into other corps' reserve units after completing compulsory service. Service personnel are recruited into the Nahal as members of volunteer Garinim (cells) affiliated with civilian youth movements. They combine military service with agricultural work in border settlements, and their express purpose is to join a settlement at the end of their service (Heymont, 1967: 316-317; Levitas, 1967: 20-33).[10] Recently, some urban Garinim have also been formed, combining military service with community work and settlement in new towns (Bamahane, May 14, 1980: 5; Sharir, interview in Bamahane, Nov. 9, 1977: 24).

Service in agricultural (or urban) settlements is interspersed with periods of full military training and duty. About one-third of the service is spent in settlement work or preparation for it, including in the military-agricultural "footholds" (*Heachzut*) set up in areas of strategic importance for security and/or in preparation for civilian habitation (Bamahane, Nov. 8, 1978: 204; Bowden, 1976: 149-150). The great majority of the Garin members serve together throughout the military service but in the course of service military needs force some dispersion. Each Garin has to send 15 percent of its members to NCO and officer training, who do not return to their Garin for the rest of the service. Unlike other military units, command positions are not appreciated among Nahal soldiers, since they cause detachment from the Garin. The Garin and the civilian movement supporting it are not interested in sending their best elements to command courses, because the same people are also the most indispensable to the Garin's operation as an effective and solidary unit. The secretary of the Garin, for example, is never taken to command courses, even though, in most cases, he is the best suited for leadership positions. A number of Garin members are also sent back to civilian life to work as youth leaders in their respective movements (Levitas, 1967: 11; Bamahane, Nov. 2, 1977: 9).

Nahal has been portrayed in the literature mostly in terms of its contribution to agriculture and rural settlement (Levitas, 1967: 10-11; Bamahane Nahal, Sept. 1979). Without denying the importance of this contribution, it should be stressed that the original reason for Nahal's formation was to keep members of collective settlement movements together and maintain their ties with the movement during military service. Nahal's existence is anchored in the traditional Zionist ideology which grants predominance to national redemption through rural development, but it was originally formed to satisfy the particularistic interests of a powerful interest group in Israeli society (Kimmerling, 1979a: 33).

Since Nahal's inception, cross-pressures have been exerted between the military and the settlement movements on the use of Nahal soldiers' time and capabilities. The issue of commander training already mentioned is a clear example of such cross-pressure. Even though Nahal units are a high-quality manpower pool for the military, only a fraction of their time and qualifications is used for central military goals. Also, since the Garin members are recruited *en bloc*, the military makes no individual selection and cannot prevent the ensuing misallocation of skills (Schiff, 1974: 101). In the course of time the military pressure for the better exploitation of the Nahal soldiers led to the extension of their military duty periods at the expense of settlement work and to their integration in other military units (Kimmerling, 1979a: 33; Haaretz, Nov. 24, 1974: 2; Bamahane, Nov. 6, 1974: 6, 20). Over the years there have also been attempts to abolish Nahal altogether, but these were foiled by the counterpressure of the settlement movements. The agricultural sector has enjoyed considerable symbolic bargaining power because of its association with the main tenets of Zionist ideology (Peri, 1980: 543; Schiff, 1974: 97; Kimmerling, 1979a: 33-34). Furthermore, Nahal embodies the national service image of the IDF; it carries a special mission of assisting in worthy civilian causes. It is therefore considered to be of great cultural-educational value to both the IDF and the parent society.

Yeshivot Hahesder (Arrangement Yeshivot) are similar to Nahal even though regarded differently in Israeli public opinion. They enable some Yeshiva students to be conscripted without having to interrupt their religious studies. Soldiers belonging to Yeshivot Hahesder are collectively recruited in preinduction groups similar to Nahal's Garinim. They serve in special units of the Armored Corps for a period of 19 months stretched over four years and interrupted by periods of continuing Yeshiva education. Each group is expected to send some of its members to command courses similar to Nahal, but unlike Nahal commanders, Yeshivot Hahesder commanders are not completely cut off from their group; they return to their Yeshivot for part of the study period. Yeshivot Hahesder do not form a separate military command like Nahal. They are more dispersed among different armored units and are commanded by regular military personnel. However, in contrast with their greater military dispersion, they keep greater separation and organizational autonomy with regard to their religious studies. Over the years the period consecrated to military duty was extended at the expense of the religious study period, but still the portion of religious studies in overall military service is longer than Nahal's comparable portion of settlement work (Bamahane, Apr. 7, 1976: 10-11, Nov. 24, 1976: 20-21, June 25, 1980: 18-19).

The combination of combat and religious studies is a fairly new phenomenon in Israeli society. For many years military service and religious studies were mutually exclusive, and most Yeshiva students are still exempt from service until the completion of their studies. Yeshivot Hahesder were conceived as a means by which nationalistic religious youth could reconcile their political-ideological views with their lack of service in the armed forces. The proposed arrangement responded to their desire to participate in the defense effort without relinquishing their religious studies and their separate communal network (Bamahane, June 25, 1980: 18; Kimmerling, 1979a: 29, 34-35).

Yeshivot Hahesder have been heralded in the Israeli public as instruments which enable the conscription of Yeshiva students. Rather than focusing on the cross-pressures between the military and nonmilitary aspects of their service (as with Nahal), reports on Yeshivot Hahesder tend to emphasize their integration in the military framework and the quality of their performance as soldiers (Bamahane, Feb. 25, 1976: 3, Oct. 27, 1976: 9, Nov. 24, 1976: 20). The alternative to the special arrangement under which these people serve is no service at all, while in Nahal's case no such exemption is contemplated. The Yeshivot Hahesder, unlike Nahal, are not portrayed in terms of the IDF's role expansion into the civilian sphere. They are not expected to contribute to a given civilian scheme. The only expectation from them is their integration into military life. Notwithstanding this important difference, Nahal and Yeshivot Hahesder are both special arrangements which accommodate military service obligations with the particular educational needs of certain civilian sectors.

Nahal and Yeshivot Hahesder expose their personnel to more education than ordinary military units, even in the properly military part of their service. Education is oriented to postservice life, and the respective civilian movements exert considerable control over it (Sharir, interview in Bamahane, Nov. 9, 1977: 19). In Nahal, movement representatives in civilian clothes accompany their respective Garin throughout the military service. They hold weekly orientation meetings and intervene with military authorities on behalf of the soldiers. Civilians sent by the movements offer agricultural training and technical assistance on running the Nahal "footholds." Seminaries are organized for each Garin in the prospective settlement or in the movement's education center in a completely civilian atmosphere with no intervention or even presence of non-Garin military. But the Nahal units are also exposed to the IDF's general education series, which counteracts the particularistic education of the movements. I have little information on the educational activities conducted in the Yeshivot Hahesder. It seems that they are more closely incorporated in the soldiers' religious studies and hence are more insulated from the IDF's general civic education.

Since 1972 Nahal has been invested with a new educational task: the special basic training of recruits who did not meet the minimal induction requirements. These recruits have tenuous ties with the rest of Nahal. They do not constitute Garinim and are not prepared for settlement. They are not affiliated with civilian youth movements. After their training, some of them stay in Nahal and fill service jobs (as drivers, cooks, maintenance personnel in headquarters), but most are sent to other units and retain no ties with Nahal (Kimmerling, 1979a: 30; Bowden, 1976: 84; Bamahane

Nahal, Sept. 1979: 48, 63). The task of administering this rehabilitation program was given to Nahal purportedly because of its "expertise" in matters of education. Nahal has a better developed educational apparatus than other military units; it was formed to create the conditions for maintaining education during military service. It was also the pacesetter in more indirect education by means of entertainment and cultural activities (Levitas, 1967: 27; Heymont, 1967: 320). Since its military output was limited, it was convenient for the IDF to transform Nahal into a specialized instrument of education. Finally, Nahal represents the IDF's social service image, and this rehabilitation program is just another auxiliary service offered to the parent society in the best national service tradition (Bamahane, Nov. 6, 1974: 7, 20).

Conclusion

I hope to have shown in this chapter that the IDF's civic education activities are characterized by the primacy of their civilian orientation. In Western democratic societies civic education conducted by the military is discussed mainly in terms of its possible influence on troop morale and related military performance. This issue does not seem to be a crucial one in Israel because of its different civil-military ties. The renewed debate found in the literature on the relative importance of political beliefs and ideology versus small unit solidarity and/or career opportunities of enlistment is raised in the context of passage to all-volunteer military forces and the rising ambiguity about citizenship obligations.[11] In both aspects the Israeli case differs sharply from its contemporary Western counterparts.

This is not to say that the IDF does not stress civic education. We have seen a highly developed educational apparatus and an abundance of formal programs in the IDF. However, these programs are directed toward the society at large. They are intended to influence the entire society's "performance," not just that of people under arms. Most of the civic education programs do not address specifically service personnel, but even those which do appeal to the larger society. The IDF acts as the supreme carrier of collective goals and values and transmits them to both civilians and military. The nation-building theme (unlike the linkage between military service and citizenship) is not taken for granted. It is repeatedly stressed and held at a high level of consciousness because of the conflict with neighboring countries and the international controversy surrounding the society's basic goals. In this respect as well Israel differs from most Western societies. For this reason the IDF's civic education stresses national ties and patriotism much more than the taken-for-granted issue of the military's place in society.

For most conscripts civic education is recreation in disguise, and its effect on military performance should be seen as similar to other entertainment activities. For some especially disadvantaged groups civic education is much more than recreation—it is mixed with overcoming some basic deficiencies in comprehensive knowledge—but the utility of this education for the military is limited because these recipients occupy peripheral positions in the armed forces. The principal aim is to contribute to their civilian citizenship role and individual development rather than to their military role. This also applies to the special education supplied to the highly promising soldiers of Nahal and Yeshivot Hahesder. But these units are discordant notes in the IDF's civic education effort since, instead of exposing their soldiers to common national values, they continue to give them the particularistic education of the respective civilian sectors with which they are affiliated.

Civilian-oriented education creates less cross-pressure on the soldier's scarce training time needed for military proficiency. Therefore it creates less bureaucratic resistance on the part of other military branches. It also continues the national service image of the armed forces, which is politically beneficial to both the military and the civilian leadership. Civilian-oriented civic education, as well as other extramilitary tasks, strengthens the link between the people and the armed forces. The IDF remains a cultural model for society and maintains its perceived superiority over the civilian sector in effectiveness and dedication to national causes. This role of the military is acknowledged and legitimized by the whole society, including the civilian leadership, insofar as it remains at the cultural-symbolical level and does not lead to political interference. It is also interesting to note that, besides its instrumental value, the military's role expansion strengthens the sense of national solidarity and increases popular support for the civilian authorities as well. It enhances the feeling that certain problem areas are being taken care of by the institution which best represents the common values and is best geared to getting things done.

NOTES

1. For the different goals of civic education conducted by the armed forces, see Wesbrook (this volume, Chapter 1).

2. See Luckham (1971: 5-35). For the relationship between Luckham's classification and the convergence-divergence model see Biderman and Sharp (1968: 383), Moskos (1970: 166), and Peri (1980: 52-43).

3. Religious, married, and pregnant women are exempt from service. Among Jewish men found fit to serve, exemptions are granted to people with severe welfare problems, to Yeshiva students, and to members of certain ultra-religious groups. Arabs are exempt from service, though not Druzes. Beduins, Cherkeses, and Christian Arabs can serve on a voluntary basis (see Peri, 1980: 19 and Kimmerling, 1979: 27-38).

4. The current affairs topics can sometimes be of singularly civilian nature. Newspaper reports have recently indicated, with a touch of amusement, that a special issue of the pamphlets sent to assist commanders in their weekly conversation hours discussed the operation of the stock exchange and financial investment opportunities. As one newspaper put it, when soldiers talk of parachuting these days, their minds are set on what happens to their stocks and not on their fellow combatants (see Yedioth Ahronoth, Mar. 12, 1981).

5. In fall 1980, however, some tension surfaced between the IDF and the Ministry of Education, the latter accusing the armed forces of exaggerating their role and success in youth rehabilitation programs at the expense of the ministry's own accomplishments. The dispute became an issue of debate at the parliament's Education Committee (Yedioth Ahronoth, Nov. 17, 1980).

6. The naming of the school after Colonel Marcus is of great symbolic significance and dramatizes the importance of the Hebrew language in the army. Colonel Marcus was an American volunteer who had served with the Israeli troops during the War of Independence. He was killed near Jerusalem by one of his sentries when, not knowing Hebrew, he failed to respond to the sentry's warning (see Roumani, 1978: 52). For details on Camp Marcus see Bar On (1967: 158-159), Bowden (1976: 55, 80-81), Rolbant (1970: 211-213), and Brig. Gen. Avner Shalev (interview in Bamahane, Mar. 14, 1979: 22).

7. The IDF has gradually expanded its special education programs to the postelementary level. Secondary school courses are given at Camp Marcus for soldiers who prolong their service by four months. Evening classes and correspondence courses are offered for study for matriculation exams (Lissak, 1971: 329-332; Bar On, 1967: 164; Roumani, 1978: 51-60; Bamahane, Feb. 9, 1977: 8).

8. For example, see the interview with Lt. Gen. Raphael Eitan on Israeli television, September 10, 1980.

9. For an earlier poll showing Galei Zahal in second place see Limor (1979: 2-3).

10. Only about 30 percent of the Nahal soldiers remain in their prospective settlements a year after their release from compulsory service. However, almost 80 percent of the new rural settlements established between 1948 and 1979 were formed by former Nahal members. See an interview with Lt. Col. Raanan Sharir in *Bamahane* (Nov. 9, 1977: 18-19), *Haaretz* (Nov. 24, 1974: 2), and Lissak (1971: 333-334).

11. On citizenship obligations see Janowitz (1980: 1-24).

BIBLIOGRAPHY

AL-QAZZAZ, A. (1973) "Army and society in Israel." Pacific Sociological Review 16, 2. *(Discussion of the military's centrality in society leads the author to conclude that Israel is indeed a garrison state; data on universal conscription, the background of senior officers, and the integration of army and society. Some basic factual inaccuracies and erroneous use of Hebrew terms show lack of firsthand familiarity with the subject matter.)*

AMIR, Y. (1969) "The effectiveness of the kibbutz-born soldier in the Israeli Defense Forces." Human Relations 22 (August). *(Quantitative study showing the superiority of the kibbutz-born soldiers over comparable non-kibbutz counterparts in the extent of their volunteering for special combat units, their assessed suitability for command positions, and their success in military training courses.)*

——— A. BIZMAN, and M. RIVNER (1973) "The effects of inter-ethnic contact on friendship choices in the military." Journal of Cross Cultural Psychology 4 (September). *(Soldiers are asked about their friendship choices before and after interethnic contact in the army. Results indicate that at the beginning of basic training soldiers of European origin reveal significant preference for friends of their own group, while soldiers of Middle Eastern origin show no ethnic preference. Little change occurs in preferences after interethnic contact.)*

AZARYA, V. and B. KIMMERLING (1980) "New immigrants in the Israeli Armed Forces." Armed Forces and Society 6 (Spring). *(The extent of integration of new immigrants in the IDF is studied in terms of their rising in ranks and their entering high-status military units. The article is based on quantitative data from the 1970s and updates earlier literature based on the 1950s; it also assesses the effect of military service on the new immigrants' general integration in the Israeli society.)*

BAR ON, M. (1967) "Education processes in the Israeli Defense Forces," in S. Tax (ed.) The Draft. Chicago: University of Chicago Press. *(Detailed account of the education programs conducted by the Israeli military [primary and secondary education completion, academic reserves, Nahal, Gadna, etc.], written by a former chief education officer in the IDF.)*

BEN DOR, G. (1973) "The military in the politics of innovation and integration: the case of the Druze minority in Israel." Asian and African Studies 9, 3. *(Discussion of the impact of military service among Druzes, indicating the emergence of a new elite which attempts to challenge the traditional leadership but still lacks its own power base.)*

BEN SHAUL, M. (1978) Generals of Israel. Tel-Aviv: Hadar. *(Biographies of the principal military figures who engendered the 1967 victory.)*

BIDERMAN, A. D. and L. SHARP (1968) "The convergence of military and civilian occupation structures: evidence from studies of military retired employment." American Journal of Sociology 73 (January).

BOWDEN, T. (1976) Army in the Service of the State. Tel Aviv: University Publishing Projects. *(Detailed discussion of the Israeli military's role expansion and service to the society at large, in education, immigrant absorption, working with the underprivileged, agriculture, rural development, etc.)*

EATON, J. W. (1969) "Gadna: Israel's youth corps." Middle East Journal 23 (Autumn). *(The structure and activities of the military-organized Youth Battalion, including the compulsory preinduction military training of secondary school pupils and the voluntary youth movement activities.)*

ERAN, M. (1974) "The selection of commanders in the Israel Defence Force." Public Administration in Israel and Abroad 14. *(Discussion of the psychological testing procedure used in selecting commanders in the IDF, written by a former chief military psychologist in the IDF.)*

GLICK, E. B. (1967) Peaceful Conflict: The Non-Military Use of the Military. Harrisburg, PA: Stackpole Books. *(Comparative study of the peacetime civic action undertaken by the military of different countries. Includes chapters on*

North and South America, the Far East, Africa, and the Middle East, the latter with emphasis on Israel.)

HALPERN, B. (1962) "The role of the military in Israel," in J. J. Johnson (ed.) The Role of the Military in Underdeveloped Countries. Princeton: Princeton University Press. *(Historical survey of the development of Jewish military organizations in Palestine and their transformation into the IDF after Israel's independence, leading to a discussion of the reasons for the IDF's nonintervention in Israeli politics, unlike many underdeveloped countries.)*

HANNING, H. (1967) The Peaceful Uses of Military Forces. New York: Praeger. *(Comprehensive comparative study of supplementary peaceful uses of armed forces in 16 countries including Israel; discussion of civic action, disaster and emergency relief, education and training, economic and social projects, and international peacekeeping.)*

HEYMONT, I. (1967) "The Israeli Nahal program." Middle East Journal 21 (Summer). *(The Nahal program of the IDF, its internal structure, its contribution to development projects in the larger society, and its applicability to other countries.)*

HOROWITZ, D. (1977) "Is Israel a garrison state?" Jerusalem Quarterly 4 (Summer). *(The centrality of the military-security sphere in Israel is discussed in terms of the recognition given to the security issue in the general public, the allocation of resources, the social status of those occupying central military positions, the close ties between civilian and military elites. The author shows how, despite such centrality of the security issues, Israel manages to remain an open society.)*

——— (1974) "The Israeli concept of national security." Public Administration in Israel and Abroad 14. *(The Israeli strategic thought is based on a pessimistic anticipation of the behavior of other actors in the international arena. This leads to an emphasis on self-reliance, an inclination toward "worst-case" analyses necessitating the pursuit of the broadest possible margin of security, a "power politics" orientation which downplays moral and legal considerations in international relations. Also, because of the constant danger situation, Israeli strategy displays a nondichotomous perception of war and peace.)*

——— (1970) "Flexible responsiveness and military strategy." Policy Sciences 1. *(The Israeli Army tends to adopt military strategies which are likely to result in increasing complexity and uncertainty of battlefield conditions, based on the assumption that it has a comparative advantage over its enemies in operational flexibility.)*

——— and B. KIMMERLING (1974) "Some social implications of military service and the reserves system in Israel." Archives Européenes de Sociologie, 15, 2. *(Studying the Israeli reserve duty system, with comparative reference to Switzerland, the authors show that military service defines the collectivity's boundaries in Israel, and military role has a strong impact on one's overall position in the society's stratification.)*

HUREWITZ, J. C. (1969) Middle East Politics: The Military Dimension. New York: Praeger. *(Comparative study of the military's social role and political involvement in Middle Eastern countries, including Israel.)*

JANOWITZ, M. (1980) "Observations on the sociology of citizenship: obligations and rights." Social Forces 59 (September).

KIMMERLING, B. (1979a) "Determination of the boundaries and frameworks of conscription. Two dimensions of civil-military relations in Israel." Studies in Comparative International Development 14 (Spring). *(Despite universal conscrip-*

tion, certain sectors of the Israeli society are exempt from service or have a strong influence on the type and duration of their service. The author examines the bargaining power of such groups [religious groups, collective settlement movements, border settlements, etc.] and the cross-pressures exerted on the universal draft system.)

——— (1979b) Social Interruption and Besieged Societies: The Case of Israel. Amherst: SUNY Buffalo, Council on International Studies. *(The routine periods of Israeli society are compared with its "interrupted phase" when the bulk of its manpower is mobilized to deal with an immediate military threat. The two periods are analyzed with reference to an ideal type of "besieged society.")*

——— (1978) "The Israeli civil guard," in L. A. Zurcher and G. Harries-Jenkins (eds.) Supplementary Military Forces. Beverly Hills, CA: Sage. *(The author examines the emergence of an auxiliary security force as a phenomenon of citizen voluntarism in response to increasing concern over the threat of terrorist activities.)*

——— (1974) "The influence of land and territorial factors on the Jewish-Arab conflict regarding the formation of the Jewish society in Eretz Israel." Ph.D. dissertation, Hebrew University.

LEVITAS, G. (1967) Nahal: Israel's Pioneer Fighting Youth. Jerusalem: Ha'Omanim Press. *(The history, organization, and various functions performed by the IDF's collective settlement units, written, with a favorable bias, by a person who served in one of these units.)*

LIMOR, Y. (1979) "The race for network surveys." Maariv—Weekend Supplement, March 8.

LISSAK, M. (1980) "The defense establishment in Israel: boundaries and institutional linkages." Presented at the IUS Conference, Chicago, 1980. *(Comprehensive discussion of the exact configurations of linkages between the Israeli military and civilian sectors in different institutional spheres [political, economic, educational and cultural, symbolic and communication networks, etc.]. Makes use of Luckham's fragmented, permeable, and integral boundary trilogy and adds to it further criteria, such as the degree of institutionalization of the linkage, the control exerted by each sector over its representatives, the relative status of each sector vis-à-vis the other.)*

——— (1970) "The Israel Defense Forces as an agent of socialization and education: a research in role expansion in a democratic society," in M. R. Van Gils (ed.) The Perceived Role of the Military. Rotterdam: Rotterdam University Press. *(The IDF's role expansion in the field of education is discussed in terms of the client's identity [civilian or military] and the content of the educational service [professional or comprehensive civic education].)*

LITTLE, R. W. (1969) "Procurement of manpower: an institutional analysis," in Selective Service and American Society. New York: Russell Sage.

LUCKHAM, A. R. (1971) "A comparative typology of civil-military relations." Government and Opposition 6 (Winter).

LUTTWAK, E. and D. HOROWITZ (1974) The Israeli Army. London: A. Lane. *(A sociological history of the Israeli armed forces, from its preindependence predecessors to the 1970s. Includes issues of military strategy as well as the social structure of the armed forces.)*

MOSKOS, C. C. (1970) The American Enlisted Man. New York: Russell Sage.

PERI, Y. (1980) "Some aspects of the relationship between the military and the polity in Israeli society." Ph.D. dissertation, London School of Economics. *(Challenges the assumption of depoliticization of the Israeli military. Shows the military elite's strong influence on high-level civilian policy-making and suggests the emergence of a "civilian-military partnership" rather than the military's absolute subordination to civilian control.)*

——— (1977) "Ideological portrait of the Israeli military elite." Jerusalem Quarterly 3 (Spring). *(Senior officers of the IDF do not display a distinctive "military mind." Their attitudes on nationalism, economics, state and religion, attitude to democracy, are similar to that of the larger society and contain the same heterogeneity as in the civilian sector. In some respects they even have a more "liberal" tendency than the civilian sector.)*

——— and M. LISSAK (1976) "Retired officers in Israel and the emergence of a new elite," in G. Harries-Jenkins and J. Van Doorn (eds.) The Military and the Problem of Legitimacy. Beverly Hills, CA: Sage. *(Studying colonels who retired from the IDF, the authors find that the high prestige and employment opportunities available to them in the larger society enable retired officers to choose a civilian career equal in status to their military one, hence preventing the crystalization of a separate elite with a distinctive ideology.)*

PERLMUTTER, A. (1978) Politics and the Military in Israel, 1967-77. London: Frank Cass. *(A sequel to the 1969 book; covers the 1967-1977 period and shows continued support to the basic thesis of civilian dominance over the military.)*

——— (1969) Military and Politics in Israel: Nation Building and Role Expansion. London: Frank Cass. *(Further development of the points made in the World Politics article. Detailed study of the IDF's role expansion and of the civil-military relations in the political sphere.)*

——— (1968) "The Israeli Army in politics: the persistence of the civilian over the military." World Politics 20 (July). *(Despite the centrality of the military in society and the various extramilitary roles performed by the armed forces, civilian control over the military has persisted and the military has undergone a process of formalization, professionalization, and depoliticization.)*

ROLBANT, S. (1970) The Israeli Soldier: Profile of an Army. London: Thomas Yoseloff. *(Comprehensive study of the development, internal structure, and sociological portrait of the Israeli armed forces; detailed examination of its different corps, the draft and mobilization system, military training and leadership, the social diversity and solidarity of servicemen, educational processes, etc.)*

ROTHENBERG, G. E. (1979) The Anatomy of the Israeli Army. New York: Hippocrene Books. *(A history of the Israel Defense Forces from its preindependence origins to 1978, with special emphasis on more narrowly military matters such as internal organization, development of military doctrine, problems of arms procurement, and military campaigns.)*

ROUMANI, M. M. (1978) From Immigrant to Citizen: The Contribution of the Army in Israel to National Integration. The Hague: Foundation of Plural Societies. *(Discussion of the difficulties encountered by first- and second-generation Oriental Jews in the military. Serious doubts are raised about the military's ability to be a channel of integration and upward mobility for Jews of non-European backgrounds. Includes detailed study of the educational services provided by the IDF, but concludes that the services are not effective because they force a European mentality on soldiers from a different cultural background.)*

SCHIFF, Z. (1974) A History of the Israeli Army: 1870-1974. San Francisco: Straight Arrow Books. *(History of the Israeli armed forces, originally written in Hebrew [hence for an Israeli audience] by the military correspondent of the*

Israeli daily Haaretz. *Emphasizes military strategy, internal organization and development, weaponry, and accounts of military campaigns.)*

SCHILD, E. O. (1973) "On the meaning of military service in Israel," in M. Curtis and M. Chertoff (eds.) Israel: Social Structure and Change. New Brunswick, NJ: Transaction Books. *(Discussion of the main characteristics of military service in Israel showing how different it is from "total institution" properties. Stresses the closeness between military and civilian sectors, the importance of informal ties in command relations, training which prepares for independent thinking and improvisation, and the "combatant" rather than "manager" image of the officers.)*

TADMOR, Y. (1976) "Conceptions of education in the Gadna." Ph.D. dissertation, Tel Aviv University.

WAKENHUT, R. (1979) "Effects of military service on the political socialization of the draftees." Armed Forces and Society 5 (Summer).

ZERTEL, I. (1980) "A kiss of death." Haaretz–Weekend Supplement, November 28.

9.

Universities in Israel: Dilemmas of Growth, Diversification, and Administration

Joseph Ben-David

ABSTRACT

Roots and background of the Israeli university: the Hebrew University (1925) and the Haifa Technion (1924) reflect the twin roots of Israeli HE, the revitalisation of Jewish culture and the Zionist programme of building up the country physically. Germany provided the academic models for both institutions. The emphasis was on research; there was little need for professional training since many immigrants were already well qualified professionally. The American private university provided the organisational model.

The emergence of a university system in the fifties and sixties: five more institutions were founded between 1949 and 1972; they tended to imitate each other, and the two older institutions, in style. The universities had to adapt to the educational needs of a steadily increasing number of students. The research tradition, however, remained strong. Students emerging from the selective Israeli high school system also appreciated the value of research. The country, however, was too small to sustain up-to-date research institutions on its own. Israel was able to benefit from American aid and many research workers received part of their training abroad.

The institutional structure of the Israeli university: Israel's involvement, through American aid, in a cosmopolitan system of learning enabled her universities to avoid the utilitarian approach of first degree and professional mass higher education and retain a commitment to research. Academic appointments are based on research attainments and publications, and institutions are marked by academic self-government.

The academic profession and research: the growth of the academic profession in Israel since 1948 has been one of the most rapid in the world. The fact that many Israeli research workers have done part of their training abroad has ensured that there was little need to recruit directly from abroad or by lowering standards at home. It has also reinforced the research tradition of the Israeli university, although some of the best research work undertaken by Israelis is done abroad. The higher education system cannot support seven research universities, yet each is organised as a research university. This perpetuates dependence upon foreign universities as research centres. There is a need for more emphasis on teaching as a career in higher education.

Students and studies: the transition between school and university for those academi-

cally qualified is relatively easy in Israel. Degree courses in professional subjects, however, are oversubscribed. The system worked well until the early sixties since those matriculating were a select group with intellectual interests. Student numbers have since increased and student interest has changed. Universities have responded by developing professional studies.

The changing character of the student body and of career opportunities has developed since 1963 a flexible programme of studies for the Israeli first degree. Since the end of the rapid growth in student numbers in 1972/73, universities have tried to attract students by satisfying student demand for the development of professional courses.

The oversubscribed professional courses are able to take the best students, which results in the most able students being taught in departments which do not present them with an intellectual challenge. The basic disciplinary departments, where most of the research workers teach, are full of students who cannot cope with the intellectual challenge. The decline in student numbers means that these disciplinary departments cannot recruit staff, which in turn threatens their research programmes.

It is suggested that a change in the student selection process would redistribute talent between the professional and the disciplinary departments. The present academic score system should be used to establish a student's suitability for study, but places should then be allocated by lottery and/or by social considerations.

Satisfying student demand for professional purpose in their degrees could be achieved by changing the educational attitudes of students and teachers. Students should be shown how academic disciplines prepare for work. First and second degree studies should be analysed to show their relationship to the careers for which they might be useful. The example of teacher training is given.

The way the system works: there is now a need for diversity in academic styles and traditions. The higher education system has been starved of funds for several years. Because of strong traditions of academic self-government, there are no professional academic administrations in Israel. This discourages academic planning. In the smaller universities of the past, academic leadership could emerge. Now excessive participatory democracy prevents this, and it has become difficult, since the expansion of the universities has halted, to shift resources from one unit to another. There is growing support for establishing effective planning and policymaking on the university and national levels.

Higher education and Israeli society: access to HE has never been a political issue in Israeli society because universities admit all minimally qualified candidates. 20% of 21–24 year-olds in 1976/77 were receiving university education, and 30% some form of HE. HE is not a source of class or economic privilege in Israeli society.

Students enter HE after military service. They receive little support from the state; the majority combine work with study. The rewards of an academic career are also limited, which has helped to preserve elements of the traditional Jewish attitude to sacred learning.

The low rewards of academic study help to explain the difficulty in recruiting students from Afro-Asian backgrounds.

I. The Roots and Background of the Israeli University

Higher education in Israel has two roots, both connected with the Zionist idea of national revival. One was the idea of the revitalisation of the Hebrew language and Jewish culture. From having been mainly a language of ritual and religious learning, Hebrew was to become the language of everyday life. Jews who participated intensively in the cultural life of many nations while narrowing down their own to the cultivation of the Biblical and Talmudic tradition, were to develop a new secular Hebrew culture. One branch of the Zionist movement, led by the philosopher Ahad Ha'am, saw the establishment of a cultural ('spiritual') centre in Israel as the main purpose of Zionism. Although the large majority of the movement did not accept Ahad Ha'am's views, and wanted not only a spiritual centre but also a full-fledged state, the programme of cultural revival and the desire to make Israel into a spiritual centre for world Jewry (and an important cultural centre in general) was incorporated into the movement's political programme.

The idea of a Hebrew University in Jerusalem, first propounded in 1882 by Hermann Schapira, a professor of mathematics in Heidelberg, and subsequently by Martin Buber, Berthold Feiwel and Chaim Weizmann (1902), Dr Israel Abrahams (1908) and H. Sacher (1918) [1] was part of this Ahad Ha'amian programme. When the Hebrew University was established in 1925, it was intended to serve as a world centre of Jewish science and scholarship.

According to this programme, the main task of the university was to advance knowledge [2]. It was assumed that the creation of new scientific and scholarly knowledge would also serve the economic and political needs of so-called 'society', and the educational needs of individuals in society, but this kind of service was to be subordinated to the main task. Scientific and scholarly advancement was considered an autonomous value, one of the aims for which society and people existed, and it was taken for granted that in the hierarchy of the aims or values of the Jewish people, this aim stood very high. This assumption was not without foundation. For 2000 years, Jews were a people of learning, and since the destruction of the Second Temple in 70 AD, the unity of the Jewish people was maintained through the adherence to, and the cultivation of, Talmudic tradition and learning.

The Haifa Technion, Israel Institute of Technology, established in 1924, was related to a second, more worldly Zionist purpose of building up the country physically. It was to be a pragmatic institution devoted to technological and technical needs, first and foremost to train engineers and architects.

The models of both of these institutions were the universities and technological high schools in Germany, which were considered at that time as the best in the world, and were the best known to the teachers recruited to the new institutions. The large majority of teachers were trained in German (including Austrian, Swiss and Czech German) universities or institutes of technology, or in other Central or Eastern European institutions of higher education which followed the German model. So strong was the influence of the German model, that when the first plans were made for the establishment of the Haifa Technion in 1913, it was envisaged that the language of instruction would be German. The idea was dropped only as a result of determined opposition by the teachers of the Hebrew school system.

The curriculum in those European institutions required in most cases four years of study and the diploma obtained at the end was recognised as evidence of the acquisition of all the scientific knowledge needed for a professional career. There were usually additional requirements for state licensure in law, medicine or teaching, but these were requirements of practical experience and knowledge, and not further academic studies. Even for those wishing to enter academic or other research careers, there were no further graduate studies. Possession of a university diploma was considered sufficient qualification to work on one's own on a doctorate and subsequently on a more advanced thesis, the *Habilitationsschrift*. Of course, one often needed to acquire further knowledge for these purposes through private study, or course work, but these were not formal requirements. Essentially, as far as the teaching programme was concerned, universities taught for only a single degree, although they also conferred higher degrees [3].

The practice that universities taught only for a single degree of an advanced kind was based on two assumptions, namely that the students were intellectually and morally mature people in possession of a well-rounded general education and adequate preparation for scientific and scholarly work, much of it to be done on their own; and that the university teachers were productive research workers whose courses and seminars were not primarily intended to cover their fields of speciality in a didactically effective way, but to share with the students their own original interpretation of knowledge in their fields and acquaint them with their own style of thought and research. The students had much freedom in the choice and attendance of their courses, and there were few examinations before the final ones. For students who were as well prepared and motivated as the universities expected them to be, this was an ideal curriculum. For the majority who were less prepared, it was not very satisfactory. These latter survived the system by a variety of compromises, such as choosing relatively undemanding subjects, or passing with low grades which were not too difficult to obtain.

The academic administration of the German, or German-type university was based on the principle of freedom of instruction and study. Academic teachers had virtually complete freedom in offering courses and seminars of their choice (but there were effective financial incentives to teach the large introductory courses), and conducting their examinations. This academic laissez-faire reduced the need for administration. Whatever academic administration there still existed was left to collegiate bodies (faculty councils and senate) and to elected representatives of the faculty (deans, rector). Financial administration and management of the physical plant were taken care of by civil servants, since universities were state institutions.

In the process of its implantation to what was then the semi-autonomous Jewish community of Palestine, the German model underwent important changes, especially in the Hebrew University. While, as has been pointed out, the curriculum of the German university was organised as if all the students intended to be trained as researchers, in fact the large majority prepared for careers in law, medicine, civil service and gymnasium teaching. In practice, the universities often adapted their curricula to the requirements of professional careers: they conferred degrees based on examinations and seminar papers alone without a thesis. In professional studies in which the acquisition of a doctoral degree was the accepted practice, such as law and medicine, universities frequently conferred the degree on the basis of rather rudimentary theses. This was a compromise, since the educational philosophy of the universities considered higher studies and research as inseparable.

In Israel, training professional people was not an important function of the university. Immigration brought to the country more than enough professionals, and any addition to their number could only have made worse an already poor employment situation [4]. Therefore, the university was conceived not only in principle (like in Germany), but also in fact, as primarily a research institution. As a result, the Hebrew University degree was a master's degree requiring—in addition to examinations in one major and two minor subjects—the writing of a thesis on a level which was equivalent to a (serious) German doctorate. Before 1949, the curriculum of the Hebrew University was constructed as if its sole purpose was to train students for research in the basic arts and sciences.

Because it was a financially weak and numerically small (about 1000 students in the mid-forties) institution, it could not attain significant international standing. But in spite of its poverty and peripherality, its staff included a few scholars and scientists of great eminence and high international reputation, such as Saul Adler, Martin Buber, Ladislaus Farkas, Michael M. Fekete, Abraham A. Fraenkel, Richard Koebner, Joel J. Racah, Yitzhak Baer, Gershom Scholem and others. They were attracted to Jerusalem partly because of their belief in Zionism and partly because of their fear of increasingly violent anti-Semitism, especially on the continent of Europe. The presence of these people on the small campus gave credibility to the emphasis on research at the small university. This research emphasis was accepted by the students. Because, as has been pointed out, employment opportunities for university graduates were poor, the only students who took the university seriously were those who had genuine personal interest in science and scholarship, even at the cost of economic sacrifice. The best of the students included a large percentage of immigrants who registered only in order to obtain immigration certificates. Many of them dropped out of the university as soon as they were legally allowed to do so without forfeiting their right for residence and citizenship. Due to these circumstances, the Hebrew University in about 1940 probably adhered to the Humboldtian idea of unity of research and teaching more than had any university anywhere in the world (including Germany) before [5].

While academically the model for the Hebrew University was the Humboldtian German university, the model for its organisation was the American private university. The Hebrew University was a private institution supported mainly by foreign, especially American, donors, and the pattern of a corporation run by a President elected by a Board of Governors formally responsible for the corporation seemed to be a suitable form of governance. However, the attempt of the first President of the University, J. L. Magnes, to manage the institution in the autocratic American fashion of the early 1920s was not accepted by the largely Continental European faculty accustomed to academic self-government. In the ensuing clash, in which the rebellious faculty was strongly supported by illustrious academic members of the Board of Governors, especially Albert Einstein, the faculty won out. The result was a private presidential university in which the role of the president was restricted to fundraising and financial management, with virtually no say in—although occasionally some influence on—academic matters. The new pattern was more like the German than the American one, since the functions of the president resembled those of the *Kurator* of the German universities, rather than those of the American university president.

As a matter of fact, academic self-government at the Hebrew University was more complete than in Germany, since in Germany self-government was controlled and frequently interfered with by the directors of higher education in the different federal states. Some of these ruled the universities under their jurisdiction in the manner of American university presidents. In the absence of such a directorate, self-government in academic matters became almost complete. In principle the Board of Governors could have exercised similar powers as those of the German states, but it never had the administrative machinery to actually do so.

These socio-historical circumstances also explain why the Haifa Technion did not develop an alternative tradition competing with the Humboldtian-Ahad Ha'amian tradition of the Hebrew University. The Technion too was modeled to a large extent on the German institutes of technology, which by the 1920s had assimilated many of the ideas and ideals of the Humboldtian university. It was quite willing to train relatively high grade engineers and do applied research, but it did not adopt a policy like that of some of the American land grant institutions which searched actively for potential users of their services, and were willing to initiate unconventional programmes of training and research according to the needs and tastes of their public. Since the economy was backward, industry hardly in existence, and the supply of immigrant engineers more than plentiful, there probably would have been little scope for the adoption or development of such a policy anyway. Therefore, instead of generating an alternative tradition of higher education, the Technion also became a high level technological university. Only in its organisation did the Technion differ somewhat from the Hebrew University. Its director, now president, fulfilled the functions of academic as well as administrative leadership, and its ties to the official Jewish institutions were initially closer than those of the University.

II. The Emergence of a University System in the Fifties and Sixties

Since the establishment of the State the following new institutions were founded: the Weizmann Institute of Science in Rehovoth (1949); Bar-Ilan University, Ramat Gan (1955); Tel Aviv University (1956); University of Haifa (1972); and Ben-Gurion University, Beersheba (1972). The Weizmann Institute began as a research institute, but in 1958 also became a graduate school; Bar-Ilan was meant to serve the religious sector; and the other three universities grew out of local initiatives. These three began as evening institutes usually run by the older institutions (the Hebrew University and the Technion, and in Beersheba also the Weizmann Institute) and—in the case of Ben-Gurion—also an important local research institute, the Negev Research Institute.

In spite of these distinct origins, in the first two decades of their existence the institutions tended to imitate, and to become increasingly similar to, each other. As will be shown below, the reasons for this were the direct supervision exercised by the Hebrew University on Tel-Aviv and Haifa universities, and of the Hebrew University and the Technion and Weizmann Institute on Ben-Gurion University, in the early stages of their development; the fact that most of the teachers in the new institutions were graduates of the older ones; and the strength and success of the research orientation during the fifties and sixties. Therefore, it is possible to describe the main developments for the system as a whole without, at this stage, having to go into the differences between the institutions.

The fact that the universities taught as best as they could the serious scholarly student, and did not care much about the rest, was considered acceptable to professors hailing from the continent of Europe. But the few who came from England and the United States (or knew the Anglo-American tradition intimately) were dissatisfied with the situation. They conceived of the university as an institution responsible for the education of all its students, and did not believe in the freedom of students to study or waste their time at their own discretion. They were also dissatisfied with the purely specialised disciplinary education received by the serious students. Many of the students came from traditional religious backgrounds with more or less Talmudic education, but without sufficient background in general studies. Others came from good humanistic gymnasia in Central or Eastern Europe, but had little if any knowledge of the Jewish cultural tradition. To cater to all these types of students, they considered it necessary to create an Israeli version of a liberal arts programme, conferring a first degree with much less specialisation than the existing master's degree, with no requirement of independent research, and with a considerable complement of general education.

These plans were adopted by the Hebrew University in 1947, but because of the 1947/48 War of Independence were put into effect only in the 1949/50 academic year.

By this time the student population, as well as the function of the university, had undergone considerable change. The proportion of students who had completed Israeli high schools increased, and the students now came to the university at the age of 20 or 21, after the completion of their army service. Unlike their predecessors during the Mandate, graduates were easily absorbed into the newly founded and expanding system of secondary education. The institution of the new BA degree—the BSc was introduced only in 1957 and became generally accepted only in 1959—proved to be very useful under the new conditions. Although, as will be shown below, it did not provide the students with the kind of education which the initiators of the degree had envisaged, and its structure had to be modified on several occasions under various pressures, it made possible the admission and education of a steadily increasing number of students (see Table I), which would have been inconceivable had the earlier research-oriented course for a master's degree been the only curriculum offered by the university.

The growth in the number of first degree students was the most conspicuous feature of

TABLE I. Number of first degree students in universities for selected years 1948/49–1977/78

Academic year	Number of students	Index base (I) 1950/51	Population end of '48, '50, etc. (thousands)	Rates per 10,000 of population
1948/49	1635	54	827.7	20
1950/51	3022	100	1370.1	22
1954/55	5514	132	1717.8	32
1959/60	9275	306	2088.7	44
1964/65	18.368	608	2525.6	73
1969/70	36.239	1199	2929.5	124
1974/75	52.088	1724	3421.6	152
1977/78	54,060	1789	3653.2	148
1983/84	64.605	2138	4148.5	155

Source: Central Bureau of Statistics, *Statistical Abstract of Israel*, no. 9 (1957/58), Table XIX/20–23, pp. 360–362: no. 19 (1968), Table XX/23, p. 543: no. 25 (1974), Table XXII/24, p. 630: no. 29 (1978), Table XXII/38, p. 685: no. 30 (1979), Table II/1, p. 31, no. 35 (1985), Table XXII/37, p. 659: Summary Table "A", p. 3.

(I) 1950/51 was chosen as a base year because in the years 1948/49 the country was in a state of war.

the expansion of the higher educational system. It was not, however, the most important element determining the character of the system's development. That part was played by the growth of university research. This may seem surprising, since in the fifties Israel was a very poor country with practically no industry and—at the beginning of the decade —with a rather backward agriculture, and was engaged in the absorption of immigrants, many of whom came from educationally underdeveloped backgrounds. But there were circumstances which made possible the development of higher education in relative independence from its surroundings.

The most important of these was the tradition of the unity of research and study established and firmly embedded in the structure of the Hebrew University under the Mandate. Of course, without adequate resources this tradition could not have had much influence on anything, but had there been a different tradition the resources—which were never plentiful—could easily have been used for other purposes. In accordance with this tradition, the Hebrew University, and subsequently all other universities, continued to recruit their teachers mainly on the basis of research attainments, and refrained from the creation of a career of college professors. The fact that the first new academic institute founded after the establishment of the State, the Weizmann Institute, was a pure research establishment engaged mainly in basic research (although the founders believed that this research would be of utmost benefit to the development of the country) was also a manifestation of the strength of the research tradition.

This tradition drew its strength not only from its historical roots, but also from the conditions prevailing in the fifties and sixties. Although the majority of students now prepared for a first degree, there were many among them who accepted research as a value, and quite a few who considered it as a personal goal. Thus, teachers who were creative researchers were usually appreciated not only because of their prestige but because there was a sufficiently large elite among the students who genuinely enjoyed, and identified with, research. And those who did not, accepted the values of this elite and of the university.

That the student body was so sympathetic to research was a result of the character of the Israeli high school up until the fifties. This was a rather selective type of school, enrolling in the fifties between 13–23% of the 15–18 age group, and providing about 10% of the 18-year-olds in the Jewish population with a matriculation certificate [6]. Many of its teachers were competent scholars. Therefore students came to the university with attitudes and values which conformed with those of the research university.

There was also no serious pressure on the universities from the sources of finance to change their philosophies. Until 1955/56 more than half of the budget of the universities came from private sources, principally from donors all over the world. For them the main function of the universities in Israel was to serve as an attractive centre of intellectual life, which was consistent with a research orientation. But even the government, which covered an increasingly large portion of the current expenditure (now about 75%) did not put pressure on the universities to comply with policies of its own, because it had none, and was by and large satisfied with what the universities did [7].

The only aspects of university life in which the government had an interest to impose its views were conditions of employment and salaries. Governments in the fifties were anxious to extend political patronage to all kinds of public employment, and to force on all public services conditions of employment and pay similar to those in the civil service. But even in this respect, the pressure on the universities was relatively mild. There was no serious attempt at political patronage, and little interference with the conditions of work of academic teachers. Only with regard to pay did governments insist on linking academic salaries to the low scales of pay prevailing in the civil service.

These conditions were sufficient to ensure the continued maintenance of Humboldtian ideals, but not the realisation of those ideals in practice. The country was too small and too poor to create and maintain research universities on an up-to-date level. And even if the material resources had been available, there would not have been the people to make use of them. Although, as has been pointed out, there were outstanding scientists and scholars in several fields, those fields were few; in many fields there were no individuals able to live up to the high ideals of scholarship adopted by the universities, and some important specialities were not represented at all. Furthermore, the number of good scientists and scholars was too small for the creation of a scientific community in the country.

The absence of resources and a local scientific community was more than compensated for by the support of the international, particularly the American, scientific community. American and British science emerged from the War greatly strengthened by the attainments of wartime research, and the idea that science was a new economic and military resource, equal or superior in importance to the traditional factors of production, had become accepted by increasingly large numbers of people in the fifties and sixties. The expanding universities and research institutes, especially in the United States, generously accepted and supported practically all advanced students or postgraduate researchers from anywhere in the world, and American foundations and agencies were also willing to fund research outside the United States on a generous scale. There was particularly great sympathy and generosity towards countries which gained independence after the War. Israel belonged to this category and was one of the first beneficiaries of American aid.

The ties with the United States were of decisive importance in keeping alive and realising in practice the ideal of the research university under the changing conditions of the fifties and sixties. Israeli university research became probably the most cosmopolitan on earth, since the majority of the research workers who began their careers in that period received at least some of their training abroad, and Israeli scientists published their papers abroad. The existence of an international scientific community, providing moral support, intellectual stimulation, research funds and an appreciative public, enabled Israeli universities to develop in a way—a system emphasising research as the supreme goal of higher education to which all the other tasks of the university have to be subordinated—that would have been impossible had they had to depend entirely on their local environment.

III. The Institutional Structure of the Israeli University

These circumstances explain how continuity was maintained between the single, somewhat anachronistic Humboldtian and Ahad Ha'amian university and the single Technion of the 1940's, and the higher educational system consisting of seven institutions which emerged in the fifties and sixties. The establishment of the State could have led—in principle—to discontinuity. As has been pointed out, in the new setting the university assumed important functions of training people for the professions and public services. This could have justified the change-over to a much more utilitarian system, modelled on the more practically oriented American state systems of higher education, or the systems of the communist countries of Eastern Europe.

The opportunities of linking Israeli institutions into a new cosmopolitan system of learning (created by American generosity) offered an alternative to the utilitarian solution. They led the universities to accept the functions of training professionals in an increasing variety of fields, and of teaching masses of students of rather heterogeneous qualifications on the assumption that these functions were to be integrated with and subordinated to research. This is manifested in two important ways. Appointments to academic positions are primarily based on attainments in research and publications, in principle irrespective of whether one teaches in a professional or basic field. The teaching load (6–8 hours a week) is such that it allows time for research, and the universities also consider it as their duty to provide facilities and some funds for research.

The other relevant feature is the existence of academic self-government. In appointments and all matters concerning the curriculum the decisive power is in the hands of senior faculty acting in assemblies, or through elected representatives. This means that the highest priority given to contributions to research in the scale of professional values of this faculty is also accepted as the highest value of the system of higher education as a whole.

Thus Israeli universities have operated, as it were, in and for two different markets: a domestic market for which they have supplied instruction mainly on a first degree level in the arts, sciences and the professions, and an external or international market for which they have supplied graduate research workers and research papers. In the domestic market they have a monopoly, and are remunerated for their services by fixed salary; the external market is competitive, and the remuneration for the services also includes scientific reputation, which is of decisive importance for advancement in an academic career. In addition, foreign systems provide training and research facilities for Israelis, as well as grants for research.

The structure of rewards inherent in these two markets until the early seventies had much to do with the continued supremacy of research as a goal of the system. The monopolistic domestic market for undergraduate education or professional training required no particular excellence from the universities or their teachers. As a market regulated by egalitarian social democratic governments it offered few differential rewards for excellence. The international market for research required excellence in research and rewarded it differentially. This enabled the universities and their teachers (because of academic self-government there is little difference between the two) to emphasise research.

This institutional structure is a key to the understanding of the way higher education has grown and functioned in Israel. It has to a great extent determined the character of the academic profession, deeply influenced the curriculum and the degree structure, and has set limits to institutional diversity among Israeli universities.

IV. The Academic Profession and Research

The growth of the academic profession in Israel since the establishment of the State in 1948 has been among the most rapid in the world (see Table II). Such rapid growth from such a narrow base would ordinarily require either massive importation of foreign teachers or drastic reduction of standards.

TABLE II. Professors and lecturers at Israeli universities: 1948/49–1975/76*

Academic year	No. of professors and lecturers	index base 50/51**
1948/49	118	85
1950/51	138	100
1953/54	301	218
1958/59	532	385
1963/64	976	707
1968/69	2814	2039
1973/74	4389	3180
1975/76	4388	3180
1980/81	4379	3173

* The number of assistants and instructors increased, between 1948 and 1976, 24 times. The increase in their numbers continued also after 1975.

** 1950/51 was chosen as a base year because in the years 1948/49 the country was in a state of war.

Source: Central Bureau of Statistics, *Students in Academic Institutions 1964/65, 1965/66*, Special Series no. 249 (1968), Table 1, pp. 4–7; no. 418 (1973), Table 1, pp. 4–6; and *Statistical Abstract of Israel*, no. 26 (1975), Table XXII/35, p. 629; no. 28 (1977), Table XXII/41, p. 629; and no. 35, Table XXII/46, p. 669.

Neither of these happened. Of the senior staff of the Israeli universities in 1976 [8] only about 29% completed all their formal training abroad. Less than 50% of these were recruited directly from abroad, or immediately upon their arrival in the country. Furthermore, direct recruitment actually decreased during the period of the greatest expansion of the system, in the sixties, although there has been a sharp increase again in the seventies (see Table III).

TABLE III. Academic staff (professors and lecturers) educated abroad by period of first employment (percentages)

Degrees abroad	Total	Year of First Employment			
		up to 1950	1951–60	1961–70	1971–76
First and last	29[1]	28	25	24	40
Last only	26	9	15	29	31
First only	6	11	9	5	3
None	39	52	51	42	25
Total	100	100	100	100	100
(N)	2596	106	488	1229	773

[1] 49% of these entered academic employment immediately upon arrival, and 65% within two years of their arrival in Israel.

Source: Yehudith Nevo, An unpublished survey of 'Israeli Academics, 1976'.

This shows that the expansion of the system took place with little need to recruit qualified people from abroad. About 80% [9] of the need could be covered from locally available people, although some of the latter were also originally immigrants trained abroad.

However, the fully trained immigrants and those directly recruited from abroad do not fully represent the dependence of the system on outside sources. In addition to the 29% trained abroad, another 32% received either their first or last degrees (usually the latter) abroad. If we add to these the academic teachers who did post-graduate work abroad; it turns out that self-sufficiency in the recruitment of academic personnel was possible only as a result of the previously described close links between the Israeli and foreign, especially American, systems of higher education. The small institutions which had existed before the establishment of the State, namely the Hebrew University and the Technion, graduated an exceptionally large proportion of potential academics without providing them with places to work, and, in many cases, also without giving them sufficient training for research. As the opportunity to enter academic careers suddenly expanded, beginning in 1949, they were ready to enter these careers. Those who began their careers in the 1940s (the category 'up to 1950' in Table III includes only a few individuals who obtained an academic post in Israel before 1940) were mainly people who came to the country in their late teens and early twenties and received all their training or their advanced training in Israel. Only a small fraction were Israeli-trained students who went abroad for advanced studies. With the expanding opportunities for training abroad since the end of the World War, this last category increased from 9% in the 1940s to 31% of the total entrants to academic positions in the seventies. Among the new entrants in the seventies there was an increase also in those fully trained abroad.

The overwhelming emphasis on training future research workers at Israeli universities, which, as has been shown above, began much before the expansion of the fifties and sixties, was no act of providence or uncanny foresight which anticipated future academic needs. Nor was the integration with foreign systems an unmixed blessing. In spite of its rapid expansion, Israeli higher education could not absorb all the Israeli PhDs trained at foreign universities and in 1967 over one-fourth of the science students studying in the United States remained abroad [10]. On the other hand, the close links between Israeli and American universities have also made reverse migration possible. The rise in the percentage of foreign recruits to Israeli universities during the seventies is partially the result of such a reverse movement.

Because of the plentiful supply of trained research workers, there was no need to reduce standards of qualification. It is practically impossible to enter an academic career in Israel without a PhD, and Israeli universities have recruited their teachers mainly from institutions with relatively high prestige in research. Of those with foreign last degrees, a large majority received their degrees in institutions with high academic prestige. Thus, the educational characteristics of newly recruited academic personnel predisposed them to maintain the traditions of emphasising research.

This state of affairs is being perpetuated by the institutional procedures of appointments and promotions. These are based primarily on publications evaluated by committees of professors, and written reports of outside (as a rule, foreign) referees. These procedures, which had been originally established in the old institutions (the Hebrew University and the Technion), were also adopted by the new ones, partly because accreditation of departments in the new universities by the Council for Higher Education depends to a large extent on the qualifications of their teachers as ascertained by the traditional criteria.

This kind of procedure, institutionalised in the entire system, has ensured the continuity of the research tradition. However, the maintenance of the tradition is dependent on very precarious conditions. The main problem is the dependence on the international system, not only in training but also in research. As has been noted by Derek de Solla Price and others, the number of research scientists in Israel with publications relative to the size and the resources of the country is exceptionally high; while the population of the country in 1967 was 0.08% of the total world population, and its GNP 0.15% of the world total, Israeli scientists were 0.9% of the world's publishing scientists [11]. The explanation of this is—as has been pointed out above—that a large part of this work is supported and much of it is actually done abroad. It is difficult to estimate the size of this part; however, one's impression is that for many teachers such work is very important, and that quite a few do their most important work abroad.

There are several reasons for this. Conditions of work in Israel are difficult and facilities (e.g. libraries) poor; the number of good doctoral students compared to that in first rate departments in the United States is small (partly because of the difficult economic conditions and reserve service of the students); and salaries abroad are very much higher than in Israel.

Since the opportunity to work abroad is most available to teachers with relatively high reputations as research workers, this transfers the seat of some of the best research done by Israelis to foreign universities. Of course, this is not the case in every department. But work abroad is a sufficiently important phenomenon to make a discernible difference between the reputation of Israeli universities, based on the published work of their teachers and the quality and quantity of research actually performed in these institutions. In other words, the large number of good research workers employed by the Israeli universities, and the numbers of their publications, do not correctly reflect the amount and quality of work done in those institutions. There are a few outstanding research units in Israel, but with the possible exception of the Weizmann Institute at Rehovot, Israeli universities—even the old ones—have a considerable way to go to create the physical conditions, administrative and technical support, and organisational and social atmosphere required for efficient research work.

The problem is exacerbated by the very institutional structure designed to safeguard academic standards. As has been pointed out, essentially similar procedures and standards have been enforced throughout the system. However, the system cannot support seven research universities, since there are neither sufficient material resources nor enough qualified advanced students for this. There are no more than two or three departments in any field and less than two in many fields with adequate resources and enough graduate students to serve as centres of research, or which have a reasonable prospect of obtaining such resources and recruiting enough students in the foreseeable future. However, largely as a result of the insistence of the older institutions on safeguarding standards (and thus preventing competition for undergraduates by lower-grade institutions), all the institutions are staffed by people who are qualified to do research, are allowed time to do it, and whose advancement depends on research publications. Consequently, all the universities consider it part of their birthright to establish research facilities and confer higher degrees in as many fields as possible, and are actually engaged in doing so. Resources and good graduate students are spread very thin, and there is little prospect of concentrating them in the two or three most promising departments.

Thus the very success of the system in training (with foreign aid) and absorbing large numbers of research workers is now preventing it from developing effective centres of research, thereby perpetuating its dependence on foreign centres.

Of course, there are also advantages to this dependence, since it compels Israeli scientists to maintain their ties with the international scientific community, and gives them access to larger, and a greater variety of, resources than a country of Israel's size could ever obtain. Given the propensity of Israelis to engage in research, there is perhaps no way of providing employment to Israeli researchers other than by exporting part of their services.

However, there are still two questions: is the major part of the work of academic researchers, which is done in Israel, done under optimal conditions; and is the dependence on 'export of research services' not excessive? The two questions are interrelated, since more first-rate research centres in the country would mean better conditions of work for at least some academics as well as less dependence on work abroad for maintaining the quality of research in Israel.

The establishment of such centres would require the introduction of some differentiation among institutions and/or departments, and perhaps also the establishment of more than a single type of academic career. The feasibility of this is, of course, dependent also on the needs of teaching, and the organisation and politics of the system. As a matter of fact, there are beginnings of such alternative careers. Experienced practitioners in professional fields, such as medicine, law or clinical psychology, can be appointed to regular or clinical academic ranks on the basis of achievements other than research. In addition, there is a career line of 'teachers' and 'senior teachers', who are not required to engage in research, for the non-academic teaching of languages and technical skills. However, none of these contributes significantly to the teaching of the bulk of the undergraduates. They are taught—in principle—by teacher-researchers who are in the regular academic career line, although many of these are junior people without tenure, a considerable fraction of whom are discharged after a few years.

The advantages of the present arrangement are that it enables young research workers to finance their doctoral and post-doctoral research; creates a pool of candidates for permanent academic appointments; and provides well-trained, up-to-date teachers for undergraduates. The problem is that although some of the young research workers are excellent, lively teachers, few of them have either the time or the opportunity to develop their teaching skills beyond the initial level. Moreover, there is a scarcity of career openings for those junior research workers and teachers who are not given permanent university positions. Both of these problems require attention; there has to be a careful investigation of the teaching arrangements and the suitability of the various kinds of teachers for the undergraduate level, and of the adequacy of training and career planning for those graduate assistants who are not promoted to a tenured rank, and have to enter non-academic careers.

V. Students and Studies

As is evident from Table IV, practically every Israeli who has the formal qualification to do so studies in an academic institution. This is not to say that everyone possessing a matriculation certificate enters a university immediately upon completing his or her army service. A number stay in the army as career officers, or enter non-academic post-secondary education or civilian employment. However, many eventually go to university, some of them in their thirties or forties. In addition, some of those not possessing a matriculation certificate enter universities after making up for this deficiency in courses recognised by the universities as equivalent to matriculation, such as special preparatory classes organised by universities (which had an enrolment of 2219 students in 1977/78) [12] or certain post-secondary diplomas. There is also an open university, entry into which is not dependent on any prior qualification. And, of course, anyone can sit for an external matriculation at any age. These second and third chance opportunities account for the fact that the entering class is always greater than could be expected on the basis of matriculations and foreign students.

TABLE IV. Graduates of matriculation examinations and first year university students (selected years between 1950/51–1977/78)*

Academic year	Graduate of matriculation examinations	First year students in universities (including foreign students)	First year students as percentage of matriculants three years before (I)
1950/51	942		
1954/55		1729	183
1955/56	2299		
1959/60		2892	126
1960/61	3558		
1964/65		5944	167
1965/66	8182		
1969/70		9817	120
1970/71	11,843		
1973/74		10,246	87
1974/75	12,500		
1977/78		13,330	107

(I)* The reason for comparing matriculants in a given year with registrants three years later is due to the three year compulsory military service which intervenes between matriculation and entry to the university. This is not a very exact procedure since women serve only two years, and some of them do not serve at all; and some men and women are allowed to complete their studies before their military service. Furthermore, there were periods when the compulsory military service was shorter than today. These qualifications have to be borne in mind in reading this table. The phenomenon in the fifties and sixties of first year registrations exceeding the total number of matriculations from three years before by up to 83% is probably due partly to immigration and partly to the fact that many people who were qualified to study at the universities postponed their studies because of military service and membership in collective settlements. The ratio of first year students to those who passed their matriculation examination decreased during the sixties. They still tend to exceed 100% by several percentages, because of the large number of foreign students and a smaller number of students who enter through the special preparatory courses of the universities.

Source: Central Bureau of Statistics. (a) *Statistical Abstract of Israel*, no. 8 (1957), Table XVII/9, p. 237; no. 23 (1972), Table XX/20, p. 593; no. 27 (1976), Table XXII/26, p. 611; no. 28 (1977), Table XXII/30, p. 619 and Table XXII/33, p. 622. (b) *Students in Academic Institutions* Special Series no. 249 (1968), Table 1, pp. 4–7, and no. 418 (1973), Table 1, pp. 4–6. (c) *Monthly Bulletin of Statistics, 1978*, Supplement no. 9, Table A, p. 78.

This means that transition from secondary to higher education in Israel is not an event to arouse much anxiety. This is not to say that everyone is accepted for the programme of their first preference. Professional programmes, such as medicine, law, accountancy, engineering and even social work and education are heavily over subscribed, and only a fraction, sometimes quite a small one, of the applicants are admitted. However, the distinction between admission to different programmes is not so invidious as that between admission and non-admission to university. From the point of view of mobility the main selection takes place following the nine years of compulsory schooling, between the ninth and twelfth grades of high school, when the class continuing its studies drops every year, so that only about 25–27% of the original class obtains a matriculation certificate at the end of its studies or later (see Table V).

There is further selection in the universities, since a considerable portion, perhaps one-third, do not obtain any degree, and only about 31% of those with a first degree obtain a second, and 0.7% a third degree [13].

This pattern of relatively easy movement from high school to the universities was well suited to the conditions prevailing up until the early sixties. As has been pointed out, at that time the number of those passing the matriculation examination was relatively small. It was a select group which contained a relatively large number of students with

TABLE V. Matriculants compared to ninth grade students three and four years before

Number of students in the ninth grade		Internal only		Including internal and external	
		N	%	N	%
1969/70	43,926	1972/73 10,000	23	12,000	27
		1973/74 9600	22	11,800	27
1971/72	48,090	1974/75 10,100	21	12,030	25
		1975/76 10,200	21	12,350	26

Source: Central Bureau of Statistics. *Statistical Abstract of Israel*, no. 24 (1973), Table XXII/13, p. 636; no. 27, Table XXII/26, p. 611; no. 28, Table XXII/30, p. 619.

fairly pronounced intellectual interests. They could afford to study any field they were interested in, because there were many opportunities in the rapidly expanding public services for people with a university degree, irrespective of the field of study, and for those seriously interested and successful in their studies there were good opportunities to enter research and academic teaching. Furthermore, this kind of student, choosing his programme of studies on the basis of intellectual interests, was well suited to the research-oriented universities' efforts to develop their arts and science faculties.

While the propensity of high school graduates to study at universities has remained as high as it was, the character of students and the conditions of employment have changed considerably. In 1964/65 students constituted about 13% of the 21–24 age group. This increased to about 20% in 1976/77 [14]. Twenty percent of an age cohort may not be too high a percentage, but it must include a large number of people who are unlikely to do advanced intellectual work. Their preparation may also be poorer than that of their predecessors, since the attractions of high school teaching as a profession had declined during the period in question (due to competing opportunities in research, academic teaching, and the civil service), which probably affected both the quality of high school teaching and the intellectual atmosphere of the schools, especially the newer ones.

The outlook of the students has also changed, especially in the seventies. Opportunities in research and the civil service have declined, and both ceased to be as attractive employments as they were in the fifties and sixties. As a result, there has been a growing preference for professional studies.

The universities responded to this situation by accelerating development of professional studies, especially in fields related to the humanities and social sciences, such as education, social work, and business administration, and in auxiliary medical sciences, such as pharmacy, speech therapy, and nursing (Table VI).

The demand for professional training is also discernible among graduate students. In the social sciences there is a concentration of master's level students in business administration and psychology (and within the latter in clinical psychology), which are professional fields *par excellence*. Those who study for a master's degree in other fields are also interested in courses with a practical professional content.

This is not to say that intellectual interest has disappeared among Israeli students. About half of the candidates still choose basic arts and science disciplines as their first preference in their applications for admission. If we count all those choosing economics, psychology and computer science as practical professional rather than disciplinary choices, the percentage of disciplinary choices drops to 36, which is still quite a high percentage in comparison to the availability of teaching and research careers. However,

TABLE VI. Applicants for admission and students in selected professional fields

	1964/65 students*	1970/71		1975/76		1977/78	
		Applicants	Students	Applicants	Students	Applicants	Students
N	17,178	16,181	36,136	24,190	48,565	25,699	49,514
thereof, in selected professional fields (percentages):	4.1	—	9.0	14.2**	13.7	17.9	13.5
Auxiliary medical profession	0.5	—	0.7	1.9	1.0	2.1	1.3
Social work	0.9	—	1.8	—	2.6	4.3	2.9
Education and teaching	1.5	—	3.4	9.8	7.2	7.7	5.9
Business administration and accounting	1.2	—	3.1	2.5	2.9	3.8	3.4

* Number of applicants not available.
** Not including data on Social Work.
Source: Central Bureau of Statistics. *Students in Academic Institutions* Special Series, no. 249, Table 13, pp. 40–43; no. 418, Table 10, pp. 32–35; and preprint, December, 1976. *Monthly Bulletin of Statistics*, 1978, Supplement no. 9, Table 7, pp. 86–87; and no. 11, Table 7, p. 30.

probably only a part of these choose basic arts and science because of specific interest in a disciplinary field. Some choose disciplinary studies as a kind of general education. Partly, they feel an emotional and intellectual need for further schooling, and partly they consider study at a university as a way to enter the middle and upper status groups. The university is the place where one establishes, or reinforces, personal contacts which may become useful later in life, and where one gets into interesting social circles and meets desirable companions and prospective marriage partners.

Thus the universities cater to a student body with very heterogeneous educational and occupational plans. The following seem to be the major types.

(1) Students choosing basic arts and sciences as their first preference, who have a special intellectual interest in one or several disciplinary fields. They probably intend to become high school or academic teachers, or research workers.

(2) Students studying for a disciplinary first degree probably with the intention of continuing for a second degree with pronounced professional orientation (economics, psychology, statistics, and some of the students in natural sciences, especially in chemistry and biology).

(3) Students studying for a disciplinary first degree after having been refused admission to professional courses which they chose as their first preference.

(4) Students choosing a disciplinary first degree for general educational purposes, without particular interest in any disciplinary speciality.

(5) Students taking professional first degrees of three years' duration which prepare them for a loosely defined set of professional and managerial occupations, such as education, social work, business administration, etc. Many of these keep their occupational options free, but prefer a professional course of study in order to have a practically useful qualification.

(6) Students studying for professional first degrees of four or more years' duration, such as engineering, law, medicine. These are probably highly committed to the specific career which they are training for, since their studies are intensive and highly technical.

The traditions of the higher educational system developed up until the 1950s with a view to catering only to the first, second and, to some extent (in the Technion), the sixth type of student. Education for the fifth type of student began only in the fifties, and the needs of the third and fourth types have still not been properly articulated.

The professional schools of four or more years' duration developed in the Technion and in faculties of law, medicine and engineering established since 1949. There are many questions which can be asked about the kind and quality of training provided in them; about the need for all or some of them, such as whether the country really needs three law and four medical schools; and about the desirability of having only one or several types of engineering education in the country. But these are the kind of questions that can be asked about any system of higher education and discussion of them in the Israeli context is of no special interest.

All the other types of students are educated in the basic arts and science (including social science faculties, and the professional schools of social work, education and business administration which are parts of, or closely related to, the faculties of humanities and social sciences.

Because of the great changes of the last 20 years—the transformation of the student population of the faculties of arts, social science, and science, and the establishment and growth of the professional schools affiliated to them—the programmes of these schools have been in constant flux. The changes began with the introduction of the three year bachelor's degree in the arts and newly established social sciences at the Hebrew University in 1950. As pointed out above, the original intention was to create a modified liberal arts programme. But neither students nor teachers were interested in this. The former, because after two/three years of army service they were in a hurry to learn something that would confer on them proficiency in a given field; the latter, because as research workers they had little interest in teaching students who did not specialise in their field. Therefore, as long as the intellectual orientation prevailed among the students, namely until the late fifties, the first degree became increasingly specialised, resembling the English honours degree.

However, the changing character of the student body and of career opportunities created pressures to relax the requirements for the first degree. These were not external political pressures, but a feeling of frustation in the university community in view of the large number of students unable to complete their studies in time, dragging them out for 5–6 years or more (instead of three). Beginning in 1963, this led to a series of curricular reforms which changed the character of the Israeli first degree fundamentally.

Today, this is a very flexible programme of studies which includes concentration in one or two disciplinary fields, and a varying number of courses and sequences from other fields. In some concentrations, especially in the natural sciences and some humanities, the choice between these other fields is very limited; in other concentrations, especially in the social sciences, the choice is much more wide-ranging. The aim of the studies is to give the students a good grasp of the problems, basic concepts, and ways of thinking prevailing in their field of concentration, but there are very limited requirements of mastery of techniques, acquaintance with scientific literature, and independent inquiry. The degree is more specialised than an American, and less specialised than an English Honours degree, comparable perhaps to an Australian 'pass' degree.

The evolution of this degree has been the result of compromise between what the average student was willing and able to invest in his studies and what the teachers could teach with more or less good conscience. Given the particular mix of students, which includes those choosing basic arts and sciences out of genuine interest and those choosing them as a last resort, this was probably a reasonable, perhaps even the best possible outcome. In principle the programme is flexible enough to provide opportunities for the better students to choose serious and challenging courses and become quite proficient in their field, or fields, of concentration, and at the same time to allow the weaker students to complete their studies. This, however, is not how studies for the first degree have in fact developed. The opportunity to study in depth is rarely taken advantage of, and the requirements, it seems, have been reduced to a level suitable to the weaker students; rather than aiming at excellence, the better students prefer to have an easy time.

The main reason for this is probably the decline in employment opportunities in academic teaching, scientific research, and civil service jobs requiring a first degree without further specification. This led to the previously mentioned turning away from the basic arts and sciences, and to professional fields, such as law, social work, agriculture or business administration. Since the rapid growth of student numbers came to an end, about 1972/73, the newly extended university system found itself with much unused capacity, and the universities have been anxious to attract students by satisfying student demand. This is being done through the extension of professional studies, especially those which are relatively inexpensive and in which there are no strong professional organisations to limit expansion (social work, education, agriculture, etc.). It seems that these fields are chosen by many students who previously opted for arts and sciences, not necessarily because they are genuinely interested in these professions, but because they want a degree which can be obtained in three years without too much effort, and which also confers on them a professional qualification to fall back on in case of need.

This presents a serious problem for the faculties of science, social science and humanities. Since the professional courses are oversubscribed and selection for admission is based on educational attainments, the oversubscribed professional schools get the better students, while the disciplinary fields get the weaker ones, those who obtained lower grades in the entrance examinations. This, of course, reduces the prestige and morale of the students and teachers in the basic arts and sciences. In principle, this problem could be corrected by graduate studies, but in practice this rarely occurs, because, as has been pointed out previously, in the large majority of fields there are too few prospective research workers in Israel to populate the graduate departments in the country at an adequate level.

The problem, then, is as follows. The large bulk of students who study arts, sciences and social sciences are on the average scholastically less able and less motivated than those who study in the professional schools. However, the teachers engaged in original research are primarily in the basic fields, and not in the professional schools. What is more, the educational atmosphere of the professional schools does not primarily reward intellectual originality and scholarship, but rather professional skills. Consequently, some of the best students are brought up in university schools and departments which do not present them with intellectual challenge and do not open to them scientific horizons, while the basic arts and science departments, which could present such challenge, are overrun with students who cannot cope with intellectual challenge.

Furthermore, because of declining or stagnant student numbers, the old and large departments of science and humanities cannot hope to expand and recruit new staff, and their prospects of keeping abreast with new developments in research are in jeopardy.

These developments present a problem to the Israeli research university. The ideal of combining research with teaching is only partially realised in professional schools, and it will be increasingly difficult to realise in the basic disciplinary fields, if the decline in the level of studies in them continues.

I shall attempt to make a few tentative suggestions which may help to reverse these trends. One would be to change the criteria of selection. With few exceptions, these are similar in all fields and consist of a combination of matriculation grades and test scores which is said to be a good predictor of success in academic studies. Scarce places are allocated to these scores, so that the greater the demand for a certain type of study the higher the minimum score required for admission.

This means that a selection procedure, originally designed to determine the prospects of students to succeed in a certain type of academic course, is used both to set the aptitude level of students admitted to different departments and as a means of administering social justice, namely to determine who among many suitable candidates for a course should actually be admitted.

The only argument in favour of allocating places in professional schools to the best students is that since the public cost of training students in professional schools is higher than in comparable basic fields (e.g. medical training is more expensive than training in biology), it is justifiable to allocate to these schools students who are least likely to fail. This would be a valid argument on the condition that the higher test scores (say between medicine and biology) significantly reduce likelihood of failure. This question has not been investigated, but it is likely that there is in every field a limit beyond which the likelihood of failure cannot be significantly reduced. Furthermore, this argument is valid only in fields in which graduates are almost sure to remain in their field of training, such as medicine. In fields in which the commitment of graduates is low, because of the relatively narrow scope and low prestige of the specific professional careers to which they lead, such as agriculture, education and social work, those with the highest ability may in effect be the ones most likely to change occupation, and thus waste their relatively expensive training. It is, therefore, doubtful that the present selection or, rather, allocation procedures are either rational or just.

It seems that the selection procedures should be used only for the purpose they were designed to serve, namely as a tool to determine the subjects a student can study with reasonable prospect of success. He or she should then have free choice between these subjects. In subjects in which demand for admission exceeds the capacity of the departments, places should be allocated by lottery, and/or by social considerations, e.g. army service, or—where applicable—by suitability judged on the basis of other than scholastic or intellectual attainments, such as relevant experience in the past.

In addition to being more just, such a procedure for the allocation of scarce places would create a more even distribution of talents between professional and basic fields, and thus enable the latter to improve their educational atmosphere. The elimination of the present invidious distinction between selective professional and non-selective basic departments might also help to restore some of the importance of intellectual values in the choices of fields made by students.

However, such change would not satisfy the need of students for a professional purpose in their studies. Some Israeli students may be interested in some kind of liberal arts programme, in postponing preparation for a profession to studies for the second degree or in-service training. But it is evident that the majority would like to have a professional goal quite early in their studies.

This could be provided in a number of ways. One would be to try to change educational attitudes among both students and teachers. Attempts could be made to explain to students in high schools, to candidates for admission, and to employers, that a good scientific and scholarly education is a valuable preparation for many kinds of work, even if the subject matter of the studies is not directly related to the prospective employment. Such things as the ability to find, analyse and summarise documentary material, to conceptualise an everyday problem or social situation, to define the considerations relevant for a rational decision, or a deep knowledge and mastery of language are important assets in many kinds of work. Making students and employers aware of the importance of these skills, and university teachers more conscious of the function of higher studies for students who do not intend to become professional scientists and scholars, would be one step towards changing the educational atmosphere and towards replacing the present concerns of students about passing examinations and the practical applicability of their studies with concerns about the intellectual contents of the studies. Of course, this recommendation for changing attitudes and behaviour may be regarded as merely a pious wish. However, the amount of criticism and self-criticism university education has been arousing suggests that there is a search for change among teachers and students, so that some pious wishes may actually spark action. Moreover, the kind of change suggested here has the advantage that it can be accomplished without complicated decisions or organisational restructuring.

A second measure for dealing with the developments cited above would be reconceptualisation of first and second degree studies in arts and science faculties, including articulation of their relationship to professional studies. All first and second degree programmes should be analysed from the point of view of the careers for which they may be useful, or to which they may directly lead; the programmes should be arranged so that students would have an idea how the different parts of the programme are related to different occupational plans.

The most obvious case for reform is the training of high school teachers. Although teaching is the destination of many graduates in the humanities and sciences [15], there is no awareness among the students that they are being trained for a profession (which may be why these fields find it difficult to compete with professional fields). The reason for this is the way one is trained for high school teaching in Israel. Today all major fields in the humanities and natural science faculties can lead to a career in high school teaching. The student can usually register for the two-year diploma course in teacher training in his third (last) year for the first degree, so that he or she can complete the BA or BSc course. If the student's grades are high enough he can also be admitted to graduate school; there he can follow simultaneously a one-year teacher training course, and after one additional year earn a master's degree. The latter is most useful for a teacher and in principle is a requirement for teaching in the eleventh and twelfth grades of academic high schools; the principle, however, is not always observed. Thus, the student's possibilities are: a bachelor's degree in three years; a bachelor's degree plus a teaching diploma in four years; the first or both of these two plus a master's degree in five years.

Entering students can find out about these possibilities, but it requires of them some effort to do so. There is certainly no one to draw their attention to these possibilities. Furthermore, at no point in their disciplinary studies will anyone aid these students in understanding how the mastery of certain courses, the ability to write a good term paper or to set up an experiment, may be of direct or indirect value to their future performance as teachers. The whole programme is designed so as not to identify the studies in the humanities with preparation for teaching. This is justified on the ground that intelligent students will make their own connections, and that adjusting disciplinary programmes to specific professional needs would destroy their intellectual coherence and jeopardise their value for those preparing for other professions. However, the idea that students can make their own connections is pure wishful thinking. How could they be able to make them when they do not yet have any experience of teaching or other professional work? Similarly, the threat to intellectual, coherence is imaginary, since (a) there are many ways to safeguard intellectual coherence in each discipline, and having a practical purpose in one's studies may be one of them; (b) even without any adjustments of the programmes, the mere awareness of the students and the teachers of how some parts of existing programmes might be related to career plans could greatly improve the motivation of the students and the performance of both teachers and students. Allowing some professional preparation into the degree programme would only raise the intellectual level of the first degree studies. The possibility of building in some professional training into the programme also exists at the master's level. A bachelor's degree is not sufficient disciplinary preparation for those who intend to teach in academic high schools, and the existing teacher training diploma is not a sufficient preparation for teachers in schools in which the problem of how to arouse any motivation to learn among students from pre-scientific cultural backgrounds is much more salient than the effective transmission of knowledge in specific fields. Two professional master's programmes—one combining the present disciplinary master's programme with practical preparation for teaching, and the other complementing the disciplinary background of the teacher not only with didactic skills but also with a thorough study of the psychological and sociological processes of education and cultural change—would be far more effective than the present approach according to which the student acquires pieces of his training separately and then puts them together as best as he or she can.

This model of disciplinary study for a first and second degree with built-in and explicit professional options can also be applied to other fields, such as linguistics oriented towards work in translation, biology oriented towards work in clinical microbiology or wildlife preservation. In these fields, as in teaching—and, of course, *a fortiori* in research—it is relatively easy to articulate disciplinary programmes with professional training.

Such reform might be capable of reinvigorating the existing arts and science programmes. They would still leave two categories of students difficult to accommodate in the existing frameworks, namely those more interested in receiving a liberal education consisting of a broader range of fields than provided in the present curriculum, and those refused admission to a specific first degree course and uninterested in anything else, but who still attend a university in order to gain a degree. The first category could be catered for in the universities. Although it is difficult to organise and teach a liberal arts course, it might be a worthwhile experiment to start such a programme.

There is little that the universities can do for students whose interests are purely vocational—at least at the stage of entry to the university—but cannot be admitted to the schools of their choice. They should be encouraged to attend not universities but other post-secondary colleges. With some of these now obtaining the right to confer bachelor's degrees, this alternative may become more attractive, so that this category of students may be diverted to a channel more suited to their needs than the university. Having acquired a first degree in these post-secondary schools, and perhaps also some work experience, some of these students may eventually develop an interest in the intellectual foundations or ramifications of their work and seek entrance to the university, which could be granted on as easy terms as possible.

VI. The Way the System Works

As has been pointed out, up until recently Israeli universities tended to become more and more similar to each other, or rather to the two old institutions. This imitativeness we have attributed to the strength of the research tradition represented by the old institutions and transmitted to the new ones in various ways. The difficulties encountered by the basic disciplinary fields and the rising demand for professional studies may alter the homogeneity of this tradition. The competition between institutions, which in the past led the newer institutions to attempt to build up research capacities and obtain rights to confer higher degrees, is giving way to competition for first degree students. This is taking the form of offering professional courses, providing university preparatory courses for the unqualified, and reforming the first degrees in ways which have made it an increasingly flexible course of study. Also, the proportion of graduates of the pre-State institutions—

mainly the Hebrew University—among the faculties of the newer universities is declining. All this creates needs, as well as possibilities, for the emergence of a greater diversity of academic styles and traditions than have existed until now. As has already been indicated, without some diversification of the system the present shortage of funds for expansion may seriously undermine the quality of research and instruction in the system, if it has not already done so. At present, one can only speak of the emergence of different styles. This is particularly noticeable in the smaller institutions. Bar-Ilan and Ben-Gurion are both trying to emphasise community service as an important university function, the former in combination with religious values and religious education, the latter with an orientation to the local community and its vicinity. Haifa has been trying to pioneer a small scale liberal arts course designed for outstanding students and there is a small independent school, the Jerusalem College of Technology, which combines advanced study of Talmud with engineering training, and unlike the traditional sequence of teaching basic disciplinary studies first to be followed by a technical course, teaches the technical courses first and leaves the training in the basic fields to the later stages. These are the only experiments in Israeli higher education which constitute significant departures from the prevailing pattern.

The Hebrew University of Jerusalem and Tel-Aviv University are large comprehensive universities with research facilities. They are rather similar in structure, but Jerusalem tries to emulate an elitist style of insistence on quality and tradition while the Tel Aviv style is innovative and entrepreneurial. These differences in style do not always correspond to practice, but probably have some effect on it.

So far these differences in style have not led to the emergence of significantly different academic programmes and methods of study. The reasons for this may be that the preparation of such alternatives requires free resources, careful planning and effective leadership, and all of these are extremely scarce in the Israeli academic system today. The system has been starved of funds for several years, and universities which are struggling to meet existing obligations have neither free funds nor the initiative and drive needed for launching new developments.

The institutions also have very limited resources for academic planning. Because of the strong traditions of academic self-government, there are no professional academic administrations in Israel. All positions of power and prestige are monopolised by temporary officials elected by the faculty from its own ranks. This limits the career expectations and horizon of personnel working full-time in academic administration. Their tasks are limited to registration of students, organising timetables, allocation of space, and keeping records, but do not extend to curricular and research policy. In these matters they provide staff services to the deans and rectors, but these are of limited value, because the discontinuity of policies resulting from the constant rotation of office-holders—few of whom have either the time or the incentive to become experts in academic administration and politics—discourages the investment of staff efforts in planning.

The same circumstances also prevent the emergence of effective academic leadership. The problem in this respect is not only amateurism and the short-term incumbency of officers, but also excessive participatory democracy. The veto power of the faculty assemblies and senates—consisting in the larger universities of up to about 500 people—is practically unlimited, and the behaviour of these unwieldy bodies, which operate in a completely informal manner inadequate even for meetings of 20–30 people, is completely unpredictable. To take care of routine business—some of which, such as appointments, has far-reaching policy implications—these assemblies work through a large number and extremely complicated system of committees. The complexity of the system is the result of representation and checks and balances insisted upon by the faculties in the name of participatory democracy. They make academic administration extremely time-consuming and cumbersome.

These problems were much less severe in the past. During the fifties and sixties, when the universities, even the old ones, were small and expanding rapidly, some academic leaders could attain real power. For example, during most of the fifties, the rector of the Hebrew University, Professor B. Mazar, also served as president (1953–61; he was first elected as rector in 1952). The establishment of new departments and the recruitment of relatively large numbers of new people to the university gave the rector-president enough power and support to counterbalance—at least temporarily—the endemic opposition in the university to the exercise of academic leadership. More or less similar situations existed in other institutions during their period of rapid growth.

In units of the universities, such as departments, schools and faculties, effective leadership could exist even longer. Depending on the personal relations between members of such units and their success in teaching and research, many of these could cooperate and manage their affairs reasonably well throughout the entire period. In fact, the main justification of the insistence on participatory self-government and opposition to professional administration has been the argument that the university is, and should be, no more than a loose coalition of self-governing departments. However, once expansion was halted and actually cut back, the lack of academic authority above the department level made it very difficult to shift resources from one unit to another. In principle, this can be done since deans and faculty committees have power over departments, but because these bodies are ineffective it is likely to be done in a halting and haphazard manner.

There is still widespread reluctance to curtail the prevailing participatory democracy, because the system has some compensatory advantages. Lack of effective academic leadership is to some extent counterbalanced by the relatively large number of people with some administrative and policy-making experience, and the even more widespread experience in public debate and in reaching democratic compromises. This allowed the system to be dynamic and flexible in adjusting to the expanding and changing student population during the sixties and early seventies, and to take advantage of the opportunities in research which existed at that time.

However, if the present analysis is correct, then the conditions which allowed the system to function reasonably well (although never very efficiently) in the past have now changed. There is, in fact, considerable support for the view that the universities and/or the Planning and Financing Committee of the Council for Higher Education will have to create a system which allows for effective planning and policymaking at the university and national levels. This is being manifested in various ways. Universities have set up planning units and committees during the last ten years, and the Planning and Financing Committee has been active in studying the problem. They are, justifiably, proceeding with caution, but there seems little doubt that if no decisions are reached on these issues in the very near future, the problems created by the gradual, across-the-board reduction of support for all academic activities (except courses leading to professional undergraduate level degrees) will seriously reduce the quality of education and research in the country.

VII. Higher Education and Israeli Society

There are innumerable links between higher education and society at large. One of the most important of these is the use of university studies as a channel of social mobility. University graduates expect to receive professional or administrative jobs, and in most countries, including Israel, indeed have a monopoly on such jobs. Equal opportunity of access to university studies is thus a matter of great importance in every society, and in most Western countries has been a frequent source of political controversy during the last decade or so.

The fact that access to higher education has never been an important political issue in Israel is an important key to understanding the place of higher education in this society. It was not an issue for two reasons. First of all, the policy of Israeli universities has always been to admit all minimally qualified candidates. Many university departments, but no university in Israel, have tried to pursue a policy of gaining reputation through restriction of access [16]. Indeed, as has been shown above, every minimally qualified student has always been admitted to a university, and universities have always done their best to facilitate access.

This orientation of providing everyone an opportunity to obtain education up to the highest level has been at the very core of the Israeli university tradition. As has been pointed out, the Hebrew University and the Haifa Technion—the first two institutions —were founded at a time when the country had an excess of academically trained people. This policy of building ahead of demand continued in the fifties and sixties, when the new universities were founded. As a result, access has never been a real problem. Furthermore, as has been seen, universities were quite flexible in adjusting their academic programme to the changing character and demands of the students by introducing a bachelor's degree of a rather popular kind and introducing a great variety of professional first degree courses.

As a result of these liberal policies, in 1976/77 about 20% of the cohort aged 21–24 received or were receiving university education and about 30% received some form of higher education [17]. These percentages are high by any except American standards. The rate of growth since the fifties has been one of the highest in the world. This expansion occurred without any political conflicts in, or in relation to, the universities, because the universities have always been in favour of expansion.

This tendency of the system to spread higher education in excess of economic demand has had much to do with the fact that higher education has not become an important source of class or even economic privilege in the country. For example, in 1974, salaried employees who studied for 16 years or more (that is frequently beyond a first degree) earned 48% more, and those with 13–15 years of schooling (post-secondary diplomas or first degree) earned 12% more than people with 9–12 years of education [18] (which is now the standard).

Neither is higher education a source of privilege in other spheres. Students or graduates have no privileges in the military, as they do in many countries. Except for a small number of highly selected students learning subjects approved by the army, in order to serve in jobs needed by the armed services after completion of their studies, there is no deferment of military service for academic studies. Young men and women have to serve first and study later and, subsequently, as students and graduates they have to do their reserve service under exactly the same conditions as everyone else.

Thus, the majority of students enter universities at least 2–3 years older than elsewhere. Nevertheless, they receive little support from the State. There are few and meagre stipends and these are given only to needy students with high academic attainments. Tuition fees are low, but no negligible burden for the majority of the students. A large proportion of the student body works full time and studies (officially or unofficially) part time, and of the remainder another large proportion works part time. The majority of students thus combine work with study. Services for students, such as housing, cafeterias, etc. are scarce and of medium to low standards. Student life is far from carefree.

The rewards of an academic career are also limited. Salaries have never been high, and have deteriorated considerably during the last six years in comparison to incomes from professional and administrative work. The standard of secretarial and other services which academics receive for their work is modest.

As a result of these low rewards, the attitude to higher learning has retained some of the elements of the traditional Jewish attitude to sacred learning, namely, it is considered a right and duty of everyone capable of benefiting from it and not just a means of advancement. It is an area more of shared values than of individual competition, in the sense that intellectual achievements are not regarded as a kind of self-advancement but as a contribution to a collective purpose. These circumstances have removed much of the invidiousness from educational advancement. However, in view of the increasing tendency to professionalism in higher education, these attitudes may change in the near future.

Awareness of these circumstances helps place in proper perspective one of the alleged failings of the system, namely its lack of success in recruiting students from Afro-Asian backgrounds. Between 1969 and 1974 the percentage of students from such backgrounds rose from about 13.5 to about 16 and to more than 20 in 1978/79 [19] as compared with a constant percentage fluctuating between 50–60 in compulsory elementary education. These are very low percentages and represent very slow advance. However, the interpretation of this apparently unsatisfactory performance has to take into consideration the fact that the advantages obtained through higher education are limited. Because of the great effort involved in university studies and the low rewards obtained for them, young people from poor and uneducated backgrounds have little reason to feel either attracted to such studies or discriminated against for being excluded from them. The policy at present is to create the educational prerequisites for such study among young men and women of Afro-Asian backgrounds. This is a task mainly for primary and secondary education, and there is every indication of progress in this respect. Today students of Afro-Asian background form nearly 50% of twelfth grade pupils (although not of matriculants!) and they are increasing their participation in non-university post-secondary education. For example, in 1977/78 they were 39% of the students in teacher training colleges. There are at present no practical suggestions beyond the kinds of things already done, such as preparatory courses and educational research and experimentation about how the universities through efforts of their own can accelerate the closing of the ethnic gap. Considering the lack of knowledge about these things, the concentration of efforts to extend and improve education at all levels, and not particularly at universities, and to prevent the growth of invidious class differences between people possessing different amounts of education, is probably more promising a policy than trying to increase the participation of groups underrepresented at universities through administrative measures, such as open admission or quota systems.

NOTES

This paper was written in 1979. Since from then until now, Israeli higher education has not changed significantly. I have not made extensive changes in the paper. Some of the statistics have been updated, and some formulations slightly changed, but essentially this is the same paper as the 1979 one. The question of how it is possible to maintain high quality research and teaching in a system with an increasingly heterogeneous student population and an egalitarian teaching body—which seemed to be central in 1979—is still central today in Israel and several other countries.

I am deeply indebted to Michael Inbar for his comments and suggestions and to Judith Nevo for her assistance with the research.

[1] See M. BUBER, B. FEIWEL & C. WEIZMANN (1902) *Eine Jüdische Hochschule* (Berlin, Jüdischer Verlag); H. SACHER (1918) *A Hebrew University for Jerusalem* (The Zionist Organization, London Bureau) (first printed 1915).

[2] Buber, Feiwel & Weizmann also stressed the importance of such an institution for the absorption of Jewish students and scholars discriminated against in many European countries. All the proponents of these

schemes also referred to the services to be performed by the university to the local community, but these were expectations of only a very general nature.

[3] In this respect, there was no difference between the German and the French universities.

[4] In 1932–42 nearly 12% of the Jewish immigrants belonged to the liberal professions, which was a very high percentage by the standards of those years. D. GUREVICH, A. GERTZ & R. BACHI (1944) *The Jewish Population of Palestine: immigration, demographic structure and natural growth*, Table 28, p. 72 (Jerusalem, Department of Statistics of the Jewish Agency for Palestine).

[5] On the Humboldtian idea of the university, see SIR ERIC ASHBY (1967) The future of the nineteenth century idea of a university, *Minerva*, 6, pp. 3–17.

[6] Central Bureau of Statistics (1952) *Statistical Abstract of Israel*, no. 3 (1952), Table 10, p. 12; no. 13 (1962), Table II/12, p. 46; no. 28 (1977), Table XXII/30, p. 619. The percentage among the Arab population was even lower.

[7] See LYDIA ARAN (1970) *Government Policy Toward Higher Education in Israel: preliminary study* (Jerusalem, Center for Policy Studies) and DAN FELSENTHAL (1967) *Mediniut Memshelet Israel Klapei Ha'mosdot l'haskala Gvoha v'Hinnukh Govoah (Policy of the Israeli Government Towards Higher Education)*. Unpublished master's thesis (Hebrew), Department of Political Science, the Hebrew University, Jerusalem.

[8] The description is based on data from an unpublished study of the academic profession in Israel by Ms Yehudith Nevo.

[9] 71% who obtained at least one of their degrees in the country and 35% of the remaining 29% who were not directly recruited from abroad, but had lived and worked in the country at least three years before entering the academic career (see Table 3, in I).

[10] P. RITTERBAND (1978) *Education, Employment & Migration*, p. 5, ASA, Rose Monograph Series (London, Cambridge University Press).

[11] D. DE D. PRICE, Measuring the size of science, *Proceedings of Israel Academy of Science, 1969/70*, BOS, and Table no. 5, p. 109, Israel Academy of Science, Jerusalem, 1970.

[12] From the *Budget Proposal for Higher Education for 1979 and Explanation*, Pamphlet 22, submitted by the Minister of Education to the Knesset, Jerusalem, March 1979.

[13] In 1969/70, 4,064 obtained first degrees; 1,259 second degrees in 1972/73, and 298 obtained third degrees in 1975/76. See Central Bureau of Statistics, *Statistical Abstract of Israel*, no. 27 (1976), Table XXI/33, p. 618; no. 28, Table XXII/39, p. 628.

[14] Central Bureau of Statistics, *Statistical Abstract of Israel*, no. 16 (1965), Table II/14, p. 38 & XX/25, p. 593; no. 29 (1978), Table II/20, p. 56 & XXII/38, p. 685.

[15] According to an unpublished survey conducted by Ms Ziva Daniel of the School of Education of the Hebrew University, 14.4% of the male and 39.9% of the female students in the faculty of science, and 22.2% of the male and 41.4% of the female students in the faculty of humanities, registered in the teachers' training courses in the Hebrew University of Jerusalem in the 1976/77 academic year.

[16] The University of Haifa has recently adopted a policy of restricting entry but it still has to be seen how it will work out in the long run.

[17] Central Bureau of Statistics, *Statistical Abstract of Israel*, no. 28 (1977), Table XXII/31, p. 620; no. 29 (1978), Table II/20, p. 56, and Table XXII/38, p. 685.

[18] Central Bureau of Statistics, *Survey of Incomes of Salaried Employees*, Special Series, no. 546, Table 11/a. In the United States college graduates earned 58% more, and college graduates with at least one year of graduate school earned 78% more than high school graduates (possessing full 12 years of schooling) in 1968 —calculated from C. JENCKS, *Inequality* (New York, Basic Books), p. 222, Table 4. According to Psacharopoulos using different data, wages of those possessing higher education were 51% higher than those possessing secondary education in Israel. The corresponding differences in other countries were: US—65%; Canada—83%; Great Britain—61%; Norway—53%; The Netherlands—74%; G. Psacharopoulos with the assistance of K. Hinchliffe (1973) *Returns to Higher Education*, p. 185 (San Francisco, Jossey-Bass).

[19] Council of Higher Education, The Planning and Grants Committee, *Higher Education in Israel: Statistical Abstract*, Jerusalem, 1979, Table 10, p. 15. *Statistical Abstract of Israel*, 1984, no. 35, p. 663, Table XXII/40.

This paper, which is published for the first time in English, is part of a book on education in Israel, published in Hebrew by Hakkibutz Hamenchad Publishers and in German by Klett-Cotta, both in co-operation with the Van Leer Jerusalem Institute. We are grateful to the Van Leer Foundation for permission to publish the paper.

Part III

ACHIEVEMENT AND THE ISSUE OF EQUAL OPPORTUNITY

10.

Determinants of Early Educational Career in Israel: Further Evidence for the Sponsorship Thesis

Abraham Yogev

This paper examines the argument that school sponsorship mechanisms are, relative to significant others' influence (SOI), a more effective determinant of educational plans and attainment in societies geared toward sponsored mobility. This argument has been previously validated with respect to aspirations for higher education in Israel. The present paper analyzes the determinants of curriculum placement in Israeli high schools. In particular, it examines the relative impact of SOI versus ability grouping at the junior high level. A path analysis of longitudinal data for a representative sample of junior high students shows that their aspirations for specific high school training are determined mainly by SOI. Yet, their curriculum placement in the tenth grade is affected by ability grouping much more than by SOI or aspirations. These findings are supported by additional discriminant analyses of high school aspiration tracks and track placement. It is also found that the high school tracking of students of Oriental origin is more heavily influenced by institutional mechanisms than the tracking of their Ashkenazi counterparts. The above processes are interpreted as indicative of a transitional period in the formation of educational careers in sponsorship-oriented systems. In such systems, sponsorship mechanisms may determine educational attainment at all school levels, but their cumulative effect on aspirations is apparent only at an advanced stage of schooling. Comparative studies which may further validate this thesis are proposed.

This paper concerns a recently proposed model of educational attainment in societies geared toward sponsored mobility. The model (Yuchtman and Samuel, 1975), which compares institutional with interpersonal determinants of educational attainment, has been tested with respect to aspirations for higher education of Israeli youth. The present paper attempts to assess the validity of this model, and of its underlining propositions, for earlier stages of the educational career. Specifically, it examines the relative impact of institutional versus interpersonal variables on aspirations for secondary schooling and on curriculum placement in Israeli secondary education.

The model proposed by Yuchtman and Samuel was developed out of the "Wisconsin model" of aspiration formation. Various studies based upon longitudinal data for a cohort of Wisconsin high school seniors (Sewell, Haller and Portes, 1969; Sewell, Haller and Ohlendorf, 1970; Woelfel and Haller, 1971; Hauser, 1972; Haller and Portes, 1973; Sewell and Hauser, 1975) stress the interpersonal effects of socialization on youth's status aspirations and attainments. In particular, they show that a crucial determinant of educational aspirations is "significant others' influence" (SOI)—or the respondent's perceived encouragement for post secondary education from parents, peers and teachers. The effects of socioeconomic status, mental ability and academic performance on the aspirations of these adolescents are largely mediated by SOI, and the direct effects of the latter on aspirations exceed the impact exerted by any of the antecedent variables. Though it has been suggested that SOI may reflect in part the respondent's projection of personal goals onto the parents (Kerckhoff and Huff, 1974), the Wisconsin findings indicate that the perception of encouragement from significant reference groups is a powerful factor in the process of educational attainment.

An earlier version of this paper was presented at the 1980 annual meeting of the American Sociological Association, New York. The paper is based on data collected for the research project on Israeli junior high schools, which was sponsored by the Israeli Ministry of Education and Culture, and directed by Michael Chen, Arieh Lewy and Chaim Adler. I am grateful to Michael Chen and Drora Kfir for providing the data and for their helpful advice, to Ephraim Yaar for his comments on an earlier draft, and to the anonymous referees for their suggestions. The expressed views and any errors that remain are the sole responsibility of the author. Address correspondence to Dr. Abraham Yogev, School of Education, Tel Aviv University, Tel Aviv, Israel.

Yuchtman and Samuel argue, however, that the Wisconsin model is not universally applicable, but rather applies to contest-oriented societies. They use Turner's (1960) distinction between "contest" mobility systems, which maintain an open race in education by means of similar and relatively non-selective educational programs throughout the entire schooling process, and "sponsored" mobility systems, which regulate the participation in the schooling process from its early stages. Obviously, these two concepts constitute an ideal typology. For instance, in the United States, which is used by Turner as a model of contest orientation, means such as tracking are used as sponsorship mechanisms by the school system (Kerckhoff, 1976; Rosenbaum, 1976, 1980). Nevertheless, these concepts reflect the tendencies of various educational systems to emphasize different means of educational mobility. These different emphases may affect the cross-cultural applicability of the Wisconsin socialization model. As noted by Yuchtman and Samuel, the majority of youth in contest-oriented societies graduate from high school and are considered qualified for higher education. This situation increases the impact of socialization factors on educational plans. Encouragement from significant reference groups therefore becomes a major determinant of educational aspirations, as evidenced by the American case. In contrast, societies practicing sponsored mobility develop educational systems characterized by high selectivity of students and by different types of high schools and graduation diplomas, only some of which qualify the student for higher education. In such societies, institutional constraints—*i.e.*, passing the selection procedures of the educational system, studying in a particular high school, achieving high grades, and being accredited with the necessary diplomas—determine status aspirations much more than do the interpersonal effects of significant others. To examine this last point, Yuchtman and Samuel report on a survey of educational and occupational aspirations of Israeli youth upon termination of their compulsory military service, which precedes college enroll-

ment. A path analysis shows that, controlling for socioeconomic status and ethnicity, the educational aspirations of these youth are primarily determined by institutional factors (type of high school, years of schooling and attainment of a governmental matriculation diploma), whereas the effect of SOI on aspirations is minor.

These findings have been supported by a later study of Israeli urban high school students (Nachmias, 1977), whose aspirations were also found to be only moderately determined by SOI. There is also some cross-cultural evidence for the sponsorship thesis of career-formation in education. Studies of high school students in Costa Rica, where a highly selective educational system is maintained, have found that SOI does not exert a significant effect on educational aspirations (Hansen and Haller, 1973; Yogev and Schrift, 1979). Recent studies on educational attainment in France, characterized by sharp mechanisms of selection and sponsorship (Bourdieu and Passeron, 1977), have established curriculum tracking in the secondary school as a major institutional mechanism of the sponsorship process. These studies (Garnier and Hout, 1976; Hout and Garnier, 1979) have shown that the direct effect of socioeconomic status on curriculum placement, and of the latter on subsequent educational attainment, are stronger than those found by studies on curriculum tracking in the United States (Heyns, 1974; Alexander and McDill, 1976; Alexander, Cook, and McDill, 1978). Even in the United States, it has been found that interpersonal determinants of educational attainment are less significant for groups which presumably experience a sponsored educational process. The effect of SOI on educational aspirations is much less pronounced for black than for white adolescents (Porter, 1974).

Most of the studies sustaining the sponsorship thesis report on students who are already in high school or who have completed their secondary education. Yuchtman and Samuel suggest that institutional effects would be stronger than the corresponding SOI effects in a sponsored education system, especially in the attainment of higher education. In their words, "within a sponsored-mobility context, the more advanced one is in the schooling process, the greater the cumulative effect of institutional directives and the less the relevance of interpersonal guidance for future career plans" (1975:522–3). According to this rationale, institutional effects would be more pronounced on plans for higher education while SOI would be a relatively more effective determinant of aspirations for secondary schooling. One should nevertheless consider the fact that sponsorship systems tend to develop mechanisms of educational sponsorship, such as differential training programs, at all levels of the schooling process. The student's experience of sponsorship thus starts at a relatively young age. It is therefore reasonable to hypothesize that in sponsorship systems, the effects of institutional selection would still be stronger than the corresponding SOI effects even with respect to aspirations for and placement in secondary schools. In this paper we examine this hypothesis in the context of the Israeli system of secondary education.

SPONSORSHIP IN ISRAELI SECONDARY EDUCATION

Until a decade ago, the Israeli system of education consisted of three levels: primary school (eight years of study, between the ages 6–14), secondary school (2–4 years of study, varying by type of school), and higher education, including both undergraduate and graduate academic training. The school reform of 1968 reduced primary schooling to six years and divided the secondary system into two levels: junior high schools, known as "intermediate schools" (3 years of study, between the ages 12–15, corresponding to the Israeli law of compulsory education up to the age of 15), and high schools (3 additional years of study, up to the age of 18). About half of Israeli schools already operate according to the reformed system.

The sponsorship mechanisms applying to the higher level of Israeli secondary education have already been described by Yuchtman and Samuel. These consist mainly of a differential tracking system, based on three types of high schools: (a) the academic preparatory school, (b) the vocational (either technological or agricultural) high school, which both administer 3-year educational programs; and (c) the vocational training school—a broad category of schools and organized programs which provide specific occupational training until the age of 16 or 17, frequently on a work-study basis. Curricular differences among these three tracks symbolize the extent to which each prepares its students for higher education. A prerequisite for university enrollment in Israeli is the "Matriculation Diploma", provided by the Ministry of Education and Culture to citizens eighteen years old who have successfully passed a series of examinations on specific curricular subjects. Though the matriculation tests are universally open, their content is geared toward graduates of academic high schools. All such graduates take the matriculation exams, and usually have a good chance of passing them. Only the bright vocational high school students, who are selected at the age of 15 or 16 to study in a specific "vocational matriculation" track, take the government tests at the age of 18. The rest are given a high school graduation diploma, which is insufficient for university candidacy. The vocational training programs do not prepare their students at all for the matriculation examinations. As a result, an overwhelming majority of the students in Israeli universities are graduates of the academic high schools.

The three main high school tracks are usually offered in separate schools. Schools which offer both academic and vocational programs are still relatively few. The decision about the specific high school training and, indirectly about the opportunity for higher education, is therefore made between the ages 14 to 15, upon completion of studies in the junior high school. Since the school reform, this decision has actually been shifted into the hands of the educational counselors of junior high schools.

A primary objective in the establishment of junior high schools was the desegregation of students by social class and ethnicity. In the previous school structure, the majority of primary school graduates from lower strata and of Jewish Oriental origin (*i.e.*, whose parents or grandparents were immigrants from Asian or African countries) either did not pursue secondary schooling or enrolled in vocational schools. In contrast, the majority of graduates of the prestigious Ashkenazi origin (*i.e.*, whose families originated in European or American countries) enrolled in academic high schools. Junior high schools, which extended compulsary education up to the age of 15, were therefore based on the principle of intermixing students from various homogeneous neighborhoods within the municipal borders. But in order to overcome variations in students' abilities, the schools were allowed to base their educational program, in part, on ability grouping. Major subjects of study are thus frequently administered on four levels—three regular ability groups, and a fourth especially designed for slow learners. Each year students are assigned to a specific ability group in each subject according to their academic performance during the previous year. Though yearly shifts in the grouping of students do occur, curricular differences among the various groups lower the probability of such changes. Shifts in groupings within the same academic year usually require the recommendations of both the subject teacher and the school counselor.

Early in their ninth year of schooling, students are encouraged by the educational counselor to register for a specific type of high school according to their academic achievement and personal tendencies. Since the students' grades in each subject do not reflect the level on which the latter was taught, counselors tend to base their recommendations on the students' ability groupings in addition to their grades. Though the counselors do not have the power to decide students' educational careers, their recommendations are usually followed by the students and their parents. This is especially true for low status families, who have less knowledge about available educational opportunities. Empirical studies (Chen and Kfir, 1977, 1979) reveal that counselors have more contacts with students of Oriental origin and of the lower ability groups, and that

such contacts are related (after controlling for academic achievement) to subsequent decreases in students' self image and educational aspirations. Also, students who have frequent contacts with counselors tend to be placed in a lower high school track than other students with similar academic achievements.

The above description shows the significance of ability grouping as a major sponsorship mechanism at the junior high level and indicates that counseling may be one of the important mechanisms linking this institutional stratification to individual outcome. The ability groups in which students are placed may determine the type of high school in which they will later enroll and, subsequently, their opportunity for higher education. Ability grouping may be viewed as a mechanism of continuous sponsorship. It is gradually applied to the determination of students' status within the junior high school, as well as to the final evaluation of their opportunity for further schooling. For an empirical assessment of the effects of this sponsorship mechanism, therefore, it is crucial to determine the extent to which ability grouping directly affects the educational career of junior high students, relative to the direct impact of interpersonal factors such as encouragement from significant others. We shall estimate these effects with respect to (a) the high school track to which junior high students aspire, and (b) the high school track in which they are actually placed, after graduation from the junior high school.

METHODS

Sample and Data

Data analyzed in this study are taken from a large research project on junior high schools (Chen, Lewy, and Adler, 1978), the objective of which was to evaluate various aspects of the Israeli school reform. This project is based primarily on longitudinal data collected from adolescents who started their studies in junior high schools in 1972, and completed them in 1974. A stratified sample of 19 junior high schools was selected by the criteria of community type, achievement level of entering students, and school title (state

Table 1. Intercorrelations, Means and Standard Deviations of Variables (N = 1891)

	X_1	X_2	X_3	X_4	X_5	X_6	X_{6a}	X_{6b}	X_7	X_8
X_1: Father's Education	—	.392	.019	.488	.378	.293	.241	.256	.278	.375
X_2: Ethnic Origin		—	−.065	.458	.235	.168	.101	.181	.142	.267
X_3: Sex			—	−.052	.056	.166	.170	.112	.195	.210
X_4: Academic Performance				—	.665	.359	.329	.280	.379	.506
X_5: Ability Grouping					—	.414	.376	.327	.434	.567
X_6: SOI (Index)						—	.841	.854	.675	.438
X_{6a}: Parental Influence							—	.436	.684	.435
X_{6b}: Peers' Influence								—	.464	.309
X_7: High School Aspiration									—	.473
X_8: High School Placement										—
$\bar{x}$	7.94	0.48	0.52	59.3	9.18	5.08	2.55	2.53	2.49	2.31
SD	4.14	0.50	0.50	16.1	2.62	1.04	0.60	0.62	0.62	0.63

school versus religious state school). According to these criteria, the sample is representative of the 84 junior high schools which were already operating in 1972 in the Jewish sector. All 3,129 first-year students of the selected schools were included in the sample. These students were approached three times—in their seventh, eighth and ninth year of schooling. During the third trimester of each academic year they completed self-administered questionnaires concerning their attitudes toward various aspects of school experience and their future career plans. They were also examined each year through a battery of achievement tests in various curricular subjects. Additional information on the students' work or high school placement (tenth grade) in 1975 was collected from students and their schools. Altogether, there were 2,234 students on whom four-year longitudinal data were collected.[1]

Two of the 19 original schools were excluded from the present analysis as they do not practice ability grouping.[2] Respon-

dents for whom complete data on the variables specified below were unavailable were also excluded. The sample used in the present study thus consists of 1,891 respondents.

Variables and Measurements

The variables used for the construction of the path model and their specific measurements are as follows (see Table 1).

X_1: *Father's Education.* Father's schooling, the only direct common indicator of socioeconomic status available, was originally categorized by six levels, ranging from primary to higher education. The middle of the range of years of schooling was entered for each category and used in the present analysis.

X_2: *Ethnic Origin.* The various waves of Jewish immigration to Israel have created an ethnic stratification according to countries of origin. In general, a distinction is made between "Oriental" and "Ashkenazi" Jews. The former migrated during the early 1950s from Asian and African countries, primarily Moslem ones, and they constitute the less prestigious ethnic group. The latter trace their origin to European or American countries. Socioeconomic gaps between the two groups are still great. Educational inequalities between them are reflected in prevalent types of secondary schooling, in the achievement of the matriculation diploma, and in the general level of educational attainment (Smooha and Peres, 1975). In this study ethnic origin was dichotomized

---

[1] The reduction of sample size is due mainly to the high dropout rate from junior high schools. Some of these schools channel their weakest students after a year or two to special schools, while in others there is a voluntary dropout of low achievers. Comparing the first wave of respondents with the final sample, for which complete longitudinal data were obtained, Chen et al. (1978:26–28) found that the sample's attrition caused a small increase in average socioeconomic status and academic performance. The final sample should therefore be regarded as representing junior high graduates.

[2] The two excluded schools have additional unusual features, and they attract a student population which is different in several respects from the rest of the sample. It was therefore impossible to use the data from these two schools for comparison with the schools which practice ability grouping.

by the father's country of birth into Asian and African countries (coded 0) versus all other countries including Israel (coded 1).

X_3: *Sex*. This variable was coded 0 for male respondents and 1 for females. Since girls tend to prefer academic over vocational training, it is expected that this variable will exert a positive effect on the high school track aspired to and attained.

X_4: *Academic Performance (Grade 7)*. As stated, each year the respondents took a battery of tests on curricular subjects, especially designed and standardized for the assessment of their academic achievements. Given towards the end of the seventh grade, the tests were composed of items in the subjects of Hebrew, English, mathematics, science and social sciences (history, geography and civic studies). Items reflected both knowledge and the ability to comprehend, abstract and apply specific information. Inter-item reliabilities of the tests, measured by Cronbach's α, ranged from .820 to .925. For the purpose of this study, overall academic performance was measured by the percentage of items correctly answered in all standardized tests.[3] This variable reflects academic achievement, which is usually measured in status attainment studies by GPA. It may also somewhat reflect academic ability or intelligence, which was not measured separately in this study.

X_5: *Ability Grouping (Grade 8)*. An overall grouping score was constructed from the ability groups of each respondent in three major subjects: Hebrew, English, and mathematics. Grouping scores for each subject ranged from 1 (lowest ability group) to 4 (highest). A simple sum of the scores resulted in an index ranging from 3 to 12.

X_6: *Significant Others' Influence (Grade 8)*. SOI indices used in status attainment studies usually measure the perception of general encouragement for further education from parents, peers and teachers. The index constructed here reflects the perceived encouragement from parents and peers with respect to type of secondary schooling. It is based on two questions: (a) "What do your parents want you to do after graduation from the junior high school?" and (b) "What does your best friend intend to do after graduation?". Responses were trichotomized as follows: (1) work or enroll in a work-study program (*i.e.*, a vocational training school); (2) study in a vocational high school—either technological or agricultural; (3) study in an academic high school. Scores were summed up for the SOI index which ranges from 2 to 6. Individual item scores were also used in the path analysis, alternatively to the index, in order to assess separately the effects of parental influence (X_{6a}) and peers' influence (X_{6b}).

X_7: *High School Aspiration (Grade 8)*. Measured by the question, "What are your plans after graduation from the junior high school?", this variable was coded into three categories, identical to those used for SOI measurement. Aspirations were measured in the eighth grade instead of the final ninth, since high school registration preceeded data collection in the final year.

X_8: *High School Placement (Grade 10)*. The respondents' whereabouts during the first high school year were classified into three levels: (1) work, or neither work nor study; (2) study in a vocational high school or a vocational-training school;[4] and (3) study in an academic high school.

It should be noted that high school tracks are treated as an ordinal trichotomy for the last three variables (X_6 to X_8). While this treatment is based on high school stratification, as described earlier, it assumes that the tracks differ among themselves only in some hierarchal sense. This assumption will be examined later in the analysis.[5]

---

[3] The correlation between respondents' performance in the tests given during the seventh and eighth grades is .835. Academic performance in the seventh grade was used in order to facilitate the causal ordering of variables in the path model.

[4] Since shifts from vocational high schools to vocational-training schools and programs occur frequently after the freshman year, both school types were included in the same category.

[5] It should also be noted that using path analysis leads to the treatment of the track variables as interval measures, though they are not inherently interval. The aspiration- and placement-tracks are the two major dependent variables in the path model. Because of the statistical difficulties involved in ordinary least squares analysis of dichotomous dependent variables, it was impossible to recode the tracks

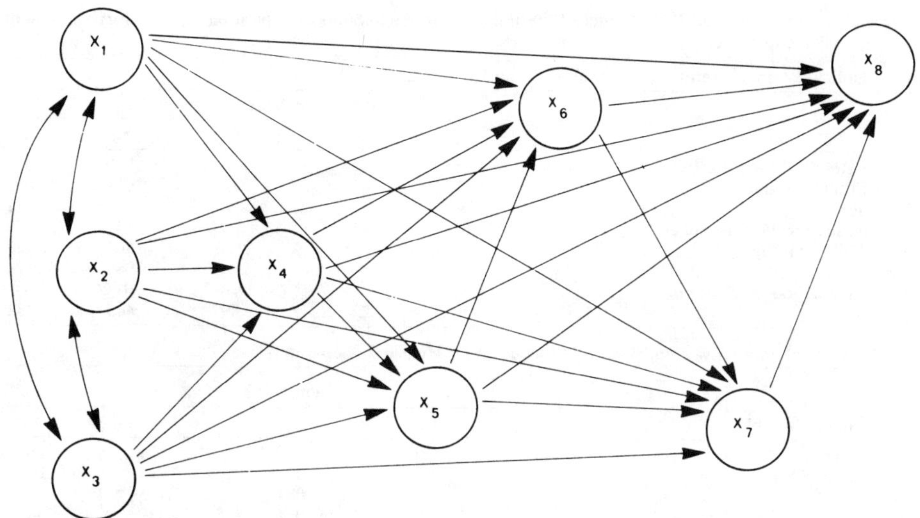

Figure 1. Path Model Depicting Determinants of High School Aspiration and Placement

X_1: Father's Education
X_2: Ethnic Origin
X_3: Sex: Female
X_4: Academic Performance (Grade 7)
X_5: Ability Grouping (Grade 8)
X_6: Significant Others' Influence (Grade 8)
X_7: High School Aspiration (Grade 8)
X_8: High School Placement (Grade 10)

ANALYSIS

The analysis includes three parts. The first examines the path model which depicts the determinants of high school aspiration and placement for the entire sample. Secondly, the assumption of linearity in the determination of aspiration and placement tracks is examined by a discriminant analysis. Finally, sex and ethnic variations in determinants of aspirations and track placement are assessed by separate regression analyses.

---

into dummy variables. Such recoding would have also greatly reduced the variation among respondents (see the discriminant analysis reported later), and it would have limited the comparisons across sex and ethnic groups, examined later in the analysis (see Goldberger, 1964, for statistical problems of regression equations involving binary dependent variables). It was therefore decided to retain the original trichotomous coding of X_7 and X_8 and, subsequently, of the SOI measure as well. The results obtained in the path analysis should therefore be regarded as merely an approximation of the determination of high school aspiration and placement.

The Path Model

The causal ordering of variables for the path analysis was based, in part, on the chronological order of data collection for specific variables. The model depicted in Figure 1 has three exogenous variables: father's education, ethnic origin, and sex. These variables, especially the first two, are expected to affect the respondent's academic performance in the seventh grade. The latter will presumably affect the respondent's ability grouping in the following year. Since ability grouping is the most overt indicator of academic status, it may be expected to exert a direct effect on SOI which, in turn, will affect high school aspiration. Finally, high school aspiration will affect the respondent's high school placement in the tenth grade. This model enables comparison of the direct effects exerted by ability grouping versus SOI on high school aspiration and placement. Such a comparison is necessary for the assessment of institutional effects (repre-

Table 2. Coefficients for Path Model: Determinants of High School Aspiration (X_7) and High School Placement (X_8)

A. Significant Others' Influence Measured by an Index (X_6)

	Dependent Variables					
Antecedent Variables	X_4	X_5	X_6	X_7	X_8	X_8[a]
X_1: Father's Education	.367	.088	.124	.026*	.089	.093
X_2: Ethnic Origin	.311	−.103	.011*	−.031*	.067	.062
X_3: Sex	−.039*	.083	.154	.096	.157	.172
X_4: Academic Performance		.673	.116	.097	.144	.159
X_5: Ability Grouping			.278	.126	.307	.328
X_6: SOI				.570	.086	.178
X_7: High School Aspiration					.162	—
R²	.324	.461	.221	.497	.445	.432

B. Parental Influence (X_{6a}) and Peers' Influence (X_{6b}) Measured Separately

	Dependent Variables				
Antecedent Variables	X_{6a}	X_{6b}	X_7	X_8	X_8[a]
X_1: Father's Education	.091	.119	.030*	.091	.095
X_2: Ethnic Origin	−.052	.067	−.009*	.074	.073
X_3: Sex	.159	.103	.084	.155	.166
X_4: Academic Performance	.157	.043*	.074	.139	.149
X_5: Ability Grouping	.240	.232	.122	.309	.326
X_{6a}: Parental Influence			.523	.126	.196
X_{6b}: Peers' Influence			.160	−.002*	.020*
X_7: High School Aspiration				.135	—
R²	.186	.142	.537	.450	.441

* Coefficient is less than twice its standard error.
[a] Reduced-form equation with X_7 excluded. See text for explanation

sented by the school experience of grouping) versus interpersonal effects on the formation of educational career at the secondary level.

The coefficients obtained for the model are presented in Table 2. The fit of the model may be judged partly by the extent of explained variance in the last two dependent variables. This model explains 50 to 54 percent of the variance in high school aspiration (depending upon whether SOI is included in the equation as an index or as separate indicators) and about 45 percent of the variance in high school placement.

Father's education and ethnic origin have a significant impact on the student's academic performance in the first junior-high grade. The gross effects of these social background variables on ability grouping in the eighth grade (see correlations in Table 1) are transmitted mainly through the strong direct effect of academic performance. Ability grouping is the most important determinant of SOI, regardless of whether the latter is measured by a composite index or by two separate indicators of perceived encouragement from parents and peers. To a much lower degree, SOI is also determined by the student's sex (females are more encouraged to pursue their schooling in the academic track), academic performance,[6] and father's education.

The most interesting findings concern the last two stages of the model. In contrast to the minor SOI effect on aspirations for higher education in Israel, the SOI measurement of this study is the best predictor of high school aspiration. The direct effects of all other antecedent variables on aspirations are much lower in comparison to the SOI impact. The perception of encouragement from significant others accounts independently for about half of the explained variance in aspirations for high school training ($R^2_{7.123456} - R^2_{7.12345} = .252$).[7]

---

[6] As shown in the bottom part of Table 2, academic performance is related to the perception of parental influence much more than to peers' influence.

[7] The independent contribution of SOI to the variance explained in aspirations is even higher when the

As shown in the bottom part of Table 2, this impact is due mainly to the direct effect of parental influence.

SOI is, however, among the least significant determinants of high school placement. Curriculum tracking in the first high school year, the tenth grade, is determined primarily by the respondent's ability grouping in the junior high school. High school aspiration, the respondent's sex and academic performance during the seventh grade also have moderate effects on high school placement. But the magnitude of the effect exerted by each of these variables is about half of that generated by ability grouping.[8]

The model thus indicates that interpersonal effects are stronger with respect to high school aspiration, while the experience of sponsorship (via the mechanism of ability grouping) has the greater effect on actual high school placement. However, the last two equations of the model are noncomparable from a statistical standpoint, due to the inclusion of high school aspiration in the latter. To overcome this comparability problem a reduced-form equation, which excludes the aspiration variable, has been computed for high school placement. The findings, presented in the last columns of Table 2, do not substantially change the results depicted above. The direct effect of SOI on curriculum placement increases from .086 to .178.[9] But this effect is still much lower than the marked influence of ability grouping on high school placement.

---

two separate SOI indicators are included in the equation simultaneously: $R^2_{7.123456_a6_b} - R^2_{7.12345} = .293$.

[8] Additional analyses were conducted in order to examine (a) the possibility that the effect of ability grouping on high school tracking is not entirely linear, and (b) the probability of an interactive influence of ability grouping and SOI on tracking. These analyses were based, first, on the inclusion of ability groups as dummy variables in the equation for high school placement. Interactions between SOI and these dummy variables were then added to a second equation. Each of these two equations increased the proportion of explained variance in high school tracking by less than one percent, in comparison with variance explained by the simpler equation in Table 2. The effect of ability grouping should therefore be regarded as linear.

[9] As shown in the bottom part of Table 2 (last two columns), the SOI effect on high school placement is due almost entirely to the perception of parental influence.

Discriminant Analysis of Tracks

The results of the path model are based on the treatment of high school aspiration and placement as ordinal trichotomous variables. This treatment assumes that the tracks differ among themselves only in some hierarchal sense. Yet, it is conceivable that the aspiration for specific tracks, or the actual placement in various tracks, is subject to different processes. It is possible that students who aspire to a specific track, or those who are placed in a certain track, are more heavily influenced by interpersonal factors, while others are more influenced by institutional variables. To examine this possibility, discriminant analysis was performed on tracks involved in both aspiration and placement. This multivariate procedure distinguishes among groups of respondents by an entered set of discriminating variables, without assuming an a-priori order of the groups (Klecka, 1975). The respondents were grouped by their aspiration and placement tracks, and each of the two sets of tracks was discriminated by variables X_1 through X_6 simultaneously.

Though two discriminant functions (one less than the number of tracks) were extracted in both analyses, only the first function of each analysis was statistically significant. The results for these first functions are presented in Table 3. The discriminating power of both functions is substantial, as indicated by the relatively low Wilks' Lambda coefficients and the high canonical correlations.[10] The results reveal, however, very similar patterns to those found in the path analysis. The discriminant function for the aspiration tracks is loaded mainly by SOI. The associated group centroids (which are the mean discriminant function scores for the tracks) indicate that the tracks are ordered with respect to the SOI-weighted function in exactly the same hierarchy as in the path model. An identical order is obtained

---

[10] The larger Wilks' Lambda is, the less discriminating power is present in the function. For comparison, each of the second functions extracted in our analyses yielded a lambda coefficient of about .99. The canonical correlations obtained are between the set of discriminating variables and two dummies constructed from the three tracks.

Table 3. Discriminant Analyses of Aspired and Attained High School Tracks: Results for First Functions

Standardized Discriminant Function Coefficients	High School Aspiration Tracks (X_7)	High School Placement Tracks (X_8)
X_1: Father's Education	.047	.177
X_2: Ethnic Origin	−.062	.117
X_3: Sex	.219	.336
X_4: Academic Performance	.172	.286
X_5: Ability Grouping	.240	.537
X_6: SOI	.836	.326
Wilks' Lambda	.486	.562
p (X^2 test)	<.001	<.001
Canonical Correlation	.712	.658
Group Centroids		
(1) Work or vocational training	−2.022	−1.705
(2) Vocational high school	−.931	−.467
(3) Academic high school	.897	.976

among the high school placement tracks, but the discriminant function, as in the path results, is weighted primarily by ability grouping and only to a lesser extent by SOI and sex. The two discriminant analyses, therefore, sustain the hierarchy of the three tracks with respect to the major SOI effect on track-aspiration versus the large direct influence of ability grouping on actual track placement.

Sex and Ethnic Variations

The above findings apply to the entire sample which contains male and female students from both the minority (Oriental) and majority (Ashkenazi) ethnic groups. Numerous studies in the United States have dealt with sex and ethnic differences in the educational attainment process.[11] Though these studies vary in sampling, measurement and variables employed, they usually indicate that SOI affects aspirations and attainment for white female students to a larger extent than for white males, and that whites of both sexes are more heavily influenced by SOI than either male or female black students. It is conceivable that sex and ethnic variations also exist in the determination of high school aspirations and placement for Israeli students. Such variations are particularly important for the assessment of interpersonal versus institutional effects on the educational careers of different groups of students. The regressions were

therefore recomputed for each of the four sex-ethnic groups separately.[12] Due to space limitations, only the last two steps of the model are presented here. The four-group regression equations for aspirations and the reduced-form equations for track-placement (from which aspirations are excluded for reasons of statistical comparability) are presented in Table 4 in both metric and standardized forms.

There are only limited group differences with respect to the major SOI influence on aspirations. Though SOI affects the aspirations of Oriental males and females to a somewhat lesser extent than those of their Ashkenazi counterparts (sex differences within each ethnic group are minor), the aspirations of all four groups are primarily and strongly influenced by SOI. More important differences exist with respect to the determination of actual tracking. It appears that the tracking of Oriental males and females is more heavily influenced by institutional mechanisms. The direct effects of ability grouping for these two groups are somewhat stronger than for Ashkenazi students, and the interpersonal effects of SOI are the weakest obtained. In addition, the tracking of Orientals (especially females) is directly affected by academic performance to a greater extent than that of Ashkenazi students. As ex-

---

[11] For a recent summary and discussion of these studies see Howell and Frese (1979).

[12] A broader analysis of the sociological and psychological determinants of sex and ethnic differences in educational attainment, which is based in part on the same source of data, is being conducted in a doctoral dissertation by Drora Kfir at the School of Education, Tel Aviv University.

Table 4. Determinants of High School Aspiration (X_7) and Placement (X_8) for Respondents Grouped by Ethnicity and Sex: Metric (b) and Standardized (β) Regression Coefficients

Independent Variables	Ashkenazi Males (N = 442)		Oriental Males (N = 537)		Ashkenazi Females (N = 471)		Oriental Females (N = 441)	
	b	β	b	β	b	β	b	β
A. Dependent Variable: High School Aspiration (X_7)								
X_1: Father's Education	.008*	.062*	−.006*	−.035*	.007*	.052*	.007*	.038*
X_4: Academic Performance	.003*	.085*	.004	.094	.003*	.085*	.004*	.088*
X_5: Ability Grouping	.032	.139	.024	.100	.027	.110	.037	.162
X_6: SOI	.369	.632	.317	.535	.368	.611	.323	.540
Constant/R^2	.111	.560	.509	.376	.015	.527	.204	.450
B. Dependent Variable: High School Placement (X_8)								
X_1: Father's Education	.018	.132	.011*	.072*	.013	.093	.019	.098
X_4: Academic Performance	.003*	.096*	.006	.138	.005	.120	.011	.233
X_5: Ability Grouping	.082	.344	.084	.399	.068	.276	.077	.316
X_6: SOI	.127	.211	.068	.129	.184	.301	.088	.138
Constant/R^2	.707	.371	.828	.348	.295	.377	.248	.353

* Coefficient is less than twice its standard error.

plained earlier, this variable reflects mainly the academic achievement of students. Since academic achievement may be regarded as an additional institutional mechanism of educational selection, this last finding strengthens the impression of stronger institutional influences on Orientals' tracking.

Ability grouping exerts the strongest effect on the tracking of Ashkenazi males as well. But while its influence for this group is almost identical to the one obtained for Oriental males, the simultaneous direct effect of SOI for Ashkenazi males is almost twice that obtained for their Oriental counterparts. For Ashkenazi females, the effect of SOI on tracking is somewhat higher than that of ability grouping. This may perhaps be explained by the general tendency of Ashkenazi female students and their parents to prefer academic over vocational secondary training in preparation for higher education.

Together the above findings suggest that institutional influences on tracking are strong for all four groups, but male and female students of the minority Oriental group tend to be more heavily tracked through institutional mechanisms.

DISCUSSION

The most significant finding of the path analysis is the differential explanatory power of antecedent variables with respect to high school aspiration, on the one hand, and high school placement on the other. This finding indicates the existence of a bifurcated process of career formation in Israeli secondary education. The perceived encouragement from significant others (especially from parents, who are presumably more influential than peers at this young age) is the major determinant of the specific high school track aspired to. But both this aspiration and SOI affect high school track placement much less than does ability grouping in junior high school. The discriminant analysis further validates the hierarchy of the three vocational and academic high school tracks with respect to these different processes of aspiration formation versus actual placement.

In order to comprehend these findings fully, one needs to interpret the three major path results: (a) the moderate direct effect of aspirations on actual placement, (b) the different direct effect of SOI on high school aspiration and on placement, and (c) the marked influence of ability grouping in the junior high school on tracking in the tenth grade.

It may be argued that the moderate effect of aspirations on placement is due to unrealistic perceptions of educational opportunities, which may prevail at this relatively young age. It should be recognized, however, that the data concerning aspirations were collected during the third trimester of the eighth school year—only a few months before the high school assignment process starts. Since the respondents were questioned about their immediate plans after junior-high graduation, it would be rather misleading to consider their aspirations unrealistic. Furthermore, a recent study of thirteen-year-old boys in Britain and the United States (Kerckhoff, 1977) has shown that educational aspirations in a society using sponsorship tend to become quite "realistic" at an earlier age than they do in a society stressing contest mobility.

The relatively low direct effects of aspirations and SOI on high school placement, in spite of the high zero-order correlations among these three variables, are caused mainly by the strong influence of ability grouping. It is the magnitude of the effect exerted by ability grouping on high school placement which depresses the direct effects of the antecedent variables. Consequently, the institutional mechanism of grouping students by their ability at the junior high level becomes the major direct determinant of their future educational career. This may be due to several reasons.

Ability grouping represents, first, the student's academic achievement in junior high school. The model shows that a large amount of the effect of ability grouping is due to academic performance, which is the major determinant of students' grouping. Since academic performance seems to represent a "contest" among students, its indirect effect on tracking through ability grouping appears to contradict our claim that the latter's impact represents a sponsorship process. But the academic performance of the Israeli students is determined to a large extent by their status of origin—father's education and ethnicity. Furthermore, the process leading to

school achievement should not necessarily serve as the major criterion for classifying a system as fostering contest or sponsored mobility. A far more important criterion is the effect exerted by academic achievement on the further educational career, relative to interpersonal effects or to the influence of personal aspirations. The findings of this study show that academic performance, through the direct effect of ability grouping, exerts a much larger impact than SOI or aspirations. A recent study of the educational career in the United States (Alexander et al., 1978) shows, in contrast to our findings, that the direct effect of one's curriculum plans (in the junior-high ninth grade) on high school curriculum placement exceeds the effect exerted by academic achievement in the ninth grade. These findings may be indicative of the differential determinants of schooling in contest versus sponsorship systems.

The effect of ability grouping on tracking cannot be attributed entirely to academic performance, however. The function of ability grouping in determining the student's status in school should be considered too. The assignment of students to specific ability groups is related to the formation of aspirations and to their perceived encouragement from significant others, as indicated by this study. Ability grouping further provides the basic rationale for counselors' recommendations with respect to high school tracking. The studies on counseling in junior high schools mentioned earlier show that students of the minority Oriental group have more contact with counselors, and that this contact is related to subsequent decreases in students' aspirations and track placement. All these findings point toward a considerable labeling effect of ability grouping on the educational career.[13]

These studies on counseling may provide a partial explanation for our finding that both male and female Oriental students are tracked more heavily by institu-

---

[13] Recently, there is an increasing awareness of the potential labeling effect of ability grouping. A noteworthy trend is the elimination of the slow-learning groups and the unification of the two highest ability levels in part of the junior high schools.

tional determinants than their Ashkenazi counterparts. These differences exist in spite of the fact that there are only minor differences between students of the two ethnic groups with respect to the SOI effect on track-aspirations. These findings provide additional support for the depiction of the Israeli educational system as based on sponsorship. Sponsorship systems of education are distinguished not only by their extensive use of institutional mobility mechanisms, but also by their use of these mechanisms for the selection of higher-status social groups and for the blocking of mobility of lower-status ones (Turner, 1960). The more vigorous application of institutional mechanisms to the tracking of the minority Oriental students exemplifies this point.

The above interpretation notwithstanding, it should be realized that SOI was found to be the major determinant of high school aspiration for all groups of students. Obviously, this strong SOI effect may be subject to a systematic error, due to its indirect measurement through students' perceptions. Yet, it supports Yuchtman and Samuel's contention that interpersonal effects on educational aspirations are more substantial than institutional effects at the lower school levels of sponsorship-oriented systems. At these levels, sponsorship experiences have not yet been accumulated to the extent of markedly influencing students' personal plans. Yet the overall picture of findings suggests the existence of a "transitional period" in the process of career-formation in such educational systems. The vigorous application of sponsorship mechanisms starts in the Israeli education system at the junior high level. These institutional mechanisms determine the students' educational career from a relatively early stage. But since the students have not yet become aware of the sponsorship process, these institutional effects are not reflected in the formation of their aspirations, largely explained at this stage by SOI. The cumulative effect of sponsorship mechanisms on aspiration-formation is apparent only in later stages of the educational process, as shown by Yuchtman and Samuel's study.

Further comparative studies are needed in order to validate the existence of this "transitional period" in educational processes of sponsorship-oriented systems. Such studies should compare the determinants of educational aspirations and attainment, at the various stages of schooling, among societies geared toward contest versus sponsored mobility. These studies may, of course, reflect the universal issue of interpersonal versus institutional determinants of education by considering the specific features of educational systems in various societies.

REFERENCES

Alexander, K. L., M. Cook and E. L. McDill
1978 "Curriculum tracking and educational stratification." American Sociological Review 43:47–66.

Alexander, K. L. and E. L. McDill
1976 "Selection and allocation within schools." American Sociological Review, 41:963–80.

Bourdieu, P. and J. C. Passeron
1977 Reproduction in Education, Society and Culture. Beverly Hills, CA: Sage Publications

Chen, M. and D. Kfir
1977 "The influence of counseling in junior high schools." Israeli Journal of Psychology and Counseling in Education 8:24–36 (Hebrew).

1979 "The students who meet the counselor in the junior high school." Israeli Journal of Psychology and Counseling in Education 10:24–9 (Hebrew).

Chen, M., A. Lewy and C. Adler
1978 Process and Result in Education: Evaluating the Contribution of the Junior High School to the Educational System. Tel Aviv and Jerusalem: Tel Aviv University and the Hebrew University (Hebrew).

Garnier, M. A. and M. Hout
1976 "Inequality of educational opportunity in France and the United States." Social Science Research 5:225–46.

Goldberger, A.
1964 Econometric Theory. New York: Wiley.

Haller, A. O. and A. Portes
1973 "Status attainment processes." Sociology of Education 46:51–91.

Hansen, D. O. and A. O. Haller
1973 "Status attainment of Costa Rican males: A cross-cultural test of a model." Rural Sociology 38:269–82.

Hauser, R. M.
1972 "Disaggregating a social psychological model of educational attainment." Social Science Research 1:159–88.

Heyns, B.
1974 "Social selection and stratification within schools." American Journal of Sociology 79:1434–51.

Hout, M. and M. A. Garnier
1979 "Curriculum placement and educational

stratification in France." Sociology of Education 52:146–56.

Howell, F. M. and W. Frese
1979 "Race, sex and aspirations: Evidence for the 'race convergence' hypothesis." Sociology of Education 52:34–46.

Kerckhoff, A. C.
1976 "The status attainment process: Socialization or allocation?" Social Forces 55:368–81.
1977 "The realism of educational ambitions in England and the United States." American Sociological Review 42:563–71.

Kerckhoff, A. C. and J. L. Huff
1974 "Parental influence on educational goals." Sociometry 37:307–27.

Klecka, W. R.
1975 "Discriminant analysis." Pp. 434–67 in N. H. Nie, C. H. Hull, J. G. Jenkins, K. Steinbrenner and D. H. Bent (eds.), Statistical Package for the Social Sciences (second edition). New York: McGraw-Hill.

Nachmias, C.
1977 "The status attainment process: A test of a model in two stratification systems." The Sociological Quarterly 18:589–607.

Porter, J. N.
1974 "Race, socialization and mobility in educational and early occupational attainment." American Sociological Review 39:303–16.

Rosenbaum, J. E.
1976 Making Inequality: The Hidden Curriculum of High School Tracking. New York: Wiley.
1980 "Track misperceptions and frustrated college plans: An analysis of the effects of tracks and track perceptions in the National Longitudinal Survey." Sociology of Education 53:74–88.

Sewell, W. H., A. O. Haller and G. Ohlendorf
1970 "The educational and early occupational attainment process: Replications and revisions." American Sociological Review 35:1014–27.

Sewell, W. H., A. O. Haller and A. Portes
1969 "The educational and early occupational attainment process." American Sociological Review 34:82–92.

Sewell, W. H. and R. M. Hauser
1975 Education, Occupation and Earnings: Achievement in the Early Career. New York: Academic Press.

Smooha, S. and Y. Peres
1975 "The dynamics of ethnic inequalities: The case of Israel." Social Dynamics 1:63–80.

Turner, R. H.
1960 "Sponsored and contest mobility and the school system." American Sociological Review 25:855–67.

Woelfel, G. and A. O. Haller
1971 "Significant others, the self-reflexive act and the attitude formation process." American Sociological Review 36:74–87.

Yogev, A. and R. Schrift
1979 "Mobility channel preference and educational aspirations in a sponsored mobility system." Unpublished manuscript, Tel Aviv University, Israel.

Yuchtman (Yaar), E. and Y. Samuel
1975 "Determinants of career plans: Institutional versus interpersonal effects." American Sociological Review 40:521–31.

11.

Classroom Intellectual Composition and Academic Achievement

Yehezkel Dar and Nura Resh

Assuming that the intellectual level of the classroom affects the quality of learning environments, it is argued that separating students into homogeneous educational frameworks enriches the environment for high-resource students and impoverishes it for low-resource students, whereas the converse occurs under heterogeneous mixing. Academic achievement consequently will be affected. This argument was subjected to an empirical analysis in two Israeli samples, one ethnically and socioeconomically heterogeneous, the other socially homogeneous. First, presuppositions concerning the impact of three dimensions of student-body composition on academic achievement were probed. It was found that (a) the intellectual component of student-body composition outweighs both ethnic and socioeconomic components; (b) classroom composition is more effective than school composition; and (c) classroom intellectual level is more effective than its variance. Subsequently, two hypotheses were supported: classroom intellectual composition positively affects the student's academic achievement, and compositional quality and personal ability interact (i.e., low-resource students are more sensitive than high-resource students to compositional quality). An educational implication follows: In separation, the low-resource students' loss is greater than the high-resource students' profit, and in mixing, the high-resource students' loss is smaller than the low-resource students' gain.

Preoccupied with the heterogeneity of student populations, educational systems manipulate student-body compositions on three levels: between

This work was supported by Ford Foundation Grant No. 845-0335, and carried out at the National Council of Jewish Women Research Institute for Innovation in Education, School of Education, Hebrew University. We wish to thank Micha Chen, Arie Lewy, and Chaim Adler for the use of the middle school research data.

schools, within the single school, and within the classroom. This manipulation includes maintaining unitrack schools versus providing for comprehensive ones; keeping segregation along ethnic or social class lines versus introducing socioeducational integration; and forming inter-class or intra-class ability groups, streams, and curricular tracks versus maintaining heterogeneous frameworks.

It is no wonder that an educational issue so controversial has been dealt with extensively, usually without conclusive evidence of the academic benefits of homogeneous or heterogeneous frameworks.[1] Perhaps the failure to reach more unequivocal conclusions should be associated not only with the weakness of the treatment (there is ample evidence that manipulation of student-body composition as such has only small effect on scholastic outcomes compared to the effect of the student's personal resources), but also with the absence of a conceptual framework appropriate for the analysis of a wide range of educational separation and mixing phenomena. Such a framework has been presented in detail elsewhere (Dar, 1986); its main points will be reproduced here to introduce an empirical investigation.

CONCEPTUAL FRAMEWORK AND HYPOTHESES

We conceptualized the independent variable as the quality of the socio-learning environment (SLE), conditioned by the intellectual level of the classroom, and affected by either separating students by personal resource level into high and low homogeneous classes, or by mixing them in heterogeneous classes.

Homogeneous differentiation in a given student cohort was seen as enriching the SLE for students with rich personal resources, who are usually placed in high trajectories, and as impoverishing the environment for students with poor resources, who are usually allocated to low trajectories. Accordingly, integration meant enriching the SLE for the low-resource student, who usually comes from a low-level environment, and impoverishing it for the high-resource student coming from a high SLE.

We thought treatment effects should be examined in terms of a hypothetical transference of low- and high-resource students from an impoverished to an enriched SLE and vice versa. Assuming that students with different amounts of personal resources react differently to environmental quality, the research should focus on the interaction of SLE quality and personal resource level on scholastic outcomes.

Note that, despite distinguishing between homogeneity and heterogene-

---

[1] The controversy associated with manipulations of student compositions is extensively treated in Yates, 1966; Husen and Boalt, 1967; Ford, 1969; Simon, 1970; Findley and Bryan, 1971; McDermott, 1976; St. John, 1975; Stephan and Feagin, 1980; Dar and Resh, 1981; Amir, Sharan and Ben-Ari, 1984.

ity, our main interest was not in the within-group, interpersonal *variance* of learning resources, but in the group *level* of these resources. Viewing separation and mixing dynamically, in terms of the transition from one composition to another of those poor or rich in personal resources, the concepts of homogeneity and heterogeneity blend with the concept of composition level.

This research paradigm rests on five assumptions. First, we assumed that student-body composition affects the quality of the student's SLE and, consequently, his or her scholastic achievement. In applying the concept of SLE we referred not only to the group aggregation of individual, learning-relevant resources, but also to group processes that were likely to be activated through the differential aggregation of these resources in higher and lower level learning trajectories. We distinguished five dimensions of the SLE that may be seen as processes mediating scholastic outcomes. The first was the *future payoff of learning*, the perceived contribution of schooling to the student's social fate as mediated through the stratification (by learning trajectory) of knowledge, credentials, and socializing power. The second dimension was the SLE's *symbolic message*, homogenization as institutional labelling that may stigmatize the low-resource student and activate a self-fulfilling prophecy of failure. *Normative influence*, the third dimension, referred to the class and school as norm-setting groups that develop group culture and educational climate, and provide behavioral role-models. It was accompanied by *comparative reference*, a dimension in which the class is a frame of reference within and through which the student locates him- or herself on subjectively important status scales and develops, accordingly, feelings of relative deprivation or gratification that may affect his or her scholastic behavior. Lastly, enrichment or impoverishment of student-body composition would affect the *quality of scholastic interaction.* Considered here were the intellectual homogeneity of the classroom, the level of learning materials, the pace of their processing, forms and standards of instruction, the availability of information and models for learning among peers, and the degree of perseverance in learning activity—all as affected by the differential aggregation of low- and high-resource students.

Our second assumption was that the intellectual component of a student body outweighs the ethnic and socioeconomic components in affecting individual scholastic outcomes, analogous to the predominance of personal ability over socioeconomic and ethnic origin in accounting for achievement (Bloom, 1976; Lavin, 1965; Madaus, Airasian, & Kellaghan, 1980). This is due not only to covariation of social and ethnic background and learning aptitude, but also to actual and attributional qualities of intellectual capacity as an important, highly convertible resource in educational and social systems (Brim, Glass, Neulinger, & Firestone, 1969). Even when a student's resource level is colored by ethnicity and socioeconomic status, the intellectual component carries the most weight in modern education. This facilitates the development of a unified conceptual framework useful in dealing with seemingly different phenomena such as ability grouping, streaming, curricular tracking, and ethnic segregation.

The third assumption was that the composition of classrooms rather than of schools affects the quality of the student's learning environment and, consequently, his or her scholastic achievement. Although many scholars have pointed to the effect of school composition and climate on scholastic behavior (Brookover, Beady, Flood, Scheitzer, and Weisenbaker, 1981; McDill and Rigsby, 1973; Rutter, Maugham, Mortimore, Oaston, & Smith, 1979), there is a strong argument for considering classrooms, the actual and proximal learning settings, as the effective context especially when school composition does not necessarily reflect class composition (Heyns, 1974; McPartland, 1969; Rosenbaum, 1976).

We also assumed that classroom ability level is more significant than variance in accounting for academic achievement. Research failed to reveal any consistent academic effect of the classroom ability variance. A more significant effect was found in studies in which composition was conceptualized as classroom ability level (Dar & Resh, 1981). Leiter (1983) convincingly demonstrated the predominance of classroom ability level over its variance in affecting student achievement, by using a design that allowed simultaneous testing of both effects.

Lastly, we assumed that high- and low-resource students reveal varying sensitivity to environmental influence. The possibility of a greater environmental dependency of low-resource students was pointed out by research on academic achievement (Coleman et al., 1966; Spady, 1973) and on academic expectations (Harp & Richer, 1969; Thornton & Eckland, 1980). It also has an intuitive feasibility. When personal resources, the stronger of the two factors in the set, are low, greater room would be left for the SLE to play its role.

Resting on the above five assumptions, we hypothesized that classroom intellectual composition positively affects the student's academic achievement; and that the classroom intellectual level interacts with personal ability level such that the lower the latter, the greater the sensitivity to the former.

RESEARCH DESIGN

The research paradigm and hypotheses were applied and examined in two separate but complementary studies. The first was carried out in an Israel-wide, ethnically and socio-economically heterogeneous sample through a re-analysis of the middle school research data of Chen, Lewy, and Adler (1978). The sample included about 3,500 8th-graders in 135 classes in 38 schools, encompassing class compositions ranging from high homogeneous (high mean achievement, high SES, high percentage of

Jewish Western-origin students), through heterogeneous to low homogeneous (low achievement, low SES, high percentage of Jewish Eastern-origin students).[2]

The sample in the second study included about 700 10th, 11th, and 12th-graders from six kibbutz high schools in Israel (Dar, 1980). In four of these schools, with 30 classes, homogeneous homeroom classes at two ability levels were formed, whereas in two schools, with 18 classes, there were heterogeneous homerooms.[3] Though fairly heterogeneous intellectually, the sample was highly homogeneous in student ethnic and socioeconomic background.

Schools in both samples practiced ability grouping in English, mathematics, and sometimes in Hebrew grammar, altogether about 25% to 30% of the curriculum. The main part of the curriculum, however, was studied in the homeroom class, which, unlike in the U. S. and Europe, constitutes the student's principal learning group, and largely determines his or her school identity.[4]

In the middle school sample the effect of a continuous variable was examined, namely, the intellectual composition as represented by the class mean academic achievement. In the kibbutz sample a quasi-experimental comparison was made between two treatments: heterogeneous homeroom classes versus homogeneous classes of low and high ability. Academic achievement in both samples was assessed cross-sectionally but earlier aptitude/achievement data were available as a control. The latent treatment variable in both studies was the SLE as determined by the classroom intellectual composition. In both cases it was possible to assess the environmental effect in terms of a hypothetical transition from a richer to a poorer SLE and vice versa.

---

[2] About half of the Jewish student population in Israel is of Asian or African origin (Orientals); the other half is of European and American origin (Westerners). Group averages of the Orientals on many socioeconomic criteria, academic achievement included, are considerably lower than the Westerners'.

[3] The within-class variance on the Milta Aptitude Test (Ortar & Murieli, 1966) of homogeneous classes is distinctly less than that of the heterogeneous classes ($p < .001$). In contrast, the difference in class variance between the high and low level homogeneous classes is insignificant (10.41 and 10.76, respectively), whereas there is a difference of more than a full standard deviation between aptitude levels of these two class types (101.93 and 87.04, respectively; $p < .01$).

[4] Despite ability grouping in both groups of the kibbutz schools, the groups differed distinctly in overall degree of homogenization. Taking into account all learning frameworks of the individual student, the average homogenization score (on a seven-point scale) in schools with heterogeneous homerooms was 2.25, compared to 5.00 in those with homogeneous homerooms. Ability grouping in the heterogeneous schools was carried out between heterogeneous homerooms, and in the homogeneous schools between parallel homogeneous homerooms, namely, within predetermined homogeneous levels.

In the middle school sample, SLE quality was straightforwardly expressed by the classroom intellectual level, but in the kibbutz sample it was implied because, in comparison to a heterogeneous class, a homogeneous one is an impoverished SLE for low-resource students and an enriched one for high-resource students. The dependent variable in both studies was the student's mean achievement on a battery of standardized tests. Using combined achievement scores on several central domains of the student's curriculum, rather than using specific test scores separately, was intended to provide a diffuse, generalized measure of academic achievement. We believe that such a measure is most responsive to the combined effect of the five SLE dimensions. This argument notwithstanding, separate analyses were also performed in the middle school sample with tests of non-grouped subjects only.

A similar regression model was applied in both studies. The interaction between personal ability and SLE quality was detected by performing separate analyses within halves of the pre-treatment aptitude/achievement distribution. The following linear equation was applied:

$$Y = a + b_1X_1 + b_2X_2 + b_3X_3 + b_4X_4 + e,$$

where Y = academic achievement as represented by a mean score on a battery of achievement tests including reading comprehension, math, English, Bible, social studies, and science in the middle school sample; and reading comprehension, social studies, history, and biology in the kibbutz sample. Both scores are percent of correct answers. In the middle school sample (8th grade), the sample mean was 58.40 with a standard deviation of 19.54. In the kibbutz sample, the sample mean was 56.03 with a standard deviation of 12.89. In the middle school sample additional analyses were made with tests of non-grouped subjects: a combination of the sub-tests in reading comprehension, social studies and science (mean = 60.51, SD = 21.05); and Bible only (mean = 54.48, SD = 21.08).

X_1 = class grade (in the kibbutz sample only: 10th grade = 1, 11th grade = 2, and 12th grade = 3); X_2 = gender (male = 1, female = 2); X_3 = pre-treatment aptitude/achievement, represented in the middle school sample by the student's mean achievement on the 7th-grade tests, which were similar to those given in the 8th grade (mean = 58.14, SD = 16.74). In the kibbutz sample the Seker score served as control, a government test administered in the 8th grade to assign students to post-elementary studies (Ortar, 1967) (mean = 78.46, SD = 9.63). X_4 = SLE. In the middle school sample, classroom intellectual composition was expressed by the classroom mean achievement. In the kibbutz sample, heterogeneous class = 1, homogeneous class = 2.

TABLE I

Increment in Explained Variance of Achievement in Two Forced Step-wise Regression Orders, Middle School Sample

	Personal resources			Compositional resources		
	Ability/ achievement	SES	Ethnic origin	Intellectual	SES	Ethnic
Step	1	2	3	4	5	6
R^2	.702	.007	.000	.049	.008	.000
Step	3	2	1	6	5	4
R^2	.340	.197	.178	.046	.003	.008

FINDINGS

Middle School Sample

Before turning to the main hypotheses, we shall take advantage of the ethnic and socioeconomic heterogeneity and the size of the middle school sample to attempt to verify three of our presuppositions: (a) among the three compositional dimensions, ethnic, socioeconomic, and intellectual, the latter is dominant; (b) classroom composition rather than school composition or student's ability group level is the most effective SLE regarding academic achievement; and (c) classroom ability level is more significant in accounting for academic achievement than is classroom variance.

The relative importance of the intellectual, socioeconomic, and ethnic dimensions, on individual and compositional levels, in accounting for academic achievement, was examined by step-wise regressions in two forced orders. Results are presented in Table I[5].

In both orders, personal resources preceded the compositional resources. However, in the first regression the intellectual dimension preceded the other two dimensions, whereas in the second it was entered last. The findings confirm the predominance of the intellectual dimension both as a personal and a classroom resource. Entering first in the regression, the pre-treatment ability/achievement factor explained 70% of the variance in academic achievement; even when entered third it remained the strongest variable, although its weight was reduced by half. The socioeconomic background of the student, when following ability, added less than one

---

[5] Personal SES was an index of father's education, number of siblings, and number of books in the home library as reported by the student. The index ranged from 3 (low) to 20 (high). The socioeconomic composition was the classroom mean of personal SES. Ethnic origin was coded thus: Western = 1, Oriental = 2. Ethnic composition was the classroom percent of Orientals ranging from 1 (below 20%) to 6 (above 95%). Westerners constituted 72% of the upper half of the ability distribution and Orientals comprised 72% of the lower half.

percent to the explained variance. Ethnic origin, as the third variable, had no effect. When first in the analysis, it contributed about 18% to the explanation, and socioeconomic background, second in the analysis, added about 20%.

When first among the compositional variables, intellectual composition added about 5% to the explanation; entered last, following ethnic and social compositions, its explanatory power was not significantly reduced. The contribution of the other two compositional dimensions ranged from zero to one percent, whether they preceded or followed intellectual composition.

The results of examining the second supposition are shown in Table II, which presents the unique contribution of the three environments (school composition, classroom composition, and the student's average ability grouping level) to the explained variance of achievement in two orders of forced step-wise regression.

In both orders, personal resources (previous ability/achievement) preceded compositional resources. However, in the first regression school composition preceded classroom composition and grouping level, whereas in the second the order was reversed. The analyses clearly verify the predominance of the classroom composition: in both orders its contribution to the explained variance approached or exceeded 5%, whereas the contribution of each of the other two environments never exceeded one percent.

The third supposition, that classroom intellectual level predominates over variance in affecting scholastic achievement, was also verified. It was accomplished through a step-wise regression with personal resources, classroom intellectual level, its intellectual variance, and an interaction term of level and variance. Pre-treatment ability/achievement accounted for 70.2% of the achievement variance, classroom level added 5.5%, classroom variance contributed only 0.3% and the interaction term did not contribute at all.

After verifying the three presuppositions, we turned to our main hy-

TABLE II

Increment in Explained Variance of Achievement for Three Compositions, Following Personal Resources in Two Forced Step-wise Regression Orders, Middle School Sample

	Personal ability/ achievement	School composition	Classroom composition	Average ability grouping[a]
Step	1	2	3	4
R^2	.702	.010	.048	.002
Step	1	4	3	2
R^2	.702	.000	.051	.010

[a] Average level of the student's ability grouping in Hebrew grammar, math, and English.

potheses, concentrating on the intellectual dimension and the classroom composition. Table III presents regression analyses in the entire aggregate and within the upper and lower halves of the distribution of personal resources.

As expected, personal intellectual resources played a decisive role in predicting academic achievement. However, when these were controlled, classroom composition still contributed distinctly to explaining student achievement. A change of one point in the mean classroom achievement conveyed a change of .43 in personal achievement, controlling for personal achievement in the previous year (and for gender). This indicated that the richer the composition, the better the student's chances for higher scholastic achievement.

Examination of the interaction between personal resource level and environmental resources by halves of the ability distribution indicated that the effect of classroom composition increased as the level of previous achievement decreased (the row regression coefficients for low- and high-resource students were .37 and .48, respectively). The poorer the student's personal resources, the more sensitive he or she was to the quality of the educational environment.

The achievement test that comprised the dependent variable in this analysis included six sub-tests: reading comprehension, Bible, social studies, science, math, and English. The last two relate to subjects that are studied in ability groups, and the soundness of their inclusion may be questionable in a test intended to tap compositional effect of the homeroom class. To face this argument, two additional analyses were performed, one with the subtests of math and English excluded from the omnibus test, the other with only the Bible test (a genuine homeroom subject). Both analyses are presented in Table IV. A similar pattern of effects appeared in both analyses, and clearly resembles that of the analysis with the general test.

Kibbutz Sample. The treatment in the middle school sample was a post-factum research definition that focused on the class intellectual composi-

TABLE III

Regression of Achievement in the Eighth Grade on Gender, Pre-treatment Ability/ Achievement (Seventh Grade), and Classroom Intellectual Composition, Middle School Sample, Metric (b) and Standardized (B) Coefficients

	X_2 Gender		X_3 7th-grade achievement		X_4 Classroom composition		R^2
	b	B	b	B	b	B	
All students	−.67	−.02	.73*	.62	.43*	.32	.76*
Upper half	.45	.02	.91*	.57	.37*	.28	.52*
Lower half	−.81	−.03	.52*	.37	.48*	.45	.50*

*$p < .001$.

TABLE IV

*Regression of Achievement in Non-Grouped Subjects in Eighth Grade on Gender,
Pre-treatment Ability/Achievement (7th grade), and Classroom Intellectual Composition,
Middle School Sample, Metric (b) and Standardized (B) Coefficients*

	X_2 Gender		X_3 7th-grade achievement		X_4 Classroom composition		R^2
	b	B	b	B	b	B	
Reading comprehension, social studies, science							
All students	−2.82*	−.07	.75*	.60	.36*	.25	.63*
Upper half	−1.89$^×$	−.06	.86*	.48	.27*	.19	.34*
Lower half	−2.62*	−.08	.59*	.35	.42*	.33	.35*
Bible							
All students	1.21†	.03	.67*	.54	.38*	.26	.55*
Upper half	2.43$^×$	.07	.89*	.45	.35*	.22	.32*
Lower half	1.10	.03	.54*	.32	.43*	.34	.32*

† $p < .05.$
$^×$ $p < .01.$
* $p < .001.$

tion as a continuous variable. In the kibbutz sample an organizational manipulation produced different types of classes, enabling a quasi-experimental examination of compositional effects within dichotomy (homogeneous/heterogeneous classes) or trichotomy (high-homogeneous/heterogeneous/low-homogeneous classes). These types differed not only in class intellectual level (as in the middle school sample), but also in class intellectual variance and in additional characteristics that are ingredients of class identity in an intentionally homogeneous situation. The social homogeneity of the kibbutz egalitarian society permits testing of the effect of intellectual composition uncontaminated by ethnic or socioeconomic factors.

Table V presents outcomes of regression analyses carried out in five categories in three groups: for the entire aggregate; within upper and lower halves of the ability distribution; and within the heterogeneous or homogeneous classes, when the treatment variable (X_4) was high or low level. In this last analysis the levels in the heterogeneous classes were determined hypothetically to be comparable to the actual levels of the homogeneous classes. This was accomplished by dividing the aggregate of the heterogeneous classes by the Seker score that optimally separated the actual high and low homogeneous classes.

Two findings were salient in the global analysis (Table V, a). First, as in the middle school sample, personal resources (pre-treatment aptitude/achievement) explained the lion's share of the student's academic achieve-

TABLE V

Regression of Achievement on Grade Level, Gender, Pre-Treatment Ability/Achievement (Seker), and Classroom Intellectual Structure in Various Ability Categories, The Kibbutz Sample, Metric (b) and Standardized (B) Coefficients[a]

Ability category	X_1 Grade level		X_2 Gender		X_3 Seker		X_4 Classroom structure		R^2
	b	B	b	B	b	B	b	B	
a. All students	4.85*	.31	−3.45*	−.13	.85*	.65	−1.75†	−.07	.53*
b. Upper half	4.69*	.39	−3.24ˣ	−.16	.80*	.35	−.76	−.04	.28*
c. Lower half	4.94*	.36	−3.95*	−.18	.68*	.39	−2.85ˣ	−.13	.35*
							X_4 = high/low level		
d. Heterogeneous	3.60*	.26	−3.42ˣ	−.15	.78†	.65	−.44	−.02	.51*
e. Homogeneous	5.54*	.32	−3.53*	−.13	.73*	.53	−4.11ˣ	−.15	.55*

[a] Negative coefficients of X_2 indicate an advantage to males, and of X_4 an advantage to heterogeneity (rows a to c) and high level (rows d and e).

† p < .05.

ˣ p < .01.

* p < .001.

ment. An increment of one point in the Seker score drew a change of .85 of achievement, and 79% of the variance explained was accounted for by this variable. Second, homogeneous classes did not provide any advantage in academic achievement; on the contrary, advantage was held by heterogeneity. However, the effect of class structure in the overall sample was weak and added little to the variance explained by the Seker score.

Interaction between SLE and personal resource level was detected through the analysis by halves of the ability distribution. A comparison of effects in the upper and lower halves revealed the expected interaction (Table V, b,c). The effect of classroom structure for the low-resource students was significantly greater than for the high-resource students (b equaled 2.85 and .76, respectively), indicating greater sensitivity of the low-resource students to SLE quality.

The positive effect of heterogeneity on both the low and high groups posed a problem in interpreting the effect in terms of SLE quality. This interpretation is valid for the low-resource students, for which a hypothetical transition from a low homogeneous class to a heterogeneous class implies improvement of SLE. However, transition from a high homogeneous class to a heterogeneous one implies SLE impoverishment for the high-resource students, which does not tally with the slight advantage in heterogeneity for this half as well. This advantage may reflect some uncontrolled difference between the research groups. This small advantage was reversed to a very small disadvantage, whereas the differential effect for the upper and lower halves was sustained when the present regression model was extended to include motivation (see Dar & Resh, 1981).

Further examination of the interaction between classroom intellectual level and personal ability was provided by regression within homogeneous classes only (Table V, e), when the treatment X_4 entered the regression as a dichotomous variable (1 = high homogeneous class, 2 = low homogeneous class). It was revealed that a hypothetical transition from a low to a high homogeneous class is associated with a four point advantage in achievement. The finding survived a complementary test, a parallel regression within the heterogeneous classes (row d), where X_4 represented the hypothetical levels. The real homogeneous classes did have a significant effect; the hypothetical levels in the heterogeneous classes did not.

The interaction between personal and classroom intellectual levels is illustrated in Figure 1. The classroom effect is presented in terms of hypothetical transition from one environment to another within levels of personal resources; the effect of personal resources is presented in terms of hypothetical transition between ability levels within environmental levels.

We assumed in the analysis that the high homogeneous class is a richer SLE for the upper half of the ability distribution, and the heterogeneous class is richer for the lower half. The effects were differences in net achievement in a hypothetical transition from low to high level of SLE or

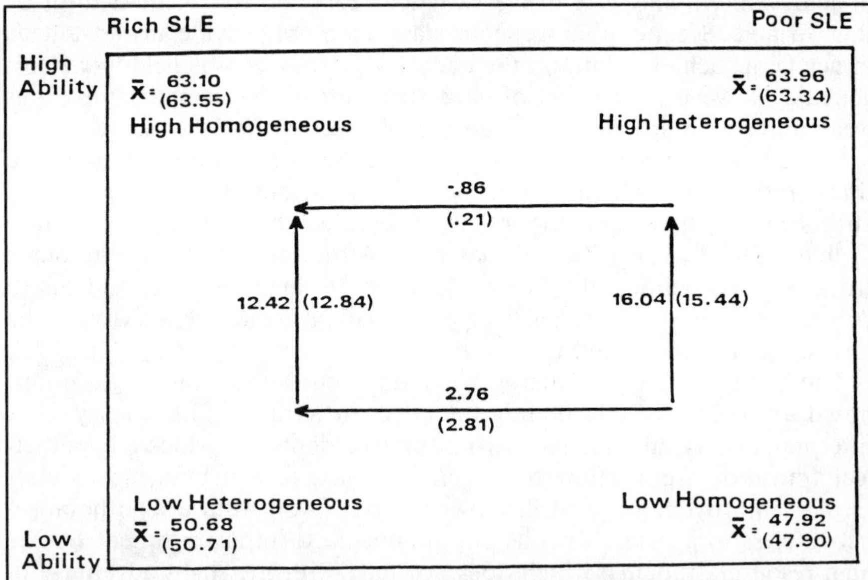

FIGURE 1. Effects of ability and SLE on achievement adjusted and raw (in parentheses) scores. (Adjusted scores were derived by co-variance analysis with grade level, sex, and Seker scores controlled.)

ability. Effects of ability in rich and poor SLE were 12.42 and 16.04, respectively; effects of SLE for high- and low-resource students were −.86 and 2.76, respectively. The ability effects in both environments were stronger than the environmental effects in either ability group, but the ability factor was stronger in a poorer environment and the environmental factor was more important for those of low ability. Both learning resources, personal ability and SLE quality, operated in the same direction, though at different intensities. However, sensitivity to one factor was greater when the other was scarce; an abundance of personal resources reduced sensitivity to environmental quality, whereas sensitivity is increased in a low resource level. Impoverishment of classroom composition thus will have a stronger effect on the low-resource student, and the high-resource student will be less affected. This implies that low-resource students transferred from a low homogeneous class to a heterogeneous class will profit more than high-resource students will lose when transferred from a high homogeneous class to a heterogeneous one.

CONCLUSIONS AND DISCUSSION

Ethnic origin per se, compared to personal ability and, to a lesser degree, to socioeconomic background, is a weak, if not insignificant, factor in explaining academic achievement as measured by objective tests. However, the tight control over the powerful variable pre-treatment achievement, whose measurement preceded that of the dependent variable by only one year, should not be overlooked. Such control minimizes the chances of independent expression of background variables because of the short interval between the two measurements and, more important, because background effects are likely to be imbedded in the pre-treatment variable as an accumulated influence. Our conclusion regarding the relative weakness of the ethnic factor in explaining achievement per se corresponds with another Israeli study that indicated the greater role played by socioeconomic background, particularly parents' education, in explaining achievement (Eshel, 1980).

The relative weakness of the ethnic factor has important implications for the implementation of educational integration and for the investigation of its scholastic outcomes. Because of sensitivity to ethnic cleavages, and the high correlation between ethnic origin, socioeconomic background, and academic ability, school integration has been conceived of primarily in terms of ethnicity. However, our analysis implies that intentional integration should be carried out primarily with regard to intellectual composition of educational frameworks. As a proxy for the intellectual dimension, socioeconomic composition is preferable to ethnic composition, at least when the principal aim of integration is educational advancement of low-resource students. (For other goals of integration, such as removing ethnic and social barriers, fostering inter-cultural contacts, and reducing prejudice, consideration of ethnic composition is of course vital.)

Our analysis corroborates the contention that to find compositional effects on scholastic outcomes, one should focus on those educational frameworks where the student's actual learning and frequent, recurrent social interaction occur. This is particularly true in the Israeli school where the homeroom class, even at the high school level, is only very partially fragmented into subject classes, and its position as the focus of learning and social activity is sustained. One cannot expect the student's various ability groups to have a very significant compositional effect beyond that of his or her homeroom class in light of its pivotal position, especially when a general achievement measure is considered.

The verification of the supposition that classroom intellectual level predominates over classroom variance in affecting individual achievement, contrasts with the prevailing preoccupation with classroom homogeneity and heterogeneity in research of compositional effects. It suggests that even when problems of heterogeneity are concerned, they should be conceptualized in terms of level rather than variance. In such terms, heterogenization is conceived as improvement of SLE for low-resource students and SLE impoverishment for high-resource students.

The main finding of this study is the corroboration of our basic hypothesis that classroom intellectual composition positively affects the student's objective academic achievement, beyond the potent effect of his or her personal intellectual resources, here tightly controlled. Implicitly it means that the classroom intellectual composition conditions, to some extent, the quality of the student's socio-learning environment.

Most interesting, however, is the confirmation of our second hypothesis that there is an interaction between personal and compositional resources, and that the compositional effect is stronger among low-resource students. Homogenization can be said to create differences in SLE quality and to cause an asymmetrical effect for low- and high-resource students. The impoverished SLE of low homogeneous classes lowers students of below-average ability, whereas a much weaker elevating effect is indicated in the enriched SLE of high homogeneous classes for the high-resource students in those classes. In other words, the loss of the low-resource students involved in impoverishment of the SLE is greater than the profit of the high-resource students accompanying SLE enrichment. Integration is not necessarily a "zero sum" game where the gain of one group equals the loss of the other. The methodological importance of this finding is that it strengthens the contention that in looking for overall compositional effects one may overlook differential effects for particular groups.

It is noteworthy that our hypotheses were supported by using a similar analytical model in two samples of very different composition. The significance of the analysis in the middle school sample is its confirmation of our hypotheses within a national, socioethnic, heterogeneous sample. A scholastic advantage to intellectual heterogeneity for low-resource students (in enriched SLE for that group), exceeding the disadvantage for the high-resource students (in impoverished SLE for them), is demonstrated here in a true socioeconomic and ethnic mix, with regard (indirectly) to the practice of ethnic integration of schools. The analysis of the kibbutz sample, on the other hand, supported our hypotheses within a socially homogeneous population, in schools that intentionally create (or refrain from creating) intellectually homogeneous classrooms. The heterogeneous class is more advantageous for low-resource students than the low homogeneous one, and there is no real disadvantage for high-resource students in the heterogeneous class versus the high homogeneous one. This replication of findings in two different social and educational contexts increases the reliability of the analysis and strengthens the contention that a unified conceptual framework is applicable in studying diverse compositional manipulations.

It is often claimed that in heterogeneous and integrated settings the low-resource student is likely to pay a social and emotional price that might affect his or her educational output. Our findings in no way support the second part of this claim. On the contrary, the low-resource students profit scholastically from heterogeneity. One may add that not only does the psychological ease achieved with separation fail to improve the academic performance of low-resource students, but even the didactic fit which separation is said to accomplish does not have the expected effect.

Though homogenization may improve didactic fit, especially at the poles of the ability distribution, this positive effect seems to be undermined by negative effects in other SLE dimensions. The gains of the low-resource students in psychological comfort and didactic fit, arguments commonly cited in favor of homogenization, do not equal their losses in quality of learning interaction, scholastically discouraging normative influence, relative deprivation due to out-of-class comparisons, stigmatic labelling inculcating a "weak" student role and frustrating prospects of a future payoff of learning.

Two qualifying remarks are warranted here. First, though the delineation of the five SLE dimensions rests on well-established theoretical models and ample empirical evidence, the interpretation of findings in terms of these processes is obviously suppositional. We feel, indeed, that a causal link between SLE quality, operationalized as classroom intellectual composition, and scholastic outcomes, may be convincingly established. That our findings may be explained in terms of these dimensions reinforces our conclusions. However, much more research is needed to validate the particular roles played by each of these dimensions in mediating compositional effects on scholastic outcomes. Steps in this direction have been made, especially in the micro-social processes of classroom learning (see Peterson, Wilkinson & Hallinan, 1984).

Second, compositional effects in our analysis emerged as moderate. Perhaps this weakness of effect enhances the mental reservation of teachers regarding fully heterogeneous frameworks, a reservation that apparently stems from real didactic difficulties (Dar, 1985). We thus feel strongly, as do many others, that the formation of heterogeneous classes should be accompanied by adaptation of teaching strategies and methods to a much greater degree than has been common. Research and field experimentation suggest that individualized instruction, activity methods, and cooperative group learning are some of the promising avenues for alleviating teaching and for enhancing positive outcomes of intellectual integration.

REFERENCES

AMIR, Y., SHARAN, S., & BEN-ARI, R. (Eds.). (1984). *School desegregation.* Hillsdale, NJ: Erlbaum.

BLOOM, B. S. (1976). *Human characteristics and school learning.* New York: McGraw-Hill.

BRIM, O. G., GLASS, D. C., NEULINGER, J., & FIRESTONE, I. J. (1969). *American beliefs and attitudes about intelligence.* New York: Russel Sage.

BROOKOVER, W., BEADY, C., FLOOD, P., SCHEITZER, I., & WEISENBAKER, J. (1981). *School social systems and student achievement.* New York: Holt, Rinehart & Winston.

CHEN, M., LEWY, A., & ADLER, C. (1978). *Halich ve toza'a be ma'ase na hinuch: Ha'arachat trumata shel hativat ha beinaim le ma'arechet ha hinuch.* [Process and outcome in education: Evaluating the contribution of the middle school to the educational system]. Tel Aviv: Tel Aviv University and the Hebrew University in Jerusalem.

COLEMAN, J. S., CAMPBELL, E. Q., HOBSON, C. J., MCPARTLAND, J., MOOD, A., WEINFELD, F. D., & YORK, R. L. (1966). *Equality of educational opportunity.* Washington, DC: U. S. Government Printing Office.

DAR, Y. (1980). *Homogeniut ve heterogeniut ba hinuch: Mashabim ishyim ve sviva limudit be hashpa'a al hesegim limudyim.* [Homogeneity and heterogeneity in education]. Unpublished doctoral dissertation, Hebrew University of Jerusalem.

DAR, Y. (1985). Teachers' attitudes toward ability grouping: Educational considerations and social and organizational influences. *Interchange, 16,* 17–38.

DAR, Y., & RESH, N. (1981). *Homogeneity and heterogeneity in education: Interaction between personal resources and the learning environment in the effect on scholastic achievement.* Jerusalem: Hebrew University, National Council of Jewish Women Research Institute for Innovation in Education.

DAR, Y., & RESH, N. (1986). *Classroom composition and pupils' achievement: Academic impact of ability based classrooms.* London: Gordon & Breach.

ESHEL, Y. (1980). Le itur ve le ivchun talmidim teuney-tipuach. [Diagnosing and locating disadvantaged students]. *E'yunim Ba'Hinuch, 27,* 143–156.

FINDLEY, W. G., & BRYAN, M. M. (1971). *Ability grouping, 1970: Status, impact and alternatives.* Athens: University of Georgia, Center for Educational Improvement.

FORD, J. (1969). *Social class and the comprehensive school.* London: Routledge & Kegan-Paul.

HARP, J., & RICHER, S. (1969). Sociology of education. *Review of Educational Research, 39,* 671–694.

HEYNS, B. (1974). Social selection and stratification within schools. *American Journal of Sociology, 79,* 1434–1451.

HUSEN, T., & BOALT, G. (1967). *Educational research and educational change: The case of Sweden.* Stockholm: Almquist & Wiksell.

LAVIN, D. E. (1965). *The prediction of academic performance.* New York: Russel Sage.

LEITER, J. (1983). Classroom composition and achievement gains. *Sociology of Education, 56,* 126–132.

MADAUS, G. F., AIRASIAN, P. W., & KELLAGHAN, T. (1980). *School effectiveness: A reassessment of the evidence.* New York: McGraw-Hill.

MCDERMOTT, J. W. (1976). *The controversy over ability grouping in American education, 1916–1970.* Doctoral dissertation, Temple University, Philadelphia, PA.

MCDILL, E. L., & RIGSBY, L. C. (1973). *Structure and process in secondary schools: The academic impact of school climates.* Baltimore: Johns Hopkins University Press.

MCPARTLAND, J. M. (1969). The relative influence of school and of classroom desegregation on the academic achievement of ninth grade negro students. *Journal of Social Issues, 25,* 93–102.

ORTAR, G. (1967). Shlosh-esrey shnot Seker: Hesegey talmidim. [Thirteen years of students' achievements (the "Seker" test).] *Megamot, 15,* 220–230.

ORTAR, G. & MURIELI, A. (1966). *Milta: Ma'arechet mivhaney miscal le kitot.* [Milta: A system of IQ tests for 4th–12th grades.] Jerusalem: Hebrew University.

PETERSON, P. L., WILKINSON, L. C., & HALLINAN, M. (1984). *The social context of instruction: Group organization and group processes.* New York: Academic Press.

ROSENBAUM, J. E. (1976). *Making inequality: the hidden curriculum of high school tracking.* New York: Wiley.

RUTTER, M., MAUGHAM, B., MORTIMORE, P., OASTON, J., & SMITH, A. (1979). *Fifteen thousand hours: Secondary schools and their effects on children.* Cambridge, MA: Harvard University Press.

SIMON, B. (1970). Classification and streaming: A study of grouping in English schools, 1860–1960. In P. Nash (Ed.), *History and education* (pp. 115–159). New York: Random House.

SPADY, W. G. (1973). The impact of school resources on students. In F. N. Kerlinger (Ed.), *Review of research in education, 1* (pp. 135–177). Itasca, IL: Peacock.

STEPHAN, W. G., & FEAGIN, J. R. (Eds.). (1980). *School desegregation, past, present, and future.* New York: Plenum.

ST. JOHN, N. (1975). *School desegregation: Outcomes for children.* New York: Wiley.

THORNTON, C. H., & ECKLAND, B. K. (1980). High school contextual effects for black and white students: A research note. *Sociology of Education, 53,* 247–252.

YATES, A. (Ed.). (1966). *Grouping in education.* New York: Wiley.

AUTHORS

YEHEZKEL DAR, Lecturer, Hebrew University of Jerusalem, School of Education, Degania Aleph, Israel 15 120. *Specializations*: Sociology of school and learning, school integration, kibbutz education.

NURA RESH, Lecturer, Hebrew University of Jerusalem, School of Education, 33a Bustenai Street, Ramat Hasharon, 47224, Israel. *Specializations*: Sociology of school integration, social aspects of counseling.

12.

Tracking and Ethnicity in Israeli Secondary Education

Yossi Shavit

Secondary education in Israel uses curricular tracking. The academic track is selective on the basis of scholastic aptitude and prepares students for higher education. The vocational tracks maintain low curricular requirements and are said to enhance educational attainment of low-aptitude students. Ethnicity is highly correlated with measured aptitude. Hence, Sephardim are typically assigned to vocational tracks whereas Ashkenazim are more likely to attend the academic track. The investigation concerns the extent to which tracking reinforces the effects of ethnic aptitude differences on ethnic inequalities in educational attainment.

An analysis of data on educational histories for a subsample of Jewish men reveals that educational persistence at the secondary level is virtually unaffected by track placement. Academic track placement enhances eligibility for higher education of all but the least able students. The availability of the vocational track does not enhance educational participation of Sephardim. Rather, it inhibits further their already low likelihood of receiving higher education.

Most secondary educational systems maintain some form of curricular tracking (e.g., Benavot, 1983). Academic tracks are often selective on the basis of scholastic aptitude and they prepare students for higher education, while vocational tracks cater to less able students and prepare them for low or intermediate positions in the socioeconomic hierarchy.

Proponents of tracking argue that it serves to resolve the tension between the conflicting functions of educational systems. The *adaptive* function requires that the school system be devoted to the production of scholastic excellence. The *integrative* function requires that education be provided to all. In order to fulfill the adaptive function, so it is argued, schools must be selective and maintain high curricular requirements. The integrative function, on the other hand, requires that the requirements be aimed at a low common denominator. Tracking is said to resolve this dilemma. The selective tracks are entrusted with the responsibility of producing scholastic excellence, while the low tracks provide educational opportunities to the "masses" (Clark, 1962; Kahane and Starr, 1976).

Direct all correspondence to: Yossi Shavit, Department of Sociology and Anthropology, University of Haifa, Mount Carmel, Haifa 31999 Israel.

This paper was written while the author was a post-doctoral Research Associate at the Institute on Aging, University of Wisconsin–Madison. David Bills, David Featherman, David Grusky, Maureen Hallinan, and Judah Matras provided helpful comments on earlier drafts of this paper. Also acknowledged are the helpful reviews by Michael Olneck and two anonymous referees.

Opponents of tracking view it as a mechanism of social exclusion. Students of subordinate social origins are typically assigned (ostensibly because of their lower scholastic aptitudes) to the low tracks, which constrains their educational and socioeconomic attainments. Upper-class students, on the other hand, are placed in tracks which lead to positions at the top of the socioeconomic hierarchy (Bowles and Gintis, 1976; Persell, 1977; see also Karabel, 1972). As such, tracking is listed among the features of formal education which inhibit social mobility and reproduce social inequality across generations.

Some previous attempts to substantiate the "exclusionary" model focus on the extent to which track placement is determined directly by the socioeconomic (or class) characteristics of students (e.g., Alexander et al., 1978). European studies often find such direct effects and conclude in favor of the model (e.g., Hout and Garnier, 1979). On the other hand, where the socioeconomic differentials in placement are fully mediated by "merit" (e.g., ability, motivation, etc.), the conclusion is often more ambiguous: While meritocratic selection conforms to accepted norms of social justice, it may also serve to reproduce social inequality, especially when ability and social origins are highly correlated (e.g., Heyns, 1974; Bowles and Gintis, 1976).

The present study examines the extent to which tracking serves to *enhance* or to *attenuate* the correlation between ethnic origin and educational outcomes among Israeli secondary school students. Ethnicity and scholastic aptitude are highly correlated in Israel. Consequently, Sephardi students are disproportionately placed in vocational tracks, while Ashkenazi students are overrepresented in the academic track. Early selection into tracks may enhance the correlation between aptitude and educational outcomes when the tracks reinforce the effect of aptitude. Reinforcement obtains where low-ability students are placed in tracks which inhibit their already low attainments (relative to other tracks) and where able students are assigned to tracks which enhance attainments beyond their already high levels. Tracking may serve to attenuate the aptitude–attainment correlation when it fulfills a compensatory function. Compensation obtains when low-ability students attend tracks which enhance their attainment relative to other tracks.

Because of the high correlation between ethnicity and aptitude, when tracking reinforces the effects of aptitude it also reinforces the correlation between ethnicity and educational attainment. If on the other hand, tracking attenuates the aptitude–attainment correlation, it may contribute to ethnic equality in education.

THE SETTING

The Structure of Israeli Education

The Israeli educational system consists of three stages: primary education (through eighth grade); secondary education (grades nine through twelve); and postsecondary education.[1] Since the mid-sixties, primary education was virtually universal, with about 95 percent of school cohorts completing eighth grade (State of Israel, 1978:14). Of primary school graduates, about 90 percent continue to some form of secondary education. Broadly defined, secondary education consists of two types of curricular tracks. The academic tracks prepare students for the matriculation exams and diploma. They offer an academic curriculum and select students on the basis of high scholastic ability. The matriculation diploma constitutes a prerequisite for admission into institutes of higher education. The diploma is obtained by passing a series of comprehensive national examinations in a variety of academic subjects. Formally, any person over the age of seventeen may take the exams independent of his or her school experience. In practice, however, the likelihood of taking the exams and passing them is much higher for students who completed the twelfth grade in academic schools. In the late sixties, about 40 percent of secondary school students attended academic tracks.

Vocational education consists of several tracks. The largest is the four-year nonmatriculating track. The curriculum in this track consists of low-level academic studies and of vocational training. The low curricular requirements of this track are said to suit the capabilities of students with low scholastic aptitudes (Kahane and Starr, in preparation; Peleg and Adler, 1977).

In addition to these two tracks, secondary education offers several other, smaller tracks. Some combine vocational (or agricultural) studies with preparation for the matriculation examinations. Others maintain short-term programs (of two or three years) and stress practical training.

Until the early seventies, the major mechanism by which students were sorted into tracks was a differentiated system of tuition subsidies. Students with high scholastic aptitudes were eligible for graded tuition subsidies in the academic tracks. (The subsidies were graded, and inversely related to parental income.) Low-ability students were encouraged to attend the nonmatriculating tracks, in which tuition fees were subsidized for all. Aptitude was assessed on the basis of national aptitude tests (hereafter, the Seker), which students were required to take during eighth grade. The Seker consisted of standardized test batteries in the following areas: vocabulary, reasoning, arithmetic, geometry, text comprehension, and composition (Ortar, 1967).

The Expansion of Vocational Education

In recent decades, most educational systems have exhibited a decline in the shares of students who attend vocational secondary education (Benavot, 1983). In Israel, by contrast, the proportion of vocational-track students has risen considerably in the past three decades. During the 1950s, only 20 percent of secondary school students attended vocational tracks. By 1970, this proportion rose to about 45 percent (Kahane and Starr, 1976). During the same period the proportion of students in the academic track declined from about 70 to 40 percent. The relative expansion of secondary vocational education is related to changes in the sociodemographic composition of the Jewish population.

Until the late 1940s the Jewish population of Palestine consisted primarily of European Jews (hereafter, Ashkenazim), most of whom had

---

[1] Since the early seventies, the Israeli educational system has been undergoing a structural reform. The data for this study pertain to respondents who attended postprimary education under the old system. Therefore, only that system is discussed. For descriptions of the reform see Kleinberger (1969) and Chen et al. (1978).

immigrated since the turn of the century (Matras, 1965). The early 1950s witnessed an influx of immigration waves, many of which originated in North Africa and the Middle East. It became apparent soon after their arrival that most Asian-African students (hereafter, Sephardim) had considerable difficulties in school. Their mean level of measured scholastic aptitude was lower than that of Ashkenazi students by almost a full standard deviation (Ortar, 1967; Minkovich et al., 1977). During the late 1960s about 40 percent of Sephardi eighth graders scored in the bottom third of the Seker score distribution and about 65 percent scored in the bottom half. Among Ashkenazim, 75 and 60 percent scored in the top half and top third of the distribution respectively. Thus, scholastic aptitude discriminatés well (in the statistical sense) between the two ethnic groups.[2]

Since primary education has been compulsory throughout the period, most Sephardim (90 percent in the late 1960s) completed eighth grade despite their low levels of scholastic aptitude. The expansion of vocational education at the secondary level is said to have been a response to the increased demand of low-ability primary school graduates for opportunities to receive secondary education (Adler, 1970; Peleg and Adler, 1977). By the late 1960s, Sephardim comprised half of all primary school graduates (State of Israel, 1978). Only 25 percent of Sephardi ninth graders, as compared with 50 percent of Ashkenazim, were placed in an academic track (Shavit-Streifler, 1983:134). Most of the ethnic difference in track placement is related to aptitude differences between

_____

[2] Scholastic aptitude is usually defined and operationalized as a cognitive construct which predicts the ability to succeed in given school systems. Its predictive efficiency is dependent on the congruence between cognitive characteristics which it measures and those which are rewarded in the schools. To the extent that schools reward characteristics which are differentially distributed among social groups, scholastic aptitude measures will also be so biased (e.g., Featherman, 1980). The "New Sociology of Education" (reviewed in Karabel and Halsey, 1977) is concerned primarily with the social constructions and definitions of knowledge and aptitude and their role in educational reproduction. In Israel (as elsewhere), research has attempted to understand the socio-cultural determinants of ethnic differences in measured aptitude (e.g., Frankenstein, 1951). The present paper takes these differences as givens. In doing so, we do not dismiss the importance of the relativity of "aptitude" in the transmission of educational and socioeconomic inequality. Rather, we accept it and are concerned with the extent to which tracking reinforces the reproductive effects of aptitude.

the groups (Nachmias, 1980; Yogev, 1981; Shavit-Streifler, 1983).

The assignment of low-ability (Sephardim) students to vocational tracks was ostensibly motivated by the assumption that academic education is ill suited to their needs, inclinations, and capabilities. It was also assumed that if placed in the academic track, most would drop out prematurely (Tzucker, n.d.). Vocational education, by contrast, was expected to increase the retention rates of low-ability students. Thus, the expansion of the vocational track was intended to enhance the overall educational participation of Sephardim.

An empirical validation of this assumption must demonstrate that the low-ability students who attend the vocational tracks are more likely to persist in secondary school than similar students in the academic track. Such evidence is not available for Israel (nor, to this author's knowledge, for other settings). Kahane and Starr (in preparation) analyze tabulated Israeli data on drop-out rates by track and find higher rates in the vocational than in the academic tracks. Yuchtman and Samuel (1975) analyze sample data and report similar findings. Neither study, however, controls for the differential aptitudes of students in the two tracks. Halsey et al. (1980:164–67) study the effects of secondary school type on the educational attainment of British respondents and find strong school-type effects even when controlling for IQ. However, their dependent variable confounds attainment at the secondary and at the post-secondary level.

American studies on tracking typically analyze data for samples of high school seniors in order to estimate track effects on a variety of educational outcomes, ignoring the differential drop-out rates by track (e.g., Alexander et al., 1978; Hauser et al., 1976; but see Heyns, 1974:1442n). Such omissions may be justified in the American setting where, in recent cohorts, relatively few students drop out before twelfth grade (e.g., Featherman and Hauser, 1978:231). In Israel, by contrast, where only about half of recent birth cohorts reach twelfth grade, a major concern is with the institutional determinants of secondary educational attainment. Thus, one objective of the present investigation is to study the determinants of persistence in secondary schools.

A second objective is to study the determinants of matriculation status. As Kerckhoff et al. (1982) demonstrate, certification can be more consequential for future socioeconomic attainment than simply the quantity of education attained, especially in educational systems which maintain qualitative forms of educational differentiation.

DATA AND VARIABLES

The data for this investigation are drawn from a life-history study of Jewish Israeli men (Matras, 1980). A systematic, stratified sample of Jewish Israeli men who were born in 1954 were interviewed when they were approximately twenty-six years old. Most members of the cohort attended eighth grade during the school year of 1968/69. Those who attended twelfth grade did so primarily during 1971/72.

The interview consisted of extensive retrospective life-history questions regarding past and present participation in numerous life domains (eg., marital, occupational, educational histories). In addition, standard socioeconomic and demographic data were collected. The interview data were then merged with eighth grade school records, which were retrieved from Ministry of Education files. The school records provide data on scholastic aptitude at eighth grade as measured by the Seker aptitude tests. School records were retrieved for 1215 of the original 2144 sample cases.[3] The sample is representative of the cohort in terms of several key variables (Shavit-Streifler, 1983). Of the 1215 cases (hereafter, the sample), about 1050 received at least some secondary education. The analysis is carried out in a subsample of respondents who followed one of the two larger tracks described earlier (hereafter, the subsample, n = 676).[4]

The dependent variables are Highest grade attended in secondary school (HIGRD) and a dummy variable (MATRIC) coded 1 if the respondent obtained the matriculation diploma. Four independent variables are employed in the analysis:

Ethnicity (SPHRD) – A dummy variable coded

1 if respondent or at least one of his parents was born in an Asian or African country.

Parental Education (PARED) – A continuous variable measuring parental education. This variable is a standardized mean of the number of school years completed by respondent's mother and father. The variable is standardized in the sample rather than the subsample.[5]

Scholastic Aptitude (APTD) – Respondent's scholastic aptitude at eighth grade. This variable is a standardized (in the sample) sum of respondent's scores on the eighth grade Seker tests.

Track Placement (VOC) – A dummy variable coded 1 if respondent attended the vocational track, and 0 if he attended the academic track.

Table 1 presents means and standard deviations of the variables by ethnicity and track. Column 5 of the table indicates that the subsample is considerably more select than the sample from which it was drawn: The mean levels of standardized parental education and aptitude are 0.17 and 0.32 respectively (as compared to 0 by construction). Similarly, the proportion of matriculants is 0.41, as compared to 0.29 in the sample (not reported), and the mean highest grade attended in secondary school is 11.4, compared to 10.8. The greater selectivity of the subsample is expected, since it excludes respondents who did not attend secondary education and those who attended the least selective, short vocational programs.

A comparison of columns 1 and 2 indicates that Ashkenazi students enjoy higher parental education, aptitude, and matriculation rates. Their mean highest grade attended is higher than that of Sephardim by two-thirds of a school year. Fifty-seven percent of Sephardim in the subsample are in the vocational track, as compared to only 22 percent of Ashkenazim.

Turning to columns 3 and 4, the intertrack difference in mean aptitudes is .84, almost a full standard deviation. Students in the academic track are more likely to matriculate than vocational students, and they persist in secondary school six months longer on the average. Are the track differences in the educational outcomes due to the differential aptitude compositions of their students or to some direct effects of the tracks themselves?

---

[3] Of the 2144 sample cases, about 200 did not reside in Israel when they attended eighth grade. An additional 150 cases did not attend eighth grade, and about 200 did not take the Seker test for a variety of other reasons (Bar-Haim, 1980). Of the remaining cases (estimated at about 1600), 20 percent were lost in the merge process.

[4] Most previous studies on the consequences of tracking distinguish between the "academic" and "all other" tracks (e.g., Alexander et al., 1978; Hauser et al., 1976; Nachmias, 1980; Yuchtman and Samuel, 1975). Such a dichotomous classification has the virtue of parsimony, but makes the strong assumption that "all other" tracks are homogeneous with respect to the process under investigation. In order to maintain parsimony but avoid making this assumption, the analysis focuses on a single contrast between the two largest tracks in the system. A more detailed analysis which contrasts the effects of the academic track with each of the remaining tracks in the system is presented elsewhere (Shavit-Streifler, 1983).

[5] In exploratory analyses additional indicators of socioeconomic background were included in the model (prestige of father's occupation when respondent was in his teens and his family size). However, controlling for parental education and ethnicity, these variables did not show significant effects on the dependent variables and were omitted from the reported analyses.

Table 1. Means and Standard Deviations (in parentheses) of Social Background, Aptitude and Educational Attainment by Ethnicity and Track[a]

| | Ethnicity | | Track | | Subsample |
	Sephardim (1)	Ashkenazim (2)	Academic (3)	Vocational (4)	Total (5)
SPHRD	—	—	.37	.73	.51
			(.48)	(.45)	(.50)
VOC	.57	.22	—	—	.40
	(.50)	(.42)			(.49)
PARED	−.35	.74	.49	−.27	.17
	(.90)	(.71)	(.89)	(.93)	(.98)
APTD	−.04	.71	.66	−.18	.32
	(.86)	(.77)	(.75)	(.86)	(.90)
MATRIC	.24	.59	.61	.12	.41
	(.43)	(.49)	(.49)	(.33)	(.49)
HIGRD	11.0	11.8	11.6	11.0	11.4
	(1.2)	(1.1)	(0.9)	(1.2)	(1.1)

[a] See text for descriptions of the subsample and of the variables.

TRACK PLACEMENT AND PERSISTENCE IN SECONDARY SCHOOL

Our first analytical objective is to assess the effect of track placement on students' persistence in secondary school. The analysis is informed by the following conceptual considerations:

1. Previous studies demonstrate that placement in the low tracks inhibits students' self-image and the encouragement which they receive from significant others. These, in turn, dampen motivation and aspirations (e.g., Heyns, 1974; Alexander et al., 1978). In addition, track placement defines quite clearly the prospects for matriculation and higher education. It is assumed that academic-track students are motivated to persist in school by the prospects of obtaining the matriculation diploma (which is perceived as crucial for future socioeconomic success). Vocational students lack this incentive and adjust their aspirations and motivations accordingly. Thus, if students' motivations and aspirations determine their persistence in school, we expect placement in the academic track to enhance persistence relative to the vocational track.

2. Track placement defines the curricular requirements to which students are exposed. Academic-track students are faced with an abstract curriculum which is, persumably, more intellectually demanding than the practical curriculum of the vocational tracks (Kahane and Starr, in preparation). This implies that aptitude is more strongly related to persistence in the academic track than in the vocational track. Mathematically, this expectation translates into an interaction between the effects of aptitude and track on persistence.

Most previous studies of educational attainment estimate regression models in which the dependent variable is highest grade attended (or completed). Given the highly skewed distribution of that variable in our data (with a mean of 11.4 and a standard deviation of 1.1, the skewness of HIGRD is −1.34), the ordinary least squares assumption of normality is grossly violated.

As an alternative to an OLS formulation, secondary educational attainment is cast as a process of grade progression (e.g., Mare, 1981). The model focuses on the determinants of continuation (versus dropping out) at each grade interval. The model consists of three equations which pertain to the continuation from grade nine to ten, ten to eleven, and eleven to twelve, respectively. The dependent variable in each equation is the probability of continuing from the grade of origin (9, 10, and 11) to the grade of destination (10, 11, and 12, respectively). Table 2 presents the gross continuation probabilities in the three grade intervals of secondary education.

The diagonal elements of the table indicate that in each of the three transitions, about 90 percent of the students persist to the following grade. The off-diagonal elements indicate that 77 percent of the subsample who attend ninth grade reach eleventh grade, and 70 percent reach twelfth grade.

Noting the extreme values of the diagonal

Table 2. Continuation Probabilities from Grade of Origin to Grade of Destination

| Grade of Origin | Grade of Destination | | |
	Tenth Grade	Eleventh Grade	Twelfth Grade
Ninth	.89	.77	.70
Tenth		.87	.79
Eleventh			.91

Table 3. Effects of Social Background, Scholastic Aptitude, and Track on Continuation to Grades Ten, Eleven, and Twelve: Logit Regression Models

	Independent Variables						
	Constant	SPHRD	PARED	APTD	VOC	A*VOC[a]	R^{2b}
Model A. Continuation from ninth to tenth grade							
A1.	2.929*	−.989*	.521*	.411*			.14
A2.	2.837*	−1.031*	.537*	.455*	.260		.14
A3.	2.775*	−.999*	.511*	.641*	.219	−.309	.15
Model B. Continuation from tenth to eleventh grade							
B1.	2.713*	−1.234*	.297*	1.090*			.25
B2.	2.852*	−1.191*	.278**	1.044*	−.323		.25
B3.	2.834*	−1.160*	.223	1.461*	−.446	−.641**	.26
Model C. Continuation from eleventh to twelfth grade							
C1.	2.478*	−.512	.628*	.379*			.17
C2.	2.565*	−.500	.604*	.347**	−.192		.17
C3.	2.417*	−.468	.583*	.666*	−.116	−.628**	.17

[a] A*VOC represents an interaction between the effects of APTD and VOC.
[b] See footnote 7 for an explanation of the R^2 statistic.
* Significant at the .05 level.
** Significant at the .10 level.

probabilities, the model is estimated in the logit framework, which is not sensitive to skewed distributions on the dependent variables (e.g., Hanushek and Jackson, 1977: Chapter 7). Each of the three equations is estimated for respondents who attended the grade of origin.[6] Thus, the equation for the continuation from grade nine to ten is estimated for the complete subsample; the equation for the continuation from grade ten to eleven is estimated only for the 89 percent of the subsample who attended tenth grade, etc. The estimates of the model are presented in Table 3.

Model A1 assumes that the continuation from ninth to tenth grade is determined solely by students' ethnicity, parental education, and aptitude. The model accounts for 14 percent of the predictive error.[7] Continuation in this

grade interval is significantly affected by the three variables.

When track is added to the model (Model A2), its effect fails to achieve significance. Nor is the interaction between track and aptitude significantly different from zero (Model A3). Thus, the continuation from ninth to tenth grade is not significantly affected by track once students' social origins and aptitude are controlled.

The same logic of model comparison is presented in panels B and C of Table 3 for continuation to grades eleven and twelve, respectively. We find small and insignificant additive effects of track on the logit continuation to both grades. The effect of track is not significant in Model B2 or C2, and the R^2 statistics of the models do not exhibit improvement over those of models B1 and C1, respectively. However, in models B3 and C3, the effects of the interactions between aptitude and track are of borderline significance. In both grade intervals continuation within the vocational track is less strongly related to aptitude than continuation within the academic track.

---

[6] Formally, the model is written as

$$\log\left(\frac{P_{gti}}{1-P_{gti}}\right) = b_g^0 + \sum_j b_{jg} X_{ij} + b_{tg} T_{gt},$$

where P_{gti} is the probability that respondent i who attended grade g in tract t will continue to grade g+1. X_{ij} is a vector of j respondent's characteristics (e.g., aptitude, ethnicity, etc.), and T_{gt} is respondent's track of placement in grade g. The model is linear and additive in the logit. In the probability scale the model is written

$$P_{gti} = \frac{\exp(b_g^0 + \sum_j b_{jg} X_{ij} + b_{tg} T_{tg})}{1 + \exp(b_g^0 + \sum_j b_{jg} X_{ij} + b_{tg} T_{tg})}.$$

The desirable properties of the model and of its functional form are discussed by Hanushek and Jackson (1977: ch. 7).

[7] "R^2" measures the proportion of predictive error under the null model (in which none of the variables affects the dependent logit) which is explained by the

estimated model. The predictive error under the null model is

$$E_y = 1 - p^p (1-p)^{1-p}$$

where p is the probability of continuing to the grade of destination. Under the estimated model the predictive error is

$$E_e = 1 - L^{1/n}$$

where L is the likelihood statistic produced by the maximum likelihood estimation of the model. "R^2" is

$$(E_y - E_e)/E_y$$

(DuMouchel, 1976; Mare, 1981).

The overall effect of track placement on secondary educational attainment is illustrated in Table 4. The table presents estimated and adjusted (for parental education and ethnicity) means of highest grade attended in secondary school by track and selected aptitude scores. The means are computed under Models A1, B3, and C3 of Table 4.[8] As the table illustrates, low-ability students persist in school somewhat longer when placed in the vocational track, while for high-ability students, persistence is greater in the academic track. Low-ability students seem to benefit from the low level of curricular requirements in the vocational track, whereas able students benefit from the positive motivational effect of the academic track. And yet the absolute magnitude of these effects should not be overstated. The differences between the two columns are small, especially at the middle ranges of the standardized aptitude distribution. For students whose standardized aptitude exceeds -1.0 (about 85 on the IQ scale and about 16 percent on the cumulative aptitude distribution in the sample), intertrack differences in secondary educational attainment do not exceed 0.09, the equivalent of about a month of school attendance.

In sum, the analysis reveals rather limited effects of track on progression in secondary schools. Placement in the vocational track enhances the progression of only the very least able students. The progression of all other students is not appreciably affected by track. Thus, tracking neither reinforces, nor considerably attenuates, the effect of aptitude in the attainment of secondary education. The major determinant of ethnic differences in attainment is the aptitude difference between the groups, and tracking does not significantly affect this relationship.[9]

---

[8] Following Mare (1981), the adjusted means of highest grade attended in secondary school (HIGRD) are computed as

$$HIGRD_{at} = 9 + P_{9at} + P_{9at} + P_{10at} + P_{9at} + P_{10at} + P_{11at},$$

where $HIGRD_{at}$ is the estimated mean HIGRD attended by students in track t and aptitude score a. P_{gat} is the adjusted probability of students in track t and ability score a continuing to grade $g+1$. The probabilities are estimated under the models and are computed for Ashkenazim at the mean of the parental education distribution.

[9] The analysis also reveals significant net effects of ethnicity and parental education on persistence in secondary school. These effects may be due either to correlates of these variables which determine educational persistence (e.g., motivation, parental encouragement) or to ethnicity-based or class discrimination in grade promotions. The data do not enable us to test these competing hypotheses.

Table 4. Estimated Means of Highest Grade Attended in Secondary School by Track and Selected Aptitude Scores, Adjusted for Parental Education and Ethnicity

Standardized Aptitude Scores	Track		Difference
	ACAD	VOC	
-2.0	10.65	11.04	.39
-1.5	11.00	11.22	.22
-1.0	11.31	11.40	.09
$-.5$	11.52	11.52	.00
0.0	11.67	11.62	$-.05$
.5	11.77	11.68	$-.09$
1.0	11.85	11.75	$-.10$
1.5	11.91	11.90	$-.11$
2.0	11.92	11.82	$-.10$

TRACKING AND MATRICULATION

Table 5 presents estimates of several logit regressions of matriculation status. As the first two models indicate, Sephardim and students in the vocational track are less likely to matriculate than Ashkenazim and academic-track students, respectively. Most of the gross effect of ethnicity is eliminated when we control for aptitude and parental education (Models 3 and 4). When track is added to the model (Model 5), the effects of socioeconomic background are reduced to insignificance. The vocational track (in which Sephardim are overrepresented) inhibits matriculation. The negative effect of track is quite considerable (at -1.908) and contributes a substantial increment to the R^2 statistic. In Model 6 the effects of ethnicity and parental education are set to zero at no loss of fit (as indicated by the R^2) or substantial change in the remaining coefficients in the model.

As Model 7 indicates, the effect of the interaction between track and aptitude on the logit of matriculation is not significant. However, inspecting Figure 1, which plots the estimated probabilities under Model 6, we note that (in the probability scale) the estimated advantage accruing to academic-track placement is most pronounced for able students: In the lowest quartile of the aptitude distribution the track effects on matriculation probabilities are small, amounting at most to a difference between .03 and .12. However, in the remaining quartiles, the magnitudes of the track effects are substantial. In the subsample, 4 percent of Ashkenazim and 20 percent of Sephardim score in the lowest aptitude quartile. (In the cohort, the respective proportions are 10 and 34 percent.) Thus, placement in the academic track can enhance the likelihood of matriculation for 80 percent of Sephardim and 96 percent of Ashkenazim in the subsample (and 65 and 90

Table 5. Effects of Social Background, Scholastic Aptitude and Track on the Likelihood to Obtain the Matriculation Diploma: Logit Regression Models

Model	Independent Variables						
	Constant	SPHRD	PARED	APTD	VOC	A*VOC	R^2
1.	.214	−1.247*					.04
2.	.361*				−2.617*		.15
3.	−.244	−.632*	.638*				.07
4.	−1.277*	−.157	.176	1.934*			.24
5.	−.759*	.049	.065	1.793*	−1.908*		.30
6.	−.725*			1.815*	−1.920*		.30
7.	−.781*			1.913*	−1.714*	−.402	.30

* Coefficient at least twice its standard error.

percent, respectively, in the cohort). In the subsample, 80 percent of Ashkenazim and only 50 percent of Sephardim who stand to benefit (in terms of the likelihood of matriculating) from placement in the academic track are so placed.

By way of illustration, Table 6 compares the relative magnitudes of the effects of ethnic differences in aptitude and track placement on the ethnic difference in matriculation rates. The first row in the table presents the expected matriculation probabilities under Model 6 (of Table 5) by ethnicity. The probabilities are computed for each group at its mean aptitude and at its proportion of vocational-track students (see Table 1 and footnote 6). Under the model, the expected proportions of matriculants are .14 and .54 for Sephardim and Ashkenazim respectively. The second row in the table presents the estimated proportions under the assumption that the mean aptitude of both groups is equal to the observed subsample mean (0.32). We note a reduction of 65 percent in the ethnic difference in the matriculation

rates (from a difference of .40 to .14). In the third row we assume that the groups are equally likely to be placed in the vocational track (at the subsample mean proportion of .40). The ethnic difference in matriculation rates is reduced by 30 percent.

In sum, the difference between Ashkenazim and Sephardim in the proportion of matriculants is due primarily to the ability differences between the groups. However, the statistical elimination of track placement differences also reduces the difference between the ethnic matriculation rates considerably. Tracking affects the ethnic difference in matriculation rates by reinforcing the positive effect of aptitude. High-ability students are typically assigned to the academic track, which enhances further their likelihood to matriculate. Ashkenazim exhibit higher levels of aptitude than Sephardim and are thus more likely to benefit from this reinforcing effect. Sephardim, on the other hand, are overrepresented in the vocational track, which inhibits further their already low matriculation rates.

SUMMARY AND DISCUSSION

To summarize, the major determinant of educational continuation in secondary education is scholastic aptitude. Given the marked difference between the ethnic groups in measured aptitude, tracking does not appreciably affect ethnic inequalities in secondary educational attainment. However, track placement is an important determinant of the likelihood to matriculate and of ethnic differences therein. Most Sephardim exhibit levels of scholastic aptitude which afford non-negligible chances to matriculate for academic-track students. Yet, most are placed in the vocational track, which prevents the realization of this potential. The low matriculation rate of Sephardim is due to no small extent to their exclusion from the academic track.

Thus, it seems that the availability of the vocational track does not fulfill its intended integrative function. Not only does it fail to

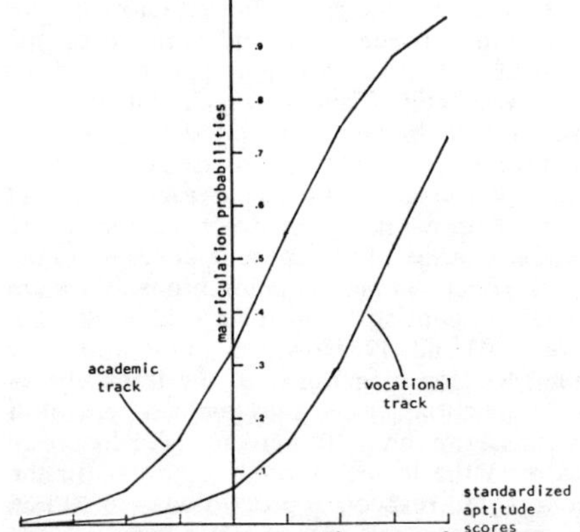

Figure 1. Estimated Probabilities of Matriculating by Track and Standardized Aptitude Scores

Table 6. Expected Proportions of Matriculants by Ethnicity Under the Model and at Selected Means of Aptitude and Track Proportions

	Ethnicity		Difference	Percent Difference Change
	Ashkenazim	Sephardim		
1. Group means of aptitude and track	.54	.14	.40	—
2. Equal aptitude means	.36	.22	.14	65
3. Equal track proportions	.45	.17	.28	30

enhance educational attainment of most low-aptitude students, it also serves to limit the supply of highly educated manpower, which is presumably necessary for economic development. It is often argued that vocational education is functional for economic development in that it supplies the economy with skilled blue-collar workers. While this assertion is still to be empirically tested, it seems inconsistent with findings of previous research that reveal small relevance of the skills acquired in secondary vocational education to those required by the ultimate labor market positions of graduates (e.g., Doron, 1968, cited in Peleg and Adler, 1977; Collins, 1979:16–17). What then is the social function of tracking?

With the help of some speculation, the findings seem to illustrate an exclusionary role of tracking which may be sketched as follows: In industrialized societies, positions of privilege are normatively allocated on the basis of educational credentials. Occupants of privileged positions attempt to retain their relative privilege by restricting the number of contenders for these positions (Parkin, 1979). This can be achieved by raising the credential entry requirements of positions (Collins, 1979) and/or by restricting the availability of opportunities to acquire credentials.

Privileged groups also attempt to transmit privilege across generations. Thus, they exert political power in support of the establishment (or perpetuation) of educational selection criteria which legitimate favorable educational opportunities to their children (Weber, 1968:342; Bourdieu and Passeron, 1977; Bowles and Gintis, 1976).

The continued hegemony of the privileged strata and the stability of the social system depend, in part, on the successful socialization of youth into the dominant value system. The socializing role of the school system is especially important in immigrant societies in which the family cannot effectively transmit the principles of the host culture. Collins (1979), for example, suggests that the expansion of mandatory schooling in the nineteenth-century United States was supported by the Anglo elites as a means to acculturate non-Anglo immigrants into the dominant Anglo value system. Similarly, in Israel, the "de-socialization" and "re-socialization" of Asian-African immigrants were paramount on the national agenda during the fifties and sixties (Bar-Yosef, 1968; Kleinberger, 1969).

For acculturation to be effectively fulfilled by the schools, educational participation must be widespread. This requirement, however, interferes with the fulfillment of the exclusionary function which requires a restriction of educational opportunities. Tracking resolves this contradiction: The academic track enables students to obtain the matriculation diploma, which presumably opens the road to socioeconomic success. The vocational track, on the other hand, serves to retain students ("keep them off the streets") and expose them to the dominant value system and ideology, but it does not confer the desirable credential. The historic decline in the relative size of the academic track may have assured a relative scarcity of matriculants and university graduates who would have contended for positions of privilege. The aptitude-based selection into tracks (and the socially accepted definition of aptitude—see footnote 2) provided Ashkenazi students with an edge in the credentialing process. It also served to legitimate the overrepresentation of Sephardim in the vocational track. In sum, tracking serves to reconcile a dilemma between an exclusionary and an integrative function of secondary education.

The "exclusionary" interpretation should be treated as an hypothesis. It is formulated in terms of ideal-typical intentions which are imputed to policymakers who were involved in processes of educational change. Clearly, intentions cannot be strictly inferred from observed consequences. Are the consequences, which were reported in this paper, intended? Or do they represent unintended consequences of well-meaning political action? An empirical evaluation of these questions should investigate the socio-political decision-making processes which resulted in the expansion of tracking in the 1950s and 1960s.

Do the findings imply that under a comprehensive, or under a non-tracked system, the observed inequality would have been substantially reduced? As Halsey et al. (1980) point out, it is not possible to predict the consequences of a change in a single variable on the outcome of a complex system of relationships. "To do so would be to fall into the classic fallacy of supposing that relationships found to hold within a given system tell what would happen if that system where changed" (Halsey et al., 1980:167). Furthermore, as Kerckhoff (1974) and Treiman and Terrell (1975) demonstrate, different educational structures can produce very similar patterns of social inequality. Thus, our findings cannot provide a solid basis for policy implications regarding alternatives to tracking as we observed it.

During the past decade, Israeli education has been undergoing far-reaching institutional changes. Most important are the democratization of the matriculation process, the postponement till tenth grade of track placement, and the expansion of a comprehensive school system. Future research will evaluate the consequences of these changes for inequalities in educational and socioeconomic attainment. Comparisons of our findings with those of future research may provide a post hoc basis for policy implications and evaluations.

REFERENCES

Adler, Chaim
1970　"The Israeli school as a selective institution." Pp. 287–301 in S. N. Eisenstadt, Rivkah Bar-Yosef and Chaim Adler (eds.), Integration and Development in Israel. Jerusalem: Israel Universities Press.

Alexander, Karl L., Martha Cook and Edward L. McDill
1978　"Curriculum tracking and educational stratification: some further evidence." American Sociological Review 43:47–66.

Bar-Haim, Yitzhak
1980　An Analysis of the Seker Files. Jerusalem: Brookdale Institute, Mimeo (Hebrew).

Bar-Yosef, Rivkah
1968　"Desocialization and resocialization—The adjustment of immigrants." International Migration Review 13:27–47.

Benavot, Aaron
1983　"The rise and decline of vocational education." Sociology of Education 56:63–76.

Bourdieu, Pierre and Jean-Claude Passeron
1977　Reproduction. Beverly Hills: Sage.

Bowles, Samuel, and Herbert Gintis
1976　Schooling in Capitalist America. New York: Basic Books.

Chen, Michael, Arle Lewy and Chaim Adler
1978　Process and Result in Education: Evaluating the Contribution of the Junior High School to the Educational System. Tel-Aviv and Jerusalem: Tel-Aviv University and Hebrew University (Hebrew).

Clark, Burton R.
1962　Educating the Expert Society. San Francisco: Chandler.

Collins, Randall
1979　The Credential Society: An Historical Sociology of Education and Stratification. New York: Academic Press.

Doron, R.
1968　Vocational Education and the Needs of Industry. Jerusalem: Szold Institute (Hebrew).

DuMouchel, William H.
1976　"On the analogy between linear and log-linear regression." Technical Report No. 67. University of Michigan, Department of Statistics.

Featherman, David L.
1980　"Schooling and occupational careers: constancy and change in worldly success." Pp. 675–738 in Orville G. Brim, Jr., and Jerome Kagan (eds.), Constancy and Change in Human Development. Cambridge: Harvard University Press.

Featherman, David L. and Robert M. Hauser
1978　Opportunity and Change. New York: Academic Press.

Frankenstein, Carl
1951　"The problem of ethnic differences." Megamot 2:261–76 (Hebrew).

Halsey, A. H., A. F. Heath and J. M. Ridge
1980　Origins and Destinations: Family, Class and Education in Modern Britain. Oxford: Clarendon Press.

Hanushek, Eric A. and John E. Jackson
1977　Statistical Methods for Social Scientists. New York: Academic Press.

Hauser, Robert M., William H. Sewell and Duane F. Alwin
1976　"High school effects on achievement." In William H. Sewell, Robert M. Hauser and David L. Featherman (eds.), Schooling and Achievement in American Society. New York: Academic Press.

Heyns, Barbara
1974　"Social selection and stratification within schools." American Journal of Sociology 79:1434–51.

Hout, Michael and Maurice A. Garnier
1979　"Curriculum placement and educational stratification in France." Sociology of Education 52:146–56.

Israel, State of
1978　Statistical Data on the Educational System. Jerusalem: Ministry of Education (Hebrew).

Kahane, Reuven and Laura Starr
1976　"The impact of rapid social change on technological education: an Israeli example." Comparative Education Review 20:165–78.
in prep.　Patterns of Vocational Socialization in Israel (Hebrew).

Karabel, Jerome
1972　"Community colleges and social stratification." Harvard Education Review 42:521–62.

Karabel, Jerome and A. H. Halsey
1977 Power and Ideology in Education. New York: Oxford University Press.
Kerckhoff, Alan C.
1974 "Stratification processes and outcomes in England and the U.S." American Sociological Review 39:789–801.
Kerckhoff, Alan C., Richard T. Campbell and Larry M. Trott
1982 "Dimensions of educational and occupational attainment in Great Britain." American Sociological Review 47:347–73.
Kleinberger, Aaron F.
1969 Society, Schools and Progress in Israel. Oxford: Pergamon Press.
Mare, Robert D.
1981 "Change and stability in educational stratification." American Sociological Review 46:72–88.
Matras, Judah
1965 Social Change in Israel. Chicago: Aldine.
1980 A Proposal for the Study of the 1954 Birth Cohort. Mimeo. Brookdale Institute, Jerusalem.
Minkovich, A., D. Davis and J. Bashi
1977 An Evaluation Study of Israeli Elementary Schools. Jerusalem: Hebrew University, School of Education.
Nachmias, Chava
1980 "Curriculum tracking: some of its causes and consequences under a meritocracy." Comparative Education Review 24:1–20.
Ortar, Gina R.
1967 "Educational achievements of primary school graduates in Israel as related to their socio-cultural background." Comparative Education 4:23–34.

Parkin, Frank
1979 Marxism and Class Theory: A Bourgeois Critique. New York: Columbia University Press.
Peleg, Rachel and Chaim Adler
1977 "Compensatory education in Israel: conceptions, attitudes and trends." American Psychologist 32:945–58.
Persell, C. Hodges
1977 Education and Inequality. New York: Free Press.
Shavit-Streifler, Yossi J.
1983 Tracking in Israeli Education: Its Consequences for Ethnic Inequalities in Educational Attainment. Unpublished doctoral dissertation, Department of Sociology, University of Wisconsin–Madison.
Treiman, Donald J. and Kermit Terrell
1975 "The process of status attainment in the United States and Great Britain." American Journal of Sociology 81:563–83.
Tzucker, David
n.d. The Vocational Education. Jerusalem: Van Leer Institute, Mimeo. (Hebrew).
Weber, Max
1968 Economy and Society. Guenther Roth and Claus Wittich (eds.). Berkeley: University of California Press.
Yogev, Abraham
1981 "Determinants of early educational career in Israel: further evidence for the sponsorship thesis." Sociology of Education 54:181–95.
Yuchtman (Yaar), Ephraim and Yitzhak Samuel
1975 "Determinants of career plans: institutional versus interpersonal effects." American Sociological Review 40:521–31.

13.

High School Attendance in a Sponsored Multi-Ethnic System: The Case of Israel

Abraham Yogev and Hanna Ayalon

INTRODUCTION

The assessment of equality of educational opportunity involves at least two distinct lines of inquiry. With some reservations, we may depict these two trends of study as presenting a "static" vs. a "dynamic" picture of the equality issue.[1]

Two major differences between these types of study are (a) the treatment of the effects of social origin (i.e., social status or ethnicity) on educational attainment as static vs. dynamic, and (b) the focus on branching points of the educational system vs. the concentration on educational attendance between branching points as critical periods for measuring equality in the educational attainment process.

Static studies usually concentrate on one or more branching points throughout the educational career. These may be points of educational selection, such as high school graduation or college entrance and graduation, or points of actual educational branching, such as the tracking of students at high school entrance. While earlier studies of this sort have focused simply on the representation of different social groups at the various branching points, more recent ones have employed sophisticated techniques, such as path analysis, to address the equality issue throughout the educational career. Such studies have assessed the effects of social origin on the educational career at consecutive branching points, or have introduced social-psychological factors which mediate and explain social origin effects on educational attainment (the Wisconsin model of status attainment, as summarized in Sewell and Hauser, 1975, is an excellent example). Their concern with consecutive stages of the educational career and the inclusion of explanatory variables create the impression of a dynamic analysis of the process of educational attainment, and hence our above reservation regarding the division to static and dynamic studies. Yet, these studies have not been dynamic at least in the sense of treating students' social origin as static "antecedent variables," which exert their effect at various branching points of the individual's career.

A different approach to inequality assessment in education was suggested about a decade ago by Boudon (1974). His approach is dynamic in the sense that he views the effects of social origins on educational attainment as ever-increasing, and not only at the branching points but also between them, concomitantly with the students' passage from one school grade to the next. Boudon proposed to divide the effects of social status on school attendance into "primary" (effect on the initial school access or on passing a branching point) and "secondary" (effect on yearly survival rates once a branching point is passed). On the basis of data from various Western European countries, he showed that the "secondary" or survival effect repeats itself year after year and thus forms an exponential effect of growing inequality in educational attainment.

In the present study we intend to elaborate Boudon's exponential model by applying it to the issue of inequality in processes of high school attendance in Israel, as related to the ethnicity and the status of origin of students. Our attempt to elaborate Boudon's model is bipolar. First, we shall examine whether ethnicity, in addition to status of origin, has an exponential effect on high school attendance in Israel. This examination elaborates Boudon's model by enabling the assessment of the joint effect of two social origin variables on students' survival at school.

Secondly, we shall employ this elaborated model to examine the effects of ethnicity and social status on survival rates in different high school tracks. This will allow us to examine differences in students' careers within separate high school subsystems with regard to the enlarged exponential model.

SPONSORSHIP AND ETHNICITY
IN ISRAELI
HIGH SCHOOLS

The proposed analysis contends to add a dynamic dimension to previous studies on Israeli secondary education, which have mainly been of the "static" mode. Yet, we shall use their findings as a starting point for the present work.

Several studies on inequality in Israeli secondary education were published during the last decade, and two major points emerge from their findings: (a) that tracking is the main institutional mechanism of educational inequality at the high school level, and that (b) this inequality is predominantly ethnic, since it is produced by a different track distribution of Jewish students of Ashkenazi (European-American) and Oriental (Asian-African) origins.

Tracking is the most distinctive feature of Israeli high schools. The two major tracks: the academic and the vocational, are usually offered in separate schools, though some comprehensive schools include both tracks.[2] During the last decade the high school students are about equally divided between the two tracks, which differ not only in their curricular program, but also in their extent of scholastic emphasis. The academic high schools, which are by far more selective, prepare all their students for the matriculation examinations. These consist of a battery of tests on various curricular subjects, given by the Ministry of Education and Culture to the students during their high school years and upon graduation. Those who successfully pass the examinations receive the "matriculation diploma," which is a prerequisite for university enrollment. While almost all the graduates of the academic track obtain this diploma, only a small portion of the vocational track students—those who specifically enroll in a vocational matriculation program—get the diploma and eventually are eligible for higher education.

The above depiction has led various scholars to use Turner's (1960) concept of educational sponsorship in analyzing the Israeli high school system. This concept relates to the elaborate construction of institutional mechanisms of selection, which help the educational system branch the students relatively early in their educational career, and thus influence their future chances of social mobility. Indeed, the tracking of students is decided upon high school entrance. This is done on the basis of previous institutional selection mechanisms, such as ability grouping at the junior high school level, rather than on the basis of personal choice or interpersonal influences of significant others, such as parents and peers (Yogev, 1981). Since tracking means going to different schools, shifting between tracks during high school years is not common, and when it occurs it usually takes the form of dropping out of the selective academic track to attend the vocational one or to attend the external schools.

While tracking by itself does not affect the chances of students for high school graduation, it strongly influences their chances of obtaining a matriculation diploma and thus of pursuing higher education (Shavit, 1984). The students must be aware of this institutional selection process, since their tracking is the major determinant of their plans for higher education, while the interpersonal encouragement of significant others (an important determinant of college plans in the United States) has no influence on the Israeli students. This has been found both with respect to high school students (Yogev and Ayalon, 1982) and to youth upon the termination of military service, which precedes university enrollment in Israel (Yuchtman and Samuel, 1975).

Sponsorship is, however, manifest not merely in the existence of institutional selection mechanisms, but also in their differential application for the social mobility of various social groups. Previous studies of Israeli secondary schools have addressed this issue mainly by examining the effects of tracking on educational inequality between Ashkenazim (Jews of European-American ancestry, who constitute the dominant ethno-cultural group) and Orientals (of Asian-African origin). It was found, first, that Oriental students are more typically placed in the vocational track, because of lower academic standing than Ashkenazim and due to the stronger influence of institutional mechanisms (ability grouping at the junior high level) on their tracking, relative to Ashkenazi students (Yogev, 1981). This is partly due to the high proportion of Oriental students in the state religious junior high schools, which emphasize scholastic excellence and thus enforce institutional selection more heavily than the secular schools (Yogev and Chen, 1985). Subsequently, Oriental students are less prone than their Ashkenazi counterparts to obtain the matriculation diploma and to pursue higher education (Smooha and Peres, 1975; Shavit, 1984).

A recent study (Yogev and Shapira, 1984) goes a step further, and reveals that high school tracking influences the occupational careers of Orientals in the younger cohort of the Israeli labor force. While higher education is the major determinant of the occupational prestige of Ashkenazi men in this cohort, the main educational determinant of the occupational attainment of young Oriental men is still high school tracking. As expected, graduates of the academic track fare better in the occupational ladder than those of the vocational high schools.

It thus appears that tracking and ethnic inequality coincide in the sponsorship process of Israeli high schools. An attempt to employ Boudon's model in the Israeli case, as well as in any other sponsored multi-ethnic system of education, should take these two factors into account.

BOUDON'S EXPONENTIAL MODEL AND ITS ELABORATION

The basic idea underlying Boudon's exponential model of school survival is rather simple. The effect of social class on educational inequality at any specific branching point, contends Boudon, will repeat itself each year, with students' advancement from one school grade to another and between school levels. Let us suppose that in a given educational system, the proportion of higher social class graduates of the junior high level who enter high school is .90. According to Boudon, the proportion of these students who will pass a year later to the junior high school class will be .81, due to the repetition of social class effect ($.90^2$ = .81). Only 73 percent ($.90^3$) of the entering students will reach the senior year. Now, if the proportion of lower class students entering high school is .70, their proportion at the junior and senior levels will be .49 and .34, respectively. This means that the inequality of educational opportunity between social classes, which is caused by the different exponential rates of yearly school survival, is ever-increasing.

Boudon's model of inequality, which was well supported by educational data from various Western countries, was acclaimed as innovative upon the publication of Boudon's major work (1974), but was hardly pursued by follow-up studies. This is perhaps due to its inevitable clash with the path-analytic status attainment models, which were then at their peak (see the exchange between Hauser, 1976, and Boudon, 1976 with respect to this point). Or maybe the reason lies in an erroneous perception of the proof of ever-rising inequality, a proof already provided by Boudon, as the only ultimate goal of the model. In any event, several years ago Halsey, Heath, and Ridge (1980) attempted to apply Boudon's exponential model to the issue of educational sponsorship in Britain's secondary education. Employing the Oxford Mobility Project data on the educational careers of 10,000 men, they have shown that in the British system of secondary education, which is sponsorship-oriented due to its tripartite division of schools, the effects of social class on secondary school attainment are mainly "primary" (at the branching point), not "secondary" (on yearly survival rates). Once social class exerts its initial influence on access to the different types of secondary schools, the survival rates of students from different social classes tend to converge. They conclude that sponsorship reduces the exponential effect of social class, and that Boudon's model probably better reflects the situation in "contest"-oriented systems of education.

Although the conclusions of Halsey and his colleagues may

well reflect the situation in Britain, they also might have resulted from their particular mode of analysis. In their attempt to contrast two single coherent models of "primary" and "secondary" class effects (based on different manipulations of the available data), they condensed the actual data of their entire sample, ex-students of different school types, into a single table of educational attendance rates. This table was then compared with the predicted "primary" and "secondary" models of class effects. Separate analyses and comparisons of survival rates within each of the school types might have resulted in somewhat different findings. The Oxford findings contradict Boudon's predictions with respect to exponential effects in a sponsored system. Boudon contends, however, that for the educational inequalities of the exponential model to be eliminated,

> either a society must be unstratified or its school system must be completely undifferentiated. It is, of course, quite unlikely that any society will ever lack social strata altogether. It is also unlikely that a school system will be completely undifferentiated, in the sense that it will offer all youngsters a common curriculum. . . . The trend in all Western societies is toward differentiation of curricula and institutions rather than toward uniformity. . . . As a consequence, we do not have to deal with the prospect of the imminent disappearance of the exponential mechanism which is largely responsible for inequality of educational opportunity (1974: 109-110).

Following Boudon, it seems that educational sponsorship causes exponential inequality by the mechanism of school tracking, which creates different educational opportunities for students of various social origins. It may therefore be worthwhile to examine the exponential effects of social origin on attendance rates within the separate school tracks. This is especially true with respect to school systems which are both sponsorship-oriented and serve a multi-ethnic clientele, the Israeli high schools being a case in point.

Both Boudon and Halsey and his colleagues have examined the exponential effects of only one type of social origin: the students' social class (as measured by father's occupational category). There is no reason why in a society such as Israel, where the ethno-cultural division of labor is a major factor of social stratification, ethnicity should not exponentially influence high school attendance rates. Similarly to social status, the effect of ethnicity on school survival may repeat itself each year. We should therefore examine the extent to which educational inequality increases exponentially with relation to each of the two social origin variables: ethnicity and social status.

Furthermore, since ethnicity and social status are inter-related in Israel, as in many other societies, it is important to assess the net exponential effect of each of the two variables by controlling for the other. This can be done by examining the exponential effects of ethnicity within social strata and, vice versa, the status effects on attendance rates within separate ethnic groups.

This leads us back to the issue of high school tracking. Due to selectivity, students of the academic track in Israeli high schools tend to be both Ashkenazim and of the middle and upper social classes, while those of the vocational schools are predominantly Orientals and of lower social status. One may therefore expect to find some differences between the effects of ethnicity and social status on the process of school attendance within the two tracks. While social status may exert the crucial effect in the more selective academic track, ethnicity may have a stronger exponential effect on students' survival in the vocational track. In the latter, ethnic affiliation may be an important distinctive feature among the predominantly lower-status students. It is thus possible that the elaboration of Boudon's model may lead to the finding of different processes of exponential inequality in the two tracks, and eventually to a more comprehensive understanding of the relationship between sponsorship and the inequality of educational opportunity.

The following analysis subsequently consists of three steps: (a) the employment of Boudon's exponential model in the examination of ethnic effects on high school attendance rates in Israel; (b) the assessment of the net effects of ethnicity and social status on high school survival, and (c) the comparison of these effects across high school tracks.

THE EXPONENTIAL EFFECTS OF ETHNICITY ON HIGH SCHOOL ATTENDANCE

To ascertain the exponential effect of ethnicity on high school attendance rates—an effect never tested before—we first examine the attendance at the various high school grades of Ashkenazim and Orientals for ten graduating classes, between the years 1969 and 1982. Our analysis is based on the yearly data published by the Central Bureau of Statistics (Israel, State of, 1967–1983), which pertains to all high school students in both the regular schools (academic and vocational) and the external ones.[3]

As Table 1 shows, we take as the basis for our calculations the number of Ashkenazi and Oriental students at the first high school grade (10th grade). A law passed in 1978 made high school education tuition-free and the 10th grade compulsory.[4] The actual branching point at the high school level has therefore become the transition from the 10th to the 11th grade, instead of the earlier branching point of high school entrance (i.e., the transition from the 9th to the 10th grade). The rate of Ashkenazi and Oriental students who passed from the 10th to the 11th grade in each graduating class is presented in the next two columns of the table. Squaring these rates, we then get the expected attendance rates at the 12th grade according to the exponential model. These are compared to the actual ("observed") attendance rates of 10th grade students who have reached the final 12th grade. The last two columns present the expected and observed rates of Ashkenazim to Orientals at the 12th grade. These were derived by dividing the exponential and actual rates of Ashkenazim to those of the Orientals, and they thus represent the expected and observed high school survival ratios of the two ethnic groups (the ratio of 1.00 signifies equality, while rates exceeding this point represent higher survival rates for the Ashkenazi students).

The major finding of the table is that the actual effects of ethnicity on high school survival and the ones predicted by the exponential model tend to converge from 1978 on. With the exception of the graduating class of 1981, the differences between the expected and observed Ashkenazi/Oriental rates since 1978 range from zero to 0.03, while before 1978 these differences are larger. This is probably due to the employment of the transition from the 10th to the 11th grade as a branching point, a procedure which reflects the reality only since the 10th grade has become compulsory.

The convergence between the exponential and actual rates may also be attributed to the rapid enlargement of the high school vocational track since the mid-1970s. As the table shows, the 12th grade actual attendance rates of Oriental students have

Table 1. Expected and Observed Attendance Rates by Ethnicity in Israeli High Schools for Ten Graduating Classes Between 1969–1982*

Graduating Class of	N of Students - Grade 10		Attendance Rate - Grade 11		Expected Attendance Rate - Grade 12		Observed Attendance Rate - Grade 12		Ashkenazi/Oriental Rate - Grade 12	
	Ashkenazi	Oriental	Ashkenazi	Oriental	Ashkenazi	Oriental	Ashkenazi	Oriental	Expected	Observed
1969	18,913	12,541	.87	.71	.76	.50	.69	.44	1.52	1.57
1970	18,682	13,390	.83	.75	.69	.56	.67	.47	1.23	1.42
1971	17,243	15,833	.87	.71	.76	.50	.72	.43	1.52	1.67
1972	15,966	15,825	.88	.72	.77	.52	.74	.48	1.48	1.54
1977	14,334	21,522	.85	.75	.72	.56	.77	.62	1.29	1.24
1978	14,087	21,611	.87	.79	.76	.62	.79	.66	1.23	1.20
1979	13,150	21,425	.87	.80	.76	.64	.80	.68	1.19	1.19
1980	12,653	22,373	.89	.82	.79	.67	.81	.69	1.18	1.17
1981	12,494	22,920	.91	.83	.83	.69	.84	.74	1.20	1.14
1982	12,695	23,640	.90	.86	.81	.74	.85	.76	1.09	1.12

*Calculations are based on data from the appropriate statistical yearbooks of Israel (Israel, State of, 1967–1983). The data relate to all high school students—in the regular (academic and vocational) and external schools. Ethnicity is defined by father's birth continent, and students whose fathers were born in Israel (undefined ethnicity) are therefore omitted. The graduating classes between 1973 and 1976 are excluded because of incomplete data.

largely increased since 1977, while being quite static and low until then. Also, the 12th grade observed attendance rates of both Ashkenazim and Orientals somewhat exceed their expected rates since 1977, thus reflecting their higher chances of school survival with the enlargement of the vocational schools.

By and large, the table shows that the effect of ethnicity on processes of high school survival has largely decreased between the late 1960s and the early 1980s. Yet, considering the fact that our analysis relates merely to the survival effect of ethnicity between the 10th and 12th grade, this effect may still be considered substantial. Furthermore, it fits quite well the exponential model, proving that ethnicity repeats its influence on educational inequality with the transition between high school grades.

The question is, of course, how much of this effect is due independently to ethnicity, rather than to its colinearity with social status. To answer that question we turn to a more elaborate examination of the 1982 graduating class.

THE NET EFFECTS OF ETHNICITY AND SOCIAL STATUS

Data on the 1982 graduating class were taken from the student data bank of the Ministry of Education and Culture. This consists of yearly information on all high school students, which is collected for administrative purposes. The data enable us to track the students' social status (indicated by father's educational level which is trichotomized here into elementary, secondary, and higher), in addition to their ethnicity (by father's birth continent) and their high school tracking. Since our main interest in this work is the comparison of attendance rates between students of the academic and vocational tracks of the regular high schools, we have excluded the external school students from the following analysis.[5]

We first examine the separate effects of ethnicity and social status on the attendance rates of the regular high school students. As Table 2 shows, the actual effect of ethnicity on survival rates at the 12th grade is much higher than the one expected by the exponential model, mainly because of the higher-than-expected survival rate of Ashkenazi students.[6] In contrast, the observed

Table 2. Expected and Observed Attendance Rates by Ethnicity and Social Status in Israeli High Schools* (Graduating Class of 1982)

	N of Students- Grade 10	*Attendance Rate - Grade 11*	*Expected Attendance Rate-Grade 12*	*Observed Attendance Rate-Grade 12*
A. Ethnicity: Father's Birth Continent				
Europe-America (Ashkenazi)	11,573	.92	.85	.96
Asia-Africa (Oriental)	22,377	.87	.76	.79
Israel (Undefined)	7,857	.93	.86	.95
Attendance Rate: Ashkenazi/Oriental			1.12	1.22
B. Social Status: Father's Education				
Elementary	19,794	.86	.74	.78
Secondary	14,415	.92	.85	.86
Higher	7,598	.96	.92	.93
Attendance Rate: Secondary/Elementary			1.15	1.10
Attendance Rate: Higher/Elementary			1.24	1.19

*Calculations are based on students of the regular schools (academic and vocational). Students of the external high schools were omitted.

effect of social status is lower than expected. This is true whether we compare the survival ratios of upper-status students or of the middle-class ones to that of the lower-status students. As the separate attendance rates for each status group show, these differences between the expected and observed odds are mainly due to the 12th grade survival rate of lower-status students (whose fathers' level of education is elementary). This rate is higher than expected. The corresponding survival rates of the middle-and upper-class students are well predicted by the exponential model.[7]

Altogether, the table shows that both ethnicity and social status, when examined separately, have quite strong effects on high school survival, though their deviations from the exponential model are in different directions: ethnicity influences the attendance rates more than expected, while social status exerts less influence than exponentially predicted. This difference further necessitates the assessment of the net effects of each of these two social origin variables. The results of this examination are presented in Table 3.

Table 3. The Net Effects of Ethnicity and Social Status on Attendance Rates in Israeli High Schools*
(Graduating Class of 1982)

	Ashkenazim				Orientals				Ashkenazi/Oriental Attendance Rate	
Father's Education	N of Students - Grade 10	Attendance Rate - Grade 11	Expected Attendance Rate - Grade 12	Observed Attendance Rate - Grade 12	N of Students -Grade 10	Attendance Rate- Grade 11	Expected Attendance Rate - Grade 12	Observed Attendance Rate - Grade 12	Expected	Observed
Elementary	3,151	.88	.77	.83	14,927	.85	.72	.77	1.07	1.08
Secondary	4,815	.93	.86	.89	6,069	.90	.81	.83	1.06	1.07
Higher	3,607	.95	.90	.93	1,381	.95	.90	.90	1.00	1.03
Attendance Rate: Secondary/Elementary										
			1.12	1.07			1.13	1.08		
Attendance Rate: Higher/Elementary										
			1.17	1.12			1.25	1.17		

* Students of the external high schools are excluded.

In this table the attendance rates are computed for student groups cross-classified by ethnicity and social status, subsequently enabling the examination of the net effects of the two variables on high school survival.[8] It appears, first, that this mode of analysis greatly reduces the uncontrolled effects of ethnicity observed earlier, while the effects of social status on survival rates are only slightly reduced. The survival ratio of Ashkenazim to Orientals, which was 1.22 for the entire ethnic groups, now ranges between 1.03 (for the upper-status students) and 1.08 (for the lower-status ones). These ratios fit the predicted exponential ones much better than the fit obtained for the gross effects of ethnicity.

In contrast, the survival ratios of status groups within the two ethnic categories are only slightly reduced in comparison to the gross status effects. The main effect of social status on inequality is revealed in the survival ratios of upper-status to lower-status students, both Ashkenazim and Orientals. While these ratios are still smaller than the ones predicted by the exponential model, they signify a substantial inequality in high school survival chances among students of different social strata.[9]

The comparison of expected and observed attendance rates of the upper- and lower-status students within ethnic groups further reveals an interesting phenomenon. The survival ratios of upper- to lower-status students, as well as the difference between model expectation and reality for these status groups, are larger among the Oriental students. This means that instead of the main net effect of ethnicity, which has been greatly reduced, we now find an interactive effect of ethnicity and social status, pronounced in the survival ratios of Orientals of higher and lower classes. Observing the separate 12th grade attendance rates of these status groups within ethnicity, this interaction seems to be the result of two factors regarding the Oriental students: (a) a close fit between the expected and observed attendance rates of both the middle- and upper-class students, while the observed rates for these groups among the Ashkenazim are relatively higher than expected, and (b) a larger difference between the attendance rates of upper- and lower-status students, compared to Ashkenazim. While the 12th grade survival rate of lower class Orientals is higher than expected, it is still lower than the one obtained by Ashkenazim of the same social status.

Put together, our findings indicate that the net effect of social status on inequality in high school survival processes is larger than that of ethnicity, though it is due in part to an interaction between the two social origin variables. The question to be answered next is whether this conclusion reflects the inequality of survival processes at both the academic and the vocational high schools.

COMPARISON OF ATTENDANCE RATES AT THE ACADEMIC AND THE VOCATIONAL TRACKS

To compare the effects of ethnicity and social status on attendance rates at the two high school tracks, we repeated the above analyses of gross and net origin effects for the students in the academic track. The results of these analyses will be compared with those of the previous section, bearing in mind that the previous findings represent the average effects for both tracks put together.[10]

The separate effects of ethnicity and social status on attendance rates at the academic track are presented in Table 4. The given

Table 4. Expected and Observed Attendance Rates by Ethnicity and Social Status in Israeli Academic High Schools (Graduating Class of 1982)

	N of Students- Grade 10	Attendance Rate - Grade 11	Expected Attendance Rate-Grade 12	Observed Attendance Rate-Grade 12
A. Ethnicity: Father's Birth Continent				
Europe-America (Ashkenazi)	7,266	.94	.88	.81
Asia-Africa (Oriental)	8,606	.91	.83	.72
Israel (Undefined)	5,329	.95	.90	.76
Attendance Rate: Ashkenazi/Oriental			1.06	1.13
B. Social Status: Father's Education				
Elementary	7,129	.89	.79	.66
Secondary	8,040	.94	.88	.78
Higher	6,002	.97	.94	.86
Attendance Rate: Secondary/Elementary			1.11	1.18
Attendance Rate: Higher/Elementary			1.19	1.30

numbers of 10th grade students in the academic track clearly indicate, that the population of this selective track is predominantly Ashkenazi (especially if the numbers of Ashkenazim and third generation Israelies are combined, as suggested in footnote 8) and of the upper and middle social strata. When these numbers are deducted from the corresponding total numbers of students in Table 2, it appears that the vocational track students are, in contrast, predominantly Oriental and of the lower-status group.

These differences in the student body of the two tracks are immediately reflected in the gross effects of ethnicity and social status on attendance rates. The effect of ethnicity on 12th grade survival, both the expected and the one actually obtained, is greatly reduced. The reason for that is the larger convergence between the attendance rates of Ashkenazim and Orientals, caused by the selectivity of the track and by the tendency of both ethnic groups to belong to the middle and upper social strata. Subsequently, a somewhat better fit is achieved between the exponential and actual influences of ethnicity, though the observed ratio of Ashkenazim to Orientals still exceeds the one predicted.

An opposite picture is revealed with respect to status effects. Comparing the findings for both tracks in Table 2 with the present ones, it is apparent that the expected attendance ratios of the middle- and upper-strata to the lower-status students are lower in the academic track than in the vocational, while the actual attendance ratios of these social strata are much higher in the academic track. The examination of the separate attendance rates of each status group in this track shows that the exponentially predicted rates of all strata are higher than the ones expected for the vocational schools. Yet, the higher-than-expected dropout rate of the academic school students before entering the final 12th grade largely reduces the actual survival rates of all students, and especially of those originating of lower-status families. This produces a stronger effect of social status on students' survival at the academic track, relative to the vocational, and also a larger deviation from the exponential prediction of status effects.

The differences in the effects of ethnicity and status on student survival chances in the two tracks are further illuminated by the examination of their net effects in the academic track, as presented in Table 5. The net effects of ethnicity, both expected

Table 5. The Net Effects of Ethnicity and Social Status on Attendance Rates in Israeli Academic High Schools (Graduating Class of 1982)

	Ashkenazim				Orientals				Ashkenazi/Oriental Attendance Rate	
Father's Education	N of Students -Grade 10	Attendance Rate - Grade 11	Expected Attendance Rate - Grade 12	Observed Attendance Rate - Grade 12	N of Students -Grade 10	Attendance Rate - Grade 11	Expected Attendance Rate - Grade 12	Observed Attendance Rate - Grade 12	Expected	Observed
Elementary	1,445	.88	.77	.69	4,848	.89	.79	.66	.97	1.05
Secondary	2,972	.94	.88	.80	2,793	.93	.86	.80	1.02	1.00
Higher	2,849	.97	.94	.88	935	.97	.94	.88	1.00	1.00
Attendance Rate: Secondary/Elementary										
			1.14	1.16			1.09	1.21		
Attendance Rate: Higher/Elementary										
			1.22	1.28			1.19	1.33		

and observed, almost completely disappear. The predicted and actual attendance rates for all status groups are either identical across ethnicities, or merely fluctuate between them (especially with respect to lower status students). The net effects of social status are, in contrast, quite dramatic. The actual chance of upper-status entering students to survive in the academic track until graduation surpasses the chance of their lower-status counterparts by 28 percent in the Ashkenazi group, and by 33 percent for the Oriental students, in spite of the much lower predicted survival ratios between the status groups of both ethnicities.

These effects are further accentuated in comparison to the vocational track. Considering the net effects of ethnicity and social status in Table 3 as average effects for both tracks, we can now compare them with the ones presented for the academic track alone in Table 5. Since there are virtually no net effects of ethnicity on the survival rates of the academic students, the net effects of ethnicity in Table 3 may be attributed solely to the vocational schools. These ethnic effects within the vocational track are seemingly more substantial than the average ethnic ratios presented in Table 3. In contrast, the average net effects of social status are much lower than the ones found for the academic track. This means that the net effects of social status may be attributed almost entirely to the academic track, while in the vocational schools the survival rates of different social strata within ethnicities approach the point of equality. In other words, ethnicity influences only the survival of the vocational school students, while social status influences mainly the attendance of students in the academic track.

CONCLUSION: SPONSORSHIP RECONSIDERED

Our findings indicate the existence of separate processes of educational inequality in the two tracks, a possibility not considered by earlier studies of high school tracking in Israel or in other countries. The fact that ethnicity influences the students' survival rates only in the vocational track, while social status exerts an inequality effect mainly in the academic track, may be attributed to two separate sources or mechanisms of inequality: institutional and interpersonal.

It is evident that the institutional emphasis of the academic schools on scholastic aptitudes, and their tendency toward selectivity on this basis throughout the high school career, may have caused the strong inequality influence of social status. After all, differences in scholastic aptitudes and achievements are quite noticeable among social strata. To the same extent, the lesser emphasis of the vocational schools on scholastic achievement and on preparation for the matriculation diploma in general might have equalized the survival rates in the vocational track.

But the differences in ethnic and status effects between the two tracks may as well be attributed to the interpersonal relations of students within each track, and to the reflection of these relations in students' perceptions of the nature of social selection in their respective schools. The predominance of Ashkenazi middle- and upper-class students in the academic schools, vs. that of the Oriental lower-class students in the vocational track, may have cultivated different student-cultures in the two tracks. While friendship patterns among students of the academic schools may have evolved mainly on the basis of social status, those among the vocational students may have evolved more on the basis of ethnicity, especially because of the ethnic differentiation of students by specific vocational programs. Such friendship patterns may, in turn, discourage the lower-status academic students and the Oriental students of the vocational track and enhance their chances of early school dropout.

Obviously, the above potential interpretations require further studies of student cultures in the two high school tracks. But whatever the specific reasons for the differences in ethnic and status inequality between the tracks are, these differences lead to two central conclusions regarding sponsorship processes in education. First, in an educational system which serves a multi-ethnic clientele, sponsorship applied to the early tracking of students may lead to a differential selection of various social groups by the separate tracks. Higher status groups tend to be selected by the academic track, while ethnicity counts more in the selection processes of the less prestigious track. The infra-structural effects of this differential process may become evident in the long run. Let us consider, for instance, the fact that most university students in Israel, who are destined for higher occupational positions, are graduates of the academic track. It is therefore possible that social reproduction by status of origin will increase in the long run, and that conflicts between social strata may eventually emerge independently of the current ethnic conflicts.

But we should also consider the fact that our finding, that the effect of ethnicity on the survival rates of vocational school students, though being substantial, was much lower than the effect of social status on inequality in the academic track. This leads to the conclusion that the concept of sponsorship should be reconsidered. High school tracking is usually regarded as a major mechanism of educational sponsorship and as the dominant factor in the making of inequality (see especially Rosenbaum, 1976). Our findings for Israel indicate, that in Western democratic societies adhering to educational sponsorship, tracking may also reflect, to some extent, the spirit of egalitarianism. While one prestigious track remains highly selective, the less prestigious one is much more egalitarian with respect to the chances of all students to graduate successfully, regardless of their social status and, to a substantial extent, regardless also of their ethnicity. Perhaps this is the token some Western democracies pay for the right to maintain educational sponsorship.

On a more general level, our analysis indicates the relevance of Boudon's exponential model to the study of specific issues of educational stratification. The employment of this model is worthwhile not merely for the general proof of ever-increasing inequality of educational opportunity. It may be applied to various questions on educational inequality. For instance, we have shown that in multi-ethnic societies, the exponential effects of ethnicity and social status on educational attainment should be assessed independently of each other. In the Israeli case, the effect of ethnicity on high school survival in general largely decreases once the social status of students is controlled for. An interaction effect between the two variables emerges instead of the main ethnicity effect. This may not be the case in other multi-ethnic societies, especially in those societies where ethnic or racial differentiation is more acute. Further comparative studies pertaining to this issue, or to similar ones, by the employment of the exponential model, may certainly introduce a new dynamic dimension to the inquiry of educational opportunities.

NOTES

1.   This study was supported by the Pinchas Sapir Center for Development at Tel-Aviv University. We are thankful to the Israeli Ministry of Education and Culture for providing the data on which the study was based, and especially to David Choresh who was most helpful in familiarizing us with the ministry's data. We also thank Nira Radum, who helped us overcome the technical difficulties involved in processing data of such a large volume.

2.   A third small track consists of the private external schools, which prepare regular-school dropouts and working youth for the matriculation examinations. Only a fraction of these external students obtain the matriculation diploma (Ayalon and Yogev, 1986).

3.   From 1983 on the Ministry of Education and Culture stopped collecting data on students' ethnicity because of ideological reasons related to the emphasis on ethnic integration. The Central Bureau of Statistics, which relies on the ministry's data for its educational statistics, thus ceased publishing new data on the ethnic distribution of high school students in the statistical yearbooks.

4.   Until then compulsory education consisted of nine years of study.

5.   We could not have fitted the external schools as a separate track into our analysis of exponential attendance rates, since their students consist mainly of regular school dropouts after completion of the 10th and 11th grades. Thus, the number of external students in the 11th and 12th grades exceeds by far their number at the 10th grade.

6.   This is mainly due to the exclusion of the external students from the present analysis. In an additional analysis which included the external students, the rates obtained were identical to those presented for the 1982 graduating class in Table 1, thus showing a better fit between the exponential and observed effects of ethnicity.

7.   Different results regarding status effects were obtained by the inclusion of external schools in the analysis. The expected and observed ratios of middle- to lower-status students in this analysis were 1.09 and 1.11, respectively. Those of upper- to lower-class students were 1.22 and 1.17, respectively. The better fit between the expected and observed ratios of middle- to lower-class students is due to the predominance of the former at the external high schools (Ayalon and Yogev, 1986).

8.   Third generation Israelis are excluded from this analysis. However, the strong resemblance of the attendance rates of students of Israeli origin to those of the Ashkenazim (see Table 2), indicates that students included in this category are predominantly Ashkenazim (since the main immigration wave of Asian-African Jews to Israel was in the early 1950s, third-generation students of Oriental ancestry are still scarce in Israeli high schools). It therefore seems that the exclusion of the group of third-generation Israelis from the present analysis, done for the sake of precision, did not significantly bias the results.

9.   The inclusion of external students in the analysis results in similar findings for the net effects of ethnicity, but further reduces the net effects of social status. For example, the expected and observed survival ratios between upper- and lower-status students are respectively reduced to 1.11 and 1.10 for Ash-

kenazim and to 1.19 and 1.15 for Orientals. These reduced net effects, and the better fits between expected and observed ratios in this analysis, are due to the relative scarcity of both upper-and lower-status students in the external schools.

10. Ideally, the comparison between the tracks should have been based on two separate analyses of the survival rates within each track. Our data prevent such an analysis, since they are based on an annual gathering of information from all high schools instead of follow-up information on individual students. Since most of the students who shift tracks during their high school career are students of the academic track who move (or are forced to move) to the less selective vocational one, a separate analysis of yearly survival rates at the vocational track is useless given our data. The comparison of the academic track with the average results obtained for both tracks is thus presented as a modus vivendi solution.

REFERENCES

Ayalon, Hanna and Abraham Yogev
  1986 "A second chance for whom? The external high schools in Israel."
        Paper presented at the 17th Annual Convention of the Israeli Soci-
        ological Society, Haifa.
Boudon, Raymond
  1974 Education, Opportunity and Social Inequality: Changing Prospects
        in Western Society. New York: Wiley.
  1976 "Comment on Hauser's review of Education, Opportunity and Social
        Inequality." American Journal of Sociology 81: 1175-87.
Halsey, A. H., A. F. Heath and J. M. Ridge
  1980 Origins and Destinations: Family, Class and Education in Modern
        Britain. Oxford: Clarendon Press.
Hauser, Robert H.
  1976 "Review essay: on Boudon's model of social mobility." American
        Journal of Sociology 81: 911-28.
Israel, State of
  1967- Statistical Yearbooks of Israel. Jerusalem: Central Bureau of Statistics.
  1983
Rosenbaum, James E.
  1976 Making Inequality. New York: Wiley.
Sewell, William H. and Robert M. Hauser
  1975 Education, Occupation and Earnings: Achievement in the Early Ca-
        reer. New York: Academic Press.
Shavit, Yossi
  1984 "Tracking and ethnicity in Israeli secondary education." American
        Sociological Review 49: 210-20.
Smooha, Sami and Yochanan Peres
  1975 "The dynamics of ethnic inequalities: The case of Israel." Social Dy-
        namics 1: 63-80.

Turner, Ralph H.
  1960   "Sponsored and contest mobility and the school system." American
          Sociological Review 25: 855-67.
Yogev, Abraham
  1981   "Determinants of early educational career in Israel: Further evidence
          for the sponsorship thesis." Sociology of Education 54: 181-95.
Yogev, Abraham and Hanna Ayalon
  1982   "Sex and ethnic variations in educational plans: a cross cultural per-
          spective." International Review of Modern Sociology 12: 1-19.
Yogev, Abraham and Michael Chen
  1985   "Sponsorship as school charter: educational mobility in religious
          versus secular schools in Israel." International Review of Modern
          Sociology 15 (in press).
Yogev, Abraham and Rina Shapira
  1984   "Ethnicity, meritocracy and credentialization in Israel: elaborating
          the credential society thesis." Paper presented at the First Interna-
          tional Conference on Education in the '90s: Equality, Equity and Ex-
          cellence, Tel Aviv.
Yuchtman (Yaar), Ephraim and Yitzhak Samuel
  1975   "Determinants of career plans: Institutional versus interpersonal ef-
          fects." American Sociological Review 40: 521-31.

Part IV
INTEGRATION AND ETHNIC DISPARITIES IN EDUCATION

14.

Interethnic Relations and Education: An Israeli Perspective

Joseph Schwarzwald and Yehuda Amir

Historical Background

Tension between ethnic groups is a common phenomenon among heterogeneous populations. Historically, Jews have not been spared the consequences of such tensions, especially in times of mass migration or religious schisms (Ben-Sasson, 1969). In Israel today, interethnic tensions are primarily the result of the massive immigration of Jews from different cultural and national backgrounds since the creation of the Jewish state in 1948. In addition to the tensions between Israeli Jews and Arabs, tensions and cleavage exist in the religiosity of observant and nonobservant Jews and in the ethnicity of Jews from multiple cultural backgrounds. This paper focuses on the consequences of the encounter between the two major Jewish ethnic categories today. Jews of North African and Asian origin (hereafter referred to as *Middle Easterners*) and Jews of European-American origin (referred to as *Westerners*).

At the foundation of the state, Israel's population was approximately 650,000. In its first decade, this society absorbed an estimated 485,000 Middle Eastern and 321,000 Western immigrants (Bentwich, 1960). The basically modern, Western cultural patterns of the absorbing society made the adjustment in the new country easier for Western immigrants but more problematic for Middle Easterners. Indeed, for Middle Easterners coming from a conservative religious and social tradition, Western cultural patterns were often strange and, at times, even objectionable (Adler, in press; Eisenstadt, 1973; Shuval, 1963). Over time, Westerners acquired positions of high-social status, whereas Middle Easterners populated the bottom of the social ladder (Smooha & Peres, 1974). This process of ethnic and social differentiation was accompanied by alienation, prejudice, and social distance in the relations between the two ethnic groups.

These problems of interethnic tensions arose despite the national aspiration to merge the various Jewish diaspora communities into a common Israeli culture. In this regard, it was clear that in order to attain a high level of technological achievement in the critical areas of defense and economy, the new Israel would have to become even more Western-oriented in its economy, social structure, and educational system (Simon, 1957). Thus, the Israeli national leadership adopted the approach (supported also by social scientists) that Middle Easterners should become Westernized through a process of resocialization (Swirsky, 1981). It was thought that resocialization would be facilitated by such factors as common Jewish nationality, religious tradition, and the relative similarity in physical appearance. Ethnic, cultural, and economic differences were considered to be temporary and of only superficial importance.

The absorption process was often accompanied by the attitude that Middle Easterners were uncultured. Counselors, supervisors, and teachers—primarily from Western background's—hurried to teach the ''primitives'' new behavior patterns. Due to their attitudes of superiority and insensitivity, these official representatives of the dominant culture showed unintentional scorn for the Middle Easterners' existing cultural values.

The ignoral and devaluation of Middle Eastern culture throughout the absorption process, as well as shortages in housing, employment, and education, often generated a feeling of powerlessness and insignificance among Middle Easterners. These absorption conditions were neither conducive for facilitating the process of integration nor for attaining national unity. In fact, the interethnic encounter was occasionally accompanied by hostility and hindered the development of the Middle Easterners' local initiatives and independent activity.

Course of the Chapter

This chapter describes the role of schools in the process of integration. In the initial section, the literature documenting the unbalanced relations between Middle Eastern and Western Jews is described. Particular attention is given to the asymmetry which characterizes these relations. Whereas Westerners accept other Westerners and reject Middle Easterners, Middle Easterners tend to prefer Westerners over themselves.

As shown in subsequent sections, this same bias is reflected within schools and poses major social and educational difficulties for Middle Eastern students.

Among the difficulties reviewed here are those of preferential standing given to Western culture in the curriculum and the negative teacher-attitudes toward Middle Easterners. The deficit in academic achievement among Middle Eastern students accompanying these conditions becomes a focal concern addressed by educators and politicians alike.

Two major stages in the school system's attempt to respond to these socioeducational problems are outlined. The first of these comprised a series of sporadic enrichment programs aimed at the Middle Eastern population, its impact fell below expectations. The second and more recent attempt involves structural Reform of the school system based upon forced desegregation. The social outcomes of this latter effort are described in detail.

For the social scientist at large, Israeli implementation of integration in a school system uniquely divided into religious and secular sectors offers unusual insight into the factors influencing integrational process. Research data demonstrating the situational contingence of effective integration are discussed in depth and are summarized from a theoretical perspective. Original intervention measures developed in Israel for improved integration are also described.

In the final section, integrational efforts within the school system are placed back into the broader social and historical perspective. A theory of perceived inequality is presented and applied to current trends in interethnic relations. This theory suggests that the differential pattern of change in cultural similarity and social standing between ethnic groups is leading to more potent feelings of inequality among Middle Easterners. The resulting activism of this group, it is concluded, may lead to renewed efforts for genuine educational integration and equality.

Patterns of Acceptance and Rejection

One persisting outcome of the unfavorable encounter between Western and Middle Eastern Jews in the absorption process is a pattern of asymmetry in acceptance and rejection between these ethnic groups. Westerners tend to evaluate people of their own community positively and Middle Easterners negatively. Middle Easterners tend to reflect the attitudes of the dominant group, evaluating people from their own ethnic category less positively than Westerners. Empirical evidence for this asymmetrical relationship appears repeatedly in studies with subjects from elementary school age through adulthood, irrespective of research methodology.

At the elementary school level, pronounced asymmetry is reflected in children's judgment of ethnic features representing the typical Israeli (Rim, 1968). Western facial features are considered more Israeli than the features of Middle Easterners. Pupils of Western origin perceive figures from their own membership group as more Israeli and like them better; Middle Eastern children also tend to view Westerners as more typically Israeli and like them more than figures from their own group.

Asymmetry in acceptance and rejection is also found among high school students. Both Westerners and Middle Easterners alike give more positive evaluations to Western than to Middle Eastern members (Amir, Sharan, Ben-Ari, Bizman, & Rivner, 1978; Peres, 1976). In addition, students from both ethnic groups are more willing to engage in activities with Westerners than with Middle Easterners (Amir, Sharan, Ben-Ari, Bizman, & Rivner, 1978). Finally, with regard to marriage, most Western students tend to have reservations about the possibility of marriage to Middle Easterners, whereas only a minority among Middle Easterners express any reservation about marriage to a Westerner (Peres, 1976).

Studies carried out among adults reveal a similar trend. Among residents of a new urban neighborhood, it is found that Westerners and Middle Easterners exhibit a good deal of rejection of various Middle Eastern ethnic groups and very little rejection of various Western ethnic groups (Shuval, 1956). Moreover, when asked who were least desirable as neighbors, more than half of the Western respondents indicated Middle Easterners, whereas only a small percentage of Middle Easterners had reservations about neighbors of Western origin. In a similar vein, Amir, Bizman, and Rivner (1975) demonstrate an identical asymmetry among soldiers. Those of Western origin tend to prefer friends of their own group, whereas Middle Easterners have no special preference—indicating Westerners and Middle Easterns equally as friends.

It appears that asymmetry in acceptance and rejection on the Middle Easterner's part is not only a reflection of the preference for Westerners but also involves a process of self-depreciation. For example, Rim's (1968) study reveals that Middle Eastern pupils have difficulty in accepting their identity and suffer feelings of alienation. Self-depreciation is also a finding emphasized by Peres (1971), who notes that Middle Easterners show a need to eliminate flaws in themselves before engaging in closer interethnic relations. The apparent feeling of inferiority and a subsequent adoption of a negative self-image undoubtedly affects the motivation and initiative of Middle Easterners in both the area of involvement of adults in community and public life and of the ability of their children to cope with the demands of school. Such outcomes are typical in encounters between majority (strong) and minority (weak) groups as shown by a series of studies in the United States on relations between blacks and whites that reveals that subjects from the minority group tend to adopt the majority's evaluation of their group and consider themselves less worthy (Ashmore, 1970; Brand, Ruiz, & Padilla, 1974).[1]

[1]Recent studies in the United States show an amelioration in this tendency (Davis, 1978; Weissbach, 1977).

Limited exceptions to the general rule of asymmetry appear in situations where Middle Easterners and Westerners share equal status. For example, Middle Eastern and Western Boy Scouts of equal social status both tend to rate members of their own ethnic group as more ideal and typically Israeli than members of the other ethnic groups (Gitai, 1972).

Schwarzwald and Yinon (1977) find a similar symmetry among middle class Western and Middle Eastern vocational high school students. The Middle Easterners tend to give higher ratings to figures of Middle Easterners than of Westerners. Westerners likewise tend to give a higher rating to figures from their own membership group. Moreover, students of mixed marriages (one parent Western and the partner Middle Eastern) tend to rate all the ethnic groups positively without distinction. Close examination of the data suggests that these more symmetric results do not reflect mutual acceptance but rather indicate a more positive self-image among Middle Easterners.

In each of these studies it is assumed that equality of social standing contributes to the reduction of asymmetrical patterns of acceptance and rejection. A more direct analysis of the influence of social status is offered in studies by Amir and colleagues with students (Amir, Sharan, Rivner, Ben-Ari, & Bizman, 1979) and soldiers (Amir, Bizman, & Rivner, 1975). Among high school students of different academic levels, less asymmetry is found in classes where Middle Easterners have a scholastic standing equal to or higher than that of Westerners. When Middle Easterners have an academic standing lower than Westerners, the typical pattern of asymmetry reappears. Among soldiers in the general army, Amir (1975) and his collaborators find typical asymmetry. However, in paratrooper units, consisting of volunteers carefully selected for martial skills and qualities pertinent to army standing, relations become more balanced.

In sum, these more recent studies suggest that the asymmetrical interethnic relations that arise during the initial encounter between Western and Middle Eastern Jews reflect objective as well as apparent status differences. Where status differences are ameliorated, patterns of acceptance and rejection become more symmetrical. Yet, even where status has been analyzed within confined settings, this tendency toward more balanced relations arises more from increased self-acceptance among Middle Easterners than from heightened acceptance between groups.

Schools before Reform

The school system is one institution that might be expected to propagate mutual acceptance and social integration. A review of the record indicates that, at least at the beginning, conditions in the Israeli schools are not conducive to these goals. The content of school curricula and the character of teachers' attitudes combine to devaluate the Middle Eastern students' self-esteem and diminish their social and academic standing.

Educational authorities adopted a curriculum that, at least until very recently, emphasized solely Western culture and almost completely ignored the heritage and history of the Middle Eastern ethnic group. For example, school texts almost entirely pass over the history of Middle Eastern Jews and their contribution to the foundation of the country. Similarly, childrens' readers generally have Western authors and present Middle Eastern figures in a disparaging light (Stahl, 1976). This tendency is clearly inconsistent with the theoretical position that equal representation of the various cultures is essential for interethnic acceptance, positive self-image of minority students, and harmony between the socialization process at home and in school (Frankenstein, 1977; Miller, 1980).

It is impossible to ignore the series of studies beginning in the 1950s and continuing to the present that indicate prejudice and disparaging attitudes of teachers toward their Middle Eastern students. Although it is difficult to estimate the extent of the phenomenon because these studies are limited in scope, a few examples should be instructive. Stahl, Agmon, & Mar-Haim (1976) present anecdotal data collected through observations that indicate insulting and belittling reactions to ethnic customs, negative and arrogant attitudes towards the disadvantaged Middle Eastern population, and feelings of frustration among teachers required to teach this population. These investigators note that teachers display ignorance and lack of interest in the traditions, customs, and beliefs prevalent among various Middle Eastern communities.

Other systematic studies also report instances of discrimination and prejudice. Stahl *et al.* (1976) also describes a laboratory experiment revealing that teachers (both Middle Easterners and Westerners) give lower grades for a composition ostensibly written by a Middle Eastern rather than a Western student. Shuval and Teichman (1972) find that kindergarten teachers are more likely to report Western than Middle Eastern children as talented, often ignoring equally talented Middle Eastern children. In a similar vein, Babad, Mann, and Mar-Haim (1975) find that graduate education students ascribe lower IQ scores to a WISC (Weschler Intelligence Scale for Children) protocol when they think it has been given by a Middle Eastern student instead of a Westerner. These studies indicate that teachers often underestimate the potential ability of Middle Eastern children, even in the face of ostensibly standardized evaluation to the contrary.

Devaluation of Middle Eastern heritage and values is reflected in a study carried out by Schwarzwald, Shoham, Waysman, and Sterner (1979). Teachers express a greater necessity to impart desirable social, personal, and educational values to "disadvantaged" Middle Eastern students than to "advantaged"

Western students. Moreover, they believe it to be less feasible to instill desirable values to the "less socialized" Middle Eastern students. Clearly, in this case, teachers hold prejudicial and stereotypic opinions about social behavior and values for which they have no objective data.

The tendency of people to behave according to beliefs and expectations that they form about themselves, others, and their social environment, even if they have little basis in reality, may lead to self-fulfilling prophecies, perpetuating a vicious cycle (Rosenthal & Jacobson, 1968). In any case, teachers' expression of such attitudes does little to improve Middle Easterners' social standing in the classroom. Teachers' perception of Middle Easterners as inferior may be one factor inhibiting latent educational potential of these students.

The major educational difficulties facing Middle Eastern students also emphasizes their social status difference from Western students. The educational gap between students of Middle Eastern origin and Western Israelis is documented in a number of studies. The most relevant of these studies tests pupils' adaptation in the early school grades (Adiel, 1968; Feitelson, 1953; Simon, 1957; Smilansky, 1957), achievement in national placement tests given in the eighth grade, which is the final elementary school class (Litwin, 1971; Ortar, 1956, 1960, 1967; Smilansky & Yam, 1969), and achievement in matriculation examinations (Smooha & Peres, 1974). These studies clearly demonstrate that many Middle Eastern students lack the most basic educational foundations, their language skills are poor, and they are bored and uninterested in school. Consequently, Middle Eastern children tend to drop out of the formal educational framework, and each successive grade contains a smaller percentage of Middle Easterners.

Clearly Middle Easterners' learning difficulties, poor achievement, and high drop-out rate are an amalgamation of home conditions as well as the transition from a traditional Middle Eastern to a modern Western culture (Adar, 1956; Simon, 1957; S. Smilansky, 1957). The Middle Eastern student frequently comes from a disadvantaged home where parents have to struggle with inadequate housing and poverty level income. In addition, the lack of Western educational experience among the Middle Eastern parents make it difficult for them to offer help and assistance to their children. Yet, whatever the reasons are, be they home or school, the resultant educational gap magnified and emphasized the social-status differences between the groups.

Introduction of School Integration

Middle Eastern students' failure in elementary school, their comparatively small numbers continuing through high school and postsecondary school education, and their subsequent difficulty adjusting to the realities and demands of social and economic life are all a source of concern to those dealing with educational policy in Israel (Adler, 1974; Eisenstadt, 1973; Peled, 1976). Consequently, these policymakers instituted a variety of planned enrichment programs to advance Middle Eastern immigrant children. Schools populated predominantly by Middle Eastern students were given preferential allocation of funds to institute special remedial programs intended to narrow the educational gap. These programs included a longer school day (the regular school day in Israel ends at about 1:00 P.M.), auxiliary teaching, and tracking in major subjects. Guidance, counseling, nutrition, and health services were expanded, and teachers specially trained to supervise the programs were placed in these schools. An effort to solve the drop-out problem was made by not allowing children to be left back and by lowering entrance requirements in order to encourage disadvantaged students to continue high school studies (Adiel, 1970; Minkovitch, Davis, & Bashi, 1982; M. Smilansky, 1973).

Certainly these efforts had some remedial effect. Illiteracy almost disappeared (Adiel, 1968). The percentage of Middle Easterners in high school and higher education increased (Smooha & Peres, 1974). The fact that the educational gap in Israel remains constant (Lewy & Chen, 1976; Minkovich *et al.*, 1980) is also a positive index when taken in contrast to the continuing growing gap found for ethnic minorities in the United States (Coleman, Campbell, Hobson, McPartland, Mood, Wernfield, & York, 1966).

Nonetheless, at the bottom line, the results of the enrichment programs are disappointing; preferential allocation of funds did not close the educational gap between Western and Middle Eastern students just as such enrichment programs in the United States have not succeeded (Orfield, 1978). A national evaluation study (Minkovich *et al.*, 1980; Razael, 1978) actually revealed that preferential treatment of schools for the disadvantaged often benefits the advantaged children. By the same token, Kfir and Chen (1980) argue that these special programs for the disadvantaged children work in reverse; it labels them with the stigma of weakness and inferiority, thereby increasing social segregation.

In light of the limited success associated with these enrichment programs, a political decision was taken in 1968 to reform the educational structure and impose ethnic integration within the schools. Instead of the division into elementary and postelementary schools, regional intermediate schools (junior high schools consisting of Grades 7, 8, and 9) were established as a first stage of high school or a transitional phase from elementary to high school. This reform plan, as it was termed, sought to fulfill two basic national goals: to bring about understanding and harmony between ethnic groups, thus helping to forge a single nation out of the varied mixture of Jewish ethnic communities; and secondly, to increase the efficacy of the educational process, raising the achievement levels of all the pupils in general and closing the educational gap.

It is important to recognize that the decision to implement a policy of integration in the schools in Israel was not a response to any legal discrimination against Middle Eastern children. The Reform in the educational system was not perceived by any explicit ethnic segregation in law or in socially accepted norms. Yet, de facto forms of ethnic segregation are prevalent, due to the fact that schools drew their student bodies from local neighborhoods generally characterized by families from similar socioeconomic levels and, often, ethnic origin. Even where student bodies are drawn from different ethnic groups and dissimilar economic strata, their proportions are not representative of the general population. Thus, the Reform plan was designed more to increase interethnic contact than to create it. The new junior high schools were established to institutionalize positive interethnic relations and ensure equal opportunity for all.

Outcomes of the Educational Reform

What was the impact of Reform? The present literature does not permit clear-cut conclusions. First, the Reform program has not been completely implemented, either at the level of the system as a whole or at the level of the individual school. Second, data on the social and educational outcomes of Reform are limited, often ambivalent, and beset by methodological problems.

From the standpoint of implementation, the Reform program has never been fully attained. Program planners feared that the wide gap in basic skills and learning achievements would make teaching difficult and would have a deleterious effect on the scholastic level. Hence, they permitted junior high-school principals to weed out problematic students, to form special classes for weak students, and to teach a small number of basic subjects (such as Hebrew, mathematics and English) in tracked classes. Of these measures, tracking was the major method used. Consequently, in the majority of junior high schools, students study most subjects in heterogeneous homeroom classes, whereas major subjects are taught in homogeneous groups formed according to scholastic level. Because of the congruence of learning achievement and ethnic origin, most higher level tracks are populated by Westerners, whereas the low level tracks are made up mainly of Middle Easterners.

Tracking is an outgrowth of an individualistic educational philosophy aimed at allowing students to progress in accordance with their ability and talents. As might be expected, in the higher-level tracks learning is more rapid than in the lower tracks (Chen, Lewy, & Adler, 1978). Hence, tracking, even in this integrated framework, undermines the educational goal of closing the achievement gap and stresses academic differences associated with ethnic origin.

Educational achievements of students in the newly integrated junior high schools are compared by Chen *et al.* (1978) with the achievements of students studying in the old system. No major advantages are noted for the integrated framework. After the Reform, the gap between Middle Easterners and Westerners remains significant and is estimated to be the equivalent of 2 school years. The achievement level of Middle Eastern students in the basic skills at the end of the ninth grade is equivalent to that of Western children completing the seventh grade. This gap has remained constant over the years—the Reform did not reduce it. The negligible achievement results in the study by Chen and his colleagues are not conclusive. These data were gathered at the onset of a program when the educational potential may not have as yet been fully realized. It is possible that the current situation is more positive, but, at present, no research data are available. In this regard it is important to note the encouraging findings that under Reform, school drop-out rates were reduced by 20%. Anecdotal testimony presented to the Public Commission on Reform (Israel Ministry of Education & Culture, 1979) also indicates more positive evaluation of learning achievements.

Has integration fulfilled the hopes for improving interethnic relations? Levin and Chen (1977) investigate social relations in ethnically-mixed classes in the junior high schools by asking two sociometric questions: "Next to which three children in your class would you like to sit?" and "With which three children do you like to play during recess?" The analysis of the combined index of the two questions reveals balanced and almost completely symmetrical interethnic acceptance. Indeed, Middle Eastern students are found to be almost as popular as Western students. The researchers note a slight tendency towards ethnic cleavage shown by the subjects' preference for members of their own ethnic group.

In another study (Amir, Rich, and Ben-Ari, 1978), interviews and observations of relations between students during class and at recess are focused on more intimate social relations. Contrary to the previous study, findings are less encouraging. They point out that children are more likely to interact with classmates of similar scholastic ability. Given that congruence between scholastic ability and ethnic origin exists, ethnic cleavage remains prevalent.

The use of different methods for collecting data and the lack of definition and strength of the interethnic dimension studied makes comparison of the findings of these two studies difficult. In a more recent study conducted by Schwarzwald and Cohen (1982), a unidimensional scale was constructed to distinguish various degrees of interpersonal acceptance for classmates, ranging from casual relations demanding little social commitment to intimate relations entailing very considerable social commitment. Interethnic acceptance was analyzed with and without regard to the academic track to which the classmate belonged. When track was included as a variable, typical asymmetry in interethnic social acceptance appeared—both Middle Easterners and Westerners showed more interpersonal acceptance for their Western classmates. When the factor of tracking was included in the analysis, the degree of social acceptance was positively related to the classmate's tracking level. The higher the tracking level of a classmate, the more students were willing to accept him or her. When tracking was held constant, neither the ethnic origin of the respondent nor the origin of classmates had any significant effect. Thus, it appears that the asymmetry revealed by the first analysis results from the unbalanced distribution of Middle Eastern classmates in the different tracks and not from ethnic origin per se. These data tend to substantiate similar claims put forth by other researchers (Amir, Sharan, Ben-Ari, Bizman, & Rivner, 1978; Hadad & Shapira, 1977).

Schwarzwald and Cohen (1982) also indicate the importance of intimacy in the assessment of interethnic acceptance. At low levels of intimacy, no ethnic cleavage is found, a result concurring with Levin and Chen's (1977) findings. However, when more intimate or demanding interethnic relations are at stake, the findings are similar to those of Amir, Rich, & Ben-Ari (1978); The students tend to show a greater degree of social acceptance for classmates of Western origin and less acceptance for Middle Eastern classmates.

Schwarzwald and Cohen's (1982) study raises major questions regarding the methodology used in earlier studies assessing interethnic acceptance. The lack of attention given to the variables of intimacy and tracking in previous work constricts the interpretation of results regarding the degree of asymmetry prior to Reform as well as change following integration. Yet, in any case, it seems that Reform did not irradicate unbalanced interethnic relations.

Integration as a Situational Contingent

Social scientists postulate that successful interethnic relations and positive results of integration are contingent on a number of conditions such as: equal status, interpersonal intimacy, social and institutional support, balanced representation of different cultures, and an atmosphere of cooperation (Amir, 1969; Miller, 1981; St. John, 1975). In Israel, the presence of two parallel public education systems—one secular and the other religious—provide a ''living laboratory'' for exploring the influence of these conditions on integration. In the following section we describe the factors differentiating between the religious and secular systems and explore their influence upon educational and social outcomes of integration.

Due to the Educational Law of 1953, the religious sector of public education enjoys a legal status equal to its secular counterpart. Under that law, state-supervised schools—religious in orientation, curriculum, and staffing—are made available to any parents aspiring to provide their children with a religious education. These schools open their doors to any student willing to adhere to basic behavior codes both in and out of school. Currently, about 21% of the entire Jewish school population is enrolled in the public religious schools.

One of the factors distinguishing the two sectors is the relative percentage of disadvantaged students, primarily of Middle Eastern descent. Disadvantaged students make up the majority in the religious system (63%), but comprise only a minority (36%) in the secular system (Egozi, 1979). This difference is accentuated by a second factor, namely the relative degree of deprivation. The disadvantaged students in the religious school system come from lower socio-economic strata than their disadvantaged peers in the secular school system (Algarebali, 1975; Lewy & Chen, 1976; Minkovich *et al.*, 1980). Consequently, the gaps in basic skills and learning achievements associated with socioeconomic and ethnic background are more apparent in the religious than in the secular schools.

A third distinguishing factor is the geographical distribution of the population. Because the religious school system comprises only about a fifth of all public Jewish education, it must recruit children from a wider geographical area. This geographical dispersion increases the heterogeneity of the classmates but limits the possibilities of contact after school hours.

The central role of religion in the religious school comprises a fourth differentiating factor between the two sectors, and the influence is quite opposite to expectation. The many aspects of religious life common to Middle Easterners and Westerners might have been supposed to act as a bridge, mitigating interethnic polarization (Leacock, Deutsch, & Fishman, 1959; Parker, 1968). But just as Israeli society generally disparages the Middle Eastern heritage and esteemed Western ways, the religious school system also gives preference to Western religious traditions, disregarding the Middle Eastern religious culture to which most of its students belong. Moreover, because parents of religious students vary greatly in their religiosity, not only the form of religious tradition but also the degree of its observance has become a point of contention. Parents of students from well-to-do neighborhoods (mainly Westerners) tend to make stricter demands than those from disadvantaged neighborhoods (mainly Middle Easterners). This arouses opposition to integration from parents of Western students who fear that contact with disadvantaged students will affect not only their children's scholastic achievements, but their religious behavior as well. In sum, the religious way of life as presented in the school has often become a disruptive factor for the Middle Eastern students by rupturing the continuity between home and school.

How did these factors affect integration under Reform? In regard to implementation, it is evident that in the religious sector the principle of interethnic integration is applied only in a formal sense at the school level. At the class level, integration is only partially instituted, applying a policy of homogeneous, academic-level homeroom classes (Chen, Lewy, & Adler, 1978). It is of interest to note that this policy of partial integration is also implemented in the secular school system in those schools in which disadvantaged students make up the majority. Conclusions regarding the influence of the relative proportion of disadvantaged students on the implementation process are self-evident.

While integration is only partially implemented in the religious school system, the conditions of the encounter there are instrumental in fostering the development of negative self-concept among Middle Eastern students. This claim is supported by data from a series of studies. Using a Hebrew version of the Fitts (1965) Self-Concept Scale, Schwarzwald (1979) compares integrated schools (Middle Easterners and Westerners) versus ethnically homogeneous (predominantly Middle Easterners) schools in both the religious and secular school systems. It appears that in the secular schools there is no difference between the self-concept of Middle Eastern and Western students. By contrast, in the integrated religious schools, the self-concept of Middle Easterners is not only more negative than that of their Western classmates but even more negative than the self-concept of Middle Eastern students in ethnically homogeneous religious as well as secular schools. This pattern is also reflected in the items on the scales measuring personality adjustment.

Further evidence of differential effects of integration was obtained in a study (Schwarzwald, 1980) investigating stereotypes in integrated and ethnically homogeneous schools in the two school systems. Using a semantic differential scale, students were asked to describe four figures from Israeli society: (1) the Middle Eastern, nonreligious Israeli; (2) the Western nonreligious Israeli; (3) the Middle Eastern, religious Israeli; and (4) the Western, religious Israeli. Based on results of a factor analysis, two evaluation indexes were computed for each student—one representing ratings of success and progress and the other for interpersonal relations. Students related both factors to ethnic background. The Western Israeli (whether religious or not) was rated as more successful and upwardly mobile than his Middle Eastern (whether religious or not) counterpart, whereas on the interpersonal relation factor, the Middle Easterner was rated higher than his Western counterpart. The differential assessment of success was found to be more extreme in integrated schools in the religious system than in the secular system. Compared to students in secular schools, students in religious schools rated Middle Eastern Israelis (whether religious or not) lower on success and progress. Middle Eastern students in integrated religious schools adopted similar assessments for the Israeli of their ascriptive group, assigning lower ratings than those of Middle Eastern students in other institutions studied. Our contention is that this ascription of traits to the various types in Israeli society reflects the difference in social reality found in the composition of the two school sectors inside and outside of school.

In respect to self-concept, therefore, integration appears to have negative consequences for the self-image of Middle Eastern students in religious schools, whereas their counterparts in secular schools are relatively unscathed. These findings are not unique in Israel—studies in the United States, testing the influence of integration on self-concept when considerable interethnic scholastic-achievement differences existed, point to similar phenomena (Armor, 1972; Gerard & Miller, 1975).

Comparing religious and nonreligious schools presents interesting findings about the attitudes of parents as well. It should be noted that the aims of integration are to reduce scholastic differences and unify ethnic groups. Chen *et al.* (1978) point out that the importance of these two goals to parents is related to the ethnic composition and academic level of students in any given school. Parents of children from low socioeconomic strata, as well as parents who fear that integration would lower the educational level, espouse the primacy of scholastic achievements and relegate social integration to secondary importance, although parents did not publicly oppose integration. Yet, because the fear of lowering the educational standards and religious norms is greater in the religious system, parents of religious students express more opposition than parents in secular schools. Investigation of the attitudes of parents to integration in schools of varying proportions of disadvantaged students have not yet been carried out in Israel. It should be pointed out, however, that in the small number of schools in which Western parents did oppose integration, the explicit fear was that educational standards would be harmed, rather than general opposition to integration per se.

From a theoretical perspective, it is possible to attribute these findings concerning self-concept, stereotypes, and parental attitudes to situational factors in the two sectors that emphasize interethnic differences. Inherent in the formation of one's self-concept are two fundamental processes that provide individuals with the basis for evaluating their ability and their social standing: first, the appraisal of the reactions and opinions of people with whom individuals are in contact, especially those he or she respects and admires, and second, the appraisal of the results of social comparisons that individuals make between themselves and others. A positive self-concept is formed when individuals are provided with positive evaluations and when social comparison indicates sufficient ability and reasonable social standing. On the other hand, the absence of positive evaluations from others and critical social comparison results can lead to the formation of a negative self-concept. In this view, poor achievements, inferior social standing, and the rejection of one's own tradition would all contribute to the development of a negative self-concept among Middle Eastern students in the religious educational system.

Yet, it is precisely these factors that are accentuated for Middle Eastern students in the religious educational system. The increased self-depreciation among these students, as well as the negative stereotypes pertaining to their ethnic group appear to demonstrate situational contingent factors surrounding the implementation of integration. Similar arguments of situational contingency can be offered concerning parental attitudes. Integration that intensifies interethnic differences arouses parental opposition, thus polluting the essential supportive atmosphere. It makes educational achievements the major focus of attention. When such polarization exists, in many cases integration is implemented only at the institutional level and not at the class level.

Supportive Intervention

Although ethnic integration has not fulfilled the great expectations held for it, social scientists continue to profer the idea as fundamentally sound. Integration, it is argued, is not a direct outcome of the interethnic encounter per se, but rather is conditional on the more comprehensive intervention plans whose purpose is to create supportive conditions for success (Amir, 1976; Cohen, 1972; Miller, 1980; St. John, 1975). Integration in the Israeli school system has been accompanied by only limited efforts of broader intervention plans and rarely guided by scientific knowledge (as in other countries facing similar problems). Yet, in recent years a number of original attempts have been made to develop supportive intervention programs aimed at the enhancement of positive interethnic relations as well as stimulation of learning.

A detailed program for teacher guidance and training in integrated schools has been developed by Amir, Rich, Ben-Ari, and Agmon (1980). Its purpose is to assist teaching staff to cope with the distinctive psychological, educational, and social problems in integrated schools. The first stage of training, conducted outside the school, presents teachers with the theoretical and practical knowledge available in professional literature. Discussions, case studies, and a series of especially developed exercises for the program touch upon such problems as the harmful effect of stereotyping and prejudice on educational initiative, barriers in communication, tensions in the school climate, and techniques for teaching heterogeneous classes. The second stage, conducted in the school, offers assistance in the implementation of the new programs learned during training sessions and solutions to problems as they arise. The training program has elicited positive reactions from both teaching staffs and students in a number of schools where it has been implemented. However, program effectiveness has not yet been systematically investigated.

Cooperative learning—another approach that has been considered by researchers in the last decade to be promising for the improvement of scholastic achievements and interethnic relations (Slavin, 1980)—has reached Israel as well. Group Investigation, a cooperative teaching method developed in Israel, is designed for teaching the scholastically heterogeneous class (Sharan & Sharan, 1976). First, the teacher presents a general subject to the class. Then, under the teacher's supervision small heterogeneous groups (consisting of two to six students) choose one component of the general topic, collect material, assist one another, decide how the material is to be summarized, and present it to the class. Finally, the work of each group is graded by the teacher as well as by other students.

Recently, Hertz–Lazarowitz, Sapir, and Sharan (1982) compare the impact of Group Investigation, the Jigsaw technique (Aronson, 1978), and traditional frontal-lecture methods on scholastic achievement and interethnic relations. The Jigsaw method raised Middle Eastern students' achievement, but provoked a more negative peer evaluation from their Western classmates. Group Investigation, on the other hand, improved interethnic acceptance. In a different study comparing small group to frontal teaching, Ben-Yitschak, Lotan, and Sharan (1980) find that Middle Easterners prefer small group teaching more than Westerners.

Research on Mexican-American students in the United States suggests that social orientation may be operating as an intervening variable in Middle Eastern students' positive experience with cooperative learning. Studies over the last 10 years have shown that a cooperative social orientation is prominent among Mexican-American children, whereas a competitive orientation is more common among Anglo-Americans (Kagan, 1977). Correspondingly, research outcomes indicate that Mexican-Americans benefit more from cooperative learning than do Anglo-Americans (Kagan, 1976; Slavin, 1980;). The argument is that the competitive orientation of Western society (Seymour, 1981) and schools is inconsistent with cooperation and the consideration for others and thus, is mismatched with the cooperative social orientation of Mexican–American students.

Similar arguments concerning a cooperative social orientation and its educational mismatch with a competitive school is adduced for Middle Eastern students in Israel. McClintock, Bayard, and McClintock (in press) contend that social orientations evolve from family structure and relations among its members. Features such as family size, mutual dependence of family members, and the extent of autonomy given to children distinguish between Mexican–American and Anglo–American families and are analogous to the features distinguishing Middle Eastern from Western families in Israel. Consequently, a more cooperative orientation may be expected from Middle Easterners. Because the orientation of the Israeli school is essentially competitive (Rich, Amir, & Ben-Ari, 1981), it may be that there is a natural affinity to the social orientation of Western children that is in conflict with Middle Eastern students' social orientation. Of course, this hypothesis requires systematic investigation. In this connection, it should be noted that Schwarzwald's (1980) study (discussed earlier) finds that Middle Eastern Israelis are indeed rated higher on the interpersonal relations factor than the Western Israeli.

A third method of intervention developed by Ben-Ari and Amir (Ben-Ari, 1982) is based on the satisfaction of the three interactional social needs outlined by Schutz (1966)—inclusion, control, and affect. Schutz assumes that a group that fulfills these needs will attract the individual and increase positive feelings among its members. Derived from this assumption, Ben-Ari and Amir maintain that an ethnically heterogeneous group providing these basic needs would improve interethnic relations and consequently, facilitate learning. With a set of original psychological exercises devised for the program, they create an atmosphere totally different than found in regular classrooms and exclude such external goals as grades and achievement. By deemphasizing scholastic achievements and previous knowledge, the exercises permit interpersonal experience in a nonroutine context and deeper interpersonal acquaintance. Ben-Ari measured the method's effect on self-concept, class climate, and the mutual evaluations and relations among group members. Relations among students improved in comparison with control groups who did not take part in the exercises. However, self-concept and class climate were not affected.

Overall, it is difficult to say that social scientific literature is rich with techniques to ensure successful ethnic integration or that methods with promise have been utilized on a significant scale in Israel. Despite the effectiveness of work in small groups and individual attention to weaker students (Klein & Eshel, 1981), traditional, basically competitive, frontal-teaching methods continue to dominate the teaching in ethnically integrated schools in Israel (Rich *et al.*, 1981).

A Look to the Future: A Theory of Perceived Inequality

A look to the future of interethnic relations in Israel suggests a greater need for the utilization of existing theoretical and practical knowledge concerning effective integration in the schools. In the past, planned integration was fueled primarily by policymakers' desire to bridge educational gaps and enhance positive social relations, with little involvement or pressure by Middle Easterners in the decision-making process. However, in the future it seems that this pattern will change; more pressure for genuine integration and equality of education will be exerted by Middle Easterners. The reasons for this projection are rooted in more global changes currently arising within the Israeli society.

As noted earlier, the encounter between Middle Easterners and Westerners in Israel must be understood against a background of the national aspiration for unity across different cultural orientations. Israelis seek to create a national Israeli culture. Peres (1971, 1976) finds expression of this desire among high school students, most of whom (75% of the Middle Easterners and 64% of the Westerners) support the blurring of ethnic differences. Along with this aspiration, both Western and Middle Eastern students wish to base the model of integration on a modern way of life that in actuality favors Western culture.

A down-to-earth expression of the wish for interethnic mingling is the percentage of mixed marriages, which rose from 9% in 1952 to 20% In 1981. Chen *et al.* (1978) evidences a different expression for mingling. Parents whose children are enrolled in integrated junior high schools generally favor integration and only a minority (15%) oppose it. Moreover, children in integrated schools currently seem to prefer classmates mainly on the basis of scholastic achievement, whereas ethnic background is of secondary importance (Amir, Sharan, Ben-Ari, Bizman, & Rivner, 1978; Hadad & Shapira, 1977; Schwarzwald & Cohen, 1982).

In the course of time, the assimilation of Middle Easterners to Western culture (Smooha, 1978) has in many respects decreased the differences between Middle Easterners and Westerners. Adoption of Western customs are evidenced by Middle Easterners having fewer children and marrying at a later age than they did in the past (Weller, Don, & Hovav, 1976). The data also show a great similarity in cultural leisure time pursuits among high school students of both Western and Middle Eastern origin (Katz & Gurevitch, 1973) and evidence of decreasing differences in language and consumer habits throughout the population as a whole.

Unfortunately, the gap in socioeconomic status has not been decreasing at the same rate as cultural differences. Peres (1982) presents evidence that the average Middle Eastern income is still appreciably less than the average Western income, although the gap has been reduced in the last decade. Similarly, because there has been an appreciable growth in Middle Eastern political representation, their number in government and political parties falls far below their proportion in the general population.

What is the social psychological significance of the increased cultural similarity on the one hand and the comparatively slow progress made in reducing the gap in socioeconomic standing on the other? Peres (1982) argues that closing the cultural gap has intensified awareness of inequality in the allocation of economic, social, and political resources and thereby, has increased the feeling of discrimination among Middle Easterners. Against the background of a tre-

mendous increase in cultural similarity between Middle Easterners and Westerners, the relatively poor improvement in the social standing of Middle
Easterners has accentuated their feelings of deprivation.

This claim is consistent with Festinger's (1954) theory of social comparison
processes that contends that only individuals with similar relevant characteristics
serve as a basis for social comparison. As long as there are significant cultural
differences, Westerners serve as a distant (and perhaps irrelevant) comparison
model for Middle Easterners. The elimination of cultural differences has made
the Westerner a relevant model for comparison. Consequently, the perception
of and objection to inequitable resource allocation has become more pronounced. The argument is graphically illustrated in Figure 4.1.

The horizontal axis in Figure 4.1 depicts the extent of cultural similarity
between Westerners and Middle Easterners in the past compared to the present;
the vertical axis represents the extent of the gap in social status. The differences
between data points for Middle Easterners in the past and present indicate that
the reduction in social-status differences is considerably smaller than that for
the cultural dimension. The slope of the diagonal in Figure 4.1 between data
points for the two ethnic groups expresses the intensity of feelings of inequality
among Middle Easterners—the steeper the slope, the stronger the feeling of
inequality expressed. Because the improvement in social standing has fallen behind the growth in cultural similarity, the slope of perceived inequality is steeper
for the present than for the past.

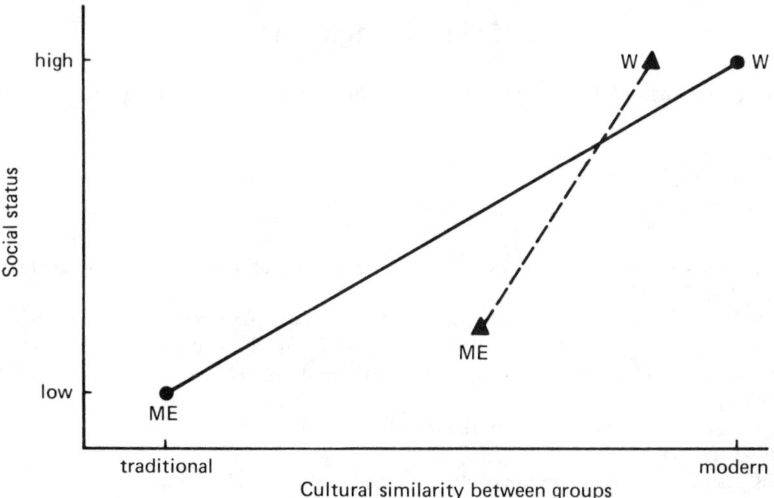

Figure 4.1.   Perceived inequality among Middle Easterners (ME) (as expressed by line slope)
in past (solid line) and present (dashed line) as a contingent of cultural and economic similarity
to Westerners (W).

There have been no systematic investigations of the theory of perceived inequality to date, but there are some supportive data for the general populace as well as for schools. In the recent 1981 national election, an ethnic party whose platform called for the elimination of interethnic differences and increased cultural and social equality succeeded in electing three members to the Israeli Knesset (or parliament). This party obtained important ministerial and governmental positions for Middle Easterners. Today, more than ever, Middle Easterners are demanding prominent and influential positions within existing political parties.

With regard to schools, in an article describing the integration process in a number of schools in Israel, Halper, Shokeid, and Weingrod (in press) conclude that pressure to institute maximal integration is exerted particularly by Middle Easterners who have made social progress. In their article, they argue that upward mobility is accompanied by previously unexpressed demands for equality. Another indication of the current pressure for equality in schools is the demand of Middle Easterners to provide more time for the study of their heritage in the educational curricula (Stahl, 1976). These reflect greater sensitivity to social inequality among Middle Easterners.

If these trends persist, greater pressure for genuine integration and educational equality should face the educational and political systems. One could only speculate as to the specific outcomes in response to these pressures. In any case, it seems that social scientists will be asked to be more intensively involved.

Acknowledgments

The authors thank Michael Hoffman for his valuable comments and suggestions on the manuscript.

References

Adar, L. Toward a study of learning difficulties of the immigrants' children. *Megamot*, 1956, 7, 139–180.(H)[*]

Adiel, S. Reading ability of culturally deprived first graders. *Megamot*, 1968, *15*, 345–356. (H)

Adiel, S. A decade of fostering the disadvantaged. In S. Adiel, G. Bergson, & A. Stahl (Eds.), *A decade of fostering the disadvantaged.* Jerusalem: Ministry of Education and Culture, 1970. (H)

Adler, C. The disadvantaged child in the formal and nonformal educational system. *Saad*, 1974, *4*, 43–49. (H)

Adler, C. School integration in the context of Israel's educational system. In Y. Amir, S. Sharan & R. Ben-Ari (Eds.), *School desegregation: Cross cultural perspectives.* Hillsdale, NJ: Lawrence Erlbaum Associates, in press.

Algarebali, M. Indices for the characterization of the social composition of schools and a system

[*](H) = published in Hebrew.

for allocation of budgets to schools with disadvantaged pupils. *Megamot,* 1975, *21,* 219–227. (H)

Amir, Y. Contact hypothesis in ethnic relations. *Psychological Bulletin,* 1969, *71,* 319–342.

Amir, Y. The role of intergroup contact in change of prejudice and ethnic relations. In P. A. Katz (Ed.), *Towards the elimination of racism.* New York: Pergamon Press, 1976, pp. 245–308.

Amir, Y., Bizman, A., & Rivner, M. Effects of interethnic contact on friendship choices in the military. *Megamot,* 1975, *21,* 287–294. (H)

Amir, Y., Rich, I., & Ben-Ari, R. Problems of school integration in the junior high school, gain and loss to pupils, and proposed solutions. *Studies in Education,* 1978, *18,* 15–36. (H)

Amir, Y., Rich, I., Ben-Ari, R., & Agmon, T. Social integration in the junior high school: An in-service staff training program. Ramat Gan, Israel: Center for Applied Manpower, Bar-Ilan University, 1980. (H)

Amir, Y., Sharan, S., Ben-Ari, R., Bizman, A., & Rivner, M. Asymmetry, academic status, differentiation, and the ethnic perceptions and preferences of Israeli youth. *Human Relations,* 1978, *31,* 99–116.

Amir, Y., Sharan, S., Rivner, M., Ben-Ari, R., & Bizman, A. Group status and attitude change in desegregated classrooms. *International Journal of Intercultural Relations,* 1979, *3,* 137–152.

Armor, D. J. The effects of bussing. *Public Interest,* 1972, *28,* 90–126.

Aronson, E. *The jigsaw classroom.* Beverly Hills, CA: Sage, 1978.

Ashmore, R. D. Solving the problem of prejudice. In B. E. Collins (Ed.), *Social psychology: Social influence, attitude change, group processes and prejudice.* Reading, MA: Addison–Wesley, 1970.

Babad, E. Y., Mann, M., & Mar-Haim, M. Bias in scoring the WISC subtests. *Journal of Consulting and Clinical Psychology,* 1975, *43,* 263.

Ben-Ari, R. *Satisfaction of interpersonal needs in desegregated schools and change in ethnic relations.* Unpublished doctoral dissertation, Bar-Ilan University, Israel, 1982. (H)

Ben-Sasson, H. H. *The middle ages.* Tel-Aviv: Dvir, 1969. (H)

Bentwich, J. S. *Education in Israel.* Tel-Aviv: Joshua Chachik Publishing House, 1960. (H)

Ben-Yitschak, Y., Lotan, M., & Sharan, S. *Developing equal-status interaction in groups of mixed-status Israel youth.* Report submitted to the Israel Ministry of Culture and Education. Ramat Gan, Israel: Sociological Services, 1980. (H)

Brand, E. S., Ruiz, R. A., & Padilla, A. M. Ethnic identification and preference: A review, *Psychological Bulletin,* 1974, *81,* 860–890.

Chen, M., Lewy, A., & Adler, C. *The junior high school study.* Jerusalem: Ministry of Education and Culture, 1978. (H)

Cohen, E. Interracial interaction disability. *Human Relations,* 1972, *25,* 9–24.

Coleman, J. S., Campbell, E. R., Hobson, C. J., McPartland, J., Mood, A. M., Wernfield, F. D., & York, R. L. *Equality of educational opportunities.* Washington, D.C.: U.S. Government Printing Office, 1966.

Davis, F. J. *Minority–dominant relations.* Arlington Heights, IL: AHM Publishing Corporation, 1978.

Egozi, M. *Statistical data on the Israeli educational system.* Jerusalem: Ministry of Education and Culture, 1979. (H)

Eisenstadt, S. N. *The Israeli society: Background, development and problems* (2nd ed.). Jerusalem: Magnes Press, 1973. (H)

Feitelson, D. Causes of failure in first grade pupils. *Megamot,* 1953, *4,* 123–173. (H)

Festinger, L. A theory of social comparison processes. *Human Relations,* 1954, *7,* 117–140.

Fitts, W. H. *Tennessee Self-Concept Scale.* Nashville, TN: Counselor Recordings and Tests, 1965.

Frankenstein, C. *Sincerity and equity.* Tel-Aviv: Sifriat Poalim, 1977. (H)

Gerard, H. B., & Miller, N. *School desegregation.* New York: Plenum, 1975.

Gitai, A. The youth movement as an agent of communal integration. *Megamot,* 1972, *18,* 401–418. (H)

Hadad, M., & Shapira, R. Commanding resources and social integration. *Megamot,* 1977, *23,* 161–173. (H)

Halper, T., Skokeid, M., & Weingrod, A. Communities, schools and integration: Some evidence from Israel. In Y. Amir, S. Sharan & R. Ben-Ari (Eds.), *School desegregation: Cross cultural perspectives.* Hillsdale, NJ: Lawrence Erlbaum Associates, in press.

Hertz-Lazarowitz, R., Sapir, C., & Sharan, S. *The effects of two cooperative learning methods and traditional teaching on the achievement and social relations of pupils in mixed ethnic junior high school classes.* Presented at the American Educational Research Association, New York, 1982.

Israel Ministry of Education and Culture. Public commission's report on the reform program in the Israeli educational system. Jerusalem: Ministry of Education and Culture, 1979. (H)

Kagan, S. *Resolutions of simple conflicts among Anglo–American, Mexican–American and Mexican children.* Paper presented at The Western Psychological Association meeting, Los Angeles, April 1976.

Kagan, S. Social motives and behaviors of Mexican–American and Anglo–American children. In J. L. Martinez (Ed.), *Chicano psychology.* New York: Academic Press, 1977.

Katz, E., & Gurevitch, M. *The culture of leisure in Israel.* Tel-Aviv: Am Oved, 1973. (H)

Kfir, D., & Chen, M. Desegregation and students' attitudes towards themselves and society. Unpublished manuscript, 1980.

Klein, Z., & Eshel, Y. *The other side of the street.* New York: Pergamon Press, 1981.

Leacock, E., Deutsch, M., & Fishman, J. A. The Bridgeview study: A preliminary report. *Journal of Social Issues,* 1959, *15,* 30–37.

Levin, J., & Chen, M. Sociometric choices in ethnically heterogeneous classes. *Megamot,* 1977, *23,* 189–205. (H)

Lewy, A., & Chen, M. Reducing or increasing educational achievement gaps in the primary schools. *Studies in Education Administration and Organization,* 1976, *4,* 3–52. (H)

Litwin, U. The allocation of resources in education in the "Seker" examination. *Megamot,* 1971, *18,* 166– 186. (H)

McClintock, E., Bayard, M. P., & McClintock, C. G. The socialization of social motivation in Mexican–American families. In E. Garcia & M. San Vargas (Eds.), *The Mexican–American child: Language, cognition and social development.* Tempe, AZ: University of Arizona Press, in press.

Miller, N. Making school desegregation work. In W. Stephan, & J. Feagin (Eds.), *School desegregation: Past, present and future.* New York: Plenum, 1980.

Miller, N. Changing views about the effects of school desegregation: Brown then and now. In M. B. Brewer & B. E. Collins (Eds.), *Scientific inquiry and the social sciences.* San Francisco, CA: Jossey-Bass, 1981.

Minkovich, A., Davis, D., & Bashi, J. *Success and failure in Israeli elementary education.* New Brunswick, NJ: Transaction Books, 1982.

Orfield, G. Research, politics and the antibusing debate. *Law and Contemporary Problems,* 1978, *42,* 141–173.

Ortar, G. General survey of the 1955 elementary school graduates—A governmental project. *Megamot,* 1956, *7,* 77–85. (H)

Ortar, G. The predictive value of the "eighth grade survey" tests: A follow-up study. *Megamot,* 1960, *8,* 209–221. (H)

Ortar, G. Educational achievements as related to socio-cultural background of primary school graduates in Israel. *Megamot,* 1967, *15,* 220–229. (H)

Parker, J. H. The integration of Negroes and whites in an integrated church setting. *Social Forces*, 1968, *46*, 359–366.

Peled, E. *Education in Israel in the 1980's.* Jerusalem: Ministry of Education and Culture, 1976. (H)

Peres, Y. Ethnic relations in Israel. *American Journal of Sociology*, 1971, *76*, 1021–1947.

Peres, Y. *Ethnic relations in Israel.* Tel-Aviv: Sifriat Poalim, 1976. (H)

Peres, Y. *Horizontal integration and vertical differentiation among Jewish ethnicities in Israel.* Unpublished manuscript, 1982.

Razael, O. *Compensatory education and welfare for whom?* Jerusalem: Ministry of Education and Culture, 1978. (H)

Rich, Y., Amir, Y., & Ben-Ari, R. Social and emotional problems associated with integration in the Israeli junior high school. *International Journal of Intercultural Relations*, 1981, *5*, 259–275.

Rim, Y. National stereotypes in children. *Megamot*, 1968, *16*, 45–50. (H)

Rosenthal, R., & Jacobson, L. *Pygmalion in the classroom.* New York: Holt, Rinehart & Winston, 1968.

Schutz, W. *The interpersonal underworld.* Palo Alto, CA: Science and Behavioral Books, 1966.

Schwarzwald, J. The self-concept of junior high school students and its significance to religious education. *Megamot*, 1979, *24*, 580–588. (H)

Schwarzwald, J. Relatedness of ethnic origin to the stereotype of the Israeli in the eyes of junior high school students. *Megamot*, 1980, *25*, 322–340. (H)

Schwarzwald, J., & Cohen, S. The relationship between academic tracking and the degree of interethnic acceptance. *Journal of Educational Psychology*, 1982, *74*, 588–597.

Schwarzwald, J., Sholam, M., Waysman, M., & Sterner, I. Israeli teachers' outlook on the necessity and feasibility of teaching values to advantaged and disadvantaged children. *The Journal of Psychology*, 1979, *101*, 3–9.

Schwarzwald, J., & Yinon, Y. Symmetrical and asymmetrical interethnic perception in Israel. *International Journal of Intercultural Relations*, 1977, *1*, 40–47.

Seymour, S. Cooperation and competition: Some issues and problems in cross-cultural analysis. In R. H. Munroe, R. L. Munroe, & B. B. Whiting (Eds.), *Handbook of cross-cultural human development.* New York: Garland STPM Press, 1981.

Sharan, S., & Sharan, Y. *Small group teaching.* Englewood Cliffs, NJ: Educational Technology Publications, 1976.

Shuval, J. T. Patterns of intergroup tension and affinity. *UNESCO International Social Science Bulletin*, 1956, *8*, 75–123.

Shuval, J. T. *Immigrants on the threshold.* New York: Atherton Press, 1963.

Shuval, R., & Teichman, Y. Conditions for intellectual growth in gifted children from varying backgrounds. In A. Ziv (Ed.), *Psychology and counseling in education.* Tel-Aviv: Tel-Aviv University, 1972. (H)

Simon, A. On the scholastic achievements of immigrant children in the lower elementary grades. *Megamot*, 1957, *8*, 343–368. (H)

Simon, U. Education of the oriental immigrant child–parent relations. *Megamot*, 1957, *8*, 41–55. (H)

Slavin, R. E. Cooperative learning. *Review of Educational Research*, 1980, *50*, 315–342.

Smilansky, M. How does the educational system cope with the problem of disadvantaged students. In H. Ormian (Ed.), *Education in Israel.* Jerusalem: Ministry of Education and Culture, 1973. (H)

Smilansky, M., & Yam, Y. The relationship between family size, ethnic origin, father's education and students' achievement. *Megamot*, 1969, *16*, 248–273. (H)

Smilansky, S. Children who fail in the first elementary grades and their parents. *Megamot*, 1957, *8*, 430–445. (H)

Smooha, S. *Israel: Pluralism and conflict.* London: Routledge and Kegan Paul, 1978.

Smooha, S., & Peres, Y. Ethnic inequality in Israel. *Megamot,* 1974, *20,* 5–22. (H)

St. John, N. S. *Social desegregation: Outcomes for children.* New York: Wiley, 1975.

Stahl, A. *Cultural integration in Israel.* Tel-Aviv: Am Oved, 1976. (H)

Stahl, A., Agmon, T., & Mar-Haim, M. Teachers' attitudes towards the culturally disadvantaged. *Studies in Education,* 1976, *11,* 45–58. (H)

Swirsky, S. *Orientals and Ashkenazim in Israel.* Haifa, Israel: Mahbarot Lemehkar Ulvikoret, 1981. (H)

Weissbach, T. Racism and prejudice. In S. Oskamp (Ed.), *Attitudes and opinions.* Englewood Cliffs, NJ: Prentice Hall, 1977, 318–338.

Weller, L., Don, Y., & Hovav, H. The impact of education on family change. *The Israel Annals of Psychiatry and Related Disciplines,* 1976, *14,* 266–274.

15.

Communities, Schools, and Integration

Jeff Halper, Moshe Shokeid, and Alex Weingrod

In his recent anthropological study of a California school, John Ogbu makes the point that relationships between the school and the community are sporadic and limited in scope. Parent and community involvement in the schools, he writes, normally mean participation in such extracurricular programs as PTA, open house, and social entertainments rather than more vital matters such as "making decisions concerning the school curriculum or new programs" (Ogbu, 1974). This is a common pattern: The extent of community participation or control over the schools may vary, but, in general, parents and other community members are content to leave schooling to the teachers and school administrators (Fein, 1971).

This traditional separation between school and community often breaks down, however, when the schools become actively involved in contemporary social and political issues. Large numbers of parents or other groups may not organize committees or attend meetings when a mathematics or history curriculum is on the agenda, but they are aroused when the topics for decision include drawing school boundary lines or busing pupils. School integration—the deliberate placing of previously separate minority and majority groups within the same school building—is surely the prime recent example of how social and political issues bring the school and its various communities into a more direct relationship. As the literature indicates, community responses to integration programs vary from total opposition to active acceptance and cooperation, with a great many shades in between (Crain, 1968; Gerard & Miller, 1975; Mayer, King, Patterson, McCullough, 1974). Community opposition has included seeking legal restraints as well as organizing demonstrations—sometimes violent—whereas cooperation may mean minority- and majority-group members coming together in various proschool activities. Whatever the response, however, the normally passive school-community relationship becomes imbued with bursts of great interest and activity.

Most of the literature tracing the response of local communities to school integration concentrates on the experience in the United States during the past quarter century. Social scientists have analyzed the complex processes that accompany integrating previously segregated Black and White schools in both the North and the South. Not surprisingly, these studies have primarily explored the *political problems and processes* arising from school integration. This point is emphasized in a recent study of integrated schools. Rist (1979) states:

> School desegregation is anything but an apolitical event. The very fact that school desegregation is profoundly political is what gives it varying approaches and programs in different communities. The political realities, the necessary compromises, the manner of external intervention by the courts or other agencies of government, and the vested interests of different groups all impinge upon the desegregation effort [p. 11].

The most ambitious study along these lines is Crain and associates' monograph entitled *The Politics of School Desegregation* (1968). Focusing on an entire city rather than a particular district or neighborhood, the authors analyze the complex interplay among civil rights advocates, boards of education, school officials, and local political and business elites in 15 U.S. cities, as they struggle and bargain with one another while seeking to implement (or delay) voluntary or court-ordered school desegregation. The authors conclude, for example, that school boards are more important than school superintendents in developing integration policies, and that the "political style of the city" and its elites is particularly critical (Crain, Inger, McWorter, & Vanecke, 1968, pp. 358–359). This emphasis upon political processes is also apparent in Gerard and Miller's (1975) longitudinal study of the outcomes of Black–White school integration in Riverside, California. Hendrick's chapter on the "Historical Setting" describes a rash of meetings, demonstrations, boycotts, and violent episodes (a school building was deliberately set on fire) that accompanied the onset of desegregation in Riverside (pp. 30–44). However, the Riverside schools were quickly integrated, and the demonstrations and meetings came to an end. Indeed, the Riverside case exemplifies rapid community acceptance and cooperation. Gerard and Miller (1975) state: "School desegregation was simply a hard issue to oppose when it involved such a minimal inconvenience and cost to the majority community [42]." On the other extreme, Collins' (1979) description of integration in Memphis, Tennessee, and Scherer and Slawski's (1979) depiction of integrated schooling in a Northern city review prolonged periods of community crisis and mutual antagonism.

The Israeli experience in school integration shares certain similarities with the United States but also has some fundamental differences. Let us begin with the differences. Although prejudice is sometimes present in relationships between Western and Middle Eastern Jews in Israel (Amir, 1969, 1976; Shuval, 1954; Smooha, 1978), the scope and depth of prejudicial attitudes and behavior is much more limited than that generally reported for Blacks and Whites in the United States. There is no tradition of racism or discrimination in Israel, and legitimization was never granted to differences between Jewish ethnic groups. On the contrary, the powerful Zionist ideology of "cultural assimilation" sought to eliminate social and cultural differences between Europeans and Middle Easterners. We would expect, therefore, that the extent of intergroup antagonism or tension accompanying school integration in Israel would be much less than in the United States. This has indeed been the case—there were no instances of rioting or other forms of violence arising from government-sponsored school integration programs.

Moreover, some potential conflicts were diffused by maintaining the school's middle-class Western orientation: Western parents whose children were to be "integrated" received assurance by the Ministry of Education that their school's curriculum would not change and that "standards" would not be lowered. They would continue to serve as "cultural models" for the Middle Easterners, who would be expected to adopt their attitudes and behavior patterns (Halper, 1977; Lewis, 1980; Weingrod, 1965). Indeed, many Middle Eastern students appear to have accepted this situation and seek to behave accordingly (Halper, 1977). Hendrick's previously cited conclusion regarding Riverside, California is therefore also applicable to Israel. As Gerard and Miller (1975) have asserted: "School desegregation was simply a hard issue to oppose when it involved such a minimal inconvenience and cost to the majority community [p. 42]."

Nevertheless, as with the American experience, school desegregation in Israel did at times provoke community opposition and lengthy political struggles. As described elsewhere in this volume, school integration was based upon the desire to eliminate structural inequalities in occupation and income between the Western and Middle Eastern segments of the population. Not all parents and community members agreed to use their neighborhood schools—or better, their own children's school—as a means to attain this goal, and consequently school integration sometimes led to intergroup political conflicts.

This chapter examines three Israeli cases of school integration in close detail. More specifically, we were interested in comparing the responses to integration in three different social settings: a Middle Eastern Jewish neighborhood in Jerusalem, a Moroccan (Middle Eastern) Jewish cooperative village in the Negev area (southern section of Israel), and a modern orthodox religious neighborhood in Jerusalem.[1] To be sure, these three instances represent only a small fraction of

---

[1]The data presented in this article grew out of three separate anthropological studies carried out by the coauthors, rather than as part of an overall comparative design. Halper's research was in Orot, Shokeid's in Romema, and Weingrod's in Yemin Shlomo. Each of the coauthors studied a variety of topics. However, in the course of the research each explored the local process of school integration and subsequently decided to utilize these separate studies jointly in this chapter.

the by now rich Israeli experience with school integration, and we make no claim that they are "typical" or representative. At the same time, however, these anthropological studies clarify some of the ways in which schools and society become articulated in the specifically Israeli context, and they point as well to trends that are likely to become more significant in the future.

THE NAVON SCHOOL: POLITICAL DISPUTE AND COMMUNITY APATHY IN A NEIGHBORHOOD OF MIDDLE EASTERN JEWS

The Navon school is situated in Orot, an older residential area located close to the center of Jerusalem.[2] The area is divided into several subneighborhoods, and the population is composed mainly of Israeli-born working-class families, whose historic origins are in southern Turkey, Iraqi Kurdistan, and Iran.

Historically, the issue of school integration did not arise in Orot, but rather in Shaarei Shalom, an adjoining neighborhood with a similar population. Shaarei Shalom's school district included a large, prestigious middle-class neighborhood called Gan v'Etz. However, children from these two neighborhoods did not attend the same elementary school but went to separate schools that shared a common playground.

This blatant segregation was obvious and disturbing to some of the Shaarei Shalom residents. Suspecting that their children were receiving inferior education, a number of parents turned to the leader of the neighborhood council that represented both Shaarei Shalom and Orot and demanded that he "do something" to integrate the schools. The local council head, Nissim Mizrachi, was a university graduate and personally dedicated to the "cause" of integration. In addition, as an elected member of the Jerusalem city council he was also in a position to campaign for desegregation within wider political circles. Mizrachi set in motion what proved to be a lengthy, bitter public dispute. Following some concessions to Gan V'Etz parents who opposed integration, the municipality, which had at first remained aloof from the dispute, recommended a plan for gradually mixing the classes.

Following his success in the Shaarei Shalom–Gan V'Etz conflict, Mizrachi decided to bring the school integration issue to the attention of parents in Orot. Surprisingly, he found that the same issue that had provoked the Shaarei Shalom residents into action received little response or attention. The Navon school had, in the past, served several generations of Orot residents; it was an accepted part of the community, arousing neither support nor condemnation. If it was a poor school, it did not differ from the expectations of the Orot residents. There was no superior Ashkenazi school nearby, and the only other comparisons were to

[2]All the names cited in this chapter are fictitious.

neighborhood religious schools whose levels were even lower. Although Mizrachi received passive support from many of the residents, integration or the quality of schooling never caught on as vital local issues.

At first Mizrachi turned to attacking the administration of the Navon school. The principal was a weak figure, but his weakness in responding to Mizrachi's attacks had the effect of blunting their force. On the other hand, the assistant principal was a forceful and energetic person who was respected by the Orot parents. Many of the teachers were also well liked: Navon presented the image of an institution valiantly seeking to cope with a difficult situation. Even though no one sprang to the school's defence, many of the residents were sympathetic to the school's problems and the efforts made to overcome them.

Mizrachi did not seem to be proposing a clear-cut program of school integration. Unlike the Shaarei Shalom–Gan V'Etz schools, there was no nearby Ashkenazi school that could be merged with Navon. Undaunted, Mizrachi suggested a different solution: The Navon school should be closed and the children bused to other, better schools in the city. Continuing his attack on the school administration, he demanded that Navon's principal be fired; this demand was rejected by the Teachers' Union. Mizrachi then publically demanded that the school be closed. At one point he even threatened to burn down the school if it were not closed! With the approach of the Knesset elections in 1973, Mizrachi, who had won a place on his party's list, distributed the following leaflet:

To the Citizens of Orot–Shaarei Shalom!

I came to Israel 37 years ago with my parents, married and have five children, and I share with you suffering and happiness. I know your needs and will struggle for you. We started a neighborhood council, and the struggle for better education was a big success. Our children who studied in backward schools now study together with the children of Gan V'Etz, and get impressive results. We must improve education at Navon, and try to replace it with a good modern school in which our children will study with children of Western origin and people who are well off. We hope that busing will be the answer.

Throughout his campaign against Navon, Mizrachi did not succeed in enlisting more than a handful of residents to support him actively. The issue of poor education at Navon was, however, an embarrassment to officials in the municipality and Ministry of Education. Under pressure from Navon's administration, the Knesset Education Committee appointed a subcommittee to investigate Mizrachi's charges. The committee held a series of hearings and submitted a report.

Their report substantiated Mizrachi's charges of poor education at the Navon school. Most of the blame was placed on Orot's "backward" population. The school administration was mildly criticized for not having developed fuller relationships with parents, and for their ineffectiveness in instructional methods. The local residents, including Mizrachi, were taken to task for their methods of protest, which, the committee charged, had undermined the morale of both pupils and teachers. The Education Committee did not recommend closing the school, as they claimed there was need for a school in the area but instead suggested some general reforms.

Nevertheless, the Navon school was in the process of being gradually phased out. Even though Mizrachi lacked grass-roots support in the neighborhood, he was influential in the Jerusalem municipality and his lobbying there had its effect. No clear decision to close the school was ever announced. Indeed, until the end there was uncertainty regarding the city's intention to maintain the Navon school. However, in 1974, the boundaries of the school district were redrawn and half the Orot neighborhood was combined with Shaarei Shalom and Gan V'Etz. By 1976 the student population at Navon, which had once stood at 1500, was reduced to 200. No new pupils were accepted for the first-grade classes that year, and students in grades two through four were reassigned to other Jerusalem schools. Finally, in 1977, the Navon school was closed entirely.

Just as they had previously accepted the school, so too the Orot residents accepted its closing without much comment or opposition. For many pupils, the educational situation had improved. This was particularly the case for those integrated with the Gan V'Etz school. Other pupils' schooling may in fact have become less effective. Many were bused to schools far from their homes, without any plans for social integration or educational assistance. On the other hand, the political agitation that had accompanied the integration conflict did subside. Mizrachi turned his attention to other issues and the neighborhoods regained their normal quiet. (For additional details, see Halper, 1977.)

FROM CONSENSUS TO CONFLICT OVER SCHOOLING IN A RURAL AREA

Located in the northern Negev, Romema is a moshav, or cooperative village, which was settled in 1956 by Moroccan immigrants from the Atlas Mountain region. Together with 11 other moshavim and a kibbutz, it composes a regional council whose responsibilities include providing education for the village children. There are four elementary schools in the region, all belonging to the national religious elementary system—three for children of the moshavim, and a separate school for the kibbutz youngsters. Together with the children of two other moshavim of North African immigrants, the Romema youngsters attended school at Gador, a nearby moshav of veteran Israelis, about two-thirds of whom were of Western origin. The teachers and administrators at this school were mainly Gador residents.

During their initial decade or so at Romema, the Moroccan settlers did not place special emphasis on questions of schooling or school integration. Their main concern was to succeed economically in agriculture, and they were also deeply involved in internal factional disputes. Throughout this period their children attended the regional school located at Gador. (For additional details of the Romema dispute, see Shokeid, 1971:1983).

The children of veteran Israeli settlers from Gador did not at first attend the local school but were instead bused to the nearby kibbutz school: In effect, the education of the children of North African immigrants was segregated from that of the children of Western veterans. Although at that time the Romemites did not protest, the national religious school authorities placed considerable pressure on the Gador parents to send their children to the local school, and, bowing to this pressure in 1966, the Gador parents agreed. However, within the school their youngsters were concentrated in a single class, and they also received additional tutoring and extracurricular activities. The arrangement adopted was one in which the Gador school included youngsters from three North African villages and from Gador itself, with the Gador children placed in a single class together with a few selected Moroccan youngsters.

This pattern prevailed for a decade. During this time important changes took place in Romema. The village became one of the most successful in the region; the earlier factional disputes were muted, and the community became increasingly stable and well managed. The village was also strikingly successful in the field of education; in 1976, more than 50% of those between the ages of 17 and 20 had completed 12 years of schooling. Quite a few of them went on to hold important positions in regional economic, organizational, and educational institutions.

It is against this brief historical background that the recent dispute between Gador and Romema regarding integrated education can be properly understood. The dispute focused on the composition of the first-grade classes. At the beginning of the 1976–77 school year, 60 pupils presented themselves for registration at the Gador regional school. Twenty-one were from Gador, and the remaining 40 came from the three North African villages in the school district. According to the agreement that had been reached 10 years earlier, all the Gador youngsters would be enrolled in the same first-grade class, whereas the others would be divided into two classes of 20 students each. In earlier years the Romema parents (as well as those in the two other immigrant villages) had accepted this, although with increasing reluctance as their economic and social status improved. By 1977 they strongly opposed this arrangement and demanded a different form of integration.

The education committee of the four villages held numerous lively meetings before the start of the school year, and two opposing plans were presented. The Gador representatives suggested that their children be divided equally into two first-grade classes, with each class having the same number of children "of good intellectual potential" from the neighboring villages. A third class would then be composed of children with a "lower intellectual level" from the other villages.

The representatives of the North African villages presented their counterproposal: Each of the three first-grade classes would have an equal number of children from each village. At the end of the school year, all the first-graders would be tested and then assigned to a second-year class.

The two sides were unable to arrive at a compromise or agree on an alternative plan. Feelings ran so high that the parents from the North African villages boycotted the school, thereby preventing the opening of the school year. The four education committees were summoned to the Ministry of Education in Jerusalem, where it was unanimously agreed that the Ministry would appoint a committee to investigate the entire matter.

Within a few days the committee met and announced its conclusions. It recommended that two equally advanced first-grade classes be established, that a third smaller class of less well-prepared first graders be set up, and that a special class also be formed for six "underdeveloped children." The committee also suggested that additional teachers be assigned, and that new educational equipment be made available for the less well-prepared students. According to this proposal, the student population of the two weaker classes would be composed entirely of North African children.

The committee's recommendations were deeply resented by the Romemites and the other North Africans. They accused the committee members of prejudice, because their conclusions were based solely on information supplied by the Gador school officials. Nevertheless, the report was finally accepted, the parents' boycott of the school was called off, and the school year began.

It is important to understand the range of attitudes expressed by the Romema parents. The older parents, particularly those who had come to Israel with young children, took a passive stance, accepting the decisions of the education committee and acting accordingly. In contrast, the younger parents, mainly persons in their 30s who had been at least partially educated in Israel, were extremely active in the dispute. The majority of these younger parents tended to favor a compromise with the Gador settlers. They acknowledged the efforts and resources invested by the people of Gador, both individually and collectively, in the education of their children. They also recognized that the environment in some Romema households was indeed such that their children were poorly prepared for school; these families were accused of slowing Romema's development. Aware of the deficiencies in their own education, these younger settlers were anxious to implement some changes, but not at the price of splitting the school. They believed that educational integration would compensate their children for the deficiencies in their own environment and provide them with equal opportunities. They often sought to calm the situation, and in meetings with Gador representatives they tried to dismiss the accusations of ethnic discrimination made by other Moroccans.

A third category was composed of men in their mid-20s who already held senior managerial positions. Most of them had completed high school in Israel, and a few had continued on to institutions of higher learning. Although their children were not yet of school age, they bitterly resented integration on Gador's terms and insisted on nothing less than complete integration. Indeed, they considered segregation preferable to a compromise that would imply that Romema students were socially or intellectually inferior. Well-acquainted with the values and techniques of higher education, and themselves "living proof" that Moroccans with their background could reach high office, they repeatedly accused the Gador committee and the ministry officials of being prejudiced and discriminatory. To be sure, the fact that their own children were not yet of school age may have served to make their attitude more extreme, but there is little doubt of the depth of their feelings.

Although the radical position in Romema advocated closing the school, radical opinion in Gador called for sending their youngsters back to the kibbutz school (even though they knew that in the kibbutz school their children would not enjoy the same high status as in the local school). Nevertheless, there were also those in Gador who had moral doubts about the village committee's refusal to have their children spread throughout the first-grade classes and asked themselves whether they had done enough to integrate their North African neighbors "into Israeli culture." In effect, the more extreme position held at Romema, plus the practical considerations of the Gador settlers, placed pressure upon the latter to agree to a compromise. In the following year both sides reluctantly agreed to assign all first graders to an appropriate class according to entrance tests. This agreement also involved some changes in the school administration, particularly the transfer of the principal who had been accused of siding with Gador. The compromise agreement has been followed by both sides. (For additional details of the Romema dispute and its implications for educational policies, see Shokeid 1983).

IDEOLOGY AND INTEGRATION IN RELIGIOUS SCHOOLING IN JERUSALEM

The events surrounding the formation of the Neot school in Jerusalem's Yemin Shlomo district represent a classic instance of how parents become involved in school integration. The background to the Neot case can briefly be summarized as follows.

During the mid-1960s a small group of friends began discussing the formation of a new type of religious school. They were all young religious parents facing The problem of enrolling their children in school. Nearly all the men were associated with the Yeshiva Harav Kook, a religious seminary that combined religious training with Zionist ideology. Western and middle class in background, Israeli born and well-educated, these parents were themselves graduates of the state religious school system. They had, in fact, been among the first graduates of a special elite religious high school program. However, they did not feel that their experience in the religious school system had been entirely satisfactory; they were critical in particular of primary schools, because they considered them to be inadequate in religious terms. One alternative might have been the schools organized by the ultrareligious Agudath Yisrael; but the parents rejected this option, because the Agudath schools emphasize neither Zionist nor national ideals.

Following lengthy discussions these parents decided to create an entirely new school, called the Neot school. Their objective was to design a school that would provide a deep religious education coupled with secondary emphasis upon secular topics such as history or mathematics. In contrast with the state religious schools, which merely taught religious topics academically, Neot was to bring the ''spirit of the Bible'' and sense of religious community to everyday life. Not only would the religious curriculum be advanced and sophisticated, but the teaching staff would be deeply committed to religious practice and hence provide a constant model for students. In addition, Neot was to develop a positive identification with the Jewish people and a commitment to Zionist ideals. Finally, registration would be selective: Only students from properly devout homes would be accepted, creating a true community among students, parents, and teachers.

Energetic, imaginative, and idealistic, the tiny band of Neot supporters set out to create their own school. Neot was at first a private school, outside the framework of the national state-supported school systems. It is important to emphasize that in the early stages (between 1966 and 1970) the issue of school integration did not figure prominently in the minds of the school's supporters or their opponents. It was only later that integration became the focus of a bitter, prolonged controversy.

The Neot school drew its support primarily from the small *yeshiva* community located in Yemin Shlomo. A few religious families from other neighborhoods who shared the school's outlook also enrolled their children there. As the number of students increased, however, opposition to the school also mounted. Some of the religious residents of Yemin Shlomo whose children were enrolled in the neighborhood state religious school, the Maimon school, were strongly opposed to Neot. These parents disapproved of the strong religious emphasis (they favored a mixed religious–secular curriculum) and were also concerned about the selective, elite stance that Neot had adopted. Moreover, the Jerusalem Education Department and the Ministry of Education also opposed the school: They saw the formation of a private religious school as a precedent that might split the entire state religious educational system. The ensuing struggle to determine the new school's legitimacy continued for 10 years.

This is not the place to document or analyze the dispute itself (described in detail by Weingrod, 1981). The Neot parents and their supporters campaigned tirelessly and effectively in favor of the new school. Indeed, following a lengthy controversy they succeeded in having their school included on the list of state-approved schools. As a result, the school received substantial state financial support, although its curriculum was not supervised by the Ministry officials.

Neot continued to grow in size—and the issue of school integration then became more intense. The reasons for this are readily apparent. The Neot school mainly attracted students from middle-income Western families; it was among this population that the school's ideology and high-quality education had its greatest appeal. Moreover, the selective criteria employed by the school appeared to rule out children of Middle Eastern origin: Prospective students were screened for their religious orthodoxy, and Middle Eastern families were thought to be less rigorous in their religious practices and consequently unsuitable as candidates. This had an immediate effect upon the local Yemin Shlomo state religious school: Its Western registration declined, and the school enrolled Middle Eastern youngsters from adjoining neighborhoods to take their place. The Maimon school therefore became more integrated, whereas the Neot school was increasingly segregated.

It soon became clear, however, that the repercussions were far wider. As an "approved state school," Neot could legally enroll students from any neighborhood in Jerusalem. As a result, Ashkenazi youngsters from schools throughout the city began streaming there. In most instances these youngsters had been enrolled in neighborhood state religious schools that had a mixed or majority Middle Eastern population. This was, indeed, the crux of the controversy: Neot was accused of causing segregation in religious education throughout the entire city of Jerusalem.

Neot's opponents joined forces to fight the school's continued growth. A committee representing eight state religious schools, as well as some influential political figures, was organized to pressure the city and state authorities and to mobilize public opinion around the banner of integration in state religious schools. At one point this group went on strike to protest Neot's selective policies. The municipal and national school authorities also joined the battle. For example, the municipal officials refused to provide Neot with larger school facilities; they accused the school of not having an adequate proportion of "underprivileged" Middle Eastern students and rejected various compromise proposals put forward by the Neot leadership.

Certain of the justice of their cause and heartened by the constant flow of new students, the Neot supporters fought back vigorously and effectively. When the authorities were slow to provide classrooms, they staged a demonstration at the Jerusalem ministry offices and "taught" in front of the television cameras; the school's lawyers kept up a lengthy correspondence with the ministries protesting the treatment they received. Sensitive to the charges of segregation, the Neot leaders claimed that they were in fact enrolling substantial numbers of underprivileged Middle Eastern youngsters. The Neot leadership even proposed a plan according to which they would, in effect, take control over several religious prekindergarten classes in predominantly Middle Eastern neighborhoods and then recruit students from this pretrained population. (The residents of these neighborhoods rejected the plan.) In this way and other ways, they sought to deal with the accusations of discrimination. However, in softer voices and behind closed doors, the school leaders expressed the view that there were "values more important than school integration"—religious values in particular—and that parents should have the right to select their children's schooling.

In the end, Neot triumphed. One of the first acts of a new (religious) Minister of Education was the allocation of funds to provide adequate space for expansion of the school. In 1978, the Neot school enrolled close to 800 students from throughout Jerusalem. Many of the religious residents in Yemin Shlomo continued to support the school, and the local state religious school adapted itself to Neot's presence. Neot had succeeded in becoming an important force in religious education in Jerusalem, and for that matter, influential throughout the whole of Israel.

DISCUSSION AND CONCLUSIONS

Although we are mindful of the problems of generalizing from a small number of cases, several trends do emerge from our analysis of the data. We suggest six closely connected conclusions regarding school integration and community in the Israeli context.

1. From the Perspective of the Community, School Integration is a Political Process Involving Local- and National-Level Agencies and Officials. In the earlier portions of this chapter, we noted the emphasis on politics in U.S. studies of the community and desegregation. Our Israeli data point in the same direction, involving political activism in each of the sample cases: At Navon the key political leader led the fight for school integration; in the Gador case the different villages mobilized as political pressure groups; and in the Neot example both sides made skillful use of various political tactics. In Israel as in the United States, opposed viewpoints, ideologies, and interests regarding school integration provoked lengthy political struggles.

There are, however, some important contrasts: In the United States these disputes tend to remain at city or local school-district level, whereas in Israel they rapidly escalate to include state agencies and national-level political organizations. For example, in Crain's study (Crain, Inger, McWorter, & Vanecko, 1968) of school integration in the United States, little attention is given to state or national-level state agencies; the key decision makers are local school-board members or important figures in the business elite. The courts at various levels are, it is true, involved in desegregation, but the issues tend to remain localized. This is in keeping with both the large scale and the power structure of U.S. society, as well as with ideological emphasis given to relatively autonomous school boards.

The Israeli pattern is, naturally, much different. Not only is the scale smaller and more compact, but state agencies and national-level political parties have considerable influence on local events (Eisenstadt, 1966). This is well exemplified in our case material. In the Navon example the Knesset Education Committee became directly involved in the dispute over local schooling, and at both Gador and Neot the Ministry of Education as well as national political party leaders took active roles in specific school-integration issues. In effect, in Israel there seems to be less distance between neighborhood and national levels.

How does this effect the Israeli school-integration process? State agencies such as the Ministry of Education are unequivocably in favor of school integration. The national political parties have also supported integration programs. Not only do these groups control crucial resources, but they are also able to generate public opinion in favor of school integration. Consequently, opponents of integration at the local level are immediately placed in a political confrontation with state-level officials, and conversely, the proponents of integration are able to enlist the active support of the government ministries and other allied agencies. This does not mean that what are essentially segregated schools cannot be established or sustained (the Neot school is a case in point). But these are probably unusual cases: The clear government prointegration policy, as well as the broad public consensus in favor of social and cultural assimilation, strongly favors the school-integration process.

2. The "Recipient" and "Applicant" Groups Differ Widely in their Success in Making Use of Political and Other Resources.   Generally speaking, those already receiving better education, the "recipient groups," are of Western origin, whereas those seeking better education (or for whom such is sought), the "applicant groups," are Middle Eastern in origin. Discussions of school integration often assume that there are major similarities within these categories. For example, the previously mentioned study by Crain and his associates suggests a certain uniformity among Blacks and Whites in the U.S. desegregation struggles (1968). However, the case material presented in this chapter shows that groups within the same category vary greatly in their access to political resources and the ways in which they employ them in particular political situations. For example, the Western parents at Neot succeeded in their battle against integration, whereas their peers at Gador failed. This is probably explained by the close ties between the Neot leadership and important national political leaders. Similarly, the Moroccan farmers at Romema successfully manipulated the religious political party as well as various national-level agencies in their battle for integration, and in this regard they resemble the Neot parents. We conclude that in conflicts over school integration both the applicant and the recipient groups are potentially able to mobilize significant support, and that the outcomes depend on particular combinations of motivation, leadership, and political skill.

3. In Certain Circumstances Applicant Groups Consider School Integration Irrelevant to Their Needs and Aspirations.   Our case material indicates that some insular urban communities are not much concerned with school integration. This is best exemplified in the case of Orot. Middle Eastern parents and community members in that neighborhood were indifferent to school integration even after having been harangued by their own political leaders and told that their children were receiving an inferior education. Within Orot, where ethnic and neighborhood social ties are powerful, feelings of relative deprivation were blunted by the self-contained nature of the neighborhood. This contrasts sharply with Shaarei Shalom, where equally strong local and ethnic ties were mixed with the realization that the children were attending an obviously segregated school.

How can this be explained? Orot's "insular character" is closely connected with its socioeconomic position: Many of its residents are occupationally linked with a series of local resources including taxi and truck driving, retailing in a large nearby open market, construction work, and the like. Entrance into these occupations is dependent on personal and family ties rather than formal educational certification. There was, therefore, no powerful incentive to insist upon school integration, and the residents themselves were not aware of the long-term importance of continuing education. For these reasons, school integration did not become a salient issue for them, and the residents rather passively accepted the proposals put forward by government education officials.[3]

4. Whereas There is General Ideological Support for School Integration, Particular Plans or Programs May Provoke Community Tension and Conflict. Our data show that an ideological commitment to integration need not prevent opposition to specific integration programs. The dispute at Gador illustrates this point: Many of the Romema students had achieved educational success before the issue of desegregation was even raised. Moreover, the Romema parents demonstrated a willingness to compromise throughout the lengthy negotiations. They also accepted the "concern for education" expressed by the Western Gador parents. Although accepting the ideology of school integration in principal, the Gador parents opposed the plan that would have distributed their children in classes with the Moroccan youngsters. In fact, they finally accepted a compromise, but the negotiations lasted more than a decade.

In this regard it is important to take note of the "educational quality" issue: In all our cases, those who opposed specific integration programs claimed that mixing the school populations would inevitably lower the quality of their children's education. Whether or not integration is detrimental to the achievements of the recipient group, the terms in which the issue is often debated are likely to provoke anxiety among Western parents. For example, the frequently discussed schooling problems of Middle Eastern children, or their designation as "culturally disadvantaged," convinces many middle-class people from Western origin

---

[3]The much stronger response of the Shaarei Shalom residents is probably explained by their close physical proximity to a middle-class Western neighborhood.

that there is little to be gained—and perhaps much to be lost—by integrating the schools. Leaving aside the merits of such concepts, a strategy that emphasizes the cultural differences and educational problems of one group of pupils is unlikely to allay the fears of others.

5. Anti-integration Sentiments May also Receive Ideological Support.   Not only have some communities opposed specific school integration plans, under certain circumstances this has also been provided with an ideological justification. This is demonstrated most clearly in the Neot case, where the emphasis given to "high religious standards" served to exclude many Middle Eastern pupils and, in effect, created school segregation. The mirror image of this position is represented in the Gador example. It is recalled that the younger, more successful Moroccan parents favored creating their own segregated school if their proposal for total classroom integration was rejected. In this case the ideological basis seems to have been that incomplete school integration would have a negative educational and psychological result, and that a high-level segregated school would therefore be preferable.

Although two cases do not necessarily signal a trend, ideological opposition to school integration may well become more insistent in the future. Discontent with the pace or results of desegregation may lead some groups to oppose continued school integration. Moreover, tensions between ethnic groups may also produce prosegregation ideologies. The process of school integration in Israel is far from complete, and any weakening of the ideological consensus will threaten the considerable progress that has already been made.

6. Upwardly Mobile Middle Easterners Are Likely to Insist upon Total School Integration.   Our data indicate that it is among this segment of the population that the demand for desegregation is especially powerful. This is best illustrated in the Gador case, where the younger, better educated Moroccans were unwilling to compromise on the integration issue. These young men and women were themselves successful graduates of the Israeli educational system, and they were affronted by the accepted pattern of segregation within the Gador school. This active concern regarding education signals a new situation, in which Middle Eastern parents will not be content with anything less than high-quality education for their children.

This is likely to be an important trend during the next decade; that is, closed urban enclaves such as Orot are becoming unusual as increasing numbers of Israeli-born Middle Easterners become absorbed within the broad Israeli middle class (Matras, 1981). Insofar as this also results in residential desegregation— and there is some evidence that this is the case—in the future many schools will become desegregated by virtue of their neighborhood population composition (Gonen, 1981). This is by no means an "automatic process," however, and it clearly depends on national and international economic, political, and social processes. Indeed, the process of upward mobility may itself sharpen tensions, as new demands and expectations are expressed by the mobile groups. The likelihood is, therefore, that school integration will continue to be an important social and political issue in the years ahead.

REFERENCES

Amir, Y. The contact hypothesis in ethnic relations. *Psychological Bulletin*, 1969, *71*, 319–342.

Amir, Y. The role of intergroup contact in change of prejudice and ethnic relations. In P. Katz (Ed.), *Toward the elimination of racism*. New York: Pergamon Press, 1976.

Collins, T. W. From courtrooms to classrooms: Managing school desegregation in a deep South high school. In R. C. Rist (Ed.), *Desegregated schools*. New York: Academic Press, 1979.

Crain, R. L., Inger, M., McWorter, G. A., & Vanecko, J. J. *The politics of school desegregation*. Chicago: Aldine, 1968.

Eisenstadt, S. N. *Israeli society*. New York: Basic Books, 1966.

Fein, L. *The ecology of the public schools*. New York: Pegasus, 1971.

Gerard, H. B., & Miller, N. *School desegregation*. New York: Plenum Press, 1975.

Gonen, A. *Some social geographic features of urban ethnic residential dispersion*, 1981. (Mimeo)

Halper, J. *Ethnicity and education: The schooling of Afro–Asian Jewish children in a Jerusalem locality*. Milwaukee: University of Wisconsin, Ph.D. thesis, 1977.

Lewis, A. *Power, poverty and education*. Ramat Gan: Turtledove, 1980.

Matras, J. *Intergenerational social mobility among different ethnic groups*. 1981. (Mimeo)

Mayer, R., King, C., Patterson, A., McCullough, J. *The impact of school desegregation in a southern city*. Lexington, Mass.: Heath, 1974.

Ogbu, J. *The next generation: An ethnography of education in an urban neighborhood*. New York: Academic Press, 1974.

Rist, R. C. *Desegregated schools*. New York: Academic Press, 1979.

Scherer, J., & Slawski, E. Color, class and social control in an urban desegregated school. In R. C. Rist (Ed.), *Desegregated schools*. New York: Academic Press, 1979.

Shokeid, M. *The dual heritage: Immigrants from the Atlas Mountains in an Israeli village*. Manchester: Manchester University Press, 1971. (Augmented edition, New Brunswick, NJ: Transaction Books, 1984.

———. Commitment and paradox in sociological research: School integration in Israel. *Ethnic and Racial Studies, 6*, 198–212.

Shuval, J. Cultural assimilation and tension in Israel. *International Social Science Bulletin*, 1954, *8*, No. 1.

Smooha, S. *Israel: Pluralism and change*. Berkeley: University of California Press, 1978.

Weingrod, A. *Israel: Group relations in a new society*. New York: Praeger, 1965.

Weingrod, A. Rashomon in Jerusalem: Ideology and power in an urban dispute. *European Journal of Sociology*, 1981, *22*, 158–169.

16.

Minority Education in Sharonia, Israel, and Stockton, California: A Comparative Analysis

Arnold Lewis

In this paper, ethnographic data from Stockton, California and Sharonia, Israel are brought to bear on the question, In what way do dominant-minority group relations affect the educational careers of poor black American and Oriental Jewish youth? Organizing the data in reference to two key concepts, power relationships and symbolic formations, it is shown that Stockton and Sharonia exhibit congruent structures of social inequality. This impinges on the organization of educational environments in each society. In both settings, minority youth must compete for educational credentials in social situations in which power relationships and symbolic formations are heavily weighted against their interests. Nevertheless, in confronting similar social situations, black American and Oriental Jewish youth have adopted divergent strategies of behavior. It is argued that alternative responses to similar educational situations can best be explained in reference to the world view and corresponding strategy for social advancement of black Americans and Oriental Jews. MINORITY EDUCATION; SOCIAL INEQUALITY; ISRAEL; BLACK AMERICANS; ORIENTAL JEWS; ETHNOGRAPHY.

Common features of complex societies are low-status minority groups that, through conquest or migration, have been incorporated into social systems dominated by others. Blacks in the United States and Oriental Jews in Israel are prominent examples of this ubiquitous social phenomenon. In comparison to others in their respective societies, they are relatively poor and powerless.

Social stratification along racial or ethnic lines is a common historical occurrence, which, as a mere consequence of its presence, need not automatically raise pressing moral or political questions. In societies with egalitarian ideologies, however, the persistence of low-status minority communities does indeed suggest a moral, if not a political, dilemma. In these circumstances, systematic social inequality suggested by the existence of poor minority communities challenges the self-image of the dominant group as a deserving elite in a just society. Likewise, an egalitarian ideal is a resource that minority group members, individually or collectively, can manipulate to their own advantage.

In response to endemic social inequality, elites in contemporary United States and Israel have looked toward publicly sponsored educational programs for relief. Blacks in the United States and Oriental Jews in Israel have been formally encouraged to compete with dominant group members for educational credentials. Toward this end, extensive efforts have been made to develop special programs designed to foster the educational careers of minority youth (see Adler 1970; Ogbu 1978:65–100; Passow et al. 1967; Smilansky and Nevo 1971:1–5).

In both societies, the educational question has been in the forefront of public discussion on ethnic-racial relations and social inequality. In political, popular, and academic forums, the debate between defenders and critics of the "culture of poverty" thesis has focused attention on cultural differences between dominant and minority groups that are thought to inhibit the ability and motivation of minority youth to compete successfully against dominant group peers for educational credentials. The culture of poverty thesis suggests that members of relatively poor minority communities in industrial societies exhibit "pathological" cultural traits, which are passed from generation to generation. Proponents of this viewpoint bring data on family structure, values, socialization habits, cognitive dispositions, and genetic heritage to support their case (see O. Lewis 1961, 1966a, 1966b; Moynihan 1965; Riessman 1962; Smilansky and Smilansky 1967). Although critics have skillfully exposed the ethnocentric bias in the culture of poverty model, the U.S. debate continues to suffer from polemics associated with its unmasking.[2] In Israel, the culture of poverty thesis remains ascendant. Both discussions suffer from a lack of careful cross-cultural comparison.

In recent years, there has been a growing discussion on the impact of the structure of dominant-minority group relations on the way of life of low-status groups (see Depres 1975; Hannerz 1974; Hechter 1975; Henry 1976; Smooha 1978). The dominant-minority group relationship can best be characterized as one of structured social inequality. This is apparent in the four sociological characteristics that distinguish minority groups. First, they are identified with physical or cultural traits held in low esteem by others in society (Wagley and Harris 1958:10). Second, membership is an ascribed, not an achieved, status (Depres 1975:195). Third, members, by choice or necessity, tend to marry among themselves (Wagley and Harris 1958:10). Fourth, minority groups are invariably associated with low-status neighborhoods and townships that have a subordinate relationship with regional and national political, economic, and social institutions (Hechter 1975).

In contrast to the culture of poverty model, emphasis on dominant-minority group relations suggests that the relatively poor life chances of minority group members are a function of the asymmetrical distribution of power in society. Thus, in competition with dominant group members for scarce resources, minority group members are relatively unsuccessful because they are relatively powerless, not because they are culturally different.

To the present, few anthropological studies have examined the educational endeavors of minority youth in reference to the structure of dominant-minority group relations.[3] This has hampered the development of a comparative anthropology of minority education. An important exception is John Ogbu's insightful account of education in Burgherside, a black and Mexican-American neighborhood of 1,700 persons on the southwest periphery of Stockton, California. Ogbu's ethnography is informed by a model suggesting that the structure of power, as well as dominant and minority perceptions of group relations, affect the educational endeavors of minority youth.

I have recently completed a study on the schooling of low-status Oriental Jews in Sharonia, a town of 3,500 persons in the highly urban central region of Israel (Lewis 1979a). Adopting a model of analysis compatible with Ogbu's, I have been struck by the congruence in the structures of social inequality in Burgherside and Sharonia. In both settings, learning environments are designed and controlled by dominant group elite who explain relatively poor academic achievements by minority youth in reference to local versions of the culture of poverty model (Ogbu 1974:13–14; Lewis 1979a:75–78). Yet the ethnographic evidence indicates sharply contrasting strategies for behavior in educational settings by Burgherside and Sharonia youth. Whereas black and Mexican-Americans in Burgherside have adopted a strategy of withdrawal from active participation in educational situations, Oriental Jews in Sharonia actively compete with one another in efforts to gain highly valued educational credentials (Ogbu 1974:81–101; Lewis (1979a:91–114).[4] These facts are in need of sociological explanation. Accordingly, the question will be examined. In what way do dominant-minority group relations in Stockton, California, and Sharonia, Israel, affect the educational careers of poor black and Oriental Jewish youth.[5]

Method of Analysis

To explore the impact of dominant-minority group relations on the educational careers of Burgherside and Sharonia youth, I propose to adopt a dialectical method of analysis. Robert Murphy captures the spirit of this approach, suggesting that

> the analyst of society question everything that he sees and hears, examine phenomena fully and from every angle, seek and evaluate the contradiction of any proposition, and consider every category from the viewpoint of its noncontents as well as its positive attributes. It requires us to look for paradox as much as complementarity, for opposition as much as accommodation. It portrays a universe of dissonance underlying apparent order and seeks deeper orders beyond dissonance. (1971:117).

If functionalism stresses consistency and order, dialectic emphasizes contradiction and conflict.

The dialectical method of analysis employed herein is a three-stage process. First, taking a lead from the French anthropologist Claude Levi-Strauss (1963:16–17), a contrasting pair of concepts that define the dominant-minority group relationship will be identified. Second, the concepts will be employed to uncover fundamental contradictions in social facts relating to the education of Sharonia and Burgherside youth. Third, out of the ethnography of contradiction, a sociological explanation of the behavior of minority youth in educational situations will be constructed.

What contrasting pair of concepts defines the dominant-minority group relationship? Central to dominant-minority group relations is the competition among social groups for scarce resources. In a provocative essay, Cohen has suggested that group competition for scarce resources takes place through the dialectical interaction of power relationships with symbolic formations (1974:13). Power relationships are grounded in the political and economic activities of people (Cohen 1974:22). Toward these ends, people organize in associations that are structured by what the sociologists Max Weber has characterized as imperative control: "the probability that a command with a given specific content will be obeyed by a given group of persons" (1947:152). In power relationships, imperative control is constantly defined and redefined.

Symbolic formations are rooted in the psychic structure of people (Cohen 1974:24). In symbolic formations (e.g., ideology, religion, and belief systems) on the nature of society, the nature of humanity, the relationship of people to the environment and to each other, collective meaning of reality is constructed. Through the manipulation of symbolic formations, social meaning is shaped and reshaped.

Power relationships and symbolic formations are not homologous, but are formed through independent processes, one social and one psychic. Yet they constantly act on one another in a dialectical fashion. If social life entails competition and cooperation among people in the exploitation of scarce resources, then culturally appropriate symbolic formations offer a medium through which individuals and groups attempt to explain their behavior and the behavior of others. Power relationships and symbolic formations both impinge on social behavior. It is in the dialectical interaction between power relationships and symbolic formations that the behavior of minority youth in educational situations can best be explained.

The ethnography of education in Sharonia and Burgherside will be organized in reference to these two key concepts. First, the structure of social inequality in Sharonia and Burgherside will be explored. It will be shown that, in terms of power relationships and symbolic formations, the structures of social inequality in the two cases are congruent. Second, educational services in each community will be examined. It will be demonstrated that the social organization of educational situations in Sharonia and Burgherside reflects underlying power relationships and symbolic formations in the wider society. Dominant group elites in Israel and Stockton share parallel assumptions regarding the relationship between education and social inequality. This affects the form and content of pedagogical curricula as well as the ideology of educators working with minority youth. Third, the belief systems by which Sharonians and Burghersiders evaluate their social situations will be explicated. It will be shown that these stand in antithetical relationship to one another. Divergent world views have spawned contrasting strategies for social advancement and attitudes toward education.

In light of these social facts, a comparative discussion of minority education in Sharonia and Burgherside will be presented.

The Structure of Social Inequality: A Comparative Ethnographic Sketch

Residents of Sharonia and Burgherside would be skeptical of the assertion that their life experiences closely resemble one another. In dismissing this suggestion, they can point to language, national identity, religious beliefs, folk histories, and social settings that separate them from one another. Indeed, cultural differences between Sharonians and Burghersiders are self-evident to native observers and the anthropologist alike. Nonetheless, close examination of the social relationships of Sharonia and Burgherside residents with other people in their societies suggests important structural similarities: (1) Residents of both communities fill working-class and underclass slots in regional economies. (2) Sharonians and Burghersiders suffer low social status in their respective social systems. (3) In pursuit of personal interests, residents of both communities interact in institutional settings that have been invented and are controlled by others. The life styles of residents in both communities are heavily subsidized by public agencies. I will examine each of these points in succession.

Sharonians and Burghersiders are relative newcomers in their contemporary environments. Both groups migrated from technologically less advanced regions to social settings with relatively advanced economic infrastructures controlled by host populations. The Oriental Jews of Sharonia immigrated to Israel between 1948 and 1953 from rural Kurdistan (Iraq) and Tripolitania (Libya). Arriving in Israel as penniless refugees, they spent months or years in shanty town immigrant camps until they were supplied with permanent housing in Sharonia by the national government. Sharing neither language nor culture in common with Ashkenazi European Jewish hosts, they made a living by working as field hands in regional citrus groves. Over the past 30 years, they and their offspring have learned Hebrew, assimilated much of the life ways of their Ashkenazi countrymen, and moved into working-class positions in the regional economy. Today, all but a few heads of households in Sharonia are employed. They make their living as construction workers, tradesmen, porters, prison guards, truck drivers, and in the services. Although a handful of Sharonians have become clerks in government bureaucracies, there are no professionals in the community. With the exception of half a dozen shopkeepers and small businessmen, Sharonians have not gained ownership of income-generating assets in their environment (Lewis 1979a:15–24).

The blacks of Burgherside came to Stockton over the past 35 years from rural areas in the southern United States in search of jobs in defense, service, and agroindustries. Facing discrimination from Anglo hosts, they settled on the edge of town in temporary huts, which over the years have been expanded into permanent housing. Today, lacking the technological skills valued in "mainstream"[6] Stockton society, Burghersiders fill semiskilled and unskilled working-class slots in the regional economy. Many work as farm laborers, adding a migrant character to their lives. Unemployment and underemployment are chronic problems. There are a few independent businessmen who operate stores, gas stations, car repair shops, hotels, and restaurants, but, on balance, Burghersiders have not gained ownership of substantial income-generating assets in their environment. Except for one teacher and a draftsman, there are no other professionals living in Burgherside (see Ogbu 1974:21–37).

Sharonians and Burghersiders are viewed as undesirable people by others in their societies. Evaluations of social status in both social settings are based on two separate, but closely correlated, status hierarchies, one based on judgments of ethnicity or race and the other based on evaluations of socioeconomic standing.

For the purpose of discussion, Israeli Jews can be divided into two ethnic categories of approximately the same number of people, Ashkenazi and Oriental. The Ashkenazim, Jews of European descent, are the dominant ethnic category in Israeli society. Included in their ranks are the Zionist pioneers who created and still dominate the political, economic, and social institutions of the state. The Orientals, Jews of North African and Near Eastern origins, are associated with stigmatized cultural and physical traits. Their traditional way of life is seen by Ashkenazim, as well as by many Oriental Jews, as being primitive. Language and life ways resembling the Arabs, among whom most Oriental Jews once lived, are looked at askance by all segments of the Jewish population. Furthermore, the relatively dark skin pigmentation of Oriental Jews is looked down upon by the lighter-skinned Ashkenazim. Although the Oriental Jews of Sharonia have rapidly assimilated the culture of their Ashkenazi countrymen, their actions are still judged against the stigmatized image of their pre-Israeli way of life (Lewis 1979a:73–78).

In Israel, as in other achievement-oriented societies, the social standing of a person is based in part on judgments of his or her economic and educational status. Sharonians are relatively poor. The average per capita consumption of townspeople is only half that of the national urban average. Few residents have finished academic high school and virtually none have higher educational credentials. Collectively, Sharonians are seen by others in their society as relatively poor, undereducated Oriental Jews (Lewis 1979a:21–22). The combination of these characteristics gives Sharonia the stigmatized status of an *azor mitzuca* (distressed area) inhabited by *te'unay tipuach* (those in need of fostering). Sharonia residents, as a category of people, are at the bottom of the Jewish Israeli social hierarchy.

The residents of Stockton can be divided into four ethnic categories: Anglos, Mexican-Americans, blacks and others.[7] The Anglos, an amalgamation of white ethnic groups, comprise nearly 80 percent of the population. Included in this category are descendants of the founders of the city and the present-day political, economic, and social elite. They view themselves as the upholders of mainstream American culture in town. Mexican-Americans occupy the second position in the local status hierarchy. Although their cultural tradition is seen as being less prodigious than that of Anglo neighbors, many Mexican-Americans have assimilated the mainstream culture (Ogbu 1974:41–42). Blacks, consistent with their subordinate social position throughout the United States, are the lowest ethnic category. Dark skin and a host of cultural traits associated with blacks are stigmatized in the Anglo-dominated social system.

Stockton residents also evaluate one another according to the socioeconomic status of the neighborhood in which one lives. Residents are considered to be either "taxpayers" or "nontaxpayers." Taxpayers include those persons who are perceived as paying property tax. Persons living in the northern section of town enjoy this status. Persons living in the southern district, whether or not they pay property taxes, are likely to be viewed as nontaxpayers. Southern Stockton is associated with blacks, poor Mexican-Americans, and others who are economic failures. Its residents are seen as lacking sufficient education. Many are welfare recipients. Burgherside is a low-status neighborhood in southern Stockton. Its black residents are viewed as nontaxpayers and are at the bottom of the Stockton social hierarchy (Ogbu 1974:38–49).

In pursuit of personal interests, Sharonians and Burghersiders interact in institutional settings that are controlled by others. The routine of daily life in Sharonia brings local citizens into constant contact with powerful national organizations and institutions. The Israeli public sector dominates the national economy to a greater extent than is the case in any other noncommunist country (Halevi and Klinov-Malul 1968:42). In relatively poor communities like Sharonia, the private sector of the economy is especially weak, and public domination of salient resources is all the more marked. Although townspeople elect a Town Council to govern the Local Authority and a Workers' Council to oversee the activities of the local branch of the powerful Histadrut Labor Federation,[8] the powers of these local institutions are relatively weak in the highly centralized Israeli political system (see Aronoff 1977:119–144; Shapiro 1976:12–20).

Control of land, working conditions, and capital in Sharonia rests with public bodies that draw their authority from a national, not a local, constituency. All development projects in town are capitalized by either the national government or the Histadrut Labor Federation. The national government is a primary supplier of educational, health, security, welfare, religious, utility, entertainment, and housing services to Sharonians. Additionally, health, legal, housing, employment, banking, entertainment, and day-care services are supplied by the Histadrut (Lewis 1979a:25–54).

Nearly all heads of household in Sharonia are employed. Nevertheless, Sharonians have relatively large families and most wives do not work. Nearly 60 percent of Sharonia families with children currently learning in elementary school have five or more children. In contrast, approximately 90 percent of Ashkenazi schoolchildren in Israel have at most one sibling (Lewis 1979a:21). To support their contemporary life style, nearly all local families must rely on welfare services or monthly subsidies from the government-sponsored National Insurance Institute.[9] Public assistance accounts for as much as 40 percent of the net incomes of many families in town (Lewis 1979a:36–42).

Civil servants working with Sharonians often find the actions of townspeople irksome. Clientele try to pressure civil servants into solving problems that are beyond their means or inclination to deal with. Government officials and middle-class observers view these attempts by local residents to find solutions to their problems as naive. These behaviors are cited in support of the argument that the Oriental Jews of Sharonia are culturally disadvantaged and incapable of fully managing their own affairs (Lewis 1979a:51–54).

Burghersiders participate directly in three neighborhood organizations that distribute a limited number of community services: the Burgherside Fire District, Community Council, and Neighborhood Service Center. These organizations sponsor fire-fighting services, neighborhood cleanup campaigns, an annual neighborhood fair, and services associated with the nationally sponsored War on Poverty of the 1960s. Nevertheless, the life style of Burghersiders is heavily dependent on resources distributed by a host of national, state, county, and city agencies over which residents have little influence.

Chronic unemployment and underemployment force many residents to rely on direct public assistance in order to survive. Community development and essential social services are controlled by Anglo taxpayers. Consequently, important decisions affecting the well-being of Burghersiders are made in accordance with Anglo social priorities and images of what is desirable for neighborhood residents. Anglo decision makers and civil servants hold negative stereotypes of Burghersiders, viewing them as socially isolated, problematic wards of the public. Social policy in Burgherside reflects this perspective (Ogbu 1974:25–37).

To this juncture, I have argued that Sharonians and Burghersiders live in social settings in which salient economic and social resources are controlled by others. Likewise, in Ashkenazi- and Anglo-dominated social systems, the Oriental Jews of Sharonia and blacks of Burgherside are identified with stigmatized physical and cultural traits. Hence, relative poverty and powerlessness are supported by dominant group belief systems stressing cultural differences between dominant and minority group members. The education of Sharonia and Burgherside youth takes place in the context of these congruent structures of social inequality.

Ashkenazim, Anglos, and Educational Services

Elites establish educational services in attempts to manipulate central aspects of the enculturation process (Lewis 1979b:102; Wallace 1961). In Sharonia and Burgherside, educational programs are sponsored by extralocal agencies controlled by Ashkenazi and Anglo authorities. In both form and content, educational services in these communities reflect the assumptions and interests of dominant group elite, not clientele.

In part, educational programs in Sharonia and Burgherside reflect dominant group conceptions of social justice in society. Social justice is a culturally specific concept. Human sacrifice among the Aztecs or social stratification by caste in classical India did not pose moral dilemmas in those societies. Indeed, persons violating traditional norms would have been morally delinquent in the eyes of their peers. In contemporary Israel and the United States, social justice is evaluated in reference to egalitarian national ideologies. In light of egalitarian dogma, unequal distribution of status and wealth between different ethnic or racial groups is a social fact in need of explanation.

The preferred explanation for social inequality by dominant group members of Israel and Stockton can best be characterized as the culturally disadvantaged argument.[10] It is assumed that social institutions generally live up to the egalitarian creed. Nevertheless, Oriental Jews and blacks, as categories of people, are seen as different in cultural orientation from their Ashkenazi and Anglo compatriots. They remain distinct in ways that violate norms valued in the wider society. Thus, their low socioeconomic status is seen as being indicative of inadequate socialization to the superior life ways of dominant group members. The folk concepts *te-unay tipuach* (in need of fostering) and "nontaxpayers" express this perspective (Ogbu 1974:13–15; Lewis 1979a:75–78).

In light of the culturally disadvantaged argument, the inferior political, economic, and social standing in society of Sharonians and Burghersiders is viewed primarily as a question of negative values and inadequate skills. It is argued that only through resocialization to dominant group values will minority youth be able to overcome culturally deficient heritages and become full-fledged members of the wider society. Hence, the answer of dominant group elites to the moral dilemma posed by the continued existence of poor minority communities in their midst is to offer minority youth opportunities to compete for educational status against dominant group peers. It is reasoned that this will maximize the chances for diligent minority youth to escape the social fate of their parents. From the culturally disadvantaged perspective, educational services become a central aspect of social policy (Ogbu 1974:133; Lewis 1979a:88–89).

Curricula in schools serving Sharonia and Burgherside youth are designed in light of the culturally disadvantaged model of how and what minority youth should learn. In Sharonia, learning is structured on the assumption that local youth are incapable of advancing as quickly as higher-status peers. Indeed, much of the curricula has been designed especially for youth designated by authorities as "those in need of fostering." In contrast to the academic emphasis at higher-status schools, learning materials in Sharonia emphasize social and cultural skills that local youth are assumed to lack. As youth advance in the educational system, curricular pluralism becomes increasingly more pronounced (Adler 1970). In the sixth, seventh, and eighth grades, youth are divided into divergent tracks, one emphasizing academic, the other vocational studies. Secondary educational programs are further divided along these lines. Sharonians invariably enter the vocational tier of the educational system (Lewis 1979a:23).

In Burgherside, curricular pluralism is less pronounced in the formal structure of educational services than is the case in the Israeli educational system. Yet similar assumptions regarding the learning abilities of minority youth have fostered congruent results. The preschool program in Burgherside, commonly referred to as Headstart, illustrates this contention. The program, instituted in Burgherside in 1966, is based on the assumption that minority youth must overcome negative cultural traits before they can learn basic academic skills. Accordingly, the program stresses three curricular goals: strengthening self-image, developing a middle-class world view, and improving self-expression through the development of motor skills (Ogbu 1974:154). To accomplish these goals, teachers rely extensively on dramatic play activities. Traditional basic skills, such as the three R's, are deemphasized.

At first, Burgherside parents eagerly supported the notion that their children would benefit from a preschool program. By 1969, however, they talked of the Headstart program with a good deal of scorn. Burgherside youth have difficulty reading at every level in the school system. Parents argue that basic reading skills should be stressed in Headstart and other learning programs. They complain that minority children are being taught how to play while Anglo youth are learning how to read. Burghersiders feel that their children want to learn to read when first entering formal educational frameworks, but educators, seeing Burghersiders as culturally disadvantaged, emphasize reading readiness as a curricular objective, not reading (Ogbu 1974:151–157).

Parents from Sharonia and Burgherside have little impact on the decision-making process by which tracking, Headstart, and other educational programs are institutionalized in their schools. Their voices are rarely heard in the major educational debates of the day. For example, the desirability of school integration has been a prominent point of discussion in the Israeli and Stockton polities. Although this reform is likely to have a profound impact on where and how minority youth learn, neither Sharonians nor Burghersiders have been asked to participate in discussions on integration schemes (Ogbu 1974:235–241; Lewis 1979a:187).

Consistent with their relative powerlessness in Ashkenazi- and Anglo-dominated societies, Sharonians and Burghersiders are not consulted regarding the assignment of teachers to neighborhood schools. In both cases, educators are socially removed from their clientele. Of the dozens of teachers assigned by the Ministry of Education to Sharonia elementary schools, only three live in town. None of the educators in regional secondary school programs are from town (Lewis 1979a:92). The situation is virtually the same in Burgherside. With one exception, none of the employees of educational institutions serving Burgherside youth are community members (Ogbu 1974:136). Professional training, certification, conditions of employment, definition of duties, rules for behavior, and evaluation of performance of educators are defined within the context of the bureaucracies for which they work. The low-status residents of Sharonia and Burgherside have few if any opportunities to affect decision-making processes in these frameworks. Their relationship to educators is one of client to patron (Ogbu 1974:142–150; Lewis 1979a:156–160). The teachers adopt the interests and attitudes of Ashkenazi and Anglo employers, not community members.

In carrying out their pedagogical duties, educators in Sharonia and Burgherside adopt the culturally disadvantaged argument. Teachers working in Sharonia insist that townspeople are culturally backward. They feel that most parents do not appreciate the value of modern education, do not supervise children's school work, and have no love for learning. Teachers believe that youth see few if any books or other cultural items at home, are intellectually understimulated, and, hence, are indolent at school. Whenever teachers feel pressure from parents, pupils, colleagues, the principal, educational inspectors, or outsiders, they support one another in gossip sessions in which they swap anecdotes on the stupidity of pupils and parents. They tell one another that they are good and dedicated educators, but that pupil performance is impaired by the inability of parents to do their share. It is argued that the home and community are the most important indicators of how children will perform in studies. Children from "good" homes learn well, while children from "bad" homes do not. From the perspective of the educators, most families in Sharonia fit into the second category (Lewis 1979a:103–105).

New teachers in town are quickly socialized to adopt the culturally disadvantaged point of view. The occasional teacher who challenges this stance quickly becomes a pariah to his or her colleagues (Lewis 1979a:105).

The negative stereotypes of clientele held by Burgherside teachers parallel those of educators in Sharonia. Burghersiders are characterized as welfare recipients with personal problems. Youth are seen as coming from father-absent broken homes. Parents are thought to be unsupportive of the educational efforts of their offspring, supplying poor personal examples. They are seen as uneducated and uncouth (Ogbu 1974:142–151, 157–159).

The negative images that educators hold of Sharonians and Burghersiders color every aspect of teacher-pupil and teacher-parent relations. Whereas educators in higher-status neighborhoods expect most students to perform well and advance in the educational system, teachers in Sharonia and Burgherside expect pupils to fail. While teachers in higher-status communities are concerned with the academic achievements of their students, educators in Sharonia and Burgherside are preoccupied with maintaining discipline (Ogbu 1974:160–163; Lewis 1979a:105–106, 112–114).

Sharonians, Burghersiders, and Educational Services

To this juncture, I have argued that the life experiences of Sharonians and Burghersiders are organized in reference to congruent structures of social inequality. Likewise, educational settings in both societies are structured by power relationships and symbolic formations that place minority youth at a disadvantage in competition with higher status peers for educational credentials. Yet Sharonians and Burghersiders interpret parallel social situations differently. This reflects the contrasting belief systems by which Sharonians and Burghersiders evaluate their place in the wider societies of which they are a part.

The impact of collective beliefs on social behavior has long been a central theoretical concern of anthropology (Geertz 1964: Leach 1954; Redfield 1953). This approach suggests that a discernible compendium of beliefs in the public domain structures the meaning that actors impute to behaviors and events in everyday life. Often expressed in myth and folklore, these root paradigms, to borrow a phrase from Turner (1974:67), "affect the form, timing and style of the behavior of those who bear them." In other words, root paradigms are collective cultural recipes for the construction of social meaning.

Zionism, a revolutionary Jewish ideology, is a central component in the self-image of Sharonians and other Jewish Israelis. From a Zionist viewpoint, the Jewish people, scattered about the world, persecuted and culturally contaminated, are obliged to return to their homeland in order to construct a Jewish utopia.[11] Each Zionist movement, religious or secular, projects a different vision of the Jewish Commonwealth and ideal Jewish person (see Fisch 1978:39–116). Common to all these images, however, is the concept of the cultural reconstruction of the Jewish people in accordance with Western cultural principles. This reflects the European origins of the various Zionish movements. Symbolically, high-status models of the new Israeli-Jewish person stand in opposition to negative stereotypes of the non-Western Oriental Jewish person (Smooha 1978:86–92).

From the Zionish point of view, Jews of different cultural backgrounds living in Israel are in the process of becoming alike. All Jewish citizens are promised full and equal share in the rewards of the new society, providing they "overcome" negative aspects of their pre-Israeli cultural heritage. This is particularly the case for Oriental Jews exhibiting stigmatized cultural traits. The government is seen as a full and active partner in this process.

Sharonians agree with Ashkenazi compatriots that upon arrival in Israel they were culturally backward in comparison to immigrants from the West. In this, they accept the basic proposition upon which the dominant group version of the culturally disadvantaged argument is constructed. In pursuit of social advancement, Sharonians attempt to distance themselves symbolically from negative images associated with Oriental Jews as a category of people. Townspeople view themselves as being well advanced in the process of becoming fully Israeli and judge one another by this yardstick. Younger residents look askance at the "primitive" folkways of their grandparents and view themselves as Israelis in all matters. They profess to few if any cultural differences between themselves and Ashkenazi countrymen. When talking of the future, they anticipate the cultural unity of the Jewish people. Neighbors who emulate cultural patterns that violate this expectation are characterized as "primitives." Thus, while each Sharonian, on completion of required cultural transformations, expects to gain an equitable share of the fruits of her or his society, Oriental Jews, as category of people, are constantly denigrated (Lewis 1979a:57–78).

In response to the structure of social inequality, Burghersiders do not find solace in utopian visions held in common with Anglo elite. Anglos and blacks do not share a belief in a process of becoming alike. Although Sharonians and Burghersiders confront similar structures of social inequality, the response of Burghersiders is not tempered by a collective perception that injustice in the present is only an interlude between an unsatisfactory past and a better future. The melting pot ideology of other ethnic minorities in the United States has not been applicable to blacks. Indeed, racial bifurcation is an endemic feature of American society.

In evaluating their role in Anglo-dominated society, Burghersiders view discrimination against blacks as the salient social fact. Rejecting the culturally disadvantaged argument of Anglo elite, Burghersiders have adopted what can be characterized as the institutional discrimination argument. Burghersiders believe that they are relatively poor because they have been deprived by Anglos from gaining good jobs, proper community services, and good educations. Looking back on a long history of systematic exclusion from Anglo institutions, they remain skeptical that the egalitarian national ideal applies to blacks in contemporary Stockton. In contrast to Sharonians, Burghersiders do not trust the intentions of dominant group members and are ambivalent toward public agencies. They do not view themselves as active participants in a process of building a better society, but rather as eternal victims of an unfair social system (Ogbu 1974:14, 231–235).

Different attitudes toward education by Sharonia and Burgherside youth reflect divergent folk images concerning the role of schooling in society. To Sharonians, educational credentials are the most important quality separating successful Israelis from persons who are culturally disadvantaged. Indeed, most parents and youth view education as the major factor separating their life chances from those of Ashkenazi peers. They accept the contention of national elite that educational programs offer the individual a fair chance to compete with higher-status peers for coveted social rewards and are eager to do so. Parents take a strong interest in the educational careers of their offspring. Some even hire private tutors to help children with lessons (Lewis 1979a:153–156).

Youth express a strong interest in learning and most feel that they work hard at school. Pupils are proud of high grades and eager to compete against friends for educational status. Youth who are diligent at school are respected by their friends and often assume leadership roles among peers (Lewis 1979a:65–73). The educational emphasis of Sharonia youth is evident in classroom behavior. Although the formal achievements of Sharonians are poor by Ashkenazi standards, this does not reflect a lack of competitive spirit at school. Indeed, the inability of teachers to direct the competitive spirit of local youth toward educational achievements is a conspicuous feature of classroom culture in Sharonia (Lewis 1979a:91–112).

Those few Sharonians who complete academic high school programs and gain higher educational credentials leave town to live in more prestigious, ethnically mixed neighborhoods. They are seen as proof by others that for the talented, schooling offers a viable means by which one can improve one's social standing in society (Lewis 1979a:184–185).

Burghersiders also believe that a good education is important in contemporary society. Youth covet "clean" white-collar jobs in contrast to the "dirty" jobs of their parents and view educational achievement as important in attaining these aspirations (Ogbu 1974:79). Nevertheless, Burghersiders do not accept the proposition that the major difference between themselves and wealthier Anglos is educational credentials. Although many feel that blacks have more opportunities in Anglo society than in the past, Burghersiders remain unconvinced that they can compete on an equal basis against Anglos for wealth, power, and social prestige. In Burgherside, social advancement is viewed as a group rather than an individual problem (Ogbu 1974:13–15).

This perspective is evident in the social behavior of Burgherside youth in educational settings. Unlike students in Sharonia, Burghersiders are reluctant to compete against one another for academic achievements. To the contrary, youth conceptualize a neighborhood "standard" and judge individual progress at school accordingly. Burgherside youth distinguish three standards of academic achievement in Stockton. The highest standard applies to wealthy Anglos. Burghersiders believe that Anglos are very diligent at school because they know that academic achievements will bring good jobs. The second standard applies to most neighborhood youth. Although neighborhood youth believe that they are as innately intelligent as Anglos, they do not work as hard as Anglos at school. This reflects their uncertainty regarding the utility of educational achievements for blacks in Anglo society. The lowest standard applies to a minority of Burgherside youth who make no pretense of learning at school. These youth are perceived as those who have not "seen the light," those who reject the principle that formal education has any inherent value at all (Ogbu 1974:89–101).

The relatively low standard of Burgherside youth at school is enforced through peer group pressure to maintain the neighborhood average. Friends encourage one another to have a good time, ignore homework, and "cut" classes. Youth who are too diligent at school are looked down upon by their peers. Those who perform above the standard are likely targets for ridicule and exclusion from peer group activities. Being too serious at school can even lead to fights with classmates (Ogbu 1974:127–132). Thus group action discourages the individual from attempting to use the educational system as a means of escaping his or her heritage.

Discussion

To this point, ethnographic data have been presented that delineate the impact of dominant-minority group relations on the educational endeavors of minority youth. In light of the evidence, what are the salient characteristics of minority youth struggles for educational status? To begin with, the social organization of the educational settings attended by minority youth reflects the structure of relations of Sharonians and Burghersiders with other Ashkenazi- and Anglo-dominated institutions. It has been shown that Sharonians and Burghersiders fill working-class and underclass slots in economic systems controlled by Ashkenazi and Anglo elites, suffer low social status in their respective social systems, and pursue personal interests through participation in social settings controlled by others.

The education of Sharonia and Burgherside youth takes place in the context of congruent structures of social inequality. In both societies, minority youth must compete for educational credentials in learning environments sponsored by extralocal agencies controlled by dominant group elites. Minority parents have little impact on important policy decisions in the educational system, nor are they consulted concerning the assignment of teachers in local schools. Educators do not live in the community and are socially removed from pupils and parents. They judge community members through the culturally disadvantaged prism, which denigrates Oriental Jews and blacks as categories of people. Thus, minority youth in both societies must contend for educational credentials in social settings in which power relationships and symbolic formations are heavily weighted against their interests. This limits their chances of competing successfully against higher-status peers for coveted educational status.[12]

In the face of similar educational situations, Sharonians and Burghersiders have adopted divergent strategies of behavior, reflecting antithetical evaluations of dominant-minority group relations. In social competition for scarce resources, Sharonians evaluate the appropriateness of potential strategies of action through Zionist eyeglasses. They accept the proposition of dominant group compatriots that social inequality in Israeli society is primarily a function of cultural differences between Ashkenazi and Oriental Jews. It follows that social advancement for Sharonians requires cultural change. When evaluating their society, townspeople see ample evidence that individual acculturated Oriental Jews can cross the ethnic line through marriage with Ashkenazim, (Peres and Scrift 1978) change of residence to ethnically mixed neighborhoods, and active participation in dominant group political, economic, and social organizations. From dominant and minority group viewpoints, this is the anticipated and preferred outcome for youth of Oriental Jewish heritage. In Sharonia, social advancement is an individual cultural quest, not a collective political struggle.

Indeed, collective action on an ethnic basis is viewed as illegitimate in the Israeli polity (see Deshen 1974). Except in the religious sphere of activity, collective organization along ethnic lines is conceptualized as a violation of basic Zionist doctrine. Collective political action by Oriental Jews is discredited by minority and dominant group members alike. An example of the salience of this perception can be seen in the reaction of Sharonians to the efforts of a group called the Israeli Black Panthers to foster collective political action by Oriental Jews (see E. Cohen 1972; Smooha 1972). The activities of this small group from Jerusalem, while causing a stir in the Ashkenazi-dominated national polity, gained little support in minority communities. Sharonians, with few exceptions, talk of the Black Panthers with great disdain. To the present, townspeople symbolically distance themselves from this movement of persons they define as "good for nothings" (Lewis 1979a:46).

The attitude of Sharonia youth in educational settings can best be understood as an extension of their world view and corresponding strategy for social advancement. Townspeople view educational achievements as an important marker variable of social progress. They pressure government agencies for more and better educational and cultural services in order to enhance the opportunity for local youth to compete with other Israelis for coveted educational status. Relative failure at school indicates to Sharonians that government and townspeople must try harder at achieving desired cultural change.

In evaluating their place in Anglo-dominated society, Burghersiders reject the assertion of dominant group members that they are relatively poor and powerless because they are culturally disadvantaged. Adopting an institutional discrimination perspective, Burghersiders reject the assertion that minority group members can advance in Anglo society through individual efforts at cultural change and social assimilation. They see little evidence that individual blacks can redefine their ethnic-racial status by gaining cultural capital in Anglo-dominated educational institutions. To the contrary, Burghersiders often cite examples of individuals who have tried this strategy and failed (Ogbu 1974:99). Persons who attempt an individualistic, assimilationist strategy are derided as "Oreo cookies," black on the outside, white on the inside (Ogbu 1974:245–246). In Burgherside, social advancement is thought to be a collective political struggle, not an individual cultural quest.

In correspondence with this world view, blacks in Burgherside and elsewhere in the United States have turned to collective political and social action. Through collective pressure on Anglo society, they hope to redefine the ethnic-racial status quo. It is thought that this will enhance the ability of minority group members as a category of persons to compete on an equal basis for coveted goods and services with dominant group members. The symbolic redefinition of Negros as black Americans and enthusiasm for black study programs are examples of symbolic actions toward this end. Collective pressure for affirmative action in the occupational sphere and ethnic-racial quotas in higher educational institutions also reflect this underlying strategy. Such actions have not been contemplated by Sharonians.

The ambivalent attitude of Burgherside youth toward formal education must be understood in this context. They recognize that technical skills gained in educational settings translate into high-status positions for Anglos, but are unconvinced that this strategy can work for individual blacks. Futhermore, they reject Anglo cultural baggage, which is an integral, if often implicit, part of school curricula. Although Burghersiders value educational credentials, youth are reluctant to make strenuous individual efforts toward this end. In dealing with a hostile environment, the option of collective resistance is more appealing than individual competition for highly desirable, but hard to achieve, goals.

What impact do divergent social perceptions and corresponding strategies for advancement in Sharonia and Burgherside have on the educational achievements of minority youth. Based on analysis herein, speculative inferences can be suggested. In synchronic perspective, the individualistic competitive strategy of Sharonians would appear to enhance the likelihood that intelligent and lucky individuals will gain highly coveted educational credentials. In contrast, the collective struggles of Burghersiders and corresponding resistance of local youth in educational settings minimize the chances of intelligent adolescents to advance in the educational system. In diachronic perspective, however, the relative impact on educational achievements of each strategy looks somewhat different. Although a few Sharonia youth will overcome a stigmatized heritage through successful participation in educational programs, most will be reconfirmed by their efforts as culturally disadvantaged Oriental Jews. This outcome is a function of the underlying structure of social inequality in educational settings, a combination of power relationships and symbolic formations that the Oriental Jewish strategy does not challenge. In contrast, the black strategy of collective confrontation with the structure of social inequality opens the possibility of basic revisions in dominant-minority group relations. Indeed, collective struggle by blacks over the past several decades has already resulted in important strides in this direction. As blacks advance as a group, the educational achievements of minority youth might be expected to improve. (Ogbu 1974:257–259).

The analysis herein uncovers social processes that place the explanatory power of the culture of poverty model of U.S. and Israeli educators in question. The culture of poverty formulation suggests that congruent social situations in Sharonia and Burgherside will produce parallel attitudes and styles of behavior in educational settings by minority youth. This expectation is based on the assumption that residents in low-status minority communities exhibit pathological cultural traits born of overcrowding, relative poverty, and apparent instability in family and community life. Youth growing up in this type of environment are expected to suffer debilitating attitudinal and learning problems that inhibit them from participating successfully in educational programs.

The culture of poverty model cannot account for the divergent strategies of behavior of Sharonia and Burgherside youth in educational settings.

Indeed, it does not sufficiently explain the social facts in either case. Alternatively, the evidence in this paper suggests that the attitude of minority youth in educational situations is closely associated with the world view and corresponding strategy for advancement of minority communities. When social advancement is perceived as an individual cultural quest, educational credentials become the salient marker variable of social progress. In contrast, the role of educational credentials is somewhat ambiguous for persons viewing themselves as involved in collective struggle against institutional discrimination. Although desirable, educational credentials are seen as a secondary factor in the process of social advancement. They are transcended in importance by communal judgments of the current state of the ethnic-racial status quo.

As long as Sharonians believe that they can gain higher status in society through individual educational efforts, the educational emphasis of Sharonia youth will continue. Likewise, as long as Burghersiders believe that minority youth cannot compete fairly in Anglo society for social status, Burgherside youth will continue to pressure peers not to violate the Burgherside "standard" in educational settings.

Endnotes

1. I would like to thank colleagues at Tel Aviv University, Emanuel Marx, Moshe Shokeid, and Hiam Hazan, as well as anonymous reviewers of *Anthropology and Education Quarterly* for making valuable comments on earlier drafts of this paper.
2. A host of academics in the United States have been sharply critical of the culture of poverty model on theoretical as well as methodological grounds. They argue that the culture of poverty formulation is ethnocentric, misuses the concept of culture, and draws on a biased data base. See, for example, Ginsburgh (1972), Harris (1979:300–304), Leacock (1971), and Valentine 1968. The polemics associated with this issue are amply apparent in a debate in *Current Anthropology* (Valentine et al. 1969:181–201) on Valentine's work.
3. Notable exceptions include Foner (1973), Hostetler and Huntington (1971), Hunt and Hunt (1970), Rosenfeld (1971), Wax et al. (1969), and Wolcott (1967).
4. In his recent book, *Minority Education and Caste*, Ogbu (1978) discusses the education of Oriental Jews and five other minority groups in reference to minority education in the United States. Generalizing from his argument on the education of black and Mexican-American youth in Burgherside, Ogbu suggests that Oriental Jews and other minority groups respond to systematic discrimination in job markets by adopting a skeptical attitude toward the value of educational credentials for minority youth (Ogbu 1978:349–354). Although I am in basic agreement with many other central points in Ogbu's argument, this particular contention is contradicted by data from Sharonia. The Israeli data on which Ogbu draws to make his case are not informed by careful ethnographic accounts of Oriental Jewish education. This is hardly Ogbu's fault as my work and Halper's (1978), the only published ethnographic studies of Oriental Jewish education, both appeared in print after the publication of Ogbu's work. My comparison of the education of Oriental Jews in Sharonia with the schooling of minority youth in Burgherside suggests that Ogbu's recently formulated model of minority education may be in need of modification.
5. The present tense is used throughout this paper to refer to data collected by Ogbu on Burgherside in 1968–1969 and information gathered by myself on Sharonia in

1975–1976. Burgherside and Sharonia are both pseudonyms. It is important to note that, in an effort to make the comparison sharper, I have excluded discussion of the Mexican-American population of Burgherside except in instances when comments on this group are central to the general argument. I am solely responsible for any misinterpretation of data from either study.

6. The folk concept "mainstream" is used by Anglos to refer to their image of white middle-class American culture (Obgu 1974:52).

7. The ethnic category "others" includes American Indians and various groups who came to Stockton from the Orient. They account for approximately 5 percent of the local population (Ogbu 1974:45).

8. After the national government, the Histadrut Labor Federation is the most powerful institution in Israeli society. It represents most of the Israeli working force, owns many of Israel's leading industrial concerns, and is a major supplier of banking, health, and other social services.

9. The National Insurance Institute, a government-sponsored agency, makes direct payments to Israeli families for each child in the household. It also disburses an assortment of other subsidies. Unemployment compensation and other welfare services are administrated by a local office of the Ministry of Welfare. On welfare services in Israel, see Greenberg and Nadler (1977).

10. It is important to distinguish between the culture of poverty model alluded to in the introduction and the culturally disadvantaged argument discussed at this juncture in the paper. The former is a scientific model proposed and debated in academic circles. The latter is a folk concept expressed by Ashkenazim and Anglos in everyday life.

11. On the Zionist movement and its ideology, see Ben-Gurion (1963), Buber (1952:109–161), Fisch (1978), Sachar (1976:3–85), and Vital (1975).

12. The debilitating consequences of negative teacher expectations on pupil performance in the classroom are suggested by Rosenthal and Jacobson (1968). For a comprehensive review of subsequent efforts to test and refine the nature of this relationship, see Persell (1977:101–121, 173–178). Berger et al. (1972) have used an experimental methodology to demonstrate the impact of external status judgments on expectation and opportunity structure in micro social situations.

References Cited

Adler, Haim
  1970 The Israeli School System as a Selective Institution. *In* Integration and Development in Israel. S. N. Eisenstadt et al., eds. 287–304. New York: Praeger.
Aronoff, Myron F.
  1977 Power and Ritual in the Israeli Labor Party. Assen/Amsterdam: Van Gorcum and Co.
Ben-Gurion, David
  1963 Vision and Redemption. *In* The Mission of Israel. Jacob Baal-Teshuva, ed. New York: Robert Speller and Son.
Berger, Joseph, Bernard P. Cohen and Morris Zelditch, Jr.
  1972 Status Characteristics and Social Interaction, *American Sociological Review* 37 (June):241–55.
Buber, Martin
  1952 Israel and Palestine. Translated by Stanley Goodman. New York: Horowitz Publishing Co.
Cohen, Abner
  1974 Two-Dimensional Man. London: Routledge & Kegan Paul.

Cohen, Eric
  1972 The Black Panthers and Israeli Society. Jewish Journal of Sociology 14 (June):93–109.
Depres, Leo, ed.
  1975 Ethnicity and Resource Competition in Plural Societies. The Hague-Paris: Mouton.
Deshen, Shlomo A.
  1974 Political Ethnicity and Cultural Ethnicity in Israel during the 1960's. In Urban Ethnicity. Abner Cohen, ed. Pp. 281–309. London: Tavistock.
Fisch, Harold
  1978 The Zionist Revolution. London: Weidenfeld and Nicolson.
Foner, Nancy
  1973 Status and Power in Rural Jamaica. New York: Teachers College Press.
Geertz, Clifford
  1964 Ideology as a Cultural System, In Ideology and Discontent. David Apter, ed. New York: Free Press, 47–56.
Ginsburgh, Herbert
  1972 The Myth of the Deprived Child. Englewood Cliffs, N.J.: Prentice-Hall.
Greenberg, Harold I., and Samuel Nadler
  1977 Poverty in Israel: Economic Realities and the Promise of Social Justice. New York: Praeger.
Halevi, Nadav, and Ruth Klinov-Malul
  1968 The Economic Development of Israel. New York: Frederick A. Praeger and the Bank of Israel.
Halper, Jeffry
  1978 Ethnicity and Education: The Schooling of Afro-Asian Jewish Children in a Jerusalem Locality Ann Arbor: University Microfilms.
Hannerz, Ulf
  1974 Ethnicity and Opportunity in Urban America. In Urban Ethnicity. Abner Cohen, ed. London: Tavistock.
Harris, Marvin
  1979 Cultural Materialism: The Struggle for a Science of Culture. New York: Random House.
Hechter, Michael
  1975 Internal Colonialism. Berkeley: University of California Press.
Henry, Frances
  1976 Ethnicity in the Americas. The Hague-Paris: Mouton.
Hostetler, John A., and Gertrude Enders Huntington
  1971 Children in Amish Society: Socialization and Community Education. New York: Hold, Rinehart and Winston.
Hunt, Robert, and Eva Hunt
  1970 Education as an Interface Institution in Rural Mexico and the American Inner City. In From Child to Adult. John Middleton, ed. Garden City, N.Y., Doubleday, 314–325.
Leach, E. R.
  1954 Political Systems in Highland Burma. Boston: Beacon Press.
Leacock, Eleanor Burke
  1971 The Culture of Poverty: A Critique. New York: Simon & Schuster.
Levi-Strauss, Claude
  1963 Totemism. Boston: Beacon Press.
Lewis, Arnold
  1979a Power, Poverty and Education: An Ethnography of Schooling in an Israeli Town. Ramat Gan, Israel: Turtledove Pub.

1979b Education Policy and Social Inequality in Israel. Jerusalem Quarterly 12 (summer):101–111.

Lewis, Oscar
1961 The Children of Sanchez: Autobiography of a Mexican Family. New York: Random House.
1966a La Vida: A Puerto Rican Family in the Culture of Poverty. New York: Random House.
1966b The Culture of Poverty. Scientific American 215 (4):19–25.

Moynihan, Daniel P.
1965 The Negro Family: The Case for National Action. Washington, D.C.: U.S. Department of Labor, Government Printing Office.

Murphy, Robert F.
1971 The Dialectics of Social Life: Alarms and Excursions in Anthropological Theory. New York: Basic Books.

Ogbu, John U.
1974 The Next Generation: An Ethnography of Education in an Urban Neighborhood. New York: Academic Press.
1978 Minority Education and Caste: The American System in Cross-Cultural Perspective. New York: Academic Press.

Passow, Harry A., et al., eds.
1967 Education of the Disadvantaged. New York: Teachers College Press.

Peres, Yochanan, and Ruth Scrift
1978 Intermarriage and Interethnic Relations: A Comparative Study. Ethnic and Racial Studies. 1(4):428–451.

Persell, Caroline Hodges
1977 Education and Inequality: A Theoretical and Empirical Synthesis. New York: Free Press.

Redfield, Robert
1953 The Primitive World and Its Transformations. Ithaca, N.Y. Cornell University Press.

Riessman, Frank
1962 The Culturally Deprived Child. New York: Harper & Row.

Rosenfeld, Gerry
1971 Shut Those Thick Lips: A Study of Slum Failure. New York: Holt, Rinehart and Winston.

Rosenthal, Robert, and Lenore Jacobson
1968 Pygmalion in the Classroom. New York: Hold, Rinehart and Winston.

Sachar, Howard M.
1976 A History of Israel. New York: Knopf.

Shapiro, Yonathan
1976 The Formative Years of the Israeli Labor Party. Beverly Hills, Calif.: Sage.

Smilansky, Moshe, and David Nevo
1971 Secondary Boarding Schools for Gifted Students from Culturally Disadvantaged Strata. Tel Aviv: Department of Educational Sciences, Tel Aviv University.

Smilansky, Moshe, and Sarah Smilansky
1967 Intellectual Advancement of Culturally Disadvantaged Children: An Israeli Approach for Research and Action. International Review of Education 13:410–429.

Smooha, Sammy
1972 Israel and Its Third World Jews: Black Panthers—the Ethnic Dilemma. Society 9(7):31–36.
1978 Israel: Pluralism and Conflict, Berkeley: University of California Press.

Turner, Victor W.
1974 Religious Paradigms and Political Action: Thomas Becket at the Council of

Northampton. *In* Dreams, Fields and Metaphors: Symbolic Action in Human Society. Victor W. Turner ed. Pp. 60–97. Ithaca: Cornell Univeristy Press.
Valentine, Charles
  1968 Culture and Poverty: Critique and Counter-Proposals. Chicago: University of Chicago Press.
Valentine, Charles, et al.
  1969 Culture and Poverty: Critique and Counter-Proposals. Current Anthropology 10:181–203.
Vital, David
  1975 The Origins of Zionism. Oxford: Oxford University Press.
Wagley, Charles, and Marvin Harris
  1958 Minorities in the New World. New York: Columbia University Press.
Wallace, Anthony
  1961 Schools in Revolutionary and Conservative Societies. *In* Anthropology and Education. F. Gruber, ed. Philadelphia: University of Pennsylvania Press.
Wax, Murray L., et al.
  1969 Indian Education in Eastern Oklahoma: A Report of Fieldwork among the Cherokee. Kansas: University of Kansas.
Weber, Max
  1947 The Theory of Social and Economic Organization. Translated by A. M. Henderson and Talcott Parsons. New York: Free Press.
Wolcott, Harry F.
  1967 A. Kwakitutl Village and School. New York: Holt, Rinehart and Winston.

17.

Ethnic Inequality in Israeli Schools and Sports: An Expectation-States Approach

Ephraim Yuchtman-Yaar and Moshe Semyonov

Ethnic inequality in educational achievement between students of European-American ("Ashkenazi") and Asian-African ("Oriental") origin in Israel has been generally attributed to the lower SES and cultural disadvantage of Oriental Jews. More recent research indicates that Israeli teachers tend to generalize the characteristics of ethnic origin so that Orientals are considered less capable intellectually and motivationally to such an extent that their handicaps are irreversible. Using the framework of expectation-states theory, this study proposes that these prevailing tendencies are an inevitable consequence of the functioning of ethnicity as a diffuse status. This interpretation suggests that ethnic prejudice in Israel is a relatively general phenomenon, not limited to the schooling process. The proposition is examined in the context of achievement in professional soccer, where intellectual prerequisites are less demanding. The findings support the proposition, showing similar patterns of ethnic inequality in terms of both actual achievement and the operation of status generalization. The Israeli case suggests that an egalitarian ideology and policies of ethnic integration cannot effectively prevent emerging inequalities so long as ethnicity functions as a diffuse status.

Ethnic differentiation in the Jewish population of Israel is a major factor in the stratification structure of that society and its underlying processes. The two main ethnic groups, commonly recognized on the basis of geocultural origin, are the Asian-Africans ("Orientals") and the European-Americans ("Ashkenazim").

The two groups are of about equal size but unequal in terms of location across the various dimensions of the social hierarchy. More specifically, Oriental Jews are doing significantly worse by almost every criterion of social, economic, and political standing, such as educational achievement

[1] An earlier draft of this article was presented at the annual meeting of the American Sociological Association, San Francisco, 1978. This research was supported in part by a grant from the Israeli Ministry of Education and Culture. We are indebted to A. Collver, W. Gamson, R. Hodge, A. Kordova, S. Messner, P. Ritterband, A. Tyree, E. Weinstein, and the anonymous referees for helpful comments.

and occupational status, income level and standard of living, and representation in the various spheres of institutional elites (see Matras 1965; Eisenstadt 1967; Lissak 1969; Yuchtman-Yaar and Fishelson 1970; Weller 1974; Hartman and Eilon 1975; Peres 1976; Smooha 1978).

The ethnic gap in socioeconomic levels and political power has been associated with manifestations of social separation and a negative attitude toward the cultural backwardness of the tradition-oriented Oriental community. Perhaps more than the extent of such ethnic disparities, their consistent and persistent pattern has facilitated the crystallization of a clear-cut hierarchical ethnic differentiation, in which the Orientals occupy the lower position (Peres 1976; Smooha 1978).

The penetration of the ethnic cleavage to the various institutional spheres of society has been particularly pronounced in the educational system. Oriental youth have been lagging behind their Ashkenazi peers, with the gap growing at the successive levels of education achievement (Prime Minister Commission 1974; Weller 1974; Peres 1976; Minkovich, Davis, and Bashi 1977). For example, although Orientals constitute fully 55% of the relevant age group, they contribute no more than 20% to the graduates of academic high schools. Correspondingly, in the mid-1970s only about 15% of undergraduates and 10% of graduate students in Israeli universities were of Oriental descent.

Extensive research devoted to the understanding of such substantial gaps in educational attainment has arrived at widely accepted conclusions. Oriental students are said to show poorer academic performance and higher dropout rates because they lag in the development of cognitive skills and motivational structure necessary for effective learning. These deficiencies are attributed mainly to the socioeconomic background of Oriental families and their traditional cultural heritage. In other words, ethnic inequality in education has been explained in terms of the "disadvantage" argument (Passow, Goldberg, and Tannenbaum 1967; Minkovich 1969; Prime Minister Commission 1974).

Implicit in this explanation is the assumption that Israeli schools are social institutions committed to universalistic standards of performance. Oriental youth are, accordingly, the victims of sociohistorical circumstances over which the educational system has little, if any, responsibility. These students suffer, therefore, from "institutional discrimination" (see Jones 1972; Butler 1976) since they fail to meet the performance criteria set by academic requirements. This form of inequality should be distinguished from social inequities, such as direct discrimination on the basis of ascription.

More recent research, however, suggests that Israeli schools are not as egalitarian in their day-to-day functioning as has been thought and that the potential for ethnic discrimination is salient in them. The most extensive and carefully documented data in support of this contention appear in the survey conducted by Minkovich, Davis, and Bashi (1977). While reaffirming the well-established connection between the lower scholastic achievements of Oriental students and their socioeconomic background, this study uncovers systematic negative stereotypes applied by Israeli teachers to these students. Such attitudes rest on widespread beliefs about intellectual incapacities of Oriental youth, who are mistakenly assumed to possess the disadvantaged syndrome on the sole basis of their descent.

Sharper undercurrents of prejudice are reported in an anthropological study of the school system in a typical Israeli development town (Lewis 1977). The data demonstrate that implicit and explicit assumptions about intellectual and motivational limitations of Orientals are shared not only by teachers but by school principals and other officials of the educational administration as well. Moreover, both studies converge in pointing out the detrimental consequences of this climate for the prospects of Oriental students in the schooling process. Thus, "Teachers in all types of schools are very pessimistic about the chances for the disadvantaged pupil to succeed in high school even if maximum educational improvements were to be introduced" (Minkovich et al. 1977, p. 141). These and related findings suggest that over and above the influence of socioeconomic background, Oriental youth are exposed to an atmosphere of prejudice and to concrete, if unintended, discrimination.

ETHNICITY AS A STATUS CHARACTERISTIC

We are concerned here with two related questions. The first is the problem of understanding the phenomena of ethnic inequality in the educational system as reported by Minkovich, Davis, and Bashi (1977) and by Lewis (1977); the second is the possibility that this social process has penetrated to other spheres of attainment as well. In addressing these questions, we are aware that Israeli society has been generally free of traditions supporting ethnic discrimination. Moreover, a policy of ethnic integration has been consistently emphasized by government and public institutions as a national goal and has enjoyed a broad base of popular support. Indeed, it is partly in the light of this atmosphere that the ethnic gap has been generally treated as a problem of imposed inequality, not social inequity (Bar-Yosef 1970; Inbar 1977; Smooha 1978).

Nevertheless, there seems to exist an a priori theoretical basis for the proposition that the manifestation of prejudice in schools could have been anticipated and, furthermore, that it is not an isolated phenomenon. The theoretical perspective we wish to adopt in this discussion is that of expectation-states theory (Berger, Cohen, and Zelditch 1972; Berger, Conner, and Fisek 1974; Berger et al. 1977). Briefly, the theory attempts to account for emerging inequalities in situations of social interaction as status-organizing processes. Its main proposition is that patterns of inequality within social groups—particularly task-oriented ones—develop typically according to initial differences in external status, which affect internal status through the operation of performance expectations. These expectations are established on the basis of cognitions and evaluations associated with the external status characteristics of individual members.

Probably the most intriguing argument of the theory is that performance expectations are always higher for group members whose external status is higher, unless there exists evidence to the contrary. This argument, referred to as the "burden of proof assumption," implies that any *diffuse* status characteristic (such as age, sex, or race) will eventually result in social inequalities at the microlevel of social interaction, regardless of relevance to specific tasks. The higher-status persons are initially expected to be competent at task performance, enjoying the opportunities that such expectations provide in ongoing interactions. In contrast, the lower-status persons have the burden of proving first that they are as capable.

We believe that the dynamics of ethnic inequality in Israel can be more fully understood in the light of these principles. The prolonged and appreciable socioeconomic gap between Ashkenazim and Orientals, coupled with social separation and with the downgraded "Oriental" culture, have facilitated their hierarchical differentiation into full-fledged status groups. In other words, ethnicity has become a diffuse status characteristic in that (1) its states are differentially evaluated (e.g., it is generally considered preferable to be Ashkenazi) and (2) Ashkenazim are assumed to be generally better at intellectually demanding tasks (adapted from Webster and Driskell 1978, p. 224). Thus, while the normative climate of society may not legitimate ethnic prejudice, the reality of a well-established cleavage between Orientals and Ashkenazim has inevitably led to such a consequence.

The data reported by Minkovich, Davis, and Bashi (1977) and by Lewis (1977) are highly consistent with this interpretation. Indeed, if we are correct in understanding these findings in terms of expectation-states theory, the perpetuation of ethnic inequality in Israeli schools is highly probable.[2] Yet it might be argued that the example of the educational system is unique. In particular, the stereotyped characteristics of the Orientals seem quite relevant to the task of academic performance. Hence the conditions of the schooling process are especially conducive to the development of ethnic prejudice. An interesting question, therefore, is whether a similar process occurs in other spheres of attainment, where intellectual abilities and aca-

[2] Webster and Driskell (1978, pp. 233–34) offer some ways of overcoming the effects of a diffuse status characteristic. A large-scale application of such techniques is yet to be attempted.

demic performance are less relevant for success. The empirical investigation reported below represents an exploration of this question.

RESEARCH AREA AND DESIGN

One of the responses of ethnic minorities to encountering inequality is the attempt to pursue careers through alternative channels of social mobility. A salient example of such an alternative is the domain of professional sports (Blalock 1967; Edwards 1973). Sport has been singled out as a prototype career track for the disadvantaged on several grounds: its tasks are not scholastically demanding and no certificates of academic performance are required to get into it (at least in Israel); also, the demonstration of excellence in sports is publicly visible, thus limiting the opportunities for discrimination. These considerations turned our attention to professional sports as an interesting area for research. In particular, since the conditions for status differentiation on the basis of ethnicity seem less favorable here than those prevailing in schools, they provide a context for the exploration of both the diffusion of ethnic inequality in Israel and the scope of applicability of expectation-states theory.

In the realm of Israeli sports, soccer represents the most established and popular enterprise, offering far greater career opportunities than any other sport. Our empirical investigation has, therefore, focused on the role of ethnicity in the attainment process of Israeli soccer players. A brief description of the main organizational features of this sport and the career patterns associated with it seems in order.

Soccer in Israel is organized through clubs scattered in various cities and communities all over the country. Each club is based in some locality and draws most of its members and attendance from its community of residence. Individual clubs are organized within a clear-cut hierarchy of discrete leagues. Each club consists of a senior ("professional") team and at least one junior team. Players in the senior teams are drafted from the junior pool, whose members' ages are under 18. Every year only a few select juniors are promoted to the senior rank, thus becoming professional soccer players.

The organizational structure of Israeli soccer provides the rationale for the assessment of achievement levels in it. First, players either succeed or fail in making the senior level. This phase implies a dichotomous distinction between those admitted and rejected. The population target for this criterion of success comprises the junior players only. Next, at least three levels of achievement exist for the senior players, depending on the ranking of their teams: Second League (low rank), First League (medium rank), and National Team (high rank). These two separate criteria of success serve as the dependent variables in our investigation.

SAMPLING AND DATA COLLECTION

In the spring of 1975, 25 soccer clubs of the two higher Israeli leagues were surveyed. They included all 16 of the First League's teams and 9 of the 32 teams in the Second League.[3] Two-thirds of the athletes were randomly selected from each club, yielding 587 junior soccer players (under the age of 18) and 385 senior soccer players. Junior players outnumber senior players because most of the clubs have more than one junior team. All respondents had belonged to their clubs at least one year prior to the survey date.

Self-administered standard questionnaires were filled out by the players under the supervision of project interviewers before or after practice sessions. Nonresponse has thus been practically eliminated. The questionnaires secured information in various areas, including background characteristics of the respondents, personal attitudes toward soccer, perceived social influences, and career planning. Some of these variables were included in the following analysis and will be presented according to their relevance.

RESULTS

Differentials of Success in Becoming Professional Players

We begin our analysis by examining the ethnic composition of the cohorts of the junior and senior teams. A comparison is meaningful because there have not been significant demographic changes in Israel during the past decade. In fact, the ethnic composition of the two age cohorts (15–19 and 20–29) in the total Jewish population does not differ significantly. Furthermore, the ethnic composition of the senior players in the present sample is similar to the 1967 distribution reported by Yaziv and Nahon (1969).

Our data show that Oriental youth are overrepresented in the junior teams. Fully 69% of the junior players belong to this ethnic group, which constitutes about 57% of the total Jewish population in the corresponding age group. The overrepresentation in junior soccer is more salient in that only 46.1% of Israeli high school students are Orientals. These figures are consistent with the expectation that Oriental youngsters turn in disproportionate numbers to professional sports as an alternative mobility track.

Turning to the senior level, however, a different trend is revealed. Only about 59% of professional players are of Oriental origin. This figure indicates that although the lower ethnic group is slightly overrepresented in professional soccer, the overrepresentation is significantly lower than ex-

[3] Teams from the Second League were selected according to a stratified sampling procedure in terms of geographical location. Three teams were randomly drawn from each of the three main regions—North, Center, and South. Since the teams of this league are underrepresented, the sample was weighted accordingly.

pected. The decrease of about 10% in the proportion of Orientals might be a misleading figure, however, since it does not take into account potential differences in motivation. More specifically, participation in junior soccer may stem from a variety of motives other than career orientation. As part of a "youth culture," involvement in junior soccer provides opportunities for fun, affiliation, social status, and sheer enjoyment of physical activities. An appropriate assessment of changes in ethnic composition from the junior to the senior levels cannot ignore the possibility that such motives are more characteristic of one ethnic group than the other.

To examine this issue, Ashkenazi and Oriental juniors were compared with respect to their aspirations of becoming professional soccer players. A significantly higher proportion of Orientals (68%) than Ashkenazim (54%) express a strong or very strong desire for such a career. These figures make it possible to "correct" for the reported discrepancy in ethnic composition between the junior and senior levels. Thus, weighting the ethnic ratios of junior players by the percentage of positive aspirations yields expected values of 73.6% and 26.4% for the Orientals and Ashkenazim, respectively. Following this adjustment, an opposed pattern of relationships between the observed and expected proportions of the two groups is obtained: 73.6% expected, versus 59.2% observed, for Orientals, and 26.4% expected, versus 42.3% observed, for Ashkenazim. These gaps point to a considerable disadvantage for Oriental youngsters who wish to choose soccer as an occupation.

As noted above, the literature on inequality in the school system has shown a substantial overlap between ethnicity and SES as a major cause for the disadvantage of Orientals. And although we did not anticipate that family SES would have similar effects on success in soccer, the possibility cannot be entirely dismissed.

In order to study this problem, we applied Goodman's (1972) model, which enables us to estimate both main and interaction effects in multidimensional contingency tables. This method is appropriate here since the dependent variable (S)—proportion of players in either the junior or senior teams—is dichotomous. The socioeconomic indicators and ethnicity were coded as follows: ethnicity (M), Orientals versus Ashkenazim. Father's education (E) was classified in two categories, according to years of schooling: 0–8 years (elementary school or less), and 9 years or more. Father's occupation (O), the second indicator of socioeconomic status, was dichotomized on the basis of Hartman's (1975) scale for occupational prestige in Israel into prestige groups 1–3 (mainly manual and blue-collar occupations) and prestige groups 4–9 (nonmanual occupations, the professions and the like).

The results of the best-fitted model obtained for our data are reported in terms of the odds ratios for each combination of the dependent variable and the background variables (see table 1). In reading the table, it should be noted that values close to 1 mean that the expected odds of cell frequencies are essentially equal. Parameters with values higher than 1 have positive effects, and those smaller than 1, negative effects.

The net effect of ethnicity, as shown in table 1, is significant and stronger than either measure of socioeconomic background or any interaction between them. The odds of success in becoming a professional player are relatively higher for the privileged ethnic group ($\gamma = 1.3$). This means that Ashkenazim are 1.3 times more likely to become professionals than Orientals, net of the effects of the socioeconomic variables studied in the model. Since the differences in occupational aspirations are not incorporated in this analysis, this figure is a conservative estimate of the Ashkenazim's advantage with respect to this criterion.

Differentials in Achievement Levels within Professional Soccer

The results reported so far deal with the first phase of a career in soccer, the transition from junior to senior teams. The next analysis is devoted to the second stage of achievement in soccer and thus will focus on the ethnic composition within the senior ranks. Table 2 presents the distribution of professional players by ethnicity and by the three levels of achievement, as defined above.

It is clear that the proportion of Orientals decreases with higher levels of attainment. Thus they are overrepresented in the lowest rank of professional soccer, while Ashkenazim are prominent at the top.

As in the preceding analysis, the gross effects of the ethnic factor should be inspected for possible overlapping with socioeconomic background. In

TABLE 1

EFFECTS OF BACKGROUND VARIABLES (Odds Ratios of Goodman's Model) IN DISTINGUISHING BETWEEN SENIOR AND JUNIOR SOCCER PLAYERS

Parameter	Estimated Effect
γ MS	1.306
γ ES	.983*
γ OS	.882
γ OES	1.168
γ DMS	1.173
γ EMS	1.000*
χ^2	.033

NOTE.—M = ethnic background, E = father's education, O = father's occupation, and S = junior versus senior dichotomy.

* N.S., excluded from the fitted model.

this analysis, however, the dependent variable is not dichotomous and was treated as a continuous, ordinal scale to enable multiple regression analysis.[4] The two measures of socioeconomic status were treated, similarly, as continuous variables: father's education was indicated by years of schooling; his occupational level was assessed in terms of Hartman's (1975) prestige scale for occupations in Israel.

In addition to socioeconomic background, however, it should be noted that Oriental families are more frequently located in relatively new and small settlements known as "development towns" (Spilerman and Habib 1976; Kraus and Weintraub 1977; Yuchtman-Yaar and Heller 1977). These are typically poorer peripheral communities, and a disproportionate number of Second League teams are associated with them. Since the distinction between the two leagues is an integral part of the scale of success, it was necessary to separate the potential effect of the community context in order to estimate more adequately the influence of ethnicity at the individual level. Two measures were selected to represent the type of community—population size and years of existence. The correlation matrix among the variables included in the analysis is given in table 3.

It is clear from this table that senior players of Oriental origin are more

TABLE 2

THE PERCENTAGE OF SENIOR PLAYERS AT THREE LEVELS OF ACHIEVEMENT IN
ISRAELI PROFESSIONAL SOCCER, BY ETHNIC BACKGROUND

| | LEVELS OF ACHIEVEMENT | | | |
ETHNICITY	Second League	First League	National Team*	N†
Asian-African	71.5	19.1	9.4	372
European-American	31.8	31.0	37.2	258

* Included in this category are players who were selected, at least once, as candidates for the National Team.
† N adjusted by weighting (see n. 3).

TABLE 3

CORRELATION MATRIX AMONG VARIABLES RELATED TO ACHIEVEMENT
IN SPORT (Senior Players Only) ($N = 508$)

Variables	E	O	C	V	A
Ethnic background (M)	.327	.415	.258	.236	.426
Father's education (E)		.445	.029	.196	.150
Father's occupation (O)			.058	.098	.277
Size of community (C)				.537	.553
Age of community (V)					.488
Achievement level (A)					

[4] For a rationale of using an ordinal scale as a continuous variable see, e.g., Labovitz (1970).

likely to have humble socioeconomic origins and to reside in smaller and more recently established towns. The figures also reveal that success in soccer is positively related to parental SES, community characteristics, and ethnicity. To examine the net effects of these variables, multiple regression analysis was performed, with the results reported in table 4.

The coefficients yielded by the regression analysis show that ethnicity retains its significant effect on level of achievement, even when we control for the other variables. Community characteristics also have a strong influence, but one should keep in mind that they, too, are related to ethnic composition and can, in part at least, be taken as an indirect measure of the contextual effect of this factor. More specifically, the chances of Orientals to reach the upper leagues are reduced because of the types of communities in which they tend to reside. Thus, in the assessment of ethnic inequality in Israeli soccer, both the direct effect of this factor and its indirect effect via the community must be recognized. These processes of ethnic inequality are very similar to those operating in Israeli schools (Minkovich et al. 1977).

SOME ADDITIONAL EVIDENCE AND INTERPRETATION

The major finding of the preceding analysis is that ethnicity is an important factor in the career prospects of Israeli soccer players. At the earlier stage of this process, Oriental youth are apparently more attracted to the potential opportunities offered by soccer, as reflected in their overrepresentation in junior teams and greater inclination to pursue a career in it. Beyond this stage, however, they are not as successful as the Ashkenazim in becoming professional players and, particularly, in reaching the top levels of soccer.

This trend can be explained in two different, though not mutually exclusive, ways. One interpretation is that ethnicity and ability in soccer are interrelated so that Orientals are not as qualified as Ashkenazim to excel at the professional level. As noticed earlier, the choice of soccer as research area was dictated largely by the consideration of prerequisites and aptitudes

TABLE 4

MULTIPLE REGRESSION ANALYSIS OF
ACHIEVEMENT FOR SENIOR PLAYERS

Independent Variables	Beta	F-ratio
Ethnicity	.238	36.0
Father's education	.072	3.6
Father's occupation	.154	16.1
Community size	.322	63.4
Community age	.230	33.8
$R^2 = .468$	...	73.6

demanded in it. Admission to professional teams is independent of educational level, and the intellectual abilities expected of players are of lower order than those pertaining to academic performance. Yet the role structure of professional soccer may be more complex than laymen realize. The limited experience we have gained in the course of our inquiry suggests that excellence in soccer involves some abstract abilities as, for example, in the comprehension of alternative game strategies. Also, decision making and good judgment are frequently called for because of unexpected developments during the game. These qualities are especially important in soccer because coaches cannot take "time-outs" (as in basketball) in order to send new instructions.[5] This feature of soccer also necessitates broader game vision and greater responsibility of individual players. More important, individual behaviors must be mutually adjusted and coordinated to achieve promotive interdependence among peers. This process consists of personal and interpersonal skills without which performance is severely impaired.

This partial description of soccer as entailing a relatively complex social role is consistent with information obtained from coaches and related personnel. The data are based on unstructured yet focused interviews aimed at getting better understanding of and insights into the determinants of success in professional soccer. In general, the interviews reveal a high degree of consensus among coaches, especially with respect to the attributes of top performers. Many of those have to do, as expected, with physical prowess and psychomotor skills, such as strength, endurance, speed, timing, and ball handling. At the same time, various cognitive skills were commonly emphasized: for example, an ability to understand an overall design in contrast to a mechanical adherence to specific instructions, or to demonstrate tactical flexibility in terms of adjustment to changing circumstances during the game. Finally, self-discipline is called for in two main respects: to suppress personal ambitions of prominence for the sake of team success and to avoid an unsportsmanlike life-style (e.g., overindulgence in extracurricular activities).

Granted the validity of this assessment, the immediate question is the relationship between role requirements and ethnicity. Is it possible that certain inaptitudes, perhaps those affecting the academic performance of Orientals, are responsible for their relative failure in soccer as well? We have no reliable evidence to support or deny such a connection. It appears, however, that its existence is widely believed in by the coaching staff—a belief on which we base the second possible interpretation of the Ashkenazi dominance of the top levels of Israeli soccer.

This phenomenon is expressed in different ways, indirect as well as direct.

---

[5] The game of soccer consists of two halves, each lasting 45 minutes. Except for an intermission of 10 minutes between the two parts, the flow of the game is continuous.

We noticed, first, that the names of players mentioned to exemplify stardom in soccer were almost invariably Ashkenazi.[6] Moreover, when confronted with the ethnic identity of their illustrations, the coaches were hardly surprised. On the contrary, most of them were aware of the greater success of Ashkenazi players and conceived that trend as "natural." Subsequently, they provided quite uniform explanations—in terms of content and terminology—for the association between ethnicity and ability in soccer. Thus Orientals were characterized stereotypically as less intelligent, too individualistic, and overemotional.

To be sure, individual Orientals were singled out as outstanding players. But status generalizations pertain to collectivities rather than individuals, and in the context of our research problem, the uncovering of their existence is of greater relevance than the question of validity. In particular, we have been impressed by the elements of similarity between coaches' attitudes in soccer and the beliefs prevailing among school teachers. The processes underlying this phenomenon and its consequences are depicted most parsimoniously by expectation-states theory, as outlined above. Notwithstanding genuine differences in performance, ethnicity serves in both situations as a basis for the attribution of distinctive abilities and behavior patterns. These perceptions and evaluations constitute the basis for performance expectations which are evidently conducive to the achievement of one group and detrimental to the other. In short, Orientals are the apparent victims of prejudice in classrooms and soccer teams alike.

The extent to which this factor accounts for the reported ethnic differences in actual attainment is difficult to assess, although its mode of operation can be reasonably understood. Given the dual function of coaches as trainers and decision makers with regard to selection and promotion, differential treatment by them is critical for actual professional development and chances of progress. This is a process well known among students of professional sports. In the United States, for example, there have been several studies pointing to systematic inequality in the allocation of black and white athletes to various positions in the major ball games (note the scarcity of blacks as quarterbacks in football and as pitchers in baseball). And although several explanations have been offered to explain this bias, it is commonly accepted that it frequently involves discrimination based on prejudice that belittles blacks' intellectual ability, leadership capacity, and dependability (see Rosenblat 1967; Eitzen and Tessendorf 1978). Finally, it is worthwhile to note that in both the United States and Israel the coaching and managerial staffs are heavily dominated by the privileged

---

[6] Ashkenazim and Orientals tend to have different names, especially last names. The distinction reflects, generally, the influence of countries of origin and, with few exceptions, is readily identifiable.

ethnic groups of these societies. In the case of Israeli soccer, for example, only one of the 16 coaches in the First League was of Oriental origin at the time of our investigation. This fact alone can be taken as another indicator of ethnic inequality as well as one of its causes.

CONCLUSIONS

The reality of socioeconomic inequality between Orientals and Ashkenazim is essentially a lasting consequence of unique historical conditions which caused the ethnic cleavage in the first place. The a priori lower SES of Oriental families, their traditional cultural heritage, and late immigration converged to create structured inequalities that could not have been substantially changed during the three decades of Israel's existence. This line of reasoning is difficult to deny, but its implications may not have been fully realized by students of the ethnic problem in Israel. The main implication of previous research, especially the disadvantage argument, is that the association between equality and ethnicity is basically spurious, since the latter apparently does not exert independent influence on opportunities. This view overlooks the existence of certain subtle social processes which facilitate the operation of ethnicity as a factor in its own right.

Expectation-states theory captures one major form of such processes. It calls attention to the universality of status generalization, especially in the case of diffuse statuses such as race, sex, or ethnicity, and to the development of performance expectations in accordance with such generalizations. These expectations may affect opportunities, encourage differential treatment at the interpersonal level, and contribute to the emergence of stable inequalities.

We believe that these processes account for at least some of the observed differences in attainment between Orientals and Ashkenazim in education and sport. This does not mean that deliberate discrimination is at work in the sense that, say, a gifted Oriental player will be rejected in favor of a less talented Ashkenazi. It does mean, however, that Oriental origin functions as a liability in terms of the "burden-of-proof" phenomenon. Ultimately, this factor suffices to reduce the chances of success.

From the viewpoint of understanding the role of ethnicity in Israel, our findings and interpretation suggest that ethnic prejudice is more pervasive than has been previously acknowledged. In this respect, the observed inequality in soccer—a career track which does not require academic credentials—is particularly indicative.

Put in a broader theoretical perspective, our study seems to stress the vulnerability of social systems to emergent inequalities even where the normative climate is in opposition to such a trend. This suggests that under conditions of structured inequality, such as a persistent and substantial overlap between ethnicity and SES, the consequences of prejudice and discrimination are difficult to avoid.

REFERENCES

Bar-Yosef, R. 1970. "Absorption versus Modernization." Mimeographed. Jerusalem: Hebrew University.

Berger, J., B. P. Cohen, and M. Zelditch, Jr. 1972. "Status Characteristics and Expectation States." *American Sociological Review* 37:241–55.

Berger, J., T. L. Conner, and M. H. Fisek. 1974. *Expectation States Theory: A Theoretical Research Program*. Cambridge, Mass.: Winthrop.

Berger, J., M. H. Fisek, R. Z. Norman, and M. Zelditch, Jr. 1977. *Status Characteristics and Social Interaction*. New York: Elsevier.

Blalock, H. M. 1967. *Toward a Theory of Minority Group Relations*. New York: Wiley.

Butler, J. S. 1976. "Inequality in the Military: An Examination of Promotion Time for Black and White Enlisted Men." *American Sociological Review* 41:807–18.

Edwards, H. 1973. *Sociology of Sport*. Homewood, Ill.: Dorsey.

Eisenstadt, S. N. 1967. *Israeli Society*. London: Weidenfeld & Nicolson.

Eitzen, S. D., and I. Tessendorf. 1978. "Racial Segregation by Position in Sports." *Review of Sport and Society* 3 (1): 109–28.

Goodman, L. A. 1972. "Modified Multiple Regression Analysis of Dichotomous Variables." *American Sociological Review* 37:28–45.

Hartman, M. 1975. "Rating of Occupations by Sociologists." [In Hebrew.] Paper presented at the annual meeting of the Israeli Sociological Association, Beer-Sheva.

Hartman, M., and H. Eilon. 1975. "Ethnicity and Class in Israel." [In Hebrew.] *Megamot* 21:129–39.

Inbar, M., and C. Adler. 1977. *Ethnic Integration in Israel*. New Brunswick, N.J.: Transaction.

Jones, J. 1972. *Prejudice and Racism*. Reading, Mass.: Addison Wesley.

Kraus, V., and D. Weintraub. 1977. "Social Differentiation and Locality of Residence, Spatial Distribution, Composition, and Stratification in Israel." Paper presented at the International Sociological Association's Stratification and Mobility Seminar, Dublin.

Labovitz, S. 1970. "The Assignment of Numbers to Rank Order Categories." *American Sociological Review* 35:515–29.

Lewis, A. J. 1977. "Sharonia: Education and Social Inequality in an Israeli Town." Ph.D. dissertation, Columbia University.

Lissak, M. 1969. *Social Mobility in Israeli Society*. Jerusalem: Israel Universities Press.

Matras, J. 1965. *Social Change in Israel*. Chicago: Aldine.

Minkovich, A. 1969. *The Disadvantaged Child*. [In Hebrew.] Jerusalem: Hebrew University and the Ministry of Education.

Minkovich, A., D. Davis, and J. Bashi. 1977. *An Evaluation Study of Israeli Elementary Schools*. Jerusalem: Bernard van Leer Foundation and the Israeli Ministry of Education.

Passow, A. H., M. Goldberg, and A. J. Tannenbaum. 1967. *Education of the Disadvantaged*. New York: Holt, Rinehart & Winston.

Peres, Y. 1976. *Ethnic Relations in Israel*. [In Hebrew.] Tel Aviv: Sifriat Hapoalin.

Prime Minister Commission. 1974. "Report of the Prime Minister's Commission on Disadvantaged Children and Youth." [In Hebrew.] 2d ed. Jerusalem: Prime Minister's Office.

Rosenblat, A. 1967. "Negroes in Baseball: The Failure of Success." *Transaction* 4:51–53.

Smooha, S. 1978. *Israel: Pluralism and Conflict*. Berkeley: University of California Press.

Spilerman, S., and J. Habib. 1976. "Development Towns in Israel: The Role of Community in Creating Ethnic Disparities in Labor Force Characteristics." *American Journal of Sociology* 81:781–812.

Webster, M., Jr., and J. E. Driskell, Jr. 1978. "Status Generalization." *American Sociological Review* 43:220–36.

Weller, L. 1974. *Sociology in Israel*. Westport, Conn.: Greenload.

Yaziv, G., and Y. Nahon. 1969. *A Social Study of Israeli Soccer*. [In Hebrew.] Jerusalem: Ministry of Education Sport Authority.

Yuchtman-Yaar, E., and G. Fishelson. 1970. "Inequality in Income Distribution." [In Hebrew.] *Economic Quarterly* 17:75–88.

Yuchtman-Yaar, E., and E. Heller. 1977. "Absorption Capacity of Development Towns and of Other Urban Settlements in Israel." [In Hebrew.] Jerusalem: Ministry of Absorption.

Part V

STUDENTS, TEACHERS, AND SCHOOL CLIMATES

18.

The Role of Models in Professional Socialization

Judith T. Shuval and Israel Adler

Abstract—Students relate to teacher-models in a variety of modes and styles. The process of modeling in professional socialization is multi-dimensional and there is no one dominant pattern that characterizes it. The pattern depends not only on qualities of the models themselves or on the structure of the situation, but on the nature of the different norms and values.

Three basic patterns of modeling appear: Active Identification, Active Rejection, as well as Inactive Orientation. The clear presence of the Rejection and Inactive patterns emphasizes the tendency of students to pick and choose selectively, to consider alternative models, and to view some of the clinical teachers as anti-models.

At the end of formal socialization, students and teaching models differ on a substantial number of the norms and values observed. Among these are certain central norms such as the importance of the People and Science components of the professional role and the Intrinsic Rewards to be gained from the profession. About a third of the norms observed were already adhered to before the starting point of formal socialization which shows considerable anticipatory socialization. Of these, some were actually abandoned over time in a process of rejection.

Classic modeling, in which students come to identify with models over time, occurs with respect to both the most idealistic and the most "cynical" of the norms observed: Idealism and Extrinsic Rewards. Students and models differed initially on these norms but students come to accept models' view.

THE RELATIONSHIP OF STUDENTS AND MODELS

The socializing agents to whom students in medical school are exposed are numerous and varied in terms of their roles, status, prestige, and amount of direct or

The research reported on here was supported by Contract No. 06-704-02 and by Grant No. HS 01857-01 and HS 01857-02 from the National Center for Health Services Research, Health Resources Administration, United States Department of Health, Education and Welfare. It was also supported by a grant from the United States—Israel Binational Science Foundation (BSF), Jerusalem, Israel.

indirect contact with students. If children are exposed to multiple models during socialization, this is *a fortiori* the case during professional socialization [1]. These agents include a variety of figures inside the medical school: teachers, both pre-clinical and clinical, nurses, paramedicals, patients, other students and additional hospital personnel. The professional role is learned in the course of interaction with all of these [2]. Influence on students during socialization may also stem from a wide variety of agents and events outside the medical school context, the effects of which on professional socialization may in some cases be considerable or even critical.

Despite the great variety of socializing agents, most attention has been focused on physician teachers as dominant figures in this process. They have been viewed as the principal models to whom students direct themselves in their attempts to learn the norms and values of the profession. Indeed, during the three years of clinical training, physician teachers serve not only as formal transmitters of skills and knowledge, but as models which are under constant scrutiny by students as they learn to act out the professional role.

From the functionalist point of view, the process of socialization involves induction of new recruits into a common core of relatively homogeneous values, norms and role definitions [3]. From this view point the process is seen as relatively smooth and orderly with students accepted by teachers in the role of junior colleagues who are gradually initiated into the intricacies of professional life. Violations of this orderly process are perceived as deviations from what is structurally defined as the normative process of socialization. Little attention is given to conflicts which are anchored in differing interests of agents and subjects or in the lack of consensus that may characterize the numerous socializing agents to which subjects are exposed.

Considering the many dilemmas and differing view points within the profession, there would seem to be some doubt as to the likelihood that students are presented with a homogenous set of norms [4]. Bucher and Strauss [5] have emphasized the segmentation of the medical profession in terms of differential values, norms, interests, colleagual relationships, and even definitions of what constitutes the core of the professional role. While agreement concerning skills and knowledge may be fairly widespread, there is generally little consensus among teachers in medical school with respect to the psycho-social resources that students need to acquire during socialization [6]. At all stages of socialization the status cues associated with various models play a major role in differentiating the effectiveness of message transmission. It is also clear that while some models may be "stars" from the student's view point, the latter tend to pick and choose traits from various models so that the values internalized are an amalgam picked up from a variety of sources [1]. It is therefore more appropriate to view the socialization process as the exposure of young recruits to a great variety of messages delivered by many agents with little necessary coherence or congruence among them.

Since medical education is a form of adult socialization, the role and effect of socializing agents is structured differently than in earlier socialization [7]. Clausen [8] has noted that socializing agents' effectiveness depends on several inter-related factors: the nature of their affective tie with subjects, their relative power, the extent of their responsibility, the specificity–diffuseness of their role, the relative primacy of teaching among the agents' sets of goals and tasks, the extent of congruence of their goals and those of their subjects, their interpersonal skills and the extent of group of contextual supports for their messages. Observation of the cultural context of medical schools indicates that the adult socialization which takes place in such settings is generally characterized by strong motivation of students to acquire the knowledge and skills of the professional role. While there tends to be less affect in the teacher–student relationship than that characterizing childhood socialization, the relationship cannot be viewed as affectively neutral. Indeed, it has been noted that a certain level of positive affect between learner and model is a *sine qua non* of occupational socialization; otherwise there is learning but no internalization of norms [9]. There may be intermittent hostility between students and teachers but more general acceptance by students of their teachers who exercise considerable power. Role relations tend to be specific rather than diffuse and teachers often have a variety of competing interests and goals in addition to teaching, e.g. research, clinical work, administration. While the manifest goals of agents and subjects are ostensibly parallel, i.e. to perform as competent physicians, the specific definitions of the components of that role often differ. Indeed, in Bloom's research he found that faculty and students had the same goals, but perceived each other as being opposed to these goals [6]. The level of teachers' interpersonal skills in communication is idiosyncratic and largely a function of chance since physician teachers are rarely selected in terms of such skills nor are they trained in them. The criteria for academic appointments in the medical school, as in other parts of the university, are the familiar ones of research and publications.

What is perhaps most important in adult socialization is the students growing tendency to pick and choose among messages by increasingly independent criteria. The elite nature of the medical student body and its self-perception in such terms, heightens the tendency to selectivity among messages in terms of their perceived appropriateness. Thus physician teachers serve not only as models to be emulated, but also as anti-models whose style of practice is sometimes rejected. It is also possible for students to ignore the formally appointed models and elect alternative models of their own choosing. What is more, the adult student is subject to a wide assortment of complementary or contradictory messages from outside the socializing institution. The role of the formally appointed socializers is therefore less exclusive and dominating than in earlier socialization.

DO STUDENTS CONFORM TO MODELS?

The material to be presented is drawn from the Israel Study of Socialization for the Health Professions and is based on a longitudinal study which started with two classes of medical students who began their studies in 1969 and who were under continuous observation with data collected before entry and at the end of each year of study. The research is continuing but the data reported here go through year six, the last year of formal training before internship. A team of anthropologists also gathered qualitative data during the entire period [2, 10–15].

The question to be considered here concerns the role of teachers in transmitting the values and norms of the profession to students during the course of socialization. This involves a process of identification during which a person comes to pattern his thoughts, feelings or actions after another person who serves him as a model [1]. The issue will be examined by observing the extent to which students come to accept their teachers' viewpoint concerning certain normative components, values and goals of the physician's role. While aware that socializing agents are numerous and differentiated, we will focus on physician teachers in view of their central role as models for future professional performance.

Socializing institutions may tend to select recruits "in their own image". This can be accomplished either by admitting students who already conform to certain of the norms and values viewed as central to the profession or by admitting the kinds of students who are thought likely to learn and accept these norms and values over the course of training. The first of these strategies is probably not too fruitful in the long run since there is evidence which shows weak correlations between attitudes measured before socialization and at later stages in the process. The correlations are weakest between attitudes measured before the start of socialization and at the start of clinical practice so that admitting conforming students does not assure output of conforming graduates [14, 15]. However on the whole educational institutions are conservative and are likely to prefer to take their chances with conformers or potential conformers rather than innovators or potential changers.

Since places in medical school are highly coveted, conformity may in some cases represent a mechanism to avoid confrontation or conflict with authority figures during socialization. If "getting through" is the major goal, nonconformity may be counter productive from the student's point of view.

Much of the socialization literature has built on the assumption that students do not know the values and norms of the profession at the time they enter medical school and that they learn these norms and values during the course of the socialization process as a result of exposure to teaching models. It has even been said that interpersonal relationships between subjects and models are not really essential to the learning process; it is sufficient for the student simply to *see* the model—provided the general context in which this occurs does not set up barriers [8].

However, there is some research evidence which questions these assumptions and which demonstrates that dental students already approximated teachers' values and norms at the starting point of professional socialization, thus suggesting a process of fairly accurate anticipatory socialization [16]. Nor do these students show a pattern of moving closer to teachers' values during the course of socialization and with respect to some values they even moved away. Manasse [17] has shown that there is no movement toward or away from teachers during socialization for pharmacy. But that research focused on a general set of value orientations rather than on norms specific to the profession [18, 19]. The former tend to crystallize during earlier stages of development, most notably during adolescence, while profession-specific values may develop later [20, 21]. Caplowitz [22] has also shown that teachers seem to have little effect in directly influencing the non-technical values and beliefs of medical students. A similar pattern has been noted with respect to socialization for a variety of other professions [23, 24]. On the other hand Shuval and Gilbert [12] have shown that students of pharmacy resemble their teachers more at the end of socialization than at its start, in terms of the priorities attributed to professional rewards.

A TYPOLOGY OF MODELING

All of the above research as well as the theoretical considerations noted suggest that the role of models is differentiated and cannot be described in terms of a single process. We may assume that students relate to norms expressed by models in a variety of styles or modes depending not only on the models' status and behavior but also in terms of the specific norm under consideration. It would therefore seem that we would do better to seek a typology of modeling rather than a single pattern.

In order to analyze the dynamics of students' identification with models' values and norms during socialization, three dimensions of the process will be considered:

1. Students' similarity to or difference from models before entry to medical school, at the starting point of socialization (T_0).
2. Extent of change in students' attitudes during socialization (T_0–T_6) and, if such change occurred, its direction with respect to models.
3. Students' similarity to or difference from models at the end point of formal socialization (T_6).

At the starting point of socialization, there are two possible patterns with regard to the similarity of students to models: different or same. Over the course of socialization, students' attitudes may change in a direction which brings them closer to the models (toward), farther from the models (away), or they may show no movement in their attitudes from the starting point to the end of socialization (no change). The outcomes of these change patterns are seen in terms of the extent of similarity between students and models at the end point of socialization. Again, students at this time may show a difference from the models or similarity in their attitudes.

Table 1 outlines a theoretical typology of modeling in terms of the logical combinations derived from these three dimensions. Three general patterns of modeling may be seen: (A) Active Identification, (B) Active Rejection, and (C) Inactive Orientation. Each of these refers to a different basic style in the relationships of students to models. The first is characterized by a mode of approach in which students' attitudes come to resemble the models over time; the second is characterized by withdrawal in which students' attitudes become less similar to models over time; the third is characterized by a pattern of relative passivity compared to the other two as students display no change in their attitudes. In a general sense A and B represent contrasting patterns.

Further differentiation by the first and third dimensions, which indicate the similarity or difference between students and models at the beginning and end of socialization, shows that the above three general modes of orientation to models are insufficient fully to characterize the various patterns that are likely to appear. Thus we see in Table 1 that there are several sub-types in each of the three basic types.

Active Identification (A) includes Classic Modeling (A_1) in which subjects were *different* from the models at the starting point of socialization, moved *toward* them during the course of socialization and ended up *similar* to the models at the end. This is one of the most familiar patterns and one that is thought to be quite frequent. Approximate Classic Modeling (A_2) is not too different from Classic Modeling (A_1) except for the fact that students, whose attitudes changed over time in a direction approaching those of the models, did not reach the latters' attitude and still differ from them at the end of socialization, although they are closer to the models than they were at the starting point of socialization. If this process continues, it is not impossible that further identification will occur at later points in time and that subjects have been caught mid-way in the course of a professional maturation process during which they are moving toward full identification with the models. On the other hand we cannot exclude the possibility that there has been a deliberate arrest in the approach pattern with students feeling that the models' attitude is in some sense too extreme so that they do identify with them but on a more moderate level.

A third form of Active Identification has been termed Over Conformity (A_3). In this pattern students who *differ* from the models at the start of socialization, move *toward* them over time in a general process of identification, but at the final stage of socialization they have already moved *beyond* the models, having adopted a more extreme position than the latter. In this case, students apparently feel that the models are in some sense inadequate: while they are perceived as adhering to attitudes which students view as generally desirable, their stance is viewed as too weak or moderate so that students adopt a more extreme position on the same attitude.

Turning to the pattern of Active Rejection (B), it is important to consider the asymmetrical power balance in medical school which structurally maintains students' dependence on teachers. Thus there are limits to the extent to which manifest active rejection can be expressed unless students are prepared to pay a real price for such independence. At the same time, Active Rejection could well occur with regard to specific areas or aspects of practice.

Two sub-types of Active Rejection may be considered and these are differentiated by the extent of students' similarity to models at the starting point of

Table 1. Typology of students' orientation to models during socialization

	Similarity of students and models at T_0		Movement of students between T_0 and T_6			Similarity of students and models at T_6	
	Different	Same	Toward	Away	None	Different	Same
A. Active identification							
A_1 Classic Modeling	×		×				×
A_2 Approximate Classic Modeling	×		×			×*	
A_3 Over Conformity	×		×			×†	
B. Active Rejection							
B_1 Total Rejection	×			×		×	
B_2 Considered Rejection		×		×		×	
C. Inactive Orientation							
C_1 Reinforcement		×			×		×
C_2 Oblivion	×				×	×	

* Students approach but do not reach models' position on the attitude continuum.
† Students approach and pass models' position on the attitude continuum.

socialization. In the first, Total Rejection (B_1) students *differed* from models at the beginning of socialization, moved farther *away* from them over time and, of necessity, ended up at the final stage of socialization quite *different* from the models. This pattern of complete rejection at all stages of socialization suggests the possibility that students are oriented to alternative extra-institutional models either real, imagined or described in the literature. What is clear is that students at no stage behaved like the models and actually changed during socialization in a manner that created a larger difference than existed initially.

The second form of Active Rejection has been termed Considered Rejection (B_2). In this pattern students were *similar* to the models at the starting point of socialization, but changed over time *away* from their early stance ending up as *different* from the models. This sub-type is characterized by some form of anticipatory socialization in the course of which candidates learned and accepted the norms characterizing their future professional role. They therefore knew the norm before the start of formal socialization but abandoned it during the course of their training. This form of rejection has been termed "considered" because subjects apparently rejected the norm after weighing its appropriateness in the context of their exposure to models and to the realities of clinical medicine.

Two further types fall under the category of Inactive Orientation (C). This title has been chosen because of the lack of change that characterizes students from the start of socialization to its end point. However it does not necessarily imply passivity. Reinforcement (C_1), for example, includes people who had already adopted the norm of the models at the start of socialization (*same*), did *not change* that orientation during the course of socialization, and ended up with the *same* attitude which conforms to that of the models. While it may be suggested that such students ignored the models and simply moved passively through the socialization process, it is equally likely that models served as systematic reinforcers of students' initial attitudes. In the latter case there could be doubt and questioning by students of their initial attitudes so that reinforcement implies active reconsideration of the continued appropriateness of such early attitudes.

In the case of the type labeled Oblivion (C_2), students started socialization as *different* from the models, did *not change* over time, and ended their socialization with the *same* norms they started with—which continue to differ from those of the models. In this case the models appear to have little effect—unless it is to convince students that they do not wish to conform to the models' norms and that their tenaciously held initial attitudes are in some sense preferable to those of the models. It is also possible that students are oriented to alternative models.

Only seven logical combinations of the possible twelve are presented in Table 1. It is illogical for example, to consider the combination in which students were the same as the models at T_0 and moved *toward* the models; or the type which differed from the models at T_0, did not change during socialization and was the *same* as the models at the end of socialization, and so on. We have organized the derived patterns in terms of the second dimension, i.e. the direction of students' movement with respect to the models, because of the centrality of this dimension in socialization theory.

PROCEDURE

We will examine the modeling process during socialization in terms of this typology in an effort to determine the empirical patterns which characterize students' orientation to models with respect to a set of eleven professional norms and values. These do not represent all possible professional norms and values nor can they be viewed as a representative sample, but they are sufficiently varied to enable us to analyze the nature of the modeling processes. They

include the three central components of the professional role, i.e. People, Status and Science, normative
idealism, expected rewards, the importance of social
factors in relations with patients, and uncertainty in
medical practice. The items used to define these
norms and values are presented in the Appendix.

Measurement of these norms and values was
obtained from students at the Hebrew University-
Hadassah Medical School (90 cases) and at the Tel-
Aviv University Medical School (70 cases) several
times during socialization and in all cases at the pre-
socialization stage (T_0) and at the end of formal socialization (T_6). The interim times varied but in all cases
permitted a mapping of change in students' attitudes
on these variable over time.

A sample of 168 clinical teachers (70 in Jerusalem
and 98 in Tel-Aviv) also indicated their attitudes to
these professional norms and values. Since it is questionable whether direct observation of models in site,
acting out their roles, can yield reliable, quantifiable
data which can be compared to systematic data gathered from students, it was decided to obtain estimates
of models' positions on the eleven norms directly
from them. We thus assume that these attitudes are
validly reflected, even if not perfectly, in models' acting out of their roles.

Comparison of the curricula and educational
approach of the two institutions reveals few differences between them. While the Tel-Aviv University
Medical School stated at its founding that it would
place more emphasis on community medicine, in
practice its program shows great similarity to the
science and research oriented Hebrew University-
Hadassah Medical School. Analysis of the selection
procedures at the two institutions also shows that the
two schools do not attract different types of applicants nor do they select different types of students
from the pools. In both institutions the population
undergoing socialization are strongly science oriented,
high scholastic achievers, 70–75% male, come from
similar types of secondary schools, and range in age

Table 2. Patterns of change among students during socialization and attitudes of clinical teachers (mean scores*)

Professional norms and values	T_0	T_1	Students T_2	T_3	T_5	T_6	Clinical teachers
People							
J†	1.8	1.7	—	2.0	2.1	2.0	1.7
TA†	1.7	1.8	—	1.9	2.0	2.1	1.7
Status							
J	3.6	3.2	—	3.1	3.3	3.4	3.3
TA	3.5	3.1	—	3.2	3.3	3.2	3.3
Science							
J	2.1	2.3	—	2.6	2.5	2.7	2.5
TA	2.1	2.4	—	2.6	2.8	3.0	2.5
Idealism							
J	3.1	3.0	—	2.8	2.9	2.8	2.8
TA	3.1	3.0	—	2.9	3.0	2.9	2.8
Intrinsic rewards							
J	1.6	—	—	—	1.8	1.9	1.7
TA	1.6	—	—	—	1.8	2.0	1.7
Extrinsic rewards							
J	2.5	—	—	—	2.8	3.1	3.2
TA	2.5	—	—	—	2.8	3.2	3.3
Family Medicine							
J	1.3	—	1.5	1.7	1.4	1.3	1.2
TA	1.3	—	1.5	1.7	1.4	1.2	1.3
Importance of patient's social background							
J	1.9	—	1.5	1.6	—	1.6	1.6
TA	1.8	—	1.9	1.9	—	1.7	1.6
Importance of permitting patient to talk about illness							
J	2.0	—	2.0	1.8	1.9	2.0	1.8
TA	2.1	—	2.1	2.0	2.0	2.0	1.8
Uncertainty: efficacy of drug							
J	2.5	—	2.7	—	2.6	2.9	2.2
TA	2.5	—	2.5	—	2.8	2.9	2.1
Uncertainty: reliability of clinical laboratory tests							
J	2.3	—	2.4	—	3.1	2.9	2.7
TA	2.3	—	2.3	—	3.0	3.0	2.7

* See Appendix for definitions of variables and direction of scores.
† J = Jerusalem Medical School, N = 90 students and 70 clinical teachers; TA = Tel Aviv Medical School, N = 70 students and 98 clinical teachers.

from 20–22 or 23 at admission. They do not differ significantly in their initial stance on the norms and attitudes considered in the study [15].

The mean scores on the norms and values of students at the various times and of the clinical teachers are presented in Table 2.

For each of these norms or values, the modeling process has been classified in terms of the types presented in Table 1 on the basis of three statistical tests.

1. Significance of the difference between the mean scores of students at T_0 and the mean scores of clinical teachers.

2. Significance of the difference between mean scores of students at T_0 and at T_6.

3. Significance of the difference between the mean scores of students at T_6 and the mean scores of clinical teachers.

The t-test for significance between means was used in all tests. 1 and 3 above were for independent samples while 2 was for matched samples.

FINDINGS

Table 3 classifies each variable into the types presented in Table 1 in terms of the significance of the three tests.

It may be seen that most of the patterns observed are replicated fully in both schools. Despite different teachers and physical settings, the basic processes observed are similar. Such patterning strengthens our confidence in the findings and reinforces our general impression of the similarity of socialization in the two institutions.

There is no evidence for completely contrasting patterns in the two schools: In no case do we find Active Identification in one and Active Rejection in the other (A and B). In the two cases in which different patterns are seen in the two schools. Inactive Orientation (C) is always one of them: Status and Importance of Social Background. We may therefore

Table 3. Observed modeling patterns (from Table 2)

	Type of modeling (by Table 1)	Similarity of students and models at T_0		Movement of students between T_0 and T_6			Similarity of students and models at T_6	
		Different $P < 0.05$	Same $P > 0.05$	Toward $P < 0.05$	Away $P < 0.05$	None $P > 0.05$	Different $P < 0.05$	Same $P > 0.05$
People								
J†	B_2		×		×		×	
TA†	B_2		×		×		×	
Status								
J	A_1	×		×				×
TA	C_1		×			×		×
Science								
J	A_3	×		×			(×)*	×
TA	A_3	×		×			×	
Idealism								
J	A_1	×		×				×
TA	A_1	×		(×)*		×		×
Intrinsic rewards								
J	B_2		×		×		×	
TA	B_2		×		×		×	
Extrinsic rewards								
J	A_1	×		×				×
TA	A_1	×		×				×
Family medicine								
J	C_1		×			×		×

TA	C_1		×			×		×
Importance of patient's social background								
J	A_1	×		×				×
TA	C_1		×			×		×
Importance of permitting patient to talk about illness								
J	C_2	×				×	×	
TA	C_2	×				×	×	
Uncertainty: efficacy of drug								
J	B_1	×			×		×	
TA	B_1	×			×		×	
Uncertainty: reliability of of clinical tests								
J	A_3	×		×			(×)*	×
TA	A_3	×		×			×	
Total		14	8	9	6	7	10	12

* Data suggest this pattern although the significance test does not hold. Classification is by this category.

† J = Jerusalem Medical School, $N = 90$ students and 70 clinical teachers; TA = Tel Aviv Medical School, $N = 70$ students and 98 clinical teachers.

conclude that the same specific pattern of modeling occurs in both schools in 9 out of 11 of the variables observed.

It is of interest to note that the overall distribution of modeling patterns (Table 4) indicates that all three basic patterns appear and all but one of the sub-patterns occur. (Only A_2 does not appear.) The clear presence of Active Rejection (B) emphasizes the freedom of selection and the discrimination exercised by students in the socialization process. The heterogeneity of the patterns points to the many different styles of modeling and to the variety of ways students relate to models or to their messages. Modeling occurs in many styles depending on the content of the message as well as on its mode of delivery.

Active Rejection (B) may be more prominent than is suggested in Table 4. It will be recalled that in Over Conformity (A_3) students, who differed from the models at T_0, moved toward them during socialization and in fact passed them on the attitude continuum, expressing a more extreme version of the models' attitude. Although this pattern has been categorized as a form of Active Identification because students move *toward* the models, it can also be viewed as a form of rejection in which models are viewed as too moderate or wishy-washy. Looked at in the latter light, the number of cases of Active Rejection (B) is augmented by four cases (from A_3) making it 10 while Active Identification is reduced to only 6 cases of Classic Modeling. Our conclusion from these findings is that Classic Modeling is certainly not the only and possibly not the modal pattern to be found and that Active Rejection by students of teachers' messages may be fairly frequent.

It is of interest to note in Table 3 that at the end of formal socialization, only 12 of the 22 observations show students and models to hold the same viewpoint on the norms and values considered. On the remaining 10 there is a significant difference between the two groups. It may therefore be concluded that professional socialization does not necessarily result in subjects accepting socializers' viewpoint in all areas. Among the areas on which there are such differences are certain values and norms that can be viewed as central to the professional role, i.e. the People component, the Science component and Intrinsic rewards of the profession.

Table 3 also indicates that there apparently is considerable anticipatory socialization of students before exposure to medical school. This is seen in the fact that on 8 of the 22 norms and values observed, there was agreement of students and teachers even before socialization commenced. In some of these cases no movement occurred during socialization but in some there was movement away—indicating conscious

Table 4. Summary of modeling patterns*

	Number*	
All A—Active Identification	10	
A_1 Classic Modeling		6
A_2 Approximate Classic Modeling		—
A_3 Over Conformity		4
All B—Active Rejection	6	
B_1 Total Rejection		2
B_2 Considered Rejection		4
All C—Inactive Orientation	6	
C_1 Reinforcement		4
C_2 Oblivion		2
	22	22

* 11 variables in two schools = 22 observations.

rejection of a norm already adhered to and apparently abandoned during the course of socialization.

It is of interest to note the content of the norms and values characterized by these patterns. These are grouped by patterns in Table 5. We will refer only to patterns which are replicated in both schools.

Classic Modeling occurs with respect to both the most idealistic and the most "cynical" of the professional norms: Idealism and Extrinsic Rewards (good income, secure employment and high occupational status). In both of these variables, students differed from the models at the starting point of socialization showing greater idealism and higher expectations of extrinsic rewards. However, they gradually come to accept the models' view until they show no difference from them at the last point in time observed. Expectations of rewards are reduced as is the level of idealism in the course of a Classic Modeling process.

The Over Conformity pattern (A_3) includes two norms which relate to the scientific backbone of medicine: the Science component of the professional role and the norm of Uncertainty with respect to laboratory results. As already noted, the Over Conformity pattern implies a certain rejection of the models' view and it therefore appears that some disillusionment with the centrality of science occurs during socialization. Emphasis on its importance is reduced as is students' confidence in the reliability of clinical laboratory findings. While students, who initially differed from models on this variable, move toward the latter during socialization, they adopt a more extreme view than the models, apparently questioning the importance and reliability of the Science component and stressing the uncertainty norm of medicine even more than the models.

In line with this pattern we find an even more extreme version of Total Rejection (B_1) with regard to the Uncertainty-drug variable. In this pattern students actually move away from the models and naturally end up at T_6 as different from them.

A pattern of Considered Rejection (B_2) characterizes certain of the most dominant professional norms, People, as well as the Intrinsic Rewards of the profession (to help, interest, challenge, responsibility and authority). In this pattern students anticipated models' stance before exposure to socialization and accepted their view of the importance of the People component as well as their view of the Intrinsic Rewards of the profession at T_0. However, during the course of the six year process, they reduced their emphasis on the importance of the People component

[2, 11] as well as their expectations for intrinsic rewards from the profession. Having considered the models' stand on these issues, they rejected it and by the end of formal socialization showed a less favorable attitude to People and more cynicism than the models with regard to expected intrinsic rewards. With respect to these central issues in the professional role, it may therefore be suggested that clinical models served as anti-models in both schools.

Reinforcement (C) of students' original stance occurs in both schools with respect to the importance of Family Medicine in Israel. We have noted that a straight-forward interpretation of this pattern suggests that models provided reinforcement for views which students already held when they entered medical school. It is also possible that views concerning the importance of Family Medicine are held tenaciously or are supported by other intra and extra-institutional elements that impinge on students during socialization. What the data show is that in the Reinforcement pattern the models' role is at most a supportive one but may be more passive.

Only one norm, encouraging patients to talk about their illness and its meaning to them, falls in the Oblivion pattern (C_2). The replication of the pattern in both schools shows that the finding is not entirely sporadic. However, the Oblivion pattern, in which students start socialization as different from the models, "ignore" or possibly reject them during the 6 year period, and end up in the same position they started, is apparently an infrequent one.

Table 5. Classification of norms and values by modeling type

Active Identification
  A_1 Classic Modeling: (Status J)*; Idealism; Extrinsic Rewards; (Social Background J).
  A_3 Over Conformity: Science; Uncertainty-lab.

Active Rejection
  B_1 Total Rejection: Uncertainty-drug.
  B_2 Considered Rejection: People; Intrinsic Rewards.

Inactive Orientation
  C_1 Reinforcement: (Status TA); Family Medicine; (Social Background TA).
  C_2 Oblivion: Importance of Patient's Talking.

* Parentheses indicate lack of replication of the pattern in both schools.

SUMMARY AND CONCLUSION

Students relate to models in a variety of modes and styles. The process of modeling is multi-dimensional and there is no one dominant pattern that characterizes it. The pattern depends not only on qualities of the models themselves or on the structure of the situation, but on the nature of the different norms and values.

The data considered refer to attitudes and do not enter into the rather complicated relationship of such attitudes to behavior. A consideration of that relationship would involve an entirely different field procedure and additional forms of data. The literature abounds with examples of the imperfect relationship between attitudes and behavior and we are certainly not assuming that there will be a direct or simple reflection in behavior of the attitudes expressed. In fact we view the behavioral context as a separate dimension and its relationship to the attitudinal dimension is a subject for further study. We would expect a variety of behaviors to accompany the attitudes—some of them ostensibly consistent and others inconsistent. However given the pressures to conformity in the student role, one might expect less Active Identification in both behavior and attitudes as dependence on teachers decreases.

The findings reported show remarkable similarity in patterns of modeling in the two medical schools. There is almost full replication of patterning and, even when the two schools do not show identical patterns, there is no evidence for contrasting modeling, such as identification in one school and rejection in the other. This lends reliability to the findings and suggests that the content of the norm itself may be the critical factor in structuring modeling during professional socialization.

All three basic patterns of modeling appear; there is no evidence for any one dominant type. Active Identification appears with considerable frequency, but so do Active Rejection and Inactive Orientation. The clear presence of the Rejection and Inactive patterns emphasizes the tendency of students to pick and choose selectively, to consider alternative models, and to view some of the clinical teachers as anti models.

At the end of formal socialization, students and teaching models differ on a substantial number of the norms and values observed. Among these are certain central norms such as the importance of the People and Science components of the professional role and the Intrinsic Rewards to be gained from the profession. While we cannot judge whether their future professional status will bring these young professionals back "into line" with their older colleagues, we can certainly conclude that they differ from them at the end of formal socialization. It is feasible that these differences will serve as the seed-bed of future social change in the medical profession. Certainly at the end point of formal socialization, it cannot be said unequivocally that the teachers are reproducing themselves.

About a third of the norms observed were already adhered to before the starting point of formal socialization which shows considerable anticipatory socialization. Of these, some were actually abandoned over time in a process of rejection.

Classic modeling occurs with respect to both the most idealistic and the most "cynical" of the norms observed: Idealism and Extrinsic Rewards. Students and models differed initially on these norms but students come to accept models' view point during the course of socialization. The lack of dominance of this pattern is of itself a central finding since it questions some of the thinking of medical educators who place their hopes on students' emulation of professional models. Students are just as prone to accept models' more "cynical" goals as their idealistic ones. Furthermore students are no less prone to reject models' values than to accept them.

In fact two of the most central norms—emphasis on the importance of the People component and the expectation of Intrinsic Rewards from the profession—are characterized by a pattern of Considered Rejection. This means that students initially did not differ from the models on these variables, but rejected the latters' viewpoint over time so that by the end of formal socialization students and models show a different stance on these issues. We have noted that in such a situation, the teachers serve as anti-models.

Models serve as reinforcers of students' original viewpoint with respect to the importance of family medicine. Anticipatory socialization made students and models similar at the starting point of socialization and there is no evidence for change among students over the six year period observed.

The scientific aspect of medicine is characterized by a pattern of Over Conformity and Total Rejection. Emphasis on the importance of science and confidence in its reliability are reduced over time among students who started their socialization with considerably more confidence in science than characterizes the models. However, students changed consistently and ended up at T_6 with significantly less confidence in science than characterizes the models. This response may reflect a boomerang effect of the strong curricular emphasis on science, especially during the preclinical years. What is clear from these data is the fact that students come to adopt a more extreme view than the teachers during the course of socialization apparently rejecting the latters' view as too conservative on this subject.

This analysis has not considered the roles of different types of models in terms of their status, "stardom", departmental affiliation, or amount of contact with students. Neither has it examined patterns of modeling among different types of students differentiated by sex, level of scholastic achievement, maturity, socio-economic status or other social characteristics. This issue will be considered in a later paper.

REFERENCES

1. Bandura A. Social-learning theory of identificatory

processes. In *Handbook of Socialization Theory and Research* (Edited by Goslin O. A.), pp. 213–262. Rand McNally, Chicago, 1969.
2. Shuval J. From "boy" to "colleague": processes of role transformation in professional socialization. *Soc. Sci. Med.* **9**, 413–420, 1975.
3. Goode W. M. Community within a community: the professions. *Am. sociol. Rev.* **XX**, 194–200, 1957.
4. Merton R. K., Reader G. G. and Kendall P. L. *The Student Physician*. Harvard Univ. Press, Cambridge, 1957.
5. Bucher R. and Strauss A. Professions in process. *Am. J. Soc.* **66**, 116–130, 1961.
6. Bloom S. W. The medical school as a social system. *Milbank mem. Fund q. bull.* **49**, 1971.
7. Brim O. G. and Wheeler S. *Socialization after Childhood*. Wiley, New York, 1966.
8. Clausen J. *Socialization and Society*. Little Brown, Boston, 1968.
9. Moore W. Occupational socialization. In *Handbook of Socialization Research and Theory* (Edited by Goslin D. A.), p. 861–883. Rand McNally, Chicago, 1969.
10. Shuval J. Socialization of health professionals in Israel: early sources of congruence and differentiation. *J. Med. Ed.* **50**, 443–457, 1975.
11. Shuval J. and Adler I. Processes of continuity and change during socialization for medicine in Israel. *Hlth Soc. Behav.* **18:2**, 112–124, 1977.
12. Shuval J. and Gilbert L. Attempts at professionalization of pharmacy. *Soc. Sci. Med.* **11**, 19–25, 1978.
13. Adler I. and Shuval J. Cross pressures during socialization for medicine. *Am. sociol. Rev.* **43**, 693–704, 1978.
14. Shuval J. and Adler I. Health occupations in Israel: comparative patterns of change during socialization. *J. Hlth soc. Behav.* **20**, 77–89, 1979.
15. Shuval J. *Entering Medicine: The Dynamics of Transition*. Pergamon Press, Oxford, 1979.
16. Quarantelli E. L., Helfrich M. and Yutsy D. Faculty and student perceptions in a professional school. *Sociol. Soc. Res.* **49**, 32–45, 1964.
17. Manasse H. R. Jr, Kabat H. F. and Wertheimen A. I. Professional socialization in pharmacy. *Soc. Sci. Med.* **11**, 653–659, 1977.
18. Allport G. W., Vernon P. E. and Lindzey G. *Study of Values: Machine Scorable Edition* (4th edn). Houghton Mifflin, Boston, 1968.

19. Springer E. *Types of Man, Manual, Study of Values.* Houghton Mifflin, Boston, 1970.
20. Konopka G. Formation of values in the developing person. *Am. J. Orthopsychiat.* **43,** 96, 1973.
21. Rokeach M. *The Nature of Human Value.* Free Press, New York, 1973.
22. Caplowitz D. Relations in Medical School: A Study in Professional Socialization. Unpublished Ph.D. dissertation, Columbia University, 1960.
23. Lortie D. C. Laymen to lawmen: law schools, careers and professional socialization. *Harv. Ed. Rev.* **29,** 352–369, 1959.
24. Schwartz A. The Engineering Student: Interaction Patterns and Orientation to Professional Values. Unpublished M.A. Thesis, Ohio State University, 1962.

APPENDIX: DEFINITION OF NORMS AND VALUES

The norms and values were defined in terms of the following sets of items presented to students several times during socialization and to clinical teachers.

The *People, Status* and *Science* components of the physician's normative role. A set of fifteen traits of the "competent" physician were rated for perceived importance in practice. The inter-item correlation matrix showed three consistent clusters of items at all times [10–15]. People-oriented items: ability to understand others' feelings and problems, desire to help others and alleviate suffering, ability to work with and get along with others, importance of a warm personality, concern with tolerance and flexibility in relations with others. Science-oriented items: knowledge and skill in the natural sciences, scientific curiosity, research ability and originality. Status-oriented items: desire to carry responsibility, emphasis on attractive external appearance, emphasis on administrative ability, and desire for prestige status. Mean scores for each component ranged over 5 categories. The lower the mean score, the more the component is viewed as important.

Idealism

"Do you think a doctor today needs to be as much of an idealist as in the past?" 4 categories. The higher the mean score, the greater the idealism.

Intrinsic rewards

"Do you expect to gain the following from your future work as a physician—opportunity to help others, interest in your work, intellectual challenge, responsibility, authority." 5 categories. The lower the mean score, the greater the expectation of reward.

Extrinsic rewards

"Do you expect to gain the following from your future work as a physician—a high income, secure job, high status?" 5 categories. The lower the mean score, the greater the expectation of reward.

Family medicine

"Do you think it is important for family medicine to be practiced in Israel?" 4 categories. The lower the mean score, the greater the importance.

Importance of patients' social background

"Do you think it is important or unnecessary for a physician to know as much as possible about a patient's social background?" 4 categories. The lower the mean score, the more important.

Importance of permitting a patient to talk about his illness

"Do you think a physician should encourage a patient to talk about his illness or should he just accept what the patient tells him?" 4 categories. The lower the mean score, the more he should encourage.

Uncertainty: efficacy of drugs

"Can a physician be certain of the clinical effects of a well tested drug?" 4 categories. The lower the mean score, the greater the certainty.

Uncertainty: reliability of clinical laboratory tests

How confident can a physician be that two laboratories doing the same tests will come up with the same results?" 4 categories. The lower the mean score, the greater the confidence.

19.
The Mechanech: Role Function and Myth in Israeli Secondary Schools

David Gordon and Walter I. Ackerman

Social scientists concerned with the workings of modern societies, organizations, and institutions have recently begun to make use of concepts previously considered the almost exclusive property of anthropologists studying primitive or exotic cultures. The concept of myth is an example. In this paper we propose to examine a particular type of myth—character myth. We will attempt to show that under certain circumstances the hidden curricula of schools perform an important function in the maintenance of character myths. Our analysis derives from Ernest Gellner's concept of conceptual incoherence,[1] and we apply that idea to the role of the *Mechanech* in Israeli secondary schools. We will devote a special section of the article to presenting an extensive description of this role. At this point it will suffice to characterize the Mechanech as an Israeli counterpart to the American homeroom teacher, whose responsibilities, however, are considerably wider and more clearly linked to pastoral care and moral education than those of the American parallel.

Our main purpose is to argue that the role of the Mechanech, aside from its intrinsic interest as an important feature of Israeli schools, is its use as the mechanism through which a character myth of Israeli society known as the *Chalutz* is maintained.

Myths and Character Myths

Anthropologists generally regard myth as a special form of narrative or story.[2] The narrative-like character of myth, however, has often been ignored in attempts to capture certain aspects of modern societies and organizations. Ellul, for instance, defines myth as an "all-encompassing, activating *image*, a sort of vision of desirable objectives that have lost their material, practical character" (emphasis added).[3] While our discussion of myth draws on Ellul's definition, there is an important difference. He is concerned with abstract images—that is, science, work, happiness, the nation, et cetera. Our interest tends to the more concrete—persons, personality types, and roles which societies transform into myths in Ellul's

---

[1] Ernest Gellner, "Concepts and Society," in *Rationality*, ed. B. Wilson (Oxford: Blackwell, 1979).
[2] Percy S. Cohen, "Theories of Myth," *Man* 4 (September 1969): 337–53.
[3] Jacques Ellul, *Propaganda: The Formation of Men's Attitudes* (New York: Knopf, 1969), p. 31.

sense. Davy Crockett in American culture and the gentlemen in English society are examples. These we call "character myths."

A detailed analysis of the reasons which inspire the creation of character myths is beyond the scope of this paper. We can, however, offer some brief suggestions: (*a*) A character myth encodes the value system of the society simply and effectively and is thus an efficient means of presenting and transmitting that system. (*b*) Because the myth is usually rooted in the society's past, it creates a sense of continuity and contributes to the strengthening of group identity. (*c*) The attributes of the character myth are always of two sorts. There are those which are genuinely moral: the mythic person has certain real virtues. Others, however, are simply external and morally neutral. This duality allows people to limit their identification with the myth to its external characteristics alone. Sustaining the myth in this way makes it possible for people to feel virtuous without their having to bother with the real virtues it represents.

Our understanding of character myths is similar to Geertz's conception of "social semantics." His detailed and sensitive analysis of the cockfight, an important feature of Balinese social life, proposes that we treat cultural forms "as texts, as imaginative works built out of social materials." This perspective views the cockfight as an art form, "*a Balinese reading of Balinese experience, a story they tell themselves about themselves*" (emphasis ours).[4] We suggest that the maintenance of the character myths of a society provides that society with "a reading of its moral experience, a story it tells itself about its own morality." We use the Chalutz as an example.

The Chalutz—an Israeli Character Myth

Chalutz means "pioneer"; this meaning stems from the biblical source (Josh. 6:13) which uses the word to denote the vanguard which leads the host on its advance. Current usage refers to those young people whose commitment to the idea of a sovereign Jewish state led them to the establishment of cooperative or collective settlements in Palestine where they sought self-fulfillment through identification with their people, their own labor, and a readiness to sacrifice their lives in defense of the land. The first Chalutzim, mainly from Eastern Europe, began to emigrate to Palestine at the end of the nineteenth century.[5]

Standard Zionist doctrine teaches that the Chalutzim came to a barren, swamp-ridden waste. Socialist zeal, love of the people and the land, courage, physical labor, and cooperative effort all combined to "make the desert bloom." Despite privation life was good and happy; days were spent in

---

[4] Clifford Geertz, *The Interpretation of Cultures* (New York: Basic, 1973), p. 448.
[5] A brief but comprehensive description of the *Chalutz* movement may be found in *Encyclopaedia Judaica* (Jerusalem: Keter, 1971), 8:247–55.

hard work accompanied by song; evenings found the Chalutzim around the campfire singing, dancing, or participating in some other group activity; in their spare time they hiked around the country they loved so much. The Chalutz was politically aware and participated in group discussions of political issues. Altogether the Chalutz was a totally group-oriented person.

The foregoing, of course, is not objective history. It is rather a stereotyped, idyllic picture in which the Chalutz has been transformed into a folk hero. The connotation of the word Chalutz is uncompromisingly positive. It has strong affective and moral overtones. The Chalutzim were idealists, good people, people to be proud of. The Chalutz was the embodiment of the ideal personality.

The Chalutz myth functions, as we have suggested, on the level of social semantics, as an Israeli reading of Israel's moral experience. Its functionality, however, may also be argued from a neo-Marxist perspective. The Chalutz myth is strikingly elitist and ethnic. It is elitist because a very high proportion of the country's leadership, both before and after the creation of the state, came from the ranks of the Chalutzim; even today the descendants of the Chalutzim are considered part of Israel's "aristocracy." It is ethnic because the Chalutzim were, by and large, Ashkenazi Jews — they came from the Jewish communities of Central and Eastern Europe. In Israel today Sephardic Jews—that is, descendants of immigrants from North Africa and the Middle East—constitute more than 50 percent of the Jewish population. The attitudes, customs, and values of the westernized Ashkenazic Jews set the standards to which the mass of Sephardic Jews which immigrated to the country during the decade of the fifties was expected to conform; the latter have yet to achieve a status commensurate with their numbers. The Chalutz is an Ashkenazic myth which may be understood as a mechanism used by the economically, politically, and socially dominant Ashkenazi Jews as a symbolic means of helping maintain their power base. Participating in activities which are associated with the Chalutz myth (hiking, communal singing of particular songs, etc.) has become part of the unquestioned adornments of the elite. Sephardic Jews with their different customs, images, and myths are at a great disadvantage here. The Chalutz myth effectively acts as a symbolic barrier to their becoming part of the elite.

Schools and Character Myths

The idea that schools are an important vehicle for the maintenance of character myths requires that we identify some of the methods and techniques they use in the process. A passage from Ernest Gellner's "Concepts in Society" suggests at least one such mechanism:

Assume that in the language of a given society, there is a word *boble* which is applied to characterize people. Research reveals that *bobliness* or *bobility* is attributed to people under either of the following conditions: (a) a person who antecedently displays certain characteristics in his conduct, say uprightness, courage and generosity, is called *boble*. (b) any person holding a certain office, or a certain social position, is also *pro facto* described as *boble* . . . but the point is: the society in question does not distinguish *two concepts*, boble (a) and boble (b). It only uses one word, boble *tout court*; and again its theories about bobility . . . only know bobility, one and indivisible. . . . Bobility is a conceptual device by which the privileged class of the society in question acquires some of the prestige of certain virtues respected in that society, without the inconvenience of needing to practice it, thanks to the fact that the same word is applied either to practitioners of these virtues or to occupiers of favored positions. It is, at the same time, a manner of reinforcing the appeal of those virtues, by associating them, through the use of the same appellation, with privilege and power. But all this needs to be said and to say it is to bring out the *internally logical incoherence of the concept—an incoherence which, indeed, is socially functional.* [Last italics ours][6]

We believe that certain school systems create particular roles which like "bobility" are "logically incoherent" and yet "socially functional." The hidden curriculum of such roles, as we shall attempt to show by the relationship we discern between the role of the Mechanech in Israeli secondary schools and the myth of the Chalutz, contains a function whose purpose is the maintenance of character myths.

The Mechanech

Pupils in Israeli high schools are assigned to specific classes. They separate for some subjects, but the class unit remains intact a good deal of the time, and a particular group of pupils may remain together as a class for a number of years. Each class has its own room, while teachers do not—they move from room to room during the day.

Each class has its own Mechanech. The Mechanech is one of the subject-matter teachers of the class; his duties as Mechanech are officially counted as one-eighth (3 hours a week) of his weekly teaching load but all Mechanchim know that the role demands much more time. The Mechanech meets with his class for 1 hour a week; that session is known either as the Mechanech or "social" hour. The content of the weekly meeting varies considerably from class to class. Some of the more usual options are discussion of current political and social issues; guest speakers on various topics; discussion of class problems—tension between different groups and pupils in the class or discipline problems with other teachers; listening to music, et cetera. The Mechanech may also use the hour for announcements, checking absenteeism, and other routine chores.

[6] Gellner, pp. 41–42.

Some Mechanchim plan the Mechanech hour by themselves. Others rely heavily on a class committee and in fact devote a great deal of time to its development. The committee's duties cover a variety of extramural activities. The class is also a social unit and once or twice a year official class parties are held. School hikes are also usually organized on a class basis, and in Israel they are extremely important. At least once a year the class (perhaps together with other classes) will go on a 3–4-day hike. In addition a class may spend 2–3 days working as volunteers on a neighboring kibbutz, and during the year there will be a number of 1-day outings as well. All these activities are organized by the class committee together with the Mechanech, who is the one teacher who will participate in all of them.

The Mechanech is also the intermediary between the class and teachers who may be having difficulties with the class as a whole or with specific pupils. Teachers feel free to report on these difficulties to the Mechanech (as long as they are not seen as indicating teaching inadequacies or failings, of course) and expect that the Mechanech will deal with them. This he will do during the Mechanech hour, as previously mentioned, or he will speak privately with particular pupils.

The Mechanech is expected to maintain a rather close relationship with each of his pupils—to meet with them on a one-to-one basis, to visit their homes, and to try and help them with their problems. If a pupil begins slacking at his studies, it is the Mechanech who will try to get him back into the groove. Toward the end of each term the Mechanech calls a meeting of all the teachers of the class to discuss the grades and behavior of each pupil. The Mechanech is expected to supply the "background" information on each pupil, and although this is not an official characteristic of his role, he will tend to act as "a friend in court" for the more problematic pupils. Report cards are distributed by the Mechanech, who will use the opportunity to give a student a pep talk if needed or to pat him on the back. Parents are invited to the school several times a year to hear about their child's progress. In most cases they will meet only with the Mechanech; he may, however, send them to speak with other teachers.

It is clear that the Mechanech is entrusted with a bewilderingly varied set of tasks; he is responsible for "pastoral care," social education in an extremely broad sense, moral education, and many other things as well. The role of Mechanech seems like an arbitrary hodgepodge of unconnected activities. Why, for instance, should the teacher who goes on hikes with kids be the one to whom other teachers turn when dealing with discipline problems?

This peculiar mix of tasks should not, however, obscure the fact that among Israeli educators the importance of the Mechanech is unquestioned, and the role has been described as "the most important function in the process of education."[7] Or as one high school principal put it, "The Mechanech is the leader . . . the glue which holds the school together . . . ; he must be open, knowledgeable, expert, sensitive. . . ." In most schools the Mechanchim, who constitute about 30 percent of the teaching staff, are clearly the elite group within the faculty. Important management decisions are considered to have been ratified by all the teachers even if in actual practice they have been approved only by the Mechanchim, who in many schools meet as a group on a regular basis.

The importance ascribed to the role of the Mechanech by people inside the school system can, it seems to us, draw on several theoretical arguments for support. One of them is central to our concern here and links the Mechanech to the Chalutz myth and to Gellner's notion of conceptional incoherence. Before addressing that issue, however, we think it advisable to point to two positive functions performed by the Mechanech.

First, there is reason to believe that the significance attached to the role of the Mechanech undoubtedly stems in part from the fact that in its attention to the individual it enables the school to refute charges of indifference and dispassion. The role provides that for every class there is one adult who really cares and is readily available to every pupil in a truly personal way. The Mechanech is thus perceived as central to the creation of a climate of personalism in Israeli high schools.

The importance attributed to the Mechanech may, second, also derive from his or her function as an interface between the official culture of the school—that represented by the administration and faculty—and the subculture of the student population.

Waller long ago called our attention to the existence of the student culture and its significance: "A . . . universal conflict between students and teachers arises from the fact that teachers are adult and students are not, so the teachers are the bearers of the culture of the society of adults and try to impose that culture upon students, whereas students represent the indigenous culture of the group of children";[8] recent events in many different parts of the world are evidence of the potential explosiveness of the special culture of the young. We have learned that the development of a productive equilibrium between the two cultures depends, in no small measure, on an awareness of the pervasiveness of the student culture, an appreciation of its contribution to the richness of life in school, the maintenance of open lines of communication, and the ability to react quickly and sensibly to its more disruptive manifestations. The Mechanech is the bridge which connects the two worlds of adults and children and attempts to transmute the negative effect of each on the other into a positive

[7] Bulletin of the Director General (in Hebrew) (Jerusalem: Ministry of Education and Culture, September 1978).
[8] Willard Waller, *The Sociology of Teaching* (New York: Wiley, n.d.), pp. 111–13.

valence. In a sense the Mechanech is a social-emotional specialist whose function is to maintain a delicate balance between the deep-seated needs of the young which seek expression in the special modes of a student culture and the equally legitimate demands of task-oriented subject-matter teachers and administrators.[9] As a middleman whose role symbolizes an institutionalized differentiation between adult claims for task accomplishment and the socioemotional needs of youngsters, the Mechanech is in a position to contribute significantly to "maintaining the internal state of the system in a steady state."[10]

These two functions of the Mechanech are readily apparent to school personnel. A third function, to which we have alluded earlier, requires an analysis of the deep structure of the role and of the seemingly unrelated and ill-matched activities of which it is composed. This deep structure is somewhat akin to the logical incoherence of "bobility." The analysis must begin with the abstract noun *chinuch*, the Hebrew word for education that is used to distinguish the work of the Mechanech from that of regular subject-matter teachers. An anthropologist studying the Israeli school system would distinguish between chinuch *a* and chinuch *b*.

Chinuch *a* consists in getting kids to engage in all the activities which draw on the Chalutz model and are associated with Chalutziut (pioneering): hiking, sitting around campfires singing, work camps, participating actively in the class's official social life, participating in the discussion of social issues in the social hour.

Chinuch *b* consists of all those activities designed to ensure that kids remain "good" (i.e., well-behaved and hardworking) pupils—preaching to the class when they misbehave, talking privately with those who are slacking, talking to other teachers about pupils who cause concern in some way or other, talking to parents about problems, et cetera. Note that the way a good pupil is conceived is not related very much to his intellectual abilities but rather to certain character traits. To put it melodramatically, Mechanech *b* is in fact the school functionary entrusted with seeing to it that his charges do not stray from the path of righteousness.

To paraphrase Gellner, Israeli educators do not distinguish between the two concepts chinuch *a* and chinuch *b*. They use one word, chinuch, and their theories about chinuch only know chinuch one and indivisible. The logical incoherence we have pointed out must serve some societal function. This, we believe, is readily apparent. Because chinuch is by virtue of chinuch *b* closely associated with righteousness, the activities associated with chinuch *a* become imbued with moral potency. Neutral

<hr>

[9] Robert Bales and Philip Slater, "Role Differentiation in Small Decision-making Groups," in *Family: Socialization and Interaction Process*, ed. T. Parsons and R. Bales (New York: Free Press, 1955), p. 305.
[10] Ibid., p. 303.

acts suddenly become moral acts; hiking changes from something one can do into something one ought to do. As a result the moral dimension of Chalutziut is reinforced and this, in turn, serves to sustain the myth of the Chalutz.

The relationship between the Chalutz and the Mechanech is, we believe, reciprocal. Not only do the Mechanech's activities maintain the Chalutz myth, but the myth itself sustains, justifies, and gives meaning to those activities. If one looks at the activities of the Mechanech "objectively," that is, divorced from the Chalutz connotation, they are rather trivial. The Mechanech is mainly concerned with the external characteristics of the Chalutz or with righteousness in the very shallow sense of being a good pupil. The role of the Mechanech gains much of its moral force from its linkage to the Chalutz myth. This helps the school in one very simple, rather cynical way: it enables schools to be involved in moral education (and feel good about this involvement) without really trying. Schools can and do expend great effort on the Mechanech role and thus, because of its tie to the Chalutz myth, convince themselves they are contributing to the moral or character education of their pupils, when to a large extent they are involved mainly in trivializing moral education. After all, seeing to it that pupils do not rag their teachers and do complete their homework is hardly on the same level as educating pupils to become the empathetic, autonomous, thoughtful kind of people that John Wilson is referring to when he talks about the "morally educated person."[11] From the point of view of the external observer this may seem unfortunate, but from the point of view of the schools themselves nothing could be better. No organization can function if it is haunted by continual failure. Real serious moral education is extraordinarily difficult. If the schools were really to get involved in moral education, they would be likely to be terribly frustrated. The Mechanech role allows the school to deal with a pseudo-moral education and to deal with it successfully—it is relatively easy to succeed with activities like a hike or class party.

Several additional considerations seem to warrant this interpretation of the role of the Mechanech and its relationship to the myth of the Chalutz.

1. While there is no dearth of research which details the shortcomings in the classroom performance of Israeli teachers, there is no empirical evidence regarding the effectiveness, or the lack of it, of the Mechanech. Despite this fact, there is widespread consensus, in and out of professional circles, that he is the solution to many of the ills which beset schools and that given the opportunity he is capable of restoring schooling to its

---

[11] John Wilson, "What Is Moral Education?" in *Introduction to Moral Education*, ed. J. Wilson, N. Williams, and B. Sugarman (Harmondsworth: Pelican, 1967), pp. 32–34.

preordained place in the forming of national character. Whenever an aspect of schooling is not subjected to empirical evaluation, there is good reason to believe that it has a symbolic and ritualistic importance. The Chalutz is beyond critical analysis in Israel; the role of the Mechanech is wrapped in the protection of the myth.

2. The activities that make up what we have called chinuch *a* are very similar to those that characterize the role of the group leader in Israeli youth movements. Most of these youth movements are quite openly geared to recruiting youngsters to join kibbutzim on completion of their army service. In other words youth leaders attempt to convince these youngsters to become bona fide Chalutzim.

3. The roots of the Mechanech role can be traced to the thought and practice of the founders of the schools of the pioneering labor movement, both in the kibbutzim and in the new urban centers created by Jewish settlement in pre-state Palestine. The work of those educators, men and women committed to the renaissance of the Jewish people in a sovereign state of its own, was profoundly influenced by the progressive example of the "New Education" of late nineteenth- and early twentieth-century Central Europe and the socially oriented philosophy of John Dewey.

Their understanding of schooling, a view whose influence extended far beyond the schools they themselves conducted, conceived of "social education" not as a mere appendage to traditional school activities but rather as the leitmotif of a new kind of educational institution and the very heart of the educational process. Respect for the integrity of childhood and adolescence was joined to a sense of civic responsibility in the forming of a learning community in which physical labor and socially oriented pupil activities provided the framework and set the tone for formal study. Their efforts proclaimed the belief that the new society they were building "required that the school change itself, its manner of operation and its characteristic pattern of relationships. . . . The school must become a community which strives to realize the ideals of the society of which it is a part. It must be guided by the aspiration to change the existing social order and to guarantee a different and better future for the child."[12]

The comprehensiveness of that vision and the range of its reach were given symbolic expression by referring to the school as a *beit chinuch* (house of education), a term which transcends the limitations implicit in the conventional appellation *beit sefer* (house of the book). Within this context it is but a short step to the enlargement of the role of the teacher from that of *moreh* (instructor) to that of Mechanech (educator). In other words, the Mechanech derives historically from the Chalutzim themselves.

---

[12] Shimon Reshef, *The Labor Movement School System in Pre-State Israel* (in Hebrew) (Tel Aviv: Tel Aviv University and Hakibbutz Hameuchad, 1980), p. 162.

Toward a General Hypothesis

Several aspects of the relationship between the role of the Mechanech and the myth of Chalutz are important for a general hypothesis regarding school systems and the maintenance of character myths:

1. The figure of the Chalutz was the complete personification of the values of the Zionist ideal. His unchallenged moral authority set a standard for all the members of the society. The transformation of the *beit sefer* into a *beit chinuch* in which all teachers are Mechanchim is an example of encompassing aspiration. Today the Chalutz represents only some of the values of Israeli society and only some teachers are Mechanchim.

2. The distinction between social education and formal study, as we have shown, draws a sharp line between the ordinary classroom subject-matter teacher and the Mechanech. It declares, among other things, that, while schools are responsible for imparting knowledge and training the intellect, they must also attend to the formation of character and the inculcation of values. It further states, at least implicitly—and this is the crucial matter—that as important as intellectual competencies may be, they really are not the stuff of which character is made. The locus of personal development and the acquisition of values, therefore, is somewhere outside the subject-matter content of the curriculum. The emphasis on social education is at its core a radically anti-intellectual stance as is the value system embodied in the idea of the Chalutz; among other things it denies the affective aspects of cognitive learning.[13] Because the activities of the Mechanech, by definition, fall largely into the sphere of social education and because he is perceived as *the* figure in the school most directly concerned with the personal development of pupils and the one with whom they are most likely to identify, he becomes, in a paradoxical mutation, a symbol of the view which questions the social efficacy of the intellective functions of schooling. Instead of maintaining a balance between the various elements which constitute the school experience, the activities of the Mechanech, as well as the expectations attached to his role, tip the scale in a direction which leads away from formal classroom activity.

3. The anti-intellectualism of the Chalutz myth and the role of the Mechanech do not, however, turn into the "anti-schoolism" described by Hofstadter in his analysis of the Davy Crocket myth.[14] Our example is a form of "pro-school" anti-intellectualism.

Schools which attempt to maintain a pro-school but anti-intellectual myth are in a paradoxical situation, and especially so when the myth is no longer pervasive but only a single thread in the fabric of a society's

[13] Israel Scheffler, "In Praise of the Cognitive Emotions," *Teachers College Record* 79 (December 1977): 171–86.

[14] Richard Hofstadter, *Anti-Intellectualism in American Life* (New York: Knopf, 1963), pp. 161–64.

system of values. One way of resolving the dilemma is to partition off some area of school life in which the myth can flourish without adversely affecting academic standards and to assign the responsibility of promoting appropriate activities to a certain member of the school staff. In Israeli secondary schools today the social life of the class may be considered that sort of special territory and the Mechanech the functionary specifically charged with the perpetuation of the myth. This is in contrast to an earlier period when the myth of the Chalutz fashioned the very nature of the school and inspired the work of all its teachers.

The foregoing leads us to a tentative suggestion: schools concerned with the maintenance of character myths appoint special functionaries for that purpose when three conditions, at least, obtain: (i) the myth is anti-intellectual, (ii) the school establishment identifies with the myth, and (iii) the myth relates to aspects of the society's past which are slowly becoming less central to its present. The validity of this hypothesis must, of course, be tested against evidence from a number of school systems. The role of the English housemaster in maintaining the myth of the gentleman and the tasks assigned the athletic coach in American high schools seem promising areas of investigation.

Conclusion

Some 50 years have passed since Waller suggested that our understanding of schools and school systems would be enlarged and enriched by an analysis of their ceremonies, myths, and rituals.[15] With few exceptions,[16] that suggestion seems to have been ignored. Our efforts here may be understood as an attempt to illustrate the usefulness of concepts such as myth in research on schools.

[15] Waller, p. 103.

[16] For example, David H. Kamens, "Legitimating Myths and Educational Organizations: The Relationship between Organizational Ideology and Formal Structure," *American Sociological Review* 42 (April 1977): 208–19.

20.

Students' Supportive Attitude toward Their Schools: The Case of the Israeli Youth Village and Its Student Society

Mordecai Arieli

Some 20% of all Jewish adolescents in Israel live in residential schools. Many of these schools are called youth villages. A youth village always includes a school. However, the students do not only learn in a youth village but lead most of their social lives in it and also work.

The schools within the youth villages resemble the wide range of regular day secondary schools in Israel. The major difference is that schools within youth villages serve proportionately more youths from disadvantaged social strata than day schools. In fact, nowadays most of the students in youth villages were placed in them because it is widely believed in Israel that schooling away from the community will benefit those whose neighborhoods are considered educationally depriving.

Social life within the youth village is usually intensive. The students are organized in co-ed peer groups. Each group has its own cottages and ample opportunities for informal interaction. In addition there are many organized extracurricular activities in the afternoons and evenings. A housefather called a 'madrich' and a house mother called a 'metapelet' lead the group. Their roles include many components: custodial and supportive, group education and individual care.

Many youth villages run farms and the students work in these farms supervized by special instructors. In almost all youth villages the students fill maintenance, cleaning and kitchen tasks. In some youth villages the student community runs these tasks in the framework of a self-governing body.

Many youth villages have traditionally adopted the pioneering and collectivist ethos of the kibbutzim. However, in the last two decades much of this ethos has been replaced by an achievement-individualistic orientation.

Various aspects of the inmate society within residential settings have been investigated, especially their relationship with the settings' formal orders (Sykes, 1958; Polsky, 1962; Ward & Kassebaum, 1965; Giallombardo, 1966; Street, Vinter and Perrow, 1966; Polsky and Claster, 1968;

Lambert, Bullock and Millham, 1975; Millham, Bullock and Cherrett, 1975). As Lambert, Bullock and Millham (1973, p.300) point out, much sociological research has encouraged policymakers to assume that the structural variables of the school are directly related to aspects of its pupil society. It is often expected that within residential schools such a relationship will be established since residential schools are "powerful environments" whose students are exposed to their regime and con-straints not only during the time devoted to schooling, but during the whole day and for a period of several years. However, Lambert, Bullock and Millham (1973), who have reviewed much of the relevant research, conclude that it is difficult to posit such relationship.

In Israel, where schooling in residential facilities is exercised as a major educational strategy for the advancement of young new immi-grants and youth from poor areas (Wolins and Gottesman, 1971; Kashti, 1979; Smilansky, Kashti and Arieli, 1982; Arieli, Kashti and Shlasky, 1983), it seems particularly important to pose the question: is there indeed a relationship between structural dimensions of residential schools and aspects of the student society? And if there is — what are its directions?

Major structural dimensions of Israeli residential schools
The degree of closedness found in educational settings is one of their major characteristics. It may be defined as the system of measures used — consciously or otherwise — by the staff to obstruct influences which may contradict or weaken their shared objectives. As theoretical models we see an extremely "closed" setting as an order whose staff use means designed to lead to the total obstruction of influences opposed to or competing with the educational direction that they wish to give their pupils, while an extremely "open" institution is an order whose staff do not employ organizational means to combat rival influences. These models remain theoretical. Staffs of residential schools are unlikely to operate their organization as an extremely open one, because removing pupils from their homes and placing them in a different geographical locus is invariably an act which gives an advantage to the culture medi-ated by the staff over the influences of the pupils' original environments such as their family and their community. But neither do staffs operate the residential educational setting as an extremely closed organization, because in every case those rival influences find their way into the setting and its culture through the pupils' latent cultures and their earlier socialization. However, each residential setting can be classified

according to its nearness to or distance from either of the two poles (openness and closedness), on the basis of characterization of its staff's goals and the processes employed by the staff to achieve these goals.

It seems that since the mid 1950's a process of change has taken place in Israeli youth villages. The process can be characterized as a gradual movement from "closedness" to "openness". More specifically, we can refer to six dimensions of change "from closedness to openness" which almost all residential schools have been undergoing, but presumably, at different levels of intensity at each school. These dimensions can be described as (a) a decrease in staff's ideological commitment, (b) the shifting of social orientation from status to role socialization, (c) an increase in the importance of instrumental aims, (d) decentralization of organizational structure, (e) increase in staff's role differentiation, and (f) increase in the centrality of professional affiliation as a teacher's frame of reference.

(a) *Decrease in staff's ideological commitment:* The directors of the youth villages have gradually ceased traditional attempts to recruit all their junior staff from among individuals who are ideologically committed to either the ethos of pioneering, or to the political movements which own the settings. Directors of party owned youth villages and their management committees have begun to recruit heads of important sub-systems from among professionals who do not identify with the party (Arieli, 1980).

(b) *Shifting of social orientation from status to role socialization:* In the past, the youth villages' educational programs aimed at extending the range of the socializing process to the overall status of the pupil, and developing his self-perception beyond his specific future roles. However, since the late 1960's it seems that the programs tend, in varying degrees, to limit the influence of the socialization process to training the pupils towards taking differentiated and specific roles in the adult society in which they are expected to participate (Kashti, 1974).

(c) *Increase in importance of instrumental aims:* In the past, expressive goals used to be considered main goals or at least equal in importance to instrumental goals, both at the stated and the implemented levels. This meant, for example, that the financial resources allotted to extra-curricular activities and the prestige allotted to the houseparents were not significantly lower than the resources allotted to schooling and the prestige allotted to teachers. At present, it seems that the latent message mediated by the senior to the junior staff and to the pupils is that schooling and schoolmasters are more highly valued than informal activities and houseparents.

(d) *Decentralization of organizational structure:* In the 1950's and 1960's the youth villages were characterized by a centralized pattern of organization. This was reflected in the nature of their internal and external organizational relations. The youth villages' decisions tended to be made by the general principal who, as he saw fit, delegated certain executive power to the heads of the sub-systems, and they, in turn, to their deputies according to a hierarchical pattern. The youth village's relations with the outside world were also largely initiated and regulated by the general principal, who served as the almost sole agent and transmitter of the norms and expectations of the external systems (the party, the management committee, placement organizations, etc.) to all ranks of the youth village. Beginning in the late 1960's these centralized features have been replaced by decentralized ones. However, youth villages have differed since then in the level of intensity of change from centralization to decentralization. The changes are reflected in the structure of internal relations within the staff. These relations are now characterized by an increasing level of autonomy of the heads of the sub-systems as regards the policy of their units, the relative freedom of decision allowed to low-ranking members of the staff and the status — of coordinator of more or less autonomous sub-systems -- assigned to the school principal. The youth villages' relations with external agencies tend to be based on the autonomy of the heads of the sub-systems in maintaining direct relationships with role partners outside the system (Kashti, 1971).

(e) *Increase in staffs' role differentiation:* In the 1950's and the early 1960's the areas of activities and the roles of the staff in all the youth villages were not highly differentiated and often even diffuse or interchangeable. In many cases the educator — a role combining formal and informal functions — acted as both schoolmaster and group counselor.

Since the mid 1960's the relations of staff members with the pupils in all schools — but again in varying degrees — have become more differentiated. This is reflected among other things in the fact that these relations have become largely delineated by the specific skill and the definition of the staff members' role.

(f) *Increase in centrality of professional affiliation as teachers' frame of reference:* In the 1950's and 1960's most teachers at the youth villages tended to consider the organization in which they worked as their most significant occupational frame of reference. This was probably partly due to the fact that teachers tended to live in the setting and partly due to their relative lack of qualifications.

At present most teachers (and other staff members such as social workers) in all the schools seem to attribute more significance to their professional identity than to their organizational affiliation. This seems to be especially so in the comprehensive and the vocational youth villages. In general, teachers are more qualified now and live outside the youth village (Arieli, 1980).

Students' attitudes to the youth village

Presenting major aspects of the student society as "an informal system" and major structural dimensions of schools as "a formal system", Lambert, Bullock and Millham (1973, p. 304) suggest that there are few clear ways in which informal student systems relate to the formal system of the school: the informal system may be (1) supportive (of the formal system), (2) manipulative (the students use features of the formal system for their own ends), (3) passive (the students ignore aspects of the formal system) or (4) rejecting (the students reject the formal system).

Rather than differentiating between four distinct ways in which student societies relate to school we suggest that student societies vary in the extent to which they support school. Students' expressions concerning their willingness to consider their youth village and its community as "home", to commit themselves to the youth village's formal objectives and to accept and observe its formal rules are different indications of the support of a given students society of its youth village.

In this work an attempt is made to find possible relationships between students' support of their youth villages and the "openness" of their youth villages.

More specifically, the relationship is investigated between (1) places student groups occupy in a rank order denoting levels of support of the youth village, and (2) the positions of these youth villages along continui denoting movement along the following directions: from much to little ideological commitment, from status to role socialization, from expressive to instrumental aims, from centralization to decentralization, from little to much staff's role differentiation and from teachers' organizational to professional affiliation as their central occupational frame of reference.

Subjects, Settings, Judges

Subjects: 46 students (31 boys and 15 girls) aged 14 - 16 were interviewed in groups of 3 - 7 members. Each group consisted of students from one student group in one youth village. There were altogether 10 groups from 10 different youth villages.

Settings: Ten co-ed youth villages were assessed. Five were agricultural schools, one a "preparatory school" which prepares students with particularly low educational achievements to attend regular secondary schools, two were schools with comprehensive programs and two were vocational schools.

Judges: Three educational supervisors who are each familiar with all the 10 youth villages were asked to evaluate the villages and the students' recorded interviews concerning the villages as explained in the following "procedure" section.

Procedure

1. The 10 groups of students from the 10 schools were interviewed in 10 separate interviews which lasted 25 to 40 minutes each. The leading question in the interview was: "It is said that the youth village is the students' second home — sometimes their first home. Can this be said about your school? " During the interviews the students were encouraged to reflect upon their attitudes toward their youth villages.

2. The three judges were asked to study the recorded contents of the interviews. They were then asked to rank the 10 groups from the most to the least supportive group of their youth village. Each of them was asked to allot rank 1 to the most and rank 10 to the least supportive group. The judges were not told in which specific youth villages the 10 groups of interviewees lived.

3. The three judges were afterwards introduced to the six above-described continui indicating the villages' movement from closedness to openness. They were then asked to jointly place each of the 10 villages on a 10 position scale (a to j) as to its place along the six continui. Position a denoted the highest level of "closedness" (highest ideological commitment, status socialization, expressive orientation, etc.), while position j denoted the highest level of "openness" (lowest ideological commitment, role socialization, instrumental enrichment, etc.).

Findings

Table 1:

Judges' Rankings of Students' Supportive Attitude Toward Schools

Youth village	Rank of Judges Ranks	Judges' mean rank	Judges' ranks		
			Judge 1	Judge 2	Judge 3
Agricultural I	1 - 2 (a)	2.0	1	4	1
Agricultural II	1 - 2 (b)	2.0	2	1	3
Preparatory	3	3.0	3	2	4
Agricultural III	4	3.7	6	3	2
Agricultural IV	5	4.7	4	5	5
Agricultural V	6	5.7	5	6	6
Vocational I	7	7.3	7	7	8
Vocational II	8	8.3	8	8	9
Comprehensive I	9	8.7	9	10	7
Comprehensive II	10	9.7	10	9	10

Table 1 shows that the five groups from the five agricultural schools support their schools' regimes — according to the judges — more than the students from the vocational and comprehensive schools. The table also shows considerable agreement between the judges concerning the rankings.

Table 2 shows that the general tendency of the judges was to place the agricultural schools (schools 1-2(a), 1-2(b), 4, 5, and 6) along the right parts of the six continui in relative proximity to the poles denoting "closedness" while the vocational and comprehensive schools (schools 7, 8, 9 and 10) were mostly placed along the left parts of the six continui in relative proximity to the poles denoting "openness".

In sum, (a) the agricultural schools were ranked in the higher positions and the comprehensive and vocational schools in the lower positions of the rank order denoting level of students' support (as assessed by the judges, table 1), (b) the former were evaluated by the judges as relatively "closed" while the latter as relatively "open" schools (table 2). In other words, schools which were considered more "closed" enjoyed higher support, while schools which were considered more "open" enjoyed lower support from students, as assessed by judges.

Table 2:
Continui denoting movement from organizational "closedness" to
"openness" and judges' joint placing of youth villages along
the continui

10(a-j) positions along continui and schools' positions, according to judges, along continui*										organizational continui
j	i	h	g	f	e	d	c	b	a	
7								1-2(a)		
8								1-2(b)		from much to little
10	9	3				6	5	4		ideological commitment
			7					1-2(b)	1-2(a)	
			8					3		from status to role
10			9			6		4	5	socialization
								1-2(b)	1-2(a)	
	7							3	5	from expressive to
10	9				8			4	6	instrumental orientation
									1-2(b)	
		7							3	from centralized to de-
	8	9	10	1-2(a)	5			4	6	centralized structure
				1-2(a)						
		6	7	4			1-2(b)			from diffuse to differ-
10	5	8	9	6			3			entiated staff roles
			4							
		9	5					1-2(b)		from organizational to
8		10	7				1-2(a)	3	6	professional frame of
										reference

* Schools are marked by their positions in judges' rankings (rank of judges' ranks)
of students' supportive attitude toward school (Table 1).

Discussion

Inference based on the judgements of three judges has inherent limitations. However, in this study it was decided to infer from few judgements for two reasons.

1. As regards the supportive attitude of students' societies toward their
youth villages, it was felt that, although unstructured interviews do not
lend themselves easily to quantifiable measures, spontaneous and diffuse expressions of support (or lack of it) toward an organization to
which one belongs may provide information which is no less meaningful

than responses to specific questions. Such expressions would require classifications made by expert judges who are familiar with the relevant organizational situations.

2. As for the assessment of the organizational dimensions, it was felt that judges who had been familiar for a considerable period of time with residential education in Israel in general and with all the 10 schools in particular would be able to develop insight into our definitions concerning the six dimensions and use them as differentiating measures of the youth villages.

According to the judges' evaluation there seems to be a relationship between the organizational dimensions and the level of the students' supportive attitude toward their youth villages; the "closed" villages enjoy more students' support than the "open" ones.

In the first years of Israel the youth village largely took the place of the kibbutz youth group of the 1930s and 1940s, and acquired some of its characteristics. The staff members' commitment to the agricultural and pioneering ideology continued to give residential education an elitist character on the pattern of the classic kibbutz youth group. In this situation the pupils tended to identify with those in charge of their education and to internalize their social concepts (Rinott, 1971). In the course of time, the reduced commitment of the staff members to any socially unifying theme led — at least partly — to reduced identification of the pupils with the staff and their social goals.

By its very nature education for settling on the land, which continued to characterize the youth village in the early years of the State, tended to avoid training the pupils in specific skills or for professional diplomas, and stressed "general education", or "education of the person". The status socialization of the "pioneer" or the "settler" entailed a life-style which encompassed every aspect of the pupils' lives — in the classroom, at work and in social activities, was consistent and limited the possibilities of internal conflicts. It seems that, as the residential schools shifted from status socialization to role socialization, namely, training pupils in specific skills, and as commitment to a unifying ideology receded, the pupils tended to resort to alternative, perhaps sometimes antagonistic social frameworks offering compensating cohesion.

The growing importance of preparing the individual for a career, a diploma and a profession limited the pupils' opportunities to engage in expressive activities. The formal status of the houseparents, who are responsible for activities of a tension-relieving nature, declined as their main function in the past, the social and ideological function, had been to some extent pushed aside.

As the staff members' commitment to a unifying social ideology decreases, and with the growing importance of instrumental training for differential roles, the centralized organizational pattern of the setting often tends to be replaced by a decentralized pattern. Hence, the youth village gradually ceases to provide the pupils with a cohesive organization having coordinated expectations. The decentralization of the organization in itself also adds to the need for an alternative or supplementary system based on the peers.

The more the education tends to take on an instrumental character, and the more differentiated its goals become, the greater seems to be the need for staff members with specific specializations. The professional with specific and esoteric specialization tends to restrict his contacts with the pupils to the area in which he is training them, a process which denies the pupils diffuse interaction with significant adults holding status.

The growing role differentiation of some of the staff members, particularly the teachers, is also apparently related to the diminished status of the setting as their occupational frame of reference. The sources of their role norms are outside the youth village, in the disciplines they specialized in, the universities where they studied, the professional associations to which they belong, or hope to belong. With the increased importance of the professional frame of reference for the staff member, his solidarity with the organization seems to decrease. He is no longer a "local" group leader, but a "cosmopolitan" professional who chances to be in a bureaucratic organization.

It seems that the more "open" the youth villages are, the more the pupils tend to feel frustration and lack of identification, leading to the creation of a compensatory and supplementary informal system which rejects the set-up of the unsatisfactory formal system.

This attitude of the pupils may be explained, at least partly, as a reaction to the differences in the structure of the youth villages, resulting from the differential changes that occurred in them.

In those residential schools where there is least commitment on the part of the staff members to an ideology, where the emphasis is on socialization for differential roles and instrumental aims, where the organizational pattern is decentralized, where many of the staff perform differentiated functions and regard their professional affiliation as their central occupational frame of reference — the pupils seem to feel somewhat abandoned by the adults.

The cost of the change expressed in the decline of "closedness" appears, therefore, to be a feeling of being deserted and a reaction of reservation or rejection on the part of the pupils towards the formal organization of the youth village and its staff.

References

Arieli M. The role of disadvantaged pupils in Israeli residential schools. Unpublished Ph.D. Thesis, University of Sussex, 1980.

Arieli M, Kashti Y, Shlasky S. Living at School: Israeli Residential Schools as People-Processing Organizations. Tel Aviv: Ramot, 1983.

Giallombardo R. Society of Women. New York: Wiley, 1966.

Kashti Y. Educational and organizational trends in the youth village. In: Wolins M, Gottesman M, eds, Group Care: An Israeli Approach. New York: Gordon & Breach, 1971.

Kashti Y. Socially disadvantaged youth in residential education in Israel. Unpublished Ph.D. Thesis, University of Sussex, 1974.

Kashti Y. The Socializing Community. Tel Aviv: Tel Aviv University, 1979.

Lambert R, Bullock R, Millham S. The informal social system: an example of the limitations of organizational analysis. In: Brown R, ed, Knowledge, Education and Culture. London: Tavistock, 1973.

Lambert R, Bullock R, Millham S. The Chance of a Lifetime? A Study of Boys and Coeducational Boarding Schools in England and Wales. London: Weidenfeld & Nicholson, 1975.

Millham S, Bullock R, Cherrett P. After Grace — Teeth: A Comparative Study of Residential Experience in Approved Schools. London: Human Context, 1975.

Polsky HW. Cottage Six. New York: Wiley, 1962.

Polsy HW, Claster DS. The Dynamics of Residential Treatment. Chapel Hill: North Carolina University Press, 1968.

Rinott Ch. Dynamics of Youth Aliyah groups. In: Wolins M, Gottesman M, eds, Group Care: An Israeli Approach. New York: Gordon & Breach, 1971.

Smilansky M, Kashti Y, Arieli M. The Residential Education Alternative. East Orange, N.J.: Institute for Humanist Studies, 1982.

Street D, Vinter RD, Perrow C. Organization for Treatment. New York: Free Press, 1966.

Sykes G. Society of Captives. Princeton: Princeton University Press, 1958.

Ward DA, Kassebaum GG. Women's Prison. London: Weidenfeld & Nicholson, 1965.

Wolins M, Gottesman M, eds, Group Care: An Israeli Approach. New York: Gordon & Breach, 1971.

21.

Open Education in Three Societies

Jo-Ann Harrison and Rivkah Glaubman

Moving into the decade of the 1980s, educators have begun to reassess the educational reforms of previous decades in order to draw lessons for the future. One of the notable characteristics of educational reform in the post–World War II period has been the advocacy of seemingly similar educational reforms in a variety of nations. As a result of this phenomenon, we have begun to witness national attempts to draw policy conclusions about certain educational reforms based on the experience of those reforms in other nations. In order to determine whether this strategy is desirable in the future, it seems important to compare the nature, origin, and degree of impact of educational reforms that have been and are being attempted in a number of different nations. An underlying question in this comparison is the relationship of educational reform to its social and cultural context and the consequences of this relationship.

This paper explores this issue in relation to open education, one of the educational reforms characteristic of the post–World War II period in several Western nations. Making sense out of this reform would entail comparing the nature of the open-education reform movement in different societies by exploring its conception, origin, and impact. This study begins such an analysis by comparing the conceptions and origin of open education in three nations—the United States, Great Britain, and Israel. The United States and Great Britain were chosen for study because they have been the spearheads of the open-education movement in the West and represent quite similar cultures. Israel is included in our comparison because it is a developing nation oriented to Western educational ideas, but it represents a clearly different national culture.

Many authorities have assumed that conceptions of open education in the United States, Great Britain, and Israel were quite similar and that these conceptions had common historical roots.[1] Recent evidence suggests that the degree of correspondence among definitions of open education

We wish to thank Vincent Rogers for his helpful comments on this paper. This research was supported by a grant from the Research Authority of Bar-Ilan University, Ramat-Gan, Israel.

[1] See, e.g., Lillian S. Stephens, *The Teacher's Guide to Open Education* (New York: Holt, Rinehart & Winston, 1974); Herbert J. Walberg and Susan Christie Thomas, *Characteristics of Open Education: Toward an Operational Definition* (Newton, Mass.: Educational Development Corp., 1971).

may have been overestimated.[2] Moreover, since there has been little objective study of the origin of these definitions, their common roots may not be assumed.

In the following pages we analyze the conceptions of open education prevalent in the three nations by comparing characteristics included in descriptions and definitions written by advocates and researchers of open education. Our analysis explores the cultural, institutional, and historical forces that appear to have contributed to the origin of these conceptions. Specifically, we test two different hypotheses of their origin. The first hypothesis proposes that the conceptions of this educational reform are the products of a selective adoption process whereby the original definition of open education was developed in British society, diffused to the other societies, and adapted to their institutional conditions. An alternative hypothesis, based on theories of the development of social movements, suggests that the development of conceptions of open education occurred in tandem in each society in response to similar cultural and historical forces.

Method

The method used to compare the definitions of open education in the societies is content analysis of major government reports, evaluation studies, descriptions, and analyses that have appeared in each society from the late 1960s until the late 1970s.[3] This method of research was used so that we could reflect on the ways those involved with the education movement have grappled in depth with the definition of open education. The 38 American and British documents chosen for analysis were mentioned in major reviews of the literature by Horwitz and were most frequently cited by other less comprehensive reviews of the literature.[4] Since there are few published materials on open education in Israel, all relevant written materials were included in our analysis.

The content analysis focused on two major aspects of open education—theoretical underpinnings (assumptions and aims) and characteristics of practices of open schooling. A comprehensive list of features of the theoretical framework and of practices was developed from a first reading of materials. Then a tally was made of those characteristics mentioned by

---

[2] Jo-Ann Harrison, Helen Strauss, and Rivkah Glaubman, *A Formative Evaluation Study of Open Classrooms in Israel* (Jerusalem: Ministry of Education, 1980); Leonard Sealey, *Open Education: A Study of Selected American Elementary Schools* (New Haven, Conn.: Edward Hazen Foundation and Ester A. & Joseph Klingenstein Fund, 1977).

[3] Documents included in the content analysis are available from the authors.

[4] Robert A. Horwitz, *Psychological Effects of Open Classroom Teaching on Primary School Children: A Review of the Research* (Grand Forks, N.D.: Study Group on Evaluation, 1976); Robert A. Horwitz, "The Psychological Effects of the Open Classroom," *Review of Educational Research* 49 (1979): 71–86; Kathleen Duvaney, *Developing Open Education in America* (Washington, D.C.: National Association for the Education of Young Children, 1974).

each report or document. In addition, we attempted to note those characteristics stressed by each document by noting the use of such adjectives as "major," "critical," "at the heart," or "most important." However, the latter comparison was not fully achieved because of the variability in the use of such adjectives by these documents. Some authors simply presented lists of most important features,[5] whereas others elaborated on certain features and not on others.[6] Consequently, the number of documents simply mentioning each feature in each society is used as the main summary statistic for our analysis. In our comparison of documents we found that some authors tend to specialize in definitions of either practices or theoretical underpinnings. Therefore, percentages were calculated separately for definitions of theoretical underpinnings and for practices of open education.

Three methods were used to analyze the origin of definitions of open education in these nations. First, the 51 documents from the three societies were analyzed to determine the acknowledged origin of definitions presented. Second, studies describing the development of open education in each society were reviewed. Third, since few Israeli sources described the development of conceptions of open education or of the open-education movement, 18 educators who are recognized as authorities on open education were interviewed about the origin of their definitions of open education and the history of the development of open education in Israel.

The final step in our procedure was checking our findings about definitions and their origin against our own personal involvement with the open-education movement in the United States and Israel and against the personal experience of other authorities acquainted with developments in more than one of the nations under discussion.

Similarities and Differences in National Definitions

Many authors contend that open education is more a set of shared attitudes than a set of shared practices.[7] The results of our content analysis of the theoretical underpinnings of definitions of open education in table 1 reveal that educators in all three nations do have common attitudes about

---

[5] See, e.g., Ruth Flurry, "Open Education: What Is It?" in *Open Education: A Sourcebook*, ed., Ewald Nyquist (New York: Bantam, 1970); Lillian G. Katz, "Research on Open Education: Problems and Issues," in *Current Research and Perspectives in Open Education*, ed. D. Dwain Hearn, Joel Burden, and Lillian Katz (Washington, D.C.: American Association of Elementary Kindergarten, Nursery Educators, 1973); Vermont State Department of Education, "Vermont Design for Education," in *Open Education: A Sourcebook*, ed. Ewald Nyquist (New York: Bantam, 1970).

[6] See, e.g., Richard M. Brandt, "An Observation Portrait of a British Infant School," in *Studies in Open Education*, ed. Herbert Walberg and Bernard Spodek (New York: Agathon, 1975); Ann Cook and Herb Mack, "The Head Teacher's Role," in *Informal Schools in Britain Today*, vol. 3 (New York: Citation, 1972).

[7] See, e.g., Anne M. Bussis and Edward A. Chittenden, *Analysis of an Approach to Open Education* (Princeton, N.J.: Educational Testing Service, 1970); Roland S. Barth, *Open Education and the American School* (New York: Schocken, 1974).

TABLE 1
DEFINITION OF ASSUMPTIONS AND AIMS OF OPEN EDUCATION
IN THE UNITED STATES, GREAT BRITAIN, AND ISRAEL

	United States		Britain		Israel	
	N	%	N	%	N	%
Aims:						
Develop whole child	6	43	9	47	8	67
Develop competence	1	7	0	0	6	50
Expand individual differences	2	14	3	16	0	0
Develop originality	1	7	7	37	0	0
Develop self-awareness	2	14	4	21	0	0
Develop responsibility	5	36	1	5	4	33
Develop thinking	3	21	5	26	5	42
Develop flexibility	2	14	2	11	3	25
Develop capacities for learning	5	36	6	32	7	58
Develop self-expression	2	14	3	16	1	8
Develop a set of values	1	7	1	5	1	8
Encourage child to produce, create	0	0	7	37	6	50
Develop compassion	0	0	1	5	2	17
Assumptions:						
Diminish distinction between work and play	2	14	4	21	4	33
Children are innately curious	5	36	2	11	5	42
Children learn through active interaction with their environment	9	64	8	42	11	92
Child can make decisions about own learning	9	64	7	37	8	67
Development proceeds through stages	3	21	3	16	2	17
Development is diverse, individual	7	50	7	37	8	67
Evaluation best done by observation	3	21	0	0	2	17
Knowledge is the result of personal integration	4	29	4	21	4	33
Education is both child centered and teacher centered	10	71	6	32	7	42
Emphasis in school should be on learning not teaching	8	57	7	37	7	42
Child learns at his own rate	4	29	7	37	10	83
An intrinsically motivated child learns best	9	50	8	42	4	33

NOTE.—Total N's: United States = 14, Britain = 19, Israel = 12.

children, development, and learning, but they differ in their attitudes about the aims of education. The relative emphasis given the 12 assumptions that appear in the literature corresponds closely in the documents. The majority of sources in all nations emphasize five assumptions in their definitions of open education: (1) children learn through active interaction with their environment, (2) children can made decisions about their own learning, (3) development is diverse and individual, (4) the emphasis in school should be on learning not teaching, and (5) education is both child centered and teacher centered. These assumptions are consistently mentioned less frequently in definitions in the three societies: (1) knowledge is a result of personal integration, (2) distinction between work and play should be diminished, and (3) evaluation is best done by observation.

The extent of discussion of the aims of open education varies among the three nations. American documents deal much less frequently than British or Israeli sources with the aims of open education. Moreover, little correspondence is found in definitions of these aims among documents of the three nations. The only aims of education that most documents in all nations propound is the development of the whole child. Even though both British and American sources mention it less frequently than Israeli sources do, a second aim of developing capacities for learning seems to be of some concern in all three societies.

To study more accurately the nature of the different national emphases, we divided the set of aims into three categories—socializing aims, individualistic aims, and intellectual aims. Figure 1 presents the differing national profiles that emerge from this analysis. American, British, and Israeli advocates of open education show somewhat different orientations to the functions of open schooling in their societies. American and British documents emphasize aims of individuality more than Israeli sources do, while Israeli authorities place a much greater emphasis on socializing aims. For example, the Vermont State Education Department proposes, "The school's function is to expand the differences between individuals and create a respect for these differences,"[8] whereas Israelis emphasize the school's role in "developing understanding of social processes and developing social behavior that is appropriate to different situations . . . such that the discipline of the group is an educational means for developing different social values."[9] British and Israeli sources mention intellectual aims more frequently than their American counterparts. However, the focuses of British and Israeli intellectual aims are quite different. The former stress original thinking, whereas the latter stress analytic thinking. For instance, Sir Alex Clegg expresses a typical British interpretation: "A child should express his own ideas rather than his teacher's and he should express them in his own rather than his teacher's way."[10] In contrast, a prominent Israeli position is that one of the goals of open education is "cognitive development and the development of concepts and basic relationships instead of the transmission of knowledge as facts. . . . This is the way to develop thinking."[11]

Content analysis of definitions of the practices of open schooling explored 28 characteristics of open-education practice in seven aspects of

[8] Vermont Department of Education (n. 5 above), p. 57.

[9] Nisan Shenin, "Work and Activity in Education: Its Meaning for a New Model of Teacher Training," *Anthology of the Yellin Teacher Seminary* (Jerusalem: David Yellin Teachers Seminary, 1970), p. 14.

[10] Sir Alex Clegg, "Revolution in the British Primary Schools," in *The Open Classroom Reader*, ed. Charles E. Silberman (New York: Vantage, 1973), p. 82.

[11] Mazal Caspi, "Active Learning: Characteristics and Approaches for the School," *B'Chinuch Hayisodi* 17 (1976): 65.

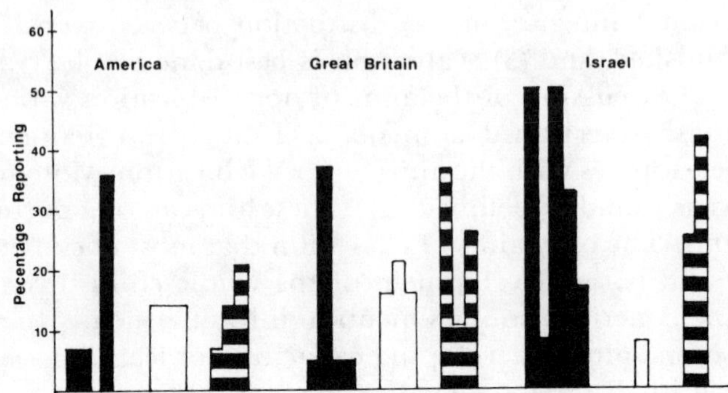

F IG. 1.—National profiles of educational aims. Solid bars = socializing aims (competence, values, production, responsibility, and compassion); open bars = individualistic aims (individual differences, self-awareness, and self-expression); striped bars = intellectual aims (originality, flexibility, and thinking).

school life: authority relations, interpersonal relations, curriculum organization, instructional methods, evaluation methods, organizing and provisioning, and supportive factors. A summary of the content analysis in table 2 shows some systematic similarities and differences among the national definitions of open-education practices.

The most apparent similarities are found in some characteristics of the three most mentioned areas of school life—namely, authority relations, instructional methods, and the organization and provisioning of the school. The majority of American, British, and Israeli documents include in their definitions the participation of students in decisions about their own learning, the use of individual and small group work as primary instructional modes, the provision of a wide variety of stimulating learning materials, and flexible use of physical space in and outside the school for learning.

However, American, British, and Israeli sources differ in their emphases on other characteristics of these areas of school life. British documents mention low teacher control, the use of discovery techniques in instruction, and flexible scheduling more than American or Israeli sources. The Plowden report states: "Children's interest varies in length according to personality, age and circumstances; it's folly either to interrupt it when it is intense or flog it when it has declined. . . . The school sets out deliberately to devise the right environment for children, to allow them to be themselves and to develop in the way and at the pace appropriate to them. . . . It lays special stress on individual discovery, on first hand experiences. . . . The visitor . . . would hear few commands and few raised voices. Children would be asked to do things more than they were told."[12]

____

[12] Central Advisory Council for Education, *Children and Their Primary Schools*, vol. 1, *The Report* (London: HMSO, 1967), par. 493–97, 501–7.

TABLE 2
DEFINITIONS OF OPEN-EDUCATION PRACTICES
IN THE UNITED STATES, GREAT BRITAIN, AND ISRAEL

Variable and Characteristic	United States		Britain		Israel	
	N	%	N	%	N	%
Authority relations:						
Student participation in decisions	14	82	12	57	6	50
Low teacher control and discipline	6	35	12	57	3	25
Interpersonal relations:						
Teacher-pupil respect, warmth	9	53	10	48	6	50
Cooperation between pupils	4	24	3	14	10	83
Cooperation among teachers	1	6	3	14	5	42
Curriculum organization:						
Informal process	5	29	6	29	3	25
Integration of subjects	6	35	13	62	5	42
Emphasis on creativity	6	35	7	33	6	50
Flexible	7	41	8	38	5	42
Instruction:						
Adapted to learning styles	4	24	5	24	4	33
Individual, small group	11	65	11	52	10	83
Informal methods	11	65	6	29	6	50
Discovery methods	2	12	10	48	4	33
Learning by doing	6	35	8	38	7	58
Free play	2	12	4	19	9	75
Evaluation:						
Emphasis on diagnosis	6	35	2	10	9	75
Student self-evaluation	2	12	0	0	6	50
Use of informal techniques	6	35	2	10	2	17
Individualized	4	24	2	10	3	25
Little grading	2	12	4	19	1	8
Organization provisioning:						
Flexible schedule	7	41	13	62	6	50
Rich varied materials	10	59	10	48	9	75
Varied human encounters	9	53	8	29	3	25
Use of space in and out of school for learning	17	65	10	48	8	67
Supportive factors:						
Supportive principal	0	0	1	5	1	8
Matched organizational structure	1	6	3	14	1	8
Provision of in-service education	4	24	4	19	1	8
Community involvement	4	24	0	0	0	0

NOTE.—Total N's: United States = 17, Britain = 21, Israel = 12.

American reports include informal guidance and extension of learning and provision of varied human encounters more than British or Israeli materials. As Barth puts it, "Implicit in all the activities of the adult in the classroom . . . is a role as ad hoc responder. . . . A teacher of young children is in a sense a travel agent. He helps a child go where the child wants to go. He counsels on the best way of getting there." In addition, "children must receive frequent and accurate responses from the personal as from the physical world; in order to learn they must be provided with the interpersonal consequences of their actions as well as the physical consequences."[13]

[13] Barth (n. 7 above), pp. 65, 107.

Israelis emphasize learning by doing and the incorporation of free play in instructional methods more than their British and American counterparts. For instance, Gidion Levine maintains, "Experimentation, learning by doing, activities, are the force of development. . . . The child who plays with blocks, and in the different corners . . . [is] going out on an adventure of problem-solving. . . . This is the process of simultaneous learning and playing."[14]

More divergence among the three nations is found in conceptions of interpersonal relations, curriculum organization, and evaluation procedures and methods.

Although some observers of the American scene have noted more American emphasis on affective elements in open education,[15] Israelis express a broader conception of affective relationships in the open classrooms than either Americans or the British. The majority of sources in all three societies include warm, respectful relationships between student and teacher. Unlike American and British documents, the majority of Israeli sources stress respect and cooperation among pupils and also frequently mention respect and cooperation among teachers.

Curriculum organization plays a more central role in discussions of open-education practice in British sources than in either Israeli or American documents. The focal point of this concern is the integration of subjects or disciplines that the British emphasize as the essential principle for organizing the curriculum. "Rigid division of the curriculum into subjects tends to interrupt children's train of thought and of interest. . . . These are among the many reasons why some work, at least, should cut across subject division at all stages of primary school."[16] Although some American and Israeli sources mention integration of subjects, more of them conceive of the curriculum as flexible and adaptable. Walberg and Thomas present a typical expression of this interpretation: "Activities are not prescribed nor constrained by predetermined curricula, but rather arise from children's interests and responses to materials."[17] In addition, Israeli authorities emphasize developing the creative aspects of the curriculum more than British or American sources do.

Evaluation procedures and methods are rarely discussed in British documents, but they are outlined in more detail in some American and Israeli documents. Both American and Israeli sources emphasize diagnosis as an important part of the evaluation system in the open classroom, but they

[14] Gideon Levine, *Activity—the Vigour of Identity* (Oranim: Study Center for Children's Activities, The School of Education of the Kibbutz Movement, 1976), p. 35.

[15] Victor Atkins, "A British View of Open Education in the U.S.," in *Open Education: Critique and Assessment*, eds. Vincent R. Rogers and Bud Church (Washington, D.C.: Association for Supervision and Curriculum Development, 1975); Sealey (n. 2 above).

[16] Central Advisory Council, p. 535.

[17] Walberg and Thomas (n. 1 above).

differ about other possible evaluation methods. The Americans stress the use of informal techniques of evaluation such as observation, whereas Israelis emphasize the incorporation of student self-evaluation in the open classroom. An example of the American orientation appears in Barth's work when he states, "Objective measures of performance may have a negative effect on learning. . . . Evidence of learning is best assessed intuitively by direct observation."[18] In contrast, an Israeli definition sees the importance of "the stepwise development of self-criticism and self-evaluation" as "an aid to students learning."[19]

The topic least mentioned in documents of all nations is the nature of organizational and community support. However, here, too, slight variations can be discerned. Some American sources include community involvement as an important element of open schooling. They advocate, "identifying the interests or capabilities of parents and bringing about their connection to the school or classroom."[20] In contrast, British reports include new models of organizing the school (family grouping, team teaching) more frequently than American reports do.

The pattern of differences among national definitions of the practices of open education seems to correspond to that found in definitions of the theoretical underpinnings of open education. The practices that American, British, and Israeli sources all include in their definitions are those most closely related to assumptions about learning and schooling shared in the three nations. On the other hand, those practices that receive differing degrees of emphasis reflect the marked differences in the nations' aims of education expressed in definitions.

Sources of Similarities and Differences in Definitions

What are the reasons for the conceptual patterns described in the previous pages? The primary hypothesis suggested in a number of sources is that current definitions originated in Great Britain, were disseminated from British sources, and then selectively adopted in both the United States and Israel.[21] As Atkins put it, "What is involved is taking ideas which have deep roots in the soil of one country and attempting to transplant them to a different society."[22] In the process of transplantation, the conception of open education was adapted to the cultural and institutional framework of the adopting society. A second possible hypothesis is that open education

[18] Barth (n. 7 above), p. 41.

[19] Caspi (n. 11 above), p. 47.

[20] Anne M. Bussis, Edward A. Chittenden, and Marianne Amarel, *Beyond the Surface Curriculum* (Boulder, Colo.: Westview, 1976), p. 130.

[21] Atkins; Ronald Podeschi and Dennis Lawrence, "The British, Americans and Open Education: Some Cultural Differences," *Peabody Journal of Education* 53 (1976): 208–15; and Sealey (n. 2 above).

[22] Atkins, p. 19.

developed as an indigenous "norm-oriented" movement in each society in response to similar periods of stress and similar patterns of internal acculturation.[23] Consequently, the cross-national similarities in definitions of open education are attributable to similarities in core values and patterns of acculturation, while differences result from uniqueness of normative systems and institutions.

The main difference between these hypotheses is their explanation of the origin of similarities in definitions of open education in the three societies. Both hypotheses agree that differences in the definitions reflect differences in dominant cultural and institutional patterns among the societies.

In the following pages we will explore the evidence for each of the hypotheses. First, we will attempt to resolve whether similarities in definition are the result of origin from a single source or the result of parallel patterns of evolution. Second, we will examine the ways that national, cultural, and institutional patterns may have shaped definitions of open education.

The Diffusion Hypothesis

In a linear diffusion/adoption process there is usually a sender system or communicator of the innovation and a receiver or adopter system.[24] The period of communication may vary greatly depending on the nature of the innovation and the situation of contact between sender and receiver. If the sender system was indeed the British educational system, the British system should acknowledge itself as the originator and disseminator of the idea, and the receiver systems, American and Israel, should acknowledge receipt of communications from it. To test this hypothesis, British, American, and Israeli literature was analyzed to determine the acknowledged origin of definitions of open education, and 18 Israeli educators who were considered the main disseminators of ideas about open education in Israel were interviewed.

British sources such as the Plowden report or studies by Gardner describe the development of informal education as a syncretistic evolutionary process.[25] Many sources attribute the elements of their definition to American sources as well as British and European psychologists and educators.[26] For instance, Gardner and Cass describe the evolution of present open-education practices to the impact of the Montessori movement, Dewey's

---

[23] The concept of "norm-oriented" movement is developed in Neil J. Smelser, *The Theory of Collective Behavior* (New York: Free Press, 1963).

[24] Ronald G. Havelock, *Planning for Innovation* (Ann Arbor, Mich.: Institute for Social Research, 1971).

[25] Central Advisory Council (n. 12 above); D. E. M. Gardner, *Experiment and Tradition in Primary Schools* (London: Methuen, 1966); D. E. M. Gardner and Joan Cass, *The Role of the Teacher in the Infant and Nursery School* (Oxford: Pergamon, 1965).

[26] John Blackie, *Inside the Primary School* (London: HMSO, 1967); Gardner and Cass.

progressive education movement, and the research and practice of Susan Isaacs.[27] Other British educators attest to the influence of American educators and critics such as John Holt and Herbert Kohl on their notions of open education as well as the accumulation of ideas based on practice in British schools.[28] Thus, British sources do not perceive themselves as the sole originators of open education.

As W. Kenneth Richmond aptly points out, "To be sure, there was no single source" of origin of the "child-centered" movement in Great Britain.[29] W. A. C. Stewart's detailed analysis of the development of the progressive schools of Great Britain substantiates this conclusion by tracing the evolution of post–World War II informal education to the British and international progressive education movements while noting the continual encorporation of American ideas during this process.[30] Armytage's *The American Influence on English Education* also documents the adoption of Deweyan ideas, the child study movement, the project method, and the Dalton plan by members of the English progressive education movement.[31]

Although catalyzed or reassured by British ideas, Americans and Israelis do not necessarily see themselves as adopters of British definitions of open education. Americans base their definitions on indigenous American orientations and sources as well as British sources. These indigenous roots were recognized in the late sixties even as Americans were becoming excited about British informal education. Barth's brief history of the emergence of the open education movement in the sixties traces the theoretical framework of the movement to American pragmatism of Dewey, Pierce, and Mead, the developmental orientations of Getzels, Halprin, Lewin, Bennis, and Rogers, and the curriculum orientations of Hawkins and Morrison.[32] It is primarily in the application of theory to practice that Barth sees the impact of British ideas. Nevertheless, even in the development of the practice of open education in the United States, a unique native component was developing in the sixties. Featherstone noted the work of Lore and Donald Rasmussen in Philadelphia, Herbert Kohl in Harlem, the street academies, and the community schools among those leading the indigenous movement.[33] Other experiments in education that supported the emergence of open education, such as nongrading, the inquiry approach, independent

[27] Gardner and Cass.

[28] Blackie; W. Z. Campbell Stewart, "Progressive Education: Past, Present and Future," *British Journal of Educational Studies* 27 (1979): 103–10.

[29] W. Kennetts Richmond, *Education in Britain since 1944* (London: Methuen, 1978), p. 25.

[30] W. A. C. Stewart, *The Educational Innovators*, vol. 2, *Progressive Schools 1881–1967* (London: Macmillan, 1968).

[31] W. H. Armytage, *The American Influence on English Education* (London: Routledge & Kegan Paul, 1967).

[32] Barth (n. 7 above).

[33] Joseph Featherstone, *Schools Where Children Learn* (New York: Liveright, 1971).

study, and fostering creativity, were already in the wind in the early sixties as Gross and Murphy's anthology, *The Revolution in the Schools*, which was published in 1964, attests.[34]

Of course, many Americans report that their visits to British schools in the sixties and early seventies provided sources of inspiration.[35] However, they also realized and warned others that the roots of American innovation are in America and that transfer of British ideas was inappropriate. British educators were invited to America to help train American teachers in a number of projects. However, as Sealey and others note, this direct intervention and dissemination of British ideas was generally limited in duration and scope.[36] It seems that the vogue for British informal education gave sanction to the work that a minority of Americans had continued since the fifties or developed in the sixties. The inspiration gained from British visitors as well as reports and visits to England catalyzed those already confirmed progressives to fight back against the behaviorists and disciplinists and to reformulate their conception of viable progressive educational practices for the public schools.

The cross-fertilization evident between the United States and Great Britain is less evident between Israel and either of the more developed nations. Most of the Israeli educators interviewed traced the evolution of their ideas to their experiences teaching the new immigrants to Israel during the late fifties and sixties. Approximately one-third were influenced in the development of instructional and organizational practices and authority relations in the classroom by their involvement in the pre-1953 kibbutzim or the workers' movement. As one of these educators put it, "To build a new country we needed to create a new 'Jewish' man who could combine work and learning and living in an egalitarian community. The kibbutz and workers' movement cherished the spirit of childhood but needed to socialize the child into their new reality of communal work." From this dual focus grew the principles of learning by doing, learning from experience, and combining the development of the individual and his or her commitment and responsibility to the collective. Thus Israelis developed their ideas of open education primarily from indigenous sources. In the late sixties after the Six-Day War, contact with American immigrants to Israel and with some British visitors to Israel encouraged more experimentation or trial of open-education practices. During the seventies the Ministry of Education sent a number of inspectors of schools, principals, and teacher trainers who were already committed to open education

---

[34] Ronald Gross and Judith Murphy, *The Revolution in the Schools* (New York: Harcourt, Brace & World, 1964).

[35] See, e.g., Vincent R. Rogers, "An American Reaction," in *Teaching in the British Primary School*, ed. Vincent R. Rogers (New York: Macmillan, 1970); Lillian Weber, *The English Infant School and Informal Education* (Englewood Cliffs, N.J.: Prentice-Hall, 1971).

[36] Sealey (n. 2 above); Atkins (n. 15 above).

and were using practices of open education on visits to England and the United States for further training. Some of these innovators went to the United States or Britain after an initial period of experimentation with open education. These individuals returned to Israel and continued their experimentation. Others journeyed abroad to confirm their opinions or develop evaluative perspectives after a longer period of experimentation.

An innovation is an idea that is defined by adopters as new to their system.[37] Adopters in Israel and America did not perceive British ideas about the integrated day or informal education as innovations because these ideas were at least in part already developed as indigenous innovations. The British exponents of open education also did not perceive themselves as innovators for they were building on past indigenous practices and ideas prevalent in America and Europe.[38] Consequently, our hypothesis that definitions of open education originated from a single source, Great Britain, and were selectively adopted from that source is not substantiated.

Parallel Patterns of Evolution Hypothesis

Smelser proposed that societal strain often activates a movement to restore or modify norms in the name of a generalized belief.[39] Supporting this notion, Levin found that educational reform is probable when a society experiences a conflict between old patterns of socialization and emerging new patterns of work or social relations.[40] If open-education movements in Great Britain, the United States, and Israel fit this notion of norm-reforming movements, their emergence should correspond to a period of internal stress, conflict, and acculturation; and they should be conceived of as movements designed to restore a similar group of core dominant values in society.

Although the development of open education in Great Britain, the United States, and Israel occurred at different times during the past 50 years, these periods were all marked by similar conflicts, social changes, and social problems. All three societies, like other Western democracies, were facing problems in realizing fraternity, liberty, and equality, the triadic values of democratic society, in times of rapid economic, political, and social change.

Britain had made considerable headway toward developing open education between the world wars, but most authorities agree that the problems and changes resulting from the Second World War catalyzed the

---

[37] Everett Rogers and F. F. Shoemaker, *The Communication of Innovations* (New York: Free Press, 1971); Gerald Zaltman, David H. Florio, and Linda A. Sikorski, *Dynamics of Educational Change* (New York: Free Press, 1977).

[38] Blackie (n. 26 above); Gardner (n. 25 above).

[39] Smelser (n. 23 above).

[40] Henry Levin, "A Taxonomy of Educational Reform," in *The Limits of Educational Reform,* ed. Martin Carnoy (New York: McKay, 1976).

growth of the open-education movement and finalized the conceptualization of informal education.[41] Zweig, Halsey, and Klein view the post–
World War II period as a time of great transitions, which placed great
stress on British society.[42] The end of the war meant the end of the British
empire and a reassessment of the British political role in the world. The
destruction of homes and institutions meant rebuilding community and
schools both physically and socially. The war had introduced a new in-
formality in relationships between different segments of the population. In
the economic sphere, new technologies produced a reshaping of economic
institutions, manual labor declined, and bureaucratization increased. Consequently, lower- and middle-class populations were undergoing substantial changes in life-style and status. Among these was an increased emphasis in their own ways on individuality and a questioning of authorities.
Thus, the fifties in Britain were characterized by a striving to create new
orientations based on the foundations of the old.

In the United States, the renaissance of the open-education movement
occurred in the late sixties and early seventies. These turbulent years were
marked by conflicts over deeply rooted social problems of equality and
popular democracy as well as by major social changes. The civil rights
movement and the antiwar movement focused American society on the
fight for social and political justice and equality. The consequences of
these movements in the late sixties were great social and political changes.[43]
The period was also characterized by technological changes, which introduced cybernation and expanded the growth of bureaucracy. Although
many movements emerged in response to these crises and social changes, a
major response focused on the reform of educational institutions.[44] The
open-education movement was closely associated with reformers who were
responding to problems of popular democracy raised by the Vietnam War
and the problem of the bureaucratization of institutional life.

The advocacy of open education in Israel began at the end of the
Six-Day War in the late sixties and was expanded after the Yom Kippur
War. During the late sixties and the seventies, Israel continued to face
periodic stress and conflict as well as social and economic changes. Israel
was moving from an agrarian society to an industrial and service-based

---

[41] See, e.g., Central Advisory Council (n. 12 above); Gardner (n. 25 above).

[42] Ferdynand Zweig, *The New Acquisitive Society* (Chichester: Rose, 1976); A. H. Halsey, *Change in British Society* (Oxford: Oxford University Press, 1978); Josephine Klein, *Samples from English Cultures*, vol. 1. (London: Routledge & Kegan Paul, 1965).

[43] Some of the changes are reported in Jerald G. Bachman and M. Kent Jennings, "The Impact of Vietnam on Trust in Government," *Journal of Social Issues* 31 (1975): 141–55; and David B. Tyack, Michael W. Kirst, and Elizabeth Hansot, "Educational Reform: Retrospect and Prospect," *Teachers College Record* 81, no. 3 (1980): 253–69.

[44] This theme is propounded in many sources. See, e.g., Geoffrey Hodgeson, *America in Our Time* (Garden City, N.Y.: Doubleday, 1976); Tyack et al.; and Robin N. Williams, Jr., *American Society*, 3d ed. (New York: Knopf, 1970).

society. New skills and orientations were required for such a development. The scarcity of the fifties, replaced by prosperity in the sixties, led to the waning of collective pioneering ideologies and the growth of materialism and individualism. These changes provided a new background for the problems facing Israeli society: survival in the face of Arab hostility, integrating the ethnic groups of Israeli society, and addressing the inequalities of society.[45] Following a pattern similar to that of the United States, one important response to the socioeconomic problems focused on the reform of educational institutions. In the early sixties the failure of the Israeli educational system to raise the educational level of the disadvantaged had been revealed.[46] A small number of Israeli educators advocated open education as a response to these challenges.

In all three societies the development of open education was conceived as a response to the pressing social and political problems and changing community and organizational environments. This educational reform reaffirmed three core cultural values—activity, individuality, and popular democracy—but gave some new interpretation to them.

The cultures of Great Britain, the United States, and Israel all emphasize directed and disciplined action in a regular occupation.[47] With the movement to industrial economies based on mechanized rather than manual labor, conceptions of activity and work were reoriented to independent individual activity and teamwork. These new interpretations of activity and work were reflected in the emphasis in open education on learning through active individual interaction with the environment. In addition, in reaction to the increased allocation from work prevalent in these societies, open education advocated the linkage of work to gratifying activity.

Émile Durkheim described Western civilization as having a "cult of the individual personality."[48] All three societies value highly the unique development of each individual as an autonomous agent who is morally responsible. They are averse to the invasion of individual integrity. Open education gave new support to this belief by advocating the development of the whole personality of the child as the primary aim of education and by focusing school practice on the individual child.

All three societies value a participative civic culture.[49] Open education in these societies proposed the development of a participative civic culture in the school as preparation for active democratic citizenship in the future.

---

[45] S. N. Eisenstadt, "Israeli Identity: Problems in the Development of the Collective Identity of an Ideological Society" and "Traditional and Modern Social Values and Economic Development," both in *Integration and Development in Israel*, ed. S. N. Eisenstadt, Rivkah Bar Yosef, and Chaim Adler (New York: Praeger, 1970).

[46] Avima Lombard, "Early Schooling In Israel," in *Early Schooling in England and Israel*, ed. Norma D. Fishbein, John I. Goodlad, and Avim Lombard (New York: McGraw-Hill, 1973).

[47] Eisenstadt, "Traditional and Modern Social Values"; Halsey; Williams.

[48] Quoted in Williams, p. 495.

[49] Gabriel Almond and Sidney Verba, *The Civic Culture* (Boston: Little, Brown, 1965).

This analysis supports the second explanation for current definitions of open education. Similar preconditions existed in each society for the emergence of a norm-oriented educational movement. These movements crystallized around similar core beliefs and attempted to restore and modify norms emanating from them. The cross-national contacts served to enhance or catalyze these national movements rather than inform them.

Sources of Definitional Divergence

Both the diffusion and evaluation hypotheses concur that the divergence of definitions of open education probably stems from the relative differences of cultural attitudes and institutions among the three nations. A number of sources give support to this notion, but few have analyzed both the relevant attitudes and institutions. Podeschi and Lawrence, as well as Atkins, propose that differences between the United States and Great Britain in attitudes toward work, privacy, fair play, authority, innovations, and freedom are reflected in differences in conceptualizations of open education in the two societies.[50] Rogers, Atkins, and Sealey attribute cross-national differences in open education to differences in the structure and culture of educational institutions.[51]

In the subsequent analysis, we discuss the relation of five cultural attitudes, attitudes toward authority, individuality, work and time, school-community relations, and holistic as opposed to segmented perspectives—to specific differences in definitions of open education. In addition, we examine the influence of the degree of bureaucratization and centralization of educational institutions on definitional divergences.

Differences in cultural attitudes.—The relative differences in the participative civic cultures of Great Britain, the United States, and Israel may be traced to differences in atittudes to authority and freedom.[52] Great Britain, the United States, and Israel vary in their relative acceptance of authority. The British maintain strong deference for independent authority, whereas the thrust of American tradition is to subject all government institutions to popular control and to distrust central authority.[53] In addition, Americans stress "inalienable rights" as unalterable by majority rule.[54] Israeli civic culture might be arrayed midway between that of Great Britain and America. It is strongly participative and allows great criticism of government institutions,[55] but at the same time large segments of the population value deference to religious and familial authorities.[56]

---

[50] Podeschi and Lawrence (n. 21 above); Atkins (n. 15 above).

[51] Rogers (n. 35 above); Atkins (n. 15 above); Sealey (n. 2 above).

[52] Almond and Verba; Atkins (n. 15 above).

[53] Almond and Verba.

[54] Williams (n. 44 above).

[55] Rita J. Simon and David Barnum, "Public Support for Civil Liberties in Israel and the United States," *Research in Law and Sociology* 1 (1968): 81–100.

[56] Eisenstadt, "Traditional and Modern Values" (n. 45 above).

These attitudinal differences find expression in the relative differences of conceptions of authority relations in definitions of open education in the three societies. Much more than British or Israeli definitions, American sources focus on the process of decision making as the central feature of authority relations in the open classroom. Moreover, Americans are in greatest consensus about the practice of student participation in decision making. In contrast, some British sources view authority relations of the open classroom as characterized primarily by less direct exercise of control by the teacher rather than by a form of more popular democracy.

Differences among Great Britain, America, and Israel can be found both in the weight given the value of individuality and in the meanings attached to it. America and Great Britain are more highly individualistic societies than Israel. Self-determination and self-development of the individual are more highly valued in both English-speaking countries than in Israel, where collective and national purposes are more emphasized. The meanings attached to individualism in Great Britain, America, and Israel also differ. Often in Britain individuality is associated with originality and intellectual elitism.[57] However, this is tempered with respect for the individual rights of others as expressed in subsidiary norms such as privacy.[58] In America of the sixties and seventies, individualism was a mass phenomenon with emphasis on individual self-expression and individual rights to the indifference of the rights of others, that is, a growth of egocentrism.[59] In Israel individuality is still associated with independence and self-reliance.[60] These differences are reflected in differing definitions of the aims of education and differing emphases on characteristics of interpersonal relations, instructional methods, and evaluation methods. British sources emphasize more than American or Israeli sources the development of originality, self-awareness, and self-expression. In addition, they conceive of curriculum organization not simply as flexible and adapted to the individual interest but also as emphasizing more intellectual strivings. This orientation is reinforced by an encouragement of learning through discovery. The practices of open education stressed by American sources are a flexible curriculum and informal methods of instruction adapted to individual interests. In contrast, Israelis stress aims of competence and production rather than self-expression. The methods of learning by doing, free play, and self-evaluation, which are mentioned more by Israelis, are seen by them as ways to achieve these aims.

[57] John White, "Conceptions of Individuality," *British Journal of Education* 28 (1980): 173–86.
[58] Podeschi and Lawrence (n. 21 above).
[59] Nathan Glazer, "Individualism and Equality in the United States," in *On the Making of America*, ed. Herbert J. Gans, Nathan Glazer, Joseph B. Gusfield, and Christopher Jencks (Philadelphia: University of Pennsylvania Press, 1979).
[60] Eisenstadt, "Traditional and Modern Values" (n. 45 above).

British, Americans, and Israelis also have somewhat different conceptions of the use of time and the meaning of work. Differences center on the stress of an instrumental relationship to work as opposed to an expressive one. The British will work long hours for the instrumental reasons of monetary return, whereas Americans—and especially Israelis—will not.[61] Yet Americans continue to express a concern for high productivity. Their propensity to account for time and work is a reaction to this ambivalence.[62] In Israeli society, tension exists between socialist and European attitudes toward work and attitudes that emerge out of the Jewish tradition. The former value productivity and efficient use of time, whereas the latter view productivity and efficiency as lesser ends compared with more familial and spiritual values.[63] Nevertheless, as a developing nation, Israel recognizes productivity as an essential national goal.

These differences may relate to the emphasis given the aim of encouraging children to be productive and the practices of flexible scheduling and of evaluation in national definitions. Although the British emphasize encouraging production, they deemphasize evaluation and stress flexible time scheduling. The Americans rarely mention encouraging production, but they are concerned that there be a clear system of evaluation. The Israelis stress both productivity and evaluation procedures.

America, Great Britain, and Israel differ in their attitudes toward school-community relations. This is reflected in the role that pressure groups outside the school play in formulating educational policy. In Britain and Israel such pressure groups play much less of a role than in the United States.[64] Although parents may have a voice in curriculum planning in both Britain and Israel, they rarely exercise their power, whereas community control of the schools was a watchword of the seventies in America.[65] These differences are reflected in conceptions of supportive factors in definitions of the practices of open education. American documents include parental involvement in open schooling more frequently than British or Israeli documents do.

The last cultural difference that influences conceptions of open education in the three societies is their emphasis on holistic or segmented orientations.[66] British, Israeli, and American perspectives might be arrayed along a continuum from more holistic to more segmented. Atkins suggests

---

[61] Zweig (n. 42 above). Support for this point may be found in Eisenstadt, "Traditional and Modern Values" (n. 45 above), and Williams (n. 44 above).

[62] Podeschi and Lawrence (n. 21 above).

[63] Eisenstadt, "Traditional and Modern Values" (n. 45 above).

[64] Maurice Kogan, *The Governance of Education* (New York: Citation Press, 1971); Tyack, Kirst and Hansot (n. 43 above); Williams (n. 44 above).

[65] Joseph S. Bentwich, *Education in Israel* (Philadelphia: Jewish Publication Society, 1965); Kogan; Marilyn Gittell, Mario Fantini, and Richard Magat, *Community Control and the Urban School* (New York: Praeger, 1970).

[66] Atkins (n. 15 above).

that these differences may result from the interplay of church and state in the different societies.[67] An alternative explanation is the development of different philosophic and scientific traditions in the different societies. Behaviorism, which proposes a segmented approach to scientific analysis, has dominated American and, to a lesser extent, Israeli thought since the end of the Second World War.[68] British thought has been less dominated by this tradition. Conceptions of curriculum in open education are clearly influenced by these trends. A considerably more unified or integrated approach to curriculum is stressed in Britain than in America or Israel.

Differences in educational institutions.—Differences in the structure of educational institutions of Great Britain, America, and Israel have also influenced aspects of the definition of open education in the three societies. Once a given institutional form exists, it may exert an influence on future educational change by constraining or facilitating certain forms of change. The interplay of four structural characteristics of educational systems of Great Britain, the United States, and Israel—the degree of centralization, the power of the teaching profession, the nature of selection processes, and the degree of bureaucratization—contributed to the emergence of different ideological emphases in the open-education reform movements.

Archer provides an insightful analysis of how these structural characteristics shape educational change.[69] According to Archer, in a highly centralized system, change must come about through the political center. It will be confined to measures that do not challenge unification and will be applied uniformly. In contrast, in a decentralized system, change will be more varied and flexible, and it may be initiated on the local as well as national level. The diversity and flexibility encouraged by a decentralized system may be enhanced or restricted by the nature of selection processes or the degree of bureaucratization in the system. If early selection is instituted and/or a highly differentiated bureaucracy exists, then the diversification encouraged by decentralization will be counteracted by a strain toward uniformity. On the other hand, late selection and/or a flexible bureaucratic structure will facilitate more diversity. In addition, the relative political power of the teaching profession in the power structure of the education system will influence the types of changes that emerge in the system. When the teaching profession is powerful, changes allowing more teacher self-determination are more likely to develop.

Of the three nations under study, Israel has the most highly centralized education system. Its strain toward uniformity is generally reinforced by a relatively early selection process and highly bureaucratized institutions.[70]

[67] Ibid.

[68] Tyack et al. (n. 43 above).

[69] Margaret Scotford Archer, *The Social Origin of Educational Systems* (London: Sage, 1979).

[70] Aharon F. Kleinberger, *Society, Schools and Progress in Israel* (Oxford: Pergamon, 1969).

Therefore, it is not surprising that the advocates of open education stressed socializing rather than individualizing aims of education and developed an evaluation component in their conceptualization of open education.

In contrast, both the American and British decentralized education systems encourage more diversity and individuality. Significant differences between these two systems are the relative power of the teaching profession and the nature of selection processes. The emergence of the open-education movement in Great Britain occurred simultaneous with the abandonment of early selection by examination and the growth in strength and status of the teaching profession.[71] These changes in educational structure facilitated the advocacy of a reorganized curriculum along integrated lines, flexible time schedules, and self-determination for the teacher. In the United States the open-education movement emerged on the heels of the Sputnik era, which emphasized identifying the talented, regularly assessing achievements through psychometric testing processes, and eliminating the teacher's role in curriculum planning. Although the open-education movement was rebelling against these characteristics of the education system, its advocacy of their reform was shaped by their very existence. Thus we find authority relations defined more in terms of student participation in decision making than in terms of an emphasis on indirect authority of the teacher, as well as an advocacy of a flexible curriculum rather than one organized totally along integrated lines.

Conclusion

This paper analyzed the definitions of open education that have become prevalent in the education literature of the United States, Great Britain, and Israel over the past decade and a half. A content analysis of 51 documents found strong commonalities among definitions of the assumptions of open education but marked differences in the definitions of aims and practices of open education among the three nations.

The majority of sources from America, Great Britain, and Israel included in their definitions similar assumptions about children, development, and learning, such as (1) children learn through active interaction with their environment, (2) children can make decisions about their own learning, (3) development is diverse and individual, and (4) education is both child centered and teacher centered. They also concurred in the inclusion of the general aim of developing the whole child and such practices as student participation in decision making, mutual warmth and respect between teacher and pupil, individual and small-group instruction, and providing a rich and stimulating environment for learning.

---

[71] A good description of the structural forces influencing the emergence of informal education in Great Britain appears in Archer.

American, British, and Israeli definitions differed in their emphases on aims of socialization, individuality, and intellectuality. American authorities tended to balance these goals. British educators placed greater stress on intellectuality and individuality. Israeli educators emphasized aims of socialization and intellectuality more than individuality. Americans, British, and Israeli educators differed as well in their inclusion of such practices as integration of the disciplines, flexible scheduling, and evaluation procedures in their definitions of the practices of open education.

This analysis focused on the written literature about open education. It would be of interest to compare teachers' conceptions of open education in the three societies under study. Since teachers have to adapt ideas to the real world of institutions, we would expect their conceptions to differ to a certain extent from those in the literature. However, we would also expect to find parallel differences among American, British, and Israeli teachers to those we found in the literature. In fact, we would hypothesize that these differences would be more pronounced because of the stronger influence of national cultural attitudes and institutional forces on a sector of the population with fewer international contacts.

Two explanations of the origin of these conceptual patterns were examined in this study. The first hypothesis proposed that current conceptions of open education originated in Great Britain and were diffused to other nations, where they were adapted to national cultures. The second hypothesis theorized that current definitions are the products of similar norm-oriented movements that evolved indigenously in each society in response to similar periods of strain and cultural acculturation. Thus, according to the first hypothesis, similarities in definitions could be explained by their common origin; according to the second hypothesis, they could be explained by their germination from similar core beliefs. Our analysis supports the latter hypothesis. Similarities are the result of parallel patterns of development and common value orientations rather than the adoption of British ideas. Differences in the definitions were traced to relatively different cultural attitudes toward authority, work, individuality, school-community relations, and perspectives, as well as differences in the structure of national educational institutions.

In analyzing the conceptualizations of open education in America, Great Britain, and Israel and their origins, this paper attempted to address the general theoretical question of the nature and origin of seemingly similar educational reforms that have emerged in different nations and the more specific question of the nature of the relationship of these educational reforms to their social and cultural context. The open-education reform movements seem to represent an example of basically autonomously generated reforms. Their similarities stem from their emergence as reaffirmations of similar core values against the background of similar cultural drifts and analogous breakdowns or changes in the social order. Their differences emerge from the adaptation of each reform movement to the unique fabric of the culture and institutions of each nation. Definitions of open education in the three societies—the ideologies of the movements—reflect a dual process of reaction and adaptation in the interaction of the movements with their societal context. It also seems that parallel, autonomously generated reforms draw on cross-national contacts with similar reform movements to facilitate the development of the reform movement, especially when the similar reform is viewed as successful. The recently developed resource mobilization approach to social movements provides a framework for understanding the nature of this catalyzation process. According to this approach, every movement needs to mobilize both tangible and intangible resources to sustain its development and impact.[72] In the case of the open-education movements, the British movement provided the American movement and, to a lesser extent, the Israeli movement with intangible resources of expertise and evidence of the workability and desirability of the reform being advocated. Thus it helped them gain support.

The policy implications of these findings seem quite clear. First, the yardsticks applied to evaluation of the implementation of open schooling in different societies need to be reexamined carefully to see that appropriate, culturally relevant criteria are being used. Second, caution should be exercised in drawing conclusions about the successes or failures of the open-education movement (or any other educational movement) in one country and applying them to another.

---

[72] The resource mobilization approach is developed in several articles in Mayer W. Zald and John D. McCarthy's anthology, *The Dynamics of Social Movements* (Cambridge, Mass.: Winthrop, 1979).

22.

Will You Sign My Autograph Book?
Using Autograph Books For a Sociohistorical Study of Youth and Social Frameworks

Hanna Herzog and Rina Shapira

ABSTRACT: This paper suggest that autograph books can be used as a tool for the study of attitudes among youth. Content analysis of 4,131 entries of 130 Israeli autograph books, written by 12-14 year-old students, during a 55 year period (1925-1980) was conducted. The analysis reveals two major changes: first, a diminishing of collective orientation coupled with an increase in individualism; second, an increase in the salience of schools and teachers coupled with a persistence in the significance of youth movements. Schooling ideology mainly serves the interests of the dominant groups, individualism raises the question of the legitimacy of the role of the state, while the youth movement ideology combines commitment to basic values of the collective with self-confidence and desire for individual careers. The findings are interpreted both in terms of normative changes in Israeli society (from quasi-socialism to advanced capitalism) and in terms of Habermas' theory of a "crisis of legitimation." The analysis also reveals a dialectic situation in which contradictory norms and values exist together.

The study of attitudes in historical perspective raises methological problems. Interviews of people with regard to the attitudes they once had are subject to distortion. When questionnaires are used, the very questioning may influence the respondent to give answers that the researcher hypothesized. These problems can be overcome by the locating of authentic material not created for the purpose of study (cf. Aires 1962, Boerdam and Warna 1980). Autograph books are such a source and can be used to examine changes in youth attitudes over time.

Young people write rhymes and sayings for one another in autograph books at the end of the school year, at graduation, or when a classmate moves away. Autograph books are written during periods of transition when people seek ways to create continuity and a sense of belonging (Turner 1969, Albert and Kessler 1976). Students write and keep these albums to remember friends and school experiences (cf.

We wish to thank S. N. Eisenstadt, W. Gamson, W. Shaffir, and the anonymous readers for valuable comments. The editors helpful editorial work is also acknowledged. Address correspondence to the authors at: Tel Aviv University, Tel Aviv, Israel.

Stern 1973: 232). Their Hebrew name—Memories Books (Sifrei Zichronot)—indicates their manifest function. Adults tend to refer to these albums as children's amusements of no significance since the writing seems ritualistic and uniform. We maintain, on the other hand, that the entry has social meaning for the parties involved—the writer and the owner of the book—and that, moreover, these books express the culture, attitudes, and social characteristics of the writers' cohort.

Although basically standardized, the set entries appear in different versions in different books, for when an item goes from person to person, it changes. Each individual uses it and makes it her or his own, consciously or not, by putting the stamp of her or his personal expression upon it (cf. Stern 1973, Dundes and Pagter 1975, Shapira and Herzog 1984). The entries reveal adolescents' attitudes toward society. The books are both a rich data source and a good tool for historical comparison since the custom of writing in and saving these books has persisted for decades (Potter 1949, Stern 1973).

The Research Design

We studied 130 Israeli autograph books, containing a total of 4,131 entries. All the books were acquired from individuals who heard that we were investigating the subject or who responded to a request in a daily newspaper (*Maariv*, 15 May 1980). It is therefore not a systematic sample of a particular population. The majority of the books we investigated belonged to girls. We do not know whether this means that more girls have autograph books and ask their friends to write in them, or that girls are simply more likely to save keepsakes of this kind or respond to requests for research materials. Both boys and girls wrote the entries in the books.

The albums studied were written by 12 to 14-year-old pupils in the years 1925-1980. The decision to study albums of these young adolescents reflects the age of the writers of most of the books received, and perhaps the most common age for writing autograph books. Limiting our data to this age group served to control the age variable. As mentioned earlier, books are traditionally exchanged on the eve of separation from a place or from friends. In Israel, elementary school graduation used to take place at the end of the eighth grade (age 14), and, since the institution of junior high schools, now takes place at the end of the sixth grade (age 12). Elementary school graduation is a very meaningful event in the adolescent's life, and represents a transitional situation.

In addition, we examined several teachers' autograph books which were signed by their students. Our analysis relied on a simple content analysis method. We coded and counted all the ideas presented in the inscriptions and compared the percentage of each theme. Our coding categories were formulated after we examined all the material we acquired. We had two major groups of categories, one concerning attitudes toward time (cf. Shapira and Herzog 1984) and the other, to social frameworks and values. For purposes of historical analysis, each ten-year period was treated as a unit and comparisons were made among the total entries of each period.

Since we do not have data about the writers or owners of the books we refer only to the age-group and not to sex, social class, ethnic and religious background or place of residence.

Findings—Changes of Social Frameworks in the Adolescent's Life

It is widely accepted that in the process of socialization the individual constructs a self-image by referring to significant others, social values, social groups and social frameworks. Inscriptions in the autograph books refer to significant others such as friends, parents, and teachers and military commanders and social groups such as the nation, the state and the human race. They also refer to values such as the use of the Hebrew language, mutual aid, cooperation, equality, personal success and others. More interesting, however, are the changes that took place over time. The most notable change is the sharp decline in national references and in references to the wider collective such as the homeland. In contrast, there is an increase in the references to school and learning, and a rising trend in references to youth and friendship.

Before the establishment of the State of Israel in 1948, references to the national collective comprised more than 30 percent of the total references to social frameworks and values. After the establishment of the State, they decreased gradually, so that in the last five years studied, they constitute only 1.6 percent of the references to social frameworks and values. In the 1930's-50's, we find entries such as the following:

> With gun on the shoulder
> And flag in the hand
> In the parade of our country
> Forward, March!

or:

> It's better to live in a hut in one's own country than in a palace somewhere else.

or:

> There are many paths open to you,
> one you must choose
> Love of our beautiful country,
> the land of the Jews.

In sharp contrast to this patriotism, a typical entry in the 1970's is the following:

> Israel is your land all right
> And its colors are blue and white
> But your husband will come from the U.S.A.
> And to New York he'll take you away.

In the 1930's attitudes toward work were expressed thus:

> Remember these words of mine: Not a knight's sword
> But the farmer's plow conquered our land.

or:

> Work is our life
> It keeps us from hunger.

In the 1970's, however, in a fairly large number of entries, we find:

> Work is our life, but that's not for us.

Another example of changing attitudes can be found vis-a-vis the Hebrew language. In the 1920's and 1930's we find demands for loyalty to the use of Hebrew, such as:

> How lovely your sounds, oh language of mine
> And how beautiful are you, my land
> For my ears are filled with your beautiful tones
> And my eyes with your beautiful views.

In 1980, however, we found entries with English expressions or lines from English popular songs when English was not the mother tongue of either the writer or the owner of the autograph book.

In general we found that before the establishment of the State, youth expressed ties with the wider collective in terms of the nation, homeland, state and even political parties. They wrote about loyalty to collective values such as the Hebrew language, work and pioneering, equality, and cooperation. These values and frames of reference almost disappear from the autograph books of recent years, and if they are mentioned at all, it is done cynically. Previous values are negated through parody and humor.

Entries conspicuously avoid reference to ethnic origin. Although ethnic relations have been defined as a social problem in Israel (Smooha 1978), youth do not refer to an ethnic community as a binding social framework. This finding corroborates those of a number of other studies that indicate that ethnic origin is not the dominant identity factor among Israeli school children (Herzog 1985).

By the end of the 1970's the only evidence of values of collective significance are in expressions of hopes for peace, and even those are few. As mentioned, along with the change in attitude toward the wider collective there is an apparent strengthening of the personal-individual dimension, a change expressed in several ways. First, there is increasing emphasis on personal success, in studies, in life, with the opposite sex, and the like. Second, the writing style changes. In contrast to the short slogan-style sayings and sentences of earlier years, the entries, particularly in recent years, have become long prose passages covering more than a single page in the autograph book. These entries deal with an analysis or the recollection of experiences common to the writer and the owner of the book. Prominent are analyses of the character of the book's owner and confessions that are startling, in view of the fact that it is known that the book will be passed around. The writing is extremely personal, even though the writer knows very well that it is not confidential. We interpret this change as the legitimization of the personality of the individual, the open and public treatment of personal problems, and the frank discussion of relations with the other sex. Below are excerpts from entries, each of which covers a number of pages:

> Girl to girl: " . . . I will never forget how we met and how much I liked you from the first moment, and how I asked myself if we were to be friends or rivals. And afterwards, when I saw that not only were you beautiful but also such a good student, I understood that even though we are rivals we would always have a special relationship."

> Another girl writes to her boyfriend: "This entry is written while our friendship is still in force. In memory of the meeting in the 'meeting room', in memory of the moonlit nights and the hands held out to each other, in memory of all the wonderful experiences we had together, in memory of our beautiful friendship which I have enjoyed so much."

The emphasis in these later inscriptions is on the connection of the individual to other individuals, in contrast to the inscriptions in the years of the formation of Israeli society when the direct connection of the individual to the wider collective framework stood out. The changes from references to the wider collective as directly connecting or mediating between the individual and society, to references to ties between separate individuals as part of the collective, can also be seen in the types of reference to past events.

Until the 1960's we find echoes of collective events: World War II, the Holocaust, illegal immigration, the War of Independence, the Sinai Campaign and in 1967 only a single mention of the Six-Day-War. There are also references to the "Ben-Gurion Prize" to encourage large families, and even to a crisis in the Labor Party (1960) which led to split. There were always references to private events, but their proportion increased from the mid-1950's on, until by the 1970's not a trace remained of the events connected with the wider collective. The personal events recalled are many and varied: volunteer work projects, trips, occurrences at school, special encounters, the viewing of a film or television show together, staying overnight together, incidents involving the opposite sex, quarrels, arguments, gossip, and more of the like. The decline of collective values was accompanied by another change—the attitude toward parents. The role of parents as mediators between the individual and society seems to be waning, at least in the extent to which it finds expression in youth culture.

Two specifically youth-oriented collective frameworks—the youth movement and the school—are continuously mentioned. Throughout the entire period, 5 to 8 percent of the entries in autograph books refer to youth movement. The relatively consistent rate of references to youth movements parallels the unchanging percentage of youth who become movement members (Shapira et al. 1979). Youth movements are social frameworks in which young people spend their free time. In Israel they are a combination of scouting and political movements (Shapira and Peleg 1980). The purpose of youth movements is to inculcate national values, political ideals and preparation for involvement in public service. In this way they serve as meaningful agents for the reproduction of the society as exemplified in the following inscription:

> A good boy scout is a good person
> A good person's way is cleared
> By our motto "Be Prepared."

Youth movements also act as elitist socialization agents which meet the need for personal achievement (Ben David 1954, Shapira and Peleg 1980, Danziger and Shapira 1981). The low but stable percentage of references to youth movements found in our data reflects its exclusive and elitist nature.

Schools and Teachers in the Adolescent's World

Israeli researchers believe there has been a decline in the status of teachers in Israeli society (cf. Ben David 1957). Logically, one might expect this trend to be reflected in a less central position of school and teachers in the adolescent's world. Our findings indicate quite the opposite, however, in a process which can be traced as far back as the 1920's. The analysis of autograph books reveals that school has become increasingly central in the youth world, as reflected in references to it, as well as to social situations related to the school. The school has also been found to be a focal point in autograph books from the United States (Stern 1973).

Three findings support this claim.   First, the percentage of entries written by teachers has increased. Figure 1 shows that in the 1920's teachers made fewer than 10 percent of the entries, while in the 1980's they contributed 25 percent. This finding suggests that teachers have become more meaningful to the youth, so that the latter want some momento to remember the former by. The custom of signing autograph books is part of the informal classroom culture. The increasing inclusion of the teacher in this informal component represents the penetration of "formal" standards into the informal social structure of the students. We assume that unless the teachers and what they represent are significant for the adolescent, they would not be asked to write an inscription. This process has developed gradually: it now involves not only the homeroom teachers, but teachers of special subjects, the school nurse, the school secretary, and in some of the books, even the school principal.

Second, the content of the inscriptions refers increasingly to school. In the entries made by teenagers, references to both school and teachers have increased. Figure 1 shows that in the 1920's the references to school and studies represented approximately 5 percent of all the references to social frameworks, while in the 1950's the respective figure reached 25 percent.

An increasing number of youth at this point of departure choose to refer to memories of school, in the style of "Remember the good old days when we sat at the same desk . . . " Third, there is a moderately increasing trend in the number of references to teachers (see Figure 1) in the text of the inscription.[1]

The increased importance of the school as a framework that mediates between the individual and the wider collective should not be

FIGURE I
The School and the Teachers in the Adolescent's World (1925-1980)

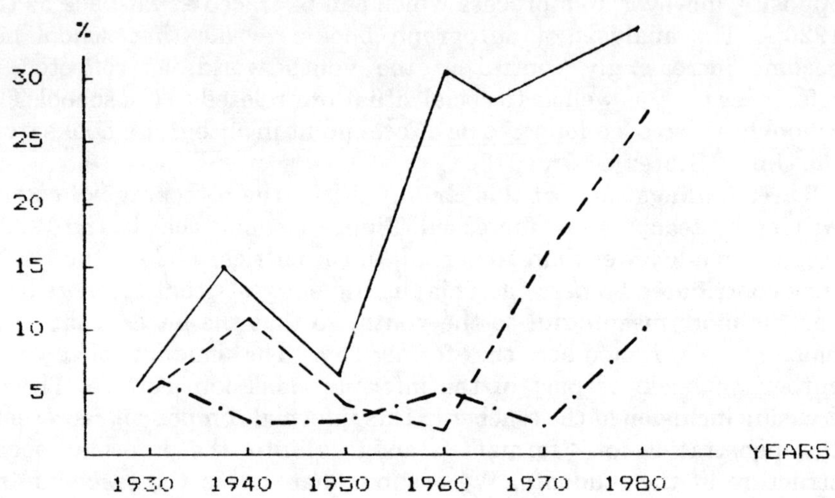

---- Percentage of entries by teachers out of all entries examined.

―――― Percentage of references to the school out of all references to social frameworks.

·—·—·— Percentage of references to teachers out of all adolescents' references to social frameworks and reference figures.

regarded as an indication of the youth's satisfaction or positive evaluation of this framework. Indeed, the entries made by the adolescents suggest ambivalence towards the school. For instance:

> Remember the good old days when you
> sat at your desk and laughed at your dear
> teachers who tried to show you the way.

The school is a source of both fond and unpleasant memories. The school is compared sometimes to oppressive frameworks such as ghettos or prisons. Teachers are remembered not only for their positive features but also for their weaknesses. Moreover, the "good" memories are not always in keeping with the goals of the educational system.

> Remember the days when we drove the teachers crazy,
> When we copied tests,
> And sometimes even got good grades.

The increasing reference to the school and teachers, then, includes an increasing criticism of this framework and its representation.

This critical tone might be interpreted as a reflection of the decline in the status of the teacher (Ben David 1957, Rinot 1981), but we suggest another possibility: The school is the most significant collective framework for youth today (as opposed to the youth movement, the nation, and the State, which dominated in the past); therefore, it receives more attention, and this includes more criticism. Accordingly, the absence of such criticism in the earlier periods which were studied does not imply that the schools were better or more appreciated at that time, but simply that the school was less central in the adolescents' world.

This complex feeling towards school can be seen in a number of entries made by students in their teacher's autograph book such as

> For two years we laughed,
> For two years we suffered,
> For two years we were one big family,
> But they've gone like a passing storm . . .

The image of the school as a big family, with both joy and suffering, clearly demonstrated that the criticism toward the school and teachers is also a result of the centrality and importance of the school in the lives of the youth.

Content analysis reveals another dual orientation toward school. On the one hand, a specific teacher-student relationship is required for the sake of achieving set goals. On the other hand, a personal affective relationship develops with the teacher, which can be measured against the entirety of interpersonal interactions in the classroom.

In each of these orientations, different characteristics are considered relevant and valuable. The achievement orientation emphasizes scholastic success and individualism. The affective orientation emphasizes the development of well-mannered and socially acceptable individuals. In the classroom, this duality is expressed in the demand for individual achievement on the one hand, and for contribution to social activities and collective projects on the other. The situation is also reflected in the demands on the teacher who is required to transmit knowledge on the one hand and to educate students towards society's values on the other. This duality is expressed particularly well in inscriptions made by teachers in students' autograph books (Herzog and Shapira 1983).

The students also perceive the complexity of the teacher's role, as indicated by a number of entries written by adolescents in their teachers' autograph books. Of the many things for which the students thank their teachers, it seems that the most appreciated element is their job of "social educator" (the specific job of the homeroom teacher). The students express gratitude to their teachers for giving them values, for teaching them good behavior and manners. They emphasize the teacher's devotion, tolerance, and understanding. But increasingly in autograph books from the 1970's on, students also thank their teachers for assistance in attaining scholastic achievements;

> For two years
> You taught us many subjects
> You gave us lots of homework
> You took us on many trips.
> You reviewed with us for exams
> So that we would succeed in them
> And in our life . . .
> Thanks for the things you did for me
> Thanks for adding some point here and there . . .

This recent emphasis on teachers' role as the transmitter of knowledge and aid to success supports the previous findings of an increasing emphasis on the individual as compared to the collective, and on personal success of the individual.

Adolescents' Social Commitments and the Social Order—Discussion

One of the main trends found in our research is a decline in national-collective values and norms among Israeli adolescents and an increase in individualistic and privately-oriented norms and values. This represents a change from references to the wider collective as directly connecting or mediating between the individual and society, to those between separate individuals within the collective. These findings can be explained in terms of functionalist theory as reflecting social change. The modernization of society has been accompanied by changes in the functions of the social institutions, and those changes are followed by changes in the normative order, changes which are expressed in youth attitudes towards their society (cf., for example, Parsons and Bales 1955, David and Moore 1967).

Scholars with a more radical view maintain that many social arrangements serve the interests of the dominant social class or the capitalist state rather than society as a whole (Collins 1972, Bourdieu 1973, Althusser 1972, Morgan 1975). Values and norms which are accepted and promoted in the capitalist state contribute to the continuation of this order. Or, in other words, they are adapted to the needs of the ruling class (cf. Marcuse 1964). According to this approach our findings should be explained as an outcome of changes in the economy of Israel, a transition from a quasi-socialist emphasis in the pre-state period and first years of the state to a more competitive capitalist emphasis over the years. The capitalist ideology which is characterized by the cult of individualism served the needs of the capitalist economy. Citizens are encouraged to seek fulfillment in personal spheres such as careers, leisure time pursuits, and consumption. This private orientation is the main motivation for working as well as consuming and as such the oil in the wheels of the capitalist machine.

The enthusiasm with the new approach has led to a new "functionalist" theory. Instead of speaking about the functions for "the society," scholars look for the functions for the ruling class. But, the normative order is not always simply a reflection of the development of the forces of production nor does it always serve the interests of the dominant class. Some of the norms and attitudes toward different social frameworks can be presented as contradictory to the interest of the rulers. Some values and norms which are sponsored mainly by agents of socialization might paradoxically negate the needs of the rulers.

We believe that Habermas in his analysis of the "legitimation crisis" (1976) illuminated this theoretical issue, while presenting a more complex and dialectic picture of the capitalist state. He claimed that there is a contradiction between the morality of self-interest and the need of the state to legitimate itself as universal. According to his analysis, capitalist society requires a shared set of cultural attitudes as boundary conditions without which it will be unstable, and in the absence of which government will be unable to find the resources to legitimate it. The problem is that the precapitalist moral values on which capitalism has hitherto relied have been progressively rendered irrelevant by the growth of the capitalist economy. Paradoxically, capitalism has failed to produce new values and norms which could act both as restraints upon economic demands and as reinforcements to a work ethic. In the development of capitalist society, individuals lose their moral identity and sense of meaning. Social integration presupposed shared meaning. Therefore, according to Habermas (1976), one of the problems facing the advanced capitalist state is the acquisition of legitimation in order to ensure a social integration. Plant (1982) argues that Habermas' interpretation of this problem is influenced by Hegel. While Hegel thought that in wider society there are mediating factors—the family, corporations, class identities, and solidarities—which provide the link between the particular and the universal, between politics and the economy, Habermas believed these mediating links have become fragmented.

This strong private orientation contradicts the need to legitimize the universal role of the state. The individualist orientation leads to an endless pressure on the state to fulfill the private needs and requests of the population. At the same time the real interest of the ruling class in state-regulated capitalism is to mobilize the population in order to support the state and its needs. Therefore crises of legitimacy and motivational commitment of the masses to the normative order of advanced capitalism are the main problems faced by the ruling class (for further consideration of this issue see Turner 1978, Plant 1982, Held 1980, and Giddens 1982). According to Habermas, the threat of anomie is endemic in late capitalism (Habermas 1976).

Following Habermas' diagnosis of the relations between the social order and the normative order, our findings could be interpreted in a deeper and more refined way. The data which were examined cover a period of 55 years (1925-1980) during which Israel became an independent state and underwent a rapid process of industrialization and other developments of modern capitalism (Eisenstadt 1967). Those changes were followed by the partial restructuring of the normative order, as reflected in the main change from collective-oriented attitudes to private-oriented norms. This trend is in line with Habermas' claim about the fragmentation of the mediating links between the individual and society, between the particular and the universal.

Our findings about the youth movements as the social framework of reference lead to a different picture, however. As was stated, private needs are fulfilled by membership in youth movements, yet at the same time the youth movements significantly influence the collectivistic conceptions of youth, the formation of a national consciousness, and political and military attitudes. Youth movements serve as elitist socialization agents which meet the need for personal achievement which is encouraged and legitimized by the capitalist normative order, but at the same time they also serve as educational elements reinforcing national universal values. As such they are an example of solving the legitimation problem of the state. But youth movements act in the informal educational system. Though about 70 percent of the youth in Israel take part in youth movement activity at some time in their life, only a small percentage persist until the age of 18.

As mentioned above, our findings reveal an increase in the importance of the school as a social reference for youth. This coincides with Collins' (1972) claim about the significance of educational frameworks as suppliers of credentials in modern society. The emphasis is on individuals and their achievements, and on self-interest as the main motivation for social actions. Bourdieu (1973), however, claims that the major role of the educational system is "culture reproduction," that is, reproduction of the culture of the "dominant class." His analysis placed particular emphasis on style, forms, and manners as important factors for which pupils are rewarded and thus become part of the process of cultural reproduction. In the Israeli case it is usually measured by ideology of contribution to the wider collective.

It seems that even in a single social institution—schools—competing and even contradictory messages are transmitted, not all of them supporting or serving "the system" or "the ruling class." The ideology of education serves the dominant class, mainly in activating the economy. It encourages individuals to compete and achieve personal success, it emphasizes private needs and achievements of the individual, elements which encourage people to take part in the capitalist economy. But this same ideology contradicts the needs of the state of legitimize itself in universal terms. As such it is a threat to the ability of the state to mobilize individuals to those aims of the state which do not contribute to the individual's success or are not so perceived. Furthermore, the state might lose its ability to persuade citizens to give up their private needs for what the ruling class defines as public needs.

Conclusions

In this article we have suggested that adolescents' autograph books can be a means for evaluating youth culture. Autograph books are part of the youth folklore which serves as a meaningful corpus of communication for the writers and the owners of the books. Viewing the adolescent period as one of transition, we see the inscription in autograph books as a social mechanism that assists the individual in coping with conditions of change. In a situation of uncertainty and insecurity regarding continuity into the future, the writing of inscriptions serves as a sort of mechanism of self-socialization which makes use of the central values of society. In making an entry, the individual transmits to the friend a message regarding continuity and continuation. Part of this continuity is constructed through the individual's bond to the social frameworks.

Our analysis also reveals that autograph books are a living, changing folklore through which one can study changes in social values and the normative order of the capitalist state. Two main trends were found. First, over the years the importance of school in youth attitudes has increased, coupled with a persistence in the significance of youth movements. The second, a change from references to the wider collective as directly connecting or mediating between the individual and society to those between separate individuals as part of the collective. Norms of individualism among Israeli youth have been strengthened and national collectivistic norms have disappeared. The increased importance of the school shows that in Israel, as in other capitalist states, students accept the dominant ideology that education is the main and the most legitimate channel for social mobility. Schooling ideology is current in Israel in all social classes and ethnic groups, regardless of the real opportunities and the factual relationship between education attainment and occupational status and income (Yogev 1981, Yogev and Shapira 1984, Yuchtman-Yaar 1985).

The second trend, that of increased individualization and the emergence of privately-oriented norms, reflects Israeli society's inclusion in the "club" of capitalist states. But while schooling ideology mainly serves the interests of the dominant group, individualization raises the question of legitimation of the universal role of the state.

From the point of view of "the whole society" or the "ruling class" it cannot be argued that these changes serve the "needs" of either. The changes in the commitments of Israeli youth to their society lead to the conclusion that the Israeli state of rulers lost part of their ability to legitimize their actions in collective terms. Instead they have to face individualist orientation and hence the same problems that other capitalist states have to legitimize their universalistic role, that is, to maintain a collective-oriented ideology and to mobilize the citizens to contribute to the state on this basis.

The Israeli political elite has failed from its point of view, to sustain the collectivist and egalitarian ideology which dominated society, as it prevailed in autograph books in the 1920's and the 1930's (See also Shapiro 1977, Eisenstadt 1967) and has not yet suggested an alternative normative order, except for privatization. The latter supports the ideology of consumption which is an inherent part of capitalist economy, but as we stated before, contradicts the need to legitimize the steering function of state capitalism. The role that the youth movements play in the Israeli society is an exception. Membership in the youth movement is a powerful mechanism of social continuity. It combines commitment to basic values of the collective with self-confidence and desire for individual careers. In this case the interests of the collective coincide with those of the individuals. Our findings indicate that the youth movement is a stable frame of reference but not the dominant one.

Analysis of youth attitudes toward social frameworks reveals a dialectic situation in which contradictory norms and values exist together. As Habermas put it, the ideology of individualism and privatization is an obstacle for state-regulated capitalism which needs legitimation in collective terms for its steering tasks. At the same time, as education and critical analysis grow, privatization can serve as a means of diffusing criticism. The ability of the youngsters to consider their commitments to different, sometimes contradictory, social frameworks might then become the key for questioning the existing social order.

Note

1. The figure demonstrates an overall increase in each of the three indicators between 1930 and 1980, and a drop in each of the indicators during the 1940's. We explain the "drop" in the following way. Before 1948 the Jewish population of Palestine was mobilized in a struggle to establish the state. National issues were important reference points for individual values and actions. Some people dropped out of school in order to join the Hachsharot (pre-military organizations) and the armed forces. School apparently declined in importance, relative to these larger national issues. However, this was a temporary decline, because when these young individuals reached the age of 30 or 40, many of them returned to school to complete their interrupted education. We interpret this to mean that education was not devalued, but rather was simply put on hold.

References

Albert, S. and Kessler, S.
  1976 "Processes for ending social encounters: The conceptual archaeology of temporal place." *Journal for the Theory of Social Behavior* 6: 147-170.
Althusser, J.
  1972 "Ideology and ideological state apparatuses." In B.R. Cosin (ed.), *Education: Structure and Society*. Harmondsworth: Penguin Books.

Aries, P.
  1962   *Centuries of Childhood*, New York: Vintage.
Ben Amos, D.
  1971   "Toward a definition of folklore in context." *Journal of American Folklore* 84: 3-15.
Ben David, J.
  1954   "Membership in youth movements and social status." *Megamot* 3: 227-247 (Hebrew).
Ben David, J.
  1957   "The social status of the teacher in Israel." *Megamot* 8: 201-212 (Hebrew).
Boerdam, J. and Wanna, O.M.
  1980   "Family photographs—A sociological approach." *The Netherlands Journal of Sociology* 16(2). October: 95-119.
Bourdieu, P.
  1973   "Cultural reproduction and social reproduction." In R. Brown (ed.), *Knowledge, Education and Cultural Change*. London: Tavistock.
Collins, R.
  1979   *The Credential Society: An Historical Sociology of Education and Stratification*. New York: Academic.
Danziger, N. and R. Shapira
  1981   "The social function of informal education structures in a development town." In *Between Center and Periphery: Education Systems in a Development Town*. Research Reports, Tel-Aviv: The Pinhas Sapir Center for Development (Hebrew).
Davis K. and W.E. Moore
  1967   "Some Principles of Stratification." In R. Bendix and S.M. Lipset (eds.), *Class Status and Power*. London: Routledge and Kegan Paul.
Dundes, A. and C. Pagter
  1975   *Urban Folklore from the Paperwork Empire*. Austin, Texas: The American Folklore Society.
Eisenstadt, S.M.
  1967   *Israeli Society*. London: Weidenfeld-Nicholson.
Giddens, A.
  1982   *Profiles and Critiques in Social Theory*. London: Macmillian.
Gumperz, J. and D. Hymes (eds.)
  1972   *Directions In Sociolinguistic—The Ethnography of Communication*. New York: Holt, Rinehart and Winston.
Habermas, J.
  1976   *Legitimation Crisis*. London: Heinemann.
Halliday, M.A.K.
  1975   "Language as social semiotic: Towards a general sociolinguistic theory." Pp. 17-46 in Makhai (ed.) *The First LACUS Forum*, Columbia, S.C.: Hornbeam Press.
Held, D.
  1980   *Introduction to Critical Theory*. London: Hutchinson.
Herzog, H.
  1985   "Social Construction of Reality in Ethnic Terms: The Case of Political Ethnicity in Israel." *International Review of Modern Sociology*, 15(1): In press.
Herzog, H. and R. Shapira
  1983   "The Teacher and the School in a Mirror: The Image of Teachers and Schools as Reflected in Autograph Books." *Studies in Education* 37-38: 241-256 (Hebrew).
Marcuse, H.
  1964   *One-Dimensional Man*, Boston: Beacon Press.
Morgan, D.J.H.
  1975   *Social Theory and the Family*. London: Routledge and Kegan Paul.
Ong, W.J.
  1971   *Rhetoric, Romance and Technology*. Ithaca and London: Cornell University Press.

Parsons, T. and R.F. Bales
1955   *Family, Socialization and Interaction Process.* New York: The Free Press.
Plant, R.
1982   "Jurgen Habermas and the idea of legitimation." *European Journal of Political Research* 10: 341-352.
Potter, C.
1949   "Autograph Album Times." In M. Leach (ed.) *Standard Dictionary of Folklore Mythology and Legend.* New York: Funk and Wagnalls.
Rinot, M.
1981   "The teacher's status in Israel in an historical perspective." *Studies in Education* 32: 5-12 (Hebrew).
Seitel, P.
1969   "Proverbs: A social use of metaphor." *Genre* II (2): 143-161.
Shapira, R., Ch. Adler, M. Lerner and R. Peleg
1979   *Blue Shirt and White Collar (The Youth Movement in Israel).* Tel Aviv: Am Oved (Hebrew).
Shapira, R. and H. Herzog
1984   "Understanding youth culture through autograph books: The Israeli case." *Journal of American Folklore* 97: 386, pp. 442-460.
Shapiro, R. and R. Peleg
1980   "From Blue Shirt to White Collar" *Forum* 38: 127-140.
Shapiro, Y.
1977   *Democracy in Israel.* Ramat Gan: Massada (Hebrew).
Smooha, S.
1978   *Israel: Pluralism and Conflict.* London and Henley: Routledge and Kegan Paul.
Stern, S.
1973   "Autograph memorabilia as an output of social interaction and communication." *New York Folklore Quarterly* 24: 219-239.
Turner, J.H.
1978   *The Structure of Sociological Theory.* Homewood, Illinois: Dorsey.
Turner, W.
1967   *The Forest of Symbols.* Ithaca: Cornell University Press.
Turner, W.
1969   *The Ritual Process: Structure and Antistructure.* Chicago: Aldine.
Yogev, A.
1981   "Determinants of early education career in Israel: Further evidence for sponsorship thesis" *Sociology of Education* 54: 181-194.
Yogev, A. and R. Shapira
1984   "Ethnicity, meritocracy and credentialization in Israel: Elaborating the credential society theses." Paper presented at the 1st International Conference on Education in the 90s. Tel Aviv.
Yuchtman-Yaar, E.
1985   "Differences in ethnic patterns of socioeconomic achievement in Israel—A neglected aspect of structured inequality." *International Review of Modern Sociology,* 15(1): In Press.

23.

Holiday Celebrations in Israeli Kindergartens: Relationships between Representations of Collectivity and Family in the Nation-State

Lea Shamgar-Handelman and Don Handelman

The object of education, contended Durkheim (1956:71), "is to arouse and to develop in a child a certain number of physical, intellectual, and moral states which are demanded of him by . . . the political society as a whole." Mechanisms of education, he added, are among the major means through which "society perpetually recreates the conditions of its very existence" (1956:123). Durkheim conjoined two themes that are salient for the modern Western nation-state. First, that the political economy of education, especially formal education, is a crucial expression of the ideology and authority of the state. Second, that the reproduction of social order depends, in no small measure, on the exercise of the power of education through the requisite apparatus of the state.

In the case of Israel the tasks of formal education were less the replication of social order than the construction of an ideological blueprint that contributed to the very creation of the state. The fusion of political ideology and formal organization, in order to influence the maturation of youngsters who were the future generation of citizenry, began in the kindergarten.[1] For example, a veteran Jewish kindergarten teacher[2] reflected, as follows, on the intimate ties that developed between the Jewish community, the *yishuv*, in pre-state Palestine and the kindergarten system. These were bonds, she enunciated, between a form of early-age education and "the ideas and aspirations that lifted the spirits of those parts of the nation that rebuilt the ruins of its homeland and rejuvenated this." The Zionist dream of returning to work the land of Israel, she added, "brought the garden into the kindergarten" (Fayence-Glick 1957:141). As in numerous other aspects of the nation-building of Israel, that of the kindergarten was linked closely to the practice of proto-national ideology.

Very young children experience and learn the lineaments of personhood and world through the family arrangements into which they are born. In these contexts they are enculturated into a sense of hierarchy and status, of order and division of labor, of sentiment and loyalty, through notions of kinship and familism that come to be the natural ordering of things. Only later is the child made to realize that parental superordination is itself subordinate to the idea of a wider social order; and that on numerous occasions loyalty and obligation to the collectivity transcends that of familial ties. This transition, however obvious, is crucial to the reproduction of the social orders of the state. It clearly is in the interests of representatives of the state to recruit the cooperation of the family in order to achieve societal goals; and thus they phrase its relationships to the family in terms of cooperation and consensus. Politicians and officials commonly liken the state and its citizenry to a great family; while the idioms of kinship and familism are used in cognate ways.

Yet this relationship between state and family is fraught with tension. This is evident in times of crisis, should officials intervene in the affairs of family; and especially when they insist that organs of the state are mandated to fulfill functions of social control and affect that the family considers its own (Shamgar-Handelman 1981; Handelman 1978). With regard to children and their maturation, state and family do have overlapping and congruent interests; but their concerns also differ and are continually negotiated.

Bluntly put, all children must learn that their parents are not the natural apex of hierarchy and authority; and that the rights of the collectivity can supercede those of familism. This is integral to the process of maturation in the nation-state. In present-day Israel the young child's entry into the kindergarten is the onset of extended periods in educational settings that are regulated and supervised by organs of the state. The youngster is moved slowly during this lengthy transition from his embeddedness within home and family until, at the age of 18, he enters the army for compulsory service. At this time he is given over wholly by his parents to the authority and service of the state. The transition is one from offspring to citizen.

With regard to this transition, kindergartens in Israel are of especial interest, since their annual round is punctuated by numerous ceremonial occasions that, on a wider scale, are of import to the religious and civic cultures of nation and state. Anthropologists are very well aware that ceremonials, whether sacred or secular, are concentrated foci of the explicit and implicit, yet selective, production, display, and manipulation of symbolic forms and sentiments (Turner 1982; Manning 1983; Moore and Myerhoff

1977). During such occasions other themes and qualities of the everyday lived-in world are held in abeyance (Handelman 1982, 1983, 1984). Whether an analysis stresses the semiotics of ceremonial structure (Geertz 1972), or the dramatistics of enactment (Turner 1974), the ritualism of ceremonialism is patterned to communicate in enhanced and pointed ways, regardless of the size or scope of the occasion.

Holiday celebrations in Israeli kindergartens are in keeping with these attributes of ceremonialism. Given the early ages of the young participants the messages of these celebrations, at least the explicit ones, are presented in quite clear-cut ways. Through such occasions children are involved, outside of their homes, in focused representations of culture that, in general, are considered to be of significance to aspects of the nation-state. On an explicit level many of these occasions celebrate versions of tradition and historicity of the Jewish people, and of the renewal and coherence of the Jewish state. Scenarios emphasize the joint effort, the consensus of cooperation, between kindergarten and parent, state and citizen, in order to inform the maturation of the child with experiences that begin to situate his personhood in relation to directives of the past and expectations of the future. On a more implicit level the "hidden agendas" of such scenarios unearth the more problematic relationship between state and family.[3] Thus numerous celebrations can be understood as versions of the relationship between representations of collectivity and family, through which youngsters are shown, and are encouraged to experience, that the superordination of the former supplants that of the latter. This sort of exposure is especially important for children in urban locales where different spheres of living are quite compartmentalized, where settings of home and work are separated, and where the access of children to the world of adults, of hierarchy and equality, is limited. The kindergarten is the first location where children learn of hierarchy and equality outside the home.

This paper discusses four cases of kindergarten ceremonials in relation to the symbolic loads they convey. It is surprising how little sociologistic analysis has been done on questions of whether and how kindergarten youngsters are exposed to the focussed manipulation of symbols and of symbolic formations of a supra-familial character, whether in Israel or elsewhere. Studies of kindergartens tend to emphasize the learning of competence in daily interaction (Jones 1969; Shure 1963; Shulz and Florio 1979). However, our argument is closer in spirit to that of Gracey (1975), who contends that the task of teachers in American kindergartens is to drill children in the role of student and, by extension, to prepare them for the rigid routines of bureaucratic corporate society. Nonetheless, work on ceremonialism in kindergartens is minimal (Heffernan and Todd 1960; Moore 1959); while there are only bare traces of such discussion on higher grades

(Kapferer 1981; Burnett 1969; Bernstein, Elvin, and Peters 1966; Waller 1932; Fuchs 1969; Weiss and Weiss 1976).[4]

We have chosen to interpret and to explicate a small number of cases, from our larger corpus of descriptions of such events, for the following reasons.[5] First, ceremonials have their own integrity of internal structure that conveys the significance of the occasion as a viable performance. This is violated if the event is not described in and of itself. The celebration, at least in part, should become the context for its own interpretation. Second, detailed description and discussion permits the reader to form interpretations alternative to those that we argue for. We hardly would insist that there are singular constructions of significance in such celebrations. Third, with so little attention given to kindergarten celebrations, it is advantageous to have available concrete examples. These may lay out some parameters of discourse for future discussions.[6]

Nonetheless, our interpretations will focus on certain structural aspects of these ceremonials that are related more specifically to our argument of explicit and implicit levels of communication in versions of the interplay of collectivity and family. In particular we give attention to the sequencing of enactments. Sequencing in ceremonial, and in other activities, probably is of signal import in cultures that, according to Lee (1959), are made coherent through lineal codifications of reality, and that have a strong sense of chronology in history and biography. Thus those acts that are placed, for example, "before" and "after" implicate the logic of organization of the whole sequence of enactment. Whether it is put together this way consciously or not, a planned occasion becomes embued with a symbolic load that, in keeping with lineal thinking, takes on much of its significance through its sequencing: through the additive accretion of symbolic acts, and so through the emergence of a more-or-less coherent story line. In addition we discuss the significance of social formations in enactments, and that of prevalent symbols. These structural aspects of enactment will be related to the three categories of person—teacher, child, and parent—whose positioning in relation to one another implicates the rudimentary conceptualizations of collectivity and family that are enacted in the kindergarten.

Therefore the next section takes up the relationships among these three categories of persons, in terms of the ideologies and goals of kindergarten educators in Palestine and Israel. In the context of this discussion, the following section discusses the celebrations themselves.

Kindergarten and Celebration in Israel

The first kindergarten in Palestine was established in 1898, and it was intended as a preparatory class for elementary school. The language of instruction was German, translated into those of the pupils. The first Hebrew-speaking Zionist kindergarten was opened in 1911. Unlike its predecessors it was an autonomous unit for early-age education. In the context of Zionism this kindergarten, its successors, and local seminaries for kindergarten teachers, all freed Hebrew early-age education from the domination of foreign theories of pedagogy. These kindergartens gave especial attention to the cultivation of the Zionist spirit: for example, to the values of working the land and building the nation (Fayance-Glick 1957:141).

By 1919 there were thirty-three Jewish kindergartens in Palestine, with a total of 2,525 pupils. Some coordination of kindergarten policy and curricula was instituted during the period of the British Mandate, on the part of the educational department of the Zionist governing bodies of the *yishuv*. Nonetheless, the prevalent pattern was of a variety of kindergarten frameworks, Zionist and other, that were subsidized in part by numerous sources, and whose programs of instruction were supervised in varying degrees.

With statehood, in 1948, kindergarten education was centralized. The Law of Obligatory Education, promulgated in 1953, made kindergarten mandatory for children at age 5, and placed the supervision of kindergartens under the aegis of the national Ministry of Education. Numerous kindergarten classes were opened for children from the age of 2 and above. From the 1920s until the present the demand for places in kindergartens almost always exceeded those available. In 1982-83 some 250,000 children, between the ages of 2 and 5, were enrolled in 2,035 kindergartens. Of those aged 2, 63.6 percent were enrolled; while for those aged 3 and above the equivalent proportions were over 90 percent (*Statistical Abstract of Israel* 1983:654).

Throughout the period of Zionist early-age education teachers insisted that the kindergarten was to be used to inculcate the meaning of Zionist existence, and to teach somewhat vague notions of Israeli "culture," not only to children but also to their parents, many of whom were recent immigrants from diverse cultural backgrounds. The kindergarten was conceived of as an instrument of national purpose: one that would help to transform the child into an Israeli person different from that of his parents. Moreover, a person who would re-enter the home to influence parents to alter their own attitudes towards the rearing of children.

Writing of the Mandatory period, Katerbursky (1962:56), a veteran educator, stated: "The obligation of the kindergarten is to uproot bad habits that the children bring from home." This was attempted, for example, through parent-teacher meetings and through instructional sessions in preparation for holiday celebrations. Katerbursky (1962:58) added: "We understand that the parents, especially the mothers, are still very distant from understanding many of the educational . . . [and] social problems of education; and we will have to educate them as well." When the occasion allowed, mothers were given instructions on how to behave towards their children, on correct attitudes towards the development of the child, on how leisure time with children should be spent, and on the kind of cooking that children would enjoy eating at home. Although such exercises were phrased in the idiom of mutual understanding between teachers and parents, it is clear that the former regarded these goals as integral to their pedagogical mandate (Katerbursky 1962:64).

These themes of inculcation hardly changed after statehood. If anything they intensified with mass immigration and a more centralized educational bureaucracy. Numerous books of instruction and advice for kindergarten teachers were published. These attest to differing perceptions over aims held by kindergarten and home: although these were ameliorated by the rhetoric of mutual cooperation disseminated by educators. We note again an emphasis on the need to educate parents as well as children (Rabinowitz 1958), and, for that matter, to enlist the youngsters as allies in this endeavor. For example, one educator put this forcefully: "Our influence on the surrounding can be great with the help of our faithful partners, the children, if only we will know how to inject into the home one common version of customs. . . . It is not the first time in the history of this country that the child fulfills an important role in educating the nation. . . . That is why we can hope that in the new assignment of the 'ingathering of the exiles' (*kibbutz galuyot*) . . . the child will fulfill his mission and will not disappoint us" (Zanbank-Wilf 1958:57). Less direct but cognate sentiments are expressed in other such didactic manuals (Naftali and Nir-Yaniv 1974; Shemer 1966; Ministry of Education and Culture 1967).

During the *yishuv* period and after, the celebration of holidays in the kindergarten was understood by educators as a signal device through which to inculcate children and parents in what Rabinowitz (1958) called the embedding of traditional contents in new patterns. Writing primarily of the *yishuv,* Fayance-Glick (1957:141) noted: "Special stress was given to holidays as a way of teaching tradition, concepts of history, and Israeli folklore to babies through the pipelines of pleasure and joy saturated with experience. And many kindergartens reached a high aesthetic level through forming the holiday and the party." Many weeks were spent in preparations that, "filled, and are filling today, most of the teaching year . . . and it is as if the kindergarten life is one long holiday with intermissions for pieces of secularity and intervals of reality" (See also Katerbursky 1962:153).

Parents were integral to these celebrations. They were lectured on the meaning of holidays; and were taught songs and dances of the kindergarten, so that they could participate fully in the celebratory education of their children (Katerbursky 1962:72). The implicit effect of such didactics was to bring parents and children together under the tutorial direction of teachers.

In more recent instruction books the teacher is featured as a touchstone of tradition. Parents, however, have undergone the traumatic social and cultural dislocations of immigration that destroyed the traditional atmosphere of holidays in the Jewish home. The teacher also is a source of modernism: of the creation of new patterns of celebration through the borrowing of elements from different Jewish traditions, in order to bring the holiday anew, through children, to homes bereft of such ceremonial occasions (Rabinowitz 1958b). No matter how naive such attitudes appear to be, they reflect the cultural melting-pot notions of Zionism. These often emphasized that immigrants would have to begin again to build a tradition in common, in order to create anew Jewish personhood in the resurgent homeland (Ben-Yosef 1957).

In such books, parents often are delineated as persons who have little information of value on ceremony in the new State. Along with their young offspring, they must be taught how to prepare the material of ceremonials (food dishes, costumes, etc.), and they must learn the symbols, songs, dances, and stories of holidays that are used and are narrated in the kindergarten (Rabinowitz 1958b). Holidays are understood by the advisors of teachers as special foci for the enculturation of the family as a whole.

In general the young child is understood, if dimly, by educators as a small-scale mediator of relationships between state and family, between public and private domains, and between "general" and more particularistic notions of culture. All of these relationships have built into them potentially conflicting loyalties, obligations, and rights—but these rarely are recognized by educators. Hidden in their writings is the premise that the control of the child, as a resource, is crucial to the reproduction of the nation-state. On the one hand the child is the citizen and culture-bearer of the future, and on the other the child as parent-to-be is essential to the formation of the family to come.

Therefore serious thought is given to the planning of ceremonials in the kindergarten; and instructional books offer various scenarios for their enactment (Rabinowitz 1958c). These are designed less to instruct didactically or to encourage reflection. Instead emphasis is placed on the arousal of emotion through symbolic forms that evoke collective sentiments. In general there is a profusion of what Langer (1953) called "presentational" symbolism: media that engage the senses more than the critical faculties of mind. Participants should experience enactments by living through their symbols, rather than as spectators. Instruction books note, for example, that the kindergarten child needs the emotional experience of a holiday, not a logical explanation or historical exposition. Ideally the celebration should be a "common experience" that "uplifts the spirit" and that encourages feelings of togetherness (Rabinowitz 1958a, 1958b).

In the views of kindergarten educators the arousal of such sentiments is induced if scenarios are well-designed, so that their enactment is left less to chance. The architectonics of celebration should be logical and holistic, with defined segments of opening, elaboration, and closing (Fayence-Glick 1948). Attention should be given to one or more major ideas or motifs, to scheduling in relation to calendrical cycles, to the sequencing and progression of the program, and to overt symbols. Often these symbols are both "living" and "lived through," such that the physical positioning of the participants itself creates symbolic formations. The symbol comes alive, and participants live through this both as a collectivity and as individuals. Such devices powerfully invoke a metonymy between motifs of celebration and their being experienced, and a synecdoche in which each part of the collective entity replicates and signifies the coherence and unity of the whole. Educators appear well aware of this more explicit level of symbolic manipulation. Yet since teachers are quite autonomous in how they plan celebrations, there is a good deal of variation in their enactments among kindergartens.

But kindergarten educators often deny that, at a more implicit level, symbolic formations in celebrations actively manipulate versions of relationships between teacher and parent, collectivity and family. Nonetheless we argue that each category of participant—teacher, child, and parent—has significance beyond the immediate persons who participate in celebrations. The teacher is a statist figure, a "gardener" whose task it is to cultivate, and so to enculturate, her young charges. In Durkheim's (1956:89) words, the teacher "is the agent of a great moral person who surpasses him: it is society . . . the teacher is the interpreter of the great moral ideas of his time." Licensed by the Ministry of Education, and subject in part to its curricula and supervision, the teacher is the first official-like figure with whom the little child comes into continuous contact outside the home. Her structural position is, in no small measure, in opposition to that of parent and home. For four to five hours a day, six days a week, she is in charge of a collection of children, indeed of a small collectivity, in which each child in theory is equal in worth and status to every other, and where she has no vested interest in the particulars of any one. Her criteria of sentiment are "objectified" in terms of more universalistic criteria, like those of a child's capabilities, capacities, and behavior. Her mandate is to help to mold the child and, through the youngster, to affect his current family of procreation and his future family of orientation.

The child's experience and knowledge, sentiment and loyalty, derive almost wholly from the encompassing primary group of the family. In the course of years of attendance in educational institutions, he ideally will be reconstituted in the image of citizen: one whose ultimate loyalties will be to the abstract idea of the nation-state. Although his attachments to family are neither attenuated nor diminished, there must occur a shift in the positional hierarchy of family and state, with the latter coming to encompass the former. This transition also is about the standardization of the biographical uniqueness of the individual and of the individual family. These processes, we believe, are begun in the kindergarten, and perhaps are most concentrated in its celebrations.

Kindergarten Celebrations

The occasions to be discussed are representative of the range of Jewish holidays celebrated in Israel, in terms of their traditional or modern roots. Given the paucity of information available on kindergarten celebrations, we prefer to inform the reader with a sense of the variation among such occasions, rather than to limit our focus to one or two categories of holiday. The first two of our cases, Hannukah and Purim, are traditional holidays, but not holy Days of Rest. Both commemorate victories: Hannukah of the Maccabees and of the rededication of the Temple in Jerusalem, and Purim the saving of the Jews of Persia through the influence of Queen Esther. Both are celebrated, in varying degrees in home and synagogue, and Purim also in the street. Our analysis of a Hannukah celebration demonstrates the implicit manipulation of hierarchy, such that the family unit is shown to be encompassed by the collectivity. The case of Purim that we discuss brings out an implicit assumption that the maturation of children moves them from a condition closer to nature to one of civilization, and so toward their assumption of citizenship in the future. The third case, Mother's Day, is borrowed from modern Western popular culture, and is a wholly secular occasion of no official standing. The implications of our case suggest that it is the collectivity that mandates the legitimacy of the family unit, and not the reverse which is closer to the viewpoint of the family. The fourth case, Jerusalem Day, is a secular state commemoration of the reunification of Jerusalem following the 1967 Six-Day War. Our analysis of this case points to the symbolic forging of direct links between the collectivity and the child as future citizen, without the mediation of the family. All of these cases offer implicit versions of hierarchical relationships between collectivity and family that should reverse the early-age experiences of the child. However, we stress here that, in the first few years of education, youngsters experience dozens of such celebrations. Explicit themes, contents, and organization vary within and among kinds of celebrations. Yet the types of implicit relationships between collectivity and family that emerge from our cases likely have a cachet of relevance that extends to numerous other kindergarten celebrations. While, for the child, it is the cumulative accretion of such experiences that has enculturative impact.

All the celebrations described took place on the kindergarten premises (although others, not discussed here, sometimes were taken outside). The kindergarten is defined as "the child's world," and the only adult that has a legitimate place within it is the teacher—the representative of the collectivity. Parents (and other adults) always are only guests in the kindergarten. Nothing better symbolizes this attitude than the chairs in the kindergarten. In all kindergartens visited, no more than one or two full-size chairs were found. That is to say, as a rule, the teacher sits in a full-size chair and, "at her feet," as it were, the children on small chairs. When parents are invited to the kindergarten, be it to a celebration, to a parent-teacher meeting or to their child's birthday party, they always are seated on children's chairs. Thus a parent in the kindergarten always occupies a child's place.

Prior to the celebrations, the children were given explanations in their respective kindergartens with regard to the character of the holiday concerned, its significance for the people of Israel or for the children themselves (as in Mother's Day), its dominant symbols, and some rudimentary historical background. Where the celebration involved more complicated enactments by the children, these were rehearsed beforehand. All the actions that took place in these celebrations were in accordance with the explicit instructions and orchestration of the teacher, unless otherwise specified.

Hannukah: Hierarchy, Family, and Collectivity

Hannukah, the Festival of Lights, commemorates the victory of the Maccabees over the Seleucids, and their rededication of the Temple in 165 B.C. According to the *Talmud,* in the Temple there was only enough undefiled oil for one day of lamp-lighting. Miraculously the oil multiplied into a supply sufficient for eight days. Hannukah is celebrated for eight consecutive days in the home, primarily by the lighting of an additional candle each day, in an eight-branched candelabrum, the *hannukiah* (pl. hannukiot). An extra candle, the *shamash,* is used to kindle the others. Hannukah celebrates liberation from foreign domination: it is a triumph of faith, of the few over the many, of the weak over the strong. In present-day Israel the martial spirit of this holiday casts reflections on the struggle of the Jewish people to create a unified national homeland.

Books of instruction suggest that the major motif be heroism in Israel. The enactment should evoke the emotional experience of the occasion. The central symbols of the celebration should be the hannukiah, candles, tops,[7] and, according to some, the national flag. The locale of the party should be filled with light, just as the shirts or blouses of the children should be white, to create an atmosphere of joyous luminosity. The best time is late afternoon or early evening, for these hours evoke the uplifting illumination of the holiday from the midst of darkness and the depths of despair; and they connect the kindergarten to the home, where candles may be lit soon after. Scenarios suggest that a central hannukiah be lit by an adult; that the parents light the small hannukiot made by their children; that the children form "living hannukiot"; and that parents and children dance or play games together (Rabinowitz 1958c). Certain of these elements were incorporated into the example described below.[8]

Description. The party began at 4:30 P.M. Thirty-two children, aged 4 to 5, and their mothers sat at tables placed along three walls of the room. Only a few fathers attended. A name-card marked the place of each child. The tables were covered by white tablecloths. At the center of each were a vase of flowers, bags of candies, and candles equal to the number of youngsters at that table. Before each child stood a little hannukiah made by that youngster. On the walls and windows were hung painted paper hannukiot, oil pitchers, candles, and tops, all of which had been prepared in the kindergarten. Against the fourth wall was a large hannukiah, constructed of toy blocks covered with colored paper, which supported eight colored candles and the shamash.

An accordionist played melodies of the holiday, and the mothers joined in singing and in clapping. The teacher welcomed all those present and, at a prearranged signal, her helper extinguished the lights. Each mother lit a candle and aided her child to kindle his own little hannukiah. The room lights were turned on. A father lit the large hannukiah of toy blocks, and recited the requisite prayers. As he did so, the teacher told the children: "Remember, when father says a blessing, you must sit quietly and listen to the blessing." More holiday songs followed.

The teacher announced: "Now we want to make a living hannukiah. A living hannukiah that walks and sings, a hannukiah of parents and children." She arranged the mothers and their children in a straight line, so that each child stood in front of his mother. An additional mother-child pair, the shamash, stood some feet to the side. Each mother held a candle, and each youngster a blue or white ribbon. Each child gave one end of his ribbon to the child-shamash. In this formation all children were attached to the shamash by their ribbons, and each mother to her own child. The mother of the shamash lit the candles held by the others. The lights were extinguished, the room lit by the living hannukiah in the gathering darkness of late afternoon. The accordionist played a melody of the holiday, "We came to chase away the darkness," as each mother walked around her child. The lights were turned on. The mothers returned to their seats as a group, followed by their children.

The children and mothers of one table returned to the center of the room and were told by the teacher: "The children will be the spinning tops. Get down, children." They fell to their knees, bent their heads, and curled their bodies forward. Each mother stood behind her child. The teacher declared: "The whole year the spinning tops were asleep in their box. From last year until this year, until now. And the children said to them, 'Wake up, spinning tops. Hannukah has come. We want to play with you.'" To a background of holiday melodies the teacher moved from child to child, touching their hand. With each contact a child awakened, stood up, raised his arms, and began to spin. Each mother spun her child, first clockwise, then counterclockwise. Next the mothers became the tops, spun by their children in one direction and then the other. The teacher told the second table: "You'll also be spinning tops. Each mother will spin her own child and when I give the signal, change roles. Alright? Let's start. . . . The children are the spinning tops . . . the parents are the spinning tops." Those at the third table followed.

Mothers and children held hands, formed an unbroken circle, and danced round and round the teacher. Only one father joined the circle. More singing, and food, followed. As 6 P.M. approached, the teacher gave the participants permission to leave; and the party broke up.

Discussion. This ceremonial is composed of three major segments, the overt symbolism of which is quite explicit. The first focuses on the serious traditionalism of the holiday, primarily through the emblem of the hannukiah. This segment brings out the connectivity between past and present. The second works through the make-believe of the spinning top, and evokes the relationship between present and future.

The initial segment proceeds through a series of candle-lightings: mother helps her child to kindle the small hannukiah, father lights the large hannukiah, and the candles are lit on the living hannukiah. These actions and others are embedded in the melodies and songs of the holiday that tell of heroism, victory, and the illumination of darkness. These themes weave together emotion and experience to carry the past into the present. The blue and white ribbons of the living hannukiah are the official colors of the modern state, and of its flag. In the living hannukiah ancient triumph is fused with modern renaissance. Collectivity is dedicated to temple, temple to collectivity.

Here the idea of family is central. The enactment replicates symbolic acts—the kindling of candles and prayers—that should take place within the home, and that delineate familial roles and an elementary division of labor. Thus it is apt for mother to help her small child, in this instance to light the hannukiah. Moreover, it is appropriate for father, the male head of household, to recite the prayers that accompany this act, on behalf of the family. Here one father does this on behalf of the assembly. The symbolism of this enactment then transcends the level of the family. The "living hannukiah" encompasses all of the mothers and children, while respecting the singularity of individual families, represented here by the dyads of mother and child. Each mother stands behind her child; and walks around and encompasses the latter, delineating the family unit. This living hannukiah is a collective symbol that also is a symbol of collectivity; while this collectivity itself is constituted of smaller family units.

The living hannukiah projects into the present the significance of past heroism and dedication. This is done through the living bodies of mothers and children, who themselves compose the shape and the significata of this central symbol. Thus the collectivity is presented as living through family units, just as the latter live within and through the former. Each is made to be seen as integral to the other. However the connotation is that the collectivity is of a higher order than the individual family, since here it encompasses the latter.

In contrast to the seriousness of the first segment, the second is playful. Its motif is the top, a child's holiday toy that itself is inscribed with Hebrew letters that denote the miraculous—the multiplication of oil, and perhaps the victory itself. But in this segment commemoration and tradition are not marked. Instead the make-believe is evoked, slumber is shattered, and the participants act joyously in the holiday mood. Again the focus is that of the family unit, represented by dyads of mother and child. The hierarchy at the close of the first segment is kept. The teacher activates each child, and the latter performs under the direction of mother.

But in this make-believe segment, mother and child reverse roles: the former becomes the sleeping top that is awakened and directed by her child. Unlike the inscription of tradition in the first segment, the playful is full of potential, as is the youngster who eventually will exchange the role of child for that of adult. As a mature adult the child will become a parent, bringing into being and controlling children of his own. This segment projects the child, as parent-to-be, towards a future in which he will replace his parents and will replicate their roles and tasks. Through the two segments past and future are joined together wilth a sense of the movement of generations. Whereas the first segment recreates family and collectivity in the images of tradition, of the enduring past, the second segment demonstrates the transitoriness of particular parents and the direction of succession. For the child the experience may evoke some feeling that his own parents are not timeless monoliths that will continue to structure his world indefinitely.

The second segment closes and the third starts with an unbroken circle dance of mothers and children who revolve about the axis of the teacher.[9] This formation is a restatement of the relationship between family and collectivity. The circle dance, however, blurs the distinctiveness of particular families and, within these, of parents and children, adults and youngsters. The delineation of family units has disappeared. Instead, all are closer to being discrete and egalitarian individuals who themselves are part of a greater and embracing collectivity. This formation connotes the connectivity of present and future citizens, and their orientation towards an axial center.

In this and in other kindergarten celebrations the teacher is the sole arbiter and the ultimate authority. She is seen by children to control parental figures before their very eyes. We argued that the teacher is a statist figure, perhaps the earliest representation of authority outside the home that very young children encounter. In these celebrations she is not an alternative source of authority to that of parents, as she may be perceived by children in the daily life of the kindergarten. Instead she is the pinnacle of hierarchy that supercedes and that subsumes the family. Thus the whole enactment is framed by the architectonics of hierarchy that are external to, but that act upon, the family unit. All actions of such celebrations, regardless of their explicit content, are embued with this quality of hierarchy.

The implicit messages of this Hannukah celebration are about hierarchy from a more statist perspective. The first segment constructs a version of the superordination of roles within the family, and then embeds the latter within a version of collectivity. The second deconstructs the centrality of family status and transforms hierarchical relationships among family members. The third emphasizes equality among citizens, all of whom are oriented towards the statist figure of the teacher.

In the first segment the child is dependent upon, and subordinate to, his mother in order to light the little hannukiah. In turn, both of them are dependent upon the figure of the father in order to light the large hannukiah and to recite prayers on behalf of the whole family. This series is an accurate rendition of the comparative status of elementary roles within the family. Family units then are made to constitute a symbol of the collectivity, the living hannukiah. The collectivity is seen to exist as a coordinated assemblage of families. Here individual families are dependent upon and are subordinate to the collectivity in order to relate to one another, and in order to create an alive and enduring vision of tradition and belief. The first segment builds up the symbol of the hannukiah in increasing degrees of encompassment and hierarchy. The apex is the living of this collective emblem. Integral to this are the ribbons, in the national colors, held by the children. Thus the hannukiah itself is embued with the symbolism of statehood; while implicit in this more traditional collective emblem is a more modern version.

The second segment begins with an expression of hierarchical family roles. The dyad of mother and child delineates the coherence of the family unit. The mother directs the movements of the spinning top, her child, in an accurate depiction of status and authority in relation to her offspring. But their reversal of roles is, at one and the same time, a representation of independence and of equality. The autonomy of children, and their founding of families, is expected to be an outcome of maturation. Through this process children partially are freed of their subordination to their family of procreation, and thereby are inculcated in their obligations of citizenship to the nation-state. As citizens, all Israelis are the theoretical equals of one another and are subordinate to the state without the intervening mediation of the family. In the third segment, the circle dance, there is no characterization of the family unit: the unbroken circle evokes egalitarianism and common effort and all the dancers are oriented towards their common center. Orchestrating their actions stands the teacher, just as the state stands in relation to its citizens.

Like the hannukiah alive, the circle dance is a living collective symbol. But each is in structural opposition to the other. The hannukiah depends on the family and on its internal hierarchy for its existence. The circle dance eliminates the specificity of the family unit and simultaneously relates each participant in equality to all others and to a statist apex of hierarchy that is not representative of family. In the sequencing of this celebration the unbroken circle with its apical center supplants the cellular hannukiah; just as, for children, with time the state will supercede their parents as the pinnacle of authority.

Purim: The Evolution of Maturity

Purim commemorates the deliverance of the Jews of Persia from the evil designs of their enemies through the persuasions of Esther, the Jewish queen of the Persian monarch. This story is read in the synagogue; and the holiday is celebrated by a festive family meal, and by the exchange of gifts of food among relatives and friends. An especially joyous holiday, it is the only time in the ritual calendar when some license in dress and behavior is encouraged. Secular celebrations take the form of dressing up in costume and attending parties.

Instruction books designate the holiday as an entertainment, with children in costume and parents in attendance. Little mention is made of the traditional significance of the holiday; and scenarios for its celebration rarely are given. It is left to the teacher to decide on the measure of organization desired. The example we discuss is in keeping with such advice. Its explicit enactment is intended to entertain and to amuse the youngsters and their mothers. However, in this there is a degree of implicit patterning that connotes the role of the kindergarten in the maturation of children. Of this the teacher denied any conscious knowledge.

Description. This celebration was held for three year-olds. Some two weeks prior, at a meeting of mothers and teacher, the teacher requested that the children be dressed in animal costumes. Her reason was that such figures were closest to the world of the child, and therefore more comprehensible to the youngsters. If this were not possible, then the child should be dressed as a clown. A few days before the party each mother informed the teacher of the costume her child would wear, so that the teacher could prepare her program.

The party took place in the late afternoon, at the onset of the holiday. Mothers and children were arranged in a wide semi-circle, facing an open area where the teacher stood. Mothers sat on the tiny kindergarten chairs, their offsprings on the floor before them. Music of the holiday played in the background.

The celebration consisted of two loosely articulated segments, separated by an intermediate segment of an unbroken circle dance. In the first the children showed their costumes before the assembly in a set order of presentation. In the second, five mothers who were dressed as clowns performed a rehearsed dance and song. The teacher, dressed as a clown, organized the presentation of costumes in terms of a simple narrative. Many years ago, she said, there was a king, and she called out a boy dressed as a king. He was joined by a girl dressed as a queen. In their court, continued the teacher, there was a zoo full of animals. She called out the inhabitants of the zoo. As each kind of character came forward a song that described its typical movements or activities was sung. The following was the order of appearance. Five cats walked on all fours and meowed. Then three rabbits hopped out. A bear fiercely lumbered forth and was introduced as a "teddy-bear." Three dainty dolls came forward and were described as living in cardboard boxes. All of these dwelled in the royal zoo. The teacher told a soldier, a policeman, and a cowboy to come out, introduced them as the "royal guard," and marched with them around the semi-circle. This ended the narrative of the zoo within the royal court. The remaining children, all dressed as clowns, were called forth. After this, all the mothers and children formed an unbroken circle, with the teacher in the center, and danced to the melody of a song about a little clown.

The teacher announced that the performance of the children had ended. She requested the performing mothers to sing. Each of their costumes was of a single color, and their song described the activities of clowns dressed in each of these colors. They sang in a line, with the teacher at their head. Food followed, and the party ended.

Discussion. Unlike the previous Hannukah celebration, this one of Purim was not considered to have any coherent scenario or explicit significance. The intention was to have fun and to give the youngsters the opportunity to play make-believe characters. The teacher had hoped that all of these characters would be animals—in her view, close to the world of the child. Faced with a mixed bag of costumes, she used a simple narrative to order their appearance. On a more implicit level this ordering is of direct relevance to our contention that kindergarten celebrations, in various ways, are engaged in the symbolic representation of rudimentary socialization, in the direction of adulthood and citizenship.

The teacher recasts the kindergarten as the court of a king and queen. This role-play is in keeping with the story of Purim, of Queen Esther and her Persian monarch. But from this point on there are no further connotations of the text of the holiday. Nonetheless, monarchy and court are emblematic of hierarchy, of moral order, and of social control. In short, these are symbols of maturity and of statehood that exist above and beyond those of home and family. A zoo is situated within the court and is filled with characters. In Israel, zoos are institutions where wild animals, instinctive and unconstrained in their nature, are locked in cages, artifacts of civilization that place external restraints on these creatures. This is a popular view of the zoo. In the teacher's view small children are close to the world of animals and so are driven by their instincts and are not governed by the obligations of maturity and by the norms of civilization. In the enactment children-as-animals are placed in a zoo, itself within a court. Through these metaphors the kindergarten is represented, on the one hand, as a locale of moral order with connotations of ultimate authority and so of statehood, and on the other as a place of confinement for those who have yet to learn internal restraint.

The order of appearance of the inhabitants of the zoo suggests strongly that the more "natural" state of youngsters is conditional. Their sequencing projects a developmental image of enculturation, of moving towards maturity within metaphors of hierarchy and control. The first animal to appear is the cat. Although cats in Israel sometimes are pets, the cities of the country are pervaded by a profusion of alley cats that are undomesticated, fierce, and wary of humans. Even as a pet the cat is a comparatively independent and autonomous creature. These are the primary stereotypes of the cat in Israel. In her narrative the teacher describes the children-as-cats as "looking for friends." That is, these make-believe cats desire to establish relationships, with the connotation of becoming more domesticated through sociation.

The next is the rabbit. In Israel this creature usually is found in the wild, and sometimes as a pet. In either case it is thought of as a timid, passive, and docile creature—a vegetarian in contrast to the more predatory cat. Although wild, the rabbit is more easily caged and controllable than is the cat. The rabbit is followed by a child dressed as a bear. However enthusiastically he plays this gruff bear, the teacher turns this wild and fierce creature into a "teddy-bear." Unlike cat and rabbit, the teddy-bear is a child's plaything. As a toy it is the human product of its natural counterpart—that is, a copy. Its animalism is man-made. A product of culture, it is a fully-controlled and domesticated creation, in contrast to cat and rabbit. Still, the teddy-bear retains its animal form.

The doll appears next. This is again a child's plaything and is man-made. Yet, unlike the teddy-bear, it is created in a human image, and its attributes of behavior are largely those of a person. According to the narrative the doll lives in a cardboard box, its own enclosure that is somewhat more akin to a home than is a cage. Where the teddy-bear is a play upon nature, the doll is a reflection of humanity and civilization. Of all the zoo creatures to appear, the doll is the most domesticated and restrained. These controls are inherent in, and emerge from, its human form and its attributes of culture. They are not a shell of strictures imposed from without, as in the case of cat and rabbit, nor an intermediate being, a domesticated animal, like the teddy-bear.

Left with a soldier, a policeman, and a cowboy, the teacher organizes them into a "royal guard." These are not inhabitants of the zoo, but stand outside it, and close and complete the framework of social control introduced by the royal figures. Like the latter the royal guards are fully human figures whose roles embody a regimentation of maturity and order. They are guardians of moral codes against the predations of more impulsive natural beings. Such associations are reinforced as the teacher takes these guardians by the arm and they march together. As she had not done with those within the zoo, the teacher identifies herself with children who, by being given roles of control and order, play themselves as they should become in the future—as mature adults.

Wittingly or not, the teacher has brought into being a small drama about the evolution and the enculturation of humanity and hierarchy that leads to maturity and the assumption of responsibility beyond that of the familial. Framed at the outset and at the close by human figures with statist and hierarchical connotations, the characters of the zoo are transposed from the wild to the tame, from creatures of instinct to artifacts of culture. Just as their mothers watch this encoding from the periphery, these youngsters see their mothers watching this happen to them. The children experience a brief metaphor of how they are perceived to be by the teacher and of what they are expected to become.

The figure of the clown was intended by the teacher as a fall-back costume for the children. Clowns were not included in court and zoo, but were presented afterward. On the face of it, these residual figures have no logical connection to prior actions in the sequence, nor to those that followed. In overt terms these clowns, like those of the clown-stereotypes that they copy, are simply unabashed figures of fun that are in keeping with the good humor of this holiday. Nonetheless, the deeper structure of the clown type likely makes these figures the most complex of the celebration (Willeford 1969).

These clown costumes, like those of numerous clown stereotypes, are composed of variegated elements that do not compose any simple pattern of symmetry and homogeneity, as do the other costumes. The elements of these clown costumes are without gender; they contrast with one another to a degree; and so, in theory, this kind of configuration should encourage an attitude of reflection toward the complexity of the overall composition. The clown is a human figure, but it is an experimental one that is constructed more self-consciously. In other words, the clown figure plays with potentials, and with the axiomatic and the taken-for-granted in human existence (Willeford 1969; Handelman 1980). Ironically, clowns are more figures of maturity than are authoritarian monarchs and regimented guards. The maturity of the clown is, in part, related to a freedom of action that accrues when self-discipline is more assured; and when one is well-aware that one is not that which one plays at. This is the maturity of adulthood, of the teacher and the performing mothers, all of whom are dressed as clowns. In our view, the appearance of the clowns, following on the characters of court and zoo, represents the completion of maturation. In a way, it signifies a reward that maturation carries with it—the freedom of action.

The appearance of the child-clowns is followed by a circle dance of all mothers and children. As noted, the connotations of this formation are of collectivity, egalitarianism, and joint effort. But there is no delineation here of the family unit, nor of the special bond between mother and child. Thus the teacher reunites the children with persons who first and foremost are adults, rather than mothers, after these little people have been represented as trained and developed in an idiom of social order. This process is validated in the second segment of the celebration. The teacher and clown-mothers perform a dance and song. The figure of the clown appears here as the apex of authority and maturity, with the teacher at its pinnacle. On this note the celebration ends.

In our view the entire enactment is an extended metaphor of a process of maturation that the child will undergo in order to turn into an adult member of a wider collectivity. The children are presented, through court and zoo, in different stages of development. These characters are super-ceded by the more complex figures of the child-clowns. The character of the clown, with its connotations of freedom tempered by self-discipline, is used to free all the children to rejoin the adults in an egalitarian circle dance. Thus the enactment is projected towards a future in which young-sters take their place of equality alongside their parents. The child-clowns also bridge the two segments. They share their figuration with teacher and performing mothers. The child-clowns blend fairly easily into the figures of the clown-mothers, who are adults indeed, and with that of the teacher-as-clown who here is at the apex of adulthood.

Mother's Day: The Creation of Family and Intimacy

This party was celebrated together by some forty children aged 3, 4, and 5, who belonged to three separate classes of the same kindergarten. The explicit aim of the teacher was to have the youngsters demonstrate their love and respect for their mothers. This included the giving of gifts by the child to his mother. However the sequencing of enactment conveys a more implicit pattern: that it is the collectivity, represented through the teacher, that brings into being the affective bonds of the mother-child relationship.

Description. During the prior week each child prepared a present for his mother: a piece of shaped dough, decorated, baked, and lacquered. A small hole allowed this to be hung on string, like a pendant. Each gift was wrapped, together with a greeting card. On the morning of the celebration vases of flowers were placed on tables, as well as an additional flower intended for each mother. The children arrived at the usual early hour; their mothers were invited for midmorning. The small kindergarten chairs were arranged in a large unbroken circle. An accordionist provided music.

Each mother was seated, with her child before her on a cushion. The teacher stood in the center of the circle. From the outset she instructed the children on how to greet and to behave towards their mothers. "Come children," she cried, "let's say a big 'hello' to mother! Let's give mother a big hug! Let's sing together, 'What a Happy Day is Mother's Day'." After the singing each child was handed a flower. They sang together, "A Fine Bouquet of Flowers for Mother." "Give the flower to mother," said the teacher, "and give kisses to mother." Each child turned, gave his mother the flower, and kissed her.

The mothers stood and were arranged in pairs. Each pair faced one another and together held their two flowers. The children formed a large circle and, holding hands, walked around all the pairs of mothers and sang. Mothers and children sat and sang together. The teacher said a few words to the youngsters on the importance of being nice to mother. The children stood, faced their mothers, and sang: "Let's bless mother, blessings for Mother's Day. Be happy in your life, for the coming year. Arise and reach 120 years."[10] The teacher instructed: "Give mother a big hug and sing, 'My dear mother loves only me, yes only me, yes only me'." After they had done so, she added: "Now smile at mother."

The mothers closed their eyes and each child gave his mother the present made especially for her; and according to instruction, gave her "a very warm kiss." The children sang together, while the mothers hung the pendants around their necks. Each mother and child formed pairs and danced and sang together. The lyrics concerned physical coordination of the "look up, look down" variety. The teacher enunciated the lyrics, so that they became instructions for movement that were followed with accuracy. All returned to their places. Since the day was Friday, said the teacher, she and the children were going to teach the mothers a song with which to welcome the Sabbath. After this singing the teacher announced that the "ceremony" was completed.

One mother stood and declared: "We want to say that it's true that we're the children's mothers. But we want to thank and to give a present to the real mother of the children while they're in the kindergarten. We want to give her this bouquet of flowers." A youngster was given the bouquet and presented it to the teacher, while the mothers applauded. Snacks were offered by the teacher, and the party closed.

Discussion. The explicit scenario of this celebration is clear. The children show their affection for their mothers in order to honor them. These qualities of emotional closeness are expressed through various media: song, dance, gifts, and numerous tactile gestures. According to the teacher the use of different media was intended to declare emphatically the strength and the vitality of the mother-child bond. The sequencing of these numerous acts was not meant to convey any implicit significance. Instead their purpose was to lengthen the celebration, and so to give the children many opportunities to demonstrate their appreciation.

In our view there is a more implicit patterning in this sequence: one that projects the creation of the familial bond out of collective formations, under the supervision of the teacher. The major social formation consists of an outer circle of mothers, an inner circle of children, and the teacher in the center. Each concentric circle constitutes a category of person—that is, mother and child. The child is situated between mother and teacher. Although each child is placed close to his mother, the affective expression of this dyad is orchestrated wholly by the teacher.

The initial stress in the ceremony is on the delineation of the social category of motherhood. Mother first is welcomed as something of a "stranger," and the youngsters are told exactly how to show affection towards her ("Let's say a big 'hello' to mother! Let's give mother a big hug!"). Such instruction may well be necessary to coordinate the actions of participants, especially when half of them are little children. Yet such directives also impress that an acquaintanceship is being formulated, that the category of children is being introduced to that of mother. It is as if, within the kindergarten, the abstract category of mother is being made real for that of the child. The intimate affection of the mother-child bond, one that precedes the kindergarten experience, is re-presented here as the creation of the teacher.

The first gift follows: a flower given to the child by the teacher, that he in turn presents to his mother. This gift is standardized for all of the mothers. Like gifts generally, its symbolic value establishes a relationship. Of common worth, this gift forges the same kind of relationship between each child and each mother. This rather impersonal gift serves to mediate into existence the category of mother and to articulate it to that of the child. This gift accords motherhood to each woman, through the proof of her status—her child who is the giver of the gift. In contrast to the developmental cycle of the family, here it is the alliance of teacher and child that forms and activates the category of motherhood. But the source of the gift is the statist figure of the teacher, and so the category of mother, and its articulation to that of the child, is shaped at her behest.

Subsequent actions support this line of interpretation. After the first gift the seamless circle of seated mothers is fragmented. The mothers form pairs: each couple holds jointly their gifts of flowers, and is connected through these. In other words, through the medium of the gift each mother is transposed: from being a member within the category of mother to becoming individuated, a person and a mother in her own right. As such she represents the motherhood and the nurturance of a family unit. Moreover, connections between families as discrete entities are delineated, as mothers jointly clasp their gifts. Yet these particular families still are denied children of their own. The youngsters are kept in their categorical formation that encircles these mothers. This implies that, from a more collectivist perspective, personhood develops within categorical boundaries: that, first and foremost, people are members of social categories, and only then are they accorded the status of persons with their own unique attributes.

The participants resume their original formation. The children stand as a category, face the mothers, and sing their blessings. They then sing, "My dear mother loves only me, yes, only me, yes, only me." This act marks the beginning of a transposition whereby each child is told to recognize the especially intimate and affective bond between himself and his mother. This shift is realized through the personalized gift that each child had prepared especially for his mother. This second gift mediates the creation of a unique relationship between a particular youngster and mother. Just as previously the mother was accorded personhood in her own right, so now is her child. The category of child is fragmented; mother and child are united, and the family unit is delineated.

This intimate bond is represented further as the concentric formation breaks up, and as each mother and child form pairs and dance and sing together. Each pair, like each family, is a separate and distinct entity. However its unity depends on the teacher, who tells each pair exactly how to coordinate their movements in unison. The special bond that is crucial to the existence and to the reproduction of the family is under her control. This is emphasized as teacher and children teach the mothers a song with which to welcome the Sabbath. The ceremony to welcome the Sabbath within the home, on behalf of family and household, is exclusively the domain of the wife and mother. Her expertise, should she do this rite, likely is garnered from sacred texts and from having watched her own mother. No external intervention is required. Here she is treated as if she were ignorant of one of the essential ritual elements that maintain the integrity of the traditional home. Instead it becomes incumbent on a representation of collectivity in alliance with its wards, the children, to impart such knowledge to mother and home.

The next occurrence is an addendum to the planned celebration, decided on by some of the mothers. It complements well the preceding sequence. One mother, on behalf of the others, thanks the teacher and calls her "the real mother of the children while they are in the kindergarten," and presents her with a gift of flowers, via a youngster. Motherhood, the special bond between mother and child, is returned through the figure of a child to its source in the enactment, the teacher. She is described as a mother and, by extension, the kindergarten becomes akin to the home, a locus of socialization that prepares the child for adulthood. Yet, in terms of this ceremony, it is through the kindergarten that the home comes into existence. And through this final gift it is to the kindergarten, embodied in the figure of the teacher, that this right is returned. The teacher is a representation of collectivity, and it is to this wider collectivity that authority is arrogated to mold these youngsters.

In other words, motherhood was delegated to the collectivity by a representative of the mothers attending the party. In Hebrew, the words "state" (*medinah*) and "motherland" (*moledet,* literally, land of birth) take the feminine form. Phrases like, "I gave my child to the state" or "I sacrifice my child for the good of the motherland" are common in describing the relationship of family-collectivity. Against this background the delegation of motherhood to a representative of the collectivity gains in depth of meaning.

From the perspective of family and home the implicit patterning of the whole ceremony recasts and reverses the normal progression of the domestic cycle: for it is the collectivity that creates the family. The usual view of parents, and the one that the little child first experiences, is that in the beginning there is the family; that into this nexus the child is born and within it matures; and that with time he leaves and establishes his own home. But here the progression is as follows: first the collectivity exists and is composed of social categories of people. Links are forged between categories, and from these there emerge discrete social units, or families. These are accorded the right to bear and to raise children; and from this there emerges the special bond between mother and child. In this process the rights of, and obligations to, the collectivity are shown to be paramount.

Jerusalem Day: Statehood and Citizenship

After the 1967 Six-Day War, Jerusalem Day was promulgated as a civil state holiday to commemorate the reunification of the capital of Israel. It is celebrated primarily through official receptions and other functions, which include a festive mass march around the environs of the city. The major thoroughfares are decorated with the national flag and with the banner of Jerusalem, a golden lion (the emblem of the ancient kingdom of Judah) rampant on a white background with blue borders. Jerusalem is the central place of the Jewish nation and state. The city was divided, from 1948 until 1967, into western and eastern sectors, the former within Israel and the latter controlled by Jordan. Within the eastern sector is Mount Moriah, the Temple Mount, the site of the first temple built by Solomon, and of the second, destroyed by the Romans in 70 A.D. This defeat spelled the onset of the Diaspora, the widespread dispersion of the Jews into exile from ancient Israel.

Circumventing part of the western and all of the southern borders of the Mount are walls that survived the Roman sack. These remnants of the outer ramparts of the second temple complex are all that was left of that edifice most sacred to Judaism. A short stretch of the western rampart is called the Wailing Wall, but is known in Israel as the Western Wall. For reasons overly complicated to discuss here, the Western Wall, long a site of worship, has become since 1967 the most significant symbol of the State and of Judaism. The Wall has become evocative of a nation whose florescence as a state awaited the return of its people. It is symbolic of a continuity that is perceived to have endured throughout the absence of Jewish sovereignty for close to 2000 years. Therefore it connects and condenses, as does no other physical presence in modern Israel, the glory and then the desuetude of the past and the national redemption of the present. We raise these points because much of the symbolism of this kindergarten celebration is focused on the Western Wall.

Description. Three classes of 3, 4, and 5 year-olds, totalling some sixty youngsters who belonged to the same kindergarten, participated. The celebration took place in the open courtyard of the kindergarten on the morning of Jerusalem Day. Parents were not invited. The courtyard was decorated with national flags and with cut-outs of the lion of Jerusalem. Most of the children were dressed, as asked to, in blue and white clothing. Each was given a small lapel pin that depicted the lion. Each class was seated along one side of the courtyard, with the teacher in the center and an accordionist nearby.

The ceremony opened with songs whose respective themes were: the ancient kingdom of Israel, rejoicing in Jerusalem, and the re-building of the temple. In a brief peroration the teacher declared that Jerusalem was and always would be the capital of Israel; that this day marked the liberation of East Jerusalem and the reunification of the city by the Israel Defence Forces; and that this day was celebrated by everyone throughout the country.

Four children of the oldest class recited a lengthy poem that told of two doves who dreamt that the people of Israel would arise. The two doves flew to Jerusalem and alighted on the Wall. The closing lines stated: "The children of Israel are singing a song; next year the city will be rebuilt." The assembly sang of the ancient longing of the Jewish people to return to Jerusalem. As this melody continued, six of the 4 year-olds danced, each holding blue and white ribbons. During the dance each child gave the ends of his ribbons to two others. As their performance ended the children were joined by the ribbons in the form of a six-pointed Shield of David (the *magen david*, commonly translated as the Star of David), the emblem on the national flag.

The teacher told a story taken from a booklet of legends about Jerusalem. The narrative spoke of a lonely wall, dark with age, and laden with the memories of the great temple, and of the free nation that dwelled here. Enemies burned the temple and drove out the Jews. They tried to destroy the wall, but their tools broke. The gentiles used the wall as a rubbish heap in order to obviate its presence. For centuries, in their hatred of the Jews, they dumped their garbage about the wall, until it disappeared from sight.

One day a diaspora Jew came to see the wall, but all denied its existence. He came to a great mound of rubbish and there learned of the custom of obliterating the Jewish wall. He swore to save it. A rumor spread that precious metals were buried there. The populace swarmed to sift through the garbage, found some coins of value, and uncovered the top stones. Happy, the Jew kissed the wall. The next morning another rumor spread that treasure was buried at its base. People excavated the rubbish and gradually the whole of the wall was revealed. No treasure was found except for that of the Jew—the Wall itself. Yet the Wall still was filthy; but a miracle occurred. Clouds gathered and rain poured, cleansing and purfying the Wall. And the Jew gave thanks for this salvation.

Dancing, and carrying toy blocks, the 3 year-olds built a wall of roughly their own height. The other youngsters formed a circle, held hands, and revolved singing and dancing around this model. With this the celebration ended.

Discussion. Unlike the previous three celebrations, in this one no reference is made to the family, nor for that matter to any social units that may mediate between nation-state and citizen. Their relationship is direct, immediate, and hierarchical. Here the family unit of the child not only is superceded but is rendered irrelevant to the nation-state. The nation is presented as the redeemer of the state, and the state as the protector of the nation. Both depend on the faith and loyalty of the citizenry.[11]

The courtyard is decorated in emblems of statehood; and it acquires the semblance of an official locale. The outfits of the youngsters are standardized through colors that shape these children into living emblems of the state. Thus their bodies are inscribed with signs of citizenship, of belonging to the collectivity. Each child appears as a small part that embodies the greater whole, itself composed of many such components. In other words, the ideal relationship between citizen and collectivity is one of synecdoche. This relationship is not manipulated during the ceremony, but is repeated in various ways.

The ceremony is divided into a preamble of songs and speech, followed by the formal enactments. The preamble enunciates themes and sentiments that are developed through the enactments. The opening songs lay out the connectivity of past, present, and future; although the words of each have in common references to verities that are held eternal. The first is about King David, who made Jerusalem the capital of ancient Israel. The second rejoices in Jerusalem eternal. The third tells that the temple, a metaphor of the nation in its reborn homeland, will be rebuilt. The words of the teacher situate these sentiments within the reality of present-day Israel. The assembly celebrates the reunification of the eternal capital of the nation-state, as do all of its citizenry on this day. Moreover this deed was accomplished by citizens in the people's army of the Israel Defence Forces, in which all these youngsters will serve on their completion of high school. Collectivity and citizenship are presented in and through one another in mutual interdependence.

The enactments begin with a poem that evokes a feeling of prophecy. The doves dream that the renewed people of Israel will rebuild the city around the central focus of the eternal Wall. In Israel the dove is an emblem of peace that harks back to the biblical story of Noah's Ark and the dove that returned with an olive branch, signifying an end to God's wrath. The poem connotes that the people of Israel will accomplish their task with God's blessing. The next song expresses the longing of people and nation to return to Jerusalem, and so to carry out this endeavor. The sense of prophecy is mated with feelings of deepest desire.

In turn, prophecy and desire are realized as six youngsters create a living Shield of David. This is a complex multivocalic symbol used by the Zionist movement to signify rejuvenation and attachment to a national homeland (See Scholem 1971). Here it is sufficient to note again that it is a preeminent emblem of the State. In this ceremony, children who sat in a loose assemblage create the precise and coordinated pattern of the emblem. As in other living symbols, just as they bring the emblem into being through their collective efforts, so its shape ties them to one another and incorporates them within a greater and encompassing design. The aesthetic and emotive effect is one of a symmetrical blending of part and whole, of the blue and white coloration of dress and of connecting ribbons. The implication is that the citizens of the future will continue together to carry out the design of the emblem, which signifies the actualization of the collectivity.

The primary message of the narrative of the rediscovery of the Wall is that the Jews must defend their patrimony, otherwise they will lose this. The tale is an allegory: the world of Israel, signified by the Wall, must be demarcated clearly from that of non-Jews who threaten its integrity and viability. This is the logic of nation and state, at their boundaries, and it is one that resonates strongly with aspects of the historical Jewish experience. In terms of nationhood then, one either is a Jew or one is not. In terms of statehood, one either is a citizen or one is not. In the ideology of the nation-state these two dimensions of inclusion-exclusion become almost isomorphic. The outer boundaries of the permissible are set by the collectivity, to which the desires of the citizen are subordinate. This is perhaps the highest level of contrast between "inside" and "outside" that is set for the Jewish citizen of modern Israel; and this is a lesson that youngsters will have reason to learn in numerous contexts beyond that of the family in years to come. At this level of contrast the hierarchy, values, and relationships of the family always are of lesser relevance.

The tale posits a series of contrasts between Jew and gentile that derive from a simple postulate: that the Wall, and by analogy the nation and state, are indestructible and enduring despite all the depredations of enemies throughout the centuries. This is its internal and eternal truth. By comparison all else is transitory. The Jew who returns to his source, across the gap of generations, is motivated by ideology. His is the wisdom of spirituality. The gentiles who try to destroy his roots are driven by materialism. He uses their cupidity to reveal the glory of the Wall; and his spirituality helps to bring about its cleansing. In the context of the celebration the qualities of Wall and Jew are those of the nation-state and its citizenry. The attributes of the gentiles are associated with all those who would deny to the Jews their homeland. The tale is at once a metaphor of renewal and a parable about boundaries of protection and national salvaton that, in the modern world, the state views itself as best able to uphold.

The closing enactment brings the message of the story into existence through the cooperative efforts of the children, just as the living Shield realized the prophecy of the poetic doves. The youngsters build the Wall from the ground up, just as modern Israel was redeemed through the joint efforts of its citizenry. The simulated labors of the children signify that which will be expected of them when they attain adulthood and full citizenship. The children dance in an unbroken circle around the completed Wall. Again their formation evokes egalitarianism, synchronization, connectivity, and perhaps the outer boundary of statehood that must be drawn and protected by its citizenry. Once more the center of the circle is filled, here by the model of the Wall—an emblem that is hierarchical and authoritative and, above all, a symbol of the Israel nation-state.

Conclusion

In the world of the little child the kindergarten celebration is among the very few categories of occasion when the order of things that structures the wider social environment directly intersects with, and dominates, that of the home. In part this is evident through explicit symbolism. Yet perhaps more profound in their impact are the architectonics of enactment. Their significance derives from the very ways in which people in unison are mobilized, organized, and synchronized in social formations in order to accomplish the more explicit scenarios of celebration. The lineal progressions of such formations constitute their own implicit sets of messages; and it is these that we have addressed here.

These celebrations, and numerous others like them, make extensive and intensive use of living formations. Some of these take the shape of explicit symbols, like the hannukiah and the Shield of David. Others, like the unbroken circle and the dyad, remain more implicit. In either instance these are highly powerful media. Through them the meaning of things is turned into the shape of things. The shape of things is graspable by the senses, as is the case of icon and emblem. Yet in such latter instances these shapes still are largely external to the human body, to the source of emotions and feelings. But one grasps the shape of things in living formations by living through them. This is a more sensual experience; one that engages the senses more fully to create a holistic experiential environment. Architects sometimes write of haptic space, of coming to know the shape of space and the feelings this engenders through the sense of touch. Through living formations the visual, the auditory, the tactile, and perhaps the olfactory senses are all "touched" by the shape of things. The meaning of form and the form of meaning become inextricable.

The sequencing of formations, in keeping with premises of lineality, are at the experiential heart of the kinds of enactments that we have addressed. Indeed, as noted, they are intended to touch the heart of the little child, and so to impress upon his being lessons that otherwise may remain more exterior to his sense of self. In particular we have stressed certain themes that will be adumbrated for the child in numerous ways and contexts in the years to come: for example, the relationship between hierarchy and equality. The interior hierarchy of the family is supplanted and is subsumed by the superordination of the collectivity. The collectivity, the nation-state, is superior to each of its citizens; yet they compose it, and it exists only through their cooperative efforts. In relation to one another, as citizens, they largely are equals. So too, as children grow, they will succeed and replace their parents, both as heads of family and as citizens. These processes depend on the proper outcome of that of maturation: the parent should infuse the child with internal restraint and with a sense of responsibility towards the collectivity and its component units. In turn, all of the above seems to evoke elementary patterns of social boundedness, and of the categories and entities that these demarcate and define. Thus boundaries between people, as members of categories and as persons, between family and collectivity, and between the nation-state and whatever lies without are taken apart, constructed anew, and, in essence, shown to exist.

Such messages are essential to the reproduction of social order. In kindergarten celebrations they are communicated in ways that make them easy to grasp for the little child. Youngsters are full of feeling, but they have yet to develop the kind of critical attitudes that can buffer personal choice against the demands of group pressure and the inducements of collective sentiments. Socialization through celebration, as instruction books for kindergartens note, is first and foremost an appeal to the emotions of little children. Thus moods and feelings about collectivity, centricity, control, and cooperation are communicated early on to Israeli youngsters. These sentiments were crucial to the periods of the *yishuv* and the early state, years of self-defense for survival and growth. Yet one should inquire whether the emphasis today on these and related values survives primarily through inertia, and through the inability of the apparatus of education and polity to check the viability of its own involution. The further growth of the nation-state may depend as much on the teaching of critical perspectives and of personal choice as it does on values that continue to close the collective circle.

Notes

1. Both in the pre-state and post-state periods there is no especial distinction between nursery school and kindergarten. Youngsters may be in kindergarten at age 2, and at age 6 continue on to elementary school.
2. The Hebrew term for kindergarten teacher, in the feminine gender, is *gannenet*. Its meaning is literally that of "gardener." The connotations of the term, as in English, are those of one who is an active agent in the processes of growing, of cultivating, and of taming. The term likely is a translation of the German *kindergertnerin*, a gardener of children, and is distinguished clearly in Hebrew from "educator" (fem. *m'khanekhet*) and "teacher" (fem. *mora*). The Hebrew term for kindergarten, *gan yeladim*, again is a translation from the German.
3. Our usage is analogous to that of "hidden curriculum" (Gearing and Tindall 1973:103), although we stress more the contested relationship between parents and state that is implicit in the maturation of youngsters, from offspring to citizens.
4. These comments hold as well for social science in Israel. The major exceptions are the study of kindergarten birthday parties by Doleve-Gandelman (1982) and the unpublished work of Shalva Weil on this topic. These occasions emphasize more the development of the child as a certain kind of social person. The ceremonials of our essay relate more to the implicit prefiguration of a statist view of social order. Therefore birthday parties are excluded from our discussion.
5. Descriptions of daily life and of ceremonial occasions in kindergartens were collected during the course of a seminar on these subjects, in urban Israel, conducted by Lea Shamagar-Handelman at the Hebrew University. The ethnographers were supervisors employed by the Ministry of Education. They observed kindergartens that they themselves supervised, and so with which they were conversant. Their observations and responses, and those of the teachers that they reported on, convinced us that the distinction between explicit and implicit agendas of ceremonials, discussed in the text, was a valid one. These educators quite consistently understood such events in terms of the obvious

occasions that they celebrated; and in terms of that which they perceived as the cooperation between teacher and parent in the attainment of a consensus on the education of the child. They did not acknowledge that the form and substance of celebratory enactments in the kindergarten implicitly communicated a statist perspective. However they did agree that the task of the teacher was to educate, not only the child, but also the parents. This is discussed in the following section of the text.

All the kindergartens observed belonged to the state secular stream of education in Israel. All their classes consisted both of boys and girls; although, for the sake of convenience, we use the masculine gender to refer to the child in general terms. These kindergartens operated six days a week, four to five hours a day.

6. We do not discuss an example of holy days, the Days of Rest, like Passover and the weekly Welcome of the Sabbath (*kabbalat shabbat*). These occasions are celebrated primarily within the family; while, within the kindergarten these, and others of the same category, are observed as rehearsals for family celebrations rather than as enactments. Their performance in earnest is permitted only on the correct ritual date and time, and in accordance with procedures laid down in texts of sacred standing. Their format of rehearsal in the kindergarten also is largely in line with such textual directives. Therefore the extent of implicit symbolic manipulation is more restricted; and so these kinds of occasion are of less concern to this paper.

7. On each of the four sides of the Hannukah top is inscribed the first letter of each of the Hebrew words, "Ness Gadol Haya Po" (There was a great miracle here). Spinning the top is a popular children's game. Regardless of which side remains uppermost when the top topples, its letter signifies the integrity and unity of the whole message, as does the top in its circular spinning.

8. In order to avoid confusion it should be noted that the *hannukiah* is distinguished from the *menorah* (the candalabrum) that appears as the official emblem of the state of Israel. The hannukiah has 8 candles (excluding the shamash) to commemorate the eight days for which the miracle of Hannukah supplied oil for the 6 candles of the menorah of the Temple on Mount Moriah.

9. In modern Israel the circle dance became a popular form through which to express egalitarianism and the dynamism of enduring bonds between persons who, through their cooperative efforts, forged the embracing collectivity of which they were a part.

10. The age to which, tradition has it, Moses lived; and a customary greeting of well-wishing.

11. We should mention that other such celebrations did not ignore the family, but involved it in the scenario. In some cases, fathers were invited to reminisce about their experiences as soldiers fighting for Jerusalem; while in others parents were asked to tell about life in Jerusalem under siege during the War of Independence. In these instances the stress was on the obligation, transferred from parents to children, to serve the country under any circumstances.

References

Ben-Yosef, Yitzhak. 1976. "Ha'khag k'besis ha'khinukh" (The Holiday as a Basis of Education). In *Sefer Hayovel Shel Histadrut Hamorim (Book of the Fiftieth Anniversary of the Teachers' Union)*. Tel Aviv: Histadrut Hamorim B'Eretz Yisrael. pp. 305-8.

Bernstein, Basil, H.L. Elvin, and R.S. Peters. 1966. "Ritual in Education." *Philosophical Transactions of the Royal Society of London* 251 (772):429-36, Series B.

Burnett, J.H. 1969. "Ceremony, Rites and Economy in the Student System of an American High School." *Human Organization* 28:1-10.

Doleve-Gandelman, Tzili. 1982. "Identité Sociale et Cérémonie d'Anniversaire dans les Jardins d'Enfants Israéliens." Unpublished Ph.D. Thesis. Paris: Ecole des Hautes Etudes en Sciences Sociales.

Durkheim, Emile. 1956. *Sociology and Education*. Glencoe: Free Press.

Fayence-Glick, S. 1948. "Khanuka B'gan Ha'yeladim" (Hannukah in the Kindergarten). *Oshiot* 2:28-39.

______. 1957. "Gan Ha'yeladim B'Eretz Yisrael" (Kindergartens in Eretz Yisrael). In *Sefer Hayovel Shel Histadrut Hamorim (Book of the Fiftieth Anniversary of the Teachers' Union)*. Tel Aviv: Histadrut Hamorim B'Eretz Yisrael. pp. 132-44.

Fuchs, E. 1969. *Teachers Talk*. New York: Doubleday.

Gearing, F.O., and B. Alan Tindall. 1973. "Anthropological Studies of the Educational Process." *Annual Review of Anthropology* 2:95-105.

Geertz, Clifford. 1972. "Notes on the Balinese Cockfight." *Daedalus* 101:1-37.

Gracy, Harry L. 1975. "Learning the Student Role: Kindergarten as Academic Boot Camp." In *Lifestyles: Diversion in American Society*, 2nd ed. Ed. S.D. Feldman and Gerald W. Thielbor. Boston: Little, Brown. pp. 437-42.

Handelman, Don. 1978. "Bureaucratic Interpretation: The Perception of Child Abuse in Urban Newfoundland." In *Bureaucracy and World View: Studies in the Logic of Official Interpretation*. Ed. Don Handelman and Elliott Leyton. St. John's: Memorial University of Newfoundland.

______. 1980. "The Ritual Clown: Attributes and Affinities." *Anthropos* 76:321-70.

______. 1982. "Reflexivity in Festival and Other Cultural Events." In *Essays in the Sociology of Perception*. Ed. Mary Douglas. London: Routledge & Kegan Paul. pp. 162-90.

______. 1983. "The Madonna and the Mare: Symbolic Organization in the Palio of Siena." In *Spectacle—An Anthropological Inquiry*. Ed. Victor Turner and Masao Yamaguchi. Tokyo: Sanseido. pp. 153-84.

______. 1984. "Inside-Out, Outside-In: Concealment and Revelation in Newfoundland Christmas Mumming." In *Text, Play, and Story* (1983 Proceedings of the American Ethnological Society). Ed. Edward Bruner. St. Paul: West Publishing.

Heffernan, Helen, and Vivian E. Todd. 1960. *The Kindergarten Teacher*. Boston: D.C. Heath.

Jones, N. Blurton. 1969. "An Ethological Study of Some Aspects of Social Behavior of Children in Nursery School." In *Primate Ethology*. Ed. D. Morris. New York: Doubleday. pp. 437-63.

Kapferer, Judith L. 1981. "Socialization and the Symbolic Order of the School." *Anthropology and Education Quarterly* 12:258-74.

Katerbursky, Zivya. 1962. *B'netivot Hagan (The Ways of the Garden)*. Tel Aviv: Otsar Hamoreh.

Langer, Susanne. 1953. *Feeling and Form*. London: Routledge & Kegan Paul.

Lee, Dorothy. 1959. "Codifications of Reality: Lineal and Nonlineal." In *Freedom and Culture*. Englewood Cliffs, N.J.: Prentice-Hall. pp. 105-20.

Manning, Frank E., ed. 1983. *The Celebration of Society*. Bowling Green: Bowling Green University Popular Press.

Ministry of Education and Culture. 1967. *Hannukah, Khag Ha'urim (Hannukah, Feast of Lights)*. Jerusalem: Ministry of Education and Culture.

Moore, Sally Falk, and Barbara Myerhoff, eds. 1977. *Secular Ritual*. Assen: Van Gorcum.

Moore, Elenora Haegele. 1959. *Fives at School*. New York: Putnam's.

Naftali, Nitza, and Nekhama Nir-Yaniv, eds. 1974. *Pirkei Hadrakha: Me'onot Yom (Subjects of Instructions: Day-Care Centers)*. Jerusalem: Ministry of Education and Culture.

Rabinowitz, Esther. 1958a. "Hakhag B'gan Ha'yeladim" (The Holiday in the Kindergarten). In *Khagim U'moadim Bakhinukh (Holidays and Times in Education)*. Ed. Esther Rabinowitz. Tel Aviv: Urim. pp. 39-44.

______. 1958b. "Hakhag, Mashmauto V'erko Bakhinukh" (The Holiday, its Meaning and Value in Education). In *Khagim U'moadim Bakhinukh*, pp. 9-57.

______. 1958c. "The Place of the Holiday in the Kindergarten." In *Khagim U'moadim Bakhinukh*, pp. 141-46.

Scholem, Gershom. 1971. "The Star of David: History of a Symbol." In *The Messianic Idea in Judaism*. New York: Schocken. pp. 257-81.

Shamgar-Handelman, Lea. 1981. "Administering to War Widows in Israel." *Social Analysis* 9:24-47.

Shemer, Aliza, ed. 1966. *Darkei Avoda B'ganei Yeladim (Ways of Work in Kindergartens)*. Tel Aviv: Tarbout V'khinukh.

Shulz, Jeffrey, and Susan Florio. 1979. "Stop and Freeze: Social and Physical Space in a Kindergarten/First Grade Classroom." *Anthropology and Education Quarterly* 10:166-81.

Shure, M. 1963. "Psychological Ecology of a Nursery School." *Child Development* 34:979-92.

State of Israel. 1983. *Statistical Abstract of Israel* (no. 34). Jerusalem: Central Bureau of Statistics.

Turner, Victor W. 1974. *Dramas, Fields and Metaphors*. Ithaca: Cornell University Press.

Turner, Victor W., ed. 1982. *Celebration: Studies in Festivity and Ritual*. Washington, D.C.: Smithsonian Institution Press.

Waller, Willard. 1932. *The Sociology of Teaching*. New York: Wiley.

Weiss, M.S., and P.H. Weiss. 1976. "A Public School Ritual Ceremony." *Journal of Research and Development in Education* 9:22-28.

Willeford, William. 1969. *The Fool and His Sceptre*. London: Edward Arnold.

Zanbank-Wilf, Aliza. 1958. "Hagan K'markiv B'yetzirat Avirat Khag Babayit" (The Kindergarten as a Component in Creating a Holiday Atmosphere at Home). In *Khagim U'moadim Bakinukh*, pp. 57-59.

24.

Education and Society in Israel: Selected Bibliography

David Glanz assisted by *Grace Hollander*

Education is one of the fundamental social institutions in any society and particularly in the establishment of a new "frontier" society such as Israel. The creation, organization, and institutionalization of schooling in a centralized nation-state is a social process that reflects a society's self-image, both as it actually is and as it wishes to be perceived. Consequently, the sociology of education in Israel provides insight into many of the country's basic dilemmas and its social structure.

The literature in both Hebrew and English on the sociology of Israeli education is very extensive. Although various bibliographies have been published in both languages, these lists confine themselves to limited and specialized areas of the discipline. We are not aware of any systematic effort made to date to organize the voluminous material that has appeared in English.

Our selected bibliography of over 750 items in English is a survey of scholarly works that have appeared on the social aspects of Israeli education in academic journals and books.* This listing, though not exhaustive, is a comprehensive summary of the English language output in the field. Its foci are the social and sociological dimensions of the education and socialization process, defined as broadly as possible. In determining whether to include a given item, we employed the most catholic criteria, including such topics as the family and education, youth culture and movements, studies in educational psychology with a social orientation, articles on social problems in special education, religious socialization, and adult education. We have, however, excluded articles dealing with purely pedagogic issues such as curriculum development, teaching methods, specific school subjects, psychological testing, research methods, and other topics that are

*Listed in accordance with a modified A.P.A. style)

not related to the social aspects of education. Unpublished dissertations, theses, social science research reports, conference papers, documents, and non-scientific popular articles were also not included.

In compiling this bibliography, our primary reference source was the Educational Resource Information Clearing House (ERIC) computerized data base. We examined all items appearing under the topic Israel from 1966, when ERIC was founded, until January 1987. Ms. Shoshanna Langerman of the Henrietta Szold National Institute for Research in the Behavioral Sciences also provided us with materials from that organization's computerized social science data base. *The Index of Articles of Jewish Studies*, a bibliographical quarterly published by the Jewish National Library and Kiryat HaSepher, was also double-checked for appropriate items.

In addition, over 200 sociologists, social psychologists, and educational researchers in Israel were queried and provided us with up-to-date listings of their publications; and journals published as recently as the spring of 1987 were examined.

As noted earlier, the bulk of the existing research and the academic work in the sociology of education in Israel appears in Hebrew. The bibliometric study of Teitelbaum, Pertz, and Langerman (1985), written in Hebrew, is the best available reference source for non-Hebrew readers who wish some insight into this Israeli literature. Drawing on the computerized data base of the Szold Institute, these authors located 1,114 research works in education published between the years 1974 and 1981. According to this study, only 9 percent of the research in the study sample was defined as theoretical-oriented, basic research, while 23 percent was categorized as applied or problem-solving, with 17 percent evaluation studies, and 51 percent descriptive studies. These findings are in part a consequence of the fact that 35 percent (387 works) of all of the research work is master's theses and 6 percent (62) are doctoral dissertations. Only 3 percent of this research was first published as books, with 34 percent appearing as articles and 23 percent as research reports in their initial publication. Excluding the master's theses and doctoral dissertations, which of course are all written in Hebrew in Israel, close to 60 percent of all other published works also appeared in that language.

The importance of Israeli universities as centers supporting educational research is clear in terms of the predominance of student theses and contractual research for the schools of education. The authors note, in conclusion, that approximately half of the research is done in teams and that most of the research in education is carried out by men despite the large number of women in the educational system. While this study does not address many of the points raised earlier in this introduction to our bibliography, it does provide a useful, if limited sketch of the realities of Israeli research in education.

While we do not view this selected bibliography as a trend report on the research in the sociology of Israeli education, it does provide an overview of what has been published. Even more importantly, it reveals those topics about which little or nothing has been published in the field in English. Initially, we thought this bibliography could be built on the foundation of earlier bibliographies of English-language materials on education. But we discovered a paucity of scholarly and strictly academic work in a number of areas, leading us to realize that future research on these topics might prove productive.

Despite the almost exclusive focus of research on the formal educational system, very little empirical matter has appeared in English on educational policy, administrators and administration, or even on teaching as a social profession and career within the school. Nor have teacher and student interaction in the classroom and the ethnographic study of education been developed in Israel as they have been in the U.S. and England. Other aspects of Israeli education that have received only limited attention include: higher education (the last major study of Israeli students was published in Hebrew in 1973, based on data collected for several previous years), Jewish religious education, education in the Arab sector, vocational education, the army as educator, and Israeli educational television. The sociology of education, knowledge, curriculum, pedagogy, and educational techniques appear to be relatively virginal territory as well. The political economy of education and questions of power and social control within the educational system have also been largely neglected.

Israeli social scientists have often tended to restrict their work in the field to questions of ethnicity and social integration, to the extent that the definition of the field of the sociology of education has been so circumscribed as to mean only that which takes place in elementary and secondary schools. Both James Coleman and Ozer Schild suggest some of the factors leading to this somewhat myopic conceptualization of the educational process. We hope readers of this volume will find in the articles presented and in the companion bibliography a broader perspective on the sociology of Israeli education and an avenue for deepening their understanding of the interaction between education and society in Israel.

Reference

Teitelbaum, R., B. Pertz, & S. Langerman
    1985.   The Research Literature on Education in Israel: A Bibliometric Study, 1974-1981. *Megamot* 29: 205-15.

Selected Bibliography

Ackerman, W.
   1973   "Reforming" Israeli education. In M. Curtis and M. S. Chertoff (Eds.), *Israel: Social Structure and Change*. New Brunswick, NJ: Transaction Books.

Adar, Z.
   1977   *Jewish Education in Israel and the United States*. (B. Chazan, Trans.). Jerusalem: Hebrew University.

Adiel, S.
   1984   Channels of communication between the residential setting and parents. In A. Zehavi et al. (Eds.), *The Integration of Immigrant Adolescents*. NY: Youth Aliyah.

Adler, C.
   1968   The Israeli school system as a selective institution. In A. M. Kazamias and E. E. Epstein (Eds.), *Schools in transition: Essays in comparative education*. Boston: Allyn and Bacon.
   1969   Education and the integration of immigrants in Israel. *The International Migration Review, 3*, 3-19.
   1974   Social stratification and education in Israel. *Comparative Education Review, 18*, 10-23.
   1976   Educational fostering and social integration: A sociologist's view. In C. Frankenstein (Ed.).
   1977   Sociology of education in Israel. *The National Directory of Sociology of Education and Educational Sociology, 1*, 14-20.
   1980   The evaluation of the Israeli school reform. In S. Goldstein (Ed.).
   1984   School integrations in the context of the development of Israel's educational system. In Y. Amir and S. Sharan (Eds.).
   1986   Israeli education addressing dilemmas caused by pluralism: A sociological perspective. In D. Rothermund and J. Simon (Eds.), *Education and integration of ethnic minorities*. London: F. Pinter.

Adler, C., and Hodge, R. W.
   1983   Ethnicity and the process of status attainment in Israel. *Israel Social Science Research, 1*, 5-23.

Adler, C., and Kahane, R.
   1984   Israeli youth in search of identity. *Youth and Society, 12*, 115-127.

Adler, C., and Peres, Y.
   1970   Youth movements and salon societies: A comparative analysis of youth cultures in Israel. *Youth and Society, 1*, 309-331.

Alpert, C.
   1983   *Technion: The Story of Israel's Institute of Technology*. New York: Hermon.

Amir, Y.
   1969   Contact hypothesis in ethnic relations. *Psychological Bulletin, 71*, 319-342.
   1975   Factors in improving ethnic relations between hostile groups. In J. W. Berry and W. J. Lonner (Eds.), *Applied Cross-Cultural Psychology*. Amsterdam: Swets and Zeitlinger.
   1976   The role of intergroup contact in change of prejudice and ethnic relations. In P. Katz (Ed.), *Towards the Elimination of Racism*. New York: Pergamon.

1985   Contact hypothesis in ethnic relations: A citation classic. *Current Contents: Social and Behavioral Sciences, 16*, 18.

Amir, Y. and Ben-Ari, R.
1985   Cognitive cultural learning, intergroup contact and change in ethnic attitudes and relations. In W. Stroebe, A. Kruglanski, M. Bar-Tal, and M. Hewstone (Eds.), *The Social Psychology of Intergroup and International Conflicts: Theory, Research and Application*. New York; Springer.

Amir, Y., and Garti, C.
1977   Situational and personal influence on attitude change following ethnic contact. *International Journal of Intergroup Relations, 1*, 58-75.

Amir, Y., and Krausz, M.
1971   Satisfaction in academic setting. *Educational Research, 13*, 141-145.
1974   Factors of satisfaction and importance in an academic setting. *Human Relations, 27*, 211-223.

Amir, Y., Rich, Y., and Ben-Ari, R.
1981   Problems of social integration in the junior high school, gain and loss to pupils, and proposed solutions. *International Journal of Intercultural Relations, 5*, 259-275.

Amir, Y., and Sharan, S., Eds.
1984   *School Desegregation: Cross Cultural Perspectives*. Hillsdale, N.J.: Lawrence Erlbaum.

Amir, Y., Sharan, S., and Ben-Ari, R.
1984   Why integration? In Y. Amir, S. Sharan, (Eds.).

Amir, Y., Sharan, S., Ben-Ari, R., Bizman, A., Rivner, M.
1978a   Asymmetry, academic status and differentiation in ethnic perception and preference of Israeli youth. *Human Relations, 31*, 99-116.
1978b   Attitude change in desegregated high schools. *Journal of Educational Psychology, 70*, 129-136.
1979   Group status and attitude change in desegregated classrooms. *International Journal of Intercultural Relations, 3*, 137-152.

Aran, L., and Ben David, J.
1968   Socialization and career patterns as determinants of productivity of medical researchers. *Journal of Health and Social Behavior, 9*, 3-15.

Arieli, M.
1972   The residential treatment center of youth aliyah. *The Forum for Residential Therapy, 2*, 331-342.
1986a   Students' supportive attitude toward their schools: The case of the Israeli youth village and its student society. In Y. Kashti and M. Arieli (Eds.), *People in Institutions: The Israeli Scene*. London: Freund.
1986b   Traditional contexts and present day realities of residential education: The case of Israel. *Paedovita* (in press).

Arieli, M. and Aviram, O.
1986   Staff roles in a total living situation: The case of an Israeli residential school. *Child and Youth Services* (in press).

Arieli, M., Cookson, P. W., Kashti, Y., Persell, C. H., and Shapira, R.
1986   Israeli Citizen and American Patrician: Total education in two societies. In Y. Kashti and M. Arieli (Eds.), *Residential Settings and the Community: Congruence and Conflict*. London: Freund (in press).

Arieli, M., & Kashti, Y.
1977   The socially disadvantaged peer group in the Israeli residential setting. *Jewish Journal of Sociology, 14*, 145-155.

Arieli, M., Kashti, Y., & Shlasky, S.
  1983   *Living at School: Israeli Residential Schools as People-Processing Organizations.* Tel-Aviv: Ramot.
Arzi, H. et al.
  1985   Proactive and retroactive facilitation of long-term retention by curriculum continuity. *American Educational Research Journal, 22,* 369-388.
Arzi, Y., and Amir, Y.
  1977   Intellectual and academic achievements and adjustment of underprivileged children in homogeneous and heterogeneous classrooms. *Child Development, 48,* 726-729.
Avgar, A., Bronfenbrenner, U., and Henderson, C. R., Jr.
  1977   Socialization practices of parents, teachers and peers in Israel: Kibbutz, moshav and city. *Child Development, 48,* 1219-1227.
Aviad, J.
  1983   *Return to Judaism: Religious Renewal in Israel.* Chicago: University of Chicago Press.
Avidor, M.
  1974   Education in Erez Israel. In *Education and Science.* Jerusalem: Keter.
Avidor, M., and Gitlin, G.
  1974   Higher Education. In *Education and Science.* Jerusalem: Keter.
Avi-Itzhak, T. E.
  1982   Teaching effectiveness as measured by student ratings and instructor self-evaluation. *Higher Education, 11,* 628-634.
  1986   Perceptions of role fulfillment: The case of fluid participation in organization. *Higher Education in Europe, 10,* 31-36.
Avi-Itzhak, T. E., and Butler-Por, N.
  1985   On perceptions of educational aims of school principals, parents and students: A cross-cultural approach. *Urban Education, 20,* 133-148.
Avi-Itzhak, T., and Kremer. L.
  1983   The effects of organizational factors on student ratings and perceived instruction. *Higher Education, 12,* 411-418.
Azarya, V.
  1983   Civic education in the Israeli armed forces. In M. Janowitz and F. Westbrook (Eds.), *The Political Education of Soldiers.* Beverly Hills, CA: Sage.
Babad, E. Y.
  1979   Personality correlates of susceptibility to biasing information. *Journal of Personality and Social Psychology, 37,* 195-202.
  1981   Performance and personality correlates of teacher's susceptibility to biasing information. *Journal of Personality and Social Psychology, 40,* 553-561.
  1982   Teacher's judgment of student's potential as a function of teacher's susceptibility to biasing information. *Journal of Personality and Social Psychology, 42,* 541-547.
  1985   Some correlates of teachers' expectancy bias. *American Educational Research Journal, 22,* 175-183.
Babad, E., and Bashi, J.
  1977   Age and coaching effects on the reasoning performance of disadvantaged and advantaged Israeli children. *Journal of Social Psychology, 102,* 169-176.

1978   On narrowing the performance gap in mathematical thinking between advantaged and disadvantaged children. *Journal for Research in Mathematical Education, 9,* 323-333.

Babad, E., Inbar, J., and Rosenthal, R.
1982   Pygmalion, Galatea, and the golem: Investigations of biased and unbiased teachers. *Journal of Educational Psychology, 74,* 459-474.

Baker, A. M.
1986   Validity of Palestinian university students' responses in evaluating their instructors. *Assessment and Evaluation in Higher Education, 11,* 70-75.

Balsi, Y.
1977   The kibbutz-integrated learning environment and informal learning experience. *Journal of Educational Thought, 11,* 224-236.

Bareli, C., and Schmida, M.
1981   Informal education in the Arab sector of Israel. *Plural Societies, 12,* 53-69.

Bar-Lev, M.
1984a   Cultural characteristics and group image of religious youth. *Youth and Society, 16,* 153-170.

1984b   Religious education in Israel. In J.M. Sutcliffe (Ed.), *A Dictionary of Religious Education.* London: SCM Press.

Bar-Lev, M., and Krausz, E.
1978   Varieties of orthodox religious behavior: A case study of Yeshiva high school graduates in Israel. *The Jewish Journal of Sociology, 20,* 59-74.

Barnea, M., and Amir, Y.
1981   Mutual attitudes and attitude change following intergroup contact of religious and nonreligious students. *Journal of Social Psychology, 115,* 65-71.

Bar-Netzer, H.
1971   Stages in the development of youth groups and the role of the madrich. In M. Wolins and M. Gottesman (Eds.).

Bar-On, E., and Perlberg, A.
1985   Facet design and smallest space analysis of teachers' instructional behavior. *Studies in Educational Evaluation, 11,* 95-103.

Bar-On, M.
1967   Education processes in Israel defense forces. In S. Tax (Ed.), *The Draft.* Chicago: University of Chicago Press.

Bar-Tal, D., and Darom, E.
1979   Pupil's attributions of success and failure. *Child Development, 50,* 264-267.

Bar-Tal, D., and Geser, D.
1980   Observing Cooperation in the Classroom Group. In S. Sharan et al., *Cooperation in Education.* Provo, UT: Brigham Young University Press.

Bar-Tal, D., and Guttmann, J.
1981   A comparison of teachers', pupils', and parents' attributions regarding pupils' academic achievements. *British Journal of Educational Psychology, 51,* 301-311.

Bar-Tal, D., Nadler, A., and Blechman, N.
1980   The relationship between Israeli children's helping behavior and their perception of parents' socialization practices. *Journal of Social Psychology, 111*, 159-167.

Bar-Tal, D., Raviv, A. and Goldberg, M.
1982   Helping behavior among preschool children: An observational study. *Child Development, 53*, 371-376.

Bar-Tal, D., Raviv, A., Raviv, A., and Bar-Tal, Y.
1982   Consistency of pupils' attributions regarding success and failure. *Journal of Educational Psychology, 74*, 104-110.

Bar-Tal, D., Raviv, A., Raviv, A., and Levit, R.
1981   Teachers' reactions to attributions of ability and effort and their predictions of students' reactions. *Educational Psychology, 1*, 231-240.

Bar-Yam, M., Kohlberg, L., and Algiris, N.
1980   Moral reasoning of students in different cultural, social and educational settings. *American Journal of Education, 88*, 345-362.

Bar-Yosef, R.
1983   On the status of the illiterate in modern society. In O. Grebelsky and R. Tokatli (Eds.).

Bar-Yosef, R. and Weiss, R.
1968   Desocialization and resocialization: The adjustment process of immigrants. *International Migration Review, 2*, 27-42.

Beit-Hallachmi, B.
1974   Self reported religious concerns of university underclassmen. *Adolescence, 9*, 333.

Beit-Hallachmi, B., and Rabin, A. I.
1977   The kibbutz as a social experiment and as a child rearing laboratory. *American Psychologist, 32*, 532-541.

Beker, J. and Eisikovits, Z.
1985   Residential group care in community context: Generalizing the Israeli experience. *Child and Youth Services, 7*, 159-165.

Belding, R. E.
1972   A private training mission in Israel. *School and Society, 100*, 319-321.

Ben-Ari, R. and Amir, Y.
1986   Contact between Arab and Jewish youth in Israel: Reality and potential. In M. Hewstone and R. Brown (Eds.), *Contact, Conflict and Intergroup Encounters*. Oxford: Basil Blackwell (in press).

Ben-Baruch, E., and Neumann, Y. (Eds.)
1982   *Educational Administration and Policy Making: The Case of Israel*. Herzilia: Unipress.

Ben-Baruch, E., and Shane, P.
1982   Autonomy and delegation of authority. In E. Ben-Baruch and Y. Neumann (Eds.).

Ben-David, J.
1962   Scientific endeavor in Israel and the United States. *The American Behavioral Scientist, 6*, 12-16.
1986   Universities in Israel: Dilemmas of growth, diversification and administration. *Studies in Higher Education, 11*, 105-130.

Bendor, S.
1977   University education in Israel. In A. S. Knowles (Ed.), *International Encyclopedia of Higher Education*. San Francisco: Jossey-Bass.

Ben-Gal, S., and Gershon, A.
1983   Culturally-disadvantaged children benefit from properly-prepared teachers. In P. Tamir, A. Hofstein, and M. Ben-Peretz (Eds.).

Ben-Peretz, M.
1980   Teacher involvement and cooperation in curriculum development. In S. Sharan et al.

Ben-Peretz, M., and Bar-Yoav, B.
1983   Social issues and science teacher education. In P. Tamir, A. Hofstein, and M. Ben-Peretz (Eds.), *Preservice and Inservice Training of Science Teachers.*

Ben-Perez, M., and Kremer, L.
1982   Value education as perceived by parents, teachers and pupils in Israel. *Journal of Moral Education, 11*, 259-265.

Ben-Perez, M., and Lavi, S.
1982   Interaction between the kibbutz community and the school. *Interchange on Educational Policy, 13*, 97-102.

Ben-Rafael, E.
1978   Higher learning and scholarship in Israel. In B. Martin (Ed.), *Movements and Issues in World Jewry 1945-1975*. CT: Greenwood.
1982   *The Emergence of Ethnicity: Cultural Groups and Social Conflict in Israel*. London: Greenwood.

Bentwich, J.
1965   *Education in Israel*. London: Routledge and Kegan Paul.

Bentwich, N.
1961   *The Hebrew University of Jerusalem, 1918-1960*. London: Wiedenfeld and Nicolson.

Bentwich, N., Dori, Y., Weisgal, M., Atzmon, D., and Editorial staffs of Tel-Aviv, Bar-Ilan, and Ben-Gurion Universities
1974   Institutions of higher learning. In *Education and Science*. Jerusalem: Keter.

Bernstein, D.
1980   Immigrants and society: A critical view of the dominant school of Israeli sociology. *British Journal of Sociology, 31*, 246-265.

Bernstein, J., and Antonovsky, A.
1981   The integration of ethnic groups in Israel. *The Jewish Journal of Sociology, 23*, 5-23.

Bettelheim, B.
1969   *The Children of the Dream: Communal Childrearing and American Education*. New York: Macmillan.

Bien, Y.
1972   The kibbutz: A working and learning society. In Y. Kalman (Ed.).
1983   A league of co-operating schools creates an educational and communal "self renewal process." *Research in Education, 27*, 23-39.

Biniaminov, I., and Glasman, N. S.
1982   Possible determinants of holding power in Israeli secondary schools. *Journal of Educational Research, 76*, 81-88.
1983   School determinants of student achievement in secondary education. *American Educational Research Journal, 20*, 251-268.

Bizman, A., and Amir, Y.
1984   Integration and attitudes. In Y. Amir and S. Sharan (Eds.).

Bizman, A., and Schwarzwald, S.
  1984   Effects of the power to retaliate on physical aggression directed toward Middle Eastern Jews, Western Jews, and Israeli Arabs. *Journal of Cross-Cultural Psychology, 15*, 65-78.
Blackstone, T.
  1971   Education and underprivileged in Israel. *The Jewish Journal of Sociology, 13*, 173-187.
Blasi, J. R.
  1976   The kibbutz as a learning environment. In O. K. Oliver (Ed.), *Education and Community*. Berkeley, CA: McCutchen.
Blass, N.
  1982   The evaluation of the educational reform in Israel: A case study in evaluation and policy making. *Studies in Educational Evaluation, 8*, 3-37.
Blass, N., and Amir, B.
  1984   Integration in education: The development of a policy. In Y. Amir and S. Sharan (Eds.).
Blum, A. A., et al.
  1981   The militant teacher: A case study in Israel. *Journal of Collective Negotiations in the Public Sector, 10*, 191-197.
Boocock, S. P.
  1974   Youth in three cultures, *School Review, 83*, 93-111.
Bowden, T.
  1976   *Army in the Service of the State*. Tel-Aviv: University Publishing Projects.
Boyd, M., Featherman, D. L., and Matras, J.
  1980   Status attainment of immigrant and immigrant origin categories in the United States, Canada, and Israel. *Comparative Social Research, 3*, 199-228.
Braham, R. L.
  1960   *Israel: A Modern Educational System*. Washington, DC: U. S. Government Printing Office.
Bruckheimer, M., and Hershkowitz, R.
  1983   Inservice teacher training: The patient, diagnosis, treatment and cure. In P. Tamir, A. Hofstein, and M. Ben-Peretz (Eds.).
Bruen, H.
  1984   Old-new land: Cultural integration and polyaesthetic education in modern Israel. *Journal of Aesthetic Education, 18*, 17-29.
Butler, R., and Nisan, M.
  1975   Who is afraid of success? And why? *Journal of Youth and Adolescence, 4*, 259-270.
Carlebach, J.
  1971   Some aspects of residential child care and the role of the Madrich. In M. Wolins and M. Gottesman (Eds.).
Carmin, A.
  1980   Problems in coping with the holocaust experiences with students in a multinational program. *The Annals of the American Academy of Political and Social Sciences, 450*, 227-236.
Caspi, M. D.
  1976   Some remarks on the training of school principals. In C. Frankenstein (Ed.).

Chen, M.
1976   Educational fostering schemes and integration. In C. Frankenstein (Ed.).
1980   Some outcomes of school reform in Israel. In S. Goldstein (Ed.).
Chen, M., and Fresko, B.
1980   The interaction of school environment and student traits. *Educational Research, 20*, 114-121.
Chermesh, R.
1977   Students' ratings of their faculty: Primary impression or dynamic process. *Sociology of Education, 50*, 290-299.
1979   Student evaluations of teaching and higher level cognitive learning: Do they conflict? *Educational Research Quarterly, 4*, 61-67.
Chermesh, R., and Neumann, Y.
1982   The construct and predictive validities of several instruments of instructional evaluation. In E. Ben-Baruch and Y.Neumann (Eds.).
Chermesh, R., and Zalgov, Y.
1979   The college instructor as leader: Some theoretical derivations from a generalization of a causal model of students' evaluations of their instructors. *Journal of Educational Research, 73*, 209-215.
Chill, A. S.
1983   Following footsteps. *Social Education, 47*, 279-280.
Coburn, A. S.
1974   Development of primary care physician manpower in England and Israel. *Journal of Medical Education, 49*, 575-583.
Cohen, A., Adoni, H., and Dror, G.
1983   Adolescents' perceptions of social conflicts in television news and social reality. *Human Concern Research, 10*, 203-225.
Cohen, E.
1976   The structural transformation of the kibbutz. In G. K. Zollscham and W. Hirsch (Eds.), *Social Change*. Cambridge, Mass: Schenkman.
Cohen, E., and Rosner, M.
1970   Relation between generations in the kibbutz. *Journal of Contemporary History, 5*, 73-86.
Cohen, E., and Sharan, S.
1980   Modifying status relations in Israeli youth: An application of expectation states theory. *Journal of Cross-Cultural Psychology, 11*, 364-384.
Cohen, Y.
1972   Towards the coming decade. In Y. Kalman (Ed.).
Danziger, N.
1982   Sex related differences in the aspirations of high school students. *Sex Roles, 9*, 683-695.
Dar, Y.
1985   Teachers' attitudes toward ability grouping: Educational considerations and social and organizational influences. *Interchange, 16*, 17-38.
Dar, Y., and Resh, N.
1986a   *Classroom Composition and Pupil's Achievement: Academic Impact of Ability Based Classrooms*. London: Gordon and Breach.
1986b   Classroom intellectual composition and academic achievement. *American Educational Research Journal, 23*, 357-374.

Darom, E., and Bar-Tal, D.
1981   Causal perception of pupils' success or failure by teachers and pupils: A comparison. *Journal of Educational Research, 74*, 233-239.

Darom, E., and Rich, Y.
1983   A measure for pupils' inconsistency of response to self-report instrument of attitudes. *Journal of Experimental Education, 51*, 160-164.

Darom, E., Sharan, S., and Lazarowitz, R.
1978   The development and validation of a multidimensional scale for assessment of teachers' attitudes toward small-group teaching. *Educational and Psychological Measurement, 38*, 1233-1238.

Devereux, E. C., Shuval, R., Bronfenbrenner, U., Rodgers, R. R., Kav-venaki, S., Kiely, E., and Karson, E.
1974   Socialization practices of parents, teachers and peers in Israel: The kibbutz versus the city. *Child Development, 45*, 269-281.

Diamond, S.
1975   Personality dynamics in an Israeli collective: A psychohistorical analysis of two generations. *History of Childhood Quarterly, 3*, 1-41.

Dobbert, M. L. et al.
1984   Cultural transmission in three societies: Testing a systems-based field guide. *Anthropology and Education Quarterly, 15*, 275-311.

Dor-Shav, Z.
1986   Jewish culture and sex differences in psychological differentiation. *Journal of Social Psychology, 124*, 15-25.

Dreman, S. B.
1976   Sharing behavior in Israeli school children: Cognitive and social learning factors. *Child Development, 47*, 186-194.

Dreyfus, A.
1983   The devil's advocate as teacher trainer. In P. Tamir, A. Hofstein, and M. Ben-Peretz (Eds.).

Dreyfus, A., Kushnit, T. and Keiny, S.
1984   Self renewal in the school and role expectations of teachers: A basic conflict. *School Organization, 4*, 41-48.

Dreyfus, A. et al.
1985   Biology education in Israel as viewed by the teachers. *Science Education, 69*, 83-93.

Dreyfus, T., and Eisenberg, T.
1984   Intuitions on functions. *Journal of Experimental Education, 52*, 77-85.

Drory, A.
1980a   Occupational considerations in the choice of academic training among Israeli students. *Vocational Guidance Quarterly, 29*, 125-133.
1980b   Expectancy theory prediction of students' choices of graduate studies. *Research in Higher Education, 13*, 213-223.

Dutter, I. E., and Seliktur, O.
1979   Attitudes of Israeli youth toward the Middle East conflict. *Journal of Peace Research, 16*, 137-153.

Eaton, J. W., and Chen, M.
1970   *Influencing the Youth Culture: A Study of Youth Organizations in Israel*. Beverly Hills, CA: Sage.

Eflal, A.
1971a   The preparatory groups (*Mechinot*). In M. Wolins and M. Gottesman (Eds.).

1971b   Youth centers. In M. Wolins and M. Gottesman (Eds.).

Eisenberg, T., Fresko, B., and Carmeli, M.

1981   An assessment of cognitive changes in socially disadvantaged children as a result of a one-to-one tutoring program. *Journal of Educational Research, 74,* 311-314.

1982   Affective changes in socially disadvantaged children as a result of one to one tutoring. *Studies in Educational Evaluation, 8,* 141-151.

1983   A follow-up study of disadvantaged children two years after being tutored. *Journal of Educational Research, 76,* 302-306.

Eisenberg, Y.

1986   The effects of computer-based instruction on college students' interest and achievement. *Educational Technology, 26,* 40-43.

Eisenstadt, S. N.

1965   The changing institutional setting and social problems of the Israeli educational system. *Acta Sociologica, 9,* 58-75.

1967   *Israeli Society.* London: Weidenfeld and Nicolson.

1973   *The Israeli Society.* (2nd ed.). Jerusalem: Hebrew University.

1976   Education as a tool for social advancement. In C. Frankenstein (Ed.).

1985   *The Transformation of Israeli Society.* London: Weidenfeld and Nicolson.

Eisikovits, R. A.

1983   Socialization behind convent gates. *Religious Education, 78,* 62-75.

1985   Children's institutions in Israel as mirrors of social and cultural change. *Child and Youth Services, 7,* 21-29.

Eisikovits, R. A., and Adam, V.

1984   Student responses to paradigmatic change: An Israeli experiment in educational anthropology. *Higher Education, 13,* 99-112.

Eisikovits, R., and Kashti, Y.

1985   Qualitative research in group care of children and youth: A cross-cultural perspective. *Child and Youth Services, 7 (Special issue).*

Eisikovits, R. et al.

1982   Models of effective youth organization: A comparative study. *New Decisions, Nov.-Dec.,* 9-19.

Elboim-Dror, R.

1958   Educational normative standards in Israel-A comparative analysis. *International Review of Education, 4,* 389-408.

1962   Problems of educational administration in Israel. *Public Administration in Israel and Abroad, 1961,* 69-76.

1963   Educational research in Israel. *Studies in Education-Scripta Hierosolymitana, 13,* 156-186.

1970   Some characteristics of the education policy formation system. *Policy Sciences, 1,* 231-253.

1971   The management system in education and staff relations in education. *Journal of Educational Administration and History, 4,* 37-45.

1973   Organizational characteristics of the education system. *The Journal of Educational Administration, 2,* 3-21.

1981   Conflict and consensus in educational policy-making in Israel. *International Journal of Political Education, 4,* 219-232.

1982a   Israel: Sysyphean reform cycles. In G. Caiden and H. Seidenkopf (Eds.), *Strategies for Administrative Reform.* Lexington, Mass.: D.C. Heath.

1982b   Main education policy-making actors. In E. Ben-Baruch & Y. Neu-
          mann (Eds.).
1982c   Some features of education legislation in the Knesset. In E. Ben-Bar-
          uch and Y. Neuman (Eds.).
Eli, I., and Shuval, J.
1982   Professional socialization in dentistry. *Social Science and Medicine,
          16*, 951-955.
Eliram, T., and Schwarzwald, J.
1986   School orientation among Israeli youth: A cross-cultural perspective.
          Journal of Cross-Cultural Psychology, (in press).
Elizur, A., and Rosenheim, E.
1982   Empathy and attitudes among medical students: The effects of group
          experience. *Journal of Medical Education, 57*, 675-683.
Elkana, Y.
1983   Elitism versus egalitarianism in higher education. *Neue Sammlung, 4*,
          366-374.
Erez, M., and Goldstein, J.
1981   Organizational stress in the role of the elementary school principal in
          Israel. *Journal of Educational Administration, 19*, 33-43.
Erez, M., and Israeli, R.
1980   Work-value orientations and their relationships to teachers' activities.
          Journal of Educational Administration, 18, 88-97.
Eshel, Y., and Klein, Z.
1978   The effects of integration and open education in the primary grades of
          elementary school. *American Educational Research Journal, 15*,
          319-323.
1981   Development of academic self concept of lower-class and middle-class
          primary school children. *Journal of Educational Psychology, 73*,
          287-293.
1984   School segregation and achievement. In Y. Amir and S. Sharan (Eds.).
Etzioni-Halevy, E., and Shapira,R.
1976   The Jewish identification of Israeli students: What lies ahead? *Jewish
          Social Studies, 37*, 251-266.
Fanshel, D.
1971   Research in youth aliyah: Some general views. In M. Wolins and M.
          Gottesman (Eds.).
Fassa, N.
1983   The labour federation leads the struggle. In O. Grebelsky and R.
          Tokatli (Eds.).
Feitelson, D.
1978   Research in early childhood education—Israel. In M. Chazan, (Ed.),
          International Research in Early Childhood Education. London: Social
          Science Research Council.
Feitelson, D., Weintraub, S., and Michaeli, O.
1972   Social interactions in heterogeneous preschools in Israel. *Child De-
          velopment, 43*, 1249-1259.
Feuerstein, R.
1971a   Low functioning children in residential and day settings for the de-
          prived. In M. Wolins and M. Gottesman (Eds.).
1971b   The redevelopment of the socio-culturally disadvantaged adolescent in
          group care. In M. Wolins and M. Gottesman (Eds.).

Feurerstein, R., Krasilow, D., and Rand, Y.
  1974   Innovative educational strategies for the integration of high-risk adolescents in Israel. *Phi Delta Kappan, 55,* 556.
Florian, V., and Har Even, D.
  1984   Cultural patterns in the choice of leisure time activity frameworks. *Journal of Leisure Research, 16,* 320-337.
Forte, M.
  1972   Parent-group education of the disadvantaged. In Y. Kalman (Ed.).
Fox, S., and Krausz, M.
  1982   An extension of the realistic preview concept to various career transitions. *Higher Education, 11,* 147-154.
Frankenstein, C.
  1976a   The complexity of the concept of integration. In C. Frankenstein (Ed.).
Frankenstein, C. (Ed.)
  1976b   *Teaching as a Social Challenge.* Jerusalem: Hebrew University School of Education.
Frankenstein, C., Frey, J. S., Fisher, S. H. (Eds.)
  1976a   *They Think Again.* Jerusalem: Hebrew University School of Education.
  1976b   *Israel.* Washington, D. C.: AACRAO World Education Series.
Fresko, B. and Kfir, D.
  1985   Introducing course evaluation in a teachers' college. *Higher Education in Europe, 10,* 52-59.
Frieman, L.
  1980   Education as a form of welfare: Legal and social problems. In S. Goldstein (Ed.).
Fuchs, I., Eisenberg, N., Hertz-Lazarowitz, R., and Sharabany, R.
  1986   Kibbutz, Israeli city and American children's moral reasoning about prosocial moral conflicts. *Merrill Palmer Quarterly, 32,* 37-50.
Gamson, Z. F.
  1973   College and the kibbutz. *Change, 5,* 22-24.
  1975   The kibbutz and higher education: Cultures in collision? *Jewish Sociology and Social Research, 2,* 10-28.
Gamson, Z., and Horowitz, T.
  1983   Symbolism and survival in developing organizations: Regional colleges in Israel. *Higher Education, 12,* 171-190.
Gamson, Z. F., and Palgi, M.
  1982   The "over-educated" kibbutz: Shifting relations between social reproduction and individual development on the kibbutz. *Interchange on Educational Policy, 13,* 55-67.
Gati, I.
  1984   On the perceived structure of occupations. *Journal of Vocational Behavior, 25,* 1-29.
Gaziel, H. H.
  1979   Role set conflict and role behavior in an educational system: An empirical study of the Israeli general inspector of schools. *Journal of Educational Administration, 17,* 58-67.
  1982a   Staff participation elementary school: Decision making and job satisfaction. In E. Ben-Baruch and Y. Neumann (Eds.).

1982b   Perceived ideal supervisory behavior and teachers' motivation orientation in an Israeli educational setting. In E. Ben-Baruch and Y. Neumann (Eds.).

1982c   Urban policy outputs: A proposed framework for assessment and some empirical evidence. *Urban Education, 17*, 139-155.

1984   Determinants of educational expenditure policy on the local level: A causal model. *Planning and Changing, 15*, 67-79.

Giladi, M. and Reed, H.

1985   Nonformal education unifies life-functions in the kibbutz. *Community Development Journal, 20*, 10-17.

Ginat, Y.

1971   Problems of policy and its implementation. In M. Wolins and M. Gottesman (Eds.).

Glanz, D.

1984   Aging and education in Israel. *Educational Gerontology, 10*, 245-267.

Glanz, D., and Harrison, M.

1978   Varieties of identity transformation: The case of newly orthodox Jews. *Jewish Journal of Sociology, 20*, 129-141.

Glanz, D., and Tabory, E.

1985   Higher education and retirement: The Israeli experience. *Educational Gerontology, 11*, 101-111.

Glasman, N. S.

1969a   Major planning activities in Israeli education. *The Journal of Educational Thought, 3*, 29-40.

1969b   Dilemmas in the process of educational administration in Israel. *School and Society, 97*, 392-395.

1970   The structural change proposal in the Israeli schools: Conflict and conquest. *Journal of Education Administration, 8*, 88-108.

1971a   Bargaining and its effect on administration and policy: Education in Israel. *Journal of Educational Administration and Policy, 4*, 46-54.

1971b   The rise of a junior high school movement: American and Israeli experiences compared. *Paedagogica Historica, 11*, 388-413.

1972   Religion through politics in Israeli education. *Jewish Education, 41*, 33-40.

1973   Decentralization and change in Israeli education. *Intellect, 192*, 122-125.

1981   Studies of secondary education finance in Israel and theoretical implications. *International Education, 2*, 15-28.

1983   Israel: Political roots and effects of two educational decisions. In R. M. Thomas (Ed.), *Politics and Education: Cases from Eleven Nations.* Oxford: Pergamon.

Glasman, N. S., and Biniaminov, I.

1981   Empirical relationships between organizational means and ends in Israeli secondary schools. *Journal of Educational Administration and History, 18*, 62-69.

Glasman, N. S., and Shani, M.

1973   On public funds and private education in Israel. *International Education, 3*, 21-39.

Globerson, A.

1978   *Higher Education and Employment: A Case Study of Israel.* New York: Praeger.

Globerson, T. et al.
1985   Teasing out cognitive development from cognitive style: A training study. *Developmental Psychology, 21*, 682-691.

Golan, S.
1958   Collective education in the kibbutz. *American Journal of Orthopsychiatry, 28*, 549-556.

Goldberg, H. E.
1979   A program for disadvantaged youth in an Israeli development town: An evaluation. *Anthropology and Education Quarterly, 10*, 21-42.
1984a   Evaluation, ethnography and the concept of culture: Disadvantaged youth in an Israeli town. In D. Fetterman (Ed.), *Ethnography in Educational Evaluation*. Beverly Hills, CA: Sage.
1984b   Disadvantaged youngsters and disparate definitions of youth in a development town. *Youth and Society, 16*, 237-256.

Golden, S. F.
1982   Religion in the schools. *Principal, 62*, 40-41.

Goldman, R.
1973   Cross-cultural adaptation of a program to involve parents and their children's learning. *Child Welfare, 52*, 521.

Goldstein, J.
1975   The elementary school principalship in Israel. *Journal of Education Administration, 13*, 118-138.
1976   Professional mobility in Israel's secondary schools: The results of survey attitudes. *Educational Administration, 12*, 51-67.

Goldstein, S. (Ed.)
1980a   *Law and Equity in Education*. Jerusalem: Academic.
1980b   Judicial intervention in educational decision making: An Israeli-American comparison. In S. Goldstein (Ed.).

Gonen, A., and Shilhav, Y.
1979   Spatial competition between school systems: The case of state religious education in Israel. *Geoform, 10*, 203-208.

Goodman, R.
1974   Israeli preschool children during wartime stress: Their knowledge and interpretation of the 1973 war. *Social Education, 38*, 367-370.

Goor, A., and Rapoport, T.
1977   Enhancing creativity in an informal educational framework. *Journal of Educational Psychology, 69*, 636-643.

Goralnik, I.
1972   Vocational training. In Y. Kalman (Ed.).

Gordon, D.
1982a   The concept of the hidden curriculum. *Journal of Philosophy of Education, 16*, 187-198.
1982b   Teacher training and ostriches. In E. Ben-Baruch & Y. Neumann (Eds.).

Gordon, D., and Ackerman, W. I.
1984   The Mechanech: Role function and myth in Israeli secondary schools. *Comparative Education Review, 28*, 105-115.

Goshen, E.
1984   Growing up in "Geulah": Socialization and family living in an ultra-orthodox Jewish subculture. *Israel Journal of Psychiatry and Related Sciences, 21*, 37-55.

Gottesman, M.
1971   An immigrant youth group and its absorption in a kibbutz. In M. Wolins and M. Gottesman (Eds.).

Gottlieb, Avi
1986   Rehabiliating disattached youths in residential centers: Problems and prospects. In Y. Kashti and M. Arieli (Eds.).

Grebelsky, O.
1972   The individual approach in life-long education. In Y. Kalman (Ed.).
1983   A second chance: A new beginning. In O. Grebelsky and R. Tokatli (Eds.).

Grebelsky, O., and Tokatli, R. (Eds.)
1983   *Literacy in Israel: Widening horizons.* Jerusalem: Ministry of Education and Culture.

Grebelsky, O., and Yaron, K.
1972   Trends in Adult Education in Israel. In Y. Kalman (Ed.).

Gross, M. B.
1970   The Israeli disadvantaged. *Teachers' College Record, 72*, 105-110.

Gross, R.
1978   Everyman's university: Open learning in Israel. *Change, 10*, 19-21.

Grunis, A. D.
1975   Legal education in Israel: The experience of Tel-Aviv law school. *Journal of Legal Education, 27*, 203-218.

Grupper, E., and Eisikovits, R. A.
1986   Student self-governance in three Israeli youth villages: An ethnographic evaluation. In Y. Kashti and M. Arieli (Eds.).

Guri, S.
1986   Equality and excellence in higher education—Is it possible? *Higher Education, 15*, 59-71.

Guttmann, J.
1982a   Pupils', teachers' and parents' causal attributions for problem behavior at school. *Journal of Educational Research, 76*, 14-21.
1982b   Israeli children's reactions to moral judgment dilemmas as a function of pressures from adults and peers: A developmental study. *Journal of Genetic Psychology, 140*, 161-168.
1984   Cognitive morality and cheating behavior in religious and secular school children. *Journal of Educational Research, 77*, 249-254.

Guttmann, J., and Bar-Tal, D.
1982   Stereotypic perceptions of teachers. *American Educational Research Journal, 19*, 519-528.

Halper, J., Shokeid, M., and Weingrod, A.
1984   Communities, schools and integration. In Y. Amir and S. Sharan (Eds.).

Halpern, S.
1984   *Every Home a Campus: Everyman's University of Israel.* Jerusalem: Institute for Educational Leadership and Jerusalem Center for Public Affairs.

Hamburger, M.
1971   The milieu is the message: Some observations on powerful environments. In M. Wolins and M. Gottesman (Eds.).

Hanegbi, R.
1971   Toward a theory of counselling techniques. In M. Wolins and M. Gottesman (Eds.).

Harman, D.
1972   Pre-academic studies. In Y. Kalman (Ed.).
Harman, Z.
1972   Multiple aspects of women's voluntary activities. In Y. Kalman (Ed.).
Harpaz, Y.
1983   The community school: Development of an idea: An ideological framework. In O. Grebelsky and R. Tokatli.
Harrison, J., and Glaubman, R.
1982   Open education in three societies. *Comparative Education Review, 26*, 352-373.
Harrison, J., Glaubman, R., and Strauss, H.
1981   Who benefits from the open classroom? The interaction of social background with class setting. *Journal of Educational Research, 74*, 87-94.
Harrison, J., Strauss, H., and Glaubman, R.
1981   The impact of open and traditional classrooms on achievement and creativity: The Israeli case. *The Elementary School Journal, 82*, 27-36.
Hedin, D., and Eisikovits, R.
1982   School and community participation: A cross-cultural perspective. *Childhood Education, 59*, 87-94.
Herman, S. N.
1962   American Jewish students in Israel: A social psychological study in cross-cultural education. *Jewish Social Studies, 24*, 3-29.
1970   *American Students in Israel*. Ithaca, NY: Cornell University Press.
1976   American students in Israel: The changing salience of an ethnic role. In A. Dashefsky (Ed.), *Ethnic Identity in Society*. New York: Rand McNally.
Hertz-Lazarowitz, R.
1983   Prosocial behavior in the classroom. *Academic Psychology Bulletin, 5*, 319-338.
Hertz-Lazarowitz, R., Feitelson, D., and Zahavi, S.
1981   Social behavior and social interaction of Israeli five to seven year olds. *International Journal of Behavioral Development, 4*, 143-155.
Hertz-Lazarowitz, R., and Sharan, S.
1979   Self esteem, locus of control and children's perception on classroom climate: A developmental perspective. *Contemporary Educational Psychology, 4*, 154-161.
1984   Enhancing pro-social behavior through cooperative learning in the classroom. In J. Karylowski et al. (Eds.), *The Development and Maintenance of Pro-Social Behavior*. New York: Plenum.
Hertz-Lazarowitz, R., Sharon, S., and Steinberg, R.
1980   Classroom learning style and cooperative behavior of elementary school children. *Journal of Educational Psychology, 72*, 99-106.
Herzberg, A. A.
1970   The relevance of education to the stratificational possibilities of the contemporary youth culture. *Urban Education, 5*, 253.
Herzog, H. and Shapira, R.
1986   Will you sign my autograph book? Using autograph books for a sociohistorical study of youth and social frameworks. *Qualitative Sociology, 9*, 109-125.
Hoffman, A. M.
1980   Workers' education in Israel. *Lifelong Learning: The Adult Years, 3*, 4-7.

Hofman, J. E.
1977   Identity and intergroup perception in Israel. *International Journal of Intercultural Relations, 1*, 79-102.
Hofman, J. E., Beit-Halachmi, B. and Hertz-Lazarowitz, R.
1982   Self-concept of Jewish and Arab adolescents in Israel: A factor study. *Journal of Personality and Social Psychology, 43*, 786-792.
Hofman, J. E., and Kremer, L.
1980   Attitudes toward higher education and course evaluation. *Journal of Educational Psychology, 72*, 610-617.
1983   Course evaluation and attitudes toward college teaching. *Higher Education, 12*, 186-190.
Hofstein, A. et al.
1986   What students say about science teaching, science teachers, and science classes in Israel and the U.S. *Science Education, 70*, 21-30.
Horowitz, T. R.
1980   Integration and the social gap. *Jerusalem Quarterly, 15*, 133-144.
1981a   The two worlds of childhood in Israel and the USSR (the Soviet child in a state of dissonance). *Crossroads, 7*, 169-181.
1981b   Assimilation v. integration: Immigrant absorption in the Israeli educational system. In J. Bhatnagar (Ed.), *Educating Immigrants*. London: Croom Helm.
1985   Professionalism and semi-professionalism among immigrant teachers from the U.S.S.R. and North America. *Comparative Education, 21*, 297-307.
1986   *Between the Two Worlds-Soviet Children in Israel*. Washington, D.C.: University Press of America.
Horowitz, T. R., and Kraus, V.
1984   Patterns of cultural transmission: Soviet and American children in a new environment. *Journal of Cross-Cultural Psychology, 15*, 399-416.
Horowitz, T. R., and Zak, I.
1980   A study of the teacher life cycle. In E.M. Ottobre (Ed.), *Assessing Teacher Effectiveness*. Princeton, NJ: International Association of Educational Research.
Hoz, R., and Nisan, M.
1979   The effects of the Yom Kippur war on values of Israeli female students. *Journal of Youth and Adolescence, 8*, 161-169.
Ichilov, O.
1977   Youth movements in Israel as agents for transition to adulthood. *Jewish Journal of Sociology, 19*, 21-32.
1981   Citizenship orientations of city and kibbutz youth in Israel. *International Journal of Political Education, 4*, 305-317.
Ichilov, O., and Chen, M.
1982   School-club activity and social integration in two educational frameworks in Israel. *International Journal of Comparative Sociology, 23*, 105-114.
Ichilov, O., and Even-Dar, S.
1984   Interethnic contacts in an alternative educational environment: The Israeli Shelef project. *Journal of Youth and Adolescence, 13*, 145-161.
Ichilov, O. and Harel, O.
1986   Patterns of discipline enforcement and the perception of justice in two educational frameworks in Israel. *Adolescence* (in press).

Ichilov, O., and Nisan, N.
1981   "The good citizen" as viewed by Israeli adolescents. *Comparative Politics, 13*, 361-376.
Ichilov, O., and Rubinek, B.
1980   Israeli adolescents' aspirations concerning some aspects of their future families. *International Journal of Society and Family, 10*, 81-97.
Ichilov, O., and Shacham, M.
1984   Interethnic contacts with gifted, disadvantaged students: Effects on ethnic attitudes. *Urban Education, 19*, 187-200.
Inbar, D.
1977   Perceived authority and responsibility of elementary school principals in Israel. *Journal of Educational Administration, 15*, 80-91.
Inbar, D. E.
1980a   Educational planning: A review and a plea. *Review of Educational Research, 50*, 377-392.
1980b   Organizational climates: Success-failure configurations in educational leadership. *Journal of Educational Administration, 18*, 232-244.
1981   The paradox of feasible planning: The case of Israel. *Comparative Education Review, 25*, 13-27.
1982a   The training of educational administrators: An holistic approach. *International Journal of Educational Development, 2*, 185-191.
1982b   Educational planning: Symbols and language. In E. Ben-Baruch & Y. Neumann (Eds.).
1984   Educational planning problems, decision making and communication. *Prospects, 14*, 489-495.
1986   Educational policy making and planning in a small centralized democracy. *Comparative Education, 22*, 271-281.
Inbar, D., Resh, N., and Adler, C.
1984   Integration and school variables. In Y. Amir and S. Sharan (Eds.).
Inbar, M.
1976   *The Vulnerable Age Phenomenon*. New York: Russell Sage Foundation/Basic Books.
1977   Immigration and learning: The vulnerable age. *Canadian Review of Sociology and Anthropology, 14*, 218-234.
1981   Some effects of stress during grade school years. In S. Bresnitz (Eds.), *Stress in Israel*. NY: Van Nostrand Reinhold.
Inbar, M., and Adler, C.
1976   The vulnerable age: A serendipitous finding. *Sociology of Education, 49*, 193-199.
1977   *Ethnic Integration in Israel: A Comparative Case Study of Moroccan Brothers Who Settled in France and in Israel*. New Brunswick, NJ: Transaction Books.
Iram, Y.
1980   Higher education in transition: The case of Israel: A comparative study. *Higher Education, 9*, 81-95.
1983a   Vocational training systems in West Germany and Israel: A comparative analysis of two models. *World Conference on Cooperative Education, 1*, 146-158.
1983b   Pedagogy as a discipline in higher education institutions: The case of Israel: Historical and comparative perspectives. *Journal of Abstracts in International Education, 2*, 29-36.

1983c   Vision and fulfillment: The evolution of the Hebrew University, 1901-1950. *History of Higher Education Annual, 3*, 123-143.

1983d   Alternative models of vocational education—Israel-Switzerland: Historical and contemporary perspectives. In K. S. Dent & P. J. Cunningham (Eds.), *Science, Technology, Education and Society since 1945*, (Vol. 6). Oxford: Westminister College.

1985a   Education Policy and Cultural Identity in Israel. In C. Brock and W. Tulasiewicz (Eds.), *Education Policy and Cultural Identity*. London: Croom Helm.

1985b   Higher education traditions of Germany, England, the U.S.A. and Israel: An historical perspective. *Paedagogica Historica, 22*, 93-118.

1986   Policy issues in the education of minorities: A worldwide view. *Education and Urban Society, 18*, 461-476.

1987a   Social policy and education for work in Israel. *Issues in Education*, (in press).

1987b   Changing patterns of immigrant absorption in Israel: Educational implications. *Canadian and International Education*, (in press).

Iram, Y., and Balicki, C.
1980   Vocational education in Switzerland and Israel: A comparative analysis. *Canadian and International Education, 1*, 95-105.

Iram, Y., and Bernstein, N.
1987   Early childhood education of the Basques in Spain and the Druze in Israel: A comparative perspective. *International Journal of Early Childhood*, (in press).

Iram, Y., and Masemann, V.
1987   Right to education for multicultural development: Canada and Israel. In N. Bernstein-Tarrow (Ed.), *Human Rights and Education*. Oxford: Pergamon.

Israeli, E.
1980   Arabic adult education in Israel: The present and the challenge. *Journal of Comparative Education, 10*, 47-53.

1981a   Adult education in community centres (*Matnasim*) in disadvantaged areas in Israel: The observed and desired. In J. H. Knoll (Ed.), *International Yearbook of Adult Education, 9*, 16-22.

1981b   Arabic adult education in Israel: The present and the challenge. *International Yearbook of Adult Education, 9*, 23-32.

1983   An attempt to "rehabilitate" a declining moshav in Israel: Phase one. *Journal of Rural Cooperation, 11*, 29-42.

Izraeli, D., and Tabory, E.
1986   The perception of women's status in Israel as a social problem. *Sex Roles, 14*, 663-678.

Izraeli, D. et al.
1979   Student self-selection for specializations in engineering. *Journal of Vocational Behavior, 15*, 107-117.

Jacobowitz, J., and Shanan, J.
1982   Higher education for the second half of life: The state of the art and future perspectives. *Educational Gerontology, 8*, 545-564.

Jacobson, H.
1983   Of chances and risks. In O. Grebelsky and R. Tokatli (Eds.).

Jaffe, E.
1985   Trends in residential and community care for dependent children and youth in Israel: A policy perspective. *Child and Youth Services, 7,* 123-141.

Jarus, A., Marcus, J., Oren, J., and Rapaport, C.
1970   *Children and Families in Israel.* New York: Gordon Breach.

Javetz, R., and Shuval, J. T.
1984   Drug use among high school students in Israel: A syndrome of social vulnerability. *Youth and Society, 16,* 171-194.

Jungwirth, E.
1983   Outspoken and hidden ideologies in science education and their implications for science teaching. In P. Tamir, A. Hofstein, and M. Ben-Peretz (Eds.).

Kagan, S., Zahn, G. L., Widaman, K., Schwarzwald, J., and Tyrrell, G.
1984   Classroom structural bias: Impact of cooperative and competitive classroom structures on cooperative and competitive individuals and groups. In R. Slavin et al. (Eds.), *Learning to Cooperate, Cooperating to Learn.* New York: Plenum.

Kahane, R.
1975   The committed: Preliminary reflections on the impact of the kibbutz socialization on adolescents. *The British Journal of Sociology, 24,* 343-353.
1986   Informal agencies of socialization and the integration of immigrant youth into society: An example from Israel. *International Migration Review, 20,* 21-39.

Kahane, R., and Starr, L.
1976   The impact of rapid social change on technological education: The Israeli example. *Comparative Education Review, 20,* 165-178.
1986   Technological knowledge, curriculum and occupational role potential. *Sociological Review* (in press).

Kalekin-Fishman, D.
1983   Implications of teacher burnout for the training of science teachers. In P. Tamir, A. Hofstein, and M. Ben-Peretz (Eds.).
1986a   Performances and accounts: Reflections on the kindergarten experience. In P. Adler and P. Adler (Eds.), *Sociological Studies of Child Development, 2,* (in press).
1986b   Burnout or alienation? A context-specific study of occupational fatigue among secondary school teachers. *Journal of Research and Development in Education* (in press).
1986c   Music and not-music in kindergartens. *Research in Music Education, 33,* (in press).
1986d   De-alienation: A problem of education for a liberated consciousness. In S.G. Shoham (Ed.), *Alienation and Violence.* London: Science Reviews Limited.

Kalman, Y. (Ed.)
1972   *Life-long education in Israel.* Jerusalem: Ministry of Education and Culture.

Kashti, Y.
1971   Educational and organizational trends in the youth village. In M. Wolins and M. Gottesmann (Eds.).

1978a   Stagnation and change in Israeli education. *Comparative Education, 14*, 151-161.

1978b   The residential setting and its influence on change in attitudes and values among disadvantaged youth. *Canadian and International Education, 7*, 81-94.

1979   *The Socializing Community: Disadvantaged Adolescents in Israeli Youth Villages.* Tel Aviv: Monograph Series, School of Education, Tel Aviv University.

Kashti, Y., and Arieli, M.

1977   Residential schools as powerful environments. *Mental Health and Society, 3*, 223-232.

1979   Israel residential education. In C. J. Payne and K. J. White (Eds.), *Caring for Deprived Children.* London: Croom Helm.

1985   Social conditions and pupils' responses in Israeli residential schools. *Child and Youth Services, 7*, 51-70.

Kashti, Y., and Arieli M. (Eds.)

1986   *People in Institutions: The Israeli Scene.* London: Freund.

1987   *Residential Settings and the Community: Congruence and Conflict.* London: Freund.

Kashti, Y., Arieli, M., and Harel, Y.

1984   Classroom seating as a definition of situation: Observations in an elementary school in one development town. *Urban Education, 19*, 161-181.

Kashti, Y., and Shalev, U.

1986   The educational institution of the kibbutz as a socializing organization. In Y. Kashti and M. Arieli (Eds.).

Katriel, T. and Nesher, P.

1986   "Gibush": The rhetoric of cohesion in Israeli school culture. *Comparative Education Review* (in press).

Katz, E., and Adoni, H.

1972   Functions of the book for society and self. In Y. Kalman (Ed.)

Katz, Y. J., and Ronen, M.

1986   A cross-cultural validation of our conservatism scale in a multi-ethnic society: The case of Israel. *Journal of Social Psychology* (in press).

Katz, Y. J., Schmida, M., and Dor-Shav, Z.

1986   Two different education structures in Israel and social integration. *Educational Research, 28*, 141-146.

Katznelson, S.

1972   The ulpan and its students. In Y. Kalman (Ed.)

Kedem, P., and Bar-Lev, M.

1983   Is giving up traditional religious culture part of the price to be paid for acquiring higher education? Adaptation of academic western culture by Jewish Israeli university students of Middle Eastern origin. *Higher Education, 12*, 373-388.

Kedem, P., and Cohen, D.

1987   The effects of religious education on moral judgment. *Journal of Psychology and Judaism, 11*, (in press).

Keiny, S.

1985   Action research in the school: A case study. *Cambridge Journal of Education, 15*.

Keiny, S. and Jungwirth, E.
  1982   Changing science teacher's role perception and teaching behavior, by means of an experimental course in human relations. *Science Education, 66*, 789-797.

Klaff, V.
  1977   Residence and integration in Israel: A mosaic of segregated peoples. *Ethnicity, 4*, 103-121.

Klein, P. S.
  1982   Preschoolers' temperament ratings in relation to their performance on cognitive tasks. *Israel Journal of Psychiatry and Related Sciences, 19*, 199-214.

Klein, Z., and Eshel, Y.
  1977   *The Open Classroom in Cross Cultural Perspective*. Jerusalem: Hebrew University.
  1980a   The open classroom in cross cultural perspective. *Sociology of Education, 53*, 114-121.
  1980b   *Integrating Jerusalem Schools*. New York: Academic Press.
  1980c   The Nachlaoth project: An Israeli experiment in school integration. In S. Goldstein (Ed.)
  1981   Development of academic self concept of lower class and middle class primary school children. *Journal of Educational Psychology, 73*, 287-293.

Kleinberger, A. F.
  1966   *Society, Schools and Progress in Israel*. New York: Pergamon.
  1975   A comparative analysis of compulsory education laws. *Comparative Education, 11*, 219-230.

Kodesh, S.
  1972   Diffusion of hebrew. In Y. Kalman (Ed.)

Kohen-Raz, R.
  1972   *From Chaos to Reality: An Experiment in the Re-education of Emotionally Disturbed Immigrant Youth in a Kibbutz*. New York: Gordon and Breach.

Krausz, E. and Bar-Lev, M.
  1978   Varieties of orthodox religious behavior: A case study of Yeshiva high school graduates in Israel. *The Jewish Journal of Sociology, 20*, 59-74.

Kremer, L.
  1978   Teachers' attitudes toward educational goals as reflected in classroom behavior. *Journal of Educational Psychology, 70*, 993-997.
  1982a   Locus of control, attitudes toward education and teaching behaviors. *Scandinavian Journal of Educational Research, 26*, 1-11.
  1982b   Professional development of elementary school principals: A case study of in-service training of Israeli principals. In E. Ben-Baruch and Y. Neumann (Eds.).
  1983   The role of the elementary school principal as perceived by Israeli principals: An attempt at role analysis. *International Review of Education, 29*, 37-46.

Kremer, L., and Ben-Peretz, M.
  1981   Personal characteristics of teachers, situational variables and deliberations in the process of planning instruction. *Research in Education, 26*, 21-30.

Kremer, L., and Moore, M.
1978   Changes in attitudes toward education during teacher training. *International Review of Education, 24*, 511-513.

Kremer-Hayon, L., and Avi-Yitzhak, T. E.
1986   Roles of academic department chairpersons at the university level. *Higher Eduation, 15*, 105-112.

Kugelmass, S.
1981   Considerations toward a policy of evaluation research: The case of the chief scientist at the Israeli ministry of education. *Studies in Educational Evaluation, 7*, 161-171.

Kugelmass, S., Levy, A., et al.
1981   *Decision Oriented Evaluation in Education: The Case of Israel.* Philadelphia: International Science Services.

Kugelmass, S., Lieblich, A., and Bossik, D.
1974   Patterns of intellectual ability in Jewish and Arab children in Israel. *Journal of Cross-Cultural Psychology, 5*, 184-198.

Kuperman, A.
1980   Training trainers for small-group teaching in Israel. In S. Sharan et al. (Eds.).

Kurtz, C., and Kremer, L.
1982   Personality characteristics and teaching behavior. *Education, 102*, 359-365.

Kurzweil, Z. E.
1964a   *Modern trends in Jewish education.* NY: T. Yoseloff.
1964b   The educational philosophy of A. D. Gordon. In Kurzweil, Z. E.
1964c   The revival of Hebrew and the foundation of the Tarbut schools. In Kurzweil, Z. E.
1964d   Some aspects of kibbutz education. In Kurzweil, Z. E.
1964e   Rabbi Kook (His influence on Jewish education). In Kurzweil, Z. E.
1964f   How Jewish are Israeli general schools? In Kurzweil, Z. E.
1964g   Some aspects of kibbutz education. In Z. E. Kurzweil.

Lamm, Z.
1978   Ideological tensions in education. *Jerusalem Quarterly, 6*, 94-110.

Laufer, Z.
1985   Institutional placement: An interim stage or an end in itself? The role criteria in the continuum of care. *Child and Youth Services, 7*, 33-50.

Laufert, L.
1983   Theory and practice in the planning of studies for adults. In O. Grebelsky and R. Tokatli (Eds.).

Lavi, Z.
1982   Toward an alternative evaluation for kibbutz schools. *Interchange on Educational Policy, 13, 92-96.*

Lazarowitz, R. See also Hertz-Lazarowitz, R.
1982   Teaching biology concepts to disadvantaged fourth-grade pupils. *Journal of Biological Education, 16*, 59-64.

Lazarowitz, R., and Hertz-Lazarowitz, R.
1979   Choices and preferences of science subjects by junior high school students in Israel. *Journal of Research in Science Teaching, 16*, 317-323.

Lazarowitz, R., Sharan, S., and Steinberg, R.
1980   Classroom learning styles and cooperative behavior of elementary school children. *Journal of Educational Psychology, 72*, 97-104.

Lazarowitz, R. et al.
 1983   Comparative-investigative learning (CIL) approach for science class-
          rooms: Workshop guide. In P. Tamir, A. Hofstein & M. Ben-Peretz
          (Eds.).

Lazin, F. A.
 1982   Education policy in Israel: The reality of implementation. In E. Ben-
          Baruch and Y. Neumann (Eds.).

Levenston, H.
 1982   Teaching English to the "disadvantaged": What do teachers think and
          how does this affect their classroom relationships? *English Teachers'
          Journal (Israel), 28*, 27-32.

Leviatan, U.
 1982   Higher education in the Israeli kibbutz: Revolution and effect. *Inter-
          change, 13*, 68-82.

Leviatan, U., and Orchan, E.
 1982   Kibbutz ex-members and their adjustment to life outside the kibbutz.
          Interchange on Educational Policy, 13, 16-28.

Levin, G.
 1982   Early childhood education in the kibbutz. In Nir-Yaniv et al. (Eds.).

Levin, T.
 1980   Classroom climate as criterion in evaluating individualized instruction
          in Israel. *Studies in Educational Evaluation, 6*, 291-292.

Levine, S.
 1984   Alienated Jewish youth and religious seminaries—An alternative to
          cults? *Adolescence, 19*, 183-199.

Levy, A., and Chen, M.
 1976   Closing or widening of the achievement gap. *Studies in Administration
          and Organization, 4*.

Levy, S.
 1984   Structure and dynamics of proscriptive values of Israeli high school
          youth. *Youth and Society, 16*, 217-235.

Lewin, T.
 1980   Patterns of classroom interaction in individualized and traditional in-
          structional strategies. *Journal of Classroom Interaction, 15*, 15-20.

Lewis, A.
 1979   Educational policy and social inequality in Israel. *The Jerusalem
          Quarterly, 12*, 101-111.

 1980   *Power, poverty and education.* Ramat-Gan: Turtledove.

 1981   Minority education in Sharonia, Israel and Stockton, California: A
          comparative analysis. *Anthropology and Education, 12*, 30-50.

Lewy, A.
 1981   Student achievement in Israel of immigrants from developed and de-
          veloping countries. *American Educational Research Journal, 18*,
          113-118.

 1985   Minimum requirement program: A potential device for promoting
          equality. *Studies in Educational Evaluation, 11*, 315-320.

Lewy, A., and Chen, M.
 1977   Differences in achievement: A comparison over time of ethnic group
          achievement in the Israeli elementary school. *Evaluation in Educa-
          tion, 1*, 3-72.

Lieblich, A., and Kugelmass, S.
1981   Pattern of intellectual ability of Arab school children in Israel. *Intelligence, 5,* 311-320.
Lieblich, A., Kugelmass, S., and Ehrlich, C.
1975   Patterns of intellectual ability in Jewish and Arab children in Israel. *Journal of Cross-Cultural Psychology, 6,* 218-226.
Liegle, L.
1980   Some remarks on deficiencies and perspectives of research on socialization in the kibbutz. In K. Bartolke, T. Bermann, and L. Liegle (Eds.), *Integrated Cooperatives in the Industrial Society: The Example of the Kibbutz.* Assen: Van Gorcum.
Linn, R.
1984   Practising moral judgement within the day care center: A look at the educator's moral decision under stress. *Early Child Development and Care, 15,* 117-132.
Lipset, S. M.
1974   Education and equality or inequality: Israel and the United States compared. *Society, 11,* 56-61.
Lissak, M.
1977   The Israeli defense forces as an agent of socialization and education: A research in role expansion in a democratic state. In M. R. Van Gils (Ed.), *The Perceived Role of the Military.* Rotterdam: Rotterdam University Press.
Lombard, A. D.
1971   Preschool education in Israel. *International Journal of Early Childhood, 3,* 82-89.
1981a   Hippy: Home instruction program for preschool youngsters. In N. Nir-Yaniv, B. Spondek, and D. Steg (Eds.), *Early Childhood Education: International Perspectives.* New York: Plenum.
1981b   *Success begins at home: Educational Foundations for Preschoolers.* Lexington, Mass: D. C. Heath.
1983   Home instruction for preschool youngsters. In O. Grebelsky and R. Tokatli (Eds.).
Lubling, A., and Zorman, R.
1982   The educational enrichment center: A holistic community approach model. *Gifted Child Quarterly, 26,* 74-76.
Mahler, S. et al.
1986   The class size effect upon activity and cognitive dimensions of lessons in higher education. *Assessment and Evaluation in Higher Education, 11,* 43-59.
Majteles, D. H.
1977   Child care in Israel: Is this a model for America? *Day Care and Early Education, 5,* 33-37.
Malkin, Y.
1972   Adult education and the Arab population of Israel. In Y. Kalman (Ed.).
Manneberg, E.
1973   Change in the structure of continuing education in the Israeli elementary and secondary Hebrew public educational system. *International Journal of Continuing Education and Training, 3,* 37-53.

Margalit, M.
1986a   Perception of parents' behavior, familial satisfaction and sense of co-
          herence in hyperactive children. *Journal of School Psychology, 23*,
          355-364.
1986b   Role perception of therapeutic teaching. *Journal of Special Education,
          19*, 205-213.
Margalit, M., and Miron, M.
1983   The attitudes of Israeli adolescents toward handicapped people. *The
          Exceptional Child, 30*, 195-200.
Margalit, T.
1983   Teaching geography in adult basic education programme. In O. Gre-
          belsky and R. Tokatli (Eds.).
Mar'i, S. K.
1978   *Arab Education in Israel.* Syracuse, NY: Syracuse University Press.
Markus, E., and Barasch, M.
1982   Assessing ethnic integration in the classroom. *Journal of Research and
          Development in Education, 5*, 1-10.
Meier, P.
1985   Community schools in Israel: The potential for integration with group
          care institutions for troubled children and youth. *Child and Youth
          Services, 7*, 91-108.
Menis, Y.
1984   Improvement in student attitudes and development of scientific curi-
          osity by means of computer studies. *Educational Technology, 24*,
          31-32.
Metzer, D.
1983   Adult education in the Israel defense forces. In O. Grebelsky and R.
          Tokatli (Eds.).
Mevarech, Z., and Rich, Y.
1985   Effects of computer-assisted mathematics instruction on disadvan-
          taged pupils' cognitive affective development. *Journal of Educational
          Research, 79*, 5-11.
Milgram, N. A.
1980   Educable mentally retarded pupils in Israel-policy and research.
          School Psychology International, 1, 28-30.
Milgram, R. M., and Milgram, N. A.
1976   Personality characteristics of gifted Israeli children. *Journal of Genetic
          Psychology, 129*, 185-194.
Miller, J.
1976   Learning under siege on the West Bank. *Change, 7*, 18-21.
Miller, N.
1984   Israel and the United States: Comparisons and commonalities in
          school desegregation. In Y. Amir and S. Sharan (Eds.).
Minkovich, A.
1975   Failures and risks in the education of the disadvantaged. In C.
          Frankenstein (Ed.).
1980   An evaluation study of elementary education in Israel. In S. Goldstein
          (Ed.).

Minkovich, A., Davis, D., and Bashi, J.
   1982   *Success and Failure in Israeli Elementary Education: An Evaluation Study with Special Emphasis on Disadvantaged Pupils.* New Brunswick, NJ: Transaction Books.
Minkovich, A., Davis, D., Bashi, J., et al.
   1977   *An Evaluation Study of Israeli Elementary Schools.* Jerusalem: Hebrew University School of Education.
Miron, M.
   1983   What makes a good teacher? *Higher Education in Europe, 8*, 45-53.
   1985   The "good professor" as perceived by university instructors. *Higher Education, 14*, 211-215.
Miron, M., and Segal, E.
   1978   "The good university teacher" as perceived by the students. *Higher Education, 7*, 27-34.
Munk, M.
   1971   The residential Yeshiva. In M. Wolins and M. Gottesman (Eds.).
Nachmias, C.
   1977a   The issue of saliency and the effect of tracking on self-esteem. *Urban Education, 12*, 327-344.
   1977b   The status attainment process: A test of a model in two stratification systems. *The Sociological Quarterly, 18*, 589-607.
   1980   Curriculum tracking: Some of its causes and consequences under a meritocracy. *Comparative Education Review, 24*, 1-20.
Nachmias, C., and Sadan, E.
   1977   Individual modernity, schooling and economic performance of family farm operators in Israel. *International Journal of Comparative Sociology, 18*, 268-279.
Nachmias, S.
   1982   Law of education and freedom of the individual. In E. Ben-Baruch and Y. Neumann (Eds.).
Nadler, A. et al.
   1982   Density does not help: Help-giving, help seeking and help-reciprocating of residents of high and low student dormitories. *Population and Environment, 5*, 26-42.
Near, H.
   1982   Kibbutz education: An historical approach. *Interchange on Educational Policy, 13*, 3-15.
Neubauer, P. B. (Ed.)
   1965   *Children in Collectives: Childrearing Aims and Practices in the Kibbutz.* Springfield, IL: Thomas.
Neuman, S., and Ziderman, A.
   1985   Do universities maintain common standards in awarding first degrees with distinction? The case of Israel. *Higher Education, 14*, 447-459.
Neumann, L., and Neumann, Y.
   1981   The effects of the academic program on students' perception of university goals. *Journal of Instructional Psychology, 8*, 154-164.
   1982a   Measurement problems and rating scales in educational research. In E. Ben-Baruch and Y. Neumann (Eds.).
   1982b   Work value of students in several career preparation. In E. Ben-Baruch and Y. Neumann (Eds.).

1982c   The goals of medical school: Differences between student and faculty perceptions. *Journal of Medical Education 57*, 557-559.

1983   Faculty perceptions of deans' and department chairmen's management functions. *Higher Education, 12*, 205-214.

1984   Discriminant analysis of students' work values: Differences between engineering. *Journal of Experimental Education, 52*, 41-46.

Neumann, M., and Elizur, A.

1979   Group experience as means of training medical students. *Journal of Medical Education, 54*, 714-719.

Neumann, Y. and Neumann, L.

1981   Determinants of students' satisfaction with course work: An international comparison between two universities. *Research in Higher Education, 14*, 321-333.

1982a   The assessment of organizational climate in an Israeli university. In E. Ben-Baruch and Y. Neumann (Eds.).

1982b   Student assessment of university goals: A comparative approach. In E. Ben-Baruch and Y. Neumann (Eds.).

1982c   Students' satisfaction with course work and its predictors: Differences among four academic programs. In E. Ben-Baruch and Y. Neumann (Eds.).

1982d   Faculty work orientations as predictors of work attitudes in the physical and social sciences. *Journal of Vocational Behavior, 21*, 359-365.

1983   Characteristic of academic areas and students' evaluation of instruction. *Research in Higher Education, 19*, 323-334.

1984   Equity theory and students' commitment to their college. *Research in Higher Education, 20*, 269-280.

Nevo, D.

1979   *The Gifted Disadvantaged: A Ten Year Longitudinal Study of Compensatory Education in Israel.* New York: Gordon and Breach.

Nichols, W. T.

1979   Impressions of social studies in Israel. *Social Studies Journal, 8*, 32-38.

Ninio, A.

1979   The Naine theory of infant and other maternal attitudes in two subgroups in Israel. *Child Development, 50*, 976-980.

Nir-Yaniv, N.

1974   Parent-teacher co-operation: Teachers learn from disadvantaged parents. *International Understanding at School, 28*, 13-15.

1982   Parent-school cooperation in a changing society: Teachers' learning from disadvantaged parents. In P. Tamir, A. Hofstein and M. Ben-Peretz (Eds.).

Nir-Yaniv, N., Spodek, B., and Steg, D. (Eds.)

1982   *Early Childhood Education: An International Perspective.* NY: Plenum.

Nisan, M.

1976   Delay of gratification in children: Personal versus group choices. *Child Development, 47*, 195-200.

1984   Distributive justice and social norms. *Child Development, 55*, 1020-1029.

Nkomo, M.

1983   Israel. *Integrated Education, 20*, 15-17.

Novick, S., and Duvdavani, D.
1976   The relationship between school and student variables and the attitudes toward science of tenth grade students in Israel. *Journal of Research in Science Teaching, 13*, 259-265.

Offer, D., Ostrov, E., and Howard, K. E.
1977   The self-image of adolescents: A study of four cultures. *Journal of Youth and Adolescence, 6*, 265-280.

Ormian, H. Y.
1980   The social aspects of education in Israel. *Journal of Jewish Communal Service, 56*, 316-327.

Ortar, G.
1967   Educational achievements of primary school graduates in Israel as related to their sociocultural background. *Comparative Education, 4*, 23-34.

Osterweil, Z.
1982   The development of political concepts in Israeli schoolboys. *International Journal of Political Education, 5*, 141-158.

Padan-Eisenstark, D.
1973   Girls' education in the kibbutz. *International Review of Education, 19*, 120-125.

Parzen, H.
1974   *The Hebrew University.* New York: Ktav.

Passow, A. H.
1984   Education of the gifted. *Prospects: Quarterly Review of Education, 14*, 177-187.

Pazy, A. and Lomrang, J.
1980   Value conceptions of American and Israeli youth. *Journal of Social Psychology, 111*, 181-187.

Peled, E.
1973   Education: The social challenge. In M. Curtis and M. S. Chertoff (Eds.), *Israel: Social Structure and Change.* New Brunswick, NJ: Transaction Books.
1979   The case of Israel (on the Israel educational system). In F. Williams (Ed.), *Government in the Classroom: Dollars and Power in Education.* New York: Praeger.
1981   Israeli education. In E. Ignas and R. J. Corsini (Eds.), *Comparative Educational Systems.* Itasca, IL: Peacock.
1982   The educational reform in Israel: The political aspect. In E. Ben-Baruch and Y. Neumann (Eds.).
1984   The concept of equality in Israel's educational policy. *Jerusalem Quarterly, 30*, 17-28.
1985   Welfare policy in Israel: The domain of Education. In S. N. Eisenstadt and O. Ahimeir (Eds.), *The Welfare State and its Aftermath.* London: Croom Helm.

Peled, M.
1982   Student alienation from Israeli secondary schools. In E. Ben-Baruch and Y. Neumann (Eds.).

Peleg, R., and Adler, C.
1977   Compensatory education in Israel: Conceptions, attitudes and trends. *American Psychologist, 32*, 945-958.

Peres, J.
1963   Youth and youth movements in Israel. *Jewish Journal of Sociology, 5*, 95-110.

Peres, Y., Ehrlich, A., and Yuval-Davis, N.
1970   National education for Arab youth in Israel: A comparative analysis of curricula. *Jewish Journal of Sociology, 12*, 147-164.

Perlberg, A.
1983a   When professors confront themselves: Towards a theoretical conceptualization of video self-confrontation. *Higher Education, 12*, 633-663.
1983b   Instructional evaluation and the improvement of teaching-learning processes. *Higher Education in Europe, 8*, 56-63.

Perlberg, A., and Keinan, G.
1986   Sources of stress in academe: The Israeli case. *Higher Education, 15*, 73-88.

Perlberg, A., and Navon, E.
1972   A profile of applicants to a leading engineering school. *Higher Education, 1*, 321-331.

Perlberg, A., and Rom, Y.
1969   A compensatory program on the higher education level: An Israeli case study. *Education Forum, 33*, 307-319.

Pincus, C.
1972   Family and school: Some preliminary observations on adolescent Russian immigrants in Israel. *Jewish Social Studies, 34*, 248-265.

Preston, D. L.
1976   The German Jews in secular education, university teaching and science: A preliminary inquiry. *Jewish Social Studies, 38*, 99-116.

Pur, D., and Gordon, D.
1982   Conservatism and centralization in school systems: The case of the Israeli high schools. In E. Ben-Baruch and Y. Neumann (Eds.).

Quarter, J.
1982   Kibbutz education and its relevance to the west: Progressive education reconsidered. *Interchange on Educational Policy, 13*, 29-44.
1984   The development of political reasoning on the Israeli kibbutz. *Adolescence, 19*, 569-593.

Rabin, A. I.
1964   Kibbutz mothers view collective education. *American Journal of Orthopsychiatry, 34*, 140-142.
1965   *Growing Up in the Kibbutz*. New York: Springer.

Rabin, A. I., and Beit-Halachmi, B.
1982   *Twenty Years Later: Kibbutz Children Grow Up*. NY: Springer.

Rabin, A. I., and Hazan, B. (Eds.)
1973   *Collective Education in the Kibbutz-From Infancy to Maturity*. NY: Springer.

Rabinowitz, D.
1972   Israel universities in time of siege. *Change, 4*, 42-47.

Ramon, S.
1974   The inter-relations between success in academic studies and patterns of thinking, personal traits and social background in Israel. *Bulletin of the British Psychological Society, 27*, 176.

Rand, Y.
1982   Towards education of a new generation: Some thoughts. In Nir-Yaniv et al. (Eds.).

Rappaport, C., and Arad, R.
1971   Evaluation of the educational process in Mechinot. In M. Wolins and M. Gottesman (Eds.).

Rappaport, Y.
1971   The educational path of youth aliyah. In M. Wolins and M. Gottesman (Eds.).

Raviv, A.
1979   Reflections on the role of the school psychologist in Israel. *Professional Psychologist, 10*, 820-826.
1984   School psychology in Israel. *Journal of School Psychology, 22*, 323-333.

Raviv, A., Bar-Tal, D., Raviv, A., and Bar-Tal, Y.
1980   Causal perceptions of success and failure by advantaged, integrated and disadvantaged pupils. *British Journal of Educational Psychology, 50*, 137-146.

Raviv, S., Sharan, S., and Strauss, S.
1973   Intellectual development of deaf children in different educational environments. *Journal of Communication Disorders, 6*, 29-36.

Reiter, S., Friedman, L. and Levi, A. M.
1982   Mentally handicapped children in special schools in Israel: A focus on social behavior. *International Journal of Rehabilitation Research, 5*, 477-485.

Reshef, S.
1980   Progressive education in pre-state Israel society, 1915-1939. *Paedigogica Historica, 20*, 153-170.
1981   National aims and educational policy. *Jerusalem Quarterly, 20*, 96-104.

Reshef, S., and Silbert, Y.
1983   The Palestine government and Jewish education 1920-1933. *History of Education, 12*, 39-52.

Rich, Y.
1986   Curriculum development for cooperative learning in the heterogeneous class. *Journal of Curriculum Studies* (in press).

Rich, Y., Amir, Y., and Ben-Air, R.
1981   Social and emotional problems associated with integration in the Israeli junior high school. *International Journal of Intercultural Relations, 5*, 259-275.

Rich, Y., Amir, Y., and Ben-Air, R., and Mevarech, Z.
1986   Cooperative strategies for mixed ethnic groups in the Israeli desegregated classroom. In L. Ekstrand (Ed.), *Ethnic Minorities and Immigrants in a Cross-Cultural Perspective*. Lisse, Holland: Swets and Zeitlinger.

Rich, Y., and Darom, E.
1981   Pupils, perceptions of the quality of life in advantaged and disadvantaged schools. In J. Epstein (Ed.), *The Quality of School Life*. Boston: Lexington Books.

Rich, Y., Linor, M., and Shalev, M.
  1984   Perceptions of the quality of school life among mainstreamed physically handicapped children. *Educational Resesarch, 26*, 27-32.

Rimon, S.
  1975   Interrelations between academic success and background factors: The Israeli case. In J. W. Berry and W. Lonner (Eds.), *Applied Cross-Cultural Psychology*. Amsterdam: Swets.

Rinott, C.
  1971   Dynamics of youth aliyah groups. In M. Wolins and M. Gottesman (Eds.).

Rinott, C., and Schachar, B.
  1974   Education in the state of Israel. In *Education and Science*. Jerusalem: Keter.

Ritterband, P.
  1969   The determinants of motives of Israeli students studying in the United States. *Sociology of Education, 42*, 330-349.
  1978   *Education, Employment and Migration: Israel in Comparative Perspective*. Cambridge: Cambridge University Press.

Rofe, Y., and Weller, L.
  1981   Ethnic groups, prejudice and class in Israel. *The Jewish Journal of Sociology, 23*, 101-111.

Rom, Z.
  1980-1981 Interaction of vocational and family factors in the career planning of teen-age girls: A new developmental approach. *Interchange, 11*, 13-24.

Ron-Polany, Y.
  1965   The parent-child relationship in collective education in Israel. *International Review of Education, 11*, 224-228.

Room, T.
  1984   Sexual stereotypes in the Israeli classroom: Theoretical conceptualization and observations. *Israel Social Science Research, 2*, 42-54.

Rosenstein, C.
  1981   The liability of ethnicity in Israel. *Social Forces, 59*, 667-686.

Rosenthal, M. K.
  1980   Developing leadership for integrated early childhood programs in Israel. *Young Children, 35*, 21-26.

Rotenberg, M., London, P., and Cooper, L. M.
  1976   Achievement motivation, socialization and hypnotic susceptibility among youths from four Israeli subcultures. *Journal of Youth and Adolescence, 3*, 89-100.

Rothman, R. C.
  1972   Education and participation in the Israeli defense forces. *Jewish Social Studies, 34*, 155-172.

Rumble, G., and Keith, H. (Eds.)
  1982   *The Distance Teaching Universities*. London: Croom Helm.

Ryback, D., Sanders, A., Lawrence, G., and Kestenblatt, M.
  1980   Child rearing practices reported by students in six cultures. *Journal of Social Psychology, 110*, 153-162.

Sabar, N.
  1979   Science and society: New trends in science teaching. *Science Education, 63*, 38-47.

1983   School based science curriculum: Myth or reality? *European Journal of Science Education, 5*, 457-462.

Safir, M. P.
1986   The effects of nature or of nurture on sex differences in intellectual functioning: Israeli findings. *Sex Roles, 14*, 581-590.

Salomon, G.
1977   Effects of encouraging Israeli mothers to co-observe 'Sesame Street' with their five-year-olds. *Child Development, 48*, 1146-1151.

1984   Television is "easy" and print is "tough": The differential investment of mental effort. *Journal of Educational Psychology, 76*, 647-658.

Salomon, G., and Leigh, T.
1984   Predispositions about learning from print and television. *Journal of Communication, 34*, 119-135.

Schachter, H. L.
1972   Educational institutions and political coalitions: The case of Israel. *Comparative Education Review, 16*, 462-473.

Schatzker, C.
1982   The holocaust in Israeli education. *International Journal of Political Education, 5*, 75-82.

Scheintuch, G. and Lewin, G.
1981   Parents' attitudes and children's deprivation: Child-rearing attitudes of parents as a key to the advantaged-disadvantaged distinction in pre-school children. *International Journal of Behavioral Development, 4*, 125-142.

Scher, D., Nevo, B., and Beit-Hallachmi, B.
1979   Beliefs about equal rights for men and women among Israeli and American students. *Journal of Social Psychology, 109*, 11-15.

Schmida, M.
1981   Extra curricular activities in the Israeli high school. *Jewish Education, 49*, 18-27.

1982   Informal education in Israel: The case of the community center. *Jewish Education, 51*, 19-24.

Schmida, M., and Katz, Y. J.
1987   The differential effect of three educational structures on the realization of academic and social variables. *Research in Education, 37*, 1-11.

Schmida, M., Katz, Y. J., and Cohen, A.
1986   Ability grouping and students' social orientations. *Urban Education, 21*, 421-431.

Schneller, R.
1980   Continuity and change in ultra-orthodox education. *The Jewish Journal of Sociology, 22*, 35-46.

1982a   Training for critical TV viewing. (1982). *Educational Research, 24*, 99-106.

1982b   The science religion problem: Attitudes of religious Israeli youth. *Youth and Society, 13*, 251-282.

1985   Heritage and change of the non-verbal language of Ethiopian immigrants. *Israel Social Science Research, 3*, 33-54.

1986   Informal agencies of socialization and the integration of the immigrant youth into society: An example from Israel. *International Migration Review (in press).*

Schoneveld, J.
1976   *The Bible in Israeli education: A study of approaches to the Hebrew Bible and its teaching in Israeli educational literature.* Assen: Van Gorcum.
Schwarzwald, J.
1984   Integration as a situational contingent: Secular versus religious public education. In Y. Amir and S. Sharan (Eds.).
Schwarzwald, J., and Amir, Y.
1984   Interethnic relations and education: An Israeli perspective. In N. Miller and N. Brewer (Eds.), *Groups in Contact: The Psychology of Desegregation.* NY: Academic Press.
Schwarzwald, J., and Cohen, S.
1982   Relationship between academic tracking and the degree of interethnic acceptance. *Journal of Educational Psychology, 74,* 588-597.
Schwarzwald, J., Fridel, S., and Hoffman, M.
1985   Carry-over of contact effects from acquainted to unacquainted targets. *Journal of Multilingual Development, 6,* 297-311.
Schwarzwald, J., Laor, T., and Hoffman, M.
in press   Impact of sociometric method and activity content on assessment of intergroup relations in the classroom. *British Journal of Education, 56,* 24-31.
Schwarzwald, J., Moisseiev, O., and Hoffman, M.
1986   Similarity versus social ambition in assessment of interpersonal acceptance in the classroom. *Journal of Educational Psychology, 78,* 184-189.
Schwarzwald, J., Shoham, M., Waysman, M., and Sterner, I.
1979   Israeli teachers' outlook on the necessity and feasibility of teaching values to advantaged and disadvantaged children. *Journal of Psychology, 101,* 3-9.
Schwarzwald, J., and Yinon, Y.
1977   Symmetrical and asymmetrical interethnic relations. *International Journal of Intercultural Relations, 1,* 40-47.
Seginer, R.
1986   Mothers' behavior and son's performance: An initial test of an academic achievement path model. *Merril-Palmer Quarterly, 32,* 153-166.
Seligman, D.
1982   Everyman's university Israel. In G. Rumble and H. Keith (Eds.), *The distance teaching universities.* London: Croom Helm.
Seliktar, O.
1980   Continuity and change in the attitudes toward the Middle East conflict: The case of Young Israelis. *International Journal of Political Education, 3,* 141-161.
Shachar, B.
1972   Workers' education. In Y. Kalman (Ed.).
Shaffir, W.
1983   The recruitment of *Baale Tshuvah* in a Jerusalem yeshivah. *The Jewish Journal of Sociology, 25,* 33-46.
Shafir, G.
1983   Organic intellectuals and the renaissance of the Hebrew language. *Sociologia Internationalis, 21,* 215-242.

Shahar, B.
1967   Adult education in Israel and other countries. *International Review of Community Development, 17-18*, 233-246.
Shamgar-Handelman, L., and Handelman, D.
1986   Holiday celebrations in Israeli kindergartens: Relationships between representations of collectivity and family in the nation-state. In Myron J. Arnoff (Ed.), *The Frailty of Authority-Political Anthropology*, (Vol. 5). New Brunswick, NJ: Transaction Books.
Shapira, A.
1980   Educational liberty and equality: Some Israeli constitutional law perspectives. In S. Goldstein (Ed.).
Shapira, R., and Enoch, Y.
1974   Ivory tower or social involvement? University professors in Israel. *Universities Quarterly, 28*, 437-450.
Shapira, R., and Etzioni-Halevy, E.
1970a   Individual and collective values of Israeli students: The impact of youth movements. *Jewish Journal of Sociology, 12*, 165-180.
1970b   Attitudes of Israeli students toward emigration. *Comparative Education Review, 14*, 162-173.
1976   Jewish identification of Israeli students: What lies ahead. *Jewish Social Studies, 37*, 251-266.
1977   The many faces of the Israeli student. In S. Shoham (Ed.), *Youth Unrest*. Jerusalem: Jerusalem Academic Press.
Shapira, R., Etzioni-Halevy, E., and Barak, A.
1986   Political attitudes of Israeli students: A comparative perspective. *Higher Education, 15*, 231-246.
Shapira, R., Etzioni-Halevy, E., and Tibon, S.
1978   Occupational choice among Israeli academics. *Journal of Comparative Family Studies, 9*, 69-81.
Shapira, R., and Hadad, M.
1982   Commanding resources and patterns of association. *Journal of Classroom Interaction, 18*, 28-35.
Shapira, R., and Herzog, H.
1984   Understanding youth culture through autograph books: The Israeli case. *American Journal of Folklore, 97*, 442-460.
Shapira, R., and Peleg, R.
1980   From blue shirt to white collar. *Forum, 38*, 127-140.
1984   From blue shirt to white collar. *Youth and Society, 16*, 195-216.
Shapira, R., and Yuchtman, E.
1975   Parental influence on achievement attitudes and performance of Israeli students. *International Journal of Comparative Sociology, 16*, 291-295.
Shapiro, L.
1980   *The History of ORT: A Jewish Movement for Social Change*. New York: Schocken.
Sharabany, R., and Hertz-Lazarowitz, R.
1981   Do friends share and communicate more than non-friends? *International Journal of Behavioral Development, 4*, 45-59.
Sharan, S.
1980   Cooperative learning in small groups: Recent methods and effects on achievement, attitudes and ethnic relations. *Review of Educational Research, 50*, 241-271.

Sharan, S., Amir, Y., and Ben-Ari,R.
 1984   School desegregation: Some challenges ahead. In Y. Amir and S. Sharan (Eds.).
Sharan, S., Darom, E., and Lazarowitz, R.
 1979   What teachers think about small-group teaching. *British Journal of Teacher Education, 5,* 49-62.
Sharan, S., Hare, P., Webb, C. D., and Hertz-Lazarowitz, R.
 1980   *Cooperation in Education.* Provo, UT: Brigham Young University Press.
Sharan, S., Hertz-Lazarowitz, R., and Ackerman, Z.
 1980   Academic achievement of elementary school children in small group versus whole class instruction. *The Journal of Experimental Education, 48,* 125-129.
Sharan, S., Hertz-Lazarowitz, R., and Kussel, P.
 1984   Social attitudes. In S. Sharan, P. Kussel, R. Hertz-Lazarowitz, Y. Bejerano, S. Raviv, Y. Sharan, T. Brosh, and R. Peleg (Eds.).
Sharan, S., Hertz-Lazarowitz, R., and Reiner, T.
 1979   Television for changing teacher behavior. *Journal of Educational Technology System, 7,* 119-131.
Sharan, S., Kussel, P., Hertz-Lazarowitz, R., Bejerano, Y., Raviv, S., and Sharan, Y.
 1985   Cooperative learning effects on ethnic relations and achievement in Israeli junior high school classrooms. In Slavin et al. (Eds.), *Learning to Cooperate, Cooperating to Learn.* NY: Plenum.
Sharan, S., Kussel, P., Hertz-Lazarowitz, R., Bejerano, Y., Raviv, S., Sharan, Y., Brosh, T., and Peleg, R.
 1984   *Cooperative Learning in the Classroom: Research in Desegregated Schools.* London: Lawrence Erlbaum.
Sharan, S. and Lazarowitz, R.
 1980   A group investigation method of cooperative learning in the classroom. In S. Sharan et al. (Eds.).
 1982   Effects of an instructional change program on teachers' behavior attitudes and perceptions. *Journal of Applied Behavioral Science, 18,* 185-201.
Sharan, S., Raviv, S., Kussel, P., and Hertz-Lazarowitz, R.
 1984   Cooperative and competitive behavior. In S. Sharan, P. Kussel, R. Hertz-Lazarowitz, Y. Bejerano, S. Raviv, Y. Sharan, T. Brosh, and R. Peleg (Eds.).
Sharan, S., and Rich, Y.
 1984   Field experiments on ethnic integration in Israeli schools. In Y. Amir and S. Sharan (Eds.).
Sharan, S., and Weller, L.
 1971   Classification patterns of underprivileged children in Israel. *Child Development, 42,* 581-594.
Sharan, S., and Yaakobi, D.
 1985   Teacher beliefs and practices: The discipline carries the message. *Journal of Education for Teaching, 11,* 187-199.
Sharni, S.
 1979   From alienation to admiration: Developmental stages of group leaders in encounters with culturally deprived mothers. *Human Relations, 32,* 737-749.
 1980   Groups of culturally deprived parents: A multidimensional intervention model. *Small Group Behavior, 11,* 345-356.

Sharon, N.
  1985   A policy analysis of issues in residential care for children and youth in Israel: Past, present, future. *Child and Youth Services, 7,* 111-122.

Shatzman, I.
  1984   Everyman's university of Israel: Original aims, interim results and new projects. *Bulletin of International Council for Distance Education, 5,* 28-38.

Shavit, Y.
  1984   Tracking and ethnicity in Israeli secondary education. *American Sociological Review, 49,* 210-220.

Shavit, Y., and Williams, R. A.
  1985   Ability grouping and contextual determinants of education expectations in Israel. *American Sociological Review, 50,* 62-73.

Sherer, M.
  1983   The incarceration period and educational achievement of juvenile delinquents. *Criminal Justice and Behavior, 10,* 109-120.
  1985   Effects of group intervention on moral development of distressed youths in Israel. *Journal of Youth and Adolescence, 14,* 513-526.

Shinar, D.
  1972   Tele-clubs in Israel. In Y. Kalman (Ed.).

Shokeid, M.
  1983   Commitment and paradox in sociological research: School integration in Israel. *Ethnic and Racial Studies, 6,* 198-212.

Sholonsky, H.
  1980   Formal education in Israel: A social welfare perspective. *Journal of Educational Thought, 14,* 196-208.

Shuval, J. T.
  1975a   The socialization of health professionals in Israel: Early sources of congruence and differentiation. *Journal of Medical Education, 50,* 443-457.
  1975b   From 'boy to colleague': Processes of role transformation in professional socialization. *Social Science and Medicine, 9,* 413-420.
  1976   Some issues in cross-national research on socialization of medical students. In M. Pflanz and E. Schach (Eds.), *Cross-National Sociomedical Research: Concepts, Methods, and Practice.* Stuttgart: Thieme.
  1980   *Entering Medicine: The Dynamics of Transition: A Seven Year Study of Medical Education in Israel.* Oxford: Pergamon.

Shuval, J. T., and Adler, I.
  1977   Processes of continuity and change during socialization for medicine in Israel. *Journal of Health and Social Behavior, 18,* 112-124.
  1979   Health occupations in Israel: Comparative patterns of change during socialization. *Journal of Health and Social Behavior, 20,* 77-89.
  1980   The role of models in professional socialization. *Social Science and Medicine, 14a,* 5-14.

Shye, S.
  1980   A structural analysis of achievement orientation derived from a longitudinal study of students in Israeli schools. *American Educational Research Journal, 17,* 281-290.

Silber, J., and Berrebi, Z. M.
  1986   Mobility and formal education in the human capital accumulation process: The case in Israel. *European Journal of Education, 20,* 399-410.

Silberman, C. E.
  1970   Give slum children a chance: A radical proposal. *Viewpoints, 46,* 69-87.
Simon, R., James, R., and Gurevitch, M.
  1971   Some intergenerational comparisons in two ethnic communities in Israel. *Human Organization, 30,* 79-88.
Smilansky, J.
  1982   Problem areas in the relationship of school psychologists and teachers. *School Psychology International, 3,* 23-28.
  1984   External and internal correlates of teachers' satisfaction and willingness to report stress. *British Journal of Educational Psychology, 54,* 84-92.
Smilansky, M.
  1979   Systems development: Planning in education: An Israeli perspective. In D. A. Wilkerson (Ed.), *Educating All Our Children: An Imperative for Democracy.* Westport: Mediax.
Smilansky, M., Kashti, Y., and Arieli, M.
  1982   *The residential alternative.* Haifa: Ach Publishing House.
Smilansky, M., and Nevo, D.
  1979   *The Gifted Disadvantaged: A Ten Year Longitudinal Study of Compensatory Education in Israel.* London: Gordon and Breach.
Smilansky, M., and Sanders, D.
  1974   Education of disadvantaged adolescents. *The Educational Forum, 38,* 411-431.
Smilansky, S., and Smilansky, M.
  1970   The role program of preschool education for socially disadvantaged children. *International Review of Education, 16,* 45-66.
Smooha, S.
  1978   *Israel: Pluralism and Conflict.* Los Angeles: University of California Press.
Sohlberg, S.
  1986   Similarity and dissimilarity in value patterns of Israeli kibbutz and city adolescents. *International Journal of Psychology, 21,* 189-202.
Soll, L., and McCall, C.
  1984   Israel and New York: Educating the nontraditional college student. *Improving College and University Teaching, 31,* 40-44.
Stachel, D.
  1982   Some factors affecting teacher behavior and pupil performance. In Y. Nir-Yaniv et al. (Eds.).
Stahl, A.
  1978   Children and childhood in the view of the traditional Jewish-Oriental family. *Journal of Comparative Family Studies, 9,* 346-354.
  1979   Adopting the curriculum to the needs of a multi-ethnic society: The case of Israel. *Curriculum Inquiry, 9,* 361-371.
  1980   Boy meets girl: Change and continuity among oriental Jews. *Adolescence, 15,* 355-360.
  1981a   The educational system of Israel: An overview. *Internationales Jahrbuch der Erwachsehenbildung 9,* 1-10.
  1981b   The Americanization of educational research in Israel. *Teachers College Record, 82,* 623-634.
  1982   Training teachers for the army disadvantaged in Israel. *Journal of Education for Teaching, 8,* 242-251.

1985   Introducing ethnic materials to the classroom: Problems B Challenge. *Urban Education, 20,* 257-272.

Stein, C. B.
1985   Israeli policy toward Sephardi schooling. *Comparative Education Review, 29,* 204-215.

Streiter, A.
1976   At ease in Zion: Some reflections on teaching English literature in Israel. *College English, 38,* 68-74.

Tadmor, S.
1975   *Education in Israel: Towards a New Society.* New York: Appleton-Century Crofts.

Tamir, P.
1983   Cognitive preferences of Jewish and Arab high school students. *Research in Science and Technological Education, 1,* 217-226.
1985   Homework and science learning in secondary schools. *Science Education, 69,* 605-618.
1986   Stability and change in inquiry orientation of high school biology teachers. *Educational Research, 28,* 51-55.

Tamir, P., and Ben-Peretz, M.
1983   Evaluation practices in teacher education in Israel. *Singapore Journal of Education, 1,* 6-13.

Tamir, P., Hofstein, A., and Ben-Peretz, M. (Eds.)
1983   *Preservice and Inservice Education of Science Teachers.* Philadelphia: Balaban International Science Service.

Tannenbaum, A. J.
1976   Research on the disadvantaged in the U.S.A.: Some comments. In C. Frankenstein (Ed.).

Taus, R.
1971   The social services. In M. Wolins and M. Gottesman (Eds.).

Tidhar, C. E. and Ostrowitz-Segal, L.
1985   Teletext in Israel: A new instructional tool. *Journal of Educational Television, 11,* 161-169.

Tokatli, R.
1983   Democratization of adult education in Israel. In O. Grebelsky and R. Tokatli (Eds.).

Toren, N., and King, J.
1982   Scientists' orientation toward their work: The relative effect of socialization versus situation. *International Journal of Comparative Sociology, 23,* 1-2.

Tsivion, A.
1983   Adult education in Jewish culture: At the crossroads. In O. Grebelsky and R. Tokatli (Eds.).

Twite, R.
1978   The first three years of an open university. *Educational Broadcasting International, 11,* 40-43.

Tyler, R. W.
1981   The U.S. versus the world: A comparison of educational performance. *Phi Delta Kappan, 62,* 307-310.

Weiner, A.
1985   Institutionalizing institutionalization: The historical roots of residential care in Israel. *Child and Youth Services, 7,* 3-19.

Weingrod, A.
  1981   Rashomon in Jerusalem: Ideology & power in an urban dispute. *Archives Europeenes de Sociologie, 22*, 158-169.
Weinstein, B.
  1985   Ethiopian Jews in Israel: Socialization and re-education. *Journal of Negro Education, 54*, 213-224.
Weiss, S.
  1972   Educating the disadvantaged, Israeli style. *Urban Education, 7*, 181-197.
Weller, L., and Levi, S.
  1981   Social class, I.Q., self-concept and teachers' evaluations in Israel. *Adolescence, 16*, 569-576.
Weller, L., and Luchterhand, E.
  1983   Family relationships of "problem" and "promising" youth. *Adolescence, 18*, 93-100.
West, H.
  1974   Early peer group interaction and role taking skills: An investigation of Israeli children. *Child Development, 45*, 1118.
Wexler, P.
  1979   Educational change and social contradiction: An example. *Comparative Education Review, 23*, 240-255.
Wilson, S.
  1969   Educational changes in the kibbutz. *Comparative Education, 5*, 67-72.
Winter, M.
  1979   Arab education in Israel. *Jerusalem Quarterly, 12*, 112-122.
Wolf, R. M., and Lerner, B.
  1983   The educational achievement controversy. *Public Interest, 72*, 124-132.
Wolins, M.
  1971a   Youth aliyah: Cause and function. In M. Wolins and M. Gottesman (Eds.).
  1971b   The kibbutz as foster mother: Maimonides applied. In M. Wolins and M. Gottesman (Eds.).
Wolins, M., and Gottesman, M. (Eds.)
  1971   *Group Care: An Israeli Approach: The Educational Path of Youth Aliyah*. New York: Gordon and Beach.
Wozner, Y.
  1986   The intensive educational internat. In Y. Kashti and M. Arieli (Eds.).
Wolowelsky, J. B.
  1981   Jewish education. *Tradition, 19*, 196-272.
Yaakobi, D., and Peterson, K.
  1981   Self-concept and perceptions of behavior: Comparisons between U.S. and Israeli science students. *Science Education, 65*, 329-334.
Yaakobi, D., and Sharan, S.
  1981   Classroom learning environment of city and kibbutz biology classrooms in Israel. *European Journal of Science Education, 3*, 321-328.
  1985   Teacher beliefs and practices: The discipline carries the message. *Journal of Education for Teaching, 11*, 187-199.
Yaar   See Yuchtman, E.
Yadlin, A.
  1974   Youth movements. In *Education and Science.*

Yaron, K.
1983   Adult education in the Arab population. In O. Grebelsky and R. Tokatli (Eds.).

Yavetz, R., and Shuval, Y.
1984   Drug use among high school students in Israel: A syndrome of social vulnerability. *Youth and Society, 16*, 171-194.

Yogev, A.
1981   Determinants of early educational career in Israel: Further evidence for the sponsorship thesis. *Sociology of Education, 54*, 181-194.
1987   Modernity and ethnic affiliation in Israeli schools: A dependence approach. *Ethnic and Racial Studies, 10*, 203-223.

Yogev, A., and Ayalon, H.
1982   Sex and ethnic variations in educational plans: A cross-cultural perspective. *International Review of Modern Sociology, 12*, 1-19.
1986   High school attendance in a sponsored multi-ethnic system: The case of Israel. In A. C. Kerckhoff (Ed.), *Research in Sociology of Education and Socialization) (Vol. 6)*. Greenwich, CT: JAI Press.

Yogev, A., and Chen, M.
1987   Sponsorship as school charter: Educational mobility in religious versus secular schools in Israel. *International Review of Modern Sociology* (in press).

Yogev, A. and El-Dor, J.
1987   Attitudes and tendencies toward return to Judaism among Israeli adolescents: Seekers or drifters? *The Jewish Journal of Sociology* (in press).

Yogev, A., and Ilan, Y.
1987   Does self-esteem affect educational aspirations? The case of the ethnic enclave. *Urban Education, 22*, (in press).

Yogev, A., and Jamshy, H.
1983   Children of ethnic intermarriage in Israeli schools: Are they marginal? *Journal of Marriage and Family, 45*, 965-974.

Yogev, A., and Roditi, H.
1987   School counselors as gate keepers: Students' guidance in poor versus affluent neighborhoods. *Adolescence* (in press).

Yogev, A., and Ronen, R.
1982   Cross-age tutoring: Effects on tutors' attributes. *Journal of Educational Research, 75*, 261-268.

Yogev, A. and Shapira, R.
1987   Ethnicity, meritocracy and credentialism in Israel: Elaborating the credential society thesis. In Robert Robinson (Ed.), *Research in Social Stratification and Mobility, Vol. 6*. Greenwich, CT: JAI Press.

Yuchtman (Yaar), E., and Samuel, Y.
1975   Determinants of career plans: Institutional versus interpersonal effects. *American Sociological Review, 40*, 521-531.

Yuchtman (Yaar), E., and Semyonov, M.
1979   Ethnic inequality in Israeli schools and sports: An expectation-states approach. *American Journal of Sociology, 85*, 576-590.

Zadok, M.
1984   The Israeli planning and grants committee at the crossroads: From shock absorber to steering wheel. *Higher Education, 13*, 535-544.

Zak, I.
1981a   The evaluation of school organization climate. In A. Lewy and D. Nevo (Eds.), *Evaluation Roles in Education.* New York: Gordon and Breach.
1981b   Continuous self-selection processes in teacher education: The way for survival. *Journal of Education for Teaching, 7,* 263-273.

Zak, I., and Birenbaum, M.
1980   Kerlinger's criterial referents theory revisited. *Educational and Psychological Measurement, 40,* 923-930.

Zak, I., and Glasman, N. S.
1979   State aid, voter power and local control in education. *National Tax Journal, 32,* 371-373.

Zak, I. and Kaufman, S.
1977   Sex-stereotypes in Israeli primers: A content analysis approach. *Studies in Educational Evaluation, 3,* 27-37.

Zakay, D., and Barak, A.
1984   Meaning and career decision-making. *Journal of Vocational Behavior, 24,* 1-14.

Zeidner, Moshe
1986   Are scholastic aptitude tests in Israel biased towards Arab college student candidates? *Higher Education, 15,* 507-522.

Ziderman, A.
1984   External examination versus internal assessment: The Israeli maturity certificate. *Comparative Education Review, 28,* 477-484.

Ziv, A., Green, D., and Guttmen, J.
1978   Moral judgment: Differences between city kibbutz and Israeli Arab preadolescents on the realistic-relativistic dimension. *Journal of Cross-Cultural Psychology, 9,* 215-226.

Ziv, A., Guttmann, J., and Green, D.
1981   Exposure to social variates and moral judgment of Israel adolescents in city, kibbutz and Arab villages. *Journal of Genetic Psychology, 139,* 69-78.

Ziv, A., Shulman, S., and Schleifer, A.
1979   Moral development: Parental and peer group influences on kibbutz and city children. *Journal of Genetic Psychology, 134,* 233-240.

Zuckerman-Bareli, C.
1975   The religious factor in opinion formation among Israeli Youth. In E. Kraus and S. Poll (Eds.), *Ethnic and Religious Diversity in Israel.* Israel: Institute for the Study of Ethnic Groups, Bar-Ilan University.

Contributors

Walter I. Ackerman is professor of education and director of the School of Continuing Education at Ben Gurion University of the Negev, Beer Sheva, Israel. His principal areas of interest are the history of Jewish education and curriculum theory.

Chaim Adler is professor in the School of Education and in the Department of Sociology and Anthropology at the Hebrew University, Jerusalem, Israel, and director of the National Council of Jewish Women's Institute for Innovation in Education.

Yehuda Amir is professor of psychology at Bar-Ilan University, Ramat-Gam, Israel. His major areas of interest are ethnic relations, intergroup conflicts, school desegregation, and cross-cultural psychology.

Mordechai Arieli is lecturer at Tel Aviv University, School of Education, Ramat Aviv, Israel. He has published research on residential institutions, classroom interaction, and the school as a social organization.

Channa Ayalon is an instructor in the Department of Sociology and Social Anthropology and in the School of Education at Tel Aviv University, Ramat-Aviv, Israel. Her chief areas of interest are sociology, social stratification, and methodology.

Victor Azarya is senior lecturer in the Department of Sociology and Social Anthropology at the Hebrew University, Jerusalem, Israel. His main interests are military sociology, urban communities, ethnicity, and religion.

Mordechai Bar-Lev is senior lecturer in the School of Education and in the Department of Sociology and Social Anthropology at Bar-Ilan University, Ramat-Gan, Israel. His main interests are the sociology of religious education, youth, leisure, and the kibbutz.

Joseph Ben-David (died 1986) was professor of sociology at the Hebrew University, Jerusalem, Israel and the director of the Edelstein Institute for the History of Science, Technology, and Medicine.

James Coleman is professor of sociology at the University of Chicago,

Illinois, U.S., and one of the outstanding figures in the field of sociology of education since the publication of his classic work, *Equality of Educational Opportunity*. He has written widely in the field and is particularly well-acquainted with the Israeli scene as the result of his frequent visits to Israel.

Yehezkel Dar is senior lecturer in the School of Education at the Hebrew University, Jerusalem, Israel. His areas of interest are sociology of education, effects of student-body compositions, kibbutz society, and education.

Rachel Elboim-Dror is professor in the School of Education, Hebrew University, Jerusalem, Israel. Her main areas of interest are education policy and politics, organization and planning of education, and Zionist education policy.

David Glanz is executive coordinator of the Bar-Ilan University Brookdale Program in Applied Geronology, and associate editor of *Studies of Israeli Society*. He is a Ph.D. candidate at Bar-Ilan University, Ramat-Gan, Israel. His interests include social gerontology, the sociology of religion, political sociology, the sociology of education, and the sociology of organizations.

Rivka Glaubman is lecturer in the School of Education at Bar-Ilan University, Ramat-Gan, Israel. Her key areas of interest are early childhood education, observational methods, human ethnology, school-based curriculum development, and open education.

David Gordon is senior lecturer in the Education Department of Ben Gurion University of the Negev, Beer Sheva, Israel. His areas of interest are planned change, educational philosophy, and sociology.

Jeff Halper is lecturer in the Institute for Urban Studies of the Hebrew University, Jerusalem, Israel. His main areas of interest are urban anthropology, ethnicity, anthropology and education, and social history.

Don Handelman is professor in the Department of Sociology and Anthropology at the Hebrew University, Jerusalem, Israel. His primary areas of interest are ritual, play, public events, symbolism, and bureaucratic organization.

Jo-Ann Harrison is senior lecturer in the School of Education at Bar-Ilan University, Ramat-Gan, Israel. Her principal area of interest is the sociology of education.

Hanna Herzog is senior lecturer in the Department of Sociology at Tel-

Aviv University, Ramat-Aviv, Israel. Her major areas of interest are political sociology, ethnic relations, political communication, women in politics, and minor parties.

Reuven Kahane is professor in the Department of Sociology and Social Anthropology and in the School of Education at Hebrew University, Jerusalem, Israel. His main areas of interest are social change and modernization.

Ernest Krausz is professor of sociology at Bar-Ilan University, Ramat-Gan, Israel. His main areas of interest are ethnic relations, the sociology of religion, and the methodology and philosophy of the social sciences.

Arnold Lewis is an independent scholar whose major interests are Israeli politics and social problems.

Sami Khalil Mar'i (died 1986) was head of the counseling department at Haifa University, Haifa, Israel and director of the Jewish-Arab Research Institute at Haifa University. His key areas of interest were Arab education, counseling, and creativity.

Nura Resh is lecturer in the School of Education at the Hebrew University, Jerusalem, Israel. Her main areas of interest are sociology of schooling, integration, and school effectiveness.

E. Ozer Schild is professor of psychology and sociology at the Haifa University, Haifa, Israel, where he has served as dean of the School of Education and as rector of the university. He formerly held the post of Chief Scientist and Senior Scientific Advisor to the Minister of Education and Culture. He has served on numerous public boards and is at present director of the Institute for Public Policy Analysis at Haifa University.

Joseph Schwarzwald is associate professor in the Department of Psychology at Bar-Ilan University, Ramat-Gan, Israel. His chief areas of interest are interethnic relations and methodology.

Moshe Semyonov is associate professor in the Department of Sociology at the University of Nebraska, Lincoln, U.S., and senior lecturer at Tel-Aviv University, Ramat-Aviv, Israel. His primary areas of interest are comparative stratification systems, social mobility, and gender and ethnic inequality.

Lea Shamgar-Handelman is senior lecturer in the Department of Sociology and in the School of Education at the Hebrew University,

Jerusalem, Israel. Her main areas of interest are sociology of family, parenthood, one-parent families, and the sociology of death.

Rina Shapira is professor of sociology in the Department of Sociology and Anthropology and the School of Education at Tel Aviv University, Ramat-Aviv, Israel, where she is director of the research unit of sociology of education and community. Her major interests are the sociology of youth, educational organizations and their social environments, and social and political stratification as related to education.

Yossi Shavit is senior lecturer in sociology at the Haifa University, Haifa, Israel. He is currently conducting research on the role of institutional and structural factors in the processes of educational and occupational stratification. He is also interested in the transition of Israeli men and women from youth to adulthood.

Moshe Shokeid is professor in the Department of Sociology and Social Anthropology at Tel-Aviv University, Ramat-Aviv, Israel. His main areas of interest are immigration and ethnicity.

Judith T. Shuval is lecturer in the Department of Sociology and in the School of Public Health at the Hebrew University, Jerusalem, Israel. Her main areas of interest are sociology of the professions, professional socialization, and the sociology of health and illness.

Laura Starr is lecturer in the School of Education at the Hebrew University, Jerusalem, Israel. Her primary areas of interest are technological education and training, and the transition from school to work.

Alex Weingrod is professor of anthropology in the Department of Behavioral Sciences at the Ben-Gurion University of the Negev, Beer Sheva, Israel. His main research interest is the interaction between politics and culture in anthropological analysis.

Abraham Yogev is senior lecturer in the School of Education and in the Department of Sociology and Anthropology at the Tel-Aviv University, Ramat-Aviv, Israel. His major areas of interest are sociology of education, social stratification and mobility, social change, and comparative survey methods.

Ephraim Yuchtman Yaar is professor of sociology at Tel-Aviv University, Ramat-Aviv, Israel. His key areas of interest are social inequalities, organizations and industrialization, and the Israeli-Arab conflict.